Competing for the Internet

Competing for the Internet

ICANN Gate – An Analysis and Plea for Judicial Review Through Arbitration

Flip Petillion
Jan Janssen

Wolters Kluwer

Published by:
Kluwer Law International B.V.
PO Box 316
2400 AH Alphen aan den Rijn
The Netherlands
Website: www.wklawbusiness.com

Sold and distributed in North, Central and South America by:
Wolters Kluwer Legal & Regulatory U.S.
7201 McKinney Circle
Frederick, MD 21704
United States of America
Email: customer.service@wolterskluwer.com

Sold and distributed in all other countries by:
Turpin Distribution Services Ltd
Stratton Business Park
Pegasus Drive, Biggleswade
Bedfordshire SG18 8TQ
United Kingdom
Email: kluwerlaw@turpin-distribution.com

Printed on acid-free paper.

ISBN 978-90-411-8252-4

e-Book: ISBN 978-90-411-8276-0
web-PDF: ISBN 978-90-411-8277-7

Printed in the United Kingdom.

About the Authors

Flip Petillion is a partner with the law firm Crowell & Moring. Over the past twenty years, he has advised on and resolved disputes concerning regulatory and competition issues in newly liberalized industries including telecommunications, postal, media, energy, transportation and the Internet. He has an impressive background in alternative dispute resolution, having served as chairman, sole arbitrator and party-appointed arbitrator, as well as counsel, in arbitration proceedings conducted by different arbitration institutions.

In particular, Flip advised new carriers on the opening of the EU Telecoms market in the 1990s. He represented a major U.S. telecommunications and media company when it took a majority participation in the newly created first alternative carrier in Belgium. For many years, he advised the new carrier on the preparation and implementation of its operations and services in the liberalized telecommunications market. He negotiated what became the reference interconnection agreement between incumbent operators and new comers all over Europe. He advised and represented alternative carriers and incumbents from many other European countries.

Flip was also closely involved in the liberalization of the African telecommunications market. Working on a project supported by the World Bank, in cooperation with renown financial advisors in French Congo, Flip rethought and put in place the new regulatory telecommunications framework, and organized the procedure to search for investors and assisted the Office National des Postes et Télécommunication (ONPT) in the selection of its foreign investors.

Flip subsequently obtained postgraduate degrees from the universities of both Leuven and Ghent on legal, technical and strategic aspects affecting the telecommunications industry. He also followed a program on negotiation and mediation lead by Harvard Law School Professor R.H. Mnookin.

Flip was selected to represent the Belgian Institute for Postal services and Telecommunications for many years in procedures brought by alternative operators against the regulatory authority. He co-authored a book on the EU and local regulatory framework.

Flip also advised new entrants on regulatory issues in the media, energy and transportation sectors inside and outside the EU.

Most recently, Flip has represented Internet companies, online services companies and multinationals from other, more traditional, sectors in arbitrations before ICDR, the international division of the American Arbitration Association in New York, and before ICC in Paris and WIPO in Geneva.

Jan Janssen, a senior associate at Crowell & Moring, has worked mainly on national and international disputes with a focus on intellectual property, information technology and the liberalization of sectors like the postal sector and the Internet's naming space. Through his work with Flip Petillion, he has acquired a profound, detailed knowledge of the regulatory framework in these sectors, and has had an excellent opportunity to perfect his arbitration skills.

Table of Contents

Foreword

From the creation of hieroglyphics in ancient Egypt, to the invention of the printing press by Gutenberg in the Middle Ages, to the development of computers in the 20th Century, advancing technology has revolutionized the world's ability to record and share information. These developments in information technology have come fast and furious. They all have been disruptive to existing orders, but the disruption is worth it: The result in every case has been an explosive improvement in the human condition.

The Internet - first developed as a military application but now firmly at the center of world commerce - has been just as disruptive as these other leaps in information technology, and just as enriching as well. But, unlike these earlier developments, the Internet's ability to achieve its true potential requires careful management of the technological underpinnings that permit seamless communication. Among the critical components of those underpinnings - at least in today's Internet - is effective and efficient management of the Internet's addressing system and domain name system (DNS).

And that brings us to ICANN. This unusual, non-profit, public-interest entity plays a critical role in ensuring a stable platform for facilitating communications globally across the web. Yet ICANN is no longer accountable to any centralized governmental or regulatory oversight. Instead, it is run through a highly complex, multi-stakeholder system.

In order to ensure that ICANN's management of the DNS is both effective and fair, ICANN has put in place procedural protections, seemingly designed to enhance due process and basic fairness. Navigating the ICANN rules and procedures, though, is extraordinarily difficult. That challenge is made all the more difficult when the ICANN Board sometimes takes steps that seem inconsistent with ICANN's guiding principles, including its promise of ensuring fairness and equality. An entire cottage industry has arisen to help domain name registrants, new gTLD applicants, registrars, registries, and brand owners protect and enforce their sometimes-competing rights and interests.

Finally, there began what was perhaps the most thought-provoking phase of all: resolving disputes with the Internet Corporation for Assigned Names and Numbers (ICANN). I handled many of the Independent Review Process (IRP) cases related to the third application round. To date, we have handled six IRPs, and we have been contacted in relation to two other cases by counsel requiring assistance with regard to procedural issues and in the development of their strategy and arguments. In view of multiparty representations and the consolidation of cases on identical claims, we have in fact represented some 70% of all IRP claimants.

And I truly never expected there to be so many issues, so many obstructions to open competition, so many 'nos' to the often elementary requests from my clients who saw no alternative but to initiate an IRP. My experience has allowed me to form my own vision of how the New gTLD Program should operate. Through the cases I have worked on, I have seen a recurrence of particular issues underlining the importance of certain legal principles and their application, and I have been lucky enough to work on cases that have allowed me to support my clients in accordance with my own vision of the best way forward. I am honored to say that some IRP panels have already expressed their gratitude for the contributions we have been able to make to the debate – in the interest of improving the Internet.

While the cataloguing of experience is perhaps already reason enough for a book, it is my belief in a better system for the future that is the driving force behind this publication. I want to share my experience with all applicants and future interested parties, and by doing so give something valuable back to the Internet community.

It was under Bill Clinton's administration that ICANN was established. The U.S. Government's aim was to increase competition and that aim is reflected in ICANN's own description of the New gTLD Program:

> The Internet Corporation for Assigned Names and Numbers, founded in 1998, has as its mission to ensure a stable and unified global Internet. One of its key responsibilities is introducing and promoting competition in the registration of domain names, while ensuring the security and stability of the domain name system (DNS).[1]

Achieving that aim requires ICANN to take some crucial steps. I must acknowledge here that ICANN has already admitted some of its mistakes. Of course, it would have been better had they not occurred in the first place, but in any event, avoiding future mistakes is now the priority. This is primarily what this book is about and I hope it contributes to much-needed, concrete initiatives and promotes change in the interests of the Internet community.

It is perhaps appropriate here to acknowledge that this book is based largely on our personal experiences with the IRP process and our involvement on behalf of claimants.

1. ICANN, *New Generic Top-Level Domains – About the Program*, https://newgtlds.icann.org/en/about/program.

Despite this personal involvement, however, every attempt has been made to ensure objectivity and to suggest improvements for the future that are for the general good of the system.

Furthermore, I hope that this book will help to reassure applicants in the fourth application round (which may be an open window). These new applicants may well look at the existing process and its implementation with suspicion in the light of the third, somewhat imperfect, application round; and applicants of the third round who themselves already are (or soon will be) active registries can also expect to be under even more scrutiny when the next round is launched. After all, the number of applicants in the third round was not that great, and as they will all directly or indirectly participate in the preparation and approval of the future regulatory framework, there is a very real possibility that without effective accountability there will be challenges based on perceived or real anticompetitive practices and abusive restriction of competition.

You will notice that the different chapters of this book are easily accessible separately. If you want to know the whole story, it helps to read this book from the beginning to the end. Enjoy it.

Finally, I would like to express my thanks to Jan Janssen, whom I introduced to this world, and who has the potential to become a leading thinker in this field. Together we have advised many international organizations and multinationals, and we have taken part in some of the most fascinating disputes ever launched on subjects related to Internet governance. It has been a joy to share long days and weekends with Jan. I invited Jan to co-author this book as a testimony to the great team we have formed over the years. My thanks also go to Diego Noesen for his unwavering support and to all my other Crowell & Moring colleagues who have made this project possible. I would like to single out Mariet Nelissen, Alexander Heirwegh and especially Penelope Turner for their invaluable help in putting this book together.

Lastly, I want to thank both of our home fronts. Jan and I have missed valuable family time over recent years and we are so grateful to Liszl and Peter for all the support they have given us at times inconvenient to them: at weekends, during the night, while on vacation. This achievement is as much theirs as it is ours and it is to them that we dedicate this book

Flip Petillion
1 November 2016

List of Abbreviations

AAA	American Arbitration Association
ADR	Alternative Dispute Resolution
AGB	gTLD Applicant Guidebook
ALAC	At-Large Advisory Committee
AoC	Affirmation of Commitments
AoI	Articles of Incorporation
APDIP	Asia-Pacific Development Information Programme
ARPA	Advanced Research Project Agency
ASEP	ICANN's Accountability Structures Expert Panel
ASO	Address Supporting Organization
AUC	African Union Commission
BGC	Board Governance Committee
BGG	Board Governance Guidelines
BWG	Boston Working Group
CCG	Code of Conduct Guidelines
ccNSO	country code Names Supporting Organization
ccTLD	country code Top Level Domain
CEP	Cooperative Engagement Process
CoIP	Conflicts of Interest Policy
CORE	International Council of Registrars
CPE	Community Priority Evaluation
DCA	DotConnectAfrica Trust
DIDP	Documentary Information Disclosure Policy
DNS	Domain Name System
DNSO	Domain Name Supporting Organization (predecessor of GNSO)

DoC	U.S. Department of Commerce
DR(S)P	Dispute Resolution (Service) Provider
ECJ	European Court of Justice
ERC	Committee on ICANN Evolution and Reform
EIU	Economist Intelligence Unit
EU	European Union
FTP	File Transfer Protocol
GAC	Governmental Advisory Committee
GNP	Geographic Names Panel
GNSO	Generic Names Supporting Organization
GPML	Globally-Protected Marks List
GSO	Generic Supporting Organization
gTLD	generic Top Level Domain
IAB	Internet Advisory Board
IANA	Internet Assigned Numbers Authority
ICANN	Internet Corporation for Assigned Names and Numbers
ICC	International Chamber of Commerce
ICDR	International Center for Dispute Resolution
ICDR Rules	International Center for Dispute Resolution's International Arbitration Rules
ICJ	International Court of Justice
ICG	IANA Stewardship Transition Coordination Group
IDN	Internationalized Domain Name
IETF	Internet Engineering Task Force
IGO	Intergovernmental Organization
IMP	Interface Message Processor
INTA	International Trademark Association
IO	Independent Objector
IOC	International Olympic Committee
IPv4	Internet Protocol version 4
IPv6	Internet Protocol version 6
IRP	Independent Review Process
ISI	Information Sciences Institute
ISO	International Standardization Organization
ISOC	The Internet Society
ISP	Internet Service Provider

ITU	International Telecommunications Union
JAS	JAS Global Advisors
JPA	Joint Project Agreement
LRO	Legal Rights Objection
Manwin	Manwin Licensing International
Merck	Merck KGaA
MIT	Massachusetts Institute of Technology
MOU	Memorandum of Understanding
MSD	Merck & Co., Inc.
NCP	Network Control Protocol
NGO	Non-governmental Organization
NGPC	New gTLD Program Committee
NIC	Network Information Center
NOC	Network Operations Center
NSF	National Science Foundation
NSFNET	National Science Foundation NET
NSI	Network Solutions, Inc.
NTIA	National Telecommunications and Information Administration
ORSC	Open Root Server Confederation
PCIJ	Permanent Court of International Justice
PDP	Policy Development Process
PICs	Public Interest Commitments
Procedural rules	The Bylaws, the ICDR Rules, and the Supplementary Procedures
RAA	Registrar Accreditation Agreement
RFP	Request for Proposals
RM	Reference Material
RSSAC	Root Server System Advisory Committee
RySG	Registry Stakeholder Group
SCO	String Confusion Objection
SO	Supporting Organization
SRI	Stanford Research Institute
SRS	Shared Registration System
SSAC	Security and Stability Advisory Committee
SSEP or SSP	String Similarity (Evaluation) Panel
sTLD	Sponsored Top Level Domain

Supplementary Procedures	(ICDR) Supplementary Procedures for ICANN Independent Review Process (or ICDR IRP Supplementary Procedures)
TCP/IP	Transmission Control Protocol/Internet Protocol
TLD	Top Level Domain
Trademark PDDRP	Trademark Post-Delegation Dispute Resolution Procedure
UCLA	University of California, Los Angeles
UDRP	Uniform Domain Name Dispute Resolution Policy
UN	United Nations
URS	Uniform Rapid Suspension procedure
USC	University of Southern California
WIPO	World Intellectual Property Organization
WTO	World Trade Organization
WWW	World Wide Web

List of Regulatory Documents

ICANN's Articles of Incorporation
ICANN's Bylaws
gTLD Applicant Guidebook
NTIA, *Registration and Administration of Internet Domain Names – Summary of Comments*
NTIA, *A Proposal to Improve Technical Management of Internet Names and Addresses - Discussion Draft ('Green Paper')*
NTIA, *Management of Internet Names and Addresses: statement of policy* ('White Paper')
Memorandum of Understanding between the U.S. Department of Commerce and the Internet Corporation for Assigned Names and Numbers
Affirmation of Commitments between the Department of Commerce and ICANN
IANA Functions Contract between the Department of Commerce and ICANN
Cooperative Agreement between the Department of Commerce and VeriSign (Network Solutions)

List of Independent Review Process Cases

RELATED TO THE REQUESTIONING OF AN EARLIER DELEGATION

Parties	*Extension*	*Relevant Decision*	*Case No.*	*Status*
ICM Registry v. Internet Corporation for Assigned names and Numbers	xxx	Questioning the reconsideration of previous ICANN Board 2005 decision in view of a GAC Advice	50 117 T 00224 08	IRP Declaration finding in favor of the Complainant TLD was delegated
Manwin Licensing International v. Internet Corporation for Assigned names and Numbers	xxx	Requestioning the delegation following the IRP Declaration in the *ICM Registry* case	50 117 T 00812 11	Joint Dismissal of IRP

RELATED TO A STRING SIMILARITY EVALUATION FINDING CONFUSING SIMILARITY

Parties	*Extension*	*Relevant Decision*	*Case No.*	*Status*
Booking.com BV v. Internet Corporation for Assigned Names and Numbers	hotels v. .hoteis	Questioning the outcome of the String Similarity Evaluation (SSP held that .hotels is confusingly similar to .hoteis; as a consequence, both applications were put in one contention set)	50-20-1400-0247	IRP Declaration naming ICANN the prevailing party and finding partially in favor of the Complainant TLD .hotels was delegated following a successful auction

RELATED TO A STRING CONFUSION OBJECTION DETERMINATION FINDING CONFUSING SIMILARITY

Parties	*Extension*	*Relevant Decision*	*Case No.*	*Status*
Vistaprint Limited v. Internet Corporation for Assigned Names and Numbers	webs v. .web	Questioning the outcome of the String Confusion Objection (ICDR Expert considered Web.com's objection to be successful)	01-14-0000 -6505	IRP Declaration naming ICANN the prevailing party and finding partially in favor of the Complainant TLDs.webs and.web were delegated following a successful auction

RELATED TO A COMMUNITY PRIORITY EVALUATION REFUSING TO GRANT PRIORITY TO THE APPLICATION

Parties	*Extension*	*Relevant Decision*	*Case No.*	*Status*
Dot Registry, LLC v. Internet Corporation for Assigned names and Numbers	inc, .llc, .llp	Questioning the outcome of the Community Priority Evaluation (EIU refused to grant community priority to Dot Registry's applications)	01-14-0001-5004	IRP Declaration naming Dot Registry the prevailing party; majority decision with a dissenting opinion

RELATED TO A COMMUNITY OBJECTION DETERMINATION DENYING THE APPLICATION

Parties	*Extension*	*Relevant Decision*	*Case No.*	*Status*
Corn Lake, LLC v. Internet Corporation for Assigned names and Numbers	charity	Questioning the outcome of the Community Objection (ICC Expert accepted the objection by the Independent Objector, even though another ICC Expert had rejected an almost identical Community objection)	01-15-0002-9938	IRP Declaration naming Corn Lake, LLC the prevailing party
dot Sport Limited v. Internet Corporation for Assigned Names and Numbers	sport	Questioning the outcome of the Community Objection (ICC Expert denied dSL's application as it was considered detrimental to SportAccord's community interests which the Expert recognized)	01-15-0002-9483	Pending

Parties	*Extension*	*Relevant Decision*	*Case No.*	*Status*
Donuts Inc. v. Internet Corporation for Assigned names and Numbers	sports, .ski and .rugby	Questioning the outcome of the Community Objection (ICC Expert denied Donuts' applications as these were considered detrimental to SportAccord's, Ski Federation's and Rugby Federation's respective community interests, which the expert recognized)	01-14-0001-6263	IRP Declaration finding in favor of ICANN Majority decision with a dissenting opinion

RELATED TO A LEGAL RIGHTS OBJECTION DETERMINATION DENYING AN OBJECTION TO AN APPLICATION

Parties	*Extension*	*Relevant Decision*	*Case No.*	*Status*
Merck KGaA v. Internet Corporation for Assigned names and Numbers	merck and .merckmsd	Questioning the outcome of the Legal Rights Objection (WIPO Expert denied Merck KGaA's objections)	01-14-0000-9604	IRP Declaration finding in favor of ICANN

RELATED TO A PUBLIC INTEREST OBJECTION DETERMINATION DENYING AN OBJECTION TO AN APPLICATION

Parties	*Extension*	*Relevant Decision*	*Case No.*	*Status*
Gulf Cooperation Council (GCC) v. Internet Corporation for Assigned names and Numbers	persiangulf	Questioning the outcome of a Community Objection (ICC Expert denied GCC's objection) and ICANN's alleged failure to protect geographic names adequately	01-14-0002-1065	Pending

RELATED TO A GAC ADVICE

Parties	*Extension*	*Relevant Decision*	*Case No.*	*Status*
DCA Trust v. Internet Corporation for Assigned names and Numbers	africa	Questioning the Board's acceptance of the GAC Advice to deny DCA Trust's application for .africa	50-2013-001083	IRP Declaration finding in favor of the Complainant
Amazon EU S.à.r.l. v. Internet Corporation for Assigned names and Numbers	amazon	Questioning the Board's acceptance of the GAC Advice to deny Amazon's application for .amazon	01-16-0000-7056	Pending
Better Living Management Co, Ltd. v. Internet Corporation for Assigned names and Numbers	thai	Questioning the Board's acceptance of the GAC Advice to deny the application for .thai	50-2014-000189	Closed
Asia Green IT System Bilgisayar San. ve Tic. Ltd. Sti. v. Internet Corporation for Assigned names and Numbers	islam and .halal	Questioning the Board's putting on hold the delegation of the .islam and .halal extensions following non-consensus GAC Advice	01-15-0005-9838	Pending

RELATED TO THE 2000 PROOF OF CONCEPT ROUND AND A COMMUNITY PRIORITY EVALUATION REFUSING TO GRANT PRIORITY TO THE APPLICATION

Parties	*Extension*	*Relevant Decision*	*Case No.*	*Status*
Commercial Connect v. Internet Corporation for Assigned names and Numbers	shop	Questioning ICANN's refusal to award the application in the 2000 proof of concept round and the outcome of the Community Priority Evaluation (EIU refused to grant community priority to Commercial Connect's application)	01-16-0000-2315	Pending

List of ICC Cases Related to Registries

Parties	*Extension*	*Relevant Decision*	*Case No.*	*Status*
Employ Media v. ICANN	jobs	Questioning ICANN's notice of breach of the Registry Agreement following an alleged change in the mission and purpose of the TLD operation	17917/VRO	Settled Employ Media continued the operation of the TLD

List of ICDR Cases Related to Registrars

Parties	*Extension*	*Relevant Decision*	*Case No.*	*Status*
Open TLD B.V. v. ICANN	N/A	Questioning ICANN's suspension of Open TLD B.V. as an ICANN-accredited registrar	01-15-0004-1379	Voluntary dismissal by Open TLD B.V. Suspension lifted

At the core of our analysis are the cases that have resulted in an Independent Review Process (IRP) decision. We do not systematically discuss or evaluate the approach taken by ICANN's evaluators during the application phase, nor by expert determinators appointed by Dispute Resolution Service Providers (DRSPs) to handle disputes related to applications. Rather, we concentrate on: (1) ICANN's actions or inactions after receiving requests for reconsiderations, (2) ICANN's arguments during IRPs when challenged on its actions and inactions, and (3) ICANN's handling of the remaining issues after an Independent Review Process (IRP) panel had rendered a decision.

In the light of this analysis of ICANN's approach, we can then suggest changes to the regulatory framework in view of the lessons learned, in order to prevent similar problems arising in the next round of gTLD applications. We will also comment on ICANN's recent efforts to improve its accountability within the framework of the so-called transition talks with the U.S. Government regarding the Internet Assigned Numbers Authority (IANA) functions.[3] We will focus in particular on the latest amendments to ICANN's Articles of Incorporation and Bylaws.

C. THE BOOK'S APPROACH

We first explain the regulatory framework governing applications, how they are evaluated, and how the affected parties can initiate and conduct any attendant objections and disputes (Chapter 2). The regulatory framework evolved over time and must be seen in the historic context of the creation of the Internet and of the policies that have shaped, and continue to shape, the Internet's governance. That is why Chapter 2 starts with a historic overview that will help understanding the applicable legal framework.

In Chapter 3, we explain the legal remedies available to applicants or any other interested party in relation to an application or its evaluation.

The next chapter, Chapter 4, comments on issues raised by the regulatory framework, independent of any specific case brought by applicants or other interested parties.

Chapter 5 is the most substantive part of this book. It contains a detailed description of each IRP case, and includes a summary of the claimant's main arguments, ICANN's response, the view of the IRP panel, and our own analysis.

Chapter 6 then sums up the concrete lessons learned from the discussion of the issues related to the regulatory framework as set out in REF Chapter 2 and in particular as they came to light during and after the IRP cases described in Chapter 5.

3. The Internet Assigned Numbers Authority (IANA) is responsible for the global coordination of the DNS Root, IP addressing and other Internet protocol resources. Until 30 September 2016, it was controlled by the U.S. Government who abandoned its oversight role to the benefit of ICANN.

In Chapter 7, we take on the ambitious task of making a list of action points and concrete proposals which would, in our view, result in an improved regulatory framework. Our approach is twofold: we propose textual changes to the current accountability framework, and in Chapter 8 we propose more fundamental changes of a structural nature, which are intended to improve the entire operational environment for Internet governance.

As we proceeded with the preparation of this book, a Cross Community Working Group on Accountability (CCWG-Accountability) was installed which has also suggested changes to the regulatory framework. However, the context within which this CCWG was established, and within which it operated (*i.e.*, in relation to a transitioning of the IANA functions) was completely different from the context in which we made our analysis and developed suggestions to amend the framework (the IRP cases).

On 27 May 2016, the Board approved the draft amendments to the Articles of Incorporation and Bylaws. These were intended to become applicable after the transitioning of the IANA functions, which took place on 1 October 2016. They contain several of our suggestions, and we are, of course, happy about this. We will comment in more detail on this latest development in Chapter 7 and Chapter 7, where we discuss additional changes that we consider necessary.

D. FUTURE EDITIONS

This edition inevitably contains errors, omissions and confusions, which will require correction, clarification and further development in future editions, to keep pace with the ongoing developments in the field. Corrections, comments and questions are encouraged, by email to flippetillion@gmail.com.

CHAPTER 2
The Regulatory Framework

A. ICANN AND ITS ROLE

1. Introduction

ICANN is the abbreviation for 'Internet Corporation for Assigned Names and Numbers', a not-for-profit public-benefit corporation formed in September 1998.[4] ICANN's primary mission is to coordinate, at the highest level, the Internet's systems of unique identifiers globally,[5] and in particular to ensure the stable and secure operation of the Internet's unique identifier systems, the Domain Name System or 'DNS'.[6]

The DNS is a hierarchical structure that permits the use of a stable and orderly system of unique identifiers, allowing computers to communicate over the Internet. The Internet is a network of computer networks. Every computer on this network has a unique identifying Internet Protocol address or 'IP address'. Each IP address can be substituted with an easy to remember set of characters or letters which becomes the domain name. Domain names have become part of website addresses, email addresses and File Transfer Protocol (FTP) servers. The DNS helps make the Internet more accessible by allowing users to type in a domain name instead of an IP address, for example typing 'www.wolterskluwer.com' rather than typing '85.17.2.5'. Even in a world where applications can be a substitute for more traditional webpages, and where the majority of traffic is generated via search engines and not via direct navigation, domain names have retained much of their original appeal. A domain name can provide a source of recognition and serve as an anchor of trust. When visiting the website of a brand owner, the domain name in the browser's address bar may give

4. *See* California Secretary of State, Business information for entity number 2121683, available on http://kepler.sos.ca.gov/.
5. ICANN, Articles of Incorporation, Article 3; ICANN, Bylaws, Article I(1).
6. ICANN, Bylaws, Article I(1).

assurance that the visitor is dealing with the true brand owner. The DNS also enables a single domain name to be linked to multiple servers, making it possible to offer a redundancy solution in case a server is down. The DNS also offers crucial support for the technological developments known as the 'Internet of things'. Developed in the 1980s,[7] the DNS remains a critical backbone supporting the Internet and the digital economy.

As the invention of the Internet and the DNS predates the existence of ICANN by many years, it is interesting to look at how ICANN became the custodian of this critical infrastructure.

2. History of the Internet

a. *The Invention of the Internet and the DNS*

It is hard to imagine a world where computers are stand-alone devices unable to communicate with each other. In today's world, we are constantly connected to a vast network of computers and servers via our smartphones, personal computers and tablets. In modern households, refrigerators, home appliances and other electronic devices are also connected and monitored via the Internet. The Internet has fundamentally changed the way we live. However, it may come as a surprise to many that the origins of the Internet can be traced back as far as the 1960s.

Until the late-1960s, long-distance communications occurred over circuit-switched networks. In a circuit-switched network, a continuous physical connection is created between the sender and the receiver, which lasts for the duration of the communication. In a circuit-switched network, there can be only one communication session per circuit at any one time. The main advantage of a circuit-switched network is that it provides for a continuous stream of data or bits and that, for the duration of the connection, maximal use can be made of the available bandwidth. Once the connection has been established, there will be no delays caused by other users of the network.

But, its main advantage is also its biggest weakness: excess bandwidth in a circuit-switched network is unavailable to other connections on the same network, making the network inefficient for the communication of mass data among a broad user network. Already in the early to mid-1960s, researchers were developing a communication method using packets rather than circuits. The first paper on this so-called packet

7. P. Mockapetris, *Domain names – concepts and facilities*, Network Working Group Request for Comments # 882, November 1983, https://tools.ietf.org/html/rfc882; P. Mockapetris, *Domain names – implementation and specification*, Network Working Group Request for Comments # 883, November 1983, https://tools.ietf.org/html/rfc883; Paul Mockapetris, *Domain Names – Concepts and Facilities*, Network Working Group Request For Comments # 1034, November 1987, http://www.ietf.org/rfc/rfc1034.txt; Paul Mockapetris, *Domain Names – Implementation and Specification*, Network Working Group Request For Comments # 1035, November 1987, http://www.ietf.org/rfc/rfc1035.txt.

switching theory was published in 1961.[8] Via packet switching technology, the data is divided into smaller packets and these packets are sent through the network independently.[9] The packets are distributed over multiple communication sessions, allowing for a more efficient use of the network's capacity and the communication of bigger data, divided in small packets. When, in 1965, researchers managed to make the first long distance communication between a computer at the Massachusetts Institute of Technology (MIT) and a computer in California, they used a low speed dial-up telephone line.[10] The experiment showed that computers could work together over long distances, but reaffirmed the need for packet switching technology as the circuit switched telephone system proved to be inadequate for communicating computer data efficiently over long distances.[11] Researchers quickly understood that packet switching technology would be more efficient and would allow for the communication of data in excess of the maximum capacity of single telephone lines.

The U.S. Department of Defense was quick to recognize the military potential of a computer communication network. Already back in 1951, the U.S. Air Force had commissioned MIT to design an early-warning network to guard against a Soviet nuclear bomber attack. The network was to include a network of computers capable of communicating data about airplane movements in 'real time'.[12] The technical developments in the mid-1960s created an ideal environment for the Department of Defense, through its Advanced Research Project Agency (ARPA) to invest in a research project to build a decentralized communication network, and it did not take long for researchers to obtain USD 1 million in funding.[13] In 1967, the first plan for this communication network, the ARPANET, was published.[14] The plan was later refined to include packet switching technology, and the design was put into practice in September 1969 when the first packet switch, called Interface Message Processor (IMP), and a host computer were connected at the University of California, Los Angeles (UCLA). One month later, a second host computer and IMP were connected at the Stanford Research Institute (SRI), and on 29 October 1969, the first successful host-to-host message was sent from UCLA to SRI using the ARPANET.[15] Other institutions soon joined, connecting universities, the military and industries. In December 1970, researchers finished the

---

8. L. Kleinrock, *Information Flow in Large Communication Nets*, July 1961, M.I.T. RLE Quarterly Progress Report, http://www.lk.cs.ucla.edu/data/files/Kleinrock/Information%20Flow%20in%20Large%20Communication%20Nets0.pdf.
9. NTIA, *Telecommunications: Glossary of Telecommunication Terms*, Business & Economics 1997, P-1.
10. Barry M. Leiner et al., *A Brief History of the Internet*, http://www.internetsociety.org/internet/what-internet/history-internet/brief-history-internet.
11. Leiner et al., *supra* n. 10.
12. Mitch Waldrop, *DARPA and the Internet revolution*, http://www.darpa.mil/attachments/%282015%29%20Global%20Nav%20-%20About%20Us%20-%20History%20-%20Resources%20-%2050th%20-%20Internet%20%28Approved%29.pdf.
13. Jonathan Weinberg, *ICANN and the Problem of Legitimacy*, 50 Duke Law Journal 187, 198 (2000); Waldrop, *supra* n. 8.
14. Leiner et al., *supra* n. 10.
15. Jessica Savio, *Browsing history: A heritage site has been set up in Boelter Hall 3420, the room the first Internet message originated in*, Daily Bruin, http://dailybruin.com/2011/04/01/browsing_history/.

development of a communication protocol, called the Network Control Protocol (NCP), which was implemented on the ARPANET throughout 1971 and 1972 and allowed ARPANET users to develop applications.[16] In 1972, email was introduced and quickly became one of the most popular applications on the ARPANET, allowing researchers to communicate better over long distances.[17] Also in 1972, the File Transfer Protocol (FTP) was developed, allowing the efficient and reliable transfer of files between host computers at remote locations and creating the possibility to store and access files at remote locations.[18]

However, the ARPANET was not the Internet, nor did it evolve into the Internet. It was a research project that connected at most about 200 people in a twenty-one-node network, and it was not very user-friendly.[19] The ARPANET's biggest achievement is probably that it brought together the people who later played a role in the technical development of the Internet.[20]

By the mid-1970s, many other computer networks emerged. *E.g.*, NASA established a computer network, the U.S. Department of Energy set up two, and the U.S. National Science Foundation (NSF) provided a grant to the Computer Science community to set up yet another network.[21] The majority of these early networks was intended for use within closed communities. Each network had its own design and characteristics with many different communication protocols, which made them incompatible with one another. In the early 1970s, researchers working on the ARPANET had been looking for ways to integrate radio and satellite networks into the ARPANET computer network.[22] The networks were largely incompatible; they operated in a completely different environment, using completely different transmission speeds and infrastructure. The researchers realized that the best way to integrate these networks was by establishing a gateway between the networks that would operate as a sort of translator between them. The idea of a router was born. Both networks would need to comply with the – yet to be developed – standards of the router, and the router's sole job would be to translate ARPANET packets into radio/satellite packets and *vice versa*.[23] The use of routers and the adoption of a universal protocol made interconnection between a virtually infinite number of networks possible.

16. Leiner et al., *supra* n. 10.
17. Leiner et al., *supra* n. 10.; Waldrop, *supra* n. 12.; Jim White, *A Proposed Mail Protocol*, RFC # 524, https://tools.ietf.org/html/rfc524 (accessed 5 April, 2016); Abhay Bhushan, Ken Pogran, Ray Tomlinson & Jim White, *Standardising Network Mail Headers*, Request for Comments # 561, https://tools.ietf.org/html/rfc561.
18. Abhay Bhushan, *The File Transfer Protocol*, Request for Comments # 354, https://tools.ietf.org/html/rfc354.
19. Milton Mueller, *Ruling the Root : Internet Governance and the Taming of Cyberspace*, 74 (MIT Press 2002).
20. Mueller, *supra* n. 19.
21. Leiner et al., *supra* n. 10; Weinberg, *supra* n. 13, p. 193.
22. Waldrop, *supra* n. 12.
23. Waldrop, *supra* n. 12.

The first version of a universal inter-networking protocol, or 'Transmission Control Protocol/Internet Protocol' (TCP/IP) was developed from 1974 onwards[24] and was deployed for military networks in 1982–1983.[25] Other networks also started using the TCP/IP to connect with each other in an expanding network of networks, which became known as the Internet.[26] From its early stages, the scope of this emerging Internet was international; the network of networks included the ARPANET and several U.S. research centers and universities as well as European institutes, such as University College London, the French Cyclades network, the British Post Office, etc.[27]

The connection between computers on the network was established using a unique numbering system. Such a system was first proposed by Jon Postel, who wrote in 1972:

> 'I propose that there be a czar (me?) who hands out official socket numbers for use by standard protocols. This czar should also keep track of and publish a list of those socket numbers where host specific services can be obtained.'[28]

Jon Postel became the first 'czar' for handing out unique numbers to network computers on the emerging Internet, and he refined the numbering system throughout the 1970s and the beginning of the 1980s.[29] In 1981, the addresses had a fixed length of four octets or 32 bits.[30] This addressing system became known by the name Internet Protocol version 4 (IPv4),[31] and was the first version that was effectively implemented on the ARPANET.[32] IPv4 has been replaced by Internet Protocol version 6 (IPv6),

24. Vinton Cerf and Robert Kahn, *A Protocol for Packet Network Interconnection*, COM-22 V 5 IEEE Transactions on Communications Technology 627, 641 (1974).
25. Waldrop, *supra* n. 12.
26. Waldrop, *supra* n. 12.
27. Jon Postel, *Assigned Numbers*, Network Working Group Request for Comments # 790, http://www.ietf.org/rfc/rfc0790.txt.
28. Jon Postel, *Proposed Standard Socket Numbers*, Network Working Group Request for Comments # 349, https://tools.ietf.org/html/rfc349.
29. Jon Postel, Nancy Neigus, *Socket Number List*, Network Working Group Request for Comments # 433, 22 December 1972, https://www.ietf.org/rfc/rfc0433.txt; Nancy Neigus, Jon Postel, *Socket Number List*, Network Working Group Request For Comments # 503, 13 April 1973, http://www.ietf.org/rfc/rfc0503.txt; Jon Postel, *Assigned Link* Numbers, Network Working Group Request For Comments # 604, 26 December 1973, http://www.ietf.org/rfc/rfc0604.txt; Jon Postel, *Assigned Numbers*, Network Working Group Request For Comments # 739, http://www.ietf.org/rfc/rfc0739.txt; Jon Postel, *Assigned Numbers*, Network Working Group Request For Comments # 750, 26 September 1978, http://www.ietf.org/rfc/rfc0750.txt; Jon Postel, *Assigned Numbers*, Network Working Group Request For Comments # 755, 3 May 1979, http://www.ietf.org/rfc/rfc0755.txt; Jon Postel, *Assigned Numbers*, Network Working Group Request For Comments # 758, August 1979, http://www.ietf.org/rfc/rfc0758.txt; Jon Postel, *Assigned Numbers*, Network Working Group Request For Comments # 762, January 1980, http://www.ietf.org/rfc/rfc0762.txt; Jon Postel, *Assigned Numbers*, Network Working Group Request For Comments # 770, September 1980, http://www.ietf.org/rfc/rfc0770.txt; Jon Postel, *Assigned Numbers*, Network Working Group Request For Comments # 776, January 1981, http://www.ietf.org/rfc/rfc0776.txt; Jon Postel, *Assigned Numbers*, Network Working Group Request For Comments # 790, September 1981 http://www.ietf.org/rfc/rfc0790.txt.
30. Jon Postel (ed.), *Internet Protocol DARPA Internet Program Protocol Specification*, Request for Comments # 791, http://www.ietf.org/rfc/rfc0791.txt.
31. Jon Postel (ed.), *supra* n. 30 p. 11.
32. Jon Postel, *Assigned Numbers*, Network Working Group Request for Comments # 790, September 1981 http://www.ietf.org/rfc/rfc0790.txt, p. 3.

which uses 128 bits, theoretically allowing 2^{128} IP addresses,[33] which is far more than the soon to be exhausted 2^{32} (approximately 4.29 billion) IP addresses available under IPv4. IPv4 however remains responsible for the majority of Internet traffic today,[34] and the transition to IPv6 creates technological challenges as demonstrated by the large number of publications dealing with transition mechanisms.[35]

Throughout the 1980s, the assignment of IP addresses remained in the hands of individuals; first the 'czar', Jon Postel,[36] who handed over the assigning authority to fellow researcher Joyce Reynolds in 1983.[37] The first steps towards making the

33. S. Deering and R. Hinden, *Internet Protocol, Version 6 (IPv6) Specification*, Network Working Group Request for Comments # 2460, https://www.ietf.org/rfc/rfc2460.txt.
34. Border Gateway Protocol, *Analysis Report*, http://bgp.potaroo.net/index-bgp.html.
35. *See e.g.*, C. Huitema et al., *Unmanaged Networks IPv6? Transition Scenarios*, Network Working Group Request for Comments # 3750, April 2004, https://www.ietf.org/rfc/rfc3750.txt; C.Huitema et al., *Evaluation of IPv6 Transition Mechanisms for Unmanaged Networks*, Network Working Group Request for Comments # 3904, September 2004, https://www.ietf.org/rfc/rfc3904.txt; M-K. Shin (ed.), Y-G. Hong et al., *Application Aspects of IPv6 Transition*, Network Working Group Request for Comments # 4038, March 2005, https://www.ietf.org/rfc/rfc4038.txt; E. Normark and R. Gilligan, *Basic Transition Mechanisms for IPv6 Hosts and Routers*, Network Working Group Request for Comments # 4213, October 2005, https://tools.ietf.org/html/rfc4213; J. Wiljakka (ed.), *Analysis on IPv6 Transition in Third Generation Partnership Project (3GPP) Networks*, Network Working Group Request for Comments # 4215, October 2005, https://tools.ietf.org/html/rfc4215; E. Davies, S. Krishnan and P. Savola, *IPv6 Transition/Coexistence Security Considerations*, Network Working Group Request for Comments # 4942, September 2007, https://www.ietf.org/rfc/rfc4942.txt; G. Camarillo, K. El Malki and V. Gurbani, *IPv6 Transition in the Session Initiation Protocol (SIP)*, Internet Engineering Task Force Request for Comments # 6157, April 2011, https://tools.ietf.org/html/rfc6157; J. Arkko and F. Baker, *Guidelines for Using IPv6 Transition Mechanisms during IPv6 Deployment*, Internet Engineering Task Force Request for Comments # 6180, May 2011, https://tools.ietf.org/html/rfc6180; X. Li et al., *The China Education and Research Network (CERNET) IVI Translation Design and Deployment for the IPv4/IPv6 Coexistence and Transition*, Internet Engineering Task Force Request for Comments # 6219, May 2011, https://tools.ietf.org/html/rfc6219; S. Jiang, D. Guo and B. Carpenter, *An Incremental Carrier-Grade NAT (CGN) for IPv6 Transition*, Internet Engineering Task Force Request for Comments # 6264, June 2011, https://tools.ietf.org/html/rfc6264; Jason Livingood, *Considerations for Transitioning Content to IPv6*, Internet Engineering Task Force Request for Comments # 6589, April 2012, https://tools.ietf.org/html/rfc6589.
36. Jon Postel, *Assigned Numbers*, Network Working Group Request For Comments # 790, September 1981 http://www.ietf.org/rfc/rfc0790.txt; Jon Postel and James Vernon, *Assigned Numbers*, Network Working Group Request For Comments # 820, January 1983, http://www.ietf.org/rfc/rfc0820.txt.
37. Joyce Reynolds and Jon Postel, *Assigned Numbers*, Network Working Group Request For Comments # 870, October 1983, http://www.ietf.org/rfc/rfc0870.txt; Joyce Reynolds and Jon Postel, *Assigned Numbers*, Network Working Group Request For Comments # *900*, June 1984, http://www.ietf.org/rfc/rfc0900.txt; Joyce Reynolds and Jon Postel, *Assigned Numbers*, Network Working Group Request For Comments # *923*, October 1984, http://www.ietf.org/rfc/rfc0923.txt; Joyce Reynolds and Jon Postel, *Assigned Numbers*, Network Working Group Request For Comments # 943, April 1985, http://www.ietf.org/rfc/rfc0943.txt; Joyce Reynolds and Jon Postel, *Assigned Numbers*, Network Working Group Request For Comments # 960, December 1985, http://www.ietf.org/rfc/rfc0960.txt (accessed 22 April 2016); Joyce Reynolds and Jon Postel, *Assigned Numbers*, Joyce Reynolds and Jon Postel, *Assigned Numbers*, Network Working Group Request For Comments # 990, November 1986, http://www.ietf.org/rfc/rfc0990.txt; Joyce Reynolds and Jon Postel, *Assigned Numbers*, Network Working Group Request For Comments # 1010, May 1987, http://www.ietf.org/rfc/rfc1010.txt.

assigning authority more institutionalized came with the creation of IANA. IANA is mentioned for the first time in a publication of 1988.[38] Joyce Reynolds remained IANA's contact until the 1990s.[39]

Computers on the Internet were able – as they still are today – to communicate efficiently via the IP addresses. The numeric IP addresses are less easily recognizable for humans. Every IP address that was assigned to a network was also assigned to the name of the network.[40] In the early stages, with a fairly limited number of computers on the network, it was relatively easy to navigate through the directory of names and numbers and to identify the correct computer. But as the network expanded, the directory became difficult to manage; the master file of the directory required constant updating, and all computers on the network needed a copy of the master file, which resulted in errors and slowness caused by the continual need to download the master file.[41] A more structured approach, adapted to the growing size of the Internet was required. In 1981, the idea to create a hierarchical name-space and to partition the name-space into different domains was brought forward.[42] The idea was further developed,[43] and ultimately resulted in the crystallization of a hierarchical structure, which became known as the DNS.[44]

At the top of the DNS hierarchical structure is a single unique root. The unique root distinguishes the Internet from alternative networks. The root contains the root zone file and thirteen clusters of root name servers.[45] The root zone file is the list of Top Level Domains (TLDs), with references to the name servers for each TLD (the TLD name server). TLDs, such as .com, .org, .mil, .gov, .us, .eu, .fr, etc., appear at the right of the rightmost dot in an Internet address or domain name. The root name servers are

38. Jon Postel, *IAB official protocol standards*, Network Working Group Request for Comments # 1083, December 1988, http://www.ietf.org/rfc/rfc1083.txt.
39. Joyce Reynolds, Jon Postel, *Assigned Numbers*, Network Working Group Request For Comments # *1700*, October 1994, http://www.ietf.org/rfc/rfc1700.txt; Joyce Reynolds (ed.), *Assigned Numbers: RFC 1700 is Replaced by an On-line Database*, Network Working Group Request For Comments # 3232, January 2002, http://www.ietf.org/rfc/rfc3232.txt.
40. Jon Postel, *Assigned Numbers*, Network Working Group Request for Comments # 790, September 1981 http://www.ietf.org/rfc/rfc0790.txt.
41. A. Yasuda and T. Thompson, *TELNET Data Entry Terminal Option DODIIS Implementation*, Network Working Group Request for Comments # 1043, February 1988, http://www.ietf.org/rfc/rfc1043.txt. J. Klensin, *Role of the Domain Name System (DNS)*, Network Working Group Request for Comments # 3467, February 2003, https://tools.ietf.org/html/rfc3467.
42. D.L. Mills, *Internet Name Domains*, Network Working Group Request for Comments # 799, September 1981, https://tools.ietf.org/html/rfc799.
43. Zaw-Sing Su and Jon Postel, *The Domain Naming Convention for Internet User Applications*, Network Working Group Request For Comments # 819, August 1982, http://www.ietf.org/rfc/rfc819.txt; Zaw-Sing Su, *A Distributed System for Internet Name Service*, Network Working Group Request For Comments # 830, October 1982, http://www.ietf.org/rfc/rfc830.txt; J. Klensin, *Role of the Domain Name System (DNS)*, Network Working Group Request For Comments # 3467, February 2003 https://tools.ietf.org/html/rfc3467.
44. Paul Mockapetris, *Domain Names – Concepts and Facilities*, Network Working Group Request For Comments # 1034, November 1987, http://www.ietf.org/rfc/rfc1034.txt; Paul Mockapetris, *Domain Names – Implementation and Specification*, Network Working Group Request For Comments # 1035, November 1987, http://www.ietf.org/rfc/rfc1035.txt.
45. Mueller, *supra* n. 19, p. 47.

specialized computers that provide connections between physical networks;[46] they operate as the place where the query for a unique IP address starts. The process is as follows: computers connect to the Internet, using a modem, Ethernet or other communication line. Connections are provided by Internet Service Providers (ISPs). When a computer wants to access a specific computer or server on the Internet (*e.g.*, the server on which Google's search engine is available or the server of Wolters Kluwer's website), the ISP will initiate a query for the unique IP address. For example, when an Internet user wants to access Wolters Kluwer's website using *wolterskluwer.com*, the ISP's name server will start its query at one of the root name servers. The root name server will respond by giving the location of the TLD name server – the .com name server in our example – as it appears in the root zone file. The ISP's name server will then query the TLD name server. The TLD name server, in turn, maintains records of all Second Level Domains (SLDs) in a specific TLD. In our example, 'wolterskluwer' is the SLD within the .com TLD. The operator of the TLD, named the 'registry' or 'registry operator', is responsible for maintaining accurate records of all SLD name servers, and will provide the ISP's name server with the location of the SLD name server. The SLD name server is generally controlled by the domain name holder, who can use the domain name for *e.g.*, the exchange of emails, file sharing or, since the invention of the World Wide Web (WWW) in 1989 and its implementation in 1990,[47] the publication of websites. The SLD name server can also operate as a second-level registry and refer to a sub-level domain.

The obvious benefit of the DNS hierarchical structure is that it is no longer necessary for each computer to have a full list of addresses for every other computer. Each computer needs only the address of an official root name server.[48] In practice, the root name servers will not be queried for every domain name request. The ISP's servers will cache the information and rarely revisit the root name servers.

Another advantage of the DNS is that multiple IP addresses can be linked to a single domain name, allowing for redundancy and better performance.

b. *Evolution of Governance Structure*

(1) The Rapid Expansion of the Internet

In the early stages of the Internet, one of the most important networks was the National Science Foundation NET (NSFNET), developed with the backing of the National Science Foundation (NSF). The NSF is a U.S. Government agency that has the statutory mission 'to promote the progress of science; to advance the national health, prosperity and welfare; to secure the national defence.'[49] Unlike most other early computer networks, the NSFNET was designed to be open to all academic users and not limited

46. Mueller, *supra* n. 19, p. 47.
47. CERN, *The birth of the web*, http://home.cern/topics/birth-web.
48. Mueller, *supra* n. 19, p. 47.
49. *NSF Act of 1950*, Pub. L. 81-507 (codified at 42 U.S.C. 1862).

to mere handfuls of specialized contractors and researchers.[50] The NSFNET essentially provided the technical backbone to establish a fast growing network of networks. Between 1991 and 1992 the network almost doubled in size, going from connecting over 3,500 networks to over 6,000 networks.[51] The amount of data transferred increased from 1.3 trillion bytes per month in 1991 to 17.8 trillion bytes per month in 1994.[52] The popularity of the Internet was boosted by the invention of the WWW and the use of the Internet for commercial purposes.

Between 1991 and 1992, the NSF had assumed responsibility for coordinating and funding the management of the non-military part of the Internet infrastructure.[53] The NSF was granted statutory authority to allow commercial activity on the NSFNET in 1992,[54] and this created interest in the private sector. On 31 December 1992, the NSF entered into a cooperative agreement with Network Solutions, Inc. (NSI).[55] NSI took over responsibility for the coordination and maintenance of the DNS, and registered domain names in the generic gTLDs on a first come, first served basis.[56]

(2) The Commercialization of the Internet and Its Challenges

On 13 September 1995, the NSF allowed NSI to charge user fees for the registration of domain names.[57] NSI was authorized to impose an annual fee of USD 50 per second level domain name in .gov, .edu, .com, .net and .org, 30% of which was to be deposited into a separate account for the preservation and enhancement of the intellectual infrastructure of the Internet.[58] Nevertheless, NSI's monopoly over domain name registrations gave rise to criticism: concern grew over the stability and regulation of the DNS, and the number of trademark disputes regarding the Internet's naming system rapidly increased.[59] It was not long before the U.S. Government took steps to address the growing dissatisfaction about the absence of competition, the commercialization of the Internet and the lack of a formal and accountable structure to manage the Internet's critical infrastructure and functions.[60] The cooperative agreement between the NSF and NSI was set to expire on 30 September 1998.[61] The growing criticism and the

50. National Science Foundation, *The Launch of NSFNET*, https://www.nsf.gov/about/history/nsf0050/internet/launch.htm.
51. National Science Foundation, *supra* n. 50.
52. National Science Foundation, *supra* n. 50.
53. NTIA, *Management of Internet Names and Addresses: statement of policy*, https://www.ntia.doc.gov/files/ntia/publications/6_5_98dns.pdf.
54. *Scientific and Advanced-Technology Act of 1992*, Pub. L. 102-476 Section 4(9), 106 Stat. 2297, 2300 (codified at 42 U.S.C. 1862).
55. NTIA, *supra* n. 53.
56. NTIA, *supra* n. 53.
57. ICANN, *Amendment 4 to Cooperative Agreement Between NSI and U.S. Government*, https://archive.icann.org/en/nsi/coopagmt-amend4-13sep95.htm.
58. ICANN, *supra* n. 57.
59. U.S. GAO, *Letter regarding Relationship with the Internet Corporation for Assigned Names and Numbers*, http://www.gao.gov/new.items/og00033r.pdf.
60. NTIA, *supra* n. 53.
61. ICANN, *Cooperative Agreement No. NCR-9218742*, http://archive.icann.org/en/nsi/coopagmt-01jan93.htm.

upcoming expiry date created a clear incentive for the U.S. Government to affirm its authority over the Internet and to have an alternative Internet Governance system installed before the expiration of the contract.

(3) Privatizing Internet Governance

In response to the growing criticism concerning Internet Governance, and in anticipation of the expiry date of the cooperative agreement, the Clinton administration began privatization efforts in July 1997 in an attempt to increase competition and to promote international participation in the DNS.[62] The U.S. Department of Commerce (DoC) issued a request for comments to ascertain the views of the public regarding various DNS management proposals as well as the underlying policy issues.[63] The U.S. Government received 432 comments,[64] and it was clear from the start that the U.S. Government and the public recognized the global significance of the Internet, and that they were looking for an accountable and fair governance structure, aimed at increasing competition and relying on market mechanisms and self-governance by the private sector, with input from governments.[65] The tension between private sector-led self-governance and governmental input was apparent from the very start, and commentators asked for clarification about the role of governments and the limitation of their involvement.[66] To promote competition, there was immediate and considerable support for 'cautiously and judiciously' adding gTLDs once the new governance structure was in place. The public was concerned, however, about the stability of the system and the potential for a significant increase in domain name and trademark disputes, and it was wary of new governance mechanisms.[67] Almost twenty years later, these concerns are still very much alive.

(a) Creating Policy: The Green Paper

On 30 January 1998, the DoC issued a proposal to improve the technical management of Internet names and addresses.[68] The proposal, which became known as the 'Green Paper', was published on 20 February 1998,[69] and a public comment period ran until 23

62. NTIA, *supra* n. 53.
63. NTIA, *Registration and Administration of Internet Domain Names – Summary of Comments*, https://www.ntia.doc.gov/other-publication/1997/registration-and-administration-internet-domain-names-summary-comments-docket.
64. NTIA, *Domain Name Comments Index*, https://www.ntia.doc.gov/legacy/ntiahome/domainname/email/list.htm.
65. NTIA, *supra* n. 63.
66. NTIA, *supra* n. 63.
67. NTIA, *supra* n. 63.
68. NTIA, *A Proposal to Improve Technical Management of Internet Names and Addresses – Discussion Draft*, https://www.ntia.doc.gov/files/ntia/publications/dnsdrft.txt ('Green Paper').
69. NTIA, *Federal Register Online: Improvement of Technical Management of Internet Names and Addresses*, https://www.ntia.doc.gov/files/ntia/publications/022098fedreg.txt.

March 1998.[70] The Green Paper set out a plan whereby the U.S. Government would gradually transfer existing IANA functions, the root system and the appropriate databases to a new not-for-profit corporation.[71] The plan was for the U.S. Government to transfer operational responsibility to the new entity, but to maintain policy oversight 'to assure stability until the new corporation is established and stable, phasing out as soon as possible'.[72]

Many commentators from the international community criticized the Green Paper, emphasizing the international scope of the Internet and the importance for the U.S. Government to acknowledge the Internet's inherently global nature and to involve the global community.[73] The European Community (now, the European Union) called for a more international approach in Internet governance, and expressed their concern that, 'in the name of the globalization and privatization of the Internet' the U.S. would claim and consolidate 'permanent US jurisdiction over the Internet as a whole.'[74] The United Nations, in connection with its Asia-Pacific Development Information Programme (APDIP) called for increased transparency and for the further progress and administration of the Internet 'in partnership with an organization which unmistakably represents the international community of Internet regulators, providers and users.'[75] It also warned that '[t]he call to relinquish government control over this critical resource may be premature and counter-productive', as 'in the vast majority of countries, access to the Internet depends wholly on Government engagement, participation and support'.[76] The Japanese Telecommunications Bureau shared the call for internationalization of the Internet's management and emphasized the need for democratic decision-making and fairness.[77] Similar concerns were expressed by the Internet industry and civil society in Asia, Australia and New Zealand.[78] The International Trademark Association (INTA) also noted 'the importance of incorporating and

70. NTIA, *Statement of Policy on the Management of Internet Names and Addresses*, https://www.ntia.doc.gov/federal-register-notice/1998/statement-policy-management-internet-names-and-addresses.
71. NTIA, *supra* n. 68.
72. NTIA, *supra* n. 68.
73. As mentioned above, the scope of the emerging Internet was international from the beginning. Moreover, one of the Internet's most important applications, the world wide web, was invented by Tim Berners-Lee, a British scientist at CERN in Europe. It is fair to say that the invention of the world wide web and CERN's decision in 1993 to introduce it into the public domain contributed significantly to the success, the further development and the international appeal of the Internet.
74. NTIA, *Comments of the Generic Top Level Domain Memorandum of Understanding Policy Advisory Body on Green Paper*, https://www.ntia.doc.gov/legacy/ntiahome/domainname/130dftmail/03_20_98.htm.
75. NTIA, *Comments of the US Council for International Business to the Department of Commerce on the 'Proposal to Improve Technical Management of Internet Names and Addresses'*, https://www.ntia.doc.gov/legacy/ntiahome/domainname/130dftmail/03_23_98-10.htm.
76. NTIA, *supra* n. 75.
77. NTIA, *Comments on NTIA's green paper by Ministry of Posts and Telecommunications of Japan*, https://www.ntia.doc.gov/legacy/ntiahome/domainname/130dftmail/03_23_98-2.htm.
78. *See* NTIA, *FICPI Discussion Draft on 'A Proposal to Improve Technical Management of Internet Names and Addresses'*, https://www.ntia.doc.gov/legacy/ntiahome/domainname/130dftmail/03_21_98.htm (21 March 1998); NTIA, *Australian Internet Industry Response to NTIA's Green Paper*, https://www.ntia.doc.gov/legacy/ntiahome/domainname/130dftmail/03_23_98-1.htm

being mindful of the international and commercial nature of the Internet.'[79] In the U.S. itself, academics, companies and associations voiced a similar plea to include the international community.[80]

A significant number of commentators expressed their support for a proposed plan to hand substantial authority over Internet policy to a Swiss not-for-profit organization called CORE (International Council of Registrars).[81] The plan, that came to be known

(23 March 1998); NTIA, *Asia Network Research Response to NTIA's Green Paper*, https://www.ntia.doc.gov/legacy/ntiahome/domainname/130dftmail/04_06_98.htm (6 April 1998).

79. NTIA, *INTA Response to the U.S. Government Paper on the Improvement of Technical Management of Internet Names and Addresses*, https://www.ntia.doc.gov/legacy/ntiahome/domainname/130dftmail/scanned/INTA.htm.

80. *See* NTIA, *Comments by IBM Corporation on Docket Entitled 'Improvement of Technical Management of Internet Names and Addresses'*, https://www.ntia.doc.gov/legacy/ntiahome/domainname/130dftmail/03_22_98.htm (23 March 1998): '[I]t is important that this plan be, and be seen as, a global and not a U.S. plan. To that end, the U.S. should actively seek and obtain the support of other countries and relevant international organizations for this approach. At the same time, the expectation that non-U.S. citizens would have unfettered access to the governing bodies envisioned in the plan, and would indeed have major representation on them, needs to be both clarified and emphasized.'; NTIA, *Disney Online Response to NTIA's Green Paper*, https://www.ntia.doc.gov/legacy/ntiahome/domainname/130dftmail/scanned/Disney.htm (20 March 1998): Comments by Disney Online, the online division of The Walt Disney Company of 20 March 1998, highlighted the importance of including the international community and expressed the wish that, within the new not-for-profit corporation, the 'Board is truly reflective of the online community and includes representatives from end users, trademark holders, international entities and governments.'; NTIA, *U.S. Civil Liberties Organizations Response to NTIA's Green Paper*, https://www.ntia.doc.gov/legacy/ntiahome/domainname/130dftmail/03_23_98-8.htm (23 March 1998): comments by U.S. civil liberties organizations such as the Electronic Frontier Foundation (EFF) and the Computer Professionals for Social Responsibility; NTIA, *MIT's Analysis of the Domain Name System Policy by a Private Institution*, https://www.ntia.doc.gov/legacy/ntiahome/domainname/130dftmail/03_17_98.htm (17 March 1998): comments by researchers at MIT of 17 March 1998, stating that, in the framework of Internet governance 'Conscientious international consultations are imperative (tedious as they may be, the alternative is much worse).'

81. *See e.g.*, NTIA, *Comment on "green paper" (Pat Forresta)l*, 31 January 1998, https://www.ntia.doc.gov/legacy/ntiahome/domainname/130dftmail/01_31_98.htm; NTIA, *A proposal to improve technical management of internet names and addresses (Robert M. Rutherford)*, 31 January 1998, https://www.ntia.doc.gov/legacy/ntiahome/domainname/130dftmail/01_31_98.htm; NTIA, *Oversight of the Non-Profit Corp. (Amit Mehrotra)*, 2 February 1998, https://www.ntia.doc.gov/legacy/ntiahome/domainname/130dftmail/02_02_98.htm; NTIA, *Comments on support of monopolies in the Green Paper (Kent Crispin)*, 9 February 1998, https://www.ntia.doc.gov/legacy/ntiahome/domainname/130dftmail/02_09_98.htm; NTIA, *Get out of the way! (Matthias Tschakert)*, 11 February 1998, https://www.ntia.doc.gov/legacy/ntiahome/domainname/130dftmail/02_11_98.htm; NTIA, *Our comments in opposition to exclusive ownership of generic Top Level Domains (Paul Stahura)*, 11 February 1998, https://www.ntia.doc.gov/legacy/ntiahome/domainname/130dftmail/02_11_98.htm; NTIA, *Comments on the US Dept. of Commerce Green Paper on Internet Names (European Telecommunication Standards Institute)*, 12 February 1998, https://www.ntia.doc.gov/legacy/ntiahome/domainname/130dftmail/02_12_98.htm; NTIA, *I Support CORE (Paul Preston)*, 12 February 1998, https://www.ntia.doc.gov/legacy/ntiahome/domainname/130dftmail/02_12_98.htm; NTIA, *Global administration for a global net (Carsten Reinke)*, 16–17 February 1998, https://www.ntia.doc.gov/legacy/ntiahome/domainname/130dftmail/02_16_98.htm, https://www.ntia.doc.gov/legacy/ntiahome/domainname/130dftmail/02_17_98.htm; NTIA, *Domain Farce (Louis Fischer)*, 18 February 1998, https://www.ntia.doc.gov/legacy/ntiahome/domainname/130dftmail/02_18_98.htm; NTIA, *Comments on US Government Draft (Shaun Dolan)*, 18 February 1998, https://www.ntia.doc.gov/legacy/ntiahome/domainname/130dftmail/02_18_98.htm; NTIA, *Domains*

as the 'Generic Top-Level Domain Memorandum of Understanding' or 'gTLD-MoU' received support from the International Telecommunications Union (ITU), a UN

(Norman Fall), 23 February 1998, https://www.ntia.doc.gov/legacy/ntiahome/domainname/130dftmail/02_23_98.htm; NTIA, *Comments on the Green Paper (Simon White)*, 24 February 1998, https://www.ntia.doc.gov/legacy/ntiahome/domainname/130dftmail/02_24_98.htm; NTIA, *1/30/98 U.S. Gov. proposal (Tom Murphy)*, 26 February 1998, https://www.ntia.doc.gov /legacy/ntiahome/domainname/130dftmail/02_26_98.htm; NTIA, *The plan to wreck the Internet (J. Williams)*, 27 February 1998, https://www.ntia.doc.gov/legacy/ntiahome/domainname /130dftmail/02_26_98.htm; NTIA, *Name proposal (Nikolaj Nyholm)*, 2 March 1998, https:// www.ntia.doc.gov/legacy/ntiahome/domainname/130dftmail/03_02_98.htm; NTIA, *Comme nts on the Technical Management of Internet Domain Names (Eurotel GmbH Internom)*, 2 March 1998, https://www.ntia.doc.gov/legacy/ntiahome/domainname/130dftmail/03_02_98.htm; NTIA, *Unbelievelable? [sic] (Denis Bucher)*, 4 March 1998, https://www.ntia.doc.gov/legacy/ ntiahome/domainname/130dftmail/03_04_98.htm; NTIA, email of Leonard Werbes to NTIA, 4 March 1998, https://www.ntia.doc.gov/legacy/ntiahome/domainname/130dftmail/03_04_98. htm; NTIA, *Do not ignore Core (Bradley Jacobsen)*, 5 March 1998, https://www.ntia.doc.gov/ legacy/ntiahome/domainname/130dftmail/03_05_98.htm; NTIA, *Response to Green Paper From Demon Internet (Stuart Berman)*, 5 March 1998, https://www.ntia.doc.gov/legacy/ ntiahome/domainname/130dftmail/03_05_98.htm; NTIA, *Give freedom a chance (Donald Smits)*, 5 March 1998, https://www.ntia.doc.gov/legacy/ntiahome/domainname/130dftmail/ 03_05_98.htm; NTIA, *Re: discussion draft (Monica Crawford)*, 6 March 1998, https://www.ntia .doc.gov/legacy/ntiahome/domainname/130dftmail/03_06_98.htm; NTIA, *Where is the CORE of your proposal? (Richard Fromme)*, 6 March 1998, https://www.ntia.doc.gov/legacy/ ntiahome/domainname/130dftmail/03_06_98.htm; NTIA, *New gTLD input (Phillip Davies)*, 6 March 1998, https://www.ntia.doc.gov/legacy/ntiahome/domainname/130dftmail/03_06_98. htm; NTIA, *Comment to discussion draft (Site Leader, Inc.)*, 8 March 1998, https://www.ntia. doc.gov/legacy/ntiahome/domainname/130dftmail/03_08_98.htm; NTIA, *Green Paper response (Capital Networks)*, 10 March 1998, https://www.ntia.doc.gov/legacy/ntiahome/ domainname/130dftmail/03_09_98.htm; NTIA, *Mediafusion's response on the Green Paper (Jacques Bernier)*,9 March 1998, https://www.ntia.doc.gov/legacy/ntiahome/domainname/13 0dftmail/03_09_98.htm; NTIA, *Re: TLDs (Mark Kavana)*, 9 March 1998, https://www.ntia.doc .gov/legacy/ntiahome/domainname/130dftmail/03_09_98.htm; NTIA, *Please correct your Green Paper (Albert Y. Boud)*, 10 March 1998, https://www.ntia.doc.gov/legacy/ntiahome/ domainname/130dftmail/03_10_98.htm; NTIA, *Support the CORE plan (John Mozena)*, 12 March 1998, https://www.ntia.doc.gov/legacy/ntiahome/domainname/130dftmail/03_12_98. htm; NTIA, *Proposal to improve T.M.I.N.A. (Robert Ridgeway)*, 13 March 1998, https://www. ntia.doc.gov/legacy/ntiahome/domainname/130dftmail/03_13_98.htm; NTIA, *Green Paper comments (Joe Angiolillo)*, 13 March 1998, https://www.ntia.doc.gov/legacy/ntiahome/ domainname/130dftmail/03_13_98.htm; NTIA, *Listen to the Internet community (Joseph Yeung)*, 13 March 1998, https://www.ntia.doc.gov/legacy/ntiahome/domainname/130dftmail/0 3_13_98.htm; NTIA, *Re: Draft on Technical Management of Internet Domain Names (Angelo González*, 16 March 1998, https://www.ntia.doc.gov/legacy/ntiahome/domainname/130 dftmail/03_16_98.htm; NTIA, *Reasons why I support CORE (Charles Liu)*, 16 March 1998, https://www.ntia.doc.gov/legacy/ntiahome/domainname/130dftmail/03_16_98.htm; NTIA, *Comments of the Internet Society in regards to the Department Of Commerce National Telecommunications and Information Administration 15 CFR Chapter XXIII [Docket No. 980212036-803 6-01] Improvement of Technical Management of Internet Names and Addresses ("Green Paper")*, 17 March 1998, https://www.ntia.doc.gov/legacy/ntiahome/domainname/130dftmail/03_17_ 98.htm; NTIA, *MARQUES response to the US discussion draft of 30 January 1998 entitled "Proposal to improve technical management of Internet names and addresses"*, 20 March 1998, https://www.ntia.doc.gov/legacy/ntiahome/domainname/130dftmail/03_20_98.htm; NTIA, *CORE solution (Jeffrey Masters)*, 20 March 1998, https://www.ntia.doc.gov/legacy/ntiahome/ domainname/130dftmail/03_20_98.htm; NTIA, *Comments on Green Paper--- For Development of the Internet Governance (Internet Association of Japan)*, 22 March 1998, https://www.ntia.doc .gov/legacy/ntiahome/domainname/130dftmail/03_21_98.htm; NTIA, *Domain Names (Garth Krock)*, 21 March 1998, https://www.ntia.doc.gov/legacy/ntiahome/domainname/130dftmail /03_21_98.htm.

agency. However, in May 1997, the U.S. Government had already indicated that it would not support the gTLD-MoU.[82] Although the gTLD-MoU received broad international support, there was no consensus concerning CORE's proposal, and the U.S. Government did not change its mind about the gTLD-MoU. But the U.S. Government responded to the call for internationalization by transferring important policy decisions to the private sector rather than the U.S. Government.[83]

(b) Finalizing Policy: The White Paper

The final plan for privatization was laid down in a statement of policy, which became known as the 'White Paper'. The White Paper acknowledged the concerns of the international community and the call for fairness and transparency in the decision-making.[84] This plan was a compromise – it proposed increased involvement of the international community and the private sector, while maintaining U.S. leadership – and it was positively received.[85] As a result, the U.S. Government was able to reaffirm its handling of the transition to private sector management. The U.S. Government believed – and rightfully so, in view of the lack of an elaborated international legal framework on Internet governance – that 'it would be irresponsible to withdraw from its existing management role without taking steps to ensure the stability of the Internet during its transition to private sector management.'[86] The U.S. Government insisted that the corporation responsible for DNS policy-making be located in the U.S., officially '[b]ecause of the significant U.S.-based DNS expertise and in order to preserve stability',[87] although according to some, this was mainly inspired to respond to Congressional concerns.[88] In any event, the concern for stability and sufficient DNS expertise seemed legitimate, and the U.S. Government argued that 'the mere fact that the new corporation would be incorporated in the United States would not remove it from the jurisdiction of other nations.'[89] Nevertheless, the U.S. Congress continued to insist until much later that there be U.S. oversight. On 16 November 2005, the U.S. House of Representatives unanimously adopted a resolution stating that 'the authoritative root zone server should remain physically located in the United States and the Secretary of Commerce should maintain oversight of ICANN.'[90] The U.S. Senate also

82. Milton Mueller, *Ruling the Root: Internet Governance and the Taming of Cyberspace*, 158 (MIT Press 2002).
83. NTIA, *Management of Internet Names and Addresses: statement of policy*, https://www.ntia.doc.gov/files/ntia/publications/6_5_98dns.pdf, (White Paper).
84. NTIA, *supra* n. 83.
85. *See* Commission of the European Communities, *Internet governance, management of Internet names and addresses, Analysis and assessment from the European Commission of the United States Department of Commerce White* Paper, 29 July 1998, COM(1998) 476 final.
86. NTIA, *supra* n. 83.
87. NTIA, *supra* n. 83, p. 31745.
88. The U.S. Congress never specifically authorized the U.S. Government to privatize DNS management, although it held hearings on the topic (*see* Stephen Ryan, *Governing Cyberspace: ICANN a Controversial Internet Standards Body*, 1 October 1999, http://www.fed-soc.org/publications/detail/governing-cyberspace-icann-a-controversial-internet-standards-body).
89. NTIA, *supra* n. 83, p. 31745.
90. U.S. House of Representatives, H Con Res 268 (16 November 2005).

asked that the President 'continue to oppose any effort to transfer control of the Internet to the United Nations or any other international entity.'[91] Some considered, maybe naively, that the physical location in the U.S. had mainly symbolic relevance.[92] More skeptical voices considered it a 'myth that U.S. oversight is completely neutral and intrinsically harmless'; they warned against the opportunities for misuse and denounced the non-transparency of the power wielded.[93]

The White Paper maintained the guiding principles of the Green Paper for management and oversight of the DNS, namely stability, competition, private bottom-up coordination and representation.[94] The entity that was going to take over the management of the DNS had to commit to these principles. With respect to ensuring stability, the White Paper stated:

> 'The introduction of a new management system should not disrupt current operations or create competing root systems. During the transition and thereafter, the stability of the Internet should be the first priority of any DNS management system. Security and reliability of the DNS are important aspects of stability, and as a new DNS management system is introduced, a comprehensive security strategy should be developed.'[95]

Recognizing the success of the Internet, which because of its decentralized nature encourages innovation and maximizes individual freedom, the U.S. Government wanted a clear commitment from the corporation that was to manage the DNS that it would rely on competition and free market mechanisms:

> 'Where possible, market mechanisms that support competition and consumer choice should drive the management of the Internet because they will lower costs, promote innovation, encourage diversity, and enhance user choice and satisfaction.'[96]

The White Paper further stressed the importance of bottom-up governance and the need for the DNS custodian to operate for the benefit of the Internet community as a whole, and to develop sound, fair and widely accepted policies for the management of the DNS.[97] This could only be achieved through transparent decision-making. In this

91. U.S. Senate, S Res 323 (18 November 2005).
92. *See* Jovan Kurbalija, *International inviolability for the root zone ?*, 9 December 2013 http://www.diplomacy.edu/blog/international-inviolability-root-zone; Jovan Kurbalija, *There is a practical solution for global inviolability of the Internet root zone*, October 2014 DiploFoundation Policy Brief, http://www.diplomacy.edu/sites/default/files/DiploFoundation%20Policy%20Brief%20No%204%20WEB%20v1.pdf.http://www.diplomacy.edu/sites/default/files/DiploFoundation0PolicyBriefNo4WEBv1.pdf.
93. Milton Mueller et al., *Political Oversight of ICANN: A Briefing for the WSIS Summit – Concept Paper by the Internet Governance Project*, 1 November 2005, http://www.internetgovernance.org/wordpress/wp-content/uploads/political-oversight.pdf, p. 5.
94. NTIA, *supra* n. 83, pp. 31743, 31749.
95. NTIA, *supra* n. 83, p. 31749.
96. NTIA, *supra* n. 83, p. 31749.
97. NTIA, *supra* n. 83, p. 31749.

respect, the U.S. Government required that the new corporation's processes be 'fair, open and pro-competitive, protecting against capture by a narrow group of stakeholders.'[98] The U.S. Government clarified:

> 'Typically this means that decision-making processes should be sound and transparent; the basis for corporate decisions should be recorded and made publicly available. Super-majority or even consensus requirements may be useful to protect against capture by a self-interested faction.'[99]

(c) The Challenges for Implementing Policies

Of course, it was not sufficient for the U.S. Government simply to formulate policies asserting control over the DNS. The U.S. Government needed to make sure that it effectively controlled the Internet's unique identifiers and that the stability of the DNS was maintained during the transition of DNS management to an accountable and fair governance structure.

The IANA functions – these include administrative tasks such as the allocation and assignment of IP address blocks, the assignment of technical protocol parameter numbers and maintenance of assigned values, and oversight of the operation of the Internet root server system[100] – were still performed by the Information Sciences Institute (ISI) of the University of Southern California (USC), where IANA was created[101] as part of a research project.[102] The IANA functions would have to be transitioned to the future DNS custodian. And, as mentioned above, the operational aspects of the Internet root server system were performed by NSI according to an agreement which was about to expire.[103] It was to be anticipated that the researchers at USC would continue to take care of IANA, and that they would be cooperative in the transition. But to guarantee the cooperation of NSI, a commercial entity, was a bigger challenge. On 7 October 1998, the U.S. Government managed to extend the cooperative agreement with NSI, and NSI accepted that the U.S. Government would transfer its DNS obligations under the cooperative agreement to a new corporation, as was foreseen in the White Paper.[104] With this extension, the U.S. Government and NSI agreed to an amendment in which the U.S. Government affirmed its authority over the

98. NTIA, *supra* n. 83, p. 31750.
99. NTIA, *supra* n. 83, p. 31750.
100. USC/ICANN Transition Agreement, https://www.icann.org/resources/unthemed-pages/usc-icann-transition-2012-02-25-en; Internet Activities Board, *IAB Official Protocol Standards*, Network Working Group Request for Comments # 1083, December 1988, https://tools.ietf.org/html/rfc1083.
101. Internet Engineering Task Force, *Request for Comments # 1083*, http://www.ietf.org/rfc/rfc1083.txt.
102. USC/ICANN Transition Agreement, https://www.icann.org/resources/unthemed-pages/usc-icann-transition-2012-02-25-en.
103. NTIA, *supra* n. 83, p. 31742; Network Information Services Manager(s) for NSFNET and the NREN: INTERNIC Registration Services Cooperative Agreement No. NCR-9218742, 1 January 1993, http://archive.icann.org/en/nsi/coopagmt-01jan93.htm.
104. ICANN, *Amendment 11 to Cooperative Agreement Between NSI and U.S. Government*, http://archive.icann.org/en/nsi/coopagmt-amend11-07oct98.htm.

Internet's root zone.[105] The amended cooperative agreement also laid down the basis for a more competitive environment among domain name registrars by requiring NSI to develop a Shared Registration System (SRS), allowing multiple registrars to provide registration services within the gTLDs for which NSI acted as a registry.[106] The introduction of an SRS, together with equal access for accredited registrars to NSI's registry services, was necessary in order to introduce appropriate competition in the sales of domain names. Before the SRS, NSI was the sole registrar for the existing open gTLDs. A transitioning of the technical IANA functions performed by NSI to a new corporation was not part of the deal. As a result, the U.S. Government and the new corporation would remain dependent on NSI for the performance of these critical functions.

(d) ICANN Becomes the Internet's Steward

In response to the White Paper, the U.S. Government received a proposal from the Internet Corporation for Assigned Names and Numbers (ICANN), a Californian non-profit organization that was created upon the instigation of Jon Postel.[107] Jon Postel's involvement was critical. His 'U.S.-based DNS expertise' was used to justify the U.S. Government's decision to keep DNS management within the U.S., and the U.S. Government expressed the belief 'that the private sector organizers will want Dr. Postel and other IANA staff to be involved in the creation of the new corporation' for the management of the DNS.[108] But rather than the private sector contacting Jon Postel, it was Jon Postel and his lawyer who laid the foundations of this new corporation, and who reached out to a geographically diverse group of individuals to serve on the first (interim) ICANN Board.[109] The first ICANN Board members had little expertise in relation to DNS matters,[110] but that may have been seen by Jon Postel more as an advantage than an inconvenience; Jon Postel would serve as ICANN's CTO,[111] and a Board with less expertise would undoubtedly make technical coordination easier. Jon Postel was reputedly seen as a trusted figure 'by almost everyone interested in DNS

105. ICANN, *supra* n. 104.
106. ICANN, *supra* n. 104.
107. David Lindsay, *International Domain Name Law: ICANN and the UDRP*, 2007 Hart Publishing, p. 46; *See* NTIA, *Letter from Jon Postel to NTIA regarding Management of Internet Names and Addresses*, 2 October 1998, https://www.ntia.doc.gov/legacy/ntiahome/domainname/proposals/icann/Letter.htm.
108. NTIA, *supra* n. 83, p. 31745.
109. *See* the declarations of these first ICANN Board Members at the ICANN public meeting of 14 November 1998 (Berkman Center for Internet and Society, *ICANN Public Meeting Transcript* 7, 14 November 1998, http://cyber.law.harvard.edu/icann/cambridge-1198/archive/transintro.html).
110. *See* Berkman Center for Internet and Society, *supra* n. 109; Michael Froomkin, *Wrong Turn in Cyberspace: Using ICANN to Route Around the APA and the Constitution*, 50 Duke Law Journal 17, 73 (2000).
111. *See* Froomkin, *supra* n. 110.

policy.'[112] The formation of ICANN was near completion,[113] and negotiations between the U.S. Government and ICANN were at an advanced stage, when Jon Postel died suddenly on 16 October 1998.[114]

Despite the fact that ICANN had lost the figurehead on which its legitimacy and trust was based,[115] the negotiations with the U.S. Government continued. On 20 October 1998, the National Telecommunications and Information Administration (NTIA) informed ICANN that the DoC 'regards the ICANN submission as a significant step towards privatizing management of the domain name system.'[116] However, the U.S. Government indicated that there were remaining concerns *inter alia*, 'in the area of accountability (representational and financial), transparent decision-making processes, conflict of interest.'[117] The U.S. Government recommended that ICANN consult with the Boston Working Group (BWG), the Open Root Server Confederation (ORSC) and others who commented critically on ICANN's proposal.[118]

On 25 October 1998, ICANN installed its first interim Board, Chairman, President and CEO.[119] Not long thereafter, the members of the newly installed ICANN Board discussed changes to the draft Bylaws and decided to hold a conference call with representatives of the BWG and the ORSC on 31 October 1998.[120] Following these discussions, the ICANN Board unanimously adopted its original Bylaws on 6

112. *See* Froomkin, *supra* n. 110; *see also* Internet Society, *A Ten Year Tribute to Jon Postel*, http://www.internetsociety.org/what-we-do/grants-and-awards/awards/postel-service-award/ten-year-tribute-jon-postel (16 October 2008).
113. When Jon Postel submitted ICANN's proposal to the U.S. Government on 2 October 1998, ICANN was formally incorporated, but it had not yet elected a Board of directors or adopted Bylaws. The ICANN Board and Bylaws would only be adopted following completion of the negotiations with the U.S. Government. *See* NTIA, *Letter from Jon Postel to NTIA regarding Management of Internet Names and Addresses*, 2 October 1998, https://www.ntia.doc.gov/legacy/ntiahome/domainname/proposals/icann/Letter.htm.
114. *See* Internet Society, *IANA's Statement on Postel Service Award*, 2008 http://www.isoc.org/postel/iana.shtml.
115. *See* Froomkin, *supra* n. 110, pp. 73, 74.
116. NTIA, *Becky Burr, Associate Administrator of NTIA for International Affairs sends letter to the Internet Corporation for Assigned Names and Numbers*, 20 October 1998, https://www.ntia.doc.gov/press-release/1998/becky-burr-associate-administrator-ntia-international-affairs-sends-letter-intern.
117. NTIA, *supra* n. 116.
118. NTIA, *supra* n. 116; *see* NTIA, Comments on the Proposals for a New Corporation to Manage Internet Domain Name System Functions, between 30 September 1998 and 15 October 1998, https://www.ntia.doc.gov/legacy/ntiahome/domainname/proposals/comments/comments.html.
119. ICANN, *Minutes of Organizational Meeting October 25, 1998*, https://www.icann.org/resources/board-material/minutes-1998-10-25-en; NTIA, *NTIA Reviewing ICANN November 6 Submission*, https://www.ntia.doc.gov/press-release/1998/ntia-reviewing-icann-november-6-submission.
120. ICANN, *Minutes of Special Meeting October 29, 1998*, https://www.icann.org/resources/board-material/minutes-1998-10-29-en; ICANN, *Notes from October 31 conference call between several members of the ICANN board and representatives of the Boston Working Group and Open Root Server Confederation*, https://www.icann.org/resources/board-material/notes-1998-10-31-en; ICANN, *Transcript from October 31 conference call between several members of the ICANN board and representatives of the Boston Working Group and Open Root Server Confederation* https://www.icann.org/resources/board-material/transcript-1998-10-31-en.

November 1998,[121] and informed the NTIA the same day.[122] On 14 November 1998, ICANN organized a public meeting to explain its operating principles to the Internet community, and allowed the public to express its concerns. On 19 November 1998, a representative of the U.S. Government had a conference call with ICANN, which resulted in ICANN amending its Articles of Incorporation and Bylaws on 21 November 1998.[123]

Four days later, the U.S. Department of Commerce and ICANN entered into a Memorandum of Understanding (MOU), which was intended to allow ICANN to give the U.S. Government the necessary assurances 'that the private sector has the capability and resources to assume the important responsibilities related to the technical management of the DNS.'[124] The MOU – which was later also referred to as the Joint Project Agreement (JPA) – set various milestones for ICANN: it emphasized the importance of accountability to and representation of the global and functional diversity of the Internet and its users,[125] and required ICANN's collaboration on a plan for the possible expansion of the number of gTLDs, which was to take into account *inter alia*, the recommendation by the World Intellectual Property Organization (WIPO) concerning the development of a uniform approach to resolving trademark/domain name disputes involving cyberpiracy.[126]

The USC, which had been operating IANA as a research project, agreed to transfer the IANA functions to ICANN, subject to the approval of the U.S. Government.[127] Probably the most important aspect of the agreement was that the USC and ICANN recognized the authority of the U.S. Government over the IANA functions (rather than that of the USC's ISI, where IANA had been created). The recognition in this agreement of U.S. Government authority is what allowed the U.S. Government to transfer control gradually to the private sector. On 8 February 1999, the U.S. Government authorized ICANN to perform the IANA functions.[128]

On 26 February 1999, the DoC officially recognized ICANN as the new corporation envisioned in the White Paper, and authorized ICANN to take over the obligations of

121. ICANN, *Minutes of Special Meeting 6 November 1998*, https://www.icann.org/resources/board-material/minutes-1998-11-06-en.
122. NTIA, *NTIA Reviewing ICANN November 6 Submission*, https://www.ntia.doc.gov/press-release/1998/ntia-reviewing-icann-november-6-submission.
123. ICANN, *Minutes of Special Meeting 21 November 1998*, https://www.icann.org/resources/board-material/minutes-1998-11-21-en.
124. NTIA, *Memorandum of Understanding between the U.S. Department of Commerce and Internet Corporation for Assigned Names and Numbers*, https://www.ntia.doc.gov/other-publication/1998/memorandum-understanding-between-us-department-commerce-and-internet-corporat.
125. MOU, Clause V(C)(8).
126. MOU, Clause V(C)(9).
127. USC/ICANN Transition Agreement, https://www.icann.org/resources/unthemed-pages/usc-icann-transition-2012-02-25-en.
128. IANA Functions Contract of 8 February 1999, https://www.ntia.doc.gov/files/ntia/publications/ianacontract.pdf.

the U.S. Government under the cooperative agreement with NSI.[129] Thus, on that date, the U.S. Government effectively granted management authority over the DNS to ICANN.

(e) Keeping Control over the Internet's Governance Structure

The U.S. Government kept its oversight role until recently. Paradoxical as it may seem, the U.S. Government's oversight role was intended to avoid overregulation and interference by governments; the U.S. Government felt it had to assert authority over the Internet in order to avoid a situation where a more international governance structure would allow European or other countries to impose new and more invasive controls on the Internet.[130] It was intended that the U.S. oversight be limited in time. The very purpose of the MOU was to allow a coordinated transition to the private sector and enable ICANN to show that it was capable of carrying out the DNS management functions in accordance with the principles of stability, competition, private bottom-up coordination, and representation.[131] The original MOU was scheduled to come to an end on 30 September 2000.[132] It was expected that, by then, ICANN would have matured into a representative and accountable organization, able to promote competition in the DNS, while maintaining its stable operation.[133] However, the U.S. Government has not relinquished its oversight role until 30 September 2016. The MOU remained in place until 2009,[134] when it was replaced by an Affirmation of Commitments (AoC) between the DoC and ICANN.[135]

In essence, the Internet governance structure has not changed since February 1999. Since that time, ICANN has been in charge of the IANA functions, and therefore responsible for creating the policies that govern the root zone. ICANN also manages important aspects of the cooperative agreement between the DoC and NSI, later Verisign, Inc. (Verisign). Verisign acquired NSI in 2000. After the acquisition, NSI continued to perform its registrar activities, but Verisign took over the registry operator business and the operational control of the Internet's root zone. Verisign kept the registry business when it sold NSI in 2003 and also continued its operational control of

---

129. NTIA, *Letter from J. Beckwith Burr to Network Solutions, Inc. regarding Cooperative Agreement No. NCR-921874, as amended*, 26 February 1999, https://www.ntia.doc.gov/legacy/ntiahome/domainname/icannnewco.htm.
130. Jack Goldsmith and Tim Wu, *Who Controls the Internet?: Illusions of a Borderless World*, 41-42 (Oxford University Press 2008).
131. MOU, Clauses II(B) and II(C).
132. MOU, Clause VII.
133. *See* NTIA, *Press Conference Remarks by Becky Burr*, https://www.ntia.doc.gov/files/ntia/publications/DNSBURR.pdf.
134. The MOU has been amended seven times between 1999 and 2009 (*infra*, Chapter 2.A.3).
135. Affirmation of Commitments by the United States Department of Commerce and the Internet Corporation for Assigned Names and Numbers, 30 September 2009, https://www.ntia.doc.gov/files/ntia/publications/affirmation_of_commitments_2009.pdf.

the Internet's authoritative root zone. As a result, when ICANN approves a change to the Internet's authoritative root zone, the U.S. Government directs Verisign to implement the change in the root.

The U.S. authority over the root has been severely criticized and characterized as a 'provocation to other governments.'[136] Critics denounce the fact that contract negotiations between the U.S. Government, ICANN and Verisign are largely non-transparent, and they condemn ICANN for favoring U.S.-based economic interests (as evidenced by the redelegation of .org to the Internet Society (ISOC), of .net (and more recently .com) to Verisign).[137]

On 14 March 2014, the NTIA announced the U.S. Government's renewed intent to relinquish its oversight role and conclude the privatization that had begun in 1997.[138] The aim was to complete the transition by 30 September 2015, the expiry date of the then current contract concerning IANA functions. However, the IANA functions contract has been extended until 30 September 2016 to allow ICANN more time to prepare for the transition. Until the transition was completed on 30 September 2016, the joint project between the U.S. Government and ICANN continued.

3. Evolution of ICANN's Role

a. *The Early Days of ICANN*

During the first year of the joint project between the DoC and ICANN to privatize DNS management, ICANN was able to maintain stability and set up a structure within ICANN to allow for the representation of different stakeholders. Already in August 1999, ICANN adopted the Uniform Domain Name Dispute Resolution Policy (UDRP), which changed the domain name landscape forever and dramatically improved the protection of trademarks on the Internet.[139] The UDRP was developed by WIPO, and provided for the establishment of a 'mandatory administrative procedure concerning abusive registrations' to be adopted 'uniformly across open gTLDs.'[140] The procedure is mandatory in the sense that the registration agreement requires all domain name

136. Milton Mueller et al., *Political Oversight of ICANN: A Briefing for the WSIS Summit – Concept Paper by the Internet Governance Project*, 1 November 2005, http://www.internetgovernance.org/wordpress/wp-content/uploads/political-oversight.pdf, p. 5.
137. Milton Mueller et al., *Political Oversight of ICANN: A Briefing for the WSIS Summit – Concept Paper by the Internet Governance Project*, 1 November 2005, http://www.internetgovernance.org/wordpress/wp-content/uploads/political-oversight.pdf, pp. 5–6.
138. NTIA, *NTIA Announces Intent to Transition Key Internet Domain Name Functions*, 14 March 2014, https://www.ntia.doc.gov/press-release/2014/ntia-announces-intent-transition-key-internet-domain-name-functions.
139. Uniform Domain Name Disputed Resolution Policy, adopted 26 August 1999, https://www.icann.org/resources/pages/policy-2012-02-25-en; For an overview of international domain name cases prior to the adoption of the UDRP, *see* Diane Cabell, *Foreign Domain Name Disputes 2000*, Computer & Internet Law (2000).
140. WIPO, *The Management of Internet Names and Addresses: Intellectual Property Issues – Final Report of the WIPO Internet Domain Name Process*, 30 April 1999, http://www.wipo.int/export/sites/www/amc/en/docs/report-final1.pdf.

registrations in an open gTLD to be subject to the administrative procedure if there is a claim initiated against the registration by a third party. Although the UDRP does not exclude the jurisdiction of the courts, the exemplary case administration carried out by WIPO (and later also by other dispute resolution providers) has meant that only a small fraction of the cases have in fact been re-tried in court.

This progress stands in sharp contrast to the concerns regarding accountability and competition. On 15 June 1999, ICANN issued a first status report identifying the progress made so far and the main challenges going forward.[141] ICANN was clearly dismayed and very critical about the lack of NSI cooperation in transforming the DNS into a more competitive environment. ICANN complained that NSI had failed to comply with its deadlines for creating a Shared Registration System (SRS) interface for its .com, .net and .org TLDs,[142] which should have ensured that competitive registrars could use the registry on the same terms as NSI's registrar branch.[143] ICANN saw NSI's behavior as an impediment to competition, and it criticized both the fact that NSI had challenged ICANN's authority regarding policy, and also the manner in which it did so. In this respect, ICANN stated:

> 'Finally, as a general proposition, NSI has to date refused to accept the policy authority of ICANN, although it continues to "participate" in the creation of ICANN institutions and policies. It has funded and encouraged a variety of ICANN critics, including some whose only common cause with NSI would appear to be unhappiness with ICANN. In short, NSI has generally been an impediment, not a help, in the transition from government controlled monopoly to a private competitive DNS.'[144]

Despite ICANN's complaints, NSI's deadline under the Cooperative Agreement to deploy the SRS was pushed back several times.[145] Nevertheless, when ICANN made its second status report in June 2000, ICANN considered that it had completed its task of ensuring competition in registration services for gTLDs.[146] ICANN reported that the

141. First Status Report to the Department of Commerce, 15 June 1999, https://www.ntia.doc.gov/report/1999/first-status-report-department-commerce-icann.
142. At the time, NSI operated the .com, .net and .org TLDs. The .com and .net TLDs are currently operated by NSI's successor, Verisign. In 2003, the operation of the .org TLD was transferred to Public Interest Registry, who operates the TLD with the technical support of Afilias.
143. ICANN, First Status Report to the Department of Commerce, 15 June 1999, https://www.ntia.doc.gov/report/1999/first-status-report-department-commerce-icann.
144. ICANN, First Status Report to the Department of Commerce, 15 June 1999, https://www.ntia.doc.gov/report/1999/first-status-report-department-commerce-icann.
145. Amendment 14 to the DOC/NSI Cooperative Agreement of 15 June 1999 extended the deadline until 16 July 1999 (https://www.ntia.doc.gov/legacy/ntiahome/domainname/amends/amend14rev.htm); Amendment 15 to the DOC/NSI Cooperative Agreement of 15 July 1999 extended the deadline until 6 August 1999 (https://www.ntia.doc.gov/legacy/ntiahome/domainname/amends/amend15rev.htm); Amendment 16 to the DOC/NSI Cooperative Agreement of 10 August 1999 extended the deadline until 10 September 1999 (https://www.ntia.doc.gov/legacy/ntiahome/domainname/amends/amend16.htm); Amendment 18 to the DOC/NSI Cooperative Agreement of 5 October 1999 extended the deadline until 5 November 1999 (https://www.ntia.doc.gov/legacy/ntiahome/domainname/amends/amend18.htm).
146. Second Status Report to the Department of Commerce, 30 June 1999, https://www.ntia.doc.gov/report/2000/second-status-report-department-commerce-icann.

share of net new domain name registrations attributable to the NSI registrar dropped from 100% to under 50%, and that the retail registration pricing dropped from USD 35 per year to USD 10.[147]

ICANN also looked to increase competition at a registry level, and posted a call for new gTLD applications on 15 August 2000, shortly before the initial expiration date of the MOU. This first round of new gTLD applications is discussed in more detail in Chapter 2.C.1 and Chapter 4.A.

b. *Extending the Timeframe for Privatization*

In spite of the progress made, the U.S. Government did not consider that the young ICANN was ready to take on the critical responsibility of managing the DNS without government oversight. On 11 September 2000, the MOU was extended until 11 September 2001 and amended to include specific tasks for ICANN, for example, to improve its accountability, enhance the root zone architecture and increase competition between TLD registries.[148] ICANN was asked to develop and test an independent review process to address claims by members of the Internet community who considered that they had been adversely affected by decisions in conflict with ICANN's bylaws or contractual obligations.[149] On 24 September 2001, the MOU was extended for yet another year.[150] And one year later, on 20 September 2002, the U.S. DoC reported that the terms of the MOU were to be extended again until 30 September 2003. This time, the U.S. Government and ICANN revised their commitments in detail.[151] The U.S. DoC expressed its concerns and disappointment about the progress made by ICANN:

> 'Clearly, ICANN's progress to date has been slower than expected and the organization still has much to accomplish before maturing into the stable and accountable entity necessary to complete transition of DNS management functions.
>
> [...] The Department has frankly been disappointed that ICANN's progress on the MOU tasks has moved so slowly. In fairness, the accomplishment of many of these tasks requires more than ICANN's unilateral effort. Further, it is not surprising that the completion of certain tasks has proven difficult or that initial thoughts on processes and structure require rethinking based upon experience. Nevertheless,

147. Second Status Report to the Department of Commerce, 30 June 1999, https://www.ntia.doc.gov/report/2000/second-status-report-department-commerce-icann.
148. MOU, Amendment 2, 11 September 2000, https://www.ntia.doc.gov/page/2000/icann-ammendment-2.
149. MOU, Amendment 2, 11 September 2000, https://www.ntia.doc.gov/page/2000/icann-ammendment-2.
150. MOU, Amendment 4, 24 September 2001, https://www.ntia.doc.gov/page/2001/icann-ammendment-4.
151. MOU, Amendment 5, 20 September 2002, https://www.ntia.doc.gov/page/2002/icann-ammendment-5.

> the variety of criticisms expressed by the Internet community is of concern to the Department - and should be instructive to ICANN.'[152]

This latest 2002 one-year term extension of the MOU was considered critical for ICANN 'to make substantial progress on the remaining transition tasks.'[153] Progress was lacking with respect to critical tasks. *E.g.*, ICANN had made only little progress in concluding agreements with the root server system operators (that would stabilize ICANN's relationship with them) and in enhancing the root server system's architecture and security.[154] With respect to its accountability, ICANN had not yet implemented an independent review process 'for decisions that purport to conflict with the corporation's bylaws', and ICANN's reconsideration process that was put in place had had 'limited success in resolving the type of disputes it was intended to address.'[155] ICANN also failed in opening up the market for generic TLDs. The U.S. DoC complained that ICANN had 'not yet defined the process, procedures, and standards for ensuring predictability and transparency in the gTLD selection process long-term (including the timeframe within which new gTLDs were to be made available).'[156]

One year later, and although ICANN had implemented an independent review process, the U.S. Government did not consider ICANN's progress sufficient to justify it relinquishing its oversight role. Much work was still needed if ICANN were to evolve into 'an independent, stable, and sustainable DNS management organization.'[157] New, specific aims were added to the express goals of previous MOUs.[158] Among these aims was the definition and implementation of 'a predictable strategy for selecting new TLDs using straightforward, transparent, and objective procedures that preserve the stability of the Internet.'[159] The strategy development was to be completed by 30 September

152. U.S. Department of Commerce, Statement regarding extension of Memorandum of Understanding with ICANN (Amendment 5), https://www.ntia.doc.gov/page/2002/statement-regarding-extenstion-memorandum-understanding-icann-ammendment-5.
153. U.S. Department of Commerce, Statement regarding extension of Memorandum of Understanding with ICANN (Amendment 5), https://www.ntia.doc.gov/page/2002/statement-regarding-extenstion-memorandum-understanding-icann-ammendment-5.
154. U.S. Department of Commerce, Statement regarding extension of Memorandum of Understanding with ICANN (Amendment 5), https://www.ntia.doc.gov/page/2002/statement-regarding-extenstion-memorandum-understanding-icann-ammendment-5.
155. U.S. Department of Commerce, Statement regarding extension of Memorandum of Understanding with ICANN (Amendment 5), https://www.ntia.doc.gov/page/2002/statement-regarding-extenstion-memorandum-understanding-icann-ammendment-5.
156. U.S. Department of Commerce, Statement regarding extension of Memorandum of Understanding with ICANN (Amendment 5), https://www.ntia.doc.gov/page/2002/statement-regarding-extenstion-memorandum-understanding-icann-ammendment-5.
157. U.S. Department of Commerce, Statement regarding extension of Memorandum of Understanding with ICANN (Amendment 6), https://www.ntia.doc.gov/page/2003/statement-regarding-extension-mou-icann-ammendment-6.
158. MOU, Amendment 6, https://www.ntia.doc.gov/page/2003/icann-ammendment-6; U.S. Department of Commerce, Statement regarding extension of Memorandum of Understanding with ICANN (Amendment 6), https://www.ntia.doc.gov/page/2003/statement-regarding-extension-mou-icann-ammendment-6.
159. MOU, Amendment 6, Article II, introducing the new Article V(C)(8), https://www.ntia.doc.gov/page/2003/icann-ammendment-6.

2004, and its implementation was to commence by 31 December 2004.[160] The U.S. Government also continued to stress the need for more transparency and accountability and a formalization of ICANN's relationship with the root server system operators.[161] Unlike previous years, where the U.S. Government had allowed for a one-year extension of the MOU, ICANN was now given a three-year extension to accomplish these goals.[162]

At the end of this three-year period, the U.S. Government and ICANN agreed to amend the MOU on 29 September 2006. ICANN's efforts in defining and implementing strategies for selecting new TLDs were still limited to specific categories of TLDs and had shown that ICANN's evaluation process needed adjustment and took much longer than expected (*infra*). In 2006, the U.S. Government and ICANN agreed to extend the MOU/JPA for another three-year period. A few days before the execution of the amendment, an almost unanimous ICANN Board approved an 'Affirmation of Responsibilities', in which ICANN confirmed its commitment 'to the private sector management of the Internet DNS, by promoting the security and stability of the global Internet, while maintaining and promoting competition through its multi-stakeholder model.'[163] ICANN also affirmed and agreed to be guided by responsibilities in relation to security and stability, transparency, accountability, etc.,[164] and it agreed to the inclusion of the Affirmation of Responsibilities in the MOU/JPA with the U.S. DoC.[165]

At the beginning of 2008, the U.S. Government conducted a review of the MOU/JPA and received numerous comments from the Internet community.[166] The U.S. DoC observed that 'there was general consensus on the need to preserve the security and stability of the DNS and the recognition that ICANN is the appropriate technical

160. MOU, Amendment 6, Article II, introducing the new Article V(C)(8), https://www.ntia.doc.gov/page/2003/icann-ammendment-6.
161. MOU, Amendment 6, Article II, introducing the new Articles V(C)(4) and V(C)(5), https://www.ntia.doc.gov/page/2003/icann-ammendment-6; U.S. Department of Commerce, Statement regarding extension of Memorandum of Understanding with ICANN (Amendment 6), https://www.ntia.doc.gov/page/2003/statement-regarding-extension-mou-icann-ammendment-6.
162. MOU, Amendment 6, Article III, introducing the new Article VII, https://www.ntia.doc.gov/page/2003/icann-ammendment-6; U.S. Department of Commerce, Statement regarding extension of Memorandum of Understanding with ICANN (Amendment 6), https://www.ntia.doc.gov/page/2003/statement-regarding-extension-mou-icann-ammendment-6.
163. ICANN, *Board Resolution 06.71*, 25 September 2006, https://www.icann.org/resources/board-material/minutes-2006-09-25-en; ICANN, *Voting Transcript of Board Meeting of 25 September 2006*, https://www.icann.org/resources/board-material/voting-transcript-2006-09-25-en; Annex A to the Joint Project Agreement between the U.S. Department of Commerce and the ICANN Corporation for Assigned Names and Numbers, 29 September 2006, https://www.ntia.doc.gov/files/ntia/publications/signedmou290906.pdf.
164. Annex A to the Joint Project Agreement between the U.S. Department of Commerce and the ICANN Corporation for Assigned Names and Numbers, 29 September 2006, https://www.ntia.doc.gov/files/ntia/publications/signedmou290906.pdf.
165. Joint Project Agreement between the U.S. Department of Commerce and the ICANN Corporation for Assigned Names and Numbers, 29 September 2006, https://www.ntia.doc.gov/files/ntia/publications/signedmou290906.pdf.
166. NTIA, *Comments received by the NTIA*, published at *NTIA Seeks Public Comments Regarding Joint Project Agreement with ICANN*, 29 October 2007, https://www.ntia.doc.gov/other-publication/2007/ntia-seeks-public-comments-regarding-joint-project-agreement-icann.

coordinator of the Internet DNS.'[167] However, most commentators agreed that 'important work remain[ed] to increase institutional confidence through implementing effective processes that will enable: long term stability; accountability; responsiveness; continued private sector leadership, stakeholder participation; increased contract compliance; and enhanced competition.'[168]

c. *Working Towards a Transition to the Private Sector: From a Joint Partnership to an Affirmation of Commitments*

During a public meeting in February 2006 concerning the U.S. Government's review of the MOU/JPA, ICANN announced its intention to prepare a plan for developing a transition framework.[169] The ICANN Board believed that ICANN was meeting its responsibilities under the MOU/JPA and that the conditions had been 'sufficiently met [to allow] that the [MOU/]JPA conclude during the months up to September 2009.'[170] After this meeting, ICANN publicly stated on several occasions – somewhat optimistically, and possibly with a view to boosting the development of a transition plan – that the MOU/JPA would conclude by 30 September 2009.[171] In anticipation of a possible transition, ICANN developed a so-called implementation plan for improving institutional confidence[172] and sought public input. Between June 2008 and May 2009, ICANN organized no fewer than three public comment periods.[173] The third public comment phase coincided with the request for public comments by the U.S. Government 'regarding the progress of the transition of the technical coordination and management of the Internet DNS to the private sector, as well as the model of private sector leadership and bottom-up policy development which ICANN represents.'[174]

167. NTIA, *Statement on the Mid-Term Review of the Joint Project Agreement (JPA) Between NTIA and ICANN*, 2 April 2008, https://www.ntia.doc.gov/press-release/2008/statement-mid-term-review-joint-project-agreement-jpa-between-ntia-and-icann.
168. NTIA, *Statement on the Mid-Term Review of the Joint Project Agreement (JPA) Between NTIA and ICANN*, 2 April 2008, https://www.ntia.doc.gov/press-release/2008/statement-mid-term-review-joint-project-agreement-jpa-between-ntia-and-icann.
169. ICANN, *Address by ICANN Chairman to Public Meeting on the Midterm Review of the JPA*, 28 February 2008, https://archive.icann.org/en/jpa/chairman-address.html.
170. ICANN, *Address by ICANN Chairman to Public Meeting on the Midterm Review of the JPA*, 28 February 2008, https://archive.icann.org/en/jpa/chairman-address.html.
171. NTIA, *Notice of Inquiry: Assessment of the Transition of the Technical Coordination and Management of the Internet's Domain Name and Addressing System [docket no. 090420688-9689-01]*, 24 April 2009, Federal Register Vol. 74, No. 78, 18689 and references there.
172. *See*, ICANN, *Draft Implementation Plan for Improving Institutional Confidence*, 26 February 2009, https://archive.icann.org/en/jpa/iic/draft-iic-implementation-26feb09-en.pdf.
173. *See* ICANN, Summary and analysis of second IIC comment period (18 September to 20 October 2008), https://archive.icann.org/en/jpa/iic/summary-iic-second-public-comment-period-en.pdf; ICANN, Summary and analysis of third IIC comment period (12 March 2009 to 11 May 2009), https://archive.icann.org/en/jpa/iic/summary-iic-third-public-comment-period-en.pdf.
174. NTIA, *Notice of Inquiry: Assessment of the Transition of the Technical Coordination and Management of the Internet's Domain Name and Addressing System [docket no. 090420688-9689-01]*, 24 April 2009, Federal Register Vol. 74, No. 78, 18688–18690.

Although strong support existed for a full transition to the private sector,[175] many agreed that there were insufficient guarantees for accountability, protection against capture, transparency, etc., to terminate the oversight by the U.S. DoC.[176] ICANN's first president and CEO, Michael M. Roberts, participated in the U.S. Government's inquiry, and encapsulated the situation quite well:

> 'One overarching problem – accountability – still dominates the relationship between ICANN and the U.S. Government, and between ICANN and its broader community, as documented in the comments that ICANN's own outreach has received. Accountability is the predominant and common factor in ICANN's Presidential Strategy Committee's public comment process. If a solution can be found to the accountability dilemma, many other issues will be more manageable.
>
> In 1998, the White Paper described an early termination of U.S. involvement in the affairs of ICANN:
>
> > "the U.S. Government would continue to participate in policy oversight until such time as the new corporation was established and stable, phasing out as soon as possible, but in no event later than September 30, 2000."
>
> But after ten years, this goal has not been realized and ICANN is still saddled with not one, but two contracts tying it to the Department of Commerce. It is clear that accountability and independence are intertwined, and a decision on independence is also a decision on accountability. In this context, accountability means clarity with respect to process and structure such that governments and private sector stakeholders are assured of fair and equitable treatment in ICANN decisions. It is possible that the delays and related stakeholder concerns in ending the MOU/JPA are more a reflection of unease over the accountability problem than they are a lack of accomplishment on the various tasks set forth in these documents.'[177]

So accountability concerns remained, and ICANN started focusing on the role of governments quite late in the development of its proposed implementation plan for improving institutional confidence. It was not until 26 June 2009 that the ICANN Board decided that a joint working group must be established between the ICANN Board and the Government Advisory Committee (GAC) to review the GAC's role within ICANN.[178]

175. *See e.g.*, ISOC, *Internet Society comments submitted to the United States Department of Commerce, National Telecommunications and Information Administration, Notice of Inquiry "Assessment of the transition of the technical coordination and management of the Internet's domain name and addressing system [docket no. 090420688-9689-01]"*, https://www.ntia.doc.gov/files/ntia/comments2009/012.pdf; Letter from SIDN to the U.S. Department of Commerce, National Telecommunications and Information Administration, 5 July 2009, https://www.ntia.doc.gov/files/ntia/comments2009/014.pdf.

176. *See e.g.*, Letter from the International AntiCounterfeiting Coalition to the U.S. Department of Commerce, National Telecommunications and Information Administration, 5 July 2009, https://www.ntia.doc.gov/files/ntia/comments2009/015.pdf; Thomas M. Lenard and Lawrence J. White, *ICANN at a crossroads: a proposal for better governance and performance*, June 2009, https://www.ntia.doc.gov/files/ntia/comments2009/017.pdf.

177. Michael M. Roberts, *The ICANN Accountability Dilemma – A Response to the 2009 ICANN Notice of Inquiry Issued by the National Telecommunications and Information Administration*, 8 June 2009, https://www.ntia.doc.gov/files/ntia/comments2009/034.pdf p. 1.

178. ICANN, *ICANN Board Resolution 2009.06.26.23*, https://www.icann.org/resources/board-material/resolutions-2009-06-26-en.

This working group was also to engage with the broader ICANN community in a fully consultative process on the GAC's role within ICANN.[179]

The discussions on improving ICANN's accountability and on a possible full transition to the private sector came at a pivotal time for ICANN. After the ICANN Board had adopted the recommendations of ICANN's policy-making body, the Generic Names Supporting Organization (GNSO), for the introduction of new gTLDs in June 2008,[180] ICANN started detailed discussions on transforming these recommendations into a concrete process for opening up the Internet's name space. An enormous amount of energy was devoted to the development of this process, which became known as the new gTLD Program. Also in June 2008, ICANN's accountability mechanisms were put to the test, as ICANN was facing its first legal challenge for which the claimant used ICANN's Independent Review Process (IRP).[181] Both events – the development of the new gTLD Program and the IRP – together gave ICANN the opportunity to show that it was finally moving towards the opening up of the Internet's naming space in a predictable, transparent and accountable manner. They provided ICANN with the chance to demonstrate that a transition could actually work.

The MOU/JPA between the U.S. DoC and ICANN was not renewed when it finally expired in September 2009. It was replaced by an Affirmation of Commitments (AoC), which was intended to be a longstanding agreement between the U.S. DoC and ICANN.[182] The AoC reaffirmed ICANN's commitments to *inter alia*: (i) ensure accountability, transparency and the interests of global Internet users, (ii) preserve security, stability and resiliency, and (iii) promote competition, consumer trust and consumer choice.[183] The AoC requires ICANN to perform regular compliance reviews and to improve its mechanisms so as to live up to its commitments on a continuing basis.

ICANN considered that the execution of the AoC completed the transition that had started in 1998.[184]

However, the AoC confirmed ICANN's relationship with the U.S. Government, and the U.S. Government did not relinquish its control over the IANA functions. ICANN continued to perform the IANA functions on behalf of the U.S. Government according to an agreement: the IANA functions contract with the NTIA. As a result, the AoC did not in fact complete the transition. Through the IANA functions contract, the U.S. Government maintained its control over changes in the authoritative Internet's root zone. The IANA functions contract has been up for renewal each year, providing the U.S. Government with remote, but real, oversight. Without control over the IANA

179. ICANN, *ICANN Board Resolution 2009.06.26.23*, https://www.icann.org/resources/board-material/resolutions-2009-06-26-en.
180. ICANN, *ICANN Board Resolution 2008.06.26.02-03*, https://www.icann.org/resources/board-material/resolutions-2008-06-26-en.
181. ICM Registry case.
182. Affirmation of Commitments, *supra* n. 135, Article 11.
183. Affirmation of Commitments, *supra* n. 135, Articles 9.1, 9.2 and 9.3.
184. ICANN, *ICANN CEO Talks About the New Affirmation of Commitments*, 30 September 2009, https://www.icann.org/news/announcement-2009-09-30-en.

functions, ICANN has no access to the Internet's root, and it would be impossible for ICANN to implement new policies affecting the root.

d. *Completion of the Transition to the Private Sector*

On 14 March 2014, in the aftermath of ICANN's most ambitious plan to date for introducing new gTLDs to the Internet's root, the NTIA announced its intent to transition out of its role as administrator of changes to the authoritative root zone file and as the historic steward of the DNS.[185] According to the NTIA, '[t]he timing [was] right to start the transition process.'[186] The NTIA invited ICANN to develop a transition plan and to propose it to the NTIA. The NTIA informed ICANN that the transition proposal 'must have broad community support and address the following four principles:

- Support and enhance the multistakeholder model;
- Maintain the security, stability, and resiliency of the Internet DNS;
- Meet the needs and expectation of the global customers and partners of the IANA services; and
- Maintain the openness of the Internet.[187]

The NTIA's role was to remain unchanged while ICANN and the Internet community prepared their proposal for a transition plan. At the time of the NTIA announcement, the IANA functions contract was set to expire on 30 September 2015,[188] and the Internet community started working towards this informal[189] deadline.

On 17 and 18 July 2014, a multistakeholder group met in London with the purpose of supporting and coordinating the development of a proposal on the IANA functions stewardship transition.[190] By the beginning of September 2014, the group, named the

185. NTIA, *NTIA Announces Intent to Transition Key Internet Domain Name Functions*, 14 March 2014, https://www.ntia.doc.gov/press-release/2014/ntia-announces-intent-transition-key-internet-domain-name-functions.
186. NTIA, *NTIA Announces Intent to Transition Key Internet Domain Name Functions*, 14 March 2014, https://www.ntia.doc.gov/press-release/2014/ntia-announces-intent-transition-key-internet-domain-name-functions.
187. NTIA, *NTIA Announces Intent to Transition Key Internet Domain Name Functions*, 14 March 2014, https://www.ntia.doc.gov/press-release/2014/ntia-announces-intent-transition-key-internet-domain-name-functions.
188. Amendment Modification No. 002 to IANA Functions Contract, 30 April 2013, https://www.ntia.doc.gov/files/ntia/publications/sa1301-12-cn-0035001.pdf.
189. The NTIA had not set a deadline for the transition and made clear that, should the community need more time, the NTIA can extend the current IANA functions contract for up to four years. *See* Remarks by Lawrence E. Strickling Assistant Secretary of Commerce for Communications and Information, PLI/FCBA Telecommunications Policy & Regulation Institute, Washington, DC, 4 December 2014, https://www.ntia.doc.gov/speechtestimony/2014/remarks-assistant-secretary-strickling-plifcba-telecommunications-policy-regula.
190. ICANN, *Statement from the first meeting of the IANA Stewardship Transition Coordination Group*, 18 July 2014, https://www.icann.org/en/system/files/files/draft-icg-statement-18jul14-en.pdf.

IANA Stewardship Transition Coordination Group (ICG) had adopted a charter[191] and issued a Request for Transition Proposals for each of the three primary IANA functions to be developed by the communities and parties most directly affected by each of the primary functions.[192] The ICG also adopted a timeline to work towards a transition by September 2015.[193] The ICG's aim was to have a proposal concerning the IANA functions transition ready for final community review by 19 June 2015. This would allow the proposal to be finalized by 31 July 2015 for submission to the NTIA.

But the Internet community was expecting more than a simple acknowledgment by ICANN of its role facilitating its technical functions; the Internet community was expecting ICANN to affirm its accountability.[194] When the U.S. Government finally relinquishes its oversight role, the general expectation is that ICANN should be more accountable, not less. Therefore, concurrent with the work of the ICG, a CCWG was established within ICANN with a view to improving ICANN's accountability in light of the anticipated transition.[195]

On 4 May 2015, the CCWG published its initial draft proposal for public comment.[196] Commentators criticized the proposed accountability framework for being too narrow and not powerful enough.[197] This initial proposal was very inward focused, and it was generally felt that ICANN should be accountable to all stakeholders, including those outside ICANN. Moreover, the enforceability of the accountability system needed to be assured unambiguously,[198] a topic which has been heavily debated in multiple disputes.[199]

At the end of the public comment phase, it was clear to the NTIA that the transition would not occur before the expiry of the IANA functions contract in view of the status of ICANN's proposal and the time necessary for the U.S. Government to evaluate the plan.[200] The NTIA informed ICANN that it could exercise an option to extend the IANA

191. ICANN, *Charter for the IANA Stewardship Transition Coordination Group*, 27 August 2014, https://www.icann.org/en/system/files/files/charter-icg-27aug14-en.pdf.
192. ICANN, *IANA Stewardship Transition Coordination Group Request for Proposals*, 8 September 2014, https://www.icann.org/en/system/files/files/rfp-iana-stewardship-08sep14-en.pdf.
193. ICANN, *IANA Stewardship Transition Coordination Group Process Timeline*, 8 September 2014, https://www.icann.org/en/system/files/files/icg-process-timeline-08sep14-en.pdf.
194. Flip Petillion, 'Filling the NTIA void', *TBO*, 1 May 2014.
195. ICANN, *Charter Cross Community Working Group on Enhancing ICANN Accountability*, 4 November 2014, https://community.icann.org/display/acctcrosscomm/Charter.
196. ICANN, *Cross Community Working Group (CCWG) Accountability Initial Draft Proposal for Public Comment*, 4 May 2015, https://community.icann.org/pages/viewpage.action?pageId=52897394.
197. *See* public comments available on https://community.icann.org/display/acctcrosscomm/First+Public+Comment+Review+Tool+-+comprehensive+version+-+18+August+2015.
198. *See* public comments available on https://community.icann.org/display/acctcrosscomm/First+Public+Comment+Review+Tool+-+comprehensive+version+-+18+August+2015.
199. *See* Chapter 5.
200. NTIA, *Remarks of Lawrence E. Strickling Assistant Secretary of Commerce for Communications and Information ICANN Meeting*, 21 June 2015, https://www.ntia.doc.gov/speechtestimony/2015/remarks-lawrence-e-strickling-assistant-secretary-commerce-communications-and-i;

functions contract for two years until September 2017, but feared that this would send the wrong signal to the Internet community, and give the impression either that it was not working hard to finish the transition plan or that the U.S. Government was reducing its efforts to complete the transition.[201] The NTIA subsequently negotiated a one-year extension with ICANN of the IANA functions contract.[202]

On 3 August 2015, the CCWG published a second draft proposal for public comments. And on 30 November 2015, a new public comment period was initiated on a third draft. The second and third drafts also remained inward-looking, focusing mostly on increasing accountability for existing stakeholder groups.[203] Insufficient account was taken of other parties, who, though not necessarily represented at ICANN, were nevertheless likely to be severely impacted by ICANN's decisions. Some stakeholders within the ICANN community asked for increased limitations on the rights of third parties not involved in ICANN's policy development processes.[204] Although imposing such limitations would impede, rather than improve, ICANN's accountability, interest groups within the Internet community are of course primarily concerned with the promotion and protection of their own interests, rather than with the common good. This is a major reason why efficient external control mechanisms are of paramount importance, even for communities in which a large number of critical voices can be heard.

For as long as the IANA functions contract remained in place, the U.S. Government retained its external control mechanism, and its ability to encourage ICANN to improve its internal and external accountability. The relinquishing of the U.S. stewardship role over the IANA functions was to be done with great care. If it turns out that the

---

NTIA, *Testimony of Assistant Secretary Strickling on 'Internet Governance Progress After ICANN 53'*, 8 July 2015, https://www.ntia.doc.gov/speechtestimony/2015/testimony-strickling-internet-governance-progress-after-icann-53.

201. NTIA, *Testimony of Assistant Secretary Strickling on 'Internet Governance Progress After ICANN 53'*, 8 July 2015, https://www.ntia.doc.gov/speechtestimony/2015/testimony-strickling-internet-governance-progress-after-icann-53.
202. Amendment Modification No. 0004 to the IANA Function Contract, http://www.ntia.doc.gov /page/iana-functions-purchase-order.
203. ICANN, *CCWG-Accountability 2nd Draft Proposal on Work Stream 1 Recommendations*, 3 August 2015 https://community.icann.org/pages/viewpage.action?pageId=53783460; ICANN, *CCWG-Accountability, 3rd Draft Proposal on Work Stream 1 Recommendations*, 30 November 2015, https://community.icann.org/pages/viewpage.action?pageId=56145016.
204. The Business Constituency within ICANN's GNSO expressed its concern that ICANN's accountability mechanisms 'would allow parties to introduce new arguments without first vetting them through the community's policy development channels.' It criticized the fact that the accountability mechanisms did not require 'parties to participate in public comment processes directly addressing the issue for which reconsideration or review is sought. This process may not create the right incentives: it invites parties to stand on the sidelines during the policy development process and bring their concerns to the Reconsideration or Independent Review processes after policy development has concluded. Such an approach could create operational inefficiency and could undermine the bottom-up, consensus based process for developing policy within ICANN.' (ICANN GNSO Business Constituency, *Comment on Cross Community Working Group on Enhancing ICANN Accountability (CCWG) 2nd Draft Report (Work Stream 1)*, 12 September 2015, https://community.icann.org/download/attachments/ 56136438/62.%20%20Business%20Constituency%20%28BC%29%20Comments.pdf?api=v 2,pp. 6–7).

transition has not been carried out properly, the global Internet community may face a largely introspective and unaccountable ICANN and a situation where established groups could effectively block new entrants from entering the market.

In this respect, it is not necessarily to be applauded that the NTIA has been pushing for the ICANN community *'to conclude on a proposal that is as simple as possible but still meets our conditions and the community's needs'*.[205] By insisting on simplicity, it seems that the NTIA was prepared to accept a baseline solution rather than the best solution. It is also worrying that the ICANN community had agreed to work in two different streams. The now completed Work stream 1 was dedicated to identifying those accountability mechanisms that must be in place or committed to before the IANA stewardship transition; work stream 2 is dedicated to improving ICANN's accountability mechanisms only after the IANA stewardship transition.[206] Since its creation, it has proven virtually impossible to persuade ICANN to enhance its accountability without external pressure. Moreover, as will be explained in Chapter 5 and Chapter 6, ICANN has sought to interpret changes that were made with the purpose of improving ICANN's accountability as the complete opposite: amendments to the accountability framework that weakened its accountability. Recent comments by ICANN's external legal advisors in response to the community's attempts to improve ICANN's accountability and ICANN's positions in IRPs are illustrative of ICANN's reluctance to offer effective redress mechanisms.[207] Such redress mechanisms are of particular importance when ICANN evaluates applications for new Internet extensions. As each TLD string is a unique identifier, TLDs have the potential to become a high-value asset which is difficult to substitute. The delegation of new TLDs is one of ICANN's most visible and economically relevant activities. TLD applicants are entitled to a fair, equitable, transparent and non-discriminatory process, and because of the high stakes involved in a TLD application, it is unsurprising that ICANN's accountability mechanisms are tested intensively with regard to these issues. Until now, parties relying on ICANN's accountability mechanisms have been confronted with the inadequacies of those mechanisms, rather than being provided with a meaningful redress in a streamlined manner. It is unfortunate that, despite three rounds of new gTLD applications (*infra*, Chapter 2.C), ICANN has been unable to install efficient redress mechanisms to guarantee legal certainty through the observance of fundamental rights. What is more, rather than enhancing its accountability mechanisms, ICANN has sought to do the opposite by

205. NTIA, *Remarks of Lawrence E. Strickling Assistant Secretary of Commerce for Communications and Information ICANN Meeting*, 21 June 2015, https://www.ntia.doc.gov/speechtestimony/2015/remarks-lawrence-e-strickling-assistant-secretary-commerce-communications-and-i.

206. ICANN, *Cross Community Working Group on Enhancing ICANN Accountability Charter*, 3 November 2014, https://community.icann.org/display/acctcrosscomm/Charter.

207. ICANN, *Impact Analysis of CCWG-Accountability Second Draft Proposals by external counsel*, https://community.icann.org/download/attachments/56136438/43.%20f%29%20%20ICANN%20Board%20Submission%20of%20Jones%20Day%20Impact%20Analysis.pdf?api=v2.

attempting to introduce a statute of limitations retroactively, arguing that applicants were not entitled to due process, and attempting to evade all responsibility through its commissioning of third parties.

On 10 March 2016, the ICANN Board published ICANN's IANA Stewardship Transition Proposal.[208] ICANN's proposal received general support from U.S. businesses[209] and members of civil society.[210] The ICANN Board adopted amended Bylaws on 27 May 2016[211] and prepared amended Articles of Incorporation.[212] The amended Bylaws and Articles of Incorporation entered into force when the U.S. Government relinquished its IANA stewardship role.

On 9 June 2016, the NTIA announced that ICANN's proposal met the criteria to complete privatization[213] and transmitted its assessment report on the proposal to U.S. Congress.[214] It has since defended its assessment report with U.S. Senators.[215]

In the meantime, ICANN had been testing the technical processes for managing the IANA functions without U.S. oversight.[216] On 12 August 2016, ICANN submitted an implementation status report on the IANA stewardship transition, confirming that all transition tasks are completed or will be completed in advance of 30 September 2016.[217] In response, the NTIA informed ICANN on 16 August 2016 that it intended to

208. ICANN, *Letter from ICANN to NTIA*, 10 March 2016, https://www.icann.org/en/system/files/correspondence/crocker-to-strickling-10mar16-en.pdf.
209. *Open Letter to Congress from U.S. Business*, http://blogs.intel.com/policy/files/2016/04/Business-Open-Letter-supporting-IANA-Transition-VersionV.pdf.
210. *Civil Society Statement of Support for IANA Transition*, https://www.accessnow.org/cms/assets/uploads/2016/05/CSstatementonIANAtransitionMay2016-1.pdf.
211. ICANN, *Future Bylaws for Internet Corporation for Assigned Names and Numbers, a California Nonprofit Public-Benefit Corporation, adopted by ICANN Board on 27 May 2016*, https://www.icann.org/en/system/files/files/adopted-bylaws-27may16-en.pdf.
212. ICANN, *Amended and Restated Articles of Incorporation of Internet Corporation for Assigned Names and Numbers, Draft as of 25 May 2016*, https://www.icann.org/en/system/files/files/draft-restated-articles-incorporation-25may16-en.pdf.
213. NTIA, *NTIA Finds IANA Stewardship Transition Proposal Meets Criteria to Complete Privatization*, 9 June 2016, https://www.ntia.doc.gov/press-release/2016/iana-stewardship-transition-proposal-meets-criteria-complete-privatization.
214. NTIA, *NTIA Letter to Congress Transmitting NTIA's Assessment of IANA Transition Proposal*, 9 June 2016, https://www.ntia.doc.gov/files/ntia/publications/ntia_letter_to_congress_transmitting_ntias_assessment_of_iana_transition_proposal_06.09.16.pdf.
215. NTIA, *NTIA Letter to Senators Thune and Rubio on IANA Transition*, 9 June 2016, https://www.ntia.doc.gov/files/ntia/publications/ntia_letter_to_senators_thune_and_rubio_on_iana_transition_06.09.16.pdf; NTIA, *NTIA Assistant Secretary Responds to Senators Rubio, Blunt, Johnson, Heller, and Sullivan Regarding the Transition of the U.S. Government's Stewardship of Key Internet Domain Name Functions*, 27 June 2016, https://www.ntia.doc.gov/files/ntia/publications/20160627_-_ntia_response_iana_-_rubio.pdf.
216. *See* Akram Atallah, *Root Zone Management Transition Update: Preservation of Security, Stability and Resiliency*, ICANN Blog, 28 June 2016, https://www.icann.org/news/blog/root-zone-management-transition-update-preservation-of-security-stability-and-resiliency.
217. ICANN, *ICANN Letter to Mr. Lawrence E. Strickling, Assistant Secretary for Communication and Information and Administrator of NTIA*, 12 August 2016, https://www.icann.org/en/system/files/correspondence/marby-to-strickling-12aug16-en.pdf; ICANN, *IANA Stewardship Transition Proposal Implementation Planning Status Report*, 12 August 2016, https://www.icann.org/en/system/files/files/iana-stewardship-implementation-planning-status-12aug16-en.pdf.

allow the IANA functions contract to expire as of 1 October 2016.[218] Everyone was thus getting ready for a transitioning of the IANA stewardship to ICANN, and a final attempt by some members of U.S. Congress to stop the transition failed. Four U.S. states tried to block the transition by filing a request for a restraining order at the eleventh hour.[219] Their request was turned down, and the transition moved forward.[220] Unless the court order gets reversed in appeal or proceedings on the merits result in a different outcome, it is unlikely that the complete privatization of the Internet and ICANN's control over it will be reversed any time soon. Although we may expect that ICANN will exercise its stewardship over the Internet in a responsible manner, one should not underestimate the risks associated with the complete privatization. In Chapter 7, Chapter 8 and Chapter 9, we identify these risks.

B. GOVERNING PRINCIPLES

Unless stated otherwise, we refer to the governing principles as they existed before the transition of the IANA functions to ICANN. When mention is made of ICANN's Bylaws, we refer to the version of the Bylaws that was current before the transition on 1 October 2016. However, ICANN's newest Bylaws, which entered into force on 1 October 2016, did not change ICANN's essential obligations, but rather strengthened them.

1. Compliance with General Principles of International Law

ICANN is a non-profit public benefit corporation, incorporated under the laws of California.[221] ICANN's mission and the limits to its authority are defined in ICANN's Articles of Incorporation, Bylaws, and in agreements with competent authorities. Given ICANN's public benefit mission to 'operate for the Internet community as a whole' – *i.e.*, globally – ICANN is not bound by principles of the local laws in California only, but, first and foremost, ICANN must carry out 'its activities in conformity with relevant principles of international law and applicable international conventions.'[222]

The requirement to comply with principles of international law was deliberate. The original draft of ICANN's Articles of Incorporation did not include any reference to

218. NTIA, *NTIA Letter to Mr. Göran Marby, President and CEO of ICANN*, 16 August 2016, https://www.ntia.doc.gov/files/ntia/publications/20160816marby.pdf.
219. U.S. District Court Southern District of Texas Galveston Division, *State of Arizona et al. v. NTIA et al.*, Complaint for Declaratory and Injunctive Relief and Application for Temporary Restraining Order and Preliminary Injunction, 28 September 2016, Case 3:16-cv-00274, https://www.icann.org/en/system/files/files/litigation-states-various-complaint-application-tro-injunction-28sep16-en.pdf.
220. U.S. District Court Southern District of Texas Galveston Division, *State of Arizona et al. v. NTIA et al.*, Order, 3 October 2016, https://www.icann.org/en/system/files/files/litigation-defendants-denying-motion-for-injunction-30sep16-en.pdf.
221. ICANN, Articles of Incorporation, Article 3.
222. ICANN, Articles of Incorporation, Article 4.

international law.[223] The fifth draft of ICANN's Articles of Incorporation – *i.e.*, the version of the Articles of Incorporation that ICANN submitted to the U.S. Government in response to the White Paper[224] – provided that ICANN should carry out its activities 'with due regard for applicable local and international law'.[225] This provision was added 'in response to various suggestions to recognize the special nature of [the] organization and the general principles under which it will operate.'[226] After negotiations with the U.S. Government and several Internet stakeholders,[227] ICANN augmented its obligations under international law on 21 November 1998.[228] From that date onwards, ICANN's Articles of Incorporation have provided that:

> 'The Corporation shall operate for the benefit of the Internet Community as a whole, carrying out its activities in conformity with relevant principles of international law and applicable international conventions and local law and, to the extent appropriate and consistent with these Articles and its Bylaws, through open and transparent processes that enable competition and open entry in Internet-related markets. To this effect, the Corporation shall cooperate as appropriate with relevant international organizations.'[229]

The Articles of Incorporation do not require ICANN merely to have 'due regard' for 'international law'; ICANN must act 'in conformity with relevant principles of international law and applicable international conventions'. As accepted both by legal scholars[230] and case law,[231] ICANN's requirement to act in conformity with relevant principles on international law includes conformity with 'the general principles of law recognized as a source of international law'. General principles of international law can thus be said to serve as a prism through which the various obligations imposed on ICANN under its Articles of Incorporation and Bylaws must be interpreted.

223. ICANN, *Draft Articles of Incorporation of new IANA*, http://forum.icann.org/iana/comments/formation/,,articles1.html.
224. NTIA, *Letter from Jon Postel to NTIA regarding Management of Internet Names and Addresses*, https://www.ntia.doc.gov/legacy/ntiahome/domainname/proposals/icann/Letter.htm (2 October 1998); ICANN, Articles of Incorporation of Internet Corporation for Assigned Names and Numbers, https://www.ntia.doc.gov/legacy/ntiahome/domainname/proposals/icann/Articles.htm.
225. ICANN, *Draft Articles of Incorporation – Fifth Iteration: Articles of Incorporation of Internet Corporation for Assigned Names and Numbers*, http://forum.icann.org/iana/comments/formation/,,articles5.html.
226. ICANN, *Draft Articles of Incorporation – Fifth Iteration: Articles of Incorporation of Internet Corporation for Assigned Names and Numbers*, http://forum.icann.org/iana/comments/formation/,,articles5.html.
227. *Supra*, Chapter 2.A.2.b(3)(d).
228. ICANN, *Minutes of Special Meeting 21 November 1998*, https://www.icann.org/resources/board-material/minutes-1998-11-21-en.
229. ICANN, Articles of Incorporation, Article 4.
230. Expert Report of Jack Goldsmith, *in* ICDR Case No. 50 117 T 00224 08, 22 January 2009, pp. 12–16, §§ 23–27.
231. *ICM Registry, LLC v. ICANN*, ICDR Case No. 50 117 T 00224 08, Independent Review Panel Declaration, 19 February 2010, para. 140.

2. Hierarchy of Legal Sources

In contrast with previous drafts of the Articles of Incorporation, ICANN's current version[232] puts principles of international law first, before applicable international conventions, local law and ICANN's Bylaws. ICANN reversed the order of the applicable rules in recognition of the international scope of its mission, and of the fundamental principle that international law prevails over domestic law.[233] As a result, any principles enshrined in Californian law, ICANN's Articles of Incorporation and/or ICANN's Bylaws will only apply to the extent that they are fully compatible with international law. ICANN's Articles of Incorporation and Bylaws must thus be interpreted in a way that is consistent with general principles of international law. If ICANN adopts secondary rules, such as policies and process, ICANN should warrant the compliance of these secondary rules with international law, national law, its Articles of Incorporation and its Bylaws; in that order.

In addition, we have always believed that ICANN's Articles of Incorporation and Bylaws should be interpreted in light of ICANN's AoC, which requires ICANN to comply with generally accepted good governance principles. Recent case law,[234] and, it seems, ICANN itself,[235] now accept this proposition. As a result, secondary rules, such as policies and process, must also be consistent with the AoC.

3. Applicable Norms

The applicable legal framework requires ICANN to act in good faith, to ensure fairness, non-discrimination, openness and transparency, accountability, and the promotion of competition. These requirements can be found in applicable norms of international law, domestic law, ICANN's Articles of Incorporation and its Bylaws. They are reiterated at different places in the Bylaws, and some requirements are taken up as core values that 'should guide the decisions and actions of ICANN.'[236] ICANN's Bylaws provide:

> These core values are deliberately expressed in very general terms, so that they may provide useful and relevant guidance in the broadest possible range of

---

232. Although ICANN has expressed the intention to change the Articles of Incorporation following the IANA transition, the version of 21 November 1998 is still in place.
233. *See e.g.*, PCIJ, *Interpretation of the Convention between Greece and Bulgaria respecting reciprocal emigration, signed at Neuilly-sur-Seine on November 27th, 1919 (Question of the Greco-Bulgarian 'communities')*, Advisory Opinion of 31 July 1930, *P.C.I.J. Rep., Series B*, No. 17, 32; PCIJ, *Treatment of Polish nationals and other persons of Polish origin or speech in the Danzich territory*, Advisory Opinion of 4 February 1932, *P.C.I.J. Rep., Series A/B*, No. 44, 24; ICJ, *Applicability of the Obligation to Arbitrate under Section 21 of the United Nations Headquarters Agreement of 26 April 1947*, Advisory Opinion of 26 April 1988, *I.C.J. Rep* 1988, 12, § 57.
234. *Vistaprint Limited v. ICANN*, ICDR Case No. 01-14-0000-6505, Final Declaration of the Independent Review Panel, 9 October 2015,§§ 67, 124.
235. ICANN adopted new Bylaws on 27 May 2016, which incorporate the Affirmation of Commitments.
236. ICANN Bylaws, Article I(2).

> circumstances. Because they are not narrowly prescriptive, the specific way in which they apply, individually and collectively, to each new situation will necessarily depend on many factors that cannot be fully anticipated or enumerated; and because they are statements of principle rather than practice, situations will inevitably arise in which perfect fidelity to all eleven core values simultaneously is not possible. Any ICANN body making a recommendation or decision shall exercise its judgment to determine which core values are most relevant and how they apply to the specific circumstances of the case at hand, and to determine, if necessary, an appropriate and defensible balance among competing values.'[237]

Although a balancing exercise may be appropriate in some circumstances, ICANN's discretion in applying its core values is not unfettered. While some of ICANN's core values, such as the promotion of competition, may be subject to restrictions (*e.g.*, to ensure compliance with essential requirements that preserve the stability and security of the Internet), other core values reflect more fundamental norms from which derogation must not be permitted.

a. *Act in Good Faith*

Many of the guiding substantive and procedural rules in ICANN's Articles and Bylaws – including the rules involving transparency, fairness, and non-discrimination – are so fundamental that they appear in some form in virtually every legal system in the world. One of the reasons they are so universal is that they arise from the general principle of good faith, which is considered to be the foundation of all law and all conventions. As stated by the International Court of Justice (ICJ), the principle of good faith is '[o]ne of the basic principles governing the creation and performance of legal obligations.'[238]

The principle of good faith includes an obligation to ensure procedural fairness by, *inter alia*, adhering to substantive and procedural rules, avoiding arbitrary action and recognizing legitimate expectations. The principle is considered so fundamental that it need not be explicitly stated in order to apply and no derogation is permitted. Many of ICANN's obligations which arise from the general principle of good faith are taken up explicitly in ICANN's governing documents. These obligations are discussed below (*infra*, under b, c and e).

b. *Apply Policies Neutrally, Fairly and Without Discrimination*

ICANN is subject to a fundamental obligation to act fairly and apply established policies neutrally and without discrimination. Not only does this obligation arise from general principles of international law, it is also laid down repeatedly in ICANN's governing documents. Article II(3) of ICANN's current Bylaws is entitled 'non-discriminatory treatment' and provides that:

---

237. ICANN Bylaws, Article I(2).
238. Nuclear Tests (*Austl. v. Fr.*), 1974 I.C.J. 253, 268 (20 Dec.) (merits); *see also* Land and Maritime Boundary (*Cameroon v. Nig.*), 1998 I.C.J. 275, 296 (11 June) (good faith is a 'well established principle of international law').

> 'ICANN shall not apply its standards, policies, procedures, or practices inequitably or single out any party for disparate treatment unless justified by substantial and reasonable cause, such as the promotion of effective competition.'

This prohibition on discrimination has been included in ICANN's Bylaws since the corporation submitted its application in 1998 to operate as the DNS custodian.[239] In their original version ICANN's Bylaws contained no example of a substantial and reasonable cause that could justify disparate treatment.[240] Following negotiations with U.S. Government officials and Internet stakeholders, ICANN added the promotion of effective competition as a possible justification for disparate treatment.[241] In 2002, ICANN changed the numbering of its Bylaws and added the title 'non-discriminatory treatment.'[242] Apart from these mainly cosmetic amendments, the article has never been changed, neither did it change with the entry into force of ICANN's post-IANA transition Bylaws, adopted on 27 May 2016. The fact that the article on non-discrimination has remained unchanged ever since ICANN became the DNS custodian evinces the fundamental nature of the principle of non-discrimination as regards ICANN's operations.

In addition, the prohibition on discrimination is not merely mentioned as a core value that 'should guide' ICANN's actions and decisions;[243] ICANN dedicated a separate article in its Bylaws to non-discriminatory treatment, containing conclusive language that it 'shall not' act inequitably or single out a party for disparate treatment. It follows that the principle of non-discrimination is a cornerstone for ICANN's actions and decisions.

c. *Remain Transparent*

Another cornerstone for ICANN's decision-making process is its obligation to operate in an open and transparent manner. ICANN's commitment to transparency is contained in ICANN's Articles of Incorporation, Bylaws and the AoC.

239. NTIA, *Letter from Jon Postel to NTIA regarding Management of Internet Names and Addresses*, https://www.ntia.doc.gov/legacy/ntiahome/domainname/proposals/icann/Letter.htm (2 October 1998); ICANN, *Bylaws for the Internet Corporation for Assigned Names and Numbers* – A California Nonprofit Public Benefit Corporation, https://www.ntia.doc.gov/legacy/ntiahome/domainname/proposals/icann/Bylaws.htm.
240. ICANN, *Bylaws for the Internet Corporation for Assigned Names and Numbers* – A California Nonprofit Public Benefit Corporation, Article IV(1)(c), https://www.ntia.doc.gov/legacy/ntiahome/domainname/proposals/icann/Bylaws.htm.
241. ICANN Bylaws, as adopted effective 21 November 1998, Article IV(1)(c), https://www.icann.org/resources/unthemed-pages/bylaws-1998-11-23-en.
242. ICANN Bylaws, as adopted effective 15 December 2002, Article II(3), https://www.icann.org/resources/unthemed-pages/bylaws-2002-12-15-en.
243. The requirement to act fairly has been further elaborated upon in ICANN's core values, which instruct ICANN to make '*decisions by applying documented policies neutrally and objectively, with integrity and fairness*' (ICANN Bylaws as amended on 15 December 2002, Article I(2)(8). Since the Bylaws amendment of 1 October 2016, this core value has become an ICANN commitment (ICANN Bylaws as amended on 1 October 2016, Article 1(2)(a)(v).

ICANN's transparency obligation was already included in Article 4 of the draft Articles of Incorporation it proposed in response to the U.S. Government's White Paper. Article 4, which, after adoption, remained unchanged in this respect, provided that ICANN 'shall operate for the benefit of the Internet community as a whole, carrying out its activities [...] to the extent appropriate and consistent with these Articles and its Bylaws, through open and transparent processes that enable competition and open entry in Internet-related markets'. Similarly, Article III of ICANN's Bylaws has always stated that ICANN and its constituent bodies[244] 'shall operate to the maximum extent feasible in an open and transparent manner and consistent with procedures designed to ensure fairness'.

These provisions have later been supplemented by the core values and commitments set out in ICANN's Bylaws, which specify that ICANN should employ 'open and transparent policy development mechanisms that: (i) promote well-informed decisions based on expert advice, and (ii) ensure that those entities most affected can assist in the policy development process.'[245] In addition, the AoC agreed between the U.S. DoC and ICANN also affirms ICANN's commitment to transparency, mentioning it as a key commitment.[246]

The emphasis ICANN has put on transparency is sensible. The principle of transparency arises from, and is generally seen as an element of, the principle of good faith. Indeed, transparency has itself obtained the position of a fundamental principle in international economic relations, especially in the regulatory and/or standard-setting role that ICANN occupies.[247] The core elements of transparency include clarity of procedures, the publication and notification of guidelines and applicable rules, and the duty to provide reasons for actions taken.[248]

The coupling of the terms 'open' and 'transparent' in ICANN's governing documents, and a consideration of the context within which the term has been included, confirms that ICANN intended the term to denote the most developed dimension of transparency, namely openness in decision making. During ICANN's first public meeting, Esther Dyson, ICANN's first Chair, stated the following about ICANN's commitment to openness and transparency:

> 'But to me, being open isn't simply posting your minutes out. To be honest, when I read our minutes, I'm embarrassed. Like any legal minutes, they say almost nothing. And I think it is our duty and it's – frankly, we've got to do it or we won't win anybody's trust, not just to post our minutes, but to explain what we did, what

244. ICANN's constituent bodies were named subordinate entities until ICANN's 'new' Bylaws were adopted effective 15 December 2002.
245. ICANN Bylaws, Article I(2)(7). The core values, along with the concept of core values, were introduced with the 'new' Bylaws as adopted effective 15 December 2002.
246. Affirmation of Commitments, *supra* n. 135, Articles 3, 7, 9.1 and 10.
247. *See* A. Kotera, *Regulatory Transparency*, in P. Muchlinski, F. Ortino and C. Schreuer, *Oxford Handbook of International Investment Law* 619 (2008); *see* Stacy Baird, *The Government at the Standards Bazaar*, 18 Stanford Law & Policy Review 35, 96–97 (2007).
248. *See* Sacha Prechal and Madeleine de Leeuw, *Dimensions of Transparency: The Building Blocks for a New Legal Principle?*, Review of European Administrative Law 51 (2007).

> was our reasoning. And sometimes that means we have to trust you, because we need to explain, well, we did this because, you know, there are these two points of view and we're trying to find a balance between them. And sometimes we need to make explicit things that our lawyers would prefer for us to keep implicit. But at some point, I'd rather say these things, I'd rather ask Frank[249] about his contract, I'd rather point out that there's tensions between the SO's and the rest of the community than simply try and hide it and pretend it's not there. So to me, transparency is not simply exposure, but explanation.'[250]

In 2009, when it executed the AoC, ICANN committed itself to providing a thorough and reasoned explanation of decisions taken, the rationale thereof and the sources of data and information on which ICANN had relied.[251] ICANN committed itself to being transparent, so as to ensure that the outcomes of its decision-making would reflect the public interest; its decisions were to contain both a rationale and adequate explanation.[252] Since ICANN's inception (as has been confirmed in its governing documents), ICANN has been committed to maintaining and improving, at a continuing basis, robust mechanisms to support the most developed notion of transparency.[253]

d. *Promote Competition and Innovation*

In performing its mission, ICANN is under an obligation to rely as far as possible on market mechanisms so as to promote and sustain a competitive environment. ICANN must be as non-interventionist as possible and its activities are limited to matters requiring, or significantly benefiting from, global coordination. The promotion and sustaining of a competitive environment was one of the primary reasons behind the U.S. Government's efforts to privatize the DNS management.[254] The focus on creating a more competitive environment has been present since the first MOU/JPA between the U.S. Government and ICANN,[255] and has been translated into ICANN's governing documents. Article 4 of ICANN's Articles of Incorporation calls for processes that 'enable competition and open entry in Internet-related markets'. ICANN's Bylaws focus on promoting competition and innovation in three of ICANN's core values, namely:

249. Esther Dyson referred to Frank Fitzsimmons, one of the nine initial directors of ICANN. He served on the ICANN Board from October 1998 to December 2002.
250. ICANN Public Meeting Transcript, Meeting Held in Cambridge, Massachusetts Saturday, 14 November, 9:00 am – 4:00 pm, 14 November 1998, http://cyber.law.harvard.edu/icann/cambridge-1198/archive/transtransparency.html, p. 222.
251. Affirmation of Commitments, *supra* n. 135, Article 7.
252. Affirmation of Commitments, *supra* n. 135, Article 9.1.
253. *See* Affirmation of Commitments, *supra* n. 135, Article 9.1.
254. *See* NTIA, *A Proposal to Improve Technical Management of Internet Names and Addresses – Discussion Draft*, https://www.ntia.doc.gov/files/ntia/publications/dnsdrft.txt (accessed 11 May 2016) ('Green Paper'); NTIA, *Management of Internet Names and Addresses: statement of policy*, https://www.ntia.doc.gov/files/ntia/publications/6_5_98dns.pdf, pp. 31742, 31743, 31744 at n. 18, pp. 31745–31746, 31747–31748, 31749, 31751.
255. Memorandum of Understanding between the U.S. Department of Commerce and Internet Corporation for Assigned Names and Numbers, 25 November 1998, Articles II.A, II.C.2, IV, V.C.3.

2. '2.Respecting the creativity, innovation, and flow of information made possible by the Internet by limiting ICANN's activities to those matters within ICANN's mission requiring or significantly benefiting from global coordination.
   [...]
5. Where feasible and appropriate, depending on market mechanisms to promote and sustain a competitive environment.
6. Introducing and promoting competition in the registration of domain names where practicable and beneficial in the public interest.'[256]

In addition, the promotion of effective competition is the only acceptable justification for disparate treatment explicitly provided for in the ICANN Bylaws.[257] Finally, the AoC affirms the promotion of competition as a key commitment[258] and as a main goal during the expansion of the top-level domain space.[259]

e. Remain Accountable

The fundamental principles which are considered in this Chapter 2.B.3 are not merely aspirational standards that ICANN may choose to adopt on a voluntary basis. They impose unambiguous commitments, and parties affected by ICANN's actions must be entitled to a meaningful review of ICANN's compliance with these fundamental obligations. ICANN has committed itself to ensuring accountability in the AoC,[260] and it has adopted both internal and external review mechanisms for accountability. Article IV(1) of ICANN's Bylaws sets forth that ICANN 'should be accountable to the community for operating in a manner that is consistent with the[...] Bylaws, and with due regard for the core values set forth in Article 1 of the[...] Bylaws.' One of ICANN's core values instructs ICANN to '[r]emain[...] accountable to the Internet community through mechanisms that enhance ICANN's effectiveness.'[261] As a result, ICANN has not merely committed itself to complying with its fundamental obligations; it has also committed itself to establishing mechanisms to redress any violation of those obligations.

C. ICANN'S LIBERALIZATION EFFORTS

One of ICANN's missions and principal objectives is to promote competition and develop policy concerning the Internet's unique identifiers, in particular in the gTLD

256. ICANN Bylaws as amended on 15 December 2002, Article I(2)(2), (5)-(6); The duty to '[r]espect the creativity, innovation, and flow of information made possible by the Internet by limiting ICANN's activities to matters that are within ICANN's Mission and require or significantly benefit from global coordination' has been taken up as a 'commitment in ICANN's Bylaws as amended on 1 October 2016, Article I(2)(a)(iii).
257. ICANN Bylaws as amended on 15 December 2002, Article II(3); ICANN Bylaws as amended on 1 October 2016, Article 2(3).
258. Affirmation of Commitments, *supra* n. 135, Article 3.
259. Affirmation of Commitments, *supra* n. 135, Article 9.3.
260. Affirmation of Commitments, *supra* n. 135, Articles 3 and 9.1.
261. ICANN Bylaws as amended on 15 December 2002, Article I(2)(10). With the adoption of its amended Bylaws of 1 October 2016, this core value has become a commitment.

name space. Before ICANN's formation, the gTLD name space consisted of five limited-use gTLDs[262] and three gTLDs which operated upon a first-come, first-served basis.[263]

The gTLD name space coexists with the ccTLD name space .ccTLDs or country code Top Level Domains are TLDs which consist of the two-letter country codes from ISO 3166.[264,265] ccTLDs are organized by an administrator for the country to which the ccTLD relates.[266] The public character of ccTLDs has always been recognized. Designated managers (or administrators) of ccTLDs are regarded as trustees of the TLD for both the nation and the global Internet community; they perform a 'public service on behalf of the Internet community.'[267] In 1998, there were well over 200 ccTLDs in existence administered by their corresponding governments or by private entities with the appropriate national government's acquiescence.[268]

While gTLDs and ccTLDs coexist in the Internet's name space, they are nonetheless different. National governments had – and, in the White Paper, the U.S. Government recognized that they would continue to have – authority to manage or establish policy for 'their own' ccTLD.[269] As ccTLDs used to be far greater in number than gTLDs, and because of the policy authority of national governments, there is a much wider variety in structure and use for ccTLDs than for gTLDs.[270] Because of this, ccTLDs can be perceived as a distinct market. In this regard, German courts have held that third parties wishing to sell or market products on the Internet may not treat the '.de' TLD as interchangeable with other generic or country code TLDs.[271] Key to these decisions was the fact that purchasers located in Germany prefer to search for websites using the '.de' TLD.

The original gTLD name space could also be seen as a collection of separate markets. In 1994, Jon Postel described the gTLD name space as follows:

---

262. .mil for use by the U.S. military, .gov for U.S. Government use, .edu for educational institutions (mainly in the U.S.) .int for international treaty organizations, and .arpa for infrastructional identifier spaces.
263. .com, .net and .org.
264. Jon Postel, *Domain Name System Structure and Delegation*, Network Working Group Request for Comments # 1591, March 1994, https://www.ietf.org/rfc/rfc1591.txt, p. 1.
265. ISO 3166 is a standard of the International Organization for Standardization that defines codes for the names of countries, dependent territories, and special areas of geographical interest and their principal subdivisions. The first part of ISO 3166 (referred to as ISO 3166-1 defines three sets of codes for the names of countries, dependent territories and special areas of geographical interest. ISO 3166-1 alpha-2 offers a set of two-letter country codes. It is the ISO 3166-1 alpha-2 codes that are uses for ccTLDs.
266. Jon Postel, *Domain Name System Structure and Delegation*, Network Working Group Request for Comments # 1591, March 1994, https://www.ietf.org/rfc/rfc1591.txt, p. 2.
267. Jon Postel, *Domain Name System Structure and Delegation*, Network Working Group Request for Comments # 1591, March 1994, https://www.ietf.org/rfc/rfc1591.txt, pp. 2 and 4.
268. NTIA, *supra* n. 83, p. 31742.
269. NTIA, *supra* n. 83, 31744.
270. *See* Jon Postel, *Domain Name System Structure and Delegation*, Network Working Group Request for Comments # 1591, March 1994, https://www.ietf.org/rfc/rfc1591.txt, p. 1.
271. OLG Frankfurt am Main, decision from 29.04.2008, case number 11 U 32/04 ("VW.de"); LG Frankfurt am Main, decision from 14.10.1998, case number 2/06 O 283/98 ("Ambiente").

> 'Each of the generic TLDs was created for a general category of organizations. [...]
>
> Of these generic domains, five are international in nature, and two are restricted to use by entities in the United States.
>
> World Wide Generic Domains:
>
>> COM - This domain is intended for commercial entities, that is companies. [...]
>>
>> EDU - This domain was originally intended for all educational institutions. Many Universities, colleges, schools, educational service organizations, and educational consortia have registered here. More recently a decision has been taken to limit further registrations to 4 year colleges and universities. Schools and 2-year colleges will be registered in the country domains [...].
>>
>> NET - This domain is intended to hold only the computers of network providers, that is the NIC and NOC computers, the administrative computers, and the network node computers. The customers of the network provider would have domain names of their own (not in the NET TLD).
>>
>> ORG - This domain is intended as the miscellaneous TLD for organizations that didn't fit anywhere else. Some non-government organizations may fit here.
>>
>> INT - This domain is for organizations established by international treaties, or international databases.
>
> United States Only Generic Domains:
>
>> GOV - This domain was originally intended for any kind of government office or agency. More recently a decision was taken to register only agencies of the US Federal government in this domain. State and local agencies are registered in the country domains [...].
>>
>> MIL - This domain is used by the US military.'[272]

In 1994, the TLD landscape was able to serve the needs of the Internet community. Although the popularity and the growth pattern of the .com gTLD was already a source of concern, it was thought to be 'extremely unlikely that any other TLDs [would] be created.'[273] Instead, to solve the domain name scarcity in the .com TLD, the Internet community was considering subdividing the domain and allowing future commercial registrations only in the subdomains.[274]

However, these views rapidly changed. As explained above, NSI's monopoly over domain name registrations gave rise to criticism and there was a growing dissatisfaction concerning the absence of competition and the dominance of the .com domain. In May 1996, following discussions with fellow Internet engineers, Jon Postel wrote that 'the inherent perceived value of being registered under a single top level domain (.COM) is undesirable and should be changed', and he advocated open, free-market

272. Jon Postel, *Domain Name System Structure and Delegation*, Network Working Group Request for Comments # 1591, March 1994, https://www.ietf.org/rfc/rfc1591.txt, pp. 2–3.
273. Jon Postel, *Domain Name System Structure and Delegation*, Network Working Group Request for Comments # 1591, March 1994, https://www.ietf.org/rfc/rfc1591.txt, pp. 1, 2.
274. Jon Postel, *Domain Name System Structure and Delegation*, Network Working Group Request for Comments # 1591, March 1994, https://www.ietf.org/rfc/rfc1591.txt, p. 2.

competition through the introduction of new gTLDs.[275] He considered that 'positive market forces dictate that this diversity, obtained through free competition, is the best means available to insure quality service to end-users and customers.'[276] He envisioned the creation of up to fifty new registries in 1996, each chartered to operate a maximum of three gTLDs for up to five years.[277] Although his plan for opening up the gTLD market did not deal with the issue of the (monopolistic) management of the then existing gTLDs, he did note that such gTLDs could come under the provisions of the plan when the existing sponsorship relationship came to an end[278] (and as mentioned above, the cooperative agreement between the NSF and NSI was set to expire on 30 September 1998).[279] In other words, Jon Postel and the members of the Internet community supporting his plan did not exclude the future introduction of a competitive process for the management of existing TLDs, and a re-evaluation every five years.

Jon Postel slightly reworked his draft plan following criticism from the Internet technical community.[280] He acknowledged the concern that NSI was 'apparently unconstrained by effective regulation or competition.'[281] He was not convinced that sharing a single top-level domain among competing registries would be manageable, but believed that the introduction of successful new TLDs could very quickly have a significant impact on competition and that it would in any event be beneficial:

> 'While new single registry top-level domains may allow only a limited form of competition, it is a better situation than we have now, and it can be generalized in the future. Thus there is no 'competition' argument to prevent creating new top-level domains.'[282]

However, the Internet community failed to reach consensus on the proposal, and international plans for the evolution of DNS administration failed. By the end of the 1990s, various proposals existed, all aimed at injecting competition into the gTLD system. But there was no united view on how to install a more competitive gTLD environment.[283] Some questioned whether it was possible to create a truly competitive

275. Jon Postel, *New Registries and the Delegation of International Top Level Domains*, May 1996, https://tools.ietf.org/html/draft-postel-iana-itld-admin-00, pp. 1, 3–4.
276. Jon Postel, *New Registries and the Delegation of International Top Level Domains*, May 1996, https://tools.ietf.org/html/draft-postel-iana-itld-admin-00, p. 4.
277. Jon Postel, *New Registries and the Delegation of International Top Level Domains*, May 1996, https://tools.ietf.org/html/draft-postel-iana-itld-admin-00, p. 8.
278. Jon Postel, *New Registries and the Delegation of International Top Level Domains*, May 1996, https://tools.ietf.org/html/draft-postel-iana-itld-admin-00, p. 4.
279. *Supra* Chapter 2.A.2.b(2); ICANN, *Cooperative Agreement No. NCR-9218742*, http://archive.icann.org/en/nsi/coopagmt-01jan93.htm (accessed 11 May 2016).
280. NTIA, White Paper, 31743 ; Jon Postel, *New Registries and the Delegation of International Top Level Domains*, June 1996, https://tools.ietf.org/html/draft-postel-iana-itld-admin-01.
281. Jon Postel, *New Registries and the Delegation of International Top Level Domains*, June 1996, https://tools.ietf.org/html/draft-postel-iana-itld-admin-01, p. 6.
282. Jon Postel, *New Registries and the Delegation of International Top Level Domains*, June 1996, https://tools.ietf.org/html/draft-postel-iana-itld-admin-01, p. 7.
283. For an overview and comparison of the proposals, *see*: OECD, *Internet Domain Names: Allocation Policies*, OECD Document GD(97)207, Paris 1997, https://www.oecd.org/sti/2091363.pdf.

environment.[284] However, the U.S. Government made clear that the creation of a competitive environment was one of the key tasks for the new custodian of the DNS. The U.S. Government expressed its conviction that 'competitive systems generally result in greater innovation, consumer choice, and satisfaction in the long run. Moreover, the pressure of competition is likely to be the most effective means of discouraging registries from acting monopolistically.'[285]

In recognition of this goal and with a view to promoting competition in the gTLD name space, ICANN has expanded the number of available gTLDs three times since its inception: in 2000, 2004 and 2011. Each application round has had its own distinct policies and processes, designed to enable varying degrees of competition while preserving the stability and security of the Internet's unique identifier system.

Applying for a new gTLD is a very complex process and cannot be compared with the simple registering of a domain name. In a new gTLD application, the applicant seeks to create and operate a registry business to support the Internet's DNS, and this involves a number of significant responsibilities as a successful applicant will run a critical piece of Internet infrastructure.

1. The First Round of 2000

On 30 April 1999, the World Intellectual Property Organization (WIPO) submitted a report to ICANN, which concluded that, 'on condition that [WIPO's] proposed improved practices for domain name registrations, [WIPO's] proposed administrative dispute-resolution procedure and [WIPO's] proposed measures for the protection of famous and well-known marks and for the suppression of abusive registrations of domain names are all adopted, new gTLDs can be introduced, provided that they are introduced in a slow and controlled manner which takes account of the efficacy of the proposed new practices and procedures in reducing existing problems.'[286] Upon analysis of WIPO's report and the comments it received, the ICANN Board decided on 27 May 1999 to refer the matter of introducing new gTLDs to ICANN's policy-making body.[287] In mid-April 2000, ICANN's policy-making body[288] recommended that the ICANN Board adopt a policy for the introduction of new gTLDs in a measured and responsible manner.[289] It was suggested that only a limited number of new gTLDs be introduced as a 'proof of concept' for possible future introductions.[290]

284. NTIA, *supra* n. 83, p. 31745.
285. NTIA, *supra* n. 83, pp. 31745–31746.
286. WIPO, *The Management of Internet Names and Addresses: Intellectual Property Issues – Final Report of the WIPO Internet Domain Name Process*, 30 April 1999, http://www.wipo.int/export/sites/www/amc/en/docs/report-final1.pdf.
287. ICANN, *Resolution 99.48*, Minutes of Meeting of 27 May 1999, https://www.icann.org/resources/board-material/minutes-1999-05-27-en.
288. The DNSO, *i.e.*, the predecessor of the GNSO.
289. ICANN, *ICANN Yokohama Meeting Topic: Introduction of New Top-Level Domains*, 13 June 2000, https://archive.icann.org/en/meetings/yokohama/new-tld-topic.htm.
290. ICANN, *ICANN Yokohama Meeting Topic: Introduction of New Top-Level Domains*, 13 June 2000, https://archive.icann.org/en/meetings/yokohama/new-tld-topic.htm.

On 16 July 2000, the ICANN Board adopted the recommendation to organize a 'proof of concept' round for new gTLDs.[291] The plan was to issue a formal call for proposals for new gTLDs by 1 August 2000 and to allow applications until 1 October 2000. ICANN would then organize a fifteen-day public comment period, announce which applicants were selected to enter into negotiations for the operation of new gTLDs by 20 November 2000, and complete negotiations by 31 December 2000.[292]

On 15 August 2000, ICANN published application instructions[293] and criteria for assessing new gTLD proposals.[294] Interested applicants had to pay a non-refundable fee of USD 50,000 for the application to be considered, without any guarantee that their application would be selected for negotiation.[295]

ICANN's first priority was to preserve the stability of the Internet. Therefore, ICANN requested that applicants provide comprehensive strategies to assure the security and reliability of the DNS and well-thought-out plans to assure the Internet's continuing stability.[296] In evaluating proposals, ICANN staff intended 'to place significant emphasis on the completeness of the proposals and the extent to which they demonstrate that the applicant has a thorough understanding of what is involved, has carefully thought through all relevant issues, has realistically assessed the business, financial, technical, operational, and marketing requirements for implementing the proposal, has procured firm commitments for all necessary resources, and has formulated sound business and technical plans for executing the proposal'.[297] Other evaluation criteria included the potential of the proposed TLD operation: (i) to assist in the long-range management of the DNS, (ii) to enhance competition for registration services, (iii) to enhance the utility of the DNS, (iv) to meet previously unmet types of needs, (v) to enhance the diversity of the DNS, and (vi) to protect the rights of third parties appropriately.[298]

The application window of this proof of concept round in fact ran from 5 September 2000 to 2 October 2000,[299] and ICANN received forty-seven applications for over 200

291. ICANN, *Resolution 00.47*, Regular Meeting of the Board Minutes, 16 July 2000, https://www.icann.org/resources/board-material/minutes-2000-07-16-en.
292. ICANN, *Resolution 00.47*, Regular Meeting of the Board Minutes, 16 July 2000, https://www.icann.org/resources/board-material/minutes-2000-07-16-en.
293. ICANN, *New TLD Application Instructions*, 15 August 2000, https://archive.icann.org/en/tlds/new-tld-application-instructions-15aug00.htm.
294. ICANN, *Criteria for Assessing TLD Proposals*, 15 August 2000, http://archive.icann.org/en/tlds/tld-criteria-15aug00.htm.
295. ICANN, *Resolution 00.48*, Regular Meeting of the Board Minutes, 16 July 2000, https://www.icann.org/resources/board-material/minutes-2000-07-16-en; ICANN, *New TLD Application Instructions*, 15 August 2000, https://archive.icann.org/en/tlds/new-tld-application-instructions-15aug00.htm.
296. ICANN, *Criteria for Assessing TLD Proposals*, 15 August 2000, http://archive.icann.org/en/tlds/tld-criteria-15aug00.htm.
297. ICANN, *Criteria for Assessing TLD Proposals*, 15 August 2000, http://archive.icann.org/en/tlds/tld-criteria-15aug00.htm.
298. ICANN, *Criteria for Assessing TLD Proposals*, 15 August 2000, http://archive.icann.org/en/tlds/tld-criteria-15aug00.htm.
299. ICANN, *New TLD Application Instructions*, 15 August 2000, https://archive.icann.org/en/tlds/new-tld-application-instructions-15aug00.htm, § 24.

new gTLDs.[300] By 10 November 2000, the applications had been evaluated by ICANN staff and outside advisors, and on 16 November, the ICANN Board selected seven new gTLD proposals to enter into contract negotiations.[301] Eventually, ICANN entered into registry agreements concerning these seven new gTLDs, and allowed for the .biz, .name, .info, .pro, .aero, .coop, and .museum gTLDs to be added to the Internet's root zone.

2. The Second Round of 2004

One of the ideas behind the 2000 proof of concept round was that the future introduction of additional gTLDs should be done only after careful evaluation of the initial introduction.[302] Upon the conclusion of the proof of concept round, ICANN set up a task force to devise an evaluation process and planning. In July 2002, this task force recommended that the ICANN Board consider to what extent it could start working on new gTLD rounds in parallel with this evaluation process.[303] In response to the task force's report, the ICANN Board instructed ICANN's President to produce a plan for action.[304]

On 18 October 2002, the then President of ICANN issued a 'Plan for Action regarding New gTLDs', which called for 'proposals for up to three more sponsored TLDs as an extension of the "Proof of Concept".'[305] The author of the plan for action was of the opinion that small, specialized TLDs, which were sponsored by and operated in the interest of a particular, defined community could be introduced relatively easily, whereas major issues in relation to the 'Proof of Concept' 'mostly affected unsponsored TLDs.[306] The introduction of only a few sponsored TLDs might allow ICANN to 'learn a bit more about the nature of the "market" for these kinds of new TLDs.'[307] In December 2002, the ICANN Board instructed ICANN's President to develop a draft Request for Proposals (RFP) for a limited number of new sponsored gTLDs (or sTLDs).[308] Proposed selection criteria were posted for public comment in March

300. ICANN, *Report on TLD Applications*, 9 November 2000, http://archive.icann.org/en/tlds/report/.
301. ICANN, *Resolution 00.89 – Minutes of Second Annual Meeting (in Marina Del Rey)*, 16 November 2000, https://www.icann.org/resources/board-material/minutes-annual-meeting-2000-11-16-en.
302. ICANN, *ICANN Yokohama Meeting Topic: Introduction of New Top-Level Domains*, 13 June 2000, https://archive.icann.org/en/meetings/yokohama/new-tld-topic.htm.
303. ICANN, *Final Report of the New TLD Evaluation Process Planning Task Force*, 31 July 2002, http://archive.icann.org/en/committees/ntepptf/final-report-31jul02.htm.
304. ICANN, *Resolution 02.97A*, 23 August 2002, https://www.icann.org/resources/board-material/minutes-2002-08-23-en.
305. Stuart Lynn, *A Plan for Action Regarding New gTLDs*, 18 October 2002 (published 8 November 2002), https://archive.icann.org/en/committees/ntepptf/new-gtld-action-plan-18oct02.htm.
306. Stuart Lynn, *A Plan for Action Regarding New gTLDs*, 18 October 2002 (published 8 November 2002), https://archive.icann.org/en/committees/ntepptf/new-gtld-action-plan-18oct02.htm.
307. Stuart Lynn, *A Plan for Action Regarding New gTLDs*, 18 October 2002 (published 8 November 2002), https://archive.icann.org/en/committees/ntepptf/new-gtld-action-plan-18oct02.htm.
308. ICANN, *Resolution 02.152*, 15 December 2002, https://www.icann.org/resources/board-material/minutes-annual-meeting-2002-12-15-en.

2003,[309] and a first draft RFP was published on 24 June 2003.[310] Meanwhile, ICANN had abandoned the proposed artificial limitation to three new sTLDs,[311] and had decided not to restrict the RFP for sTLDs to the applicants of the 2000 proof of concept round only.[312] The sTLD application process was to be open to both not-for-profits and other forms of entities that otherwise met the RFP criteria for a sponsoring organization, and was scheduled for completion in 2004.[313]

The sTLD application process was officially launched on 15 December 2003, when ICANN posted the final version of the RFP for sTLDs.[314] The application window lasted until 16 March 2004.[315]

Consistent with ICANN's fundamental obligations, the RFP specified that the selection procedure was based on 'principles of objectivity, non-discrimination and transparency.'[316] Applicants had to pay a non-refundable application fee of USD 45,000, and meet the following criteria:

- Sponsorship information: The proposed sTLD 'must address the needs and interests of a clearly defined community'. The application had to demonstrate: (i) support from the sponsoring organization, (ii) the appropriateness of the sponsoring organization and the policy formulation environment, and (iii) broad-based support for the sTLD from the intended community;
- Business plan information: Applicants had to demonstrate their methodology for introducing a new sTLD and their ability to implement a robust and appropriately resourced organization and submit a financial model outlining the financial, technical and operational capabilities of the organization;
- Technical standards: Applicants had to demonstrate their ability: (i) to ensure stable registry operation, (ii) to conform with best practice technical standards for registry operations, (iii) to offer a full range of registry services, and (iv) to assure continuity of registry operation in the event of business failure;
- Community value: Applicants had to demonstrate: (i) the added value of the proposed sTLD to the Internet name space, (ii) safeguards that protect the

309. ICANN, *ICANN Rio de Janeiro Meeting Topic: Criteria to be used in the Selection of New Sponsored TLDs*, 25 March 2003, http://archive.icann.org/en/meetings/riodejaneiro/stld-rfp-topic.htm.
310. ICANN, *Establishment of new sTLDs: Request for Proposals (Draft for public comment)*, 24 June 2003, http://archive.icann.org/en/tlds/new-stld-rfp/new-stld-rfp-24jun03.htm.
311. ICANN, *Establishment of new sTLDs: Request for Proposals (Draft for public comment)*, 24 June 2003, http://archive.icann.org/en/tlds/new-stld-rfp/new-stld-rfp-24jun03.htm.
312. ICANN, *Resolutions 03.169-171*, 31 October 2003, https://www.icann.org/news/advisory-2003-10-31-en.
313. ICANN, *Resolutions 03.169-171*, 31 October 2003, https://www.icann.org/news/advisory-2003-10-31-en; ICANN, *ICANN Launches Broad Strategic Initiative for New Generic Top-Level Domain*, 31 October 2003, https://www.icann.org/news/announcement-2003-10-31-en.
314. ICANN, *New sTLD Application*, 15 December 2003, https://archive.icann.org/en/tlds/new-stld-rfp/new-stld-application-parta-15dec03.htm.
315. ICANN, *New sTLD Application*, 15 December 2003, https://archive.icann.org/en/tlds/new-stld-rfp/new-stld-application-parta-15dec03.htm.
316. ICANN, *New sTLD Application – Explanatory Notes and Selection Criteria*, 15 December 2003, https://archive.icann.org/en/tlds/new-stld-rfp/new-stld-application-parta-15dec03.htm.

rights of others, (iii) assurance of charter-compliant registrations and avoidance of abusive registration practices, (iv) assurance of adequate dispute-resolution mechanisms and (v) the provision of ICANN-compliant WHOIS services.[317]

ICANN received ten applications for nine sTLDs in response to the RFP.[318] A team of independent evaluators determined that two applications[319] satisfied all of the selection criteria. The other applicants were given an opportunity to provide additional clarifying information to the evaluators and the ICANN Board.[320] The sTLD application round ultimately resulted in ICANN's approval of the .post, .cat, .asia, .jobs, .mobi, .tel, .travel and .xxx gTLDs.[321]

3. The Third Round of 2011

Well before the launch of the second round of 2004, on 24 June 2003, the leadership of ICANN's policy body, now the GNSO Council, advised the ICANN Board that 'the namespace should be market driven and that organizations [should be] free to propose names that they believed would be of use to DNS users'.[322] On 31 October 2003, the ICANN Board accepted the GNSO's recommendation, and expressed ICANN's commitment to define and implement a predictable strategy for selecting new gTLDs using straightforward, transparent and objective procedures that preserve the stability of the Internet. The Board expressed the belief that ICANN should begin immediately with the development of a long-term policy for selecting new gTLDs, and requested that implementation commence before 31 December 2004.[323]

---

317. ICANN, *New sTLD Application – Explanatory Notes and Selection Criteria*, 15 December 2003, https://archive.icann.org/en/tlds/new-stld-rfp/new-stld-application-parta-15dec03.htm.
318. DotAsia Organisation Limited applied for .asia selecting Afilias Limited to provide registry services; Fundació puntCAT, Fundació Privada, a Catalonia private foundation, applied for .cat, selecting CORE Internet Council for Registrars to provide registry services; Employ Media LLC applied for .jobs, selecting Verisign to provide registry services; The U.K. nonprofit Spamhaus Project applied for .mail, selecting Verisign to provide registry services; The Irish company DotMobi, Ltd. together with Nokia Corporation, Vodafone Group Services Limited and Microsoft applied for .mobi, selecting Afilias Limited to provide registry services; The UPU applied for .post, selecting the Swiss Academic and Research Council to provide all technical registry functions under the UPU's supervision; The U.S. company NetNumber Inc. with sponsoring organization Pulver.com applied for .tel; The U.K. company Telnic Limited also applied for .tel, selecting CORE Internet Council of Registrars to provide registry services; The New York corporation Tralliance applied for .travel, selecting NeuLevel, Inc. to provide registry services; ICM Registry LLC applied for .xxx, selecting Afilias Limited to provide registry services (ICANN, *Status Report on sTLD Application Process*, 19 March 2004, https://archive.icann.org/en/tlds/stld-apps-19mar04/PostsTLDStatusRpt.pdf).
319. For .post and .cat.
320. ICANN, *ICANN Meetings in Kuala Lumpur – ICANN Public* Forum, 22 July 2004, http://archive.icann.org/meetings/kualalumpur/captioning-public-forum-23jul04.htm.
321. ICANN did not approve the applications for .tel by NetNumber Inc. and for .mail by Spamhaus Project.
322. ICANN, GNSO Council Montreal Meeting on 24 June 2003 – minutes, http://www.dnso.org/dnso/notes/20030624.GNSOmontreal-minutes.html.
323. ICANN, *Board Resolution 03.166-168 and rationale*, 31 October 2003, https://www.icann.org/news/advisory-2003-10-31-en.

It finally took the GNSO until October 2007 to complete its policy development work on new gTLDs, and to submit a set of principles and recommendations to ICANN's Board.[324] The GNSO gave the following reasons for introducing new gTLDs:

> 'The reasons for introducing new top-level domains include that there is demand from potential applicants for new top-level domains in both ASCII and IDN formats. In addition the introduction of new top-level domain application process has the potential to promote competition in the provision of registry services, to add to consumer choice, market differentiation and geographical and service-provider diversity.'

In developing its proposed policy, the GNSO collaborated with other ICANN policy development and advisory organizations; the GNSO consulted with the GAC, At-Large Advisory Committee (ALAC), Country Code Names Supporting Organization (ccNSO), and Security and Stability Advisory Committee (SSAC).[325] The ICANN Board of Directors adopted the GNSO's proposed policy in June 2008.[326] The implementation plan needed further development and Board approval.[327]

Key to the implementation plan was the development of an applicant guidebook, which had to provide new gTLD applicants with a step-by-step procedure and to inform prospective applicants what to expect during the application and evaluation periods.[328] A first draft applicant guidebook was released for public comment on 24 October 2008.[329] It took almost three years, seven versions of the applicant guidebook, fifty-eight explanatory memoranda and nearly fifty new gTLD-related public comment sessions before the ICANN Board approved the new gTLD program.[330] The application window was planned to open on 12 January 2012 and to close on 12 April 2012.[331] In fact, the application window was extended until 30 May 2012, following technical issues with the only application portal.[332] The Board envisaged some changes to the

324. ICANN Generic Names Supporting Organization, *Final Report - Introduction of New Generic Top-Level Domains Part A*, 8 August 2007, http://gnso.icann.org/en/issues/new-gtlds/pdp-dec05-fr-parta-08aug07.htm.
325. ICANN, ICANN Generic Names Supporting Organization, Final Report - Introduction of New Generic Top-Level Domains, Part A, 8 August 2007, http://gnso.icann.org/en/issues/new-gtlds/pdp-dec05-fr-parta-08aug07.htm; ICANN Generic Names Supporting Organization, *Final Report - Introduction of New Generic Top-Level Domains, Part B*, 1 August 2007, http://gnso.icann.org/en/issues/new-gtlds/pdp-dec05-fr-partb-01aug07.htm#_Toc47680302.
326. ICANN, *ICANN Board Resolution 2008.06.26.02*, https://www.icann.org/resources/board-material/resolutions-2008-06-26-en#_Toc76113171.
327. ICANN, *ICANN Board Resolution 2008.06.26.03*, https://www.icann.org/resources/board-material/resolutions-2008-06-26-en#_Toc76113171.
328. ICANN, *Information on the Applicant Guidebook*, http://newgtlds.icann.org/en/applicants/agb.
329. ICANN, *New gTLD Program: Draft Applicant Guidebook (Draft RFP)*, 24 October 2008, http://archive.icann.org/en/topics/new-gtlds/draft-rfp-24oct08-en.pdf.
330. ICANN Resolution 2011.06.20.01, http://www.icann.org/en/groups/board/documents/resolutions-20jun11-en.htm; ICANN Board Rationales for the Approval of the Launch of the New gTLD Program, http://www.icann.org/en/groups/board/documents/rationale-board-approval-new-gtld-program-launch-20jun11-en.pdf.
331. ICANN Resolution 2011.06.20.01, http://www.icann.org/en/groups/board/documents/resolutions-20jun11-en.htm.
332. ICANN, *New gTLD Update on the close of the TLD Application system*, 30 May 2012, http://newgtlds.icann.org/en/announcements-and-media/announcement-3-30may12-en.

applicant guidebook following discussions with the GAC.[333] After the Board's approval of the new gTLD program, ICANN changed the applicant guidebook twice, once before the application window to reflect the outcome of the discussions with the GAC,[334] and a second time after the close of the application window.[335]

The applicant guidebook, named the gTLD Applicant Guidebook (AGB), sets out an application process, an evaluation process, and an objection and dispute resolution process. The AGB had to reflect the principles and recommendations of the GNSO's new gTLD policy. In particular, the AGB had to guarantee that new gTLDs would be introduced in 'an orderly, timely and predictable way.'[336] Consistent with ICANN's fundamental obligations, the GNSO recommended that evaluation and selection procedure for new gTLD registries respect the principles of fairness, transparency and non-discrimination.[337] Transparent and predictable criteria, which were objective and measurable had to be made available to the applicants prior to the initiation of the process, and, normally, no subsequent selection criteria were to be used in the selection process.[338] The GAC agreed with this recommendation and stated as a principle that 'the evaluation and selection procedure for new gTLD registries should respect the principles of fairness, transparency and non-discrimination. All applicants for a new gTLD registry should therefore be evaluated against transparent and predictable criteria, fully available to the applicants prior to the initiation of the process. Normally, therefore, no subsequent additional selection criteria should be used in the selection process.'[339] The GNSO's new gTLD policy required that there be a base contract provided to applicants at the beginning of the application process.[340]

a. *The Application Process for a New gTLD*

Reflective of the GNSO's new gTLD policy, the AGB served as a manual for the application procedure – it guides the applicant through the process detailing the

333. ICANN Resolution 2011.06.20.01, http://www.icann.org/en/groups/board/documents/resolutions-20jun11-en.htm.
334. ICANN, *New gTLD Applicant Guidebook 11 January 2012*, https://newgtlds.icann.org/en/applicants/agb/guidebook-full-11jan12-en.pdf.
335. ICANN, *New gTLD Applicant Guidebook 4 June 2012*, https://newgtlds.icann.org/en/applicants/agb/guidebook-full-04jun12-en.pdf.
336. *i.e.*, the first stated principle of the GNSO's policy on new gTLDs (*See* ICANN Generic Names Supporting Organization, *Final Report - Introduction of New Generic Top-Level Domains Part A*, 8 August 2007, http://gnso.icann.org/en/issues/new-gtlds/pdp-dec05-fr-parta-08aug07.htm).
337. ICANN Generic Names Supporting Organization, *Final Report - Introduction of New Generic Top-Level Domains Part A*, 8 August 2007, http://gnso.icann.org/en/issues/new-gtlds/pdp-dec05-fr-parta-08aug07.htm.
338. ICANN Generic Names Supporting Organization, *Final Report - Introduction of New Generic Top-Level Domains Part A*, 8 August 2007, http://gnso.icann.org/en/issues/new-gtlds/pdp-dec05-fr-parta-08aug07.htm.
339. ICANN, *GAC Principles regarding new gTLDs*, 28 March 2007, https://gacweb.icann.org/display/GACADV/2007-03-28-gTLD-2?preview=/28278822/41943559/gac-principles-regarding-new-gtlds-28mar07-en.pdf, Principle 2.5.
340. ICANN Generic Names Supporting Organization, *Final Report - Introduction of New Generic Top-Level Domains Part A*, 8 August 2007, http://gnso.icann.org/en/issues/new-gtlds/pdp-dec05-fr-parta-08aug07.htm.

requisite documents and information, the financial and legal commitments and what to expect during the application and evaluation periods. The AGB contained a base registry agreement that applicants were presumed to enter into upon the successful completion of the application and evaluation process. Having passed through all the application stages, applicants were expected to make their gTLD operational, and this is why a detailed plan for the launch and operation of the proposed gTLD had to be submitted as part of the application process. If a successful applicant did not progress the gTLD into the root system within twelve months of the gTLD being delegated, ICANN could terminate the registry agreement.

The AGB described in detail what information was required in order to apply successfully for a new gTLD. Generally speaking, ICANN required applicants for new gTLDs to describe their administrative, operational, technical and financial capability to launch and operate a new gTLD extension for a term of at least ten years. There were fifty different questions on the basis of which such capability was to be determined by external evaluators to be appointed by ICANN.

Applicants had to describe in detail their background and the mission and purpose of the applied-for gTLD. They had to demonstrate their operational and technical capability as well as their financial capacity to run the proposed gTLD registry. Applications had to include detailed business plans and contingency planning, identifying risks and worst-case scenarios. It is not surprising that ICANN asked for abundant and detailed information, given its responsibility for preserving the security, stability and global inter-operability of the Internet. As applicants apply to control a critical piece of the Internet infrastructure on which millions of Internet users may rely, extensive scrutiny of each applicant is necessary to ensure new gTLD registries will be able to comply with ICANN's contract and to follow all best practices and standards.

There are a number of distinct steps in the application process for new gTLDs:

(1) Application preparation and submission;
(2) Application evaluation;
(3) Contract negotiation and execution; and
(4) New gTLD delegation and testing.

After having completed these steps, the successful applicant for the TLD was able to start registering domain names in the TLD, allowing the introduction of websites and emails.

b. *What Was ICANN Expected to Do?*

ICANN was expected to review the applications regardless of whether or not it called upon third parties to help with the technical and financial evaluation or to solve objections. ICANN was expected to assess applicants' capabilities on the basis of objective, measurable and transparent criteria. The ICANN Board remained responsible for the new gTLD program, which implies in our view that ICANN had to perform quality controls and that it was expected to assess whether the third party advice or resolution was reasoned and meaningful, and to take the appropriate time to perform the assessments.

(1) The Evaluation Phase

After the application window, there were several evaluation stages, each with its own estimated duration. During the evaluation process, ICANN had to check whether the application met the requirements. ICANN first checked whether an application was administratively complete (Have all mandatory questions been answered? Have all required supporting documents been provided in the proper format(s)? Have the evaluation fees been received?). Unless there were exceptional circumstances, an application that was not administratively complete was rejected.

Then, ICANN performed the initial evaluation. The initial evaluation started with a background screening of the applicant. Background screening criteria were introduced in recognition of ICANN's duty 'to protect the public interest in the allocation of critical Internet resources.'[341] ICANN affirmed the right to deny an otherwise qualified application, and gave applicants a list of circumstances that would ordinarily result in the automatic disqualification of an applicant.[342] The list contains various types of criminal or cybersquatting behavior.[343] Applicants also had to provide an explanation for 'any additional background information that may be found concerning the applicant or any individual named in the application, which may affect eligibility.'[344] Finally, applicants had to warrant that statements and representations in the application were true, accurate and complete in all material respects. A change in circumstances that would render any information provided in the application false or misleading had to be notified to ICANN in writing.[345] Background screening was needed to make sure that critical Internet resources were allocated to reliable parties.

Once the background screening was completed, ICANN checked whether the application met the administrative, operational, technical and financial requirements.

If an application passed the initial evaluation and there were no objections, no GAC Advice and no identity or confusing similarity with another (applied-for) gTLD, the application immediately moved to the delegation phase.

341. ICANN, *New gTLD Applicant Guidebook 4 June 2012*, https://newgtlds.icann.org/en/applicants/agb/guidebook-full-04jun12-en.pdf, Module 1-24.
342. ICANN, *New gTLD Applicant Guidebook 4 June 2012*, https://newgtlds.icann.org/en/applicants/agb/guidebook-full-04jun12-en.pdf, Module 1-22.
343. ICANN, *New gTLD Applicant Guidebook 4 June 2012*, https://newgtlds.icann.org/en/applicants/agb/guidebook-full-04jun12-en.pdf, Module 1-22 to Module 1-24.
344. ICANN, *New gTLD Applicant Guidebook 4 June 2012*, https://newgtlds.icann.org/en/applicants/agb/guidebook-full-04jun12-en.pdf, Attachment to Module 2, A9, evaluation question 11(h).
345. ICANN, *New gTLD Applicant Guidebook 4 June 2012*, https://newgtlds.icann.org/en/applicants/agb/guidebook-full-04jun12-en.pdf, Module 6-2, Top-Level Domain Application – Terms and Conditions 1.

Applicants failing certain elements of the initial evaluation process were allowed to request an extended evaluation. In the context of an extended evaluation, the applicant was entitled to exchange additional information with the evaluators in order to clarify information contained in the application. An additional payment was required. However, the same evaluation criteria were used during the initial and the extended evaluation.

To perform the evaluations, ICANN had selected independent evaluation panels which were to use a point scoring system to assess answers to the fifty questions posed in the application form and which were to consider, among other things, what influence the applied for gTLD could have on the stability of the DNS and whether the applied for gTLD was confusingly similar to existing gTLDs or other applications.

There was a minimum pass score applicable to most sections of the application form which had to be met for the application to progress.

Since it is not possible for two or more identical strings to occupy the Internet space, the String Contention procedure would come into effect should there be applications for identical strings. The String Contention procedure aimed in the first instance at a self-resolving of the contention by the parties by mutual agreement.

Also, if there were two or more applications for confusingly similar strings, only one application could be granted and therefore the String Contention procedures would also come into effect. Again, applicants were always given the opportunity to resolve the contention in a mutually acceptable settlement amongst themselves.

ICANN selected the various evaluation panelists through a call for 'Expressions of Interest'. Each panelist had to abide by the Code of Conduct and Conflict of Interest guidelines included in the Applicant Guidebook.

These were the main evaluation panels:

- String Similarity Panel

This Panel was tasked with assessing whether a proposed gTLD string was likely to result in user confusion due to similarity with any reserved name, any existing TLD, any requested Internationalized Domain Name (IDN) ccTLD, or any new gTLD string applied for in the same application round. This assessment had to take place as part of the string similarity review at the initial evaluation stage.[346]

- DNS Stability Panel

This Panel had to determine whether the proposed *string* might adversely affect the security or stability of the DNS. This was planned to occur during the DNS stability string review at the initial evaluation stage.[347]

346. ICANN, *New gTLD Applicant Guidebook 4 June 2012*, https://newgtlds.icann.org/en/applicants/agb/guidebook-full-04jun12-en.pdf, Module 2-5–2-11; Module 2-30.
347. ICANN, *New gTLD Applicant Guidebook 4 June 2012*, https://newgtlds.icann.org/en/applicants/agb/guidebook-full-04jun12-en.pdf, Module 2-11–2-15; Module 2-30.

- Registry Services Panel

This Panel had to look for any adverse impact on security or stability of the *registry services* proposed in the application. If applicable, this review was planned to take place during the extended evaluation period.[348]

- Geographical Names Panel

This Panel was responsible for the review of each applied-for gTLD to determine whether it represented a geographic name. In the event that the string represented a geographic name and required government support, the panel was then to also review and verify the supporting documentation.[349]

- Technical Evaluation Panel

This Panel was expected to review the applicant's technical and operational capability to run a gTLD registry as proposed in its application. This review was to take place during the technical/operational reviews at the initial evaluation stage, and might also occur in the extended evaluation stage if necessary.[350]

- Financial Evaluation Panel

This Panel was asked to review the applicant's financial capability to maintain a gTLD registry against the relevant business, financial and organizational criteria contained in the Applicant Guidebook. This review was planned to take place during the financial review at the initial evaluation stage, and might also occur in the extended evaluation stage if necessary.[351]

On numerous occasions, ICANN has indicated that it followed the recommendations of its evaluation panels almost automatically. However, the lack of transparency in the selection of the panels and in their workings has given rise to severe criticism by applicants.[352]

(2) The Objection Phase

The new gTLD program also gave various categories of third parties the opportunity to challenge the application for a particular gTLD via Alternative Dispute Resolution (ADR) mechanisms. Such challenges (called 'objections') could be initiated with

348. ICANN, *New gTLD Applicant Guidebook 4 June 2012*, https://newgtlds.icann.org/en/applicants/agb/guidebook-full-04jun12-en.pdf, Module 2-24–2-26; Module 2-30.
349. ICANN, *New gTLD Applicant Guidebook 4 June 2012*, https://newgtlds.icann.org/en/applicants/agb/guidebook-full-04jun12-en.pdf, Module 2-16–2-22; Module 2-30.
350. ICANN, *New gTLD Applicant Guidebook 4 June 2012*, https://newgtlds.icann.org/en/applicants/agb/guidebook-full-04jun12-en.pdf, Module 2-22–2-23; Module 2-30.
351. ICANN, *New gTLD Applicant Guidebook 4 June 2012*, https://newgtlds.icann.org/en/applicants/agb/guidebook-full-04jun12-en.pdf, Module 2-23, 2-28; Module 2-30.
352. *Infra*, Chapter 4, Chapter 5 and Chapter 6.C.2.b(5).

so-called independent DRSP according to a pre-established set of rules.[353] Under these rules, objections could be based on the following grounds:

- String Confusion:[354] The applied-for gTLD string is confusingly similar to an existing TLD or to another applied-for gTLD string in the same round of applications. Objectors could be existing TLD operators or gTLD applicants in the current round.
- Legal Rights: The applied-for gTLD string infringes the existing legal rights of the objector. Objectors could be rights holders, for example, trademark holders.
- Community: There is substantial opposition to the gTLD application from a significant portion of the community to which the gTLD string may be explicitly or implicitly targeted. Objectors could be an established institution associated with a clearly delineated community.
- Limited Public Interest: The applied-for gTLD string is contrary to generally accepted legal norms of morality and public order that are recognized under principles of international law such as racially abusive strings.

The ground for objection dictates which DRSP was to manage the dispute process: String Confusion Objections (SCOs) were managed by the International Centre for Dispute Resolution (ICDR). Legal Rights Objections (LROs) were managed by the Arbitration and Mediation Center of the World Intellectual Property Organization (WIPO). Limited Public Interest Objections and Community Objections were managed by the International Chamber of Commerce (ICC).

Parties were not prevented from taking a matter to court. However, decisions obtained through the ADR mechanisms established within the framework of the new gTLD program were likely to be quicker and easier to execute. We are not aware of any objection to an application for which the objector did not pursue the proposed ADR mechanism. In rare instances, court action has followed the outcome of an ADR decision.[355]

In the assessment of objections and the objection grounds, it should be kept in mind that the new gTLD program was launched with the goal of enhancing competition, consumer choice and innovation through the introduction of new gTLDs. ICANN designed the objection process to protect the legitimate rights of certain specific, defined groups, while also ensuring that objectors cannot prevent the delegation of legitimate TLDs. Accordingly, objections were only permitted on four specific grounds enumerated by ICANN: string confusion, legal rights, community opposition and limited public interest.

353. ICANN, *New gTLD Applicant Guidebook 4 June 2012*, https://newgtlds.icann.org/en/applicants/agb/guidebook-full-04jun12-en.pdf, Attachment to Module 3: New gTLD Dispute Resolution Procedure.
354. 'String' refers to the sequence of letters that the gTLD is composed of.
355. *See e.g.*, U.S. District Court, C.D. California, *Del Monte International GmbH v. Del Monte Corporation*, 995 F.Supp.2d 1107 (C.D. Cal. 2014).

(3) Delegation of New gTLDs

Once an application had passed all the evaluation and selection processes, including objection processes and final approval, it entered the pre-delegation stage. During this stage, the applicant entered into an agreement with ICANN and was expected to pass technical tests before the new gTLD was delegated to the root zone.

New gTLDs are being introduced carefully so that the process does not cause instability in the Internet. A maximum of 1000 new gTLDs can be delegated per year. ICANN planned to start with the evaluation and delegation of the IDNs. Other gTLDs were to be delegated according to a prioritization number that was provided in a draw.

The successful applicant for a particular new gTLD obtains an exclusive right to operate the applied for gTLD. Having become a registry operator, the applicant becomes a 'trustee' of the top-level domain for the global Internet community.

CHAPTER 3
Legal Remedies

This chapter covers the legal remedies that parties can rely on to challenge decisions either by ICANN taken in the context of the handling of an application (*e.g.*, in the evaluation or implementation phase), or following the outcome of an objection between applicants (or between a third party and an applicant) handled by one of the Dispute Resolution Service Providers (DRSPs) described in Chapter 2.C.3.b(2).

For example, ICANN must decide whether or not an applicant has complied with various requirements of an administrative, operational, technical or financial nature. Also, on receiving a string contention report from the appointed String Similarity Evaluation Panel (SSEP), ICANN has to decide whether or not it will adopt the views in the SSEP's report. And ICANN must also take a decision following an Expert Determination of an ICC panel on the question of whether or not a party can object to an application based on community grounds. These are all examples of ICANN decisions that may give rise to the use of the legal remedies described below.

A. NEGOTIATED AGREEMENT

It is clear that parties may (and probably should) first use negotiation to attempt to solve any dispute that they have with ICANN. In principle, ICANN has an open and receptive policy regarding questions raised by unhappy applicants. It informs applicants of their options regarding the resolving of disputes and is prepared to allow applicants time to assess their situation, their available options and their respective chances of success.

However, there is ambiguity and potential conflict in ICANN's attitude. It is in ICANN's interest that disputes be sorted out as soon as possible (so as to allow the application process to continue working smoothly for the largest possible number of applicants). Nonetheless, as we will demonstrate in Chapter 5 on case studies where we discuss the claims initiated by discontent applicants, ICANN often persistently defends unreasonable outcomes and hardly ever compromises, even where there is no apparent reason for it to maintain its position. Although it has conducted numerous discussions with a multitude of applicants, and its attempt to assure uniformity and coherence in its position-taking is an honorable goal, many applicants have discovered that in practice ICANN is unwilling to concede much in negotiation.

Seen from ICANN's point of view, it would of course be problematic to concede on key issues where the knock-on effect could make ICANN's negotiating position untenable in other matters. But all too often ICANN's position seems to be inspired more by concerns about the process than by a reasoned approach based on both process and substance. To take one example, the ban on discrimination creates two clear and distinct obligations for ICANN: similar situations must be treated similarly and different situations must be treated differently. These obligations cannot be fully met if ICANN intervenes only in certain specific cases and fails to address the underlying issue that has allowed incoherent outcomes in different cases. For example, although ICANN has reacted positively in response to certain individual complaints regarding inconsistent determinations on string confusion it has failed to address the underlying reason for the inconsistencies in the determinations and has refused to intervene in the majority of cases.

It is also interesting to examine the contradiction between on the one hand ICANN's inflexibility on key issues (presumably inspired by a need for consistency), and on the other its clear opposition to the principle that Independent Review Process (IRP) declarations have precedential value. ICANN's position on this is indefensible, as we explain in more detail in Chapter 5 and Chapter 6.

These contradictions suggest that ICANN may have a tendency to switch views according to the situation in which it finds itself.

To sum up, and to end on a positive note, a negotiated agreement is a logical step in the search for a solution for a particular issue. However, it should be borne in mind that pre-litigation negotiation may well not provide the answer. Sadly, we do not know of any case in which contact with ICANN led to a pre-litigation discussion that was truly intended to result in a negotiated solution. To date, it would seem that ICANN sees negotiation as desirable only when a prevailing claimant seeks to enforce a legal decision, and even then, it has sometimes proved difficult to convince ICANN to take constructive action.[356]

356. *E.g.*, In the *ICM Registry* case, the IRP Panel issued its declaration on 19 February 2010. However, the IRP declaration was qualified as non-binding, and the registry agreement was executed only on 31 March 2011. In the *Booking.com* case, the IRP Panel issued a recommendation to the ICANN Board to improve the new gTLD Program processes both with respect to Booking.com's application and for future rounds. The ICANN Board took into account the Panel's recommendation for future rounds, but refused to reconsider its processes with respect to Booking.com's application.

B. OMBUDSMAN

1. Framework

ICANN has installed an Ombudsman's Office, managed by a single Ombudsman with staff support. The Office of the Ombudsman and the work that the Ombudsman does are established by Article V of the ICANN Bylaws.

a. Competent Authority

The Ombudsman is a full-time position, with salary and benefits appropriate to the function, as determined by the Board. The Ombudsman is appointed by the Board for an initial term of two years, subject to renewal by the Board. He or she is subject to dismissal by the Board only upon a three-fourths vote of the entire Board.

The Ombudsman must maintain neutrality and independence and have no bias or personal stake in an outcome, and must comply with all ICANN conflicts-of-interest and confidentiality policies. No ICANN employee, Board member, or other participant in a Supporting Organization (SO) or Advisory Committee is allowed to prevent or impede the Ombudsman's contact with the ICANN community (including employees of ICANN). ICANN employees and Board members must direct members of the ICANN community who voice problems, concerns, or complaints about ICANN to the Ombudsman, who advises complainants about the various options available for the review of such problems, concerns, or complaints. ICANN staff and other ICANN participants must observe and respect determinations made by the Ombudsman concerning the confidentiality of any complaints received.

b. Mandate and Scope

The principal function of the Ombudsman is to provide an independent internal evaluation of complaints by members of the ICANN community who believe that the ICANN staff, the ICANN Board or an ICANN constituent body has treated them unfairly. Considering the fact that the term 'ICANN community' is not defined, ICANN's Ombudsman *de facto* reviews each complaint received, and determines whether it meets the requirements mentioned in ICANN's Bylaws.

A party can make a complaint to the Ombudsman concerning:

- Decisions, actions, or inactions by one or more members of ICANN staff;
- Decisions, actions, or inactions by the ICANN Board of Directors which may be inconsistent with the Articles of Incorporation or the Bylaws; and
- Decisions, actions or inactions by ICANN constituent bodies.

The Ombudsman does not have jurisdiction over complaints concerning:

- Internal administrative matters;

- Personnel issues;
- Issues relating to membership of the Board; or
- Issues relating to vendor/supplier relationships.

The Ombudsman can also start an investigation on his or her 'own' motion, provided he or she has obtained authorization from ICANN's Board Governance Committee (BGC) to do so.

The Ombudsman must serve as an objective advocate for fairness, and seek to evaluate and where possible resolve complaints about unfair or inappropriate treatment by the ICANN staff, the ICANN Board, or ICANN constituent bodies, clarifying the issues and using conflict resolution tools such as negotiation, facilitation, and 'shuttle diplomacy' to achieve these results. The Ombudsman must facilitate the fair, impartial and timely resolution of problems and complaints that affected members of the ICANN community (excluding employees and vendors/suppliers of ICANN) may have with specific actions or failures to act by the ICANN Board or ICANN staff, which have not otherwise become the subject of either the Reconsideration or Independent Review processes.

The Ombudsman may not take any actions that have not been authorized in ICANN's Bylaws, and in particular, he or she may not institute, join, or support in any way any legal actions challenging ICANN's structure, procedures, processes or any conduct by the ICANN Board, staff or constituent bodies. The Ombudsman does not have the power to make, change or set aside a policy, administrative or ICANN Board of Director's decision, act or omission.

The Ombudsman does, however, have the power to investigate these matters, and to use ADR techniques to resolve them. The Ombudsman has the right to have access to (but not to publish if otherwise confidential) all necessary information and records from ICANN staff and constituent bodies to enable an informed evaluation of the complaint and to assist in dispute resolution where feasible (subject only to such confidentiality obligations as are imposed by the complainant or any generally applicable confidentiality policies adopted by ICANN).

The Ombudsman is specifically authorized to make such reports to the Board as he or she deems appropriate with respect to any particular matter and its resolution or the inability to resolve it. Reports of the Ombudsman are usually posted on ICANN's website.

Each year, the Office of Ombudsman publishes a consolidated analysis of the year's complaints and resolutions, dealing with confidentiality obligations and concerns. These annual reports include a description of any trends or common elements of complaints received during the period in question, as well as recommendations for steps that might be taken to minimize future complaints. The annual report is posted on ICANN's website.

2. Analysis

a. Independence

Today, an ombudsman can provide an efficient and easily accessible mechanism to help resolve disputes. ICANN ought to be acclaimed for having introduced an Office of the Ombudsman. Within ICANN, the Ombudsman is said to be an independent and objective advocate for fairness. However, given that ICANN's Board maintains control over the Ombudsman's Office, there is potential for that independence and objectiveness to be compromised.

First, there is the Ombudsman's salary, which is determined by ICANN's Board. ICANN's institutional documents appear to provide no limits to the Board's discretion in this respect. Although the Board needs a three-fourths majority to dismiss the Ombudsman, a simple majority suffices to reduce the Ombudsman's salary in such a way as to create an incentive for the Ombudsman to resign.

Also, the initial term of the Ombudsman is much shorter than the term of an ICANN Board member. If an Ombudsman is too critical towards the organization, he or she risks not being reappointed, and a two-year term is very short in an organization as complex as ICANN. If the Ombudsman wants to start an investigation on his or her own motion, the initiative may be curtailed by the BGC.

These institutional constraints do not give the Ombudsman a strong hand within ICANN. An Ombudsman who is excessively dependent on the organization's Board may not be able to preserve independence towards that Board.

b. Weight

The influence of the Ombudsman's institution can be seen as further weakened if one accepts the proposition, as ICANN does, that a complaint with the Ombudsman may not be pursued concurrently with another accountability mechanism. In our view, there is no legal basis to prevent the Ombudsman from carrying on his or her activities once an alternative accountability mechanism (a Request for Reconsideration (RfR) or an IRP) has been initiated.

It is true that ICANN's Bylaws establish that the Ombudsman shall act as a neutral party in matters for which the RfR and IRP have not been invoked.[357] However, while these Bylaws set forth what the Ombudsman must do; they do not prevent the Ombudsman from continuing his or her activities in connection with a complaint for which there has been a subsequent request for an RfR or an IRP. As contacting the Ombudsman does not constitute notice to ICANN of any particular action or cause of action, an aggrieved party may well feel the need to initiate an RfR or IRP as matters proceed, in order to preserve its rights.

357. ICANN's Bylaws, Articles V(2) and V(3)(1).

As the time period for filing an RfR or IRP will often have lapsed before the Ombudsman can effectively assist in finding a resolution to a problem (an RfR must be filed within fifteen days, whereas parties have a minimum of sixty days for bringing complaints to the Ombudsman), it would be counterproductive to require that the Ombudsman cease his or her activities when an RfR or request for IRP is filed.

Both RfR proceedings and IRPs allow for settlement discussions with the ICANN Board or ICANN executives. The use in these discussions of shuttle diplomacy and ADR techniques by an independent ombudsman, advocating fairness, would undoubtedly add to the efficiency of the Ombudsman's function and promote the resolution of conflicts.

c. *Confidentiality*

The confidential nature of the Ombudsman's complaint procedure can contribute to the efficient resolution of conflicts. However, in view of ICANN's openness and transparency obligations, a balance must be struck between considerations of confidentiality, fairness, due process and transparency.

The confidentiality in which the Ombudsman operates may not be used as an excuse to negotiate side deals with ICANN which could have an impact on third parties. Where conflict resolution is achieved, third parties are entitled to a detailed rationale setting out the grounds for the resolution. In cases where no conflict resolution is achieved, the complaining party may have an interest in disclosing details about the Ombudsman's involvement. In such cases, the confidentiality belongs to the complaining party, and we see no reason why a complaining party should be prevented from disclosing details about its dealings with the Ombudsman, provided the rights of third parties are respected. In this respect, the Ombudsman's reluctance to testify should apply only to information that is truly confidential, and not to information for which a complainant has waived confidentiality.

d. *The Practice of Draft Reports*

In cases where the Ombudsman makes a draft report first, he or she will request feedback from ICANN or other individuals concerned before making a final report. This practice can help avoiding misunderstandings and errors. However, there are non-transparency issues that could arise concerning such feedback. For example, a complainant may not be informed whether or not ICANN or its Board has commented on the draft report, nor will it be privy to those comments. Without the guarantee of a minimum of transparency between the parties involved – at least at this stage of the proceedings – the Office of the Ombudsman cannot be seen as an ideal dispute resolution mechanism, and the Ombudsman risks losing the trust that he or she should be able to inspire.

C. DIDP REQUEST

Parties who wish to seek legal remedies related to an ICANN action or inaction may need to first obtain all the relevant information that will allow them to assess the situation and their chances of success. Parties may issue formal requests for disclosure of documents in the framework of legal proceedings. However, most information should already be available in view of ICANN's openness and transparency obligations. Formal legal action may be cumbersome, and ICANN can be invited to disclose relevant information on a voluntary basis. This is why it is important to consider the ICANN Documentary Information Disclosure Policy (DIDP), which streamlines ICANN's voluntary disclosure practice.

1. Framework

On 15 February 2008, the ICANN Board adopted the DIDP as part of its *Accountability & Transparency Frameworks and Principles*.[358] The purpose of this policy is to 'ensure that information contained in documents concerning ICANN's operational activities [...] is made available to the public unless there is a compelling reason for confidentiality.'[359]

As required by the DIDP, ICANN proactively publishes 'a comprehensive set of materials' on the ICANN website as 'a matter of due course.'[360] ICANN organizes these materials in 'categories of documents' which ultimately relate to ICANN's operational activities. The DIDP states that the following categories of documents must be made publicly accessible:

- Annual Reports;
- Articles of Incorporation;
- Board Meeting Transcripts, Minutes and Resolutions;
- Budget;
- Bylaws (current);
- Bylaws (archives)
- Correspondence;
- Financial Information;
- Litigation documents;
- Major agreements;
- Monthly Registry reports;
- Operating Plan;
- Policy documents;

358. ICANN, *Adopted Board Resolutions | New Delhi*, February 15, 2008, http://www.icann.org/en/minutes/resolutions- 15feb08.htm#_Toc64545917.
359. ICANN, *ICANN Accountability & Transparency Frameworks and Principles*, 2008, https://www.icann.org/en/system/files/files/acct-trans-frameworks-principles-10jan08-en.pdf, p. 9.
360. The DIDP does not ascribe a definition to the term 'due course' and uses the phrases 'as a matter of due course' and 'in due course' somewhat interchangeably. *Ibid.*

- Speeches, Presentations & Publications;
- Strategic Plan;
- Material information relating to the Address Supporting Organization (ASO);
- Material information relating to the Generic Supporting Organization (GNSO);
- Material information relating to the country code Names Supporting Organization (ccNSO);
- Material information relating to the At large Advisory Committee (ALAC);
- Material information relating to the Governmental Advisory Committee (GAC);
- Material information relating to the Root Server System Advisory Committee (RSSAC); and
- Material information relating to the Security and Stability Advisory Committee (SSAC).

However, much information on ICANN's operations is not publicly available, and members of the public may request disclosure via a DIDP Request.

a. Competent Authority

DIDP Requests are evaluated by ICANN staff; in practice, they are handled by ICANN's legal department.

b. Mandate and Scope

In evaluating DIDP requests ICANN will evaluate if disclosure is appropriate. ICANN has established a long list of circumstances in which it considers no disclosure to be warranted. It is perfectly understandable and justifiable for ICANN not to disclose personal, medical or other information that would constitute an unnecessary invasion of personal privacy. It is equally justified not to disclose information that would put at risk the security and stability of the Internet. However, in addition, ICANN will not disclose information exchanged with governments or international organizations, if the information was provided in the expectation that it would be kept confidential and/or its disclosure would or is likely to materially prejudice ICANN's relationship with that party.

Moreover, internal information relating to ICANN's deliberative and decision-making processes can be kept secret if ICANN determines that the information is likely 'to compromise the integrity of ICANN's deliberative and decision-making process by inhibiting the candid exchange of ideas and communications, including internal documents, memoranda, and other similar communications to or from ICANN Directors, ICANN Directors' Advisors, ICANN staff, ICANN consultants, ICANN contractors, and ICANN agents.'[361] Neither will ICANN disclose information that was provided pursuant to a nondisclosure agreement.

ICANN's list of circumstances for non-disclosure is illustrative only. The DIDP contains a catch-all clause giving ICANN discretion to determine whether the harm in disclosing information outweighs the public interest or vice versa. ICANN must thus perform a balancing exercise for each and every DIDP request. According to the DIDP, ICANN must not respond to requests: (i) which are unreasonable; (ii) which are excessive or overly burdensome; (iii) when complying with the request would not be feasible; or (iv) which are made with an abusive or vexatious purpose or by a vexatious or querulous individual.

Similarly, ICANN is not required to create or compile summaries of any documented information, or to respond to requests seeking information that is already publicly available. Nonetheless, it is to be presumed that ICANN is aware of the impenetrable nature of its website,[362] and, perhaps because of its website's lack of transparency, ICANN often helps those requesting information to locate that information when it is already publicly available.

c. *Procedure*

The process to request document disclosure is straightforward. Requests are sent via email to a designated address and ICANN staff will respond to the request in writing. If a request is denied, ICANN must identify the reasons for non-disclosure. A denial of information may be appealed with the ICANN Board in an RfR or, if the denial is attributable to the Board, in an IRP.

d. *Timing*

ICANN will try to respond to DIDP requests within thirty calendar days. ICANN will inform the requestor in writing if it is unable to meet that timeframe. It will indicate when a response will be provided and indicate the reasons of the extension.

2. Analysis

The Berkman Center for Internet & Society at Harvard University prepared an independent review on the transparency at ICANN in 2010.[363]

361. ICANN, *Documentary Information Disclosure Policy*, https://www.icann.org/resources/pages/didp-2012-02-25-en.
362. ICANN has a tradition of creating microsites dedicated to working groups. Information is constantly added, and not always in a thematic way. While a lot of information can be found online, it proves often difficult for outside observers to retrieve relevant documents.
363. Herbert Burkert and Urs Gasser, *Accountability and transparency at ICANN – an independent review – Memorandum: Transparency and internal decision making*, available at: https://www

The overall conclusions in the report are self-explanatory. Here is an extract:

> '[...] the information flow coming from ICANN to a requester should become the object of active transparency and [...] the information should not only be received by the requester but the information should also become part of the active communication inventory to save others the need to initiate similar requests and to let the general public benefit from all requests.'
>
> 'After analyzing ICANN's various *practices* of transparency, and noting that ICANN justly emphasizes the importance of transparency as a form of accountability, one is struck by the impression of how comparatively little effort seems to have been put into an adjustment and modernization of ICANN's interface with the general public.
>
> This is particularly surprising for an institution that is seen by many to incorporate the INTERNET in the literal sense. Many of the points criticized could be addressed by a more dedicated effort to improve information design – guided by an engagement for the transparency default, keeping in mind the transparency interests and the information retrieval behavior of the user community and by looking for best practices at the sites of organizations with similar tasks. Instead, one is faced with a website that seems to have incrementally grown with the size and complexity of ICANN's activities without conceptually fully mastering them – at least in as far as their representational aspects are concerned.'
>
> 'Going through the various *policy* reconsiderations, the exemption policies or – as ICANN has chosen to call them somewhat aseptically – 'Conditions for Nondisclosure' are at the core of all deficiencies. They are comprehensive, they are overbroad, and they are driven by a 'belt-plus-suspender'-philosophy where any seemingly transparency friendly rudiment is disciplined by an all comprehensive confidentiality override. This approach to exempting information from disclosure affects active transparency (although seemingly less so because the public has no way to know what is just *not* actively made available), passive transparency (because the exemptions discourage its use and keep this important accountability instrument underdeveloped) and participatory transparency (because it makes ICANN too inhibited to engage in real dialogue instead of a series of one-way communications).
>
> The issue of exemptions will have to be addressed in the same manner as it has been addressed in the public sector: reduction of exemptions, precision of exemptions, allowing for a broad public interest override (but without a confidentiality 'over-override'), strict classification and declassification policies and some form of oversight and most of all, with less fear and more courage.
>
> If this issue is addressed properly, the most promising change should be encouraged with regard to participatory transparency. That is, implementing procedures and instruments that would allow ICANN and the interested public to engage in dialogue that would encourage all participants to reconsider their positions in the interest of the goals ICANN and its community stands for.'

.google.be/url?sa = t&rct = j&q = &esrc = s&source = web&cd = 8&ved = 0ahUKEwjx2rGRg7zNAhXLbBoKHRy9AR8QFghZMAc&url = https%3A%2F%2Fcyber.law.harvard.edu%2Fpubrelease%2Ficann%2Fpdfs%2FTransparency_Memorandum.pdf&usg = AFQjCNGuncG0Srrf-gn6vhps5QcaxTF6Fg&sig2 = 5wqXu3HhV4SZ4y3VtxTHSA.

It is surprising that, in response to this report, which was requested by ICANN with the aim to review and improve its accountability,[364] ICANN made no changes to its DIDP and many of its responses to DIDP requests remain illustrative of the criticized 'belt-plus-suspender' philosophy. ICANN's staff remains capable of using all-comprehensive confidentiality overrides.

And when confidentiality reasons are invoked abusively, a requestor's means of recourse remain limited. In fact, a requestor would have little choice but to bring the issue to the ICANN Board in an RfR. The ICANN Board would then review whether confidentiality reasons should rightfully be invoked, or whether the balance should favor disclosure.

Practice shows that the Board often adopts a process-focused position. The ICANN Board will investigate whether ICANN's staff correctly mentioned a reason for non-disclosure, and whether it balanced the potential harm of disclosure with the public interest. The Board does not substantially review whether the balancing exercise of ICANN staff is acceptable in view of ICANN's transparency obligations.[365] In other words, as long as ICANN staff make mention of a reason for non-disclosure and the fact that a balancing exercise has been performed, ICANN staff have absolute discretion to accept or deny a DIDP request. Moreover, as neither the requestor nor a third party is given access to the requested information, there is no opportunity to check whether the denial was legitimate. If a competent arbitration panel or judge does not compel ICANN to disclose the information so as to review ICANN's balancing exercise, there are no limits on ICANN's discretion to restrict transparency in this context. Such an application of the DIDP would conflict with ICANN's openness and transparency obligations.

D. REQUEST FOR RECONSIDERATION

1. Framework

Any person or entity materially affected by an action or inaction of ICANN may request reconsideration of that action by the ICANN Board. The right to request reconsideration by the Board is established by Article V of the ICANN Bylaws, which requires that the requestor show that it has been adversely affected by:

(a) One or more staff actions or inactions that contradict established ICANN policy(ies); or
(b) One or more actions or inactions of the ICANN Board that have been taken, or not taken, without consideration of material information, unless the

364. ICANN, *Accountability and Transparency Review Team – Selection of Independent Expert and Update on ATRT Review*, 10 August 2010, https://www.icann.org/news/announcement-2010-08-10-en.
365. For an example of the ICANN Board's process-focused approach, *see* BGC determination on Reconsideration Request 14-39, 11 October 2014.

requesting party could have but did not submit the information for the Board's consideration at the time of action or refusal to act; or

(c) Since 11 April 2013, one or more actions or inactions of the ICANN Board that have been taken as a result of the Board's reliance on false or inaccurate material information.

a. *Competent Authority*

The Board Governance Committee (BGC) reviews and considers Reconsideration Requests or RfRs. The BGC has investigative authority and makes recommendations to ICANN's full Board. Since 11 April 2013, the BGC is authorized to make final determinations on RfRs regarding staff actions or inactions, without reference to the full Board.

b. *Mandate and Scope*

RfRs can be filed against actions and inactions of either ICANN staff or the ICANN Board. However, ICANN also accepts RfRs against actions and inactions of third-party vendors which contradict established policies.[366]

The BGC has the authority to:

- Evaluate requests for review or reconsideration;
- Conduct whatever factual investigation is deemed appropriate;
- Request additional written submissions from the affected party, or from other parties; and
- Make a recommendation to the Board of Directors on the merits of the request.

Since the change in Bylaws of 11 April 2013, the BGC may also:

- Summarily dismiss insufficient requests;
- Evaluate requests for urgent consideration; and
- Make a final determination on RfRs regarding staff action or inaction, without reference to the full ICANN Board.

Prior to 11 April 2013, the BGC was also able to decide not to hear an RfR, giving reasons for its decision. With the amendments of 11 April 2013, the BGC is given clear guidelines for summary dismissal of an RfR. An RfR may be summarily dismissed if: (i) the requestor fails to meet the requirements for bringing a Reconsideration Request; (ii) it is frivolous, querulous or vexatious; or (iii) the requestor had notice and opportunity to, but did not, participate in the public comment period relating to the contested action, if applicable.

366. *See* BGC Recommendation on Reconsideration Request 13-5.

When making a determination relating to a staff action or inaction, the BGC's determination is final and has precedential value.

c. Procedure

All Reconsideration Requests must be submitted to an e-mail address designated by the BGC. Since the change in Bylaws of 11 April 2013, ICANN requires that requestors use a specific form that is posted on ICANN's website, and that they acknowledge and agree to the terms and conditions set forth in the form when filing.

On 11 April 2013, ICANN also introduced a clear page limit of twenty-five pages (double-spaced, twelve-point font) of argument in support of an RfR. Requestors may however submit all documentary evidence (without limitation) necessary to demonstrate why the action or inaction should be reconsidered.

The BGC will evaluate each RfR upon its receipt to determine if it is sufficiently stated or whether there are reasons for summary dismissal. For all RfR that are not summarily dismissed, the BGC must promptly proceed to review and consideration.

RfR proceedings may be consolidated if: (i) the requests involve the same general action or inaction; and (ii) the parties submitting RfRs are similarly affected by such action or inaction. ICANN clarified in 2013 that consolidated filings may be appropriate if the alleged causal connection and the resulting harm is the same for all of the requestors. However, each individual requestor has to demonstrate that it has been materially harmed and adversely impacted by the action or inaction giving rise to the request.

In handling the RfR, the BGC may request additional information or clarifications from the requestor, and may elect to conduct a meeting with the requestor by telephone, email or, if acceptable to the requestor reconsideration, in person. In 2013, ICANN clarified that a requestor may ask for an opportunity to be heard, and that the BGC has absolute discretion to grant or dismiss such a request. We are not aware of any such request being granted by the BGC.

The BGC will act on RfRs on the basis of the public written record. When a hearing is being organized, it is thus advisable to ensure that there is a written report of the hearing. The public record will include the information submitted by the requestor, but it may also include information by ICANN staff or third parties. For example, the BGC may ask ICANN staff for their views on the matter, or request a third party to supply information relevant to the RfR. The views and comments of ICANN staff are made publicly available on ICANN's website. The requestor must be provided with information collected from third parties. Information that is considered relevant must be referred to in the BGC's recommendation. Although it is not explicitly stated in the ICANN Bylaws, such information should also be included in a BGC determination.

The BGC's determinations and recommendations must be posted on ICANN's website. In cases where a recommendation is made by the BGC, the Board is not bound to follow the recommendation. In practice, the ICANN Board only exceptionally rejects a BGC recommendation. The final decision of the Board is made public as part of the preliminary report and minutes of the Board meeting at which the decision is made. The Board's decision on a BGC recommendation is considered final. As a result, no new RfR based on the exact same circumstances may be filed.[367] Such requests will be summarily dismissed. However, the Board's decision can be challenged in an IRP.

d. *Timing*

The timing for filing an RfR is relatively short (it was halved on 11 April 2013). Requests challenging staff actions must now be filed within fifteen days of the date on which the party submitting the request became aware of, or should reasonably have become aware of, the challenged staff action. Requests challenging Board actions must be filed within fifteen days of the publication of the action in a resolution, if that publication is accompanied by a rationale. If no rationale is provided, the request must be submitted within fifteen days from the initial posting of the resolution. Inactions (by ICANN staff or the ICANN Board) may be challenged within fifteen days following the date on which the affected person reasonably concluded, or should reasonably have concluded, that the action was not going to be taken in a timely manner.

The normal throughput time for a Reconsideration Request should be between thirty and sixty days. The BGC has an extendable deadline of thirty days following receipt of the request to make a final determination or recommendation to the ICANN Board. If more time is required, the BGC must report to the ICANN Board explaining the circumstances that have prevented it from reaching a decision and providing its best estimate of the time still required to produce a final determination or recommendation. Where the BGC makes a recommendation, the ICANN Board must issue its decision relating to the BGC's recommendation within sixty days of receipt of the RfR or as soon thereafter as feasible. Any circumstances that delay the Board from acting within this timeframe must be identified and posted on ICANN's website. In practice, delays occur frequently.[368]

In urgent matters, requestors may apply to the BGC for urgent consideration. However, such requests are only envisioned for Board action or inaction. Requests for urgent consideration must be made within two business days (calculated at ICANN's headquarters in Los Angeles, California) of the posting of the resolution at issue. The request for urgent consideration must include an explanation of why the matter urgently needs reconsideration and must demonstrate that the RfR is likely to succeed. The BGC must respond to the request for urgent consideration within two business

367. However, in contrast with BGC determinations, the Bylaws do not provide that a determination by the full Board on an RfR has precedential value.

368. *See e.g.*, Request for Reconsideration 13-5 took 166 days to completion; Request for Reconsideration 13-9 took 393 days to completion; Request for Reconsideration 14-10 took 107 days to completion; Request 14-27 took 102 days to completion; Request 16-3 took 131 days to completion, etc.

days after receipt of such a request. If the BGC agrees to consider the matter with urgency, it will cause notice to be provided to the requestor, who will have two business days after notification to complete the RfR. The BGC will issue a recommendation on the urgent RfR within seven days of the completion of the filing of the RfR, or as soon thereafter as feasible. If the BGC does not agree to consider the matter with urgency, the requestor may still file an RfR within the regular time frame set forth within the Bylaws.

e. Costs

ICANN will absorb the normal administrative costs of the reconsideration process. However, ICANN reserves the right to recover any costs that are deemed to be extraordinary in nature. When such extraordinary costs can be foreseen, that fact, and the reasons why such costs are necessary and appropriate for the evaluating of the RfR, will be communicated to the requestor. The requestor will then have the option of withdrawing the request or agreeing to bear such costs.

2. Analysis

Requestors have only rarely been successful in having the ICANN Board review a staff or Board action. This is because the BGC and the ICANN Board adopt a purely process-based approach in addressing RfRs. To date, ICANN has limited its reviews so as to be based purely on its policy documents without investigating whether the application of those policies is fair and in line with the more fundamental rules governing ICANN and contained in its Articles of Incorporation and Bylaws. ICANN's belief that its RfR process cannot be used to question unfair or discriminatory results following the 'correct' application of its policies seems to be deeply rooted, as is illustrated by the voting statements of some conscientious ICANN Board members. In 2013, ICANN Board Member, Mr. George Sadowsky abstained from voting on a resolution. He did not vote against the resolution, as he considered the scope of the reconsideration process to be limited to evaluating whether an established process was followed. He stated:

> 'The reconsideration process is a very narrowly focused instrument, relying solely upon investigating deviations from established and agreed upon process. As such, it can be useful, but it is limited in scope. In particular, it does not address situations where process has in fact been followed, but the results of such process have been regarded, sometimes quite widely, as being contrary to what might be best for significant or all segments of the ICANN community and/or Internet users in general.
>
> [...]

> As a Board member who is aware of ICANN's Bylaws, I cannot vote against the motion to deny reconsideration. The motion appears to be correct based upon the criteria in the Bylaws that define the reconsideration process and the facts in this particular case.'[369]

Other ICANN Board members expressed similar concerns to explain their decision to abstain, rather than reject, a Board resolution that had significant implications regarding fairness.[370] By adopting such a narrow view of the RfR process as an accountability mechanism, ICANN has missed out on the opportunity of improving its accountability towards gTLD applicants. Many legal proceedings could have been avoided if ICANN had adopted a different view to its own RfR process.

E. COOPERATIVE ENGAGEMENT PROCESS

1. Framework

On 11 April 2013, ICANN introduced the Cooperative Engagement process (CEP). The CEP is established by Article IV, Section 3, paragraphs 14, 16 and 17 of the ICANN Bylaws. The actual operation of the CEP was posted in a note on ICANN's website, and is considered to be incorporated into ICANN's Bylaws.

The CEP is a voluntary process which can be initiated before filing a Request for Independent Review (IRP).[371] The process aims to resolve the contested issue and to determine if any issues remain for the IRP, or whether the matter should be brought to the ICANN Board's attention. Although the CEP is voluntary, parties are urged to enter into a period of cooperative engagement, and if a party elects not to participate in good faith in the cooperative engagement, it could have important cost implications in future proceedings: in such cases, and provided ICANN prevails in the IRP, the IRP Panel is obliged to award ICANN all reasonable fees and costs incurred by ICANN during the proceedings, including legal fees.

The CEP process proceeds as follows: Within fifteen days of the posting of the minutes of an ICANN Board meeting, a party may file a request for CEP. The requestor should identify the Board action(s) at issue, as well as the provisions of the ICANN Bylaws or Articles of Incorporation that have allegedly been violated. The requestor is also expected to designate a single point of contact for the resolution of the issue. ICANN expects the CEP to be between ICANN and the requesting party, without reference to outside counsel. However, nothing prevents a requestor from designating outside counsel as the single point of contact if it believes that this will help to advance the process.

369. ICANN, Minutes of the Meeting of the New gTLD Program Committee, 10 September 2013, https://www.icann.org/resources/board-material/minutes-new-gtld-2013-09-10-en.
370. ICANN, Minutes of the Meeting of the New gTLD Program Committee, 10 September 2013, https://www.icann.org/resources/board-material/minutes-new-gtld-2013-09-10-en, *see* statements by Ray Plzak, Olga Madruga-Forti, Kuo-Wei Wu.
371. *Infra* Chapter 3.F.

Within three business days following the initiation of a CEP, ICANN will designate a single executive to serve as the point of contact for the resolution of the issue, and provide notice of the designation to the requestor. ICANN expects the requestor and ICANN's representative to confer (either by telephone or in person) within two business days of ICANN providing notice of its designated representatives, in order to attempt to resolve the issue, and to determine if any issues remain for the IRP or whether the matter should be brought to the ICANN Board's attention. If, during the first conference, the representatives are not able to resolve the issue or agree on a narrowing of issues, or a reference to the ICANN Board, they will be expected to meet in person at a location mutually agreed upon within seven calendar days of the initial conference. At this second conference, the parties will attempt to reach a definitive agreement on the resolution of the issue or on the narrowing of issues remaining for the IRP, or whether the matter should be brought to the ICANN Board's attention. The time schedule and process may be modified if both ICANN and the requestor agree in writing. In practice, the time schedule is often extended. This is understandable in view of the complexity of issues that can be raised within a CEP.

The CEP request suspends the deadline to file an IRP for a maximum of fourteen days, unless parties agree on a longer suspension. In practice, ICANN has consistently agreed to longer suspensions in cases when the CEP has taken longer than initially expected.

Within a CEP, all matters discussed during the cooperative engagement phase are to remain confidential and are not to be subject to discovery or used as evidence for any purpose within the IRP, and this without prejudice to either party.

2. Analysis

Participation in multiple CEPs has shown us that the CEP can be a useful mechanism for instigating open and frank discussions with ICANN's General Counsel and his team. Although a CEP may not result in a negotiated agreement in circumstances where interests and positions are diametrically opposed between parties, it remains an excellent process that can create goodwill between the parties and ensure the efficient handling of further proceedings. The CEP also offers a unique opportunity for ICANN to obtain advanced knowledge of the arguments that a party may be planning to raise as part of an IRP. However, for a party that believes in its arguments, this is a small price to pay for the increased efficiency a CEP can bring to the dispute resolution.

F. INDEPENDENT REVIEW PROCESS

1. Framework

The Independent Review Process (IRP) is established by Article IV, Section 3 of the ICANN Bylaws.

The IRP is meant to be an independent third-party review of ICANN Board actions or inactions that are alleged to be inconsistent with ICANN's Articles of Incorporation or Bylaws.

Any person materially affected by a decision or action by the Board that he or she asserts is inconsistent with the Articles of Incorporation or Bylaws may submit a request for independent review of that decision or action. On 11 April 2013, ICANN clarified that, in order to be materially affected, the person must suffer injury or harm that is directly and causally connected to the Board's alleged violation of the Bylaws or the Articles of Incorporation and not as a result of third parties acting in line with the Board's action.

a. Competent Authority

ICANN appointed the International Centre for Dispute Resolution(ICDR), a division of the American Arbitration Association (AAA) as international dispute resolution provider for IRPs. According to ICANN's Bylaws, the IRP provider may vary 'from time to time'. However, since its inception, the ICDR has always been ICANN's IRP provider. Requests for IRP must thus be filed with the ICDR, and a copy must be sent to ICANN. The ICDR administers the IRP and coordinates the appointment of the panelists who will rule on the request.

The original intention was that there be an omnibus standing panel of between six and nine members with a variety of expertise, including jurisprudence, judicial experience, ADR and knowledge of ICANN's mission and work from which each specific IRP Panel could be selected. It is the IRP provider's job to determine a procedure for assigning members from the standing panel to individual IRP panels. It was however foreseen that, if the omnibus standing panel does not have the requisite diversity of skill and experience needed for a particular proceeding, the ICDR (or any other competent IRP provider) can identify one or more panelists, as required, from outside the omnibus standing panel to augment the panel members for those proceedings.

The members of the standing panel are supposed to serve for terms that are staggered to allow for continued review of the size of the panel and the range of expertise. Individuals holding an official position or office within the ICANN structure are not eligible to serve on the standing panel. The membership of the standing panel is coordinated by the IRP provider but subject to approval by ICANN. The standing panel is to have a Chair appointed for a term not exceeding three years. An individual IRP panel will comprise one or three members. Either party may request consideration by either a one- or three-member panel. The Chair of the standing panel will make the final determination of the size of each IRP panel, taking into account the wishes of the parties and the complexity of the issues presented.

In fact, however, although the decision to have an omnibus standing panel was adopted on 11 April 2013, such a panel has never been installed. As a result, the default arbitration rules of the IRP provider (*i.e.*, the ICDR) apply. Thus, parties may agree on an appointment procedure, and, in the absence of an agreement, the IRP provider's case administrator may decide on the appointment or method of appointment of panelists.

Once appointed, the IRP panelist or panelists are responsible for managing the proceedings and for ruling upon the request for IRP. All panel members must adhere to conflicts-of-interest policy stated in the IRP provider's operating rules and procedures, as approved by the ICANN Board.

b. *Mandate and Scope*

IRP panels are charged with comparing contested actions of the ICANN Board to ICANN's Articles of Incorporation and Bylaws, and with declaring whether or not the Board has acted consistently with the provisions of the Articles of Incorporation and Bylaws. It has been broadly accepted that the IRP panel's evaluation for consistency with ICANN's Articles of Incorporation and Bylaws extends to both ICANN Board actions and inactions.

Since the adoption of the amended Bylaws of 11 April 2013, an IRP panel must apply a 'defined standard of review', focusing on:

- Did the Board act without conflict of interest in taking its decision?
- Did the Board exercise due diligence and care in having a reasonable amount of facts in front of them? and
- Did the Board members exercise independent judgment in taking the decision, believed to be in the best interests of the company?[372]

The standard of review was introduced with the stated purpose of enhancing ICANN's accountability,[373] and arguably is intended to increase scrutiny and, as a result, increase the care taken by the ICANN Board.

IRP panels must make their declarations based solely on the documentation, supporting materials, and arguments submitted by the parties. According to the ICANN Bylaws, they have the authority to:

- Summarily dismiss requests brought without standing, lacking in substance, or that are frivolous or vexatious;
- Request additional written submissions from the party seeking review, the Board, ICANN's SOs, or from other parties;
- Declare whether an action or inaction of the Board was inconsistent with the Articles of Incorporation or Bylaws;

372. The 'company' meaning ICANN.
373. *See* ICANN, *Rationale for Resolution 2013.04.11.06*, https://www.icann.org/resources/board-material/resolutions-2013-04-11-en#1.d; ICANN, *Rationale for Resolutions 2012.12.20.17 – 2012.12.20.19*, https://www.icann.org/resources/board-material/resolutions-2012-12-20-en#2.c.

- Recommend that the Board stay any action or decision, or that the Board take interim action, until such time as the Board reviews and acts upon the opinion of the IRP;
- Consolidate requests for independent review if the facts and circumstances are sufficiently similar; and
- Determine the timing for each proceeding.

IRP panels must also specifically designate the prevailing party and issue a decision on the costs of the IRP proceedings. They also have the discretion to grant a party's request to keep certain information confidential, such as trade secrets.

The question of whether an IRP panel's authority is limited to the tasks listed above, or whether this list is merely illustrative, has been the subject of debate. In our view, the authority of an IRP panel must be assessed in the light of: (i) the purpose of the IRP, which is to offer an effective and meaningful accountability mechanism, and (ii) the choice for the ICDR arbitration rules that govern the IRP procedure. These rules are designed to provide a final resolution of the dispute, and with this aim in mind, a broad interpretation on the IRP panel's authority may appear appropriate. In addition, the authority to: (i) summarily dismiss requests, (ii) consolidate requests, and (iii) determine the timing for each proceeding was added to the ICANN Bylaws on 11 April 2013, although these changes may have been intended primarily as a clarification of an IRP panel's authority, rather than an intention to modify the remit of a panel's authority. Clearly, IRP panels that were appointed prior to the 2013 amendment were undoubtedly able to determine the timing for the proceedings.

c. *Procedure*

The IRP has been designed to offer cost-efficient and lightweight proceedings. Therefore, ICANN's Bylaws specify that an IRP panel should conduct its proceedings as far as is feasible by email and otherwise via the Internet. An IRP panel may organize hearings, where these are considered necessary. However, ICANN clearly favors telephone hearings over in-person hearings. With the amendments of 11 April 2013, ICANN's Bylaws limit hearings – whether telephonic or in-person – to argument only. The Bylaws require that all evidence, including witness statements, be submitted in writing in advance. Notwithstanding this, the examination and cross-examination of witnesses has been allowed in the past, and ICANN's limitations concerning the organization of hearings (as expressed in its Bylaws)[374] have been considered excessive.

The CEP discussed above,[375] was also introduced with the purpose of streamlining IRPs. Although the CEP is voluntary, ICANN urges parties to enter into CEP prior to

374. ICANN Bylaws, Article IV(3)(12).
375. *See* Chapter 3.E.

initiating a request for IRP. If the parties do not successfully resolve their differences through the CEP, a claimant may then submit a request for IRP with the competent IRP provider.

Since 11 April 2013, and as the case for RfRs (see above), there is a page limit that applies to a request for IRP: it may not exceed twenty-five pages (double-spaced, twelve-point font) of argument. The same limit also applies to ICANN's response. Documentary evidence may be submitted without limitation. If parties submit expert evidence, ICANN requires that such evidence be provided in writing and that there be a right of reply to the expert evidence.

Consolidated requests may be appropriate when the causal connection between the circumstances of the requests and the harm is the same for each of the requesting parties.

Upon the filing of a request or consolidated requests for IRP, the parties are urged to participate in a voluntary conciliation period for the purpose of narrowing the issues that are stated within the request for IRP. If parties elect to participate in a conciliation period, a conciliator will be appointed. The appointment is supposed to be made by the Chair of the IRP omnibus standing panel. However, as no omnibus standing panel is in place, the parties must agree on a process for appointing the conciliator. As the CEP serves the exact same purpose as the conciliation period, a conciliation period will often be unnecessary, particularly if the parties have been able to sufficiently narrow the issues remaining in the independent review during the CEP. In practice, ICANN has agreed that claimants who have participated in a CEP need not enter into a conciliation period. Where parties do enter into a conciliation period, all matters discussed during that period are to remain confidential, are not subject to discovery and cannot be used as evidence for any purpose within the IRP. In addition, the conciliator will not be eligible to serve as one of the panelists presiding over the IRP in question.

As there is no omnibus standing panel in place, parties will use the early stages of IRP proceedings to have the IRP panel installed. Once appointed, the IRP panel will decide, in consultation with the parties, on the further steps of the proceedings. The course of proceedings will vary, depending on the nature of the case.

d. *Timing*

In the amended Bylaws of 11 April 2013, ICANN introduced a deadline for filing an IRP request. A request for IRP must be filed within thirty days of the posting of the minutes of the Board meeting (and the accompanying Board Briefing Materials, if available) that the requesting party contends demonstrates that ICANN violated its Bylaws or Articles of Incorporation. In accordance with Article 3 of the ICDR arbitration rules, ICANN must respond within thirty days following the commencement of the IRP. The IRP panel may impose deadlines for further written submissions and decide on a hearing date.

Since 11 April 2013, ICANN's Bylaws have stipulated that the IRP Panel should strive to issue its written declaration no later than six months after the filing of the request for IRP. In practice, more time has been needed to complete the proceedings.

An IRP panel must make its final declaration no later than sixty days from the date of the closing of the hearing, unless otherwise agreed by the parties or determined by the ICDR's administrator.[376]

Where feasible, the ICANN Board must consider the IRP panel's declaration at the Board's next meeting. The declarations of the IRP panel, and the Board's subsequent action on those declarations, are final and have precedential value.[377]

e. Costs

The party not prevailing shall ordinarily be responsible for bearing all the costs of the IRP provider. However, in an exceptional case the IRP panel may in its declaration allocate up to half of the costs of the IRP provider to the prevailing party based upon the circumstances, and depending on the reasonableness of the parties' positions and their contribution to the public interest. Each party to the IRP proceedings shall bear its own expenses. However, if the party requesting the independent review does not participate in good faith in a CEP or conciliation process, and ICANN is the prevailing party in the request for independent review, the IRP panel must award ICANN all reasonable fees and costs incurred by ICANN in the proceeding, including legal fees.

2. Analysis

As we discuss at length in this book, the IRP procedure raises many questions and calls for a detailed review and amendment. We refer to Chapter 5 and Chapter 6 where we discuss these issues in detail.

G. COURT

1. Framework

ICANN is an organization incorporated under the law of the State of California in the United States. This means that ICANN must abide by the laws of the United States and California and can be called to account by the judicial system. A party can take ICANN to court if a decision or the absence of a decision would violate federal U.S. or California law. In addition, on the basis of ICANN's own Articles of Incorporation, and bearing in mind the nature of its activities and mission, ICANN is also subject to international law.

376. Article 30(1) ICDR arbitration rules.
377. ICANN Bylaws, Article IV(3)(21).

However, ICANN's terms and conditions associated to the application process contain an explicit waiver of redress through court proceedings. Therefore, if an aggrieved applicant wishes to challenge ICANN in court, it would first have to invalidate this waiver before a court could assess any substantive arguments.

2. Cases

ICANN has frequently been involved in litigation. However, only a few cases have dealt with ICANN's liberalization efforts.[378]

H. MEDIATION PROCEEDINGS

1. Framework

The vast majority of agreements between ICANN and gTLD registry operators provide for mediation as a dispute resolution mechanism.[379] Parties must attempt to resolve a dispute in connection with the registry agreement through mediation before they may initiate arbitration.

The agreement does not appoint a pre-established mediation provider, but gives large discretion to the parties to agree on a single mediator or a mutually acceptable mediation provider that will appoint a mediator. The mediator will determine the rules and procedures of the mediation, following consultation with the parties. Mediation is not expected to last for more than ninety days, and may be terminated at any time by either party or the mediator if the parties have participated in good faith in the mediation but have been unable to resolve the dispute. The parties will bear their own costs in the mediation and share equally the fees and expenses of the mediator.

By way of comparison, the Registrar Accreditation Agreement (RAA) between ICANN and registrars provides for similar mediation proceedings to resolve disagreements related to proposed revisions of the RAA. The mediation is mandatory, and will be facilitative and non-evaluative. If the parties have not managed to resolve the dispute after ninety days, the mediation will automatically terminate (unless extended by agreement of the parties). The mediator will then deliver to the parties a definition of the issues. This could be considered during any possible future arbitration.

378. *See e.g.*, *Name.Space, Inc v. ICANN*, Opinion of U.S. District Court of Appeals of the Ninth Circuit for the Central District of California, 31 July 2015, https://www.icann.org/en/system/files/files/namespace-ninth-circuit-affirming-dismissal-31jul15-en.pdf; *Image Online Design, Inc. v. ICANN*, Order Granting Motion to Dismiss of U.S. District Court of Central District of California, 7 February 2013, https://www.icann.org/en/system/files/files/order-granting-motion-dismiss-07feb13-en.pdf; *Ruby Glen, LLC v. ICANN*, Complaint before the U.S. District Court of Central District of California, 22 July 2016, https://www.icann.org/en/system/files/files/litigation-ruby-glen-complaint-22jul16-en.pdf.
379. The.com registry agreement with Verisign does not provide for mediation, but for a form of cooperative engagement between the parties.

2. Analysis

ICANN clearly promotes the use of mediation as a dispute resolution mechanism with existing contracting parties. However, mediation is not proposed to gTLD applicants with a view to resolving disputes during the application process itself. That seems unfortunate, since mediation could have enabled applicants to better understand ICANN's position. Although ICANN's position has been clear from the start in many cases that have led to IRP proceedings, ICANN has sometimes had difficulties explaining why it has adopted certain positions. The less adversarial mediation setting could have contributed to applicants understanding the rationale behind ICANN's position. This could have led to more openness, and might in some circumstances have removed the need for litigation.

I. ARBITRATION PROCEEDINGS

1. Framework

ICANN's contracts with registries and registrars provide for an arbitration clause.

Arbitration with registries is organized by the International Chamber of Commerce (ICC). Unless the registry is an Intergovernmental Organization (IGO) or governmental entity, the seat of the arbitration is Los Angeles County, California. For registries that are intergovernmental organizations or governmental entities, the seat of arbitration is Geneva, Switzerland. The arbitral tribunal is competent for disputes concerning contractual performance and proposed amendments. Depending on the nature of the claims, the case will be heard by a single arbitrator or a panel of three arbitrators.

Arbitration does not seem to be the only binding dispute resolution mechanism for registries, however. As parties agree that irreparable damage could occur from a party's default under the agreement, the registry agreement also provides that they are entitled to seek specific performance (from the arbitrator or court of competent jurisdiction) of the terms of the registry agreement, as well as any other remedy to which each party is entitled. As a result, registries may seek specific performance in courts.

The Registrar Accreditation Agreement (RAA) also contains an arbitration clause, but with a different arbitration institute. For disputes under the RAA, the International Arbitration Rules of the American Arbitration Association (AAA) apply. The seat of arbitration is Los Angeles County, California. However, under the RAA, parties may also elect to submit their dispute to a court of competent jurisdiction. A request for injunctive relief with a competent court will not amount to a waiver of the arbitration agreement.

2. Cases

ICANN has only occasionally been involved in non-IRP arbitrations. A list of relevant arbitration cases related to TLD applications is mentioned in the Table of ICC cases related to registries.

3. Analysis

ICANN included unambiguous arbitration clauses in its contracts with both registries and registrars. Nothing prevented ICANN from offering a similar agreement to gTLD applicants. However, instead, ICANN has tried to prevent applicants from bringing disputes before a court. It has argued that the IRP, which is the alternative for applicants, is limited in scope and does not qualify as arbitration – even though ICANN's General Counsel has referred to the IRP panelists as arbitrators.[380] A lot of energy has been put into procedural arguments concerning the scope of IRPs, and this could have been avoided if ICANN had opted for unambiguous arbitration agreements with gTLD applicants.

380. ICANN, *Report on Status of Independent Review Nominating Committee*, March 2010, https://archive.icann.org/en/meetings/accra/indrev-topic.htm.

CHAPTER 4

Issues Related to ICANN's Liberalization Efforts

A. ISSUES RELATED TO THE 2000 PROOF OF CONCEPT ROUND

1. The Proof of Concept's Set Up Phase

As some of the applicants in the proof of concept round[381] recognized, ICANN was correct to proceed carefully with the introduction of Top Level Domains (TLDs). It was crucial that the security and stability of the DNS be maintained. The recommendation to introduce new gTLDs in a 'measured and responsible manner'[382] was a sensible one. In the same way, it was probably a wise decision to introduce only a limited number of new TLDs initially and to allow for the future introduction of additional TLDs only after careful evaluation of the initial introduction procedure.[383]

But what is a 'limited number', and what should be the criteria for introducing and maintaining new TLDs? ICANN has never given a straightforward answer to these questions. Its policy development was essentially flawed in that it never developed objective evaluation criteria, and, under the pretext of a '*proof of concept*' round, ICANN in fact issued long-term licenses for the operation of gTLDs to a small number of companies on the basis of subjective criteria. The idea of a proof of concept usually implies a short, often incomplete, realization of a method, idea or technology to demonstrate its feasibility. But the 2000 proof of concept round for gTLDs was not limited to demonstrating the feasibility of introducing different types of new gTLDs in

381. Group One Registry, Inc., *Request for Reconsideration 00-10*, 15 December 2000, https://archive.icann.org/en/committees/reconsideration/stahura-request-15dec00.htm.
382. ICANN, *ICANN Yokohama Meeting Topic: Introduction of New Top-Level Domains*, 13 June 2000, https://archive.icann.org/en/meetings/yokohama/new-tld-topic.htm.
383. ICANN, *ICANN Yokohama Meeting Topic: Introduction of New Top-Level Domains*, 13 June 2000, https://archive.icann.org/en/meetings/yokohama/new-tld-topic.htm.

the future; it actually turned into a RFP to administer scarce resources within the DNS. Instead of being a test run, ICANN's proof of concept round changed the DNS landscape forever, and this fundamental change created a great deal of dissatisfaction with aspiring new market entrants.

2. The Evaluation Phase

ICANN's process for evaluating and selecting new gTLDs was essentially arbitrary and left much discretion in the hands of the ICANN Board, whose decision-making procedure suffered from a lack of transparency. Not surprisingly, many applicants asked the ICANN Board to reconsider its decision not to grant their application. They complained of ICANN's arbitrariness and discriminatory treatment, and about the lack of transparency and due process.[384] However, ICANN denied all these reconsideration requests on the basis of essentially the same rationale: ICANN reasoned that 'the process of selecting new TLDs was not an effort to find the most worthy or the most attractive applications, but rather to select a "limited number" of appropriate proposals for this initial proof of concept phase. Given this objective and the large number of applications, it was likely that worthy proposals might not be selected.'[385] ICANN

384. Abacus America, Inc., *Request for Reconsideration 00-8*, 28 November 2000, https://archive.icann.org/en/committees/reconsideration/vachovsky-request-28nov00.htm; IATA, *Request for Reconsideration 00-9*, 15 December 2000, https://archive.icann.org/en/committees/reconsideration/goldberg-request-15dec00.htm; Group One Registry, Inc., *Request for Reconsideration 00-10*, 15 December 2000, https://archive.icann.org/en/committees/reconsideration/stahura-request-15dec00.htm; Sarnoff Corporation, *Request for Reconsideration 00-11*, 15 December 2000, https://archive.icann.org/en/committees/reconsideration/sarnoff-request-15dec00.htm;.TV Corporation International, *Request for Reconsideration 00-12*, 15 December 2000, https://archive.icann.org/en/committees/reconsideration/dottv-request-15dec00.htm; Image Online Design, Inc., *Request for Reconsideration 00-13*, 15 December 2000, https://archive.icann.org/en/committees/reconsideration/iodesign-request-15dec00.htm; SRI International, *Request for Reconsideration 00-14*, 15 December 2000, https://archive.icann.org/en/committees/reconsideration/sri-request-15dec00.htm; ICM Registry, *Request for Reconsideration 00-15*, 16 December 2000, https://archive.icann.org/en/committees/reconsideration/icm-request-16dec00.htm; Telnic Limited, *Request for Reconsideration 00-16*, 24 November 2000, https://archive.icann.org/en/committees/reconsideration/telnic-request-24nov00.htm; .Kids Domains, Inc., *Request for Reconsideration 01-2*, 1 February 2001, https://archive.icann.org/en/committees/reconsideration/howe-request-1feb01.htm.

385. ICANN, *Recommendation of the Committee on Reconsideration Request 00-8*, 5 March 2001, https://archive.icann.org/en/committees/reconsideration/rc00-8.htm; ICANN, *Recommendation of the Committee on Reconsideration Request 00-9*, 30 April 2001, https://archive.icann.org/en/committees/reconsideration/rc00-9.htm; ICANN, *Recommendation of the Committee on Reconsideration Request 00-10*, 5 March 2001, https://archive.icann.org/en/committees/reconsideration/rc00-10.htm; ICANN, *Recommendation of the Committee on Reconsideration Request 00-11*, 16 March 2001, https://archive.icann.org/en/committees/reconsideration/rc00-11.htm; ICANN, *Recommendation of the Committee on Reconsideration Request 00-12*, 16 March 2001, https://archive.icann.org/en/committees/reconsideration/rc00-12.htm; ICANN, *Recommendation of the Committee on Reconsideration Request 00-13*, 16 March 2001, https://archive.icann.org/en/committees/reconsideration/rc00-13.htm; ICANN, *Recommendation of the Committee on Reconsideration Request 00-14*, 16 March 2001, https://archive.icann.org/en/committees/reconsideration/rc00-14.htm; ICANN, *Revised Recommendation of the Committee on Reconsideration Request 00-15*, 7 September 2001, https://archive.icann.org/en/

considered that '*the only way*' to measure the success of the proof of concept round effectively was by its outcome: 'did it produce a "limited number" of sufficiently diverse proposals that the experience gained from their introduction will allow more educated decisions about possible future introductions.'[386] ICANN never questioned the 'inherent subjectivity of many of the criteria established for the evaluation of proposals.'[387] Instead, ICANN reasoned that, because of this inherent subjectivity, 'it was inevitable that reasonable people could conclude that some different collection of proposals would be as well (or even better) suited for th[e] proof of concept than those chosen.'[388]

In other words, the ICANN Board considered it had absolute discretion in deciding which applications it selected to enter the Internet root as a result of the proof of concept round. ICANN provided no justification for selecting one application over another. In one case, ICANN explained that the fact that none of its Board members (referred to as Directors) put forward a specific proposal for further consideration 'apparently reflected the fact than no Director felt that [the] proposal should be among the limited group of new TLDs in th[e] "proof of concept" phase.'[389] The decision not to consider a specific proposal was thus based rather on the personal opinion of ICANN's directors rather than on the facts.

By putting its Board members' opinions before the facts, ICANN subjected applicants to disparate treatment. Some applicants saw their applied-for TLD string enter the root, others saw their application considered but not selected, and still others did not even see their application considered by the ICANN Board. When asked for a justification for this disparate treatment, ICANN explained that: (i) the selection depended entirely on the opinions of its Board members (*i.e.*, whether those opinions be well reasoned or not), and (ii) it was unable to provide an exhaustive overview of the sources of information to which the Board members had access. The Board had many sources, but ICANN only named a few:

> 'Thus, the Board's decision on new TLDs was the product of many inputs from many sources. The sources of information the Board had at its disposal while making the decision on new TLDs were, among other things, the applications themselves, the comments posted on the on-line public comment forum, the independent expert evaluations of the applications, the applicants' responses to the expert evaluations, the public presentations, and a number of other reports and

---

committees/reconsideration/rc00-15-1.htm; ICANN, *Recommendation of the Committee on Reconsideration Request 00-16*, 30 April 2001, https://archive.icann.org/en/committees/reconsideration/rc00-16.htm; ICANN, *Recommendation of the Committee on Reconsideration Request 01-2*, 30 April 2001, https://archive.icann.org/en/committees/reconsideration/rc01-2.htm; ICANN, *Resolutions 01.52 – 01.59 – Special Meeting of the Board Minutes*, 7 May 2001, https://www.icann.org/resources/board-material/minutes-2001-05-07-en; ICANN, *Resolution 01.79 – Regular Meeting of the Board Minutes*, 10 September 2001, https://www.icann.org/resources/board-material/minutes-2001-09-10-en.

386. *Supra* n. 385.
387. *Supra* n. 385.
388. *Supra* n. 385.
389. ICANN, *Recommendation of the Committee on Reconsideration Request 00-8*, 5 March 2001, https://archive.icann.org/en/committees/reconsideration/rc00-8.htm.

> analyses such as those from ICANN constituencies and outside groups. The Board took into account these many different and sometimes competing information sources in seeking to achieve a reasonable proof of concept for the new TLD program.'[390]

ICANN also explained that although Board members would necessarily have received unsolicited emails pertaining to the applications, it had no indication that any Board member had relied on any such emails.[391] In our view, the requirements of openness and transparency would seem to demand that any such email communications be published, and that reasons be given for not taking them into account.

Instead of offering applicants a rationale for ICANN's disparate treatment and full transparency regarding the Board's decision-making process, ICANN relied on the *ipse dixit* that the process for selecting TLD applications 'was both designed to and did in fact comply with the requirements of openness, transparency, and fairness outlined in ICANN's Bylaws and MOU.'[392] ICANN stated its belief that the process was '*eminently fair*',[393] and that it was 'in every respect fully open and transparent.'[394] And because ICANN stood by this belief, the discussion was closed. ICANN even minimized the importance of facts or the possibility of any lack of understanding on the part of its Board members when evaluating proposed applications:

> 'Even if, for the purposes of argument, there were factual errors made, or there was confusion about various elements of a proposal, or each member of the Board did not fully understand all the details of some of the proposals, this would still not provide a compelling basis for reconsideration of the Board's conclusion.'[395]

For ICANN, the end justified the means, and all that mattered was to find a small number of acceptable proposals for the initial proof of concept round.[396] ICANN argued that 'it was clear from the beginning that only a limited number would be selected,' hence 'no applicant could have had any reason to believe that its application would definitely have been selected, and thus no one can reasonably claim that they were misled in any way by the process.'[397]

In other words, in exchange for their USD 50,000 application fee, applicants received no guarantee whatsoever that their application was going to be reviewed on the basis of objective criteria and with due regard for all the relevant facts. Even though all applicants had an equal opportunity to provide information and to react to the evaluation team's report, that did not mean that they all had an equal chance of being selected. Where applicants were in a comparable situation, ICANN did not provide a 'substantial and reasonable cause' justifying the non-selection of some and the

390. *Supra* n. 385.
391. ICANN, *Recommendation of the Committee on Reconsideration Request 00-9*, 30 April 2001, https://archive.icann.org/en/committees/reconsideration/rc00-9.htm.
392. ICANN, *Recommendation of the Committee on Reconsideration Request 00-9*, 30 April 2001, https://archive.icann.org/en/committees/reconsideration/rc00-9.htm.
393. *Supra* n. 385.
394. *Supra* n. 385.
395. *Supra* n. 385.
396. *Supra* n. 385.
397. *Supra* n. 385.

selection of others. Indeed, ICANN did not even attempt to find objective reasons, but instead proceeded on the (in our view) spurious grounds that it had absolute discretion in selecting new TLDs based on what were inherently subjective criteria. Although a subjective process such as this may be acceptable for a beauty contest, it is not appropriate for ICANN – Internet resources as crucial as TLDs, should not be delegated in this way. In selecting new TLD operators during the proof of concept round, ICANN effectively distributed control over scarce – and potentially highly profitable – Internet resources to a narrow group of companies. It's inscrutable, subjective appraisal of the applicants could not but become a source of dissatisfaction, giving rise (rightly or wrongly) to speculation about prejudice, favoritism and disparate treatment.

3. The Delegation Phase and Beyond

a. The Contribution to Free Competition of the So-Called Proof of Concept Round Was Only Modest

The market dominance of .com has long been a source of criticism, and this criticism was a driving factor in the U.S. policy that led to the creation of ICANN. The initial White Paper provided that 'NSI [(*i.e.*, the operator of. com at the time)] and the U.S. Government must reach agreement on the terms and conditions of NSI's evolution into one competitor among many in the registrar and registry marketplaces.'[398]

In the proof of concept round, ICANN approved the introduction of two gTLDs with the explicit purpose of introducing competition for .com (.info and .biz). Maybe ICANN should have approved more gTLDs designed with this purpose. It did not approve any of the applications for .web, for example, the gTLD string that was most in demand with applicants in 2000. The .web gTLD was probably the best market competitor for the dominant .com.

Indeed, the dominant position of .com did not change as a result of the proof of concept round. By the end of 2003, Verisign, the company that had acquired NSI and operated both .com and .net, acted as the registry for 85% of all gTLD registrations.[399] The .com gTLD represented about 45% of the total TLD market (*i.e.*, inclusive of ccTLDs). The .net TLD accounted for 8% of the total TLD market.[400] Therefore, with the management of these two TLDs alone, Verisign had a market share of over 50%. What is more, looking at only the gTLD market, .com had a market share of 73%, and .net and .org

398. NTIA, *Management of Internet Names and Addresses: statement of policy*, https://www.ntia.doc.gov/files/ntia/publications/6_5_98dns.pdf, (White Paper), 31751.
399. OECD, "Generic Top Level Domain Names: Market Development and Allocation Issues", *OECD Digital Economy Papers*, No. 84 (2004), OECD Publishing, Paris, p.13.
400. Summit Strategies International, *Evaluation of the New gTLDs: Policy and Legal Issues – prepared for the Internet Corporation for Assigned Names and Numbers (ICANN)*, https://archive.icann.org/en/tlds/new-gtld-eval-31aug04.pdf, p. 95.

accounted for 12% and 8.2% respectively.[401] This meant that the combined market share of the six new gTLDs that were active by then was less than 7%, while the market strength of .com, .net and .org together was more than 93%.[402]

Although the proof of concept round did not have a significant impact on market share, it did contribute to a more competitive environment. The 2004 study commissioned by ICANN concluded prudently that the introduction of new gTLDs had allowed for some competition with the incumbent registry, and it presented a positive outlook for the future on the basis of increased innovation:

> 'The new gTLDs have introduced some competition, but how much is debatable. Examining market share, extent of actual choice and price elasticity suggests that impact has been minimal. Other evidence, however, indicates that TLD expansion has attracted about 20% new registrants and led to new uses among 40 – 60% of registrants. The most significant contribution has been the development of facilities-based competition. As a result, new providers of registry services have been able to compete effectively with the incumbent registry, VeriSign, on that basis. Innovation has played a supporting role, and may become increasingly important as the three largest registries work to distinguish themselves from one another.'[403]

However, further on in the report, it was acknowledged that most new gTLD registries viewed the industry with pessimism, with one registry calling it 'moribund', and with only one new registry sounding slightly more positive by expressing the view that the industry 'continues to present opportunities.'[404] By contrast, the incumbent operators were much more optimistic in their outlook, expecting continued expansion and stable growth.[405]

The positive forecast by the incumbent operator Verisign turned out to be correct, as Verisign remains by far the largest TLD operator and the dominant position of .com has not changed since 2004.[406] The decision by ICANN not to delegate the .web gTLD (the gTLD that was most in demand by applicants in the proof of concept round, and which seemed the most natural contender for .com), certainly did not help in creating more

401. Summit Strategies International, *Evaluation of the New gTLDs: Policy and Legal Issues – prepared for the Internet Corporation for Assigned Names and Numbers (ICANN)*, https://archive.icann.org/en/tlds/new-gtld-eval-31aug04.pdf, p. 96.
402. Summit Strategies International, *Evaluation of the New gTLDs: Policy and Legal Issues – prepared for the Internet Corporation for Assigned Names and Numbers (ICANN)*, https://archive.icann.org/en/tlds/new-gtld-eval-31aug04.pdf, p. 96.
403. Summit Strategies International, *Evaluation of the New gTLDs: Policy and Legal Issues – prepared for the Internet Corporation for Assigned Names and Numbers (ICANN)*, https://archive.icann.org/en/tlds/new-gtld-eval-31aug04.pdf, p. 5.
404. Summit Strategies International, *Evaluation of the New gTLDs: Policy and Legal Issues – prepared for the Internet Corporation for Assigned Names and Numbers (ICANN)*, https://archive.icann.org/en/tlds/new-gtld-eval-31aug04.pdf, p. 96.
405. Summit Strategies International, *Evaluation of the New gTLDs: Policy and Legal Issues – prepared for the Internet Corporation for Assigned Names and Numbers (ICANN)*, https://archive.icann.org/en/tlds/new-gtld-eval-31aug04.pdf, p. 96.
406. *See* Verisign, *The Domain Name Industry Brief*, Volume 13 – Issue 3, September 2016, https://www.verisign.com/assets/domain-name-report-sept2016.pdf.

competition.[407] To create a truly competitive environment, it would arguably have been better had ICANN examined whether an entity other than Verisign could have operated .com, and to organize a RFP process for that purpose rather than arranging a controlled rush of applications for new Internet extensions.

b. *Procrastination in Terminating the Proof of Concept Round*

It took ICANN a very long time to bring the proof of concept round to an end. In response to applicants who expressed concerns about their non-selection, ICANN responded that no applications had been denied; instead, ICANN considered all applications that had not been selected to be 'suspended'.[408]

However, the 'suspended' applications seemed to be suspended indefinitely. When ICANN wanted to organize a new gTLD round in 2011, it needed to find a solution for these suspended applications. It decided to offer applicants from the 2000 proof of concept round a credit of USD 86,000 towards the evaluation fee in the 2011 new gTLD Program. The proof of concept applicants were eligible for a maximum of one credit, provided they applied for the same gTLD string as in 2000 and confirmed that they had no legal claims arising from the proof of concept process.[409] However, they were to be granted no other preferential rights in connection with their application within the 2011 new gTLD Program.

4. Lack of Efficient Legal Remedies

At the time of the proof of concept round, ICANN did not yet have an IRP in place, although this accountability mechanism was anticipated by ICANN's original Bylaws of 6 November 1998. The only specific accountability mechanism that ICANN had developed at that time was its internal reconsideration process. And, as explained above,[410] the methodology adopted by the ICANN Board in examining the reconsideration requests did not give the requesters much chance to succeed. The ICANN Board considered all reconsideration requests in bulk, and provided a 'one size fits all' rationale, which made an examination of the underlying facts redundant. The ICANN Board considered it had absolute discretion to pick and choose winners. Many of the unsuccessful applicants were startups, who could not afford court litigation with uncertain results. In view of ICANN's refusal to grant their application, these applicants were de facto left without adequate legal remedy.

407. During the latest round of new gTLDs, the application for.web was auctioned and the auction was won by an applicant who appears being under the control of Verisign to date, ICANN has not yet decided to delegate the .web extension.
408. *Supra* n. 385.
409. ICANN, *New gTLD Applicant Guidebook 4 June 2012*, https://newgtlds.icann.org/en/applicants/agb/guidebook-full-04jun12-en.pdf, Modules 1-43–1-44.
410. *See* Chapter 4.A.2.

B. ISSUES RELATED TO THE 2004 SPONSORED ROUND

1. The Sponsored Round Set Up Phase

a. *Creation of a Policy with Subjective Criteria to Limit Applications*

The proof of concept round had shown that relatively small registries could present a viable business. ICANN had gained experience in evaluating technological and financial criteria and was able to objectify the process for these criteria. As explained in Chapter 2.C.2 above, the 2004 round was limited to sponsored TLDs (sTLDs), as it was believed by the architects of this round that TLDs sponsored by and operated in the interest of a particular, defined community could be introduced relatively easily.[411]

However, some criteria for sponsorship and community value remained highly subjective. There was no clear definition of what should constitute a 'community'; there was no need for a community to be pre-established, and there were no specific guidelines as to how the evaluators should weigh the 'appropriateness' of the application's sponsoring organization. There were also no pre-established criteria or guidelines to evaluate how policies and procedures would add value to the Internet name space.[412] The use of vague and subjective evaluation criteria made it possible for ICANN to select new TLD operators arbitrarily. The statement in the RFP that the selection procedure was based on 'principles of objectivity, non-discrimination and transparency'[413] was nothing more than an *ipse dixit*. ICANN should have invested more time in developing objective criteria and in ensuring transparency for the evaluation process. But ICANN wanted to move quickly with a limited 'extension' of the proof of concept round, reserved for sTLDs only.

The decision to limit the 2004 round to sTLDs only was based on the premise that sTLDs operated in the interest of a particular, defined community and could therefore be added to the DNS 'smoothly and with little fanfare'. It was considered that 'most of the vexing problems over the course of the new gTLD process [had] arisen in connection with the unsponsored TLDs',[414] and sTLDs were believed to raise fewer business concerns than unsponsored TLDs:

> '*Sponsored* TLDs on the whole also raise fewer business concerns than *unsponsored* TLDs. Since registrants must come from a carefully defined and limited community, there are fewer worries about trademark infringement and cybersquatting. This is an assertion that needs to be tested against the reality of

411. Stuart Lynn, *A Plan for Action Regarding New gTLDs*, 18 October 2002 (published 8 November 2002), https://archive.icann.org/en/committees/ntepptf/new-gtld-action-plan-18oct02.htm.
412. ICANN, *New sTLD Application – Explanatory Notes and Selection Criteria*, 15 December 2003, https://archive.icann.org/en/tlds/new-stld-rfp/new-stld-application-parta-15dec03.htm.
413. ICANN, *New sTLD Application – Explanatory Notes and Selection Criteria*, 15 December 2003, https://archive.icann.org/en/tlds/new-stld-rfp/new-stld-application-parta-15dec03.htm.
414. Stuart Lynn, *A Plan for Action Regarding New gTLDs*, 18 October 2002 (published 8 November 2002), https://archive.icann.org/en/committees/ntepptf/new-gtld-action-plan-18oct02.htm.

> experience with the existing sponsored TLDs, at least one of which has yet to start accepting registrations via ICANN-accredited registrars. Likewise, sponsored TLDs entail fewer and less complex start-up and launch phase worries. Within the defined communities to be served by unsponsored TLDs, there is likely to be less contention among multiple applicants for the same domain name. The sponsoring organizations are well-positioned to sort out any of these issues that might arise, acting in the best interests of their particular communities. Sponsored TLDS are, by definition, limited with regard to the number of registrations, so they are unlikely to grow to the size of the largest unsponsored TLDs, although clearly even sponsored TLDs with very generic names could grow quite large quite rapidly.'[415]

These reasons to distinguish between sponsored and unsponsored TLDs were given shortly after the delegation of new gTLDs in the proof of concept round, and little research went into examining how to tackle the perceived problems with the unsponsored TLDs of the proof of concept round. While there may well be cogent arguments for protecting well-defined communities when adding new TLDs to the Internet root, organizing a new gTLD round exclusively for sTLDs was in our view not the best way to proceed. Without a clear definition of what constitutes a community, there was always going to be a risk of disparate treatment. Moreover, the delegation of a sTLD was unlikely to spur competition with the incumbent dominant registry. Given the time and effort required to set up this new gTLD round and evaluation process for sTLDs, it is appropriate to wonder whether ICANN's resources would not have been better spent in developing a broader new gTLD round which incorporated adequate protection mechanisms for well-defined communities.

Instead, ICANN organized a limited round without clear evaluation criteria for what should define a community.

b. Selection of Evaluators

ICANN admitted that there was 'unavoidably [going to be] some degree of subjectivity in the evaluation of proposals' and expressed its intention to minimize the consequences of imperfect evaluation by working with multiple evaluation teams, working independently of each other.[416] ICANN looked for teams that 'can be seen to act objectively' and that were 'not involved in ICANN activities and are not subject to ICANN political nuances and pressures.'[417] ICANN organized a RFP to engage external consultants as evaluators.[418] ICANN engaged three dedicated teams of three (internationally diverse) individuals to perform the technical, business/financial and

415. Stuart Lynn, *A Plan for Action Regarding New gTLDs*, 18 October 2002 (published 8 November 2002), https://archive.icann.org/en/committees/ntepptf/new-gtld-action-plan-18oct02.htm.
416. ICANN, *ICANN Rio de Janeiro Meeting Topic: Criteria to Be Used in the Selection of New Sponsored TLDs*, 25 March 2003, https://archive.icann.org/en/meetings/riodejaneiro/stld-rfp-topic.htm#B.
417. ICANN, *ICANN Rio de Janeiro Meeting Topic: Criteria to Be Used in the Selection of New Sponsored TLDs*, 25 March 2003, https://archive.icann.org/en/meetings/riodejaneiro/stld-rfp-topic.htm#B.
418. ICANN, *Independent Evaluators of sTLD proposals*, http://archive.icann.org/en/tlds/new-stld-rfp/panel.htm.

sponsorship/community evaluation respectively.[419] The identities of these nine evaluators were deliberately kept confidential until the conclusion of the evaluation process, so as to prevent applicants from trying to influence the evaluations.[420] Following the evaluation, ICANN disclosed the identities of the evaluators with biographical data.[421]

The disclosure of the identities of the evaluators was essential for applicants as it enabled them to verify that the evaluators had the necessary credentials and were truly independent. The decision to keep the identities secret until the end of the evaluation process seems equally justified. However, ICANN could have been more transparent about the selection process for external evaluators. We are not aware of any report detailing ICANN's efforts to attract qualified evaluators or explaining how the selected evaluators compared to other candidates, etc. Transparency in this respect would undoubtedly have increased applicant trust in the evaluation procedure.

2. The Evaluation Phase

a. *The Independent Evaluators' Restrictive Application of the Evaluation Criteria*

The evaluation criteria (vague as they were) created problems in the evaluation phase. The independent evaluators commissioned by ICANN had no clear guidelines as to how they should be interpreted,[422] and, as a result, applicants could not form a clear expectation with regard to the evaluation process. The evaluators also applied the evaluation criteria in a restrictive way. Out of ten applications (for a total of nine gTLDs), only two applications (for .post and .cat), satisfied all of the selection criteria, according to the evaluators. Three applications (for .asia, .travel and .xxx) satisfied the technical, business and financial criteria, but did not fulfill the sponsorship criteria. The applications for .jobs and .mobi satisfied the business and financial criteria, but failed the technical and sponsorship criteria. Finally, the application for .mail and the two applications for .tel failed all sets of criteria. The team that evaluated the sponsorship criteria considered that, despite not meeting the evaluation criteria, the applications for .asia, .jobs and .travel merited further discussions with ICANN.[423]

This put ICANN in an uncomfortable position. ICANN had stated that the involvement of its staff and its Board in the evaluations was going to be limited:

419. ICANN, *Status Report on the sTLD Evaluation Process*, 19 March 2004, http://archive.icann.org/en/tlds/stld-apps-19mar04/stld-status-report.pdf.
420. ICANN, *Status Report on the sTLD Evaluation Process*, 19 March 2004, http://archive.icann.org/en/tlds/stld-apps-19mar04/stld-status-report.pdf.
421. ICANN, *Status Report on the sTLD Evaluation Process*, 19 March 2004, http://archive.icann.org/en/tlds/stld-apps-19mar04/stld-status-report.pdf.
422. The evaluators were expected to have the necessary skills and experiences to assess the indistinct evaluation criteria brought forward by ICANN (*see* ICANN, *Independent Evaluators of sTLD proposals*, http://archive.icann.org/en/tlds/new-stld-rfp/panel.htm).
423. ICANN, *Status Report on sTLD Application Process*, 19 March 2004, https://archive.icann.org/en/tlds/stld-apps-19mar04/PostsTLDStatusRpt.pdf.

> 'Except to opine on legal questions and to provide administrative support, ICANN staff would not enter the evaluation process, although staff would synthesize the outcomes for presentation to the Board. Similarly, the Board would not intrude in the evaluation process itself; its options would be to accept or to reject the results of the evaluation.'[424]

Faced with a recommendation to allow only an extremely small number of applications and engage in further discussions with certain applicants, the ICANN Board decided to engage more actively in the process. It asked all the applicants to provide additional, clarifying information and to answer further questions from the evaluators and from ICANN.[425] For the technical and the business/financial evaluation, ICANN requested the evaluation teams to reconvene between October 2004 and June 2005 to review the applicants' supplementary materials.[426] The sponsorship criteria were evaluated by the ICANN Board itself, without further input by the evaluation team.[427]

The ICANN Board's involvement in the evaluation of the sponsorship criteria made the evaluation less transparent, and the ICANN Board was criticized for discriminating between applicants in its re-evaluation of previous findings. In any event, it was clear that the ICANN Board interpreted the term 'community' more broadly than the external evaluation team had done. The evaluation team considered that only two of the applications met the sponsorship criteria; in the end, the ICANN Board – upon re-evaluation – did not deny a single application for not meeting the sponsorship criteria.

b. *The ICANN Board's Reaction to Belated Governmental Intervention*

For certain extensions, it would seem natural for governments to wish to protect the interests of national minorities (*e.g.*, the Catalonian minority in Spain for .cat) or to guarantee the observance of international treaties or policies (*e.g.*, the international policies for telephone number mapping for .mobi and .tel). However, the involvement of governments should not be allowed to interfere with the legitimate expectations of applicants, and governments should be involved as early as possible in the process and the policy development.

Governments were involved in the development of the RFP for the 2004 sponsored round, and had been given the opportunity to give recommendations to the ICANN

424. ICANN, *ICANN Rio de Janeiro Meeting Topic: Criteria to Be Used in the Selection of New Sponsored TLDs*, 25 March 2003, https://archive.icann.org/en/meetings/riodejaneiro/stld-rfp-topic.htm#B.
425. ICANN, *ICANN Meetings in Kuala Lumpur – ICANN Public Forum*, 22 July 2004, https://archive.icann.org/en/meetings/kualalumpur/captioning-public-forum-23jul04.htm.
426. ICANN, *Status Report on sTLD Application Process*, 19 March 2004, https://archive.icann.org/en/tlds/stld-apps-19mar04/PostsTLDStatusRpt.pdf.
427. ICANN, *Status Report on sTLD Application Process*, 19 March 2004, https://archive.icann.org/en/tlds/stld-apps-19mar04/PostsTLDStatusRpt.pdf.

Board via the Government Advisory Committee (GAC). Already in 2000, the GAC had asked ICANN to 'avoid, in the creation of new generic TLDs, well-known and famous country, territory or place names; well-known and famous country, territory or regional language or people descriptions; or ISO 639 Codes for representation of languages unless in agreement with the relevant governments or public authorities.'[428]

The GAC received briefing papers about the RFP process, and the GAC liaison was present during the ICANN Board meetings that led to the Board authorizing ICANN to negotiate the technical and financial details of the registry agreements with applicants.[429] On 3 April 2005, the GAC informed ICANN that no members had expressed specific reservations or comments about the applications for sTLDs.[430] The GAC merely called upon ICANN to ensure that: (i) the introduction of sTLD did not interfere with established international policies for telephone number mapping, (ii) sponsors of sTLDs encompassed the entirety of the relevant user community, and (iii) eventual distortions of competition were effectively avoided.[431]

ICANN was already taking these concerns into account, as shown by the terms of its Board's resolutions authorizing contract negotiations for .mobi and .jobs.[432] The applicants for .cat and .asia had also engaged in discussions with representatives of relevant governments.[433] Although all applications for sTLDs had already been received by 16 March 2004, government and GAC representatives did not express their concerns formally with the ICANN Board about one specific sTLD application (for .xxx) until August 2005.[434] Although the ICANN Board had already completed its evaluation of the application for .xxx and had authorized contract negotiations without any specific reservation, the ICANN Board reacted to the concerns by government and GAC representatives by re-examining the sponsorship criteria. This resulted in many delays,

428. ICANN, *GAC Principles for the Delegation and Administration of Country Code Top Level Domains*, 23 February 2000, https://archive.icann.org/en/committees/gac/gac-cctldprinciples-23feb00.htm, Section 8.3.
429. *See e.g.*, ICANN, *Minutes – Special Meeting of the Board*, 3 May 2005, https://www.icann.org/resources/board-material/minutes-2005-05-03-en; ICANN, *Minutes – Special Meeting of the Board*, 18 October 2004, https://www.icann.org/resources/board-material/minutes-2004-10-18-en.
430. Letter from GAC Chairman to the ICANN CEO, 3 April 2005, https://www.icann.org/resources/pages/tarmizi-to-twomey-2005-04-03-en.
431. Letter from GAC Chairman to the ICANN CEO, 3 April 2005, https://www.icann.org/resources/pages/tarmizi-to-twomey-2005-04-03-en.
432. ICANN, *Resolutions 04.123 – 04.126 – Special Meeting of the Board*, 13 December 2004, https://www.icann.org/resources/board-material/minutes-2004-12-13-en.
433. ICANN, *Status Report on sTLD Application Process*, 19 March 2004, https://archive.icann.org/en/tlds/stld-apps-19mar04/PostsTLDStatusRpt.pdf.
434. Letter from GAC Chairman to Chairman of the ICANN Board, 12 August, 2005, https://www.icann.org/resources/pages/tarmizi-to-board-2005-08-12-en; Letter from M. Gallagher, Assistant Secretary for Communications and Information, U.S. Department of Commerce to Chairman of the ICANN Board, 11 August 2005, https://www.icann.org/en/system/files/files/gallagher-to-cerf-15aug05-en.pdf.

and finally the Board decided to reject the application for .xxx at its meeting of 30 March 2007.[435] This decision was later reversed, following a challenge by the .xxx applicant.[436]

3. The Delegation Phase and Beyond

As a result of these delays and external events, it took ICANN a very long time to enter into certain registry agreements for sTLDs. *E.g.*, the registry agreement for .post was only executed on 11 December 2009,[437] even though the application for .post had been approved on or before 27 October 2004.[438]

The introduction of special-purpose TLDs in a sponsored round never had the potential to impact the dominant position of .com significantly. Neither the proof of concept round, nor the sponsored round resulted in true alternatives for .com, and, in December 2008, the U.S. Department of Justice (DoJ) observed that 'many registrants [did] not perceive .com and other gTLDs (such as .biz and .info) and country coded TLDs ("ccTLDs," such as .uk and .de) to be substitutes' but rather as '*complements*'.[439] The DoJ concluded 'that existing gTLDs likely would not become a competitive threat to .com registrations because the network effects that make .com registrations so valuable to consumers will be difficult for other TLDs to overcome.'[440] In other words, the .com registry operator may have been profiting for too long from its first-mover advantage, resulting in high brand awareness, customer loyalty and consistent consumer behavior.

The DoJ also 'found evidence that other gTLD registry operators may possess a degree of market power.'[441] The DoJ observed that '[t]he need of many registrants to purchase domains in many or most gTLDs allows each gTLD registry operator to impose costs on

435. ICANN, *Adopted Resolution 07.18 from ICANN Board Meeting*, 30 March 2007, https://www.icann.org/resources/board-material/resolutions-2007-03-30-en.
436. ICANN, *Adopted Board Resolutions 2011.03.18.23 – 2011.03.18.25 – Silicon Valley / San Francisco*, 18 March 2011, https://www.icann.org/resources/board-material/resolutions-2011-03-18-en.
437. ICANN, *.post Sponsored TLD Agreement*, 11 December 2009, https://www.icann.org/resources/unthemed-pages/post-2015-10-30-en.
438. ICANN, *Announcement: ICANN Moves Forward in First Phase Commercial & Technical Negotiations with Two sTLD Applicants*, 27 October 2004, https://www.icann.org/news/announcement-2004-10-27-en.
439. Letter from Deborah A. Garza, Acting Assistant Attorney General (U.S. Department of Justice) to Meredith A. Baker, Acting Assistant Secretary for Communications and Information (NTIA), 3 December 2008, https://www.ntia.doc.gov/files/ntia/publications/icann_081218.pdf, p. 2.
440. Letter from Deborah A. Garza, Acting Assistant Attorney General (U.S. Department of Justice) to Meredith A. Baker, Acting Assistant Secretary for Communications and Information (NTIA), 3 December 2008, https://www.ntia.doc.gov/files/ntia/publications/icann_081218.pdf, p. 2.
441. Letter from Deborah A. Garza, Acting Assistant Attorney General (U.S. Department of Justice) to Meredith A. Baker, Acting Assistant Secretary for Communications and Information (NTIA), 3 December 2008, https://www.ntia.doc.gov/files/ntia/publications/icann_081218.pdf, p. 3.

registrants that purchase domains simply because a gTLD exists.'[442] The DoJ believed that the introduction of new gTLDs 'could impose substantial additional domain registration costs on many consumers' and that the introduction of new gTLDs [was] not likely to constrain the exercise of market power by existing gTLDs.'[443] As a result, rather than limiting market power of incumbent registries, the two first rounds of new gTLDs might simply have granted market power to newcomers.

4. The Introduction of the Independent Review Process

The Independent Review Process (IRP) was introduced as an accountability mechanism in 2002.[444] It became operational after April 2004, when ICANN elected the International Center for Dispute Resolution (ICDR) of the American Arbitration Association (AAA) as IRP provider.[445] As a result, applicants in the 2004 sTLD round had the opportunity to challenge before an independent panel the decisions of the ICANN Board. The applicant for .xxx made use of this opportunity and the proceedings initiated by this applicant are discussed in detail in Chapter 5.A below.

C. THE 2011 NEW GTLD PROGRAM

As mentioned above,[446] in 2003 the ICANN Board expressed the wish to commence the implementation of a long-term policy for selecting new gTLDs by the end of 2004.[447] However, it was only in October 2007 that ICANN developed a policy for organizing a competitive round for new gTLDs,[448] a policy that was approved by the ICANN Board in June 2008.[449] It then took the ICANN Board until June 2011 to approve the new gTLD Program going forward.[450] Applications for new gTLDs were received between 12

442. Letter from Deborah A. Garza, Acting Assistant Attorney General (U.S. Department of Justice) to Meredith A. Baker, Acting Assistant Secretary for Communications and Information (NTIA), 3 December 2008, https://www.ntia.doc.gov/files/ntia/publications/icann_081218.pdf, p. 3.
443. Letter from Deborah A. Garza, Acting Assistant Attorney General (U.S. Department of Justice) to Meredith A. Baker, Acting Assistant Secretary for Communications and Information (NTIA), 3 December 2008, https://www.ntia.doc.gov/files/ntia/publications/icann_081218.pdf, p. 3.
444. ICANN, *Bylaws as adopted effective 15 December 2002 (the 'New Bylaws')*, 15 December 2002, https://www.icann.org/resources/unthemed-pages/bylaws-2002-12-15-en.
445. ICANN, *Resolution 04.33 adopted at Special ICANN Board Meeting*, 19 April 2004, https://www.icann.org/resources/board-material/resolutions-2004-04-19-en.
446. *Supra* Chapter 2.C.3.
447. ICANN, *Board Resolution 03.166-168 and rationale*, 31 October 2003, https://www.icann.org/news/advisory-2003-10-31-en.
448. ICANN Generic Names Supporting Organization, *Final Report - Introduction of New Generic Top-Level Domains Part A*, 8 August 2007, http://gnso.icann.org/en/issues/new-gtlds/pdp-dec05-fr-parta-08aug07.htm.
449. ICANN, *ICANN Board Resolution 2008.06.26.02*, https://www.icann.org/resources/board-material/resolutions-2008-06-26-en#_Toc76113171.
450. ICANN, *Approved Board Resolutions 2011.06.20.01 – 2011.06.20.03 – Singapore*, 20 June 2011, https://www.icann.org/resources/board-material/resolutions-2011-06-20-en.

January 2012 and 30 May 2012,[451] and ICANN was still processing a fair number of these applications when we submitted this book for publishing in the Fall of 2016.

The new gTLD Program set up the first new gTLD round that was to be almost entirely focused on creating competition in the new gTLD market. There was no limitation on the number of gTLDs that could be introduced, and there were few limitations to free market mechanisms to acquire a new gTLD. However, the new gTLD Program did not offer the 'long-term policy' for selecting new gTLDs mentioned by ICANN in 2003; it set up a singular round. Although the new gTLD Program arguably offers a good basis for a long-term policy, or a continuous process for introducing new gTLDs, it remains questionable whether introducing a continuous process at this stage would yield positive net social benefits. New gTLDs are likely to create net private benefits for the majority of new gTLD operators; however, it seems unlikely that a new gTLD will break the hegemony of .com any time soon. The slowness with which new gTLDs have been introduced since the creation of ICANN has given the operator of .com plenty of opportunity to strengthen its dominant position.

1. The Program Set Up Phase

a. *Policy Versus Implementation*

Although the new gTLD Policy Development Process (PDP) was remarkably slow, the resulting policy was not particularly detailed. The underlying principles of the process were clearly expressed, the first being that new gTLDs 'must be introduced in an orderly, timely and predictable way.'[452] The policy further set forth that the 'evaluation and selection procedure for new gTLD registries should respect the principles of fairness, transparency and non-discrimination.'[453] 'All applicants for a new gTLD registry should therefore be evaluated against transparent and predictable criteria, fully available to the applicants prior to the initiation of the process.'[454] Arguably, these policy statements are nothing more than an affirmation of ICANN's essential obligations under its Articles of Incorporation and Bylaws.

In order to create a transparent and predictable application process, the policy had to set out the applicable standards and evaluation criteria in a detailed manner. This it did

451. ICANN, *Approved Board Resolutions 2011.06.20.01 – 2011.06.20.03 – Singapore*, 20 June 2011, https://www.icann.org/resources/board-material/resolutions-2011-06-20-en; ICANN, *New gTLD Update on the close of the TLD Application system*, 30 May 2012, http://newgtlds.icann.org/en/announcements-and-media/announcement-3-30may12-en.
452. ICANN Generic Names Supporting Organization, *Final Report - Introduction of New Generic Top-Level Domains Part A*, 8 August 2007, http://gnso.icann.org/en/issues/new-gtlds/pdp-dec05-fr-parta-08aug07.htm.
453. ICANN Generic Names Supporting Organization, *Final Report - Introduction of New Generic Top-Level Domains Part A*, 8 August 2007, http://gnso.icann.org/en/issues/new-gtlds/pdp-dec05-fr-parta-08aug07.htm, Recommendation 1.
454. ICANN Generic Names Supporting Organization, *Final Report - Introduction of New Generic Top-Level Domains Part A*, 8 August 2007, http://gnso.icann.org/en/issues/new-gtlds/pdp-dec05-fr-parta-08aug07.htm, Recommendation 1.

not do. So, for example, while the policy stated that applied-for strings 'must not be confusingly similar to an existing top-level domain or a Reserved Name,'[455] it did not define, nor did it identify or develop, a scientific methodology to establish what exactly constitutes 'confusing similarity'. The development of the process for dealing with issues of confusing similarity was largely left to the implementation phase. The same was true for many other aspects of the new gTLD policy. The policy provided a process for dispute resolution and for challenging decisions, but the actual criteria for challenging applications were developed only during the implementation phase.

The fact that important policy aspects were left to be determined in the implementation phase created obvious tensions. In many instances, it has been questioned whether the implementation was in fact consistent with the agreed policy. This tension between policy and implementation arose, for example, in cases such as the *Booking.com* case, the *Vistaprint* case and the *Despegar et al.* case. We discuss this issue in more detail in the next chapter.

b. *Privileges*

The blurred lines between policy and implementation created opportunities for certain stakeholders to bypass the normal course of multi-stakeholder, bottom-up policy development. One example of this was the special protection ICANN granted to the International Olympic Committee (IOC) and the International Red Cross and Red Crescent Movement (RCRC) by prohibiting the delegation of certain new gTLDs which used names related to these two organizations.[456]

The policy for the introduction of new gTLDs did not in general envision protection mechanisms for specific named organizations. The Generic Names Supporting Organization (the GNSO, the body responsible for ICANN policy development), envisioned reserving only certain specific names for technical reasons, and names related to ICANN and IANA.[457] The issue of special protection for the IOC first arose when the IOC commented on the first version of the Applicant Guidebook in December 2008.[458]

455. ICANN Generic Names Supporting Organization, *Final Report - Introduction of New Generic Top-Level Domains Part A*, 8 August 2007, http://gnso.icann.org/en/issues/new-gtlds/pdp-dec05-fr-parta-08aug07.htm, Recommendation 2.
456. ICANN, *New gTLD Applicant Guidebook 4 June 2012*, https://newgtlds.icann.org/en/applicants/agb/guidebook-full-04jun12-en.pdf, Module 2-10 and 2.11.
457. ICANN Generic Names Supporting Organization, *Final Report - Introduction of New Generic Top-Level Domains Part A*, 8 August 2007, http://gnso.icann.org/en/issues/new-gtlds/pdp-dec05-fr-parta-08aug07.htm, Recommendations 4 and 5.
458. Letter from Urs Lacotte, Director General (IOC) and Howard M. Stupp, Legal Affairs Director (IOC) to ICANN, 5 December 2008, https://forum.icann.org/lists/gtld-guide/pdf3zsyjSX1z3.pdf (note: the letter is dated 5 December 2009; however, it was attached to an e-mail of 5 December 2008, available at https://forum.icann.org/lists/gtld-guide/msg00053.html).

The American member of the International Red Cross and Red Crescent Societies (which is part of the RCRC) commented only on the fourth version of the Applicant Guidebook in July 2010.[459]

It would seem that the IOC did not initially request preferential treatment; it stressed that 'many other entities outside the Olympic Movement will most certainly have concerns regarding potential abuses of their Intellectual Property rights, similar to those expressed [...] by the IOC', and it considered it 'essential that ICANN addresses those concerns in a responsible manner.'[460] The American Red Cross advocated a fair process with a two-tiered cost structure 'in order to separate commercial uses of the new gTLDs from the charitable, humanitarian, informational, educational, and lifesaving missions executed by not-for-profit organizations using the Internet.'[461] The Red Cross movement requested ICANN to consider the particular needs of not-for-profits such as the Red Cross,[462] and equally seemed not to demand preferential treatment.

However, what followed were private discussions between ICANN's VP for Stakeholder Relations and Deputy General Counsel, and the IOC and the RCRC.[463] In May 2011, the IOC and the RCRC obtained the support of the GAC.[464] The GAC advised the ICANN Board to agree that the names requested by the IOC and the RCRC should not be delegated at the top-level until the GNSO and GAC had been able to develop policy advice for future rounds based upon the global public interest.[465] On 20 June 2011, the ICANN Board authorized its President and CEO to modify the Applicant Guidebook to this end.[466] The modifications benefiting the IOC and the RCRC were introduced without a PDP and were intended to keep effect until such policy advice had been developed.

459. Letter from Debra Y. Hughes, Esq., Senior Counsel (American Red Cross) to the ICANN Board and Staff, 21 July 2010, https://forum.icann.org/lists/4gtld-guide/pdfeuUATLzMGk.pdf.
460. Letter from Urs Lacotte, Director General (IOC) and Howard M. Stupp, Legal Affairs Director (IOC) to ICANN, 5 December 2008, https://forum.icann.org/lists/gtld-guide/pdfzGW987HUO8.pdf (note: the letter is dated 5 December 2009; however, it was attached to an e-mail of 5 December 2008, available at https://forum.icann.org/lists/gtld-guide/msg00053.html), p. 2.
461. Letter from Debra Y. Hughes, Esq., Senior Counsel (American Red Cross) to the ICANN Board and Staff, 21 July 2010, https://forum.icann.org/lists/4gtld-guide/pdfh9CC0bVt05.pdf, p. 16.
462. Letter from Debra Y. Hughes, Esq., Senior Counsel (American Red Cross) to the ICANN Board and Staff, 21 July 2010, https://forum.icann.org/lists/4gtld-guide/pdfh9CC0bVt05.pdf, p. 18.
463. *See e.g.*, Letter from ICANN to Urs Lacotte, Director General (IOC) and Howard M. Stupp, Legal Affairs Director (IOC), 23 March 2010, https://www.icann.org/en/system/files/files/beckstrom-to-lacotte-23mar10-en.pdf; Letter from counsel to IOC to ICANN, 1 July 2011, https://www.icann.org/en/system/files/files/bikoff-to-pritz-01jul11-en.pdf; Letter from Debra Y. Hughes, Esq., Senior Counsel (American Red Cross) to ICANN Board and Staff, 10 May 2011, https://www.icann.org/en/system/files/files/hughes-to-pritz-stathos-10may11-en.pdf.
464. ICANN GAC, Letter from Heather Dryden, Chair (GAC) to Peter Dengate Thrush, Chairman (ICANN Board), 12 May 2011, https://www.icann.org/en/system/files/files/dryden-to-dengate-thrush-12may11-en.pdf.
465. ICANN, *Rationale: Remaining areas of difference between ICANN's Board and Governmental Advisory Committee regarding implementation of the New gTLD Program*, https://www.icann.org/en/system/files/bm/rationale-gac-response-new-gtld-20jun11-en.pdf.
466. ICANN, *Approved Board Resolutions*, 20 June 2011, https://www.icann.org/resources/board-material/resolutions-2011-06-20-en.

On 26 March 2012, the GNSO Council recommended that the ICANN Board's New gTLD Program Committee (NGPC) extend certain protections related to the IOC/RCRC names.[467] The NGPC rejected this recommendation on 10 April 2012, as it had concerns about the timing:[468] the application window for new gTLDs had already been open for about three months and was scheduled to close on 12 April 2012. A change so late in the process would have been incompatible with the spirit of the new gTLD Program, which required the application and evaluation process to be predictable.[469]

Although ICANN did not follow this GNSO recommendation, its Board's initial decision to grant special protection to the IOC and the RCRC was severely criticized. Several voices – including ICANN's Registry Stakeholder Group (RySG, a division of the GNSO) – expressed concern that the ICANN Board had basically 'short-circuited' ICANN's PDP by implementing specific protection mechanisms without proper community input.[470] However, as the debate had shifted towards the issue of *extending* the protection of IOC/RCRC names, the ICANN Board's initial decision to grant provisional protection to the IOC and the RCRC had already become a *fait accompli.*

It seems unlikely that the IOC and/or the RCRC would have been able to achieve special protection in time through the normal bottom-up PDP had the ICANN Board not intervened in the way that it did. Moreover, when the ICANN Board discussed the issue, it emphasized that the criteria had to be tailored so as to limit special protection to a few cases with extraordinary reach and public service. Outside counsel performed preliminary research and anticipated that very few or no organizations other than the IOC and the RCRC could satisfy the criteria that were established.[471] It could be said, therefore, that the criteria were established in order to benefit only the IOC and the RCRC. Of course, there may be good reasons to establish criteria that only apply to a very narrow group of organizations. However, ICANN remained silent as to why it had introduced tailored criteria for the benefit of the IOC and the RCRC, and the criteria themselves were no justification.

The absence of a justification is all the more worthy of note, given that the ICANN Board had made the following statement on the issue shortly before: 'Even with the

467. ICANN, *GNSO Council Resolution 20120326-1*, 26 March 2012, http://gnso.icann.org/en/council/resolutions#201203.
468. ICANN, *Approved Resolutions 2012.04.10.NG4 – 2012.04.10.NG5 – Meeting of the New gTLD Program Committee*, 10 April 2012, https://www.icann.org/resources/board-material/resolutions-new-gtld-2012-04-10-en.
469. ICANN, *ICANN Generic Names Supporting Organization: Final Report - Introduction of New Generic Top-Level Domains*, http://gnso.icann.org/en/issues/new-gtlds/pdp-dec05-fr-parta-08aug07.htm, recommendations 1 and 9.
470. David W. Maher, Chair (RySG), *Comments of the RySG on the IOC/RC Names at the Top Level*, 7 March 2012, http://forum.icann.org/lists/ioc-rcrc-proposal/msg00010.html; *see also* ICANN At-Large Advisory Committee (ALAC), ALAC Statement on the Reservation of Olympic and Red Cross Namesin the gTLD Application Procedure, 23 March 2012, http://forum.icann.org/lists/ioc-rcrc-proposal/pdfogYOred2Fb.pdf.
471. ICANN, *Unredacted version of Board Workshop Paper on IOC/Red Cross Protection*, 20 June 2011, released on 28 August 2012, https://www.icann.org/en/system/files/bm/briefing-materials-unredacted-20jun11-en.pdf.

extraordinary recognition these renowned organizations have earned, the Board is not sure a separate set of protections should be afforded them.'[472]

Regardless of whether substantial and reasonable cause existed for the preferential treatment of the IOC and the RCRC, it is our view that good governance required the ICANN Board to justify its decision. Were ICANN not obliged to explain the underlying reasons for establishing ad hoc criteria there would be nothing to prevent the ICANN Board from developing tailored criteria for any organization it chose. This would open the door to arbitrary decision-making. In this instance, the sympathy felt by many for the work done by the IOC and RCRC, together with the fact that the offered protection remained relatively limited, would probably have made it fairly easy for ICANN to provide a reasonable justification that would have been acceptable to the community.

c. *Selection of Evaluators*

ICANN engaged third-party contractors to provide it with recommendations and advice concerning the applications. On 25 February 2009, ICANN started looking for providers for 'Applicant Evaluation Teams (Technical and Financial Evaluation)', 'Geographic Name Evaluation', 'String Similarity Examiners' and a 'Comparative Evaluation Panel' (which later became a 'Community Priority Evaluation Panel').[473] ICANN published calls for expressions of interest, and amended these calls on 31 July 2009.[474] At that time, the Applicant Guidebook was still in an early draft form, and the criteria to be evaluated by the third-party providers were still under development. ICANN's calls for expressions of interest did not reveal how the proposals from third-party providers were going to be evaluated either intrinsically, or vis-à-vis other contenders (if at all).

472. ICANN, *Board workshop: new gTLD Program discussion topics*, https://www.icann.org/en/system/files/bm/briefing-materials-20jun11-en.pdf, 60-61.

473. ICANN, *Call for Expressions of Interest (EOIs) – New gTLD Process: Application Evaluation Temas (Technical and Financial Evaluation)*, 25 February 2009, https://archive.icann.org/en/topics/new-gtlds/eoi-app-eval-25feb09-en.pdf; ICANN, *Call for Expressions of Interest (EOIs) for a New gTLD Geographic Names Panel*, 25 February 2009, https://archive.icann.org/en/topics/new-gtlds/eoi-geonames-25feb09-en.pdf; ICANN, *Call for Expressions of Interest (EOIs) for New gTLD String Similarity Examiners*, 25 February 2009, https://archive.icann.org/en/topics/new-gtlds/eoi-string-sim-25feb09-en.pdf; ICANN, *Call for Expressions of Interest (EOIs) for a New gTLD Comparative Evaluation Panel*, 25 February 2009, https://archive.icann.org/en/topics/new-gtlds/eoi-comparative-evaluation-25feb09-en.pdf.

474. ICANN, *Call for Expressions of Interest (EOIs) – New gTLD Process: Application Evaluation Temas (Technical and Financial Evaluation)*, 31 July 2009, https://archive.icann.org/en/topics/new-gtlds/eoi-app-eval-31jul09-en.pdf; ICANN, *Call for Expressions of Interest (EOIs) for a New gTLD Geographic Names Panel*, 31 July 2009, https://archive.icann.org/en/topics/new-gtlds/eoi-geo-names-31jul09-en.pdf; ICANN, *Call for Expressions of Interest (EOIs) for New gTLD String Similarity Examiners*, 31 July 2009, https://archive.icann.org/en/topics/new-gtlds/eoi-string-sim-31jul09-en.pdf; ICANN, *Call for Expressions of Interest (EOIs) for a New gTLD Community Priority Evaluation Panel – formerly Comparative Evaluation Panel*, 31 July 2009, https://archive.icann.org/en/topics/new-gtlds/eoi-commun-priority-31jul09-en.pdf.

On 25 October 2009, ICANN published a list of interested third-party providers.[475] There were twelve candidates in total. However, ICANN did not disclose which provider was interested in which panel role, meaning that ICANN could have had only one candidate for certain panels. ICANN also published a 'general criteria matrix', but gave no detail as to how the importance of each criterion was to be judged.[476]

On 26 October 2011, ICANN announced which seven companies it had selected as evaluation panels, and their respective roles.[477] However, ICANN did not disclose how these companies met or exceeded the minimum selection criteria. It was also unclear how ICANN had handled a case where there was only one (or only very few) potential provider(s) wishing to serve on a specific evaluation panel.

In previous rounds, ICANN had also failed to disclose detailed information about the selection process of third-party evaluators. However, transparency was of even more importance in the new gTLD Program, because the ICANN Board itself took a much more limited role in the evaluation of applications, with the third-party providers exercising much greater power. However, despite this increased need for transparency, ICANN became arguably even less transparent. As mentioned above,[478] in the 2004 sponsored round, ICANN at least disclosed the identities of the evaluators with biographical data following the evaluation.[479] In the new gTLD Program, the identities of the evaluators were not disclosed, making it impossible for applicants to verify if the evaluators had the necessary credentials and if they were independent. Inconsistent outcomes in the evaluation process then made applicants question the credentials and independence of these anonymous evaluators.

d. *The Lack of Training for Evaluators and Experts and the Lack of Effective Quality Control Mechanisms*

A precondition for both effective training and effective quality control is that the methodology used for the evaluations be documented. If nobody but the evaluator has an insight into how the evaluations are carried out, no effective training can be given to new evaluators, and there can be no quality control. Therefore, when an applicant requests documents detailing the methodology and rationale behind the evaluation, it

475. ICANN, *Announcement: Evaluators Selection for the New gTLD Program Continues*, 25 October 2009, https://www.icann.org/news/announcement-2009-10-25-en.
476. ICANN, *Announcement: Evaluators Selection for the New gTLD Program Continues*, 25 October 2009, https://www.icann.org/news/announcement-2009-10-25-en.
477. ICANN, *New gTLD Program Update*, 26 October 2011, http://archive.icann.org/en/meetings/dakar2011/bitcache/New%20gTLD%20Program%20Update-vid=29453&disposition=attachment&op=download.pdf, p. 19; ICANN, *Transcripts of Dakar New gTLD Program Update*, 26 October 2011, http://archive.icann.org/en/meetings/dakar2011/bitcache/Transcript_%20DAKAR%20New%20gTLD%20Program%20Update-vid=30087&disposition=attachment&op=download.pdf, pp. 13–14; Michael Salazar, *Preparing Evaluators for the New gTLD Application Process*, 22 November 2011, https://newgtlds.icann.org/en/blog/preparing-evaluators-22nov11-en.
478. *See* Chapter 4.B.1.b.
479. ICANN, *Status Report on the sTLD Evaluation Process*, 19 March 2004, http://archive.icann.org/en/tlds/stld-apps-19mar04/stld-status-report.pdf.

should not receive the response from ICANN that the evaluation panels are responsible for the development of their own process documentation and methodology and that many of the relevant documents are not in ICANN's hands. This has, however, happened in the past.[480]

ICANN claimed in 2011 that it had been 'building and implementing a robust training program' and that it was 'conducting simulation exercises.'[481] ICANN never provided proof for these trainings. A former Chief Strategy Officer and Senior Vice President of Stakeholders Relations of ICANN also wrote that purported experts who served as panelists in the objection phase had not received adequate training, resulting in inconsistent recommendations.[482]

When ICANN announced the name of the companies it selected to perform the evaluations, ICANN also explained that it had retained a third-party provider for quality control.[483] However, it seems that no formal selection process was put in place to appoint a third party for quality control. No criteria for performing the quality control were published. Indeed, when ICANN was looking for evaluators, no call for expressions of interest or similar document was issued for the selection of quality controllers.

JAS Global Advisors (JAS), the provider that was selected as ultimate quality controller was also selected as a provider of technical, operational and financial evaluations.[484] ICANN described JAS as a 'sort of a tertiary source for providing the financial and technical evaluation'[485] and as having experience in 'due diligence, Internet security, and global IT operations' as well as 'intimate knowledge of ICANN.'[486]

While these qualifications may be valuable for the quality review of technical, operational and financial evaluations, they are of no relevance to the performance of quality control in relation to any of the string reviews or to Community Priority Evaluations (CPEs). Indeed, although ICANN submitted that JAS performed quality control in relation to the string similarity review process,[487] this quality control was unsatisfactory; JAS did not have the necessary qualifications and the review

480. *See e.g.*, ICANN's response of 27 April 2013 to Booking.com's DIDP request, https://www.icann.org/en/system/files/files/petillion-response-27apr13-en.pdf, pp. 1–2.
481. Michael Salazar, *Preparing Evaluators for the New gTLD Application Process*, 22 November 2011, https://newgtlds.icann.org/en/blog/preparing-evaluators-22nov11-en.
482. ICDR Case No. 01-14-0001-6263, Expert Witness Statement of Kurt Pritz.
483. ICANN, *New gTLD Program Update*, 26 October 2011, http://archive.icann.org/en/meetings/dakar2011/bitcache/New%20gTLD%20Program%20Update-vid=29453&disposition=attachment&op=download.pdf, p. 19; ICANN, *Transcripts of Dakar New gTLD Program Update*, 26 October 2011, http://archive.icann.org/en/meetings/dakar2011/bitcache/Transcript_%20DAKAR%20New%20gTLD%20Program%20Update-vid=30087&disposition=attachment&op=download.pdf, p. 14.
484. Michael Salazar, *Preparing Evaluators for the New gTLD Application Process*, 22 November 2011, https://newgtlds.icann.org/en/blog/preparing-evaluators-22nov11-en.
485. ICANN, *Transcripts of Dakar New gTLD Program Update*, 26 October 2011, http://archive.icann.org/en/meetings/dakar2011/bitcache/Transcript_%20DAKAR%20New%20gTLD%20Program%20Update-vid=30087&disposition=attachment&op=download.pdf, p. 14.
486. Michael Salazar, *Preparing Evaluators for the New gTLD Application Process*, 22 November 2011, https://newgtlds.icann.org/en/blog/preparing-evaluators-22nov11-en.
487. ICANN's Response (*Booking.com*), § 30.

methodology was inadequate. Indeed, JAS only performed a limited control over a random sample of applications.[488] This control consisted of a procedural review[489] and a review of the technical, operational and financial aspects of new gTLD applications.[490]

By its nature, a quality check on a random sample of applications cannot provide effective quality control in connection with string similarity review. A string similarity review necessarily involves all applied-for gTLDs, and the quality of the review cannot be ensured by randomly checking a few applications. Indeed, a random check might only reveal obvious cases (*e.g.*, that a string similarity panel had considered the (distinctive and unique) .abudhabi string not to be confusingly similar to .paris, or any other string applied for), but this could not provide any reassurance that the standard for assessing confusing similarity had in fact been applied correctly in less obvious cases.

As a result, it seems that ICANN's process did not provide either for adequate training or effective quality review.

e. *Key Features of the Policy Were Changed after Applications Had Been Submitted*

As mentioned above,[491] the first and primary principle of the new gTLD Program was that new gTLDs 'must be introduced in an orderly, timely and predictable way.'[492] In line with this principle, ICANN developed the Applicant Guidebook for prospective applicants to make sure they understood what was required from them when applying for a new gTLD and to explain what they could expect at each stage of the evaluation process.[493] However, there were many changes made to the new gTLD Program during the evaluation process. Of course, certain developments could not have been foreseen, and some changes were required as a result of the number of applications which was

---

488. ICANN, *New gTLD Program Update*, 26 October 2011, Dakar, http://dakar42.icann.org/node/26953, pp. 14–15; ICANN's Response (*Booking.com*), § 30.
489. ICANN, *New gTLD Program Update*, 26 October 2011, Dakar, http://dakar42.icann.org/node/26953, p. 15: "*We're also doing random procedural reviews to ensure that each evaluator is running the procedures in exactly the procedural way that we've specified. This is our approach to quality assurance.*"
490. *See* ICANN, *New gTLD Program Update*, 26 October 2011, Dakar, http://dakar42.icann.org/node/26953, pp. 14–15: The process to quality control process mentions the need for consistent 'scoring' and the 'rescoring' of 15% of the applications. The scoring of applications only applies to the evaluation of the technical, operational and financial aspects of the application (ICANN, *New gTLD Applicant Guidebook 4 June 2012*, Attachment to Module 2, Evaluation Questions and Criteria, A-3 to A-4) and not to the String Similarity Review.
491. *See* Chapter 4.C.1.a.
492. ICANN Generic Names Supporting Organization, *Final Report - Introduction of New Generic Top-Level Domains Part A*, 8 August 2007, http://gnso.icann.org/en/issues/new-gtlds/pdp-dec05-fr-parta-08aug07.htm.
493. ICANN, *ICANN Board Rationales for the Approval of the Launch of the New gTLD Program*, 20 June 2011, http://www.icann.org/en/groups/board/documents/rationale-board-approval-new-gtld-program-launch-20jun11-en.pdf, p. 12; ICANN, Information on the Applicant Guidebook as published on http://newgtlds.icann.org/en/applicants/agb.

far greater than ICANN expected. So, it was normal that the process would require some flexibility, and that there would be certain delays. However, certain changes to the Guidebook amounted to a drastic departure from previously established policy and, what is more, from ICANN's obligations under its Articles of Incorporation and Bylaws.

Perhaps the most telling example of this is ICANN's decision not to allow so-called closed generic TLDs or exclusive generic TLDs in the 2011 round. A gTLD string was considered to be an exclusive generic TLD if the string represented a generic term, and domain name registrations were to be limited to the registry operator and/or its affiliates.

On 11 April 2013, the GAC advised the ICANN Board that exclusive registry access for strings representing generic terms 'should serve a public interest goal.'[494] On 21 June 2015, the ICANN Board responded to the GAC advice by issuing a resolution disallowing closed generic TLDs in the 2011 new gTLD Program.[495]

However, closed generic TLDs had always been envisioned in the policy-making of the new gTLD Program. One report that was prepared to assist the ICANN community in the development of the new gTLD Program stated:

> 'In the extreme, a company could seek delegation of a standard gTLD that would be used solely by that company (*i.e.*, it would accept no outside registrants at all).'[496]

A former Chair of the GNSO also explained that the notion of closed generic TLDs was envisioned during the development of the policy on new gTLDs:

> 'So we did have a notion of – and in fact I think if you go through all the history of the conversations, we did have conversations that presumed that there would be names that were for private usage and not be open to the general market. That was just assumed.
>
> I certainly had that assumption all along. And when this issue came up as an issue that had never been discussed, I was really shocked because I thought it was just a for[e]gone conclusion that you can open it and sell it to the public or you can close it and use it for your family.
>
> I mean, this was even before ICANN had decided that only corporations could apply for names. We had the assumption that a family could apply for its name – that I could apply for .doria and use it for my family as I wished.'[497]

---

494. ICANN, *GAC Communiqué – Beijing, People's Republic of China*, 11 April 2013, https://gacweb.icann.org/download/attachments/28278854/Beijing%20Communique%20april2013_Final.pdf?version=1&modificationDate=1367607354000&api=v2, p. 11.
495. ICANN, *Approved Resolution 2015.06.21.NG02 – Meeting of the New gTLD Program Committee*, 21 June 2015, https://www.icann.org/resources/board-material/resolutions-new-gtld-2015-06-21-en.
496. Michael L. Katz, Gregory L. Rosston and Theresa Sullivan, *Economic Considerations in the Expansion of Generic Top-Level Domain Names – Phase II Report: Case Studies prepared for ICANN*, December 2010, https://archive.icann.org/en/topics/new-gtlds/phase-two-economic-considerations-03dec10-en.pdf, 40 p. 23.
497. ICANN, *Transcription ICANN Durban Meeting, NCUC Workshop Wednesday 17 July 2013 at 13:30 local time*, 17 July 2013, http://archive.icann.org/en/meetings/durban2013/bitcache/

The template agreement that was provided to prospective applicants at the beginning of the application process allowed for the possibility of single-registrant gTLDs, and it did not distinguish between gTLD strings that were comprised of trademarks and the ones that were comprised of truly generic words.[498]

In view of the above, it was not surprising that applicants made use of this possibility and applied for single-registrant generic word TLDs. It was foreseeable – and even foreseen in the program – that they would do so. Applicants, who had invested significant resources in developing business plans for closed generic TLDs and in preparing their application, were given a legitimate expectation that they would be entitled to use their generic word TLD as a single-registrant TLD.

This legitimate expectation was infringed when the ICANN Board forced applicants for exclusive generic TLDs to do one of the following:

> 'a. submit a change request to no longer be an exclusive generic TLD, and sign the current form of the New gTLD Registry Agreement;
> b. maintain their plan to operate an exclusive generic TLD. As a result, their application will be deferred to the next round of the New gTLD Program, subject to rules developed for the next round, to allow time for the GNSO to develop policy advice concerning exclusive generic TLDs; or
> c. withdraw their application for a refund consistent with the refund schedule in the Applicant Guidebook.'[499]

As a result, an applicant for an exclusive generic TLD who wished to maintain its plan to operate the gTLD as a single-registrant TLD was obliged to wait for a next round of new gTLDs, without being sure of what the rules for that next round would be; indeed, the applicants concerned had no guarantee that exclusive generic TLDs would in fact be allowed in the next round. Moreover, it remains highly uncertain if and when a new round of gTLDs will be organized. In other words, the only viable option for applicants for exclusive generic TLDs, who wanted to generate a return on investment in the foreseeable future, was to adapt their business plan and to abandon the idea of operating an exclusive generic TLD. In view of what amounted to a fundamental ICANN policy change, we believe that ICANN should, at the very least, have provided adequate compensation to these applicants, including a full refund of the evaluation fee for those applicants electing to withdraw their application.

Transcript_%20NCUC%20-%20The%20Debate%20on%20%27Closed%27%20Generic%20Top%20Level%20Domains-vid=52845&disposition=attachment&op=download.pdf, p. 20.

498. ICANN, *New gTLD Applicant Guidebook 4 June 2012*, Attachment to Module 5 *Draft new gTLD Agreement*, Articles 2.6, 4.5, Specification 9, Clause 6.

499. ICANN, *Approved Resolution 2015.06.21.NG02 – Meeting of the New gTLD Program Committee*, 21 June 2015, https://www.icann.org/resources/board-material/resolutions-new-gtld-2015-06-21-en.

2. The Evaluation Phase

a. Outsourcing in General: Accountability Problem

The ICANN Board limited its involvement in the evaluation of new gTLD applications in the 2011 round. As explained above,[500] ICANN made extensive use of external contractors to perform the substantive parts of the evaluations. Nevertheless, ICANN reassured prospective applicants that its Board had 'ultimate responsibility for the New gTLD Program,' and that its Board reserved the right to consider any application for a new gTLD individually.[501] The fact that the ICANN Board maintained ultimate responsibility for the new gTLD Program is coherent with the requirement in Article II(1) of ICANN's Bylaws setting forth that the powers of ICANN and its business and affairs are to be conducted by, or under the direction of, the ICANN Board.

However, ICANN has adopted a restricted interpretation of its Board's responsibility for the program. As will be discussed in detail in the case descriptions in the next chapter, new gTLD applicants complaining to ICANN of perceived errors in the evaluation process, have been advised that it was not for ICANN's Board to second-guess the substantive determinations of independent third-party evaluators.[502] In our opinion, this was not the appropriate response to such complaints. The third-party evaluators were engaged to give advice to ICANN and its Board, according to the evaluation criteria and applicable standards defined by ICANN. A better response, on receiving non-frivolous allegations of erroneous or inconsistent application of these criteria or standards, would have been to examine the issues and address the alleged errors or inconsistencies in question. Instead, in most cases ICANN limited itself to reviewing whether or not the third-party evaluators had followed the accepted process – *i.e.*, without looking into whether the evaluators applied the standards correctly, fairly and consistently.

ICANN took the position that it should automatically accept the advice of its contractors, and that its own task was essentially limited to publishing the evaluation results.[503] ICANN's position, if accepted, arguably results in an accountability gap. The evaluation results are final decisions with respect to applications. However, if these decisions are effectively not being made by ICANN, the new gTLD Program excluded all possible remedies.

Indeed, ICANN's Top-Level Domain Application Terms and Conditions required applicants to release ICANN and the third-party evaluators from 'any and all claims by

500. *See* Chapter 4.C.1.c.
501. ICANN, *New gTLD Applicant Guidebook 4 June 2012*, https://newgtlds.icann.org/en/applicants/agb/guidebook-full-04jun12-en.pdf, Module 5-4.
502. *See e.g.*, ICANN, *BGC Determination on Reconsideration Request 14-5*, 27 February 2014, https://www.icann.org/en/system/files/files/determination-vistaprint-27feb14-en.pdf, p. 9 ; ICANN's Sur-Reply (*Despegar et al.*), § 15.
503. *See* ICANN, *New gTLD Applicant Guidebook 4 June 2012*, https://newgtlds.icann.org/en/applicants/agb/guidebook-full-04jun12-en.pdf, Modules 2.6, 4-8 and 4-9.

applicant that arise out of, are based upon, or are in any way related to, any action, or failure to act, by ICANN or any ICANN Affiliated Party [– the defined term ICANN Affiliated Party includes the third-party evaluators selected by ICANN –] in connection with ICANN's or an ICANN Affiliated Party's review of this application [...].'[504] ICANN required Applicants to agree 'not to challenge, in Court or any other judicial fora, any final decision made by ICANN with respect to the application, and irrevocably waive [...] any right to sue or proceed in Court or any other judicial for a [*sic*] on the basis of any other legal claim against ICANN and ICANN affiliated parties with respect to the application.'[505] Applicants were given the possibility to use the accountability mechanisms set forth in ICANN's Bylaws for the purposes of challenging 'any final decision *made by ICANN* with respect to the application.'[506] These mechanisms were not explicitly made available for 'decisions' made by ICANN's contractors. As a result, if the evaluations were not to qualify as decisions made by ICANN, and if the litigation waiver is enforceable,[507] there would be an accountability gap, with no remedies available for applicants that were treated unfairly.

In our view, it would be contrary to ICANN's obligation to remain accountable to accept that the evaluations were anything other than ICANN decision, and such an interpretation would also be at odds with ICANN's central mission to operate in a responsible manner for the benefit of the Internet community as a whole. The actions by ICANN's contractors must be attributable to ICANN, and final decisions as to whether or not to allow a particular gTLD into the Internet root are decisions that ICANN cannot outsource.[508] In short, the decisions of ICANN's contractors in the evaluation of new gTLDs can only constitute recommendations and advice.

Despite these strong arguments, however, ICANN has sought to interpret the recommendation and advice of third-party evaluators as final decisions that are not attributable to ICANN. And ICANN has taken other steps to try to avoid being held responsible. During the evaluation of new gTLDs, ICANN modified the accountability mechanisms set forth in its Bylaws. It introduced a time bar for challenging its decisions, and proceeded to invoke that time bar with retroactive effect, in an attempt, in our view, to prevent potential flaws in its new gTLD policies from being challenged. These attempts

504. ICANN, *New gTLD Applicant Guidebook 4 June 2012*, https://newgtlds.icann.org/en/applicants/agb/guidebook-full-04jun12-en.pdf, Module, 6-4.
505. ICANN, *New gTLD Applicant Guidebook 4 June 2012*, https://newgtlds.icann.org/en/applicants/agb/guidebook-full-04jun12-en.pdf, Module, 6-4.
506. ICANN, *New gTLD Applicant Guidebook 4 June 2012*, https://newgtlds.icann.org/en/applicants/agb/guidebook-full-04jun12-en.pdf, Module, 6-4 (emphasis added).
507. As we explain in Chapter 6.C.1.b(2) and Chapter 7.D, we are of the opinion that the waiver should be unenforceable, at least in the event ICANN were to invoke the litigation waiver against the enforcement of an IRP declaration.
508. However, an IRP panel or a competent court may rule that not allowing a particular gTLD application is contrary to ICANN's Articles of Incorporation or Bylaws, as the decision would be contrary to good faith or discriminatory. In such instances, ICANN should stop the violation of its Articles of Incorporation and/or Bylaws.

to limit its responsibility are completely at odds with ICANN's commitment to maintain and improve its accountability and governance.

b. *Consistency Issues*

As ICANN may not discriminate between parties, unless this is justified by reasonable and substantial cause, a consistent application of evaluation standards is of critical importance. Because of the high number of applications received during the 2011 round, and the different evaluators and evaluation companies involved, it was vital that consistency be assured through appropriate training, preparation, streamlined processes and coordination, and quality checks as the evaluations were made. However, it seems that many of these important aspects were lacking. One example concerned two applicants who submitted virtually identical applications except for their use of a different gTLD string. The two applicants received different clarification questions from the evaluation panels. Even if, in the end, both their applications were approved and the final outcome was not affected, situations such as this show that the approach of the evaluators was not always consistent or in-line with one another. This apparent lack of consistency was detrimental to applicants' confidence in the new gTLD Program and cast doubt on the methodology used in certain situations, such as the string similarity review or the CPE, where the evaluation not only concerns the individual applicant but may also impact third-party applicants.

A more coordinated approach could have avoided many of these consistency issues. Although 1,930 new gTLD applications were submitted, 90% of the applications shared one of thirteen technical infrastructures, and there were fewer than fifty different technical infrastructures in total.[509] However, all applications were processed on a stand-alone basis.[510] Even if each application needed to be considered individually, nothing would have prevented the evaluators examining the fewer than fifty different technical infrastructures first, before reviewing each application individually. This would have made the evaluation process much more efficient and coherent, and also faster.

c. *Issues with the String Similarity Review Process*

In its final report on the introduction of new gTLDs, the GNSO had recommended that 'strings must not be confusingly similar to an existing top-level domain or a Reserved Name.'[511],[512] After the ICANN Board had accepted this recommendation, ICANN

509. ICANN, *Program Implementation Review*, 29 January 2016, https://www.icann.org/en/system/files/files/program-review-29jan16-en.pdf, p. 78 (Note: according to a table provided on p. 79 of this report, 91% of applications shared on of 11 technical infrastructures).
510. ICANN, *Program Implementation Review*, 29 January 2016, https://www.icann.org/en/system/files/files/program-review-29jan16-en.pdf, p. 80.
511. ICANN, *supra* 469, Recommendation 2.
512. Reserved Names are listed names that were not available as gTLD strings. The Reserved Names list contained names such as ICANN, IANA, GNSO, WWW. For a full list, *see* ICANN, *New*

developed a process of reviewing similarity between: (i) applied-for gTLD strings, and (ii) existing TLDs, reserved names and other applied-for strings. The objective of this review was to prevent user confusion and loss of confidence in the DNS resulting from the delegation of similar strings into the Internet root zone. If applied-for strings were found to be confusingly similar to each other, the strings would be put in a contention set and only one of these strings would be delegated.

ICANN's string similarity review process resulted in two non-exact match contention sets for gTLDs in Latin script: the application for .hoteis ('hoteis' is Portuguese for 'hotels') was put in a contention set with the application for .hotels and the application for .unicom was put in a contention set with the application for .unicorn.[513]

The applicants for these strings received the following explanation from ICANN: 'After careful consideration and extensive review performed against criteria in Section 2.2.1.1 of the Applicant Guidebook, the String Similarity Panel has found that the applied-for string ([...]) is visually similarly [sic] to another applied-for string ([...]), creating a probability of user confusion. Due to this finding, the following two strings have been placed in a contention set [...].'[514]

However, ICANN gave no insight as to the reasons why it had created the .hoteis/ .hotels and .unicom/ .unicorn contention sets. No rationale was given, nor did the affected applicants receive any information as to how the string similarity panel (SSP) made its determination. The applicants were not informed as to the identity and qualifications of the evaluators, or as to how their applications were evaluated against other applications and what criteria were used by the evaluators in reaching their decisions.

The affected applicants expressed concerns about the way in which the standard for string confusion had been applied and about the way in which the string similarity process was implemented.

Many voices, including the GAC, also expressed the concern that the string similarity review did not result in a finding of confusing similarity between singular and plurals

gTLD Applicant Guidebook 4 June 2012, https://newgtlds.icann.org/en/applicants/agb/guidebook-full-04jun12-en.pdf, Module 2-9, 2-10.

513. ICANN, *New gTLD Program: String Similarity Contention Sets*, 26 February 2013, https://newgtlds.icann.org/en/announcements-and-media/announcement-26feb13-en. Later, ICANN also announced that application for non-exact match contention sets for IDN gTLDs (*i.e.*, in non-Latin script) were also put in a contention set (*see* ICANN, *String Similarity: IDN Variant Review Results*, 1 March 2013, https://newgtlds.icann.org/en/announcements-and-media/announcement-01mar13-en). However, this decision appears not to have generated the same controversy as the decision on Latin script gTLDs.

514. Letter from Christine Willett, Vice President, New gTLD Operations (ICANN) to Booking.com, 26 February 2013, not published.

of the same string.[515] With respect to singular and plural gTLDs, the ICANN Board – in our view correctly – decided that this was not for the SSP to determine.[516]

The standard for ICANN's string confusion test was as follows:

> 'standard for String Confusion – String confusion exists where a string so nearly resembles another visually that it is likely to deceive or cause confusion. For the likelihood of confusion to exist, it must be probable, not merely possible that confusion will arise in the mind of the average, reasonable Internet user. Mere association, in the sense that the string brings another string to mind, is insufficient to find a likelihood of confusion.'[517]

ICANN had indicated that the string confusion test was a high bar:

> '[T]he standard indicates that confusion must be probable, not merely possible, in order for this sort of harm to arise. Consumers also benefit from competition. For new gTLDs, the similarity test is a high bar, as indicated by the wording of the standard.'[518]

ICANN had also specified that the string similarity process was not intended to 'hobble competition or reserve a broad set of string [sic] for a first mover.'[519] In its call for expression of interest for new gTLD String Similarity Examiners, ICANN had specified:

> 'Policy discussions indicate that the most important reason to disallow similar strings as top-level domain names is to protect Internet users from the increased exposure to fraud and other risks that could ensue from confusion of one string for another. This reasoning must be balanced against unreasonable exclusion of top-level labels and denial of applications where considerable investment has all ready been made. As the top-level grows in number of registrations, drawing too large a circle of 'similarity protection' around each existing string will quickly result in the unnecessary depletion of available names. The unnecessary exclusion of names would also tend to stifle the opportunity of community representation at the top-level and innovation.'[520]

---

515. *See* Letter from Elisa Cooper, Chair (GNSO Business Constituency) to ICANN, 22 October 2013, https://www.icann.org/en/system/files/correspondence/cooper-to-new-gtld-program-committee-22oct13-en.pdf; Letter from Elisa Cooper, Chair (ICANN Business Constituency) to NGPC, 30 December 2013, https://www.icann.org/en/system/files/correspondence/cooper-to-ngpc-30dec13-en.pdf; ICANN Government Advisory Committee, *GAC Communiqué – Beijing, People's Republic of China*, 20 April 2013, https://gacweb.icann.org/display/gacweb/GAC+Announcement+Archive?preview=/27132037/30900359/Beijing%20Communique%20april2013_Final.pdf, p. 4.
516. ICANN, *Approved Resolution 2013.06.25.NG07 – Meeting of the New gTLD Program Committee*, 25 June 2013, https://www.icann.org/resources/board-material/resolutions-new-gtld-2013-06-25-en.
517. ICANN, *New gTLD Applicant Guidebook 4 June 2012*, https://newgtlds.icann.org/en/applicants/agb/guidebook-full-04jun12-en.pdf, Module 2-8.
518. ICANN, *New gTLD Draft Applicant Guidebook-Version 2: Analysis of Public Comment*, http://archive.icann.org/en/topics/new-gtlds/agv2-analysis-public-comments-31may09-en.pdf, p. 149.
519. ICANN, *New gTLD Draft Applicant Guidebook-Version 2: Analysis of Public Comment*, http://archive.icann.org/en/topics/new-gtlds/agv2-analysis-public-comments-31may09-en.pdf, p. 149.
520. ICANN, *ICANN call for expression of interest (EOIs) for new gTLD String Similarity Examiners*, 31 July 2009, http://archive.icann.org/en/topics/new-gtlds/eoi-string-sim-31jul09-en.pdf, p. 4.

As a result, ICANN's methodology used by the SSP was shown to be flawed and the outcome of the string similarity review was contradicted by empirical evidence. The string similarity evaluators remained anonymous and no rationale was given for the panel's arbitrary 'decision' finding confusing similarity.

A panel of legal experts later confirmed that there was 'no question but that that process lacked certain elements of transparency and certain practices that are widely associated with requirements of fairness.'[527] Members of the ICANN Board also raised concerns about the fairness of the string similarity process.[528] However, ICANN refused to address these problems.

d. *Issues with the Community Priority Evaluation*

The CPE was carried out later than the string similarity review in the evaluation process, and it seems that ICANN learned from the criticism it received with respect to the string similarity review process. At least, in part: ICANN posted the rationale of the CPE panel's recommendations[529] and informed applicants about the process before the start of the evaluation.[530]

However, ICANN did not communicate the identity of the evaluators or their qualifications. On the face of it at least, the outcomes of many different CPEs seem inconsistent. For example, although the majority of CPE applications for generic words associated with an industry sector were rejected, there were a few exceptions. As the scoring system was not always applied in a coherent way, this might explain why some applicants obtained a passing score while others did not.

In spite of ICANN's declarations to the contrary, it also turned out that ICANN's staff was intimately involved in the CPE and in the production of the CPE result; ICANN staff supplied continuing and important input regarding the CPE reports. However, ICANN's input was not made public, and ICANN was secretive about the fact that it gave input to the CPE panels. Therefore, it seems that the CPE panels were less independent than ICANN claimed, and that the CPE process was not transparent.

As will become clear in our discussion in the next chapter, issues with the CPE provided the subject matter for several IRP cases.

527. *Booking.com v. ICANN*, ICDR, No. 50-20-1400-0247, Final IRP Declaration, § 117 (3 March 2015).
528. ICANN, *Minutes – Meeting of the New gTLD Program Committee*, 10 September 2013, https://www.icann.org/resources/board-material/minutes-new-gtld-2013-09-10-en.
529. *See* ICANN, *CPE Results*, https://newgtlds.icann.org/en/applicants/cpe.
530. The Economist Intelligence Unit, *Community Priority Evaluation Panel and its Processes*, 6 August 2014, https://newgtlds.icann.org/en/applicants/cpe/panel-process-07aug14-en.pdf.

e. *The ICANN Board's Reaction to Belated Governmental Intervention*

As had been the case in the past, the GAC was also closely involved in the policy development for this round of new gTLDs. In March 2007, the GAC had already presented its general public policy principles related to the introduction, delegation and operation of new gTLDs.[531] ICANN's GNSO took account of these principles in the development of its policy for introducing new gTLDs.[532] However, that did not mean that the advice expressed by the GAC was adopted automatically. The GNSO made use of the GAC advice to develop its policy on new gTLDs.

An area of particular interest to the GAC – and one of the topics which has been debated the most – was the protection of geographical names. In its 2007 public policy principles, the GAC advanced that ICANN should *inter alia* avoid the delegation of 'country, territory or place names, and country, territory or regional language or people descriptions, unless in agreement with the relevant governments or public authorities.'[533] The GNSO formulated as a policy that geographical names should not be put on a list of reserved names. New gTLD applicants needed to show that the use of the proposed string would not violate the national laws of the country in which the applicant was incorporated, and national or local governments could use the objection mechanisms that were proposed under the GNSO policy.[534]

In June 2008, the GAC expressed its concerns in relation to the GNSO policy regarding the protection of geographic names.[535] The ICANN Board discussed the issue promptly with the GAC. The Board anticipated that the treatment of geographic names within the new gTLD Program was going to lead to 'the first of a number of discussions necessary to resolve the differences [between the GNSO and the GAC], and that this [was going to be] a topic of discussion with the GNSO and the broader community.'[536] As a result of its discussions with the GAC, ICANN developed additional safeguards for the protection of geographic names.[537] These safeguards were included in the first version

531. ICANN GAC, *GAC Principles regarding New gTLDs*, 28 March 2007, https://archive.icann.org/en/topics/new-gtlds/gac-principles-regarding-new-gtlds-28mar07-en.pdf.
532. ICANN, *ICANN Generic Names Supporting Organization: Final Report - Introduction of New Generic Top-Level Domains*, http://gnso.icann.org/en/issues/new-gtlds/pdp-dec05-fr-parta-08aug07.htm.
533. ICANN GAC, *GAC Principles regarding New gTLDs*, 28 March 2007, https://archive.icann.org/en/topics/new-gtlds/gac-principles-regarding-new-gtlds-28mar07-en.pdf, Section 2.2.
534. ICANN, *ICANN Generic Names Supporting Organization: Final Report - Introduction of New Generic Top-Level Domains*, http://gnso.icann.org/en/issues/new-gtlds/pdp-dec05-fr-parta-08aug07.htm, Recommendation 5 Discussion.
535. ICANN GAC, *GAC Communiqué – Paris*, 26 June 2008, https://gacweb.icann.org/download/attachments/27131940/GAC_32_Paris_Communique.pdf?version = 1&modificationDate = 1312228254000&api = v2, p. 3.
536. ICANN, *Letter from Paul Twomey, CEO & President (ICANN) to Janis Karklins, Chairman (GAC)*, 2 October 2008, https://www.icann.org/en/system/files/files/twomey-to-karklins-02oct08-en.pdf.
537. ICANN, *Letter from Paul Twomey, CEO & President (ICANN) to Janis Karklins, Chairman (GAC)*, 2 October 2008, https://www.icann.org/en/system/files/files/twomey-to-karklins-02oct08-en.pdf.

of the Applicant Guidebook.[538] They provided that applications for certain types of geographic name strings needed to be accompanied by documents of support or non-objection from relevant governments or public authorities. The proposed criteria to distinguish – on the basis of International Standardization Organization (ISO) lists and other published lists – between geographic name strings and other strings were intended to be clear and objective, and to allow for the predictable delimitation of geographic name strings as regards other strings.

The criteria were further fine-tuned in a second version of the Applicant Guidebook.[539] The ICANN Board considered that the proposed treatment of geographic names at the top level was a workable compromise between the recommendations of the GNSO and the GAC's advice, but wanted even greater specificity on the scope of protection of certain geographic names at the top level.[540] The Board also expressed its desire to continue discussions with the GAC 'to find a mutually acceptable solution,'[541] and clarified in a letter of 17 March 2009 to the GAC that these discussions would be about the protection of geographic names at the second level.[542]

The GAC, however, remained unsatisfied about the protection of geographic names at the top level. In its response of 24 April 2009, the GAC suggested that it 'would be sensible to enable Governments (or the GAC) to object to an application for a gTLD on public interests grounds without going through the time and cost of the formal objection process', as foreseen in the draft Applicant Guidebook.[543] On 18 August 2009, the GAC also asked ICANN to adopt less clearly delineated criteria to distinguish between geographic name TLDs and other TLDs.[544]

The Board replied on 22 September 2009, emphasizing its intent to provide a 'bright line rule' for applicants on geographic names. For names that did not fall under the specific protection for geographic names, the objection process could provide 'a secondary avenue of recourse.'[545]

538. ICANN, *New gTLD Program: Draft Applicant Guidebook (Draft RFP)*, version 1, 24 October 2008, http://archive.icann.org/en/topics/new-gtlds/draft-rfp-24oct08-en.pdf, Module 2-8 and following.
539. ICANN, *Draft Applicant Guidebook, Version 2*, 18 February 2009, Module 2-11 and following.
540. ICANN, *Letter from Paul Twomey, CEO & President (ICANN) to Janis Karklins, Chairman (GAC)*, 17 March 2009, https://www.icann.org/en/system/files/files/twomey-to-karklins-17mar09-en.pdf; ICANN, *Adopted Board Resolutions 2009.03.06.07 – 2009.03.06.08 – Mexico*, 6 March 2009, https://www.icann.org/resources/board-material/resolutions-2009-03-06-en.
541. ICANN, *Adopted Board Resolutions 2009.03.06.07 – 2009.03.06.08 – Mexico*, 6 March 2009, https://www.icann.org/resources/board-material/resolutions-2009-03-06-en.
542. ICANN, *Letter from Paul Twomey, CEO & President (ICANN) to Janis Karklins, Chairman (GAC)*, 17 March 2009, https://www.icann.org/en/system/files/files/twomey-to-karklins-17mar09-en.pdf.
543. ICANN GAC, *Letter from Janis Karklins, Chairman (GAC) to Paul Twomey, CEO & President (ICANN)*, 24 April 2009, https://www.icann.org/en/system/files/files/karklins-to-twomey-24apr09-en.pdf.
544. ICANN GAC, *Letter from Janis Karklins, Chairman (GAC) to Peter Dengate Thrush, Chairman of the Board (ICANN)*, 18 August 2009, https://www.icann.org/en/system/files/files/karklins-to-dengate-thrush-18aug09-en.pdf.
545. https://www.icann.org/en/system/files/files/dengate-thrush-to-karklins-22sep09-en.pdf, p. 17.

Many exchanges followed. The GAC remained of the opinion that 'names by which countries are commonly known as and which do not appear in ISO lists should also be given the same protection as country names that do appear.'[546] ICANN accepted a proposal by the GAC to expand the scope of protection to the thousands of sub-national names identified on the ISO 3166-2 list.[547] The idea of the GAC creating a list of geographic and geopolitical names was discussed between the GAC and the ICANN Board. But the GAC 'moved away from this suggestion because it would be a resource intensive effort for all governments to undertake.'[548]

The need for unambiguous evaluation criteria and clarity for potential applicants remained of quintessential importance to the ICANN Board and the ICANN community. The ICANN Board made clear to the GAC that it was not going to change its position on this issue.[549] In the end, ICANN also agreed to protect names 'by which a country is commonly known, as demonstrated by evidence that the country is recognized by that name by an intergovernmental or treaty organization.'[550] The GAC welcomed this change, as well as the possibility to issue 'Early Warnings' or 'GAC Advice' against applicants for geographic strings who avoided the 'government support requirement.'[551]

To summarize, the negotiations between the ICANN Board and the GAC had thus resulted in a clear departure from the GNSO policy that geographic names would only be protected through the new gTLD objection mechanisms. As an alternative, well-defined and predictable criteria were introduced to define which strings would qualify as a geographic name gTLD and require governmental support. The GAC and/or its

546. ICANN GAC, *Letter from Heather Dryden, Interim Chairman (GAC), to Peter Dengate Trush, Chairman (ICANN), and Rod Beckstrom, President & CEO (ICANN)*, 23 September 2010, https://www.icann.org/en/system/files/files/dryden-to-dengate-thrush-23sep10-en.pdf, p. 5; *see also* ICANN GAC, *Letter from Janis Karklins, Chairman (GAC) to Peter Dengate Trush, Chairman (ICANN)*, 10 March 2010, https://www.icann.org/en/system/files/files/karklins-to-dengate-thrush-10mar10-en.pdf.
547. ICANN, *Letter from Peter Dengate Thrush, Chairman (ICANN), to Heather Dryden, Chair (GAC)*, 5 August 2010, https://www.icann.org/en/system/files/files/dengate-thrush-to-dryden-05aug10-en.pdf, pp. 6–7.
548. ICANN, *Letter from Peter Dengate Thrush, Chairman (ICANN), to Heather Dryden, Chair (GAC)*, 5 August 2010, https://www.icann.org/en/system/files/files/dengate-thrush-to-dryden-05aug10-en.pdf, pp. 6–7.
549. ICANN, *Letter from Peter Dengate Thrush, Chairman (ICANN), to Heather Dryden, Chair (GAC)*, 5 August 2010, https://www.icann.org/en/system/files/files/dengate-thrush-to-dryden-05aug10-en.pdf; ICANN, *Adopted Board Resolutions 2010.09.25.02 – 2010.09.25.03*, https://www.icann.org/resources/board-material/resolutions-2010-09-25-en; ICANN, *Letter from Peter Dengate Thrush, Chairman (ICANN), to Heather Dryden, Chair (GAC)*, 23 November 2010, https://www.icann.org/en/system/files/files/dengate-thrush-to-dryden-23nov10-en.pdf.
550. ICANN, *New gTLD Applicant Guidebook 4 June 2012*, https://newgtlds.icann.org/en/applicants/agb/guidebook-full-04jun12-en.pdf, Module 2-17.
551. ICANN GAC, *GAC Comments on the Applicant Guidebook (April 15th, 2011 version)*, 26 May 2011, https://gacweb.icann.org/download/attachments/28278837/GAC%20Comments%20on%20the%20new%20gTLDs%20-%2026%20May%202011.pdf?version=1&modificationDate=1312360275000&api=v2, p. 11.

members could also use the new gTLD objection mechanisms for reasons of limited public interest or to protect the communities they represent.

In addition, governments could provide notifications via the application comment forum to communicate concerns relating to national laws, or they could issue GAC Early Warnings.[552] A GAC Early Warning is a notice, providing the applicant concerned 'with an indication that the application is seen as potentially sensitive or problematic by one or more governments.'[553] A GAC Early Warning could act as an incentive for an applicant to withdraw its application. Government notifications or GAC Early Warnings had to be issued within sixty days following the date on which ICANN publicly posted the applications in order to be considered by the evaluators.[554] Finally, the GAC could issue 'GAC Advice on New gTLDs'. According to the Applicant Guidebook, where the GAC advised ICANN that its consensus opinion was that a particular application should not proceed, this would create 'a strong presumption for the ICANN Board that the application should not be approved.'[555] For it to be considered by the ICANN Board during the evaluation process, the GAC had to submit its advice by the close of the objection filing period.'[556]

ICANN's objection filing period closed on 13 March 2013. However, the GAC waited until 11 April 2013 to issue its Advice on New gTLDs.[557] At that time, the GAC had reached a consensus disapproving two applications (for .africa and .gcc). The GAC had also identified certain other 'gTLD strings where further GAC consideration may be warranted', and had advised the ICANN Board not to proceed beyond the initial evaluation for those strings.[558] This advice was expressed with respect to .shenzhen (IDN in Chinese), .persiangulf, .guangzhou (IDN in Chinese), .amazon (and IDNs in Japanese and Chinese), .patagonia, .date, .spa, .yun, .thai, .zulu, .wine and .vin. Some of these gTLD strings arguably had geographic connotations, but they did not qualify as a geographic name for which the new gTLD Program offered protection. On 18 July 2013, the GAC informed ICANN that it had reached consensus that some of these gTLD applications (including for .amazon and .thai) should also not proceed.[559]

552. ICANN, *New gTLD Applicant Guidebook 4 June 2012*, https://newgtlds.icann.org/en/applicants/agb/guidebook-full-04jun12-en.pdf, Module 1-7.
553. ICANN, *New gTLD Applicant Guidebook 4 June 2012*, https://newgtlds.icann.org/en/applicants/agb/guidebook-full-04jun12-en.pdf, Module 1-7.
554. ICANN, *New gTLD Applicant Guidebook 4 June 2012*, https://newgtlds.icann.org/en/applicants/agb/guidebook-full-04jun12-en.pdf, Modules 1-5, 1-6.
555. ICANN, *New gTLD Applicant Guidebook 4 June 2012*, https://newgtlds.icann.org/en/applicants/agb/guidebook-full-04jun12-en.pdf, Module 3-3.
556. ICANN, *New gTLD Applicant Guidebook 4 June 2012*, https://newgtlds.icann.org/en/applicants/agb/guidebook-full-04jun12-en.pdf, Module 1-11, 3-3.
557. ICANN GAC, *GAC Communiqué – Beijing, People's Republic of China*, 11 April 2013, https://gacweb.icann.org/download/attachments/28278854/Beijing%20Communique%20april2013_Final.pdf?version=1&modificationDate=1367607354000&api=v2, p. 3.
558. ICANN GAC, *GAC Communiqué – Beijing, People's Republic of China*, 11 April 2013, https://gacweb.icann.org/download/attachments/28278854/Beijing%20Communique%20april2013_Final.pdf?version=1&modificationDate=1367607354000&api=v2, p. 3.
559. ICANN GAC, *GAC Communiqué – Durban, South Africa*, 18 July 2013, https://gacweb.icann.org/download/attachments/28278854/Final_GAC_Communique_Durban_20130718.pdf?version=1&modificationDate=1375798225000&api=v2.

However, this GAC advice was not submitted within the time limit given for consideration by the ICANN Board in the evaluation process. Despite this, the ICANN Board first accepted not to proceed beyond the initial evaluation stage,[560] and later decided – acting upon the GAC's belated 'consensus advice' – that the applications identified by the GAC should not be allowed to proceed.[561] The Board acted on the basis of the 'strong presumption' created by the GAC advice.

The GAC did not provide any rationale in support of its advice that the gTLD applications in question should not proceed. Moreover, the Board's acceptance of the GAC advice erased the delicate compromise that had been established, after years of discussion, between the GNSO's policy on new gTLDs and the GAC's requested protection for geographic names. In the Program Implementation Review, ICANN described its geographic names evaluation as based on established international classification lists and clear criteria, which supported a 'fair evaluation and predictable process.'[562] However, the predictability and fairness of the process was completely compromised by the ICANN's Board's adoption of the GAC's consensus advice.

What is more, legal scholars have convincingly argued that international law does not recognize sovereign, exclusive or priority rights of States to geographic names.[563] Thus, there seems to be no legal basis for ICANN to protect geographic names more than is allowed for by the Applicant Guidebook's carefully drafted compromise text on the subject. To date, this analysis has never been contested, and was even confirmed by ICANN's own appointed expert.[564]

In view of the above, it is puzzling why the ICANN Board accepted GAC advice (that was delivered outside the time limit), and refused a number of individual applications simply because the GAC advised that there was a 'strong presumption' that the applications should not proceed. The GAC did not provide a rationale for its advice, and most of the discussions between the GAC and the ICANN Board were not open to the public.

Moreover, the GAC did not only advise on individual applications; it also questioned key aspects of the new gTLD Program after ICANN had already received new gTLD applications. This led ICANN to change key features of the new gTLD Program pending

560. ICANN, *Approved Resolution 2013.06.04.NG01 – Meeting of the New gTLD Program Committee*, 4 June 2013, https://www.icann.org/resources/board-material/resolutions-new-gtld-2013-06-04-en.
561. ICANN, *Approved Resolution 2013.09.10.NG03 – Meeting of the New gTLD Program Committee*, 10 September 2013, https://www.icann.org/resources/board-material/resolutions-new-gtld-2013-09-10-en; ICANN, *Approved Resolution 2014.05.14.NG03 – Meeting of the New gTLD Program Committee*, 14 May 2014, https://www.icann.org/resources/board-material/resolutions-new-gtld-2014-05-14-en.
562. ICANN, *Program Implementation Review*, 29 January 2016, https://www.icann.org/en/system/files/files/program-review-29jan16-en.pdf, p. 75.
563. Heather Forrest, *Protection of Geographic Names in International Law and Domain Name System Policy*, Wolters Kluwer Law International 2013.
564. ICANN, *Letter from Steve Crocker, Chair (ICANN), to Heather Dryden, Chair (GAC) with expert opinion of Jérôme Passa dated 31 March 2014*, 7 April 2014, https://www.icann.org/en/system/files/correspondence/crocker-to-dryden-07apr14-en.pdf.

the evaluation phase.[565] With many of the discussions happening behind closed doors, one may seriously question whether ICANN complied with its transparency obligations in this respect, and whether ICANN allowed for the neutral and fair application of its policies.

3. The Objection Phase

a. *Inconsistent Expert Determinations and the ICANN Board's Selective Interventions*

ICANN selected world-renowned Dispute Resolution Service Providers (DRSPs) of high repute to consider objections made to applications. The DRSPs for Legal Rights Objections (LROs) (WIPO) and for Limited Public Interest Objections (ICC) had the advantage that their appointed experts could base their findings on existing legal rules, international trademark law and public international law respectively. Moreover, WIPO had long-standing experience in dealing with ICANN's regulatory framework and had access to a large pool of experts in trademark law who had experience with ICANN's processes through the handling of Uniform Domain Name Dispute Resolution Policy (UDRP) cases.

By contrast, the experts ruling on String Confusion Objections (appointed by ICDR) and those ruling on Community Objections (appointed by ICC) had to work within a completely new framework using untested objection standards that were specifically designed for the new gTLD Program. To ensure consistent outcomes, it was important for all experts to have a thorough understanding of the applicable standards and how they were developed. In view of the drawn out nature of the new gTLD Program's development, this may not have been easy to achieve for ICANN specialists, let alone for outsiders. Without adequate training and other mechanisms to ensure consistency of approach, it was almost unavoidable that divergent expert determinations on String Confusion and Community Objections would result.

The ICANN Board decided to intervene in the most obviously inconsistent or otherwise unreasonable decisions, and it created additional review mechanisms for a few limited objections.[566] However, where the inconsistencies were perhaps less blatant, the ICANN Board refused to intervene, notably even in cases where the challenged expert determination was based on one of the inconsistent or unreasonable expert determinations that had in fact caused the ICANN Board to intervene.[567]

565. *See e.g.*, ICANN's decision not to allow closed generic TLDs (*Supra* Chapter 4.C.1.e).

566. ICANN, *ICANN Board New gTLD Program Committee Resolutions 2014.10.12.NG02 – 2014.10.12.NG03*, https://www.icann.org/resources/board-material/resolutions-new-gtld-2014-10-12-en; ICANN, *Approved Board Resolutions 2016.02.03.12 – 2016.02.03.13 – Regular Meeting of the ICANN Board*, 3 February 2016, https://www.icann.org/resources/board-material/resolutions-2016-02-03-en.

567. *See e.g.*, ICANN, *BGC Determination on Reconsideration Request 14-5*, 27 February 2014, https://www.icann.org/en/system/files/files/determination-vistaprint-27feb14-en.pdf.

b. *The Independent Objector*

ICANN appointed an Independent Objector (IO) for the new gTLD Program, and granted him the authority to file objections against 'highly objectionable' gTLD applications to which no objection had otherwise been filed.[568] The IO could file community objections or limited public interest objections. The IO did not 'act on behalf of any particular persons or entities, but [...] solely in the best interests of the public who use the global Internet.'[569] He was independent from ICANN and the ICANN Board, and neither ICANN staff nor the ICANN Board was authorized 'to direct or require the IO to file or not file any particular objection.'[570] ICANN also required the IO to 'be and remain independent and unaffiliated with any of the gTLD applicants,' and considered that 'various rules of ethics for judges and international arbitrators provide models for the IO to declare and maintain his/her independence.'[571]

However, the fact that ICANN appointed a single individual as IO has made these rules of ethics potentially unworkable in certain circumstances. Indeed, it is conceivable that for particular applications, the IO would have vested interests in an unrepresented community or a party that could be affected by that application. That no one else is available to object to a 'highly objectionable' application in these circumstances, would create an ethical dilemma for the IO. If the IO were to elect not to object to the 'highly objectionable' application because of a conflict of interests, this could result in the application proceeding for want of an alternative. If, however, the IO were to object and openly state the conflict, the credibility of the objection could be reduced. And if the IO were to object without raising the conflict at all, there could be a perception of bias.

In one case, the appointed expert in a community objection considered that links between the IO and major representatives of the community on behalf of which the IO had raised an objection led to 'justifiable doubts as to his independence in the eyes of the Applicant and the broader public.'[572] The expert found that the applicant's challenge to the independence of the IO had to be upheld, given the 'importance of ensuring the perception of neutrality, independence and impartiality of the office of the IO and of the entire gTLD dispute resolution process.'[573] In this particular case, because the applicable procedures did not address the consequences of upholding the challenge

568. ICANN, *New gTLD Applicant Guidebook 4 June 2012*, https://newgtlds.icann.org/en/applicants/agb/guidebook-full-04jun12-en.pdf, Modules 3-9 and following.
569. ICANN, *New gTLD Applicant Guidebook 4 June 2012*, https://newgtlds.icann.org/en/applicants/agb/guidebook-full-04jun12-en.pdf, Module 3-9.
570. ICANN, *New gTLD Applicant Guidebook 4 June 2012*, https://newgtlds.icann.org/en/applicants/agb/guidebook-full-04jun12-en.pdf, Module 3-10.
571. ICANN, *New gTLD Applicant Guidebook 4 June 2012*, https://newgtlds.icann.org/en/applicants/agb/guidebook-full-04jun12-en.pdf, Module 3-10.
572. ICC Case No. EXP/396/ICANN/13 (c. EXP/397/ICANN/14, EXP/398/ICANN/15), *Prof. Alain Pellet, Independent Objector v. Amazon EU s.à.r.l.*, 27 January 2014, § 53.
573. ICC Case No. EXP/396/ICANN/13 (c. EXP/397/ICANN/14, EXP/398/ICANN/15), *Prof. Alain Pellet, Independent Objector v. Amazon EU s.à.r.l.*, 27 January 2014, § 53.

(according to the expert),[574] the expert nevertheless considered it appropriate to deal with the merits of the case. However, it is clear that situations like these cannot contribute to public trust in the new gTLD Program.

A further anomaly concerning the position of the IO is the link between the IO's remuneration and the number of objections raised and amount of work performed in relation to those objections.[575] This potentially promotes the raising of unnecessary objections. In fact, the IO has filed twelve admissible community objections and eleven admissible limited public interest objections. The IO was successful in four of the community objections. However, in one case the expert determination was later reversed by ICANN[576] and another case is still being disputed.[577] The IO was successful in only one of the eleven limited public interest objections, and that decision was later reversed on the grounds of its inconsistency with other expert determinations.[578] As a result, it would seem that the IO's objections were warranted in only two community objections –out of total of twenty-three objections raised. Going forward, ICANN may wish to consider a fixed compensation for the office of the IO irrespective of the number of objections raised. This may help to reduce the superfluous use of resources on unnecessary objection proceedings.

4. Other Issues

a. *Data Exposure Issue*

A security breach in ICANN's applicant portals has enabled unauthorized access to confidential applicant information. When the breach was discovered, ICANN took the portals offline to investigate the issue and to install a security patch.[579] ICANN was able to bring the portals back online quickly.[580] However, ICANN's investigations revealed that a group of individuals was 'responsible for numerous instances of suspected intentional unauthorized access to other applicants' confidential information' for a protracted period of time.[581] These individuals, who were affiliated to certain

574. ICC Case No. EXP/396/ICANN/13 (c. EXP/397/ICANN/14, EXP/398/ICANN/15), *Prof. Alain Pellet, Independent Objector v. Amazon EU s.à.r.l.*, 27 January 2014, § 54.
575. ICANN, *New gTLD Applicant Guidebook 4 June 2012*, https://newgtlds.icann.org/en/applicants/agb/guidebook-full-04jun12-en.pdf, Module 3-11.
576. ICC Case EXP/403/ICANN/20, *Independent Objector v. Medistry LLC*; ICANN, *Approved Board Resolutions 2016.02.03.12 – 2016.02.03.13 – Regular Meeting of the ICANN Board*, 3 February 2016, https://www.icann.org/resources/board-material/resolutions-2016-02-03-en.
577. ICC Case EXP/395/ICANN/12, *Independent Objector v. Corn Lake, LLC*; Dot Charity IRP Proceedings.
578. ICC Case EXP/412/ICANN/29, *Independent Objector v. Ruby Pike, LLC*; ICC Case CASE No. EXP/600, *Independent Objector v. Ruby Pike.*
579. ICANN, *Announcement: New gTLD Applicant and GDD Portal Update*, 1 March 2015, https://www.icann.org/news/announcement-2015-03-01-en.
580. ICANN, *Announcement Update – New gTLD Applicant and GDD Portal Back Online*, 2 March 2015, https://www.icann.org/news/announcement-3-2015-03-02-en.
581. ICANN, *Approved Board Resolutions 2016.08.09.14-2016.08.09.15 – Special Meeting of the ICANN Board*, 9 August 2016, https://www.icann.org/resources/board-material/resolutions-2016-08-09-en, rationale.

applicants, had been able to access trade secrets and sensitive business information relating to competitors. ICANN apparently asked them to provide an explanation for their activity, and to certify that they would delete or destroy all information obtained and that they had not used and would not use the information they had illegally accessed.[582] However, the applicants affected by the illegal access requested full transparency, and considered that a mere statement by the individuals who had accessed the confidential and proprietary information of competing applicants was an insufficient ground for ICANN to refrain from taking further action.[583] It was only after ICANN had been put under pressure by an IRP panel[584] and the applicants affected[585] that ICANN took steps to investigate the issue more thoroughly. To date, ICANN has not taken any remedial measures towards the applicants affected by the data breach.

b. *Name Collision Issue*

Alongside the Internet root zone there are alternative root zones, such as corporate intranets. When improperly configured, an attempt to resolve a name used in this private name space could result in a query being sent to the Internet's DNS. This issue is known as 'name collision'. With the delegation of new gTLDs, the name collision issue constituted a threat for ill-configured intranets. Indeed, if a corporate intranet was so configured that its network computers made the distinction between the Internet and the intranet on the basis of a TLD ascribed to the intranet, it would no longer be possible to make the distinction between the Internet and the intranet in question should the ascribed TLD become an active TLD in the Internet root zone. In such cases, the administrative boundaries between the Internet and the intranet would overlap. Due to the widespread use of certain extensions (*e.g.*, .home and .corp) for corporate intranets, a lot of corporations risked experiencing name collision issues if they did not change their configuration before these gTLDs were introduced into the Internet root zone.

At first glance, name collision poses no threat to the stability of the Internet; it only creates issues regarding the stability of ill-configured intranets. Nevertheless, ICANN intervened to address the name collision issue, and put several new gTLD applications on hold because of this. ICANN did this long after it had received the applications for new gTLDs, and even though it could have addressed the issue in the early stages of the development of the new gTLD Program. On 15 November 2010, ICANN's Security and Stability Advisory Committee (SSAC) already raised the potential issue of name collision in a report that was published for review by the ICANN community and

582. ICANN, *Announcement: New gTLD Applicant and GDD Portals Update*, 27 May 2015, https://www.icann.org/news/announcement-2015-05-27-en.
583. Letter from counsel to Despegar et al. to ICANN, 5 June 2015, https://www.icann.org/en/system/files/files/didp-request-20150605-1-petillion-redacted-05jun15-en.pdf.
584. Despegar et al. IRP Declaration, § 136.
585. Letter from counsel to Despegar et al. to ICANN, 8 March 2016, https://www.icann.org/en/system/files/correspondence/petillion-to-atallah-08mar16-en.pdf.

Board.[586] The ICANN Board considered the report on 10 December 2010, and decided to amend the DNS Stability Review in the Applicant Guidebook 'to allow the option to prohibit the delegation of problematic strings' and 'to address the potential technical and stability issues discussed in [the SSAC report].'[587] The Applicant Guidebook provided that the review to decide whether a string is problematic would take place during the initial evaluation's string review.[588] ICANN encouraged applicants 'to prepare to minimize the possibility of operational difficulties that would pose a stability or availability problem for its registrants and users.'[589] However, this was merely an advisory notice and not part of the evaluation, 'unless the string raises significant security or stability issues' as defined in the Applicant Guidebook.[590] We are not aware of any application which was later put on hold for name collision issues that did not pass the ICANN security and stability evaluation.

The name collision issue was again raised at the ICANN Board's meeting of 18 May 2013 – *i.e.*, almost a year after the close of the new gTLD application window. The ICANN Board decided at that meeting to commission a study considering the potential security impact of name collision issues created by the delegation of new gTLDs.[591] It is unclear why such a study was commissioned at the eleventh hour, rather than before the opening of the new gTLD application window.

Moreover, in February 2013, the Internet Engineering Task Force (IETF) published RFC 6762 which was likely to adversely impact the new gTLD applicants for .home and .corp. While the IETF said that it did not recommend the use in private networks of unregistered TLDs at all, it seemed to identify the .home and .corp extensions as a safe option.[592] In February 2013, it was publicly known that there were multiple new gTLD applications for .home and .corp. As a result, using .home and .corp in a private network was likely to generate name collision issues in the future.

Since then, ICANN has taken initiatives to mitigate the risk of name collisions and commissioned additional reports. However, some applications have remained on hold for over two years, and ICANN has not yet given any indication that this situation will soon change.

586. ICANN SSAC, *Invalid Top Level Domain Queries at the Root Level of the Domain Name System*, 15 November 2010, https://www.icann.org/en/system/files/files/sac-045-en.pdf.
587. ICANN, *Adopted Board Resolution 2010.12.10.22 – Cartagena*, 10 December 2010, https://www.icann.org/resources/board-material/resolutions-2010-12-10-en.
588. ICANN, *New gTLD Applicant Guidebook 4 June 2012*, https://newgtlds.icann.org/en/applicants/agb/guidebook-full-04jun12-en.pdf, Modules 2-4, 2-11 and following.
589. ICANN, *New gTLD Applicant Guidebook 4 June 2012*, https://newgtlds.icann.org/en/applicants/agb/guidebook-full-04jun12-en.pdf, Module 2-12.
590. ICANN, *New gTLD Applicant Guidebook 4 June 2012*, https://newgtlds.icann.org/en/applicants/agb/guidebook-full-04jun12-en.pdf, Module 2-12.
591. ICANN, *Approved Board Resolutions 2013.05.18.08 – 2013.05.18.11 – Regular Meeting of the ICANN Board*, 18 May 2013, https://www.icann.org/resources/board-material/resolutions-2013-05-18-en.
592. S. Cheshire, M. Krochmal and Apple Inc., *Multicast DNS*, Internet Engineering Task Force Request for Comments # 6762, February 2013, https://tools.ietf.org/html/rfc6762, p. 67.

5. The Delegation Phase and Beyond

While it is perhaps still too early to accurately assess the effects of the new gTLD Program (the program is still ongoing, and some new gTLDs are still waiting to be delegated) we can already observe some trends and developments in the domain name marketplace which are, or seem to be, inspired by the introduction of new gTLDs. Judging from the high prices that have been paid to acquire certain new gTLDs, it seems that registry operators are confident that positive net private benefits can be obtained through the operation of the new gTLDs.

The existence of positive net social benefit is less readily apparent with respect to certain new gTLDs. Since the introduction of the new gTLDs, we have witnessed an upturn in UDRP proceedings, with the proportion of cases involving new gTLDs seemingly increasing. In 2015, WIPO observed an increase of 4.6% in UDRP cases compared with the previous year. More than 10% of these cases related to new gTLDs, the most frequently recurring being .xyz, .club, and .email.[593] Between January and September 2016, WIPO assessed 1,782 domain name complaints. A total of 354 disputes related to new gTLDs, which accounted for almost 20% of the total caseload. The increase in the proportion of disputes relating to new gTLDs is remarkable, and could indicate that the rights protection mechanisms that were introduced with the new gTLD Program lack efficiency to address the social cost of illicit domain name registrations.

The new gTLD Program introduced a Uniform Rapid Suspension System (URS) as a fast and cost-effective mechanism to tackle clear-cut trademark abuse in new gTLD domain name registration. The URS provides for the temporary suspension rather than the transfer of an infringing domain name registration. Many trademark holders do not consider the URS to be an efficient mechanism for dealing with cybersquatting, as they see value in defensively registering the disputed domain name.

The increase in the number of disputes relating to new gTLDs may indicate that the introduction of certain new gTLDs led to defensive registrations or otherwise increased the costs of defending trademarks. This could arguably have been avoided if the advice of the economic experts who advised ICANN on the introduction of new gTLDs had been followed.[594]

Nevertheless, the overall outlook regarding social benefits is somewhat encouraging. A report commissioned by ICANN to assess the extent to which the new gTLD Program had resulted in changes in competition observed that some changes in the marketplace 'are consistent with what one would expect in a marketplace with increased

593. WIPO Press Release. *Cybersquatting Cases Up in 2015, Driven by New gTLDs*, 18 March 2016, http://www.wipo.int/pressroom/en/articles/2016/article_0003.html.

594. *See* Michael L. Katz, Gregory L. Rosston and Theresa Sullivan, *An Economic Framework for the Analysis of the Expansion of Generic Top-Level Domain Names*, June 2010, https://archive.icann.org/en/topics/new-gtlds/economic-analysis-of-new-gtlds-16jun10-en.pdf, 55, p. 31.

competition.'[595] But increased competition was mainly observed among registrars,[596] and this market was already much more open to competition than the market for registry operators. The market for registry operators saw newcomers enter the top fifteen based on their share of all registrations (*i.e.*, both new and legacy TLDs), but no important changes to competition could be observed.[597] Although Verisign's overall share has declined following the introduction of new gTLDs,[598] there seems to be no competitor who is likely to challenge Verisign's dominance in the near future. At the registry level, it remains to be seen whether the new gTLD Program has done much more than grant market share to newcomers.

Nevertheless, some registry operators have introduced new rights protection mechanisms which go beyond the rights protection mechanisms imposed by ICANN. This type of self-regulation, if followed by others, could give rise to important social benefits that would probably not have existed without the introduction of new gTLDs.

595. Greg Rafert and Catherine Tucker, *Phase II Assessment of the Competitive Effects Associated with the New gTLD Program*, 28 September 2016, https://www.google.be/url?sa=t&rct=j&q=&esrc=s&source=web&cd=4&ved=0ahUKEwjnx4G8pvvPAhXiKMAKHW6gBrQQFgg9MAM&url=https%3A%2F%2Fnewgtlds.icann.org%2Fen%2Freviews%2Fcct%2Fcompetitive-effects-phase-two-assessment-11oct16-en.pdf&usg=AFQjCNGBzs5_5aQGR5jjaweKCSFoF_sSfQ&cad=rja, p. 2.
596. Greg Rafert and Catherine Tucker, *Phase II Assessment of the Competitive Effects Associated with the New gTLD Program*, 28 September 2016, https://www.google.be/url?sa=t&rct=j&q=&esrc=s&source=web&cd=4&ved=0ahUKEwjnx4G8pvvPAhXiKMAKHW6gBrQQFgg9MAM&url=https%3A%2F%2Fnewgtlds.icann.org%2Fen%2Freviews%2Fcct%2Fcompetitive-effects-phase-two-assessment-11oct16-en.pdf&usg=AFQjCNGBzs5_5aQGR5jjaweKCSFoF_sSfQ&cad=rja, pp. 2, 14.
597. Greg Rafert and Catherine Tucker, *Phase II Assessment of the Competitive Effects Associated with the New gTLD Program*, 28 September 2016, https://www.google.be/url?sa=t&rct=j&q=&esrc=s&source=web&cd=4&ved=0ahUKEwjnx4G8pvvPAhXiKMAKHW6gBrQQFgg9MAM&url=https%3A%2F%2Fnewgtlds.icann.org%2Fen%2Freviews%2Fcct%2Fcompetitive-effects-phase-two-assessment-11oct16-en.pdf&usg=AFQjCNGBzs5_5aQGR5jjaweKCSFoF_sSfQ&cad=rja, p. 17.
598. Greg Rafert and Catherine Tucker, *Phase II Assessment of the Competitive Effects Associated with the New gTLD Program*, 28 September 2016, https://www.google.be/url?sa=t&rct=j&q=&esrc=s&source=web&cd=4&ved=0ahUKEwjnx4G8pvvPAhXiKMAKHW6gBrQQFgg9MAM&url=https%3A%2F%2Fnewgtlds.icann.org%2Fen%2Freviews%2Fcct%2Fcompetitive-effects-phase-two-assessment-11oct16-en.pdf&usg=AFQjCNGBzs5_5aQGR5jjaweKCSFoF_sSfQ&cad=rja, pp. 18–19.

CHAPTER 5

Case Studies: Effectiveness of the IRP as an Ultimate Remedy

The effectiveness of the remedies available to applicants in cases involving a dispute with ICANN can be best judged in the light of an in-depth study of the Independent Review Process (IRP) cases that have so far been decided. During our preparation of this chapter, we looked at each important IRP in detail so as to be able to highlight for each case the important issues that were discussed and the outcome of that discussion.

For each case we first give a brief summary explaining its background and importance, and we describe the main issues at stake.

Where appropriate, we then mention specific issues raised in the following areas:

- Points of procedure: including the applicable procedural rules, the jurisdiction of the IRP panel, standing requirements and time bar issues, the conduct of proceedings, the panel members nomination, appointment, removal and replacement, emergency proceedings, the written-arguments-only principle or otherwise, the possibility to organize hearings, admit witnesses and expert witnesses and allow document production, the timing for the decision, the duration and the costs of the procedure;
- Questions concerning the applicable law: including sources of law (international and domestic law, ICANN's Articles of Incorporation, Bylaws and governing principles such as ICANN's core values), essential rights and obligations that limit ICANN's performance of its mission (*e.g.*, under principles such as good faith, due process, fairness, non-discrimination and transparency), standard of review;
- The authority of the panel (to declare whether or not there is a violation, to indicate the prevailing party, to issue a recommendation or a summary

dismissal, to impose interim measures, to take procedural orders, to decide on costs, and to grant affirmative relief);
- The nature (binding or otherwise, with or without precedential value) and enforcement of an IRP declaration.

We describe in turn, insofar as they are available, the significant arguments of the claimant, ICANN's position, the IRP panel's findings and, where helpful, we provide our own analysis of the issues raised and discuss the implications. It should be noted that in some cases, certain points raised by the claimant were not in fact taken up by ICANN or *vice versa*, and that for some issues raised by one or both parties there was no ruling by the IRP panel.

As some of the discussion points raised are of lesser importance in terms of this book (*e.g.*, some of the procedural points), our analysis draws attention to those matters that we consider to have a particular relevance going forward. While preparing this chapter, we found to our satisfaction that many of the points that have been raised by us in the IRPs that we have handled personally, have also been raised in other cases. We hope that this chapter, containing as it does a detailed comparison of the most important IRP cases, will contribute to a better understanding of the main issues that need to be addressed.

We have finalized our analysis early November 2016. The then most recent IRP decision available on ICANN's website was the decision in the *Corn Lake* case regarding .charity. As the panel chair in that case also is the chair of the panel in then pending *dot Sport Limited* case in which we represent the claimant, we found it inappropriate to comment on the *Corn Lake* case at that point in time.

A. THE ICM REGISTRY CASE (.XXX)

1. Key Notes

- IRP under the first set of applicable rules.
- Confirmation that international law applies to ICANN.
- Confirmation that an IRP panel applies a *de novo*, objective and independent standard in examining whether the Board acted or failed to act in a manner consistent with ICANN's Bylaws and Articles of Incorporation.
- Confirmation of the non-binding nature of the IRP under the then applicable rules.
- Claimant ICM Registry was prevailing.
- xxx was delegated to Claimant.

2. Introduction

This[599] was the very first case to be initiated in the second round[600] and the only case of that round to result in a final IRP decision. The case has some, though limited, significance for the third round, because the IRP panel decided that: (i) general principles of international law apply to ICANN, and (ii) the standard of review in an IRP is an objective one. Other aspects of the case have become obsolete in view of the amended regulatory framework (*e.g.*, the precedential value of IRP decisions) and/or more recent case law (*e.g.*, the findings of the IRP panel in the *Vistaprint* case on the binding nature of IRP decisions). However, ICANN has nonetheless, and in our view incorrectly, relied repeatedly on this decision to prepare its defense in recent IRPs. Needless to say, it is imperative that all ICANN's arguments developed in more recent IRPs be carefully checked for consistency with the applicable framework and past case law.

To summarize, this case is particularly significant for the following reasons:

- The IRP decision confirms that ICANN is bound by general principles of international law, including the obligation to act in good faith;
- It also implicitly recognizes that prospective gTLD applicants are entitled to legal certainty and legitimate expectations;
- Although the panel in the *ICM Registry* case did not consider its decision to be binding, ICANN did in fact accept the panel's decision, and did not change its fundamental obligations as a result of the decision. This in itself serves as recognition that ICANN is indeed bound by general principles of international law and that it must guarantee legal certainty towards prospective gTLD applicants.

3. Case Background

In 2008, ICM Registry claimed that ICANN had yielded to the pressure of the Government Advisory Committee (GAC) when it finally decided in 2005 not to delegate the .xxx TLD to ICM Registry.

ICM Registry's application for .xxx was a very controversial one.[601] A previous application by ICM Registry for .xxx had been rejected in the 2000 Proof-of-Concept

599. We were not involved as counsel for either party in this case.
600. The 2004 round introducing gTLD, which was reserved to sponsored TLDs (*see* Chapter 2.C.2 *supra*).
601. Although the idea of a .xxx gTLD already existed before the creation of ICANN (*see* OECD, *Internet Domain Names: Allocation Policies*, OECD Document GD(97)207, Paris 1997, https://www.oecd.org/sti/2091363.pdf), opposition existed within some segments of the adult online content industry and reservations were articulated about a content-specific TLD for sex-related content, even if its content-designation is purely voluntary. The 'clear identification of a "red light district" and the stigma involved in being found there, and the concern about a "slippery slope" toward mandatory location in the gTLD' were believed to raise privacy and First

round,[602] as ICANN's evaluators concluded that other less controversial proposed TLDs (without the 'adult' element) would better serve the goals of the introduction of new TLDs.

In 2004, controversy existed: (i) as to whether ICM Registry's application met the sponsorship criteria, and (ii) concerning political sensitivities and public order considerations by the GAC. ICANN's evaluation panel initially considered that ICM Registry did not meet the sponsorship criteria. But, upon invitation by the ICANN Board and after many discussions and debate, ICM Registry was able to convince the ICANN Board that its application met them. The ICANN Board subsequently entered into contract negotiations. The contract negotiations were said to be straightforward and to focus on technical and financial aspects. However, the GAC voiced concerns about the .xxx application very late in the process, when ICM Registry and ICANN were already far advanced in the contract negotiations. ICANN stalled the contracting process and the ICANN Board eventually accepted the GAC Advice and rejected ICM Registry's application for .xxx.

ICM Registry filed a request for an IRP, and asked the Panel to issue a binding decision declaring that ICANN's rejection of the .xxx application, and the continued failure to delegate the .xxx application, was inconsistent with ICANN's Bylaws and Articles of Incorporation.

4. Points of Procedure

a. Applicable Procedural Rules

ICM Registry argued that the procedure is governed by the ICDR Rules, as supplemented by the Supplementary Procedures for IRP and ICANN's Bylaws.

ICANN did not comment.[603]

The IRP panel agreed with ICM Registry that the following procedural rules should be considered:

- The ICDR Rules;
- The ICDR Supplementary Rules for IRP; and
- The ICANN Bylaws (version of 29 May 2008).

Amendment issues. (*see* ICANN, *Report on TLD Applications: Application of the August 15 Criteria to Each Category or Group*, 9 November 2000, https://archive.icann.org/en/tlds/report/report-iiib1c-09nov00.htm).

602. The first round organized by ICANN to introduce new gTLDs, organized in 2000 (*see* Chapter 2.C.1 *supra*).

603. ICANN developed arguments in response to ICM Registry's procedural claims only, but did not challenge the applicability of the procedural rules.

b. Jurisdiction of the IRP Panel

ICM Registry considered that the IRP panel's task was to make a final, binding decision as to whether ICANN's administration of the second round, and its consideration, approval and then rejection of ICM Registry's application, were consistent with ICANN's Bylaws and Articles of Incorporation. It argued that the IRP panel should make a full, non-deferential review of ICANN's actions.[604]

ICANN did not challenge the IRP panel's jurisdiction.[605]

The IRP panel noted that '[t]he principal - and difficult - issue that the Panel must resolve is whether the rejection by the ICANN Board of the proposed agreement with ICM Registry and its denial of the application's request for delegation of the .xxx sTLD was or was not consistent with ICANN's Bylaws and Articles of Incorporation.'[606]

c. Nomination, Appointment, Removal and Replacement of Panelists

ICM Registry argued that because the ICDR did not maintain a panel of neutral arbitrators under contract for the ICANN IRP, each party should propose a panelist. The two co-panelists would then select the Chairman of the Panel. In case of their failure to appoint a panelist, the ICDR would be entitled to appoint the panelist.

ICANN expressly agreed with the appointment procedure as proposed by ICM Registry.

The ICDR accepted the appointment procedure as proposed by ICM Registry and not contested by ICANN.

d. Written/Oral Arguments, Hearing and Witnesses

ICM Registry asked for a live oral hearing with witness statements, examination and cross-examination, rather than the exclusive reliance on written arguments.

ICANN argued that written arguments should be limited to the parties filing one additional brief each.[607] It argued that no live hearing was necessary, and that this approach was 'consistent with the procedures that govern the Independent Review Process.'[608]

However, in this case, ICANN did not in fact oppose a live oral hearing.[609] ICANN proposed that the hearing be limited to closing arguments, excluding live witness testimony.

---

604. ICM's Reply, § 323.
605. However, as will be explained further below, ICANN did challenge the standard of review and the nature of the IRP Declaration.
606. ICM IRP Declaration, § 142.
607. ICANN's Response (*ICM*) § 108.
608. ICANN's Response (*ICM*), § 93, n. 161.
609. ICANN's Response (*ICM*), § 108.

The IRP panel agreed to a live hearing and organized a five-day oral hearing in Washington D.C.

Court reporters and transcripts were used during the oral hearing.

The IRP panel allowed for both written and oral witness statements. Witnesses were examined and cross-examined during the hearing.

e. Costs

ICM Registry asked that ICANN reimburse all costs incurred by ICM Registry in connection with its application, including attorneys' fees and costs, and that ICANN bear all the costs of the IRP.

ICANN did not comment.

Declaring ICM Registry to be the prevailing party, the IRP panel ruled that, pursuant to Article IV, Section 3(12) of the Bylaws, ICANN was responsible for all the costs of the IRP Provider. Each party was held responsible for its own attorneys' fees.

5. Applicable Law

a. Sources

ICM Registry argued that apart from the obligations that are explicitly mentioned in ICANN's Bylaws, ICANN must also comply (by virtue of Article 4 Articles of Incorporation) with relevant principles of International law, including compliance with general principles of law.

ICANN argued that an IRP panel need not consider a claim that ICANN violated an applicant's rights under international law and applicable international conventions, and local law, because the scope of the IRP 'is limited to ensuring that ICANN operated in a manner that is consistent with its Bylaws and Articles of Incorporation.'[610]

The IRP panel ruled that ICANN must act in conformity with general principles of international law, requiring ICANN to act in good faith:

> 'In the view of the Panel, ICANN, in carrying out its activities 'in conformity with the relevant principles of international law,' is charged with acting consistently with relevant principles of international law, including the general principles of law recognized as a source of international law. That follows from the terms of Article 4 of its Articles of Incorporation and from the intentions that animated their inclusion in the Articles, an intention that the Panel understands to have been to subject ICANN to relevant international legal principles because of its governance of an intrinsically international resource of immense importance to global communications and economies. Those intentions might not be realized were Article 4 interpreted to exclude the applicability of general principles of law.
>
> [...]

610. ICANN's Response (*ICM*), § 6, n.1.

> The paramount principle in play is agreed by both parties to be that of good faith, which is found in international law, in the general principles that are a source of international law, and in the corporate law of California.'[611]

b. Essential Rights and Obligations

ICM Registry maintained that by ultimately rejecting ICM Registry's application, ICANN had breached the general principles of international law related to acting in good faith, not abusing rights, creating legitimate expectations, and estoppel.

Further, ICM Registry argued that ICANN had violated its Bylaws and Articles of Incorporation by departing from its established procedure in its rejection of ICM Registry's application. ICANN was said to have violated its Bylaws and Articles of Incorporation by being overly deferential to the views of the GAC, which ICANN's Bylaws specify is to have only an advisory, as opposed to a mandatory or decision-making, role with respect to ICANN's activities.[612]

Specifically, ICM Registry claimed that ICANN had violated:

- 'ICANN's Core Value of '[e]mploying open and transparent policy development mechanisms';
- ICANN's Core Value of '[m]aking decisions by applying documented policies neutrally and objectively, with integrity and fairness';
- ICANN's Core Value of '[a]cting with a speed that is responsive to the needs of the Internet';
- ICANN's Core Value of '[r]emaining accountable to the Internet community';
- ICANN's Bylaws, Article II, Section 3, that 'ICANN shall not apply its standards, policies, procedures, or practices inequitably or single out any particular party for disparate treatment unless justified by substantial and reasonable cause, such as the promotion of effective competition';
- ICANN's Bylaws, Article III, Section 1, that 'ICANN and its constituent bodies shall operate to the maximum extent feasible in an open and transparent manner and consistent with procedures designed to ensure fairness'; and
- ICANN's Articles of Incorporation, Paragraph 4, that '[ICANN] shall operate for the benefit of the Internet community as a whole, carrying out its activities in conformity with relevant principles of international law and applicable international conventions and local law and, to the extent appropriate and consistent with these Articles and its Bylaws, through open and transparent processes that enable competition and open entry in Internet-related markets.'[613]

ICANN considered ICM Registry's factual assertions to be incorrect, and argued that ICANN's Bylaws and Articles of Incorporation prevented ICANN from accepting ICM Registry's application for .xxx:

---

611. ICM IRP Declaration, §§ 140–141.
612. ICM's Reply, § 412.
613. ICM's Request for IRP, § 86.

> 'ICANN could have been in violation of its mission had it approved ICM's proposed .xxx sTLD. Such conduct could have forced ICANN into a position of regulating content on the Internet, which is beyond ICANN's technical mandate.
>
> [...]
>
> ICANN's Bylaws could not be more clear that the Board is obligated to consider the opinions expressed by the GAC, and a failure to do so would itself have resulted in a violation of the Bylaws.'[614]

ICANN also argued that it had acted in good faith and complied with the requirements of Article 4 Articles of Incorporation:

> 'Without a doubt, ICANN's compliance with Paragraph 4 is easily confirmed by the time and energy afforded to ICM's proposal; ICANN spent countless hours considering the proposed .xxx sTLD and the impact the proposal would have on the Internet community as a whole.'[615]

The IRP panel found that the ICANN Board's 'reconsideration of sponsorship criteria, once the Board had found them to have been met, was not in accord with documented policy'[616] and that the Board had previously found 'that ICM's application met financial, technical and sponsorship criteria.'[617] The IRP panel concluded from the above that ICANN had violated its essential obligations.

The IRP panel also indicated that there might have been 'ground for questioning the neutral and objective performance of the Board, and the consistency of its so doing with its obligation not to single out ICM Registry for disparate treatment', but that the facts were not fully coherent in this regard.[618] The IRP panel thus recognized ICANN's obligation not to single out applicants for disparate treatment, but did not pronounce itself on the issue in the *ICM Registry* case.

c. *Standard of Review*

ICM Registry stated that ICANN's violations should be assessed objectively, not deferentially:

> '[The] term 'independent review' in itself connotes a review that is not deferential. The [...] 'independent review' consists of consideration, inspection, or reexamination of a subject or thing that is not subject to the control or influence of another.'[619]

ICANN requested the panel to adopt a deferential standard of review:

614. ICANN's Response (*ICM*), § 105.
615. ICANN's Response (*ICM*), § 105.
616. ICM IRP Declaration, § 150.
617. ICM IRP Declaration, § 149.
618. ICM IRP Declaration, § 151.
619. ICM's Reply, § 312.

> 'As long as the Board's discussions are open and transparent, its decisions are made in good faith, and the relevant parties have been given an opportunity to be heard, there must be a strong presumption that the Board's decisions are not at odds with the Bylaws or Articles.'[620]

It claimed that support for a deferential standard of review could be found in:

- The ICANN Bylaws:

> 'The Bylaws make clear that the Board should exercise *its* best judgment and employ a 'balancing' standard to determine which core values are most relevant to the specific issue before the Board. Thus, the Board may, in its discretion, determine that it must support one core value over another. Such conduct is entirely consistent with ICANN's Bylaws and should not be questioned absent a showing of bad faith, which ICM has not alleged (and truly could not allege) in these circumstances.'[621]

> 'The deference due to the ICANN Board is further reinforced by the Bylaws provision governing the independent review process itself. Article IV, Section 3 strictly limits the scope of independent review proceedings to the narrow question of whether ICANN acted in a manner 'inconsistent with' the Bylaws and Articles of Incorporation. In confining the inquiry into whether ICANN's conduct was *inconsistent with* its governing documents, the presumption is one of consistency so that inconsistency must be established, rather than the reverse. Other language in Section 3 confirms this deference. The provision charges the Panel with the duty of 'comparing contested actions of the Board to the Bylaws and Articles of Incorporation, and with declaring whether the Board has acted consistently with' those two documents. By making clear that the Panel's role is limited to finding actual and specific violations of express provisions of the Bylaws or Articles (as opposed to a broader inquiry into the propriety of Board actions more generally), the provision governing this tribunal's review makes clear that independent review is not to be used as a mechanism to upset arguable or reasonable actions of the Board.'[622]

- The drafting history of the IRP:

> 'Further with respect to the nature of the IRP's review, ICANN clearly envisioned during the creation of the current Independent Review Process that the IRP would employ a deferential standard of review. The IRP was not intended to serve as the 'supreme Court of ICANN' with 'power to revisit and potentially reverse or vacate decisions of the ICANN Board.' Such an entity would itself raise difficult questions regarding who would execute this authority and the scope of this delegated power. Instead, ICANN recognized that, given its diverse composition, the *Board* is the most appropriate body to make final decisions on ICANN policies, subject to review by this Panel with respect to claims that the Board violated its Bylaws or Articles of Incorporation.'[623]

> 'The drafters of the IRP provision (including Ms. Burr) confirmed this plain meaning in explaining the IRP's purpose and effect. In the Report that recommended the language of the IRP provision, the drafters stated that the IRP 'is not

620. ICANN's Response (*ICM*), § 87.
621. ICANN's Response (*ICM*), § 87.
622. ICANN's Sur-Reply (*ICM*), § 123.
623. ICANN's Response (*ICM*), § 88.

the 'Supreme Court of ICANN' that some in the community have urged.' The Report made clear that the limited scope of review proceedings had been decided precisely in light of the appropriate latitude of the Board to make decisions on behalf of ICANN. [...] Thus, as the drafters explained and in keeping with the plain language of the Bylaws, the narrow scope of the independent review process was designed precisely to protect the prerogatives of the Board in making decisions for which there is a range of reasonable conduct. Deference to such discretionary Board determinations is therefore inherent in the structure, as well as the text, of the Bylaws.'[624]

– The composition of the ICANN Board:

'The fact that ICANN's Board consists of volunteers – often tasked with making decisions on matters of first impression affecting issues of global concern – further suggests that considerable deference to the Board is appropriate, particularly absent evidence of fraud or other misconduct. These volunteers are not permitted to have a financial stake in the outcome of the Board's decisions and are duty bound to act consistent with ICANN's Bylaws and Articles, and in the best interests of the Internet community worldwide.'[625]

'[D]eference is particularly appropriate with respect to ICANN in light of the unusual and carefully crafted structure of its Board.'[626]

– The laws of the United States:

'The laws of the United States also provide guidance. American jurisprudence has consistently applied a presumption of good faith to the decision-making process of a corporation's board of directors. Indeed, this presumption ordinarily 'precludes judicial inquiry into actions of corporate directors taken in good faith and in the exercise of honest judgment in the lawful and legitimate furtherance of corporate purposes'. If the good faith presumption is not rebutted, a court will not substitute its judgment for that of the board.'[627]

'Basic principles of corporate law supply an independent basis for deference due to the reasonable judgments of the ICANN Board in this matter. It is black-letter law that 'there is a presumption that directors of a corporation have acted in good faith and in the best interest of the corporation'. This presumption ordinarily operates to 'preclude[] judicial inquiry into actions of corporate directors taken in good faith and in the exercise of honest judgment in the lawful and legitimate furtherance of corporate purposes,' and, if unrebutted, forecloses a reviewing court from substituting its judgment for that of the board.

In California, where ICANN is located and incorporated, these principles require deference to actions of a corporate board of directors so long as the board acted 'upon reasonable investigation, in good faith and with regard for the best interests of' the corporation, and 'exercised discretion clearly within the scope of its authority'. This includes the boards of not-for-profit corporations. As California

624. ICANN's Sur-Reply (*ICM*), § 124.
625. ICANN's Response (*ICM*), § 89.
626. ICANN's Sur-Reply (*ICM*), § 132.
627. ICANN's Response (*ICM*), § 91.

> courts have explained, this doctrine rests on the well-accepted premise that those to whom decision-making has been entrusted are better equipped to make policy and management decisions than courts.'[628]

The IRP panel agreed with ICM Registry that 'the judgments of the ICANN Board are to be reviewed and appraised by the Panel objectively, not deferentially.'[629] The panel based its reasoning on: (i) ICANN's vast regulatory authority and the 'pervasive global reach', and (ii) the provisions of ICANN's Articles of Incorporation, Bylaws and specific representations ICANN had made.[630]

6. Authority of the Panel

In ICM Registry's view, the IRP panel was authorized to declare that ICANN had acted inconsistently with its Bylaws and Articles of Incorporation.

ICANN argued that the IRP panel's task was very narrow:

> 'Th[e IRP] Panel is not being asked to substitute its judgment for that of the Board. Instead, th[e IRP] Panel is tasked with reviewing the record and determining whether the evidence provides adequate support for the Board's actions with respect to some of ICANN's most important core values.'[631]

The panel made the following declarations:

- The findings of the IRP panel are advisory in nature.
- The actions and decisions of the ICANN Board are not entitled to deference; they are to be appraised objectively.
- ICANN must act in conformity with relevant general principles of law (such as good faith).
- The ICANN Board found that ICM Registry's application for the .xxx sTLD met the required sponsorship criteria.
- The Board's reconsideration of that finding was not consistent with the application of neutral, objective and fair documented policy.

7. The Nature of the IRP Declaration

ICM Registry argued that the IRP Declaration should be final and binding on the parties.[632]

ICANN argued that its Bylaws and its drafting history made clear that IRP Declarations are not binding and that the ICDR's Supplementary Procedures on IRPs confirm the advisory nature of IRP Declarations. Specifically, ICANN argued that the ICDR IRP Supplementary Procedures do not mention that IRP Declarations must be final and

628. ICANN's Sur-Reply (*ICM*), §§ 126-127.
629. ICM IRP Declaration, § 136.
630. ICM IRP Declaration, § 136.
631. ICANN's Response (*ICM*), § 8.
632. ICM's Reply, §§ 8 and 296 and following.

binding, while the ICDR Rules do expressly mention the final and binding nature of arbitral awards. ICANN argued that this omission was made intentionally to distinguish IRP Declarations from arbitral awards.

The IRP panel concluded that its findings were advisory in nature, and did not constitute a binding arbitral award. The IRP panel found support for its conclusion in: (i) ICANN's Bylaws charging the Board with reviewing an opinion, (ii) an omission in the Supplementary Procedures adopted for IRP when compared to the ICDR Rules, and (iii) the drafting history of the IRP provisions:

> 'A board charged with reviewing an opinion is not charged with implementing a binding decision. [...] If the IRP's Declaration were binding, there would be nothing to consider but rather a determination or decision to implement in a timely manner. The Supplementary Procedures adopted for IRP, in the article on 'Form and Effect of an IRP Declaration', significantly omit the provision of Article 27 of the ICDR Rules specifying that award 'shall be final and binding on the parties'. [...] Moreover, the preparatory work of the IRP provisions summarized above in paragraph 93 confirms that the intention of the drafters of the IRP process was to put in place a process that produced declarations that would not be binding and that left ultimate decision-making authority in the hands of the Board.'[633]

For the panel, these elements outweighed other evidence that would otherwise have suggested that an IRP should be an arbitral process with a binding award (the panel mentioned, for example, the testimonies of ICANN's officers before the U.S. Congress referring to the IRP as independent arbitration, the Rules of the ICDR, the fact that it is '*unquestioned that the term 'arbitration' imports production of a binding award*', and the mandate of the panel (as specified in the Supplementary Procedures) to decide the issue(s) presented and to designate the prevailing party).[634]

8. Noteworthy Points for Analysis

a. Applicable Law: Essential Rights and Obligations

The IRP panel's statements in relation to applicable law and the parties' rights and obligations remain important for IRP cases of the third round.

The Articles of Incorporation and ICANN's fundamental obligations under its Bylaws have not changed since the *ICM Registry* case. The panel's finding that ICANN is charged to carry out its activity taking into account general principles of international law (such as good faith) is a key finding that is still relevant today.

Reading between the lines, the IRP panel considered that ICANN must act in accordance with documented policy. ICANN risks violating its Bylaws and Articles of Incorporation when deviating from documented policy.

633. ICM IRP Declaration, § 133.
634. ICM IRP Declaration, § 132.

b. Applicable Law: Standard of Review

The rules on the standard of review have changed since the *ICM Registry* case, and the panel's findings on the standard of review may therefore seem less important as a result. However, recent IRP panels have referred to the *ICM Registry* case in support of their finding that IRP panels must apply a *de novo*, objective and independent standard in examining whether the Board acted or failed to act in a manner consistent with ICANN's Bylaws and Articles of Incorporation. We particularly refer to the *Booking-.com* and *Vistaprint* cases discussed below.

c. Nature of the IRP Declaration

The IRP panel's handling of the *ICM Registry* case was consistent with the rules of international arbitration. The panel considered itself competent to analyze whether the ICANN Board acted consistently with ICANN's Articles of Incorporation and Bylaws. However, the panel did not provide a binding ruling, but considered its findings to be only advisory in nature.

The panel's view that its findings are advisory in nature was made on the basis of a balancing exercise between the then current Rules, Supplementary Procedures and Bylaws. These Rules have changed, and the New gTLD Applicant Guidebook (AGB) contains a specific dispute resolution clause. The panel might have also misinterpreted the relationship between the Rules, Supplementary Procedures and the Bylaws. Recent case law suggests that an IRP Declaration is binding (albeit only partially, according to one panel).[635]

The panel's finding on the advisory nature of its declaration may have had an impact on the relief granted by the IRP panel. The panel expressed its views on the reconsideration by the Board of the sponsorship criteria, but it remained somewhat ambiguous on the question of whether the Board acted neutrally, objectively and consistently with its obligation not to single out ICM Registry for disparate treatment. If the panel had been of the opinion that it had to issue a final and binding award, it might have expressed an unequivocal view on the issue. Instead, the panel gave leeway to ICANN to reject ICM Registry's application on other grounds than the sponsorship criteria.

In view of the controversy surrounding ICM Registry's application for .xxx, very sensitive and political issues were presented to the IRP panel. These issues may have convinced the IRP panel to rule in favor of ICM Registry. However, the panel remained careful not to offend anyone, and gave its opinion on the least controversial issues only. The panel stated it did 'not question the integrity of the ICANN Board's disposition of the ICM Registry application, still less that of any of the Board's members.'[636] The panel's cautious attitude may be attributable to the panelists' personalities, but also to

635. *See* Vistaprint IRP Declaration, §§ 130 and following.
636. ICM IRP Declaration, § 150.

the nature of the file and the fact that this was the very first IRP. This probably resulted in a wise decision; the panel would have done a disservice to the Internet community if it had issued a firm, but potentially challengeable, declaration in which the ICANN Board lost face. It is unlikely that the ICANN Board would have accepted a more controversial IRP Declaration than the one that was issued, and as a result the IRP as an accountability mechanism would have become less efficient.

In the event, despite the cautious nature of the decision, ICM Registry had to impose quite some pressure on ICANN before the ICANN Board agreed to accept the majority opinion in the IRP Declaration.

B. THE MANWIN LICENSING INTERNATIONAL CASE (.XXX)

1. Key Notes

- IRP under the first set of applicable rules.
- Case ended in a settlement.

2. Introduction

This[637] second IRP was abandoned by the parties before the panel could reach a final decision. However, interesting arguments were raised, for example in relation to the claimant's standing, time bar issues, the possible preclusive effect of a previous IRP and court case, the standard of review, etc.

Although the panel did not actually issue an IRP Declaration in this case, the panel did identify that the prior IRP proceedings involving ICM Registry possibly had preclusive effect and it invited the parties to provide additional briefing on this issue. Indeed, the panel organized a telephone hearing for arguments on both the question of standing and concerning the possible preclusive effect of the prior IRP Declaration.

Furthermore, the *Manwin* case had a direct impact on the IRP rules, possibly because ICANN wanted to prevent other requests similar to Manwin's from being filed.

3. Case Background

Manwin Licensing International (Manwin) first filed a lawsuit against ICM Registry and ICANN in November 2011. That case arose from the delegation of .xxx following the IRP between ICM Registry and ICANN. Manwin, who are owners of adult-content websites in other TLDs and producers of adult content, objected to ICANN's delegation of .xxx to ICM Registry. They brought a suit against both ICANN and ICM Registry under the U.S. antitrust laws with claims including conspiracy in restraint of trade in violation of Section 1 and conspiracy to monopolize trade in violation of Section 2 of

637. We were not involved as counsel for either party in this case.

the U.S. Sherman Act. In August 2012, the U.S. District Court of the Central District of California dismissed certain claims and allowed others to continue. It dismissed the claims that were based on an 'alleged separate market for affirmative registrations of domain names within TLDs connoting or intended exclusively or predominately for adult content'. Claims for attempted monopolization were dismissed, but Manwin maintained its claims based on a separate market for defensive registrations,[638] as well as its claims for conspiracy in restraint of trade and for conspiracy to monopolize.

In its motions to dismiss the suit, ICANN argued that it was not subject to antitrust laws. According to ICANN, because it 'does not (and cannot under its Bylaws) participate in any way in any of the markets that may exist that involve the DNS, or TLD registries or registrars', it should not be subject to antitrust laws that regulate market participants. In particular, ICANN argued that its actions in delegating the .xxx TLD fell squarely within ICANN's non-commercial, public-benefit purpose, and therefore were outside the scope of the Sherman Act.

The U.S. Court ultimately rejected this argument in August 2012, finding that ICANN's grant of the .xxx to ICM Registry, in return for the payment of fees, was 'quintessential' commercial activity. Regardless of ICANN's non-profit, public-benefit purpose, it 'may be held liable under the Sherman Act' when it engages in commercial transactions.

The Manwin plaintiffs alleged two relevant markets: the market for defensive registrations in .xxx and the market for affirmative registrations.[639] ICANN argued that there was no market for all defensive .xxx registrations, because each name within .xxx was its own individual market. The U.S. Court rejected ICANN's argument on the grounds that it was bound by the Ninth Circuit's decision in Coalition for *Internet Transparency v. VeriSign* (in which ICANN was not a party). In that case, the argument that there was no market for expiring domain names because each such name constituted its own individual market was rejected. The Court therefore found that the plaintiffs had sufficiently shown that there was a market for defensive registrations.

On the other hand, however, the U.S. Court in the *Manwin* case held that the plaintiffs had failed to adequately show the existence of a distinct market for affirmative registrations in a TLD intended for adult content, because they had failed to demonstrate why other operating TLDs were not reasonable substitutes for .xxx. The Court noted that, because one of the plaintiffs claimed to operate the most popular, free adult video websites in the .com TLD, it appeared that affirmative registration in another TLD was a substitute for affirmative registration in .xxx. Without their being a distinct market for affirmative registrations, there was no danger of monopolization of a distinct market. Accordingly, the Court dismissed all claims related to the market for affirmative registrations.

638. The defensive registration of a domain name refers to a registration that is done primarily for the purpose of preventing a third party to register the domain name in the domain.
639. The affirmative registration of a domain name in a domain is meant for an active use of the domain name in the domain, *e.g.*, to operate a website or to use the name in email addresses.

The U.S. Court found that Manwin had sufficiently shown antitrust injury and anti-competitive or predatory conduct by arguing that ICANN and ICM Registry had: (i) 'suppress[ed] or eliminate[ed] competing bids for the original .xxx TLD registry contract' and subsequent renewals, resulting in a contract with price and sales terms that 'would not exist in a competitive market'; (ii) precluded creation of other adult-content TLDs; and (iii) had set above-market prices and restrictions on output.

In November 2011, Manwin had started parallel IRP proceedings. When the U.S. court case was dismissed with prejudice on 8 May 2013, Manwin and ICANN informed the IRP panel on that same day that they had reached a settlement, and they jointly requested that the IRP be dismissed with each party bearing its own costs.

Although the *Manwin* case did not result in a final decision, below we indicate the parties' respective positions on some points of discussion. When read in light of arguments developed in more recent cases, it is interesting to see how ICANN already relied on certain arguments in the *Manwin* case that it would later use again, sometimes unsuccessfully. In particular, the *Manwin* case seems to have shaped the rules and ICANN's arguments on a party's standing, the time bar and the precedential value of IRP declarations. However, the IRP rules following the *Manwin* case were not adapted solely to benefit ICANN's argumentation, as is readily apparent from the amendments to the IRP rules on the standard of review. These regulatory changes will be discussed as from the *Booking.com* case below.

4. Points of Procedure

a. Applicable Procedural Rules

ICANN argued that the applicable procedural rules consisted of the Supplementary Procedures, ICANN's Bylaws and the ICDR Rules. It claimed that general legal principles did not apply directly to the IRP, but were there to inform the panel:

> 'Few formal rules govern ICANN's Independent Review Process. Although general legal principles – such as *res judicata*, issue preclusion, and Article III standing – inform the Panel's rulings in this IRP, those principles are not directly applicable. Rather, the Panel is guided primarily by the practical and equitable concerns forming these general principles and built into the IRP.'[640]

It argued that the Supplementary Procedures and Bylaws should take precedence over the ICDR Rules:

> '[T]o the extent that formal rules govern the IRP, those rules reinforce the need for finality. The Supplementary Procedures for the IRP incorporate the International Center for Dispute Resolution's International Arbitration Rules ("ICDR Rules") insofar as they do not conflict with the Supplementary Procedures or ICANN's Bylaws.'[641]

640. ICANN's Supplemental brief (*Manwin*), p. 4.
641. *Ibid.*

b. *Jurisdiction of the IRP Panel*

Manwin argued that the purpose of an IRP is to determine whether an ICANN decision has violated ICANN's Articles of Incorporation or Bylaws and that such a review necessarily involves a review of the merits:

> 'As an example of ICANN's loose use of historical IRP discussions, ICANN claims that IRPs 'may not 'involve a review of the merits of the particular decision'' [...] To the contrary of course, the very expressed purpose of an IRP is to determine whether the decision violated ICANN's Bylaws.'[642]

ICANN claimed that only actions or decisions by the Board could be reviewed in an IRP; not a Board's failure to act, nor third party actions or decisions:

> 'Under the *expression unius* canon, the limitation of IRP review to Board actions or decisions prevents an interpretation that permits an IRP claimant to challenge (a) the Board's failure to act, and (b) an action or decision of a party other than the Board.'[643]

It also claimed that an IRP panel may only review process failures and not the merits of a particular decision:

> '[T]he IRP is limited to complaints about alleged process failures in the Board's decision-making that directly affect parties specifically concerned with that decision-making.'[644]
>
> '[T]he IRP may not 'involve a review of the merits of the particular decision.'[645]
>
> 'Consistent with the Reform Committee's recommendation, the Board never 'broaden[ed] independent review ... to involve a review of the merits of a particular decision.' The scope of the IRP was then, as it is now, limited to a review of the consistency of the Board's procedural decision-making with the Articles of Incorporation and Bylaws.'[646]

ICANN stated that the approval or rejection of a new TLD was obviously within the mandate of the ICANN Board; such decision being exactly the sort of decision that the IRP provisions were designed to address:

> '[T]he prior IRP proceeding involving .xxx addressed a very specific Board action – there, the Board's denial of ICM's application for the .xxx TLD. The decision was exactly the sort of decision that the IRP provisions were designed to address, the approval or rejection of a new TLD obviously is squarely within the mandate of the ICANN Board.'[647]

642. Manwin's Supplemental brief, p. 15, n. 16.
643. ICANN's brief re standing (*Manwin*), p. 13.
644. ICANN's brief re standing (*Manwin*), p. 14.
645. ICANN's brief re standing (*Manwin*), pp. 16–17.
646. ICANN's Supplemental brief (*Manwin*), pp. 11–12.
647. ICANN's brief re standing (*Manwin*), p. 18.

c. *Nomination, Appointment, Removal and Replacement of Panelists*

The parties agreed that each party would select one arbitrator, and that those arbitrators in turn would select the Chairman. The parties disagreed about the order in which their respective arbitrators should be selected. Manwin asked for a simultaneous selection by both parties. ICANN wanted Manwin to select its arbitrator first. The ICDR was asked to resolve the dispute.

d. *Standing*

Manwin suggested that, in interpreting the standing requirement for a claimant to be materially affected by an ICANN Board action (or inaction), ''[m]aterially affected by' simply means significantly influenced by'[648] and a broad IRP standing must be adopted:

> 'ICANN's power over the Internet, ICANN's nature, ICANN's mission and core values, and the purpose of the IRP procedure require broad IRP standing so that the process can achieve its remedial purpose.'[649]

Manwin found support for a broad interpretation of the IRP standing provision in the drafting history of the ICANN's Bylaws and in the Bylaws' plain language:

> 'The drafting history of the standing Bylaw supports a broad interpretation of the IRP standing provision. [... The] history confirms that 'materially affected by' is an extremely low threshold designed to weed out 'frivolous or non-substantive' challenges. [... The Advisory] Committee [on Independent Review] was merely noting that essentially *every member* of the Internet community is 'affected in some quantum' by *every* ICANN decision, and that something 'more direct' *than that* should be required. The 'something more' was materiality and that simply avoided frivolous or non-substantive claims.'[650]
>
> 'ICANN cites some of its historical IRP discussions as support for restricting IRP standing. But all those discussions were superseded by the plain language ICANN subsequently adopted, and which ICANN has interpreted as equivalent to Article III standing. Nothing suggests that the superseded discussions were intended to construe the current standing provision contrary to its plain language or to ICANN's own most recent interpretation.'[651]

Manwin criticized ICANN for trying to add limitations that appear nowhere in the Bylaw texts:

> '[ICANN] seeks to rewrite 'materially affected by' to add at least two limitations that nowhere appear in the text. First, it wants the Board action not only to 'materially affect' the claimant, but also to 'specifically concern the 'materially affected' claimant.' Second, it wants the harm to be caused 'by' the Board's

648. Manwin's brief re standing, p. 7.
649. Manwin's brief re standing, p. 9.
650. Manwin's brief re standing, pp. 11–13.
651. Manwin's Supplemental brief, p. 15.

conduct, but also to be 'derived directly from ICANN Board conduct.' [...] But since neither limitation appears in the text, the Bylaw cannot be rewritten to include them.'[652]

Manwin argued that the standing threshold must be low and less demanding than a threshold applied by courts, because an IRP panel can only issue non-binding, advisory opinions:

> 'The standing threshold for a non-binding, advisory IRP opinion should necessarily be lower than for obtaining binding orders enforceable by plenary federal governmental powers.'[653]

Indeed, Manwin argued it must have standing, as a U.S. District Court in a companion Federal action had already decided that Manwin had standing.[654]

Manwin also stated that ICANN's acts were a direct cause of its harm, and that as a result it met the standing requirement:

> 'ICANN argues that [Manwin] lacks standing because its harm stems entirely from acts by ICM not ICANN. [...] The argument is silly. ICANN created the .xxx TLD, approved the ICM registry contract, empowered and authorized ICM to set anticompetitive pricing and other .xxx operating terms about which [Manwin] complains, and gets a cut of every monopoly-priced registration fee received by ICM. ICANN's acts are thus a direct cause of [Manwin]'s harm.'[655]

ICANN insisted that Manwin, in order to have standing, must show harm that is concrete, particularized and actual or imminent:

> 'Injury in fact is 'an invasion of a legally protected interest which is (a) concrete and particularized, and (b) actual or imminent, not conjectural or hypothetical.''[656]

It stated that the drafting history of the IRP supports such stringent standing requirements:

> 'When ICANN adopted revised Bylaws in December 2002 following an evolution and reform process, the concept of a 'conventional legal threshold of materiality' was adopted, limiting the availability of the IRP to persons 'materially affected' by an ICANN Board decision or action. The materiality threshold remains in place today.
>
> The constructs of the 'conventional legal threshold of materiality' requirement can be informed by the analogous constitutional 'case and controversy' jurisdictional limit placed upon the federal courts in the United States, whereby a plaintiff must satisfy three elements to have standing. First, the plaintiff must have suffered a 'concrete and particularized' injury in fact. Second, the injury must be 'fairly ... trace[able] to the challenged action of the defendant, and not ... th[e] result [of] the independent action of some third party not before the court.' Third, a court

652. Manwin's brief re standing, p. 9.
653. Manwin's brief re standing, p. 14.
654. Manwin's brief re standing, pp. 16–17.
655. Manwin's brief re standing, p. 21.
656. ICANN's Response (*Manwin*), § 109.

> decision in the litigant's favor must be likely to redress the plaintiff's claimed injuries. [Manwin] fails to satisfy *any* of the three prongs of this conventional legal test for standing.'[657]

ICANN argued that its position concerning the IRP's standing threshold was supported by International law:

> 'The contours of the 'conventional legal threshold of materiality' requirement contemplated by the Advisory Committee on Independent Review may also be informed by international law, such as the standing threshold applied to plaintiffs by the highest court of the European Union ('EU'), the Court of Justice ('ECJ'). The ECJ reviews challenges to actions taken by such institutions as the EU Council, EU Commission or European Central Bank. The standing threshold individual ECJ applicants must satisfy is dictated by the Treaty on the Functioning of the EU, which provides that: 'Any natural or legal person may ... institute proceedings against an act addressed to that person *or which is of direct and individual concern to them*, and against a regulatory act which is of direct concern to them and does not entail implementing measures.' The ECJ has strictly construed both the 'direct concern' and 'individual concern' prongs of this legal threshold for standing, despite recent challenges. [Manwin] cannot satisfy either of the threshold standing requirements under the law of the European Union, which also militates in favour of a finding that [Manwin] has not met the 'materiality threshold' set forth in ICANN's Bylaws.'[658]

ICANN also argued Manwin's interpretation of the IRP standing requirement would impair ICANN's ability to carry out its mandate:

> '[Manwin]'s interpretation of the IRP standing requirement has no limiting principles. According to [Manwin], as long as an individual or entity can identify an ICANN decision or action in the causal chain that led to its grievance, it has standing to maintain an IRP. This interpretation is wholly without merit and could result in ICANN being overrun with IRPs and impaired from carrying out its mandate.'[659]

In short, ICANN considered Manwin to lack standing to request an IRP, as it was not materially affected by a decision or action by the Board:

> 'The IRP was created to allow community participants taking part in ICANN's processes the ability to seek external, third-party review of an ICANN Board decision.
>
> As a reflection of ICANN's reliance on community participation in ICANN's multi-stakeholder model, ICANN's Bylaws expressly limit who may submit a request for an IRP proceeding. Only persons '*materially affected* by a decision or action by the Board that he or she asserts is inconsistent with the Articles of Incorporation or Bylaws may submit a request for independent review of that decision or action.'

657. ICANN's Response (*Manwin*), §§ 107-108.
658. ICANN's Response (*Manwin*), § 118.
659. ICANN's brief re standing (*Manwin*), p. 15.

> [... A]n IRP claimant must demonstrate some logical nexus or connection between the claimant's alleged harm and a decision or action of the ICANN Board. In other words, the ICANN Board's decision or action must specifically concern the 'materially affected' IRP claimant.
>
> [...] Having failed to participate in ICANN's processes, and complaining only of ICM's conduct in operating .xxx, [Manwin] cannot properly invoke the IRP.
>
> [... Manwin]'s claimed injury is thus derived entirely from actions purportedly taken by ICM, not the ICANN Board.
>
> [...] IRP proceedings must be limited in some rational way to a review of ICANN Board conduct that specifically concerns the affected party. [Manwin] here fails to make that connection.'[660]
>
> '[Manwin] is not directly affected by anything ICANN did. Rather, it is directly affected by *ICM's* adoption of pricing and other terms for registration of domain names in .xxx with which [Manwin] disagrees. This link is too attenuated to provide IRP standing against ICANN.'[661]

ICANN claimed that Manwin had itself shown that it was not 'materially affected', by requesting relief that did not redress the injury it had purportedly suffered:

> '[Manwin]'s articulation of the generic relief that it hopes will result form this IRP actually proves that [Manwin] does not have a concrete and particularized injury redressable by the IRP. [...T]he relief [Manwin] now requests, the educational and public benefits derived from the IRP process, is not 'likely' to – and in fact will not – redress the injury [Manwin] purportedly has suffered.'[662]

e. *Time Bar*

Manwin argued that it was not required to participate in ICANN processes and that it could raise issues about an ICANN decision at its convenience:

> '[N]othing in the standing Bylaw states or even suggests that the IRP claimant must participate in the ICANN processes leading to the challenged board decisions. Again, ICANN is simply asking the Panel to rewrite its standing Bylaw, something this Panel cannot do.'[663]

ICANN argued that Manwin had waited too long before it raised its concerns:

> 'In fact, [Manwin] did not raise its concerns until it filed this IRP action, six months after ICANN bound itself to the registry agreement. [... Manwin] cannot remedy its previous failures to act by invoking an IRP seeking to overturn decisions made long ago.'[664]

660. ICANN's Response (*Manwin*), §§ 6–12.
661. ICANN's brief re standing (*Manwin*), p. 20.
662. ICANN's Supplemental brief (*Manwin*), pp. 8–9.
663. Manwin's brief re standing, p. 18.
664. ICANN Supplemental brief (*Manwin*), pp. 2–3.

5. Applicable Law

Parties exchanged views on the Standard of Review issue.

Manwin argued that no deference is owed to ICANN's interpretation of the Bylaws:

> 'Whatever deference might otherwise be owed to an entity's interpretation of its Bylaws is forfeited where, as here, the entity expresses an intent for independent non-deferential review.'[665]

ICANN disagreed, and argued it was entitled to deference in interpreting its Bylaws:

> 'Over the course of several years, ICANN established the specific contours of the IRP. Thus, ICANN is in a unique position to address why the IRP was created, the expectations of how that process facilitates ICANN's mandate, and who was intended to be able to invoke the IRP. As a result, ICANN's interpretation of the Bylaws giving rise to that process deserves deference.'[666]

ICANN stated that the *ICM* IRP panel did not address the deference to which ICANN is entitled in interpreting its Bylaws:

> '[Manwin] also contends that the prior IRP Panel 'specifically rejected ICANN's deference argument', but fails to note that the prior IRP Panel did not address bylaw interpretation; rather, it addressed the application of the business judgment rule to ICANN's decision making. The business judgment rule is not at issue here, and [Manwin] provides no explanation for why the Panel should ignore California principles of bylaw interpretation when interpreting ICANN's Bylaws, particularly given its initial stance that the Bylaws section addressing IRP standing must be interpreted broadly.'[667]

6. Authority of the Panel

Manwin considered that it was entitled to affirmative relief and demanded that ICANN void the registry agreement with ICM Registry.

ICANN claimed that the Bylaws contain a clear statement regarding the limited relief available:

> 'ICANN's Bylaws permit the IRP panel to grant two forms of relief: (1) declare whether the Board's action was inconsistent with the Articles of Incorporation or Bylaws, and (2) recommend that the Board stay an action or decision, or take interim action, until the Board acts upon the IRP panel's opinion.'[668]

ICANN rejected the idea that an IRP panel can grant affirmative relief:

> '[Manwin] has requested that the Panel award certain affirmative relief, beyond the relief allowed in the IRP, which is limited to a declaration of whether the ICANN Board acted in conformance with its Bylaws or Articles of Incorporation. [... T]he Panel's authority is limited to *declaring* whether an action or inaction of

665. Manwin's Supplemental brief, p. 14.
666. ICANN's brief re standing (*Manwin*), p. 7.
667. ICANN Supplemental brief (*Manwin*), p. 10.
668. ICANN's Supplementary brief (*Manwin*), p. 15.

> the Board was inconsistent with the Articles of Incorporation or Bylaws and *recommending* that the Board stay any action or decision or take any interim action until such time as the Board reviews and acts upon the declaration of the IRP panel. There is nothing in the Bylaws or Articles of Incorporation that grants the Panel authority to award affirmative relief and to require ICANN to undertake specific conduct.'[669]

ICANN argued that the form of relief requested by Manwin that did fall within the scope of an IRP panel's authority would in fact serve no purpose, as ICANN would be unable to "act [...] upon the opinion of the IRP' panel':[670]

> 'Doing so would require ICANN to shut down the .xxx sTLD, causing the breach of thousands of contracts involving third-party registrants operating in that domain. The operation of the .xxx sTLD is too far along to allow ICANN to unilaterally halt its operation. The Panel's decision would not only be non-binding, it would be impossible to implement.
>
> [... F]or the Panel to conclude that ICANN could act upon the declaration that [Manwin] seeks, it would not only have to interpret the registry agreement between ICANN and ICM, but review the conduct of a third party (ICM) to determine if that conduct provided a basis for rescission. That is not the province of an IRP Panel.'[671]

ICANN claimed that the requested relief would be impractical:

> 'Finally, the nature of the relief sought by [Manwin] is impractical. ICANN cannot unilaterally do anything about the registry agreement to include price caps or other terms that [Manwin] apparently seeks without potentially breaching a contract. The IRP cannot issue a declaration advising ICANN to breach a contract. If it did, it is highly improbable that ICANN would be able to follow that declaration. And a declaration advising ICANN to renegotiate with ICM would not have any effect on ICM, severely constraining ICANN's bargaining position.'[672]

7. Nature and Value of the IRP Declaration

a. *Binding Nature of the IRP Declaration*

Manwin confirmed that it was in agreement with ICANN and the *ICM Registry* panel that the IRP process was not binding:

> '[T]he IRP process is not binding on ICANN or the Board. Rather, it results only in published declarations and recommendations, which can be accepted or rejected by the Board.'[673],[674]

---

669. ICANN's Response (*Manwin*), §§ 26 and 158.
670. ICANN's Supplemental brief (*Manwin*), p. 16.
671. ICANN's Supplemental brief (*Manwin*), pp. 16–17.
672. ICANN's brief re standing (*Manwin*), p. 24.
673. ICANN Bylaws, Article IV, §3(8).
674. Manwin's brief re standing, p. 10.

Manwin then argued that, because the opinions of the IRP panel were non-binding, it did not matter whether or not ICANN were able to implement the panel's recommendations:

> 'ICANN may choose not or be unable to implement th[e IRP] Panel's decisions. But ICANN and public Internet accountability cannot help but benefit from a thorough airing of its decision-making about the .xxx TLD – the most controversial top level domain name ever approved and broadly decried worldwide as an extortion scheme.'[675]

ICANN stated that the IRP panel had limited authority, and could only issue non-binding declarations:

> 'The IRP was not created to require ICANN to abdicate its decision-making authority to a third party (which it cannot legally do). Accordingly, the Panel's declaration is not binding. However, the Board is mandated to consider the Panel's declaration at the Board's next meeting, where feasible. Further, as a key component of ICANN's accountability commitment to its community, ICANN takes the process quite seriously.'[676]

b. *Precedential Value of IRP Declarations and Preclusive Effect*

Manwin argued that the previous IRP Declaration concerning ICM's application for .xxx did not preclude Manwin from asking ICANN to void the .xxx registry agreement with ICM. There should be no preclusive effect, according to Manwin, because:

- The IRP proceeding is not binding and, as a result, could not possibly interfere with a declaration in a previous IRP:

> 'Because th[e IRP] proceeding is not binding, it could not in any manner interfere with the previous IRP proceeding. Also, because this IRP and the previous one are non-binding, res judicata and collateral estoppel are inapplicable. An arbitration has no preclusive effect unless the parties have agreed it does. [...] Here, ICANN has agreed that the results of an IRP arbitration are not preclusive or binding under any circumstances.'[677]

- The IRP initiated by Manwin related to different issues between different parties. An IRP had effect *inter partes*; not *erga omnes*:

> 'Even if IRP proceedings were generally binding, the previous IRP could have not preclusive effect against [Manwin] here. A binding prior determination has preclusive effect only upon *parties* to the earlier proceeding if the new proceeding concerns the *same issues* or causes of action *actually decided* in the previous proceeding. 'Res judicata precludes parties or their privies from re-litigating a *cause of action* [finally resolved in a prior proceeding].''[678]

- No rule barred the claimants from bringing an IRP:

675. Manwin's Supplemental brief, p. 2.
676. ICANN's Response (*Manwin*), § 44.
677. Manwin's Supplemental brief, pp. 6–7.
678. Manwin's Supplemental brief, p. 7.

> 'This Panel should also permit the IRP because ICANN has adopted no rule barring them under these circumstances. ICANN could have – but did not – adopt specific rules addressing when previous IRPs would preclude or affect later IRPs. The Panel should not adopt a rule which ICANN itself did not.'[679]

> 'Finally, consistent with the different standards and functions of the IRP and lawsuit, no law precludes both from proceeding. Nor does any IRP or other ICANN rule. ICANN could have, but did not, adopt rules barring IRPs under certain circumstances where they might overlap with other actions. There is no reason for this Panel to adopt for ICANN a rule which it did not itself find appropriate, particularly where this IRP can address important Bylaw issues which will not be determined in the lawsuit.'[680]

Manwin also argued that the companion Federal action before the U.S. District Court did not bar Manwin from bringing the IRP:

> 'ICANN argues that [Manwin]'s antitrust suit bars this IRP. It does not. The proceedings are independent, address violations of different standards before different authorized bodies, and may result in different remedies.

> [...] While both the IRP and antitrust lawsuit focus on ICANN's conduct in establishing the .xxx TLD and approving the .xxx TLD registry contract, the two proceedings judge that conduct under different standards. For example, nothing in the antitrust suit will determine whether ICM has violated its Bylaws. More specifically, that suit will not determine whether ICANN violated its Bylaw obligation to adequately consider the objections to the .xxx TLD by governmental bodies and others.'[681]

In ICANN's view, Manwin was seeking 'to have a second IRP initiated for the purpose of second-guessing the declaration of the first IRP Panel and ICANN's decision to follow that Panel's declaration.'[682]

ICANN argued that Manwin's position could not be reconciled with the need for IRP decisions to be considered final:

> '[T]o the extent that [Manwin] persists in challenging ICANN's approval of ICM's application for .xxx, its position cannot be reconciled with the need for finality of IRP decisions.'[683]

It went on to argue that applicable arbitration law dictated that the findings of an IRP are final:

> 'Applicable arbitration law is instructive in this regard. [...] Indeed, as the California Court of Appeal has noted, the ''very essence' of arbitration is finality. Permitting a person to challenge an action or decision that already has been adjudicated by an arbitration panel 'would undermine the legitimacy of the arbitration award itself, and of the arbitration process'. Thus '[d]ecisions of an arbitration panel normally provide the type of finality sought by courts to be protected by collateral estoppel'.

679. Manwin's Supplemental brief, p. 10.
680. Manwin's Supplemental brief, p. 13.
681. Manwin's Supplemental brief, pp. 11-12.
682. ICANN's Response (*Manwin*), § 4.
683. ICANN brief re standing (*Manwin*), p. 1.

> Courts have applied California's strict claim preclusion rules to prevent parties from re-litigating claims that were previously addressed in arbitration, even if the party filing suit was not a party to the prior arbitration proceeding.'[684]

> 'Article 27(1) of the ICDR Rules provides that a tribunal's decision 'shall be final and binding on the parties'. Although the [ICM] IRP Panel made clear that an IRP Panel's ruling is not *binding* in the sense of compelling actions, no one [...] has disputed that an IRP Panel's ruling must be final.

> The distinction between 'final' and 'binding' is well-established. In this context, 'final' refers to whether a Board action can be subject to further IRP review, whereas 'binding' refers to the effect of an IRP declaration on ICANN's freedom to act. The importance of the distinction is that, while ICANN can decline to take action consistent with an IRP Panel's declaration, neither ICANN nor anyone else can petition the prior IRP Panel for reconsideration of its decision or seek review of that decision by another IRP Panel or any other adjudicative body. [...] Given the purpose of an IRP proceeding to bring finality to ICANN's decision-making, a third party is not permitted to second-guess a prior IRP Panel's decision simply by initiating a new IRP.'[685]

In ICANN's view, it made no sense to re-litigate issues which were addressed in a previous IRP case:

> 'Whether labeled as *res judicata*, collateral estoppel, finality of judgments or just common sense, neither [Manwin] nor anyone else has standing to re-litigate issues previously decided by a different IRP Panel. Allowing such claims would render the IRP meaningless and could put ICANN in a position where it must address repeated and inconsistent rulings.'[686]

> '[The ICM] Panel already fully considered and declared that the ICANN Board's *rejection* of ICM's .xxx application in March 2007 was inconsistent with ICANN's Bylaws and Articles of Incorporation. For [Manwin] to now claim that ICANN's *approval* of ICM's .xxx application following the Board's consideration of the Panel's Declaration is a violation of ICANN's Bylaws and Articles of Incorporation is absurd.

> Moreover, allowing [Manwin] to re-litigate ICANN's approval of .xxx would establish a precedent that controversies such as these never end; they could be subject to the second-guessing of subsequent IRP Panels. Indeed, should [Manwin] prevail in this proceeding, and should the ICANN Board somehow decide to block the .xxx TLD – a TLD that already has been implemented on the Internet – under [Manwin]'s interpretation of the rules, nothing would prevent ICM from filing yet another request for IRP proceeding. The process would become an endless loop that would make a farce out of what is otherwise a truly unique method for obtaining review of decisions by a board of directors.'[687]

ICANN also maintained that a prior IRP Declaration has preclusive effect, also for third parties:

> 'In arguing that the prior IRP Panel's decision lacks preclusive effect because [Manwin] was not a party to that IRP and had no privity with ICANN, [Manwin]

684. ICANN's brief re standing (*Manwin*), p. 4.
685. ICANN's Supplementary brief (*Manwin*), pp. 4–5.
686. ICANN's brief re standing (*Manwin*), p. 3.
687. ICANN's Response (*Manwin*), §§ 129–130.

> essentially contends that ICANN's Bylaws cannot be adequately protected by ICANN in the context of an IRP. But the purpose of the IRP is to provide a forum for parties directly affected by an action or decision of the ICANN Board to challenge that action or decision, and to bring finality to the Board's decision. If a non-party to a prior IRP were permitted to initiate a new IRP to attack a result favorable to its adversary, the IRP would become a forum for parties to wage proxy wars against one another [...], without regard to the effect on ICANN or the rest of the Internet community. That result is inconsistent with the IRP's core purposes.'[688]

Finally, ICANN asserted that the *ICM* IRP panel had found that 'any reconsideration' of ICANN's decision to approve the .xxx TLD would violate ICANN's Articles of Incorporation and Bylaws,[689] and that it would be impossible for an IRP panel to reach a decision to the contrary (*i.e.*, to find that ICM's application to operate the .xxx TLD would violate ICANN's Bylaws).[690]

The IRP panel did not discuss the issues relating to the nature of the declaration.

8. Noteworthy Points for Analysis

a. Nature of the IRP Declaration

Both parties' positions in the *Manwin* case are remarkable. First, Manwin agreed that the IRP Declaration would be non-binding, and be primarily for educational purposes, and second, ICANN relied on arbitration law, whereas it has always tried to make a distinction between IRPs and arbitration.

The *Manwin* case may not have reached a decision, but it has had an impact on the IRP rules. After the *Manwin* case, ICANN changed its Bylaws to clarify the standing requirements. It added to the Bylaws:

> 'In order to be materially affected, the person must suffer injury or harm that is directly and causally connected to the Board's alleged violation of the Bylaws or the Articles of Incorporation, and not as a result of third parties acting in line with the Board's action.'

ICANN also added language to the Bylaws to make clear that an IRP declaration and the Board's subsequent action are final and have precedential value. This seems clearly to have been inspired by the *Manwin* case, and ICANN's desire to avoid such cases being brought to IRP in the future.

ICANN also introduced a time bar to avoid a decision being challenged months after its adoption by ICANN. It added a new Article IV(3)(3) to its Bylaws, stipulating that a request for independent review must be filed within thirty days of the posting of the minutes (and the accompanying Board Briefing Materials, if available) of the Board meeting said to demonstrate ICANN's violation of its Bylaws or Articles of

688. ICANN's Supplementary brief (*Manwin*), p. 7.
689. ICANN's brief re standing (*Manwin*), p. 6.
690. ICANN's Supplementary brief (*Manwin*), p. 6.

Incorporation. The Article also provided for the consolidation of multiple requests. It appears that ICANN wanted to indicate that cases such as Manwin's should be brought in a timely fashion and that cases which deal essentially with the same facts must be consolidated.

Quite remarkably, ICANN did not add a clause to its Bylaws making it explicit that IRP claimants are not entitled to affirmative relief.

Nonetheless, we believe that the changes made to ICANN's Bylaws will not prevent a case such as *Manwin* being brought to IRP in the future (provided it is initiated in time). The *Manwin* case concerned the implementation of the IRP Declaration in the *ICM Registry* case, and the requested relief was not necessarily incompatible with the panel's declaration in the *ICM Registry* case. ICANN was offered some leeway in the implementation of the IRP Declaration (*supra*).

ICANN misrepresented the facts when it stated that the *ICM Registry* panel found that '*any* reconsideration' of its decision to approve the .xxx TLD would violate ICANN's Articles of Incorporation and Bylaws.[691] The *ICM Registry* Panel only referred to the Board's reconsideration of whether ICM met the sponsorship criteria. However, if ICANN believes that the panel found that *any* reconsideration of the decision to approve the .xxx TLD would have violated ICANN's Articles of Incorporation and Bylaws, this could be interpreted as a recognition by ICANN that TLD applicants are entitled to full legal certainty, and that there is no room for reconsideration for political reasons or on the basis of GAC Advice.

C. THE BOOKING.COM CASE (.HOTELS/.HOTEIS)

1. Key Notes

- IRP under the new set of applicable rules.
- Confirmation that the string similarity process lacked certain elements with regard to *transparency* and *fairness.*
- Confirmation that the standard of review is an objective one, requiring the appraisal of the Board's conduct independently, and without any presumption of correctness.
- Incorrect application of the time-bar rule, which was introduced only after the application window had closed.
- ICANN was the prevailing party but the panel found partially in favor of the Claimant (on cost allocation).
- Claimant Booking.com was found to have contributed to the public interest.
- ICANN was encouraged to consider whether, notwithstanding the result of the string similarity review of .hotels and .hoteis, approval of both of Booking-

691. ICANN's brief re standing (*Manwin*), p. 6.

.com's and Despegar's proposed strings would in fact be in the best interest of the Internet community; ICANN refused to consider this.
- hotels was delegated to Booking.com following a successful public auction.
- Booking.com paid USD 2,200,000 in the auction.
- Auction proceeds went to ICANN.

2. Introduction

The *Booking.com* case[692] is of central importance in any discussion concerning IRPs, and in particular regarding the disparate treatment of applicants. Although the IRP panel failed to address certain key issues, and the final ICANN board decision that was taken in response to the IRP declaration raises many concerns, several interesting points were discussed. These included the remit of a panel's authority, time-bar issues, standard of review, and the question of a party's essential rights and obligations.

Despite not really addressing the merits of the case, it is worth noting that the IRP panel considered that the nature and significance of the issues raised by Booking.com, and the contribution to the 'public interest' of its submissions, made it appropriate and reasonable for the IRP costs be shared equally by the parties, thus expressing their disapproval of ICANN's approach.

3. Case Background

Booking.com is a Dutch company, and is the premier online accommodation reservation service, facilitating bookings with almost half a million hotels and other accommodation providers worldwide.

In 2012, Booking.com made an application to ICANN for the generic top level domain (gTLD) .hotels. Around the same time, another applicant made a similar application for the gTLD .hoteis. Hoteis is the Portuguese word for hotels.

Pursuant to the ICANN Guidebook, all applications are subject to an initial evaluation.[693] As part of this process, .hotels and .hoteis underwent string similarity review. This process was conducted by a String Similarity Panel (SSP) selected, appointed and instructed by ICANN. On 26 February 2013, ICANN notified Booking.com that, because .hotels was, in the SSP's view, 'confusingly similar' to .hoteis, it had been placed in a contention set with the application for .hoteis. When prospective gTLDs are placed in a contention set, the applicants must determine between themselves which gTLD is to be permitted to proceed; where no agreement is reached the applicants must bid against each other in an auction.

692. We acted on behalf of the claimant Booking.com in this case.
693. For more information on the initial evaluation process, *see* Chapter 2.C.3.b(1) and ICANN, *New gTLD Applicant Guidebook 4 June 2012*, https://newgtlds.icann.org/en/applicants/agb/guidebook-full-04jun12-en.pdf, Modules 1-8 to 1-10 and Module 2.

On 28 March 2013, Booking.com requested that ICANN produce documents relating to the standard used to determine whether gTLDs are 'confusingly similar', and how that determination had been made in this specific instance. On the same day, Booking.com also filed a formal RfR of the decision which placed .hotels and .hoteis in a contention set.

Initially, ICANN stated that, because the SSP was independent, many of the documents Booking.com had requested were not under ICANN's control. Subsequently, ICANN released a generalized document entitled 'String Similarity New gTLD Evaluation Panel – Process Description.' In September 2013, ICANN's Board denied Booking.com's RfR.

Booking.com sought to resolve the dispute amicably in a CEP. When no resolution was forthcoming, Booking.com initiated an IRP seeking to overturn ICANN's decision to place the .hotels application in a contention set.

On the merits, Booking.com claimed that despite ICANN's finding to the contrary there was no confusing similarity between the strings .hotels and .hoteis. Booking.com argued that ICANN should not have placed the respective applications for these strings in a contention set, and that both applications should be allowed to proceed in the application program.

4. Points of Procedure

a. *Arguments Discussed*

(1) Applicable Procedural Rules

ICANN argued that its Bylaws, the IRP Supplementary Procedures and the ICDR Rules apply, and that the Supplementary Procedures take precedence over the ICDR Rules. ICANN did not discuss the order of precedence between ICANN's Bylaws and the Supplementary Procedures, but mentioned the Bylaws first:

> 'ICANN's Bylaws and the Supplementary Procedures that the ICDR has adopted specially for IRP proceedings, apply here.'[694]

> 'Absent a governing provision in ICANN's Bylaws or the ICDR's Supplemental Procedures, the ICDR Rules apply. But in the event of any inconsistency between the Supplementary Procedures and the ICDR's Rules, the Supplementary Procedures shall govern.'[695]

The IRP panel ruled that the following procedural rules apply:

- ICDR Rules (version of 1June 2009).
- ICDR Supplementary Rules for IRP.
- Bylaws (version of 11 April 2013).

694. ICANN's Response (*Booking.com*), § 25.
695. ICANN's Response (*Booking.com*), § 25, n. 32.

(2) Jurisdiction of the IRP Panel

Booking.com argued that the IRP panel's core obligation as part of an independent review consisted of 'declaring whether or not ICANN acted consistent with its Articles and Bylaws' by accepting the SSP's view and refusing to submit it to a substantive review.[696]

ICANN stated that the IRP panel is charged with reviewing ICANN Board actions for consistency with the Articles of Incorporation and Bylaws:

> 'This Independent Review Process Panel ('IRP Panel') is 'charged with comparing contested actions of the [ICANN] Board to the [ICANN] Articles of Incorporation and Bylaws, and with declaring whether the Board has acted consistently with the provisions of those Articles of Incorporation and Bylaws.''[697]

However, it stressed that the sole purpose of an IRP is to focus on the actions of the ICANN Board; not the actions of ICANN staff or third parties:

> 'The sole purpose of an IRP is to focus on the actions of the ICANN Board; it is not available as a mechanism to challenge the conduct of ICANN staff or third parties such as the third-party evaluators in the context of the New gTLD Program. Because the selection of the SSP was the decision of ICANN staff – and not the ICANN Board – Booking.com has failed to challenge any Board conduct appropriately subject to an IRP.'[698]

ICANN submitted that a '[d]emonstrated adherence to approved and documented processes cannot provide a basis for an IRP under ICANN's Bylaws.'[699]

The IRP panel confirmed that it may review actions and inactions of the ICANN Board:

> 'Lest there be any misunderstanding as regards the proper subject matter of IRP proceedings or the role of the Panel, we note that, as was clearly established during the hearing, it is common ground between the parties that the term 'action' (or 'actions') as used in Article IV, Section 3 of the Bylaws is to be understood as action(s) *or inaction(s)* by the ICANN Board. The Panel observes that this understanding comports not only with the provisions of Article IV, Section 2 of the Bylaws concerning 'Reconsideration', which expressly refer to 'actions or inactions of the ICANN Board', but with the clear intent of Section 3 itself, which stipulates at sub-section 11 that 'the IRP Panel shall have the authority to: ... (c) declare whether an action or inaction of the Board was inconsistent with the Articles of Incorporation or Bylaws.'[700]

696. Booking.com's Request for IPR, § 41.
697. ICANN's Response (*Booking.com*), § 2.
698. ICANN's Sur-Reply (*Booking.com*), § 23; *see also* ICANN's Response (*Booking.com*), §§ 3 and 9.
699. ICANN's Response (*Booking.com*), § 38.
700. Booking.com IRP Declaration, § 53.

(3) Nomination, Appointment, Removal and Replacement of Panelists

Booking.com requested that the panel be composed of three members. As ICANN had not established the omnibus standing panel described in the Bylaws and no alternative appointment procedure was in place, Booking.com suggested that each party appoint one panelist, after which the two appointed panelists could jointly select the Chairman of the panel.[701]

ICANN agreed with the appointment procedure that was proposed by Booking.com. The party-appointed panelists were nominated consecutively (Booking.com communicated its panelist first) not simultaneously. However, since the *Vistaprint* case, most claimants have favored a simultaneous nomination of panelists.

(4) Standing

Booking.com stated that it had suffered direct harm as a result of the ICANN Board's violations of the Articles of Incorporation and Bylaws, as ICANN's decision generated additional and unnecessary costs for Booking.com:

> 'This does not change the fact that Booking.com has suffered direct harm as a result of the ICANN Board's violations of its Articles of Incorporation and Bylaws. The result of that violation is that .hotels and .hoteis have been put in a contention set. Without the requested relief, Booking.com can only resolve the contention set through private negotiations with the applicant for .hoteis or through an auction. The first option is of no use, unless Booking.com is willing to buy out the applicant for .hoteis – a direct competitor of Booking.com. The second option would similarly end in a payment, to ICANN, the entity that created the contention set. Both options will generate additional and unnecessary costs for Booking.com while offering no guarantee that Booking.com will obtain the .hotels gTLD.'[702]

ICANN claimed that the IRP is only available to persons materially affected by a decision or action of the ICANN Board; not by the actions of ICANN staff or third parties:

> 'ICANN's Bylaws provide that the Independent Review Process is only available to persons 'materially affected by a decision or action of the [ICANN] Board that he or she asserts is inconsistent with the Articles of Incorporation or Bylaws.' The IRP is thus limited to challenging ICANN Board conduct, and is not available as a means to challenge the conduct of third parties, or even conduct of ICANN staff. Because the determination that .hotels and .hoteis are visually similar and properly included in a contention set was the decision of the independent String Similarity Panel – and not the ICANN Board – Booking.com has failed to challenge any Board conduct appropriately subject to the Independent Review Process.'[703]

ICANN argued, therefore, that Booking.com's IRP Request was misplaced, because it did not challenge an ICANN Board action:

701. Booking.com's Request for IRP, § 76.
702. Booking.com's Reply, § 43.
703. ICANN's Response (*Booking.com*), § 32.

> 'Booking.com's IRP Request is therefore misplaced because it challenges an action of an independent, third-party expert evaluator rather than an action of the ICANN Board.'[704]

The IRP panel accepted that Booking.com was challenging a Board action, and, as explained under Chapter 5.C.4.a(2) above, considered that the subject matter of IRP proceedings and the role of the panel covered both actions and inactions of the ICANN Board.[705] Moreover, the IRP panel defined the Applicant Guidebook as 'the crystallization of Board-approved consensus policy concerning the introduction of new gTLDs.'[706] As a result, the IRP panel agreed with Booking.com that it had standing to bring its case.

(5) Time Bar

Booking.com argued that it could not be prevented from challenging the unlawful implementation of a policy, regardless of the policy's age:

> 'It is of no relevance whether there was a debate regarding the legality of new legislation (or an ICANN policy) prior to its adoption, since such a debate could not prevent an entity that is subject to an illicit enforcement action from challenging the (unlawful) implementation of the policy in individual cases. In other words, Booking.com cannot be prevented from challenging the (unlawful) implementation of the Applicant Guidebook in the context of its .hotels application.
>
> The point is all the stronger here, since Booking.com never benefited from an initial window of opportunity during which it could challenge the legislation or policy. It was effectively barred from challenging the Applicant Guidebook at the time of its adoption by the fact that it could not – at that time – show any injury or harm. Furthermore, any challenge at that time risked causing substantial harm to Booking.com as it would have revealed its plans to apply for a new gTLD.'[707]

ICANN stated that the Bylaws require IRP Requests to be filed within thirty days of the publication of materials demonstrating the alleged violation:

> '(ICANN's Bylaws), at Art. IV, § 3.3 (requiring that IRP Requests be filed within 30 days of the publication of materials demonstrating the alleged violation).'[708]

It then argued that, as a result of this, Booking.com was time-barred from challenging the Guidebook, as the Guidebook was adopted over two years previously:

> 'However, neither the Bylaws nor the Articles require ICANN to reconsider the outcome of the Guidebook development process, a process that was started many years ago and completed over two years ago (and one for which the time for challenge has long since past).'[709]

---

704. ICANN's Sur-Reply (*Booking.com*), § 31.
705. Booking.com IRP Declaration, § 53.
706. Booking.com IRP Declaration, § 54.
707. Booking.com's post-hearing submission, email of 13 December 2014.
708. ICANN's Sur-Reply (*Booking.com*), § 24, n. 29.
709. ICANN's Sur-Reply (*Booking.com*), § 43.

The IRP panel found that an IRP must be initiated within thirty days of the establishment of the challenged process and that Booking.com should have objected at the time the Guidebook was first implemented:

> 'We add that we agree with ICANN that the time has long since passed for Booking.com or any other interested party to ask an IRP panel to review the actions of the ICANN Board in relation to the establishment of the string similarity review process, including Booking.com's claims that specific elements of the process and the Board decisions to implement those elements are inconsistent with ICANN's Articles and Bylaws. Any such claims, even if they had any merit, are long since time-barred by the 30-day limitation period set out in Article IV, Section 3(3) of the Bylaws. As ICANN expressed during the hearing, if Booking.com believed that there were problems with the Guidebook, it should have objected at the time the Guidebook was first implemented.'[710]

As we will comment below, the thirty-day limitation period was only introduced on 11 April 2013, *i.e.*, long after the new gTLD application window closed.[711] This important regulatory aspect was not properly taken into account during the discussions.

(6) Written/Oral Arguments

Booking.com requested a hearing, preferably in person. However, Booking.com did not insist on an in-person hearing, and the parties mutually agreed to organize a telephone hearing.

(7) Witnesses and Expert Witnesses

Booking.com submitted an expert report by Prof. Dr. Piet Desmet[712] to show that .hotels and .hoteis cannot be considered confusingly similar. It also submitted a second report to show that the delegation of both .hotels and .hoteis would not include any risks to any of the applicants and would even be beneficial to ICANN's mission and purpose.

(8) Costs

Booking.com argued that it should be awarded its costs in the IRP proceeding.

ICANN did not comment.

---

710. Booking.com IRP Declaration, § 129.
711. The application window closed on 30 May 2012 (*see* Akram Atallah, *New gTLD update*, 30 May 2012, https://newgtlds.icann.org/en/announcements-and-media/announcement-3-30may12-en).
712. Prof. Dr. Piet Desmet is Professor of Applied Linguistics at the KU Leuven University, Belgium.

The IRP panel decided that half the costs of the IRP provider should be allocated to ICANN (the prevailing party) in view of the extraordinary circumstances of the case (*i.e.*, the nature and significance of the issues raised by Booking.com and its contribution to the public interest):

> 'Article IV, Section 3(18) [...] of the Bylaws also states that 'in an extraordinary case the IRP Panel may in its declaration allocate up to half of the costs of the IRP Provider to the prevailing party based upon the circumstances, including a consideration of the reasonableness of the parties' positions and their contribution to the public interest. Each party to the IRP proceedings shall bear its own expenses.'
>
> [...T]he Panel considers that the nature and significance of the issues raised by Booking.com, and the contribution to the 'public interest' of its submissions, are such that it is appropriate and reasonable that the IRP costs be shared equally by the parties. We consider that the extraordinary circumstances of case - in which some members of ICANN's New gTLD Program Committee have publicly declared that, in their view, the rules on the basis of which Booking.com's claims fail should be reconsidered by ICANN - warrants such a holding.'[713]

b. *Noteworthy Points for Analysis*

Some elements of fact and certain claims made by Booking.com were arguably incorrectly summarized in the panel's description of the hearing. For example, the panel remarked that Booking.com was largely silent during the hearing on the subject of discrimination. This was a surprising observation, as discrimination was a core argument raised by Booking.com.

The panel also wrongly stated that Booking.com had emphasized that it did not challenge the validity or fairness of the process as set out in the Guidebook and that it acknowledged that the established process had been followed.[714] The panel failed to make the distinction between the establishment of the policy and its implementation. Booking.com argued that although the process as described in the Guidebook was not in itself necessarily flawed and unfair (because it left sufficient freedom for a fair and correct implementation), it had in fact not been implemented in a fair and correct manner.

When asked whether the process, as implemented, followed the process as described in the Guidebook, Booking.com's answer was that it followed the letter of the process, but not its spirit. This was because the process was described in vague terms that allowed for it to be implemented either in compliance with ICANN's fundamental obligations or in violation with ICANN's obligations. Needless to say, only the former is acceptable.

713. Booking.com IRP Declaration, §§ 149–152.
714. Booking.com IRP Declaration, § 70.

(1) Applicable Procedural Rules

In our opinion, the panel erred in ruling (without any reservation) that the Bylaws of 11 April 2013 applied to the procedure. The panel did not discuss the fact that changes to the Bylaws were introduced only after the new gTLD application window closed and after the dispute following the determination by the SSP in February 2013 had arisen.

(2) Jurisdiction of the IRP Panel

The IRP panel made a well-reasoned decision in finding that it was able to review both actions and inactions of the ICANN Board.

(3) Standing

It is significant that the panel did not reject the central premise of Booking.com's claim, namely that there was no significant risk of users being confused in the event of both .hotels and .hoteis being delegated as gTLDs. Rather, by allowing the IRP to continue, the panel implied that there was sufficient merit in this argument. In any event, the panel did not deny that Booking.com made a *prima facie* case on the merits, and the panel went on to analyze the arguments advanced by Booking.com.

(4) Time Bar

The IRP panel disregarded the fact that when ICANN adopted the Applicant Guidebook and when interested parties submitted their new gTLD applications in 2012, there was no time limit for bringing a request for IRP. Thus, prospective applicants, who considered that they risked being materially affected by ICANN's application of the Guidebook in contravention of the Articles of Incorporation and/or Bylaws, could legitimately expect to be allowed to challenge the Guidebook as well as ICANN's implementation thereof.

ICANN's decision to introduce a time bar for challenging Board decisions was introduced on 11 April 2013, *i.e.*, long after the new gTLD application window closed.[715] As a result, the time bar ought to apply to decisions taken after 11 April 2013 only.

Moreover, the panel did not draw the distinction between the adoption of the general principles and their subsequent implementation. According to case law of the U.S. Supreme Court, a policy's age or the age of an implementing regulation cannot be used as an excuse for clear inconsistency with fundamental legal principles.[716] So even if a

715. Compare Article IV(3)(3) of the previous ICANN Bylaws with Article IV(3)(3) of the amended ICANN Bylaws of 11 April 2013.
716. *See e.g.*, *Brown v. Gardner*, 513 U.S. 115, 122 (1994); *Rapanos v. United States*, 547 U.S. 715, 752 (2006).

statute of limitations is imposed on challenges to a specific policy, it should not prevent anyone affected by the application of the policy from challenging that application on the grounds that the policy conflicts with a more fundamental legal principle.[717]

(5) Witnesses and Expert Witnesses

The IRP panel largely disregarded Booking.com's expert evidence. Indeed, the Panel did not focus on the merits of the case, but struggled with the remit of its authority.

(6) Costs

The IRP panel's finding that ICANN was to bear half of the costs, despite being the prevailing party, is a clear indication of the panel's disagreement with ICANN's approach to string similarity review.

5. Applicable Law

a. Arguments Discussed

(1) Sources

Booking.com argued that the applicable law for the proceedings is contained in ICANN's Articles of Incorporation and Bylaws, which must be interpreted in light of the fact that ICANN is subject to both local and international law and must act in compliance with general principles of international law.[718]

It further argued that the IRP panel must consider any ICANN policies relevant to the dispute, including the policies set out in the New AGB.[719]

ICANN did not comment.

The IRP panel listed the same applicable sources of law as provided by Booking.com, and underlined that ICANN had to carry out its activities 'in conformity with relevant principles of international law and applicable international conventions.'[720] In its discussion of the applicable standard of review, the IRP panel stressed the international character of ICANN's mission and the applicability of principles of international law.[721]

717. *Weaver v. Federal Motor Carrier Safety Admin.*, 744 F. 3d 142, 145 (D.C. Cir. 2014).
718. Booking.com's Request for IRP, § 39.
719. Booking.com's Request for IRP, § 42.
720. Booking.com IRP Declaration, § 52.
721. Booking.com IRP Declaration, §§ 112–113.

(2) Essential Rights and Obligations

Booking.com argued that ICANN must act in *good faith*, and that this implied an obligation to ensure procedural fairness:

> 'The principle of good faith includes an obligation to ensure procedural fairness by, *inter alia*, adhering to substantive and procedural rules, avoiding arbitrary action, and recognizing legitimate expectations.'[722]

Booking.com also argued that ICANN must safeguard *due process* rights, giving applicants the right to be heard and providing them with reasoned decision-making:

> 'ICANN's obligation to safeguard due process rights covers the right to be heard by an independent and impartial adjudicator. [...] ICANN's use of faceless evaluators and its failure to disclose the criteria that were used is a blatant violation of Booking.com's right to due process.'[723]
>
> 'The requirement to document each decision is not a surprising one. Without a well-documented rationale based on a clearly established methodology, there is no basis on which decisions can be evaluated and, where appropriate, challenged. Providing such a rationale constitutes an essential due process requirement. [... T]he requirement to state reasons forms part of ICANN's general obligations and applies regardless of whether or not it is mentioned in a policy or guidebook.'[724]

Booking.com argued that ICANN must apply policies *neutrally, fairly and without discrimination*:[725]

> 'Even if a published policy or process were to explicitly derogate from fundamental due process rights (which is not the case here), ICANN could not implement that policy or process without violating its Articles of Incorporation and Bylaws.'[726]

It also pointed out that ICANN must guarantee *openness* in its decision-making:

> 'The core elements of transparency include clarity of procedures, the publication and notification of guidelines and applicable rules, and the duty to provide reasons for actions taken. The coupling of the terms '*open*' and '*transparent*', and a consideration of the context within which the term has been included, confirms that ICANN intended the term to also denote the most developed dimension of transparency, namely openness in decision-making.'[727]

ICANN argued that it was only necessary for it to adhere to established policies and processes:

> 'The fact that ICANN, following years of inclusive policy development and implementation planning, ultimately did not include a requirement that ICANN publish the rationale for the String Similarity Panel's individual determinations

722. Booking.com's Request for IRP, § 44.
723. Booking.com's Reply, §§ 26–27.
724. Booking.com's Reply, § 28.
725. Booking.com's Request for IRP, § 45.
726. Booking.com's Reply, § 41.
727. Booking.com's Request for IRP, § 50.

> does not mean that ICANN acted inconsistent with its Bylaws or Articles of Incorporation. Indeed, there is no established policy or process that requires ICANN to take such action.'[728]

ICANN argued in particular that gTLD applicants were not entitled to procedural *due process*:

> 'There is no provision in ICANN's Bylaws, Articles, or Guidebook that specifically affords any gTLD applicant a right to procedural 'due process' similar to that which is afforded in courts of law. Nevertheless, because ICANN does conduct its activities in the public interest, ICANN does provide more opportunity for parties to be heard and to dispute actions taken than most private entities, including the extensive accountability mechanisms that are set forth in the Bylaws (such as the right to file a reconsideration request and the right to file an Independent Review proceeding such as this one). There is no 'due process' right to have some other form of remedy available when an applicant disagrees with the determination of an evaluation panel and, rights of 'due process' are not normally available in a corporate setting. The due process clause in the U.S. Constitution 'protects individual rights only from *government* action, not from *private* action.' ICANN's approval and administration of the New gTLD Program is a private action, not that of a state actor.'[729]

As regards *fairness*, ICANN maintained that Booking.com had no legally protected interest and was not entitled to procedural due process:

> 'Because Booking.com has not been deprived of a legally protected interest, its invocation of alleged procedural 'due process' rights fails as a matter of substantive law and also fails to identify conduct of ICANN's Board that violated either the Bylaws or the Articles.'[730]

Furthermore, ICANN argued that the ICANN Board is not required to supervise or to control the quality of expert panel determinations:

> '[T]here is no provision in the Bylaws or Articles that requires the ICANN Board to supervise or perform a quality control review of expert panel determinations.'[731]

It stated that there is no process to allow for the substantive review of expert panel determinations:

> 'The Guidebook does not provide for any process by which ICANN (or anyone else) may conduct a substantive review of ICC's results. The only 'review' of ICC's results that was ever contemplated is procedural, in the form of a quality assurance review over a random sampling of applications to test whether the process referenced above was followed.'[732]

As a result, it argued, the ICANN Board was entitled to accept an expert panel determination without a substantive review:

728. ICANN's Response (*Booking.com*), § 37.
729. ICANN's Sur-Reply (*Booking.com*), § 18.
730. ICANN's Sur-Reply (*Booking.com*), § 19.
731. ICANN's Sur-Reply (*Booking.com*), § 35.
732. ICANN's Response (*Booking.com*), § 17.

> 'Accordingly, Booking.com's claim that the ICANN Board violated its Bylaws by 'accepting' the SSP's determination on .hotels/.hoteis without a substantive review is wrong. The ICANN Board took no action – and was not required to take any action – with respect to evaluating or accepting the SSP's determination because the Guidebook does not call for the Board to take any such action. Nor is any such action required by any Bylaws or Articles provision. Accordingly, it cannot be a violation of ICANN's Bylaws or Articles for the Board not to conduct a 'quality control' review of the SSP's determination. Because there is no Board action or decision associated with the SSP's determination, there is nothing for the IRP Panel to review.'[733]

Regarding *openness*, ICANN argued that it was under no obligation to publish the evaluation panel's methodology:

> 'Nowhere in the Guidebook is there a requirement that the SSP's methodology for performing String Similarity Review be published before the SSP commenced its evaluation process.'[734]

It also denied any obligation to publish the rationale for the evaluators' determinations:

> 'Nowhere in the Guidebook is there a requirement that the rationale for the determination(s) rendered by the independent third-party evaluators be published.'[735]

The IRP panel commented that the string similarity process lacked certain elements with regard to *transparency* and certain practices that are widely associated with the requirements of *fairness*:

> 'The Panel is not unsympathetic to Booking.com's complaints regarding the string similarity review process as established by the Guidebook. There is no question but that that process lacks certain elements of transparency and certain practices that are widely associated with requirements of fairness. For example, the Guidebook provides no means for applicants to provide evidence or make submissions to the SSP (or any other ICANN body) and so be fully 'heard' on the substantive question of the similarity of their applied-for gTLD strings to others.'[736]

However, the IRP panel found that the fact that an established process had been followed was a fundamental obstacle to Booking.com's case:

> 'However, the fundamental obstacle to Booking.com's case is that *the established process was followed* in all respects.'[737]

The panel did not consider that the ICANN Board had blindly accepted a decision of a subordinate body; rather, it felt that the Board had been thoughtful in its consideration of Booking.com's request, even if the reconsideration process was in itself perhaps limited and imperfect:

733. ICANN's Sur-Reply (*Booking.com*), § 38.
734. ICANN's Sur-Reply (*Booking.com*), § 29.
735. ICANN's Response (*Booking.com*), § 35.
736. Booking.com IRP Declaration, § 117.
737. Booking.com IRP Declaration, § 132.

> 'The Panel is struck by the extent and thoughtfulness not only of the NGPC's consideration of the issue,[738] certain aspects of which are discussed above, but of the BGC's detailed analysis and its Recommendation to the NGPC, on the basis of which Booking.com's Request for Reconsideration was denied. Contrary to Booking.com's allegations, in neither instance was this merely a blind acceptance of a decision of a subordinate body. In fact, the reconsideration process itself, however limited and perhaps imperfect it may be, is inconsistent with Booking.com's claims of lack of 'due process'.'[739]

(3) Standard of Review

Booking.com submitted that the standard of review is non-deferential, and that a restrictive interpretation of the standard of review would be inappropriate:

> 'In its Response to the Request for IRP, ICANN submits that its "Bylaws specify that a deferential standard of review be applied when evaluating the actions of the ICANN Board". This is simply wrong. No such specification is made in ICANN's Bylaws or elsewhere, and a restrictive interpretation of the standard of review would be inappropriate. It would fail to ensure accountability on the part of ICANN and would be incompatible with ICANN's commitment to maintain (and improve) robust mechanisms for accountability, as required by Article 9.1 of ICANN's Affirmation of Commitments [...] and ICANN's core values, which require ICANN to "remain accountable to the Internet community through mechanisms that enhance ICANN's effectiveness".'[740]

ICANN argued that IRP panels must apply a deferential standard of review:

> 'ICANN's Bylaws specify that a deferential standard of review be applied when evaluating the actions of the ICANN Board, and the rules are clear that the appointed IRP Panel is neither asked to, nor allowed to, substitute its judgment for that of the Board.'[741]

The IRP panel held that the standard of review is an objective one, requiring the appraisal of the Board's conduct independently, and without any presumption of correctness:

> 'Nevertheless, this does not mean that the IRP Panel may only review ICANN Board actions or inactions under the deferential standard advocated by ICANN in these proceedings. Rather, as explained below, the IRP Panel is charged with 'objectively' determining whether or not the Board's actions are in fact consistent with the Articles, Bylaws and Guidebook, which the Panel understands as requiring that the Board's conduct be appraised independently, and without any presumption of correctness.'[742]

---

738. The New gTLD Program Committee was established by the Board at its 10 April 2012 meeting.
739. Booking.com IRP Declaration, § 134.
740. Booking.com's Reply, § 6.
741. ICANN's Response (*Booking.com*), § 24.
742. Booking.com IRP Declaration, § 111.

b. Noteworthy Points for Analysis

(1) Essential Rights and Obligations

It might have been expected that once the IRP panel had recognized deficiencies in the process, it would have taken a firmer stance with ICANN.

However, in ruling that ICANN's adherence to an established process formed a fundamental obstacle to IRP review, the panel seems effectively to have accepted that ICANN could by-pass its essential obligations by adopting a generalized policy that could then be implemented arbitrarily.

(2) Standard of Review

The IRP panel's findings on the standard of review are important. They serve as strong support for the argument that the defined standard of review in ICANN's latest Bylaws is not exhaustive.

The *Booking.com* panel's view on this has also been accepted by panels in more recent cases.[743]

6. Authority of the Panel

a. Arguments Discussed

Booking.com suggested that a claimant be entitled to such relief as that would put an end to the inconsistency of ICANN's decision with the Articles of Incorporation and Bylaws:

> 'Any relief ordered must be sufficient to avoid another unfair, arbitrary and discriminatory decision. Any other outcome would leave ICANN in ongoing violation of the fundamental principles that bind it[. ...] The only way in which ICANN can act in accordance with its Articles of Incorporation and Bylaws is to reject the determination that .hotels and .hoteis are confusingly similar and to dissolve the resulting contention set.'[744]

ICANN argued that the IRP panel has no authority to grant affirmative relief, on the basis that its authority is limited to issuing opinions as to whether an action or inaction of the Board was inconsistent with the Articles of Incorporation or Bylaws and recommending interim actions or the stay of any action or decision:

> 'Booking.com's request for affirmative relief goes well beyond the IRP Panel's authority. An IRP Panel is limited to issuing its opinion as to 'whether an action or inaction of the Board was inconsistent with the Articles of Incorporation or Bylaws' and 'recommend[ing]' that the Board stay any action or decision or take

743. *See* DCA Final IRP Declaration, § 65; Vistaprint IRP Declaration, §§ 12–126.
744. Booking.com's Reply, § 45.

any interim action until such time as the Board reviews and acts upon the opinion of the IRP Panel. This IRP Panel does not have the authority to grant affirmative relief or to require ICANN to undertake specific conduct.'[745]

ICANN also argued that the IRP panel may not perform a substantive review of an evaluation panel's decision:

> 'Under ICANN's Bylaws, however, an IRP Panel does not have the authority to perform a substantive review of the String Similarity Panel's decision (even if the String Similarity Panel's conduct was deemed to be that of ICANN staff). The IRP Panel is only 'charged with comparing contested actions of the [ICANN] Board to the [ICANN] Articles of Incorporation and Bylaws, and with declaring whether the Board has acted consistently with the provisions of those Articles of Incorporation and Bylaws.' The IRP Panel is not tasked with determining whether the String Similarity Panel's decision to include .hotels and .hoteis in a contention set was wrong, and the IRP is not available as a mechanism to re-try the decisions of independent evaluation panels.'[746]

ICANN insisted that Booking.com's request to the IRP panel to act beyond its authority could not be harmonized with the language of the Bylaws:

> 'Booking.com urges the IRP Panel to act beyond its authority as established in ICANN's Bylaws. There is no way to harmonize Booking.com's position with the language of the Bylaws because the Bylaws make clear that this Panel does not have the discretion to modify or ignore the Bylaws.'[747]

The IRP panel considered the role of the IRP panel to be limited to assessing whether the applicable rules were followed; not whether such rules are appropriate or advisable:

> '[O]ur role in this IRP includes assessing whether the applicable rules — in this case, the rules regarding string similarity review — were followed, not whether such rules are appropriate or advisable.'[748]

The IRP panel did not consider itself entitled to substitute its judgment for that of the ICANN Board, nor to appraise the policies and procedures established by ICANN:

> 'That being said, we also agree with ICANN to the extent that, in determining the consistency of Board action with the Articles, Bylaws and Guidebook, an 'IRP Panel is neither asked to, nor allowed to, substitute its judgment for that of the Board.' In other words, it is not for the Panel to opine on whether the Board could have acted differently than it did; rather, our role is to assess whether the Board's action was consistent with applicable rules found in the Articles, Bylaws and Guidebook. Nor, as stated, is it for us to purport to appraise the policies and procedures established by ICANN in the Guidebook (since, again, this IRP is not a challenge to those policies and procedures themselves), but merely to apply them to the facts.'[749]

745. ICANN's Sur-Reply (*Booking.com*), § 46; *see also* ICANN's Response (*Booking.com*), § 56.
746. ICANN's Response (*Booking.com*), § 47.
747. ICANN's Sur-Reply (*Booking.com*), § 48.
748. Booking.com IRP Declaration, § 110.
749. Booking.com IRP Declaration, § 115.

> '[T]he fact is that the sort of mechanisms that Booking.com asserts are required (and which those NGPC members believe should be required) are simply not part of the string similarity review process as currently established. As to whether they *should* be, it is not our place to express an opinion, though we note that such additional mechanisms surely would be consistent with the principles of transparency and fairness.'[750]

The IRP panel believed itself able to recommend a course of action for ICANN to consider:

> 'However, we can — and we do — acknowledge certain legitimate concerns regarding the string similarity review process raised by Booking.com, discussed above, which are evidently shared by a number of prominent and experienced ICANN NGPC members. And we can, and do, encourage ICANN to consider whether it wishes to address these issues in an appropriate manner and forum, for example, when drafting the Guidebook for round two of the New gTLD Program or, more immediately, in the exercise of its authority under Section 5.1 (Module 5-4) of the Guidebook (which it may choose to exercise at any time, in its discretion) to consider whether, notwithstanding the result of the string similarity review of .hotels and .hoteis, approval of both of Booking.com's and Despegar's proposed strings would be in the best interest of the Internet community.'[751]

b. *Noteworthy Points for Analysis*

We disagree with the panel that it did not have the requisite authority to review the ICANN decision beyond its consistency with the relevant ICANN instruments. In our view, the panel was empowered to review the conformity of ICANN's processes in the context of the fundamental principles included in the relevant instruments and the wider legal framework. It remains unclear on what legal basis the panel considered that it was not empowered to perform this review. The panel based its reasoning on the time bar which ICANN had introduced only after the adoption of the process in question – a process about which the panel said there was 'no question but that that process lacks certain elements of transparency and certain practices that are widely associated with requirements of fairness.'[752] As explained above, the panel's reasoning on the time bar is flawed,[753] and the continued implementation of a process which is demonstrably non-transparent and unfair would, in our view, qualify as a violation of the Articles of Incorporation and Bylaws.

We believe that it is open to an IRP panel to issue a declaration that an ICANN action or inaction is inconsistent with the Articles of Incorporation or Bylaws, and a declaration that upholding a specific action or inaction would be a continued violation of the Articles of Incorporation and Bylaws. In such circumstances, the IRP panel's declaration would effectively grant affirmative relief.

750. Booking.com IRP Declaration, § 128.
751. Booking.com IRP Declaration, § 154.
752. Booking.com IRP Declaration, § 117.
753. *Supra*, Chapter 5.C.4.a(5) and Chapter 5.C.4.b(4).

Instead, in the *Booking.com* case, the panel opted to encourage ICANN to reconsider its decision on the basis that there were certain legitimate concerns regarding the string similarity review process. In view of the circumstances, the panel decided that each party should bear one-half of the costs. This serves as an indication that the panel wanted ICANN to reconsider its position and to use its authority to introduce fairness.

7. Nature and Value of the IRP Declaration

a. *Arguments Discussed*

Booking.com argued that IRP Declarations are binding:

> 'Since ICANN's amendment of its Bylaws on 11 April 2013, IRP declarations have precedential value [...]. The precedential value – and binding force – of IRP declarations was recently confirmed in an IRP Panel declaration that itself has precedential effect. It follows that the IRP declaration requested in this case by Booking.com would be binding upon ICANN. Any other outcome would effectively grant ICANN arbitrary and unlimited power. It would make ICANN virtually untouchable, something which was never intended and it would be incompatible with ICANN's obligation to maintain and improve robust mechanisms for accountability [...].
>
> Nor can Booking.com be considered to have waived the rights that ICANN has violated. An applicant cannot waive judicial remedies in relation to its fundamental rights. In particular, a party cannot waive its right to be heard, or to be dealt with fairly and in a non-discriminatory manner.'[754]

ICANN argued that the IRP is a specific form of dispute resolution, which is non-binding:

> 'The Independent Review Process ('IRP') is not a form of traditional dispute resolution (*i.e.*, mediation or arbitration), and is a non-binding process in which entities that deal with ICANN can have a further check-and-balance with respect to specific decisions of the ICANN Board, and specifically, whether the Board's actions are consistent with ICANN's Bylaws and Articles of Incorporation.'[755]

It suggested that the IRP declaration was non-binding because the ICANN Board was not permitted to outsource its decision-making authority:

> 'The IRP Panel's declaration is not binding because the Board is not permitted to outsource its decision-making authority. The Board will, of course, give serious consideration to the IRP Panel's declaration and, 'where feasible,' shall consider the IRP Panel's declaration at the Board's next meeting.'[756]

ICANN further argued that the plain language of the IRP provisions in ICANN's Bylaws, and their drafting history, make clear that IRP declarations are not binding on ICANN:

> 'Booking.com also incorrectly views ICANN's Bylaws as granting the IRP Panel authority to issue a declaration that would be 'binding' on ICANN. The plain

754. Booking.com's Reply, §§ 11–12.
755. ICANN's Response (*Booking.com*), § 23.
756. ICANN's Response (*Booking.com*), § 26.

> language of the IRP provisions set forth in Article IV, Section 3 of ICANN's Bylaws, as well as the drafting history of the development of the IRP provisions, make clear that IRP Panel declarations are not binding on ICANN. There is no ambiguity on this issue. In fact, the first ever IRP Panel constituted under ICANN's Bylaws recognized the proper scope and authority of an IRP panel when it correctly stated: 'The holdings of the Independent Review Panel are advisory in nature; they do not constitute a binding arbitral award.' *ICM* IRP Panel declaration.'[757]

The panel did not address the issue of the binding nature of IRP declarations. But the panel did consider the issue of precedential value, ruling that it was in no way bound by the IRP declaration in the *ICM Registry* case.[758]

b. *Noteworthy Points for Analysis*

It should be noted that the panel did not explain why it considered it was in no way bound by the IRP declaration in the *ICM Registry* case. Although we agree with the conclusion, it may be for very different reasons. At the time of the *ICM Registry* case, there was no provision in the ICANN Bylaws or elsewhere establishing that IRP declarations had precedential value. The rule that IRP declarations are final and have precedential value was introduced in ICANN's Bylaws on 11 April 2013. This rule cannot apply retroactively to IRP declarations issued before that date. As a result, the *ICM Registry* case does not create precedential value, simply because the legal basis was lacking at the date of the decision and there are no indications that the introduction of the rule in 2013 was merely an interpretative measure. The panel was thus stating the obvious in finding that it is in no way bound by the IRP declaration in the *ICM Registry* case.

Another question is why the panel explicitly ruled on the issue of precedential value (in particular in view of the fact that it was not asked to do so by the parties). A possible explanation is that the panel only looked into the latest version of ICANN's Bylaws, and that it was not aware of the fact that the rule of precedential effect did not yet exist at the time of the *ICM Registry* case. The panel's findings on the time bar shows that the panel did not pay much attention to the historical context of the applicable framework.[759] As a result, in making explicit mention of the fact that it did not consider itself bound by a previous IRP declaration, the panel showed that it considered the precedential value of IRP declarations to be persuasive rather than binding.

757. ICANN's Sur-Reply (*Booking.com*), § 49, n. 70.
758. Booking.com IRP Declaration, § 113.
759. *Supra* Chapter 5.C.4.a(5).

8. ICANN Board's Decision Following the IRP Declaration

Following the IRP declaration, the ICANN board issued a new decision on 26 April 2015, wherein it declined to reconsider its point of view.[760] A new RfR, filed jointly thereafter by Booking.com and Travel Reservations (formerly Despegar)[761] had no impact.

9. Analysis of ICANN's Final Decision

When making its decision of 26 April 2015, it is possible that the ICANN Board may not have been fully informed for the following reasons:

- The ICANN Board did not address the fact that in the IRP Declaration the panel had encouraged the Board to consider whether approval of both the .hotels and .hoteis strings would be in the best interests of the Internet community.
- At most, the ICANN Board addressed the outcome of the Declaration in the context of a review of the New gTLD Program for future rounds of new gTLD applications.
- It is not known if the ICANN Board was made aware that Booking.com had offered to engage in discussions with the ICANN Board, and, as it turned out, that Travel Reservations had accepted an invitation to participate in those discussions.
- It is also not known if the ICANN Board was made aware of the flaws in the IRP panel's reasoning on the time bar issue.

Another point of concern is the fact that it was the full ICANN Board that reconsidered the issue, rather than the New gTLD Program Committee (NGPC). The purpose of establishing the NGPC was to create a committee that excluded Board members with perceived, potential or actual conflicts of interest with respect to the New gTLD Program. ICANN puts its decision-making on IRPs at risk if it allows potential conflicts of interest to arise by allowing the entire Board to rule on an IRP involving a new gTLD application.

The ICANN Board recognized as a problem the fact that applicants were not given an opportunity to be heard fully on the substantive question of the similarity between their applied-for gTLD strings and other gTLD strings. However, the ICANN Board took no action to correct this obvious lack of due process with respect to Booking.com.

As the ICANN Board decided to take action only for future rounds, the ICANN Board effectively upheld the unfair and non-transparent treatment of Booking.com. We are of the opinion that, in doing so, the Board allowed disparate treatment of Booking.com as compared to other applicants, both in the third and future gTLD rounds.

---

760. ICANN, *Approved Board Resolutions 2015.04.26.14 – 2015.04.26.16 – Regular Meeting of the ICANN Board*, 26 April 2015, https://www.icann.org/resources/board-material/resolutions-2015-04-26-en.
761. The other party concerned by the String Similarity Panel evaluation.

10. What Happened Thereafter?

On 13 May 2015, Booking.com and Travel Reservations filed an RfR with ICANN, asking the ICANN Board to bring its string similarity review process in line with ICANN's Articles of Incorporation and Bylaws, not only for the future but also for the current new gTLD round.[762] Although the IRP panel had explicitly encouraged the ICANN Board to consider whether approval of both of Booking.com's and Travel Reservations' proposed strings would in fact be in the best interest of the Internet community, the ICANN Board refused to consider this recommendation. In their RfR, and in a letter to the ICANN Board, Booking.com and Travel Reservations explicitly asked the ICANN Board to consider the recommendation.[763]

When some Board members (finally) started a discussion on the IRP panel's suggestion, the discussion was cut short by a Board member who 'clarified that consideration of the IRP panel's suggestion is beyond the scope of the reconsideration request before the Board.'[764] However, the ICANN Board's failure to consider the IRP panel's suggestion was precisely what the reconsideration request was about. Booking.com and Travel Reservations considered that the ICANN Board's inaction on the IRP panel's suggestion created disparate treatment, and thus violated ICANN's Articles of Incorporation and Bylaws.[765] However, during the Board's discussion, ICANN's then President and CEO reduced the issue before the Board to the question of 'whether the Board violated its Bylaws or Articles of Incorporation by accepting the Booking.com Final Declaration.'[766] However, the request by Booking.com and Travel Reservations was not aimed at challenging the Board's acceptance of the IRP declaration; it mainly challenged the Board's inaction on the IRP panel's recommendation.

We do not know whether this oversimplification of the matter by some of ICANN's Board members was deliberate or whether it amounted to a lack of care. However, it is worthy of note that a majority of ICANN's Board members refused to reconsider, and thoroughly review, the decision to put the applications for .hotels and .hoteis in a contention set, a decision which was based on unreasoned advice. The point is all the stronger in view of: (i) the fact that the Board was given a reasoned expert report

762. Request for Reconsideration 15-7 by Booking.com B.V. and Travel Reservations SRL, 13 May 2015, https://www.icann.org/en/system/files/files/reconsideration-request-15-7-booking-bv-travel-reservations-srl-annexes-13mar15-en.pdf.
763. Letter on behalf of Booking.com and Travel Reservations to the ICANN Board of 16 July 2015, https://www.icann.org/en/system/files/correspondence/booking-bv-travel-reservations-srl-to-icann-board-redacted-16jul15-en.pdf.
764. ICANN, *Minutes – Special Meeting of the ICANN Board*, 28 July 2015, https://www.icann.org/resources/board-material/minutes-2015-07-28-en.
765. Request for Reconsideration 15-7 by Booking.com B.V. and Travel Reservations SRL, 13 May 2015, https://www.icann.org/en/system/files/files/reconsideration-request-15-7-booking-bv-travel-reservations-srl-annexes-13mar15-en.pdf, pp. 5–6; Letter on behalf of Booking.com and Travel Reservations to the ICANN Board of 16 July 2015, https://www.icann.org/en/system/files/correspondence/booking-bv-travel-reservations-srl-to-icann-board-redacted-16jul15-en.pdf.
766. ICANN, *Minutes – Special Meeting of the ICANN Board*, 28 July 2015, https://www.icann.org/resources/board-material/minutes-2015-07-28-en.

stating that there was no reason why .hotels and .hoteis should not co-exist, (ii) various ICANN Board members had openly declared that they found the process unfair and could see no reason why .hotels and .hoteis should not co-exist, and (iii) the only parties that were truly concerned by the underlying issue saw no reason for .hotels and .hoteis not to co-exist.

The interested parties did not take further legal action against the Board's refusal to reconsider its decision on confusing string similarity between .hotels and .hoteis. The ICANN-created string contention was finally resolved in an auction, in which Booking.com paid USD 2,200,000 to ICANN to acquire the right to operate the .hotels gTLD. Travel Reservations' application for .hoteis was denied.

D. THE DCA TRUST CASE (.AFRICA)

1. Key Notes

- IRP under the new set of applicable rules.
- With express reference to the *Booking.com* case, confirmation that the standard of review is a *de novo objective and independent* accountability process.
- Claimant DotConnectAfrica Trust (DCA) Trust was the prevailing party.
- Relevance only from a procedural point of view; no proof of material harm, which is why ICANN could have questioned Claimant's standing.

2. Introduction

As will become apparent from the case background description, and from our analysis of the question regarding standing, it is unclear why this case was started and why the claim was not dismissed in the early stages of the IRP.[767] One of the elementary conditions required when initiating an IRP is that the claimant show harm suffered as a result of the ICANN decision. In this case, DCA applied for a geographic gTLD string for which it needed the support of the relevant authorities. However, despite its claims to the contrary, DCA lacked this basic support for the geographic name TLD in question. This indisputable element of fact undermined the claimant's credibility in the application process as well as in the IRP. Although DCA prevailed in this case, it is our view that the IRP should never have been initiated in the first place. It is a puzzle why ICANN did not make this point, and argue that DCA could not prove material harm and hence had no standing to initiate the IRP. In any event, we believe the importance of this case to be limited.

Moreover, the *Booking.com* case had already addressed the key notes that were raised in the *DCA* case. The main value of the *DCA Trust* case is that it confirmed the findings of the Booking.com IRP Declaration regarding the applicable standard of review.

767. We were not involved as counsel for either party in this case.

3. Case Background

In 2009, DCA launched the idea of applying for the geographic name TLD '.africa'. An application for a geographic name TLD can only be successful if the applicant shows the necessary support or non-objection by the relevant authorities. In 2009, DCA had asked for and received the support of the African Union Commission (AUC). However, in 2010, the AUC organized a Request For Proposal (RFP) process for the application and operation of the .africa TLD, and purportedly no longer supported individual initiatives for the .africa TLD application. DCA did not participate in the AUC's RFP process, and submitted its gTLD application in 2012 together with the endorsement letter of the AUC, which it had received in 2009. Another applicant, ZACR, also applied for .africa with the support of the AUC.

It is worth reminding that DCA's application was originally formulated as an application for .dotafrica much to the amusement of the sector. DCA claimed that this was a mistake and ICANN ultimately allowed this blunder to be corrected, an initiative that it may have regretted greatly at a later stage.[768]

DCA's application for .africa passed the initial evaluation on the technical and financial criteria, and evaluation of whether or not it had the necessary support of the relevant authorities began. The Geographic Names Panel (GNP) was charged with this evaluation.

In the meantime, the GAC, upon instigation of the AUC, reached a consensus and advised on 11 April 2013 that DCA's application for .africa should not be approved.[769]

On 4 June 2013, the ICANN Board passed a resolution in which it accepted the GAC consensus advice not to accept DCA's application.[770]

DCA challenged this resolution and asked the Board to reconsider its position. According to DCA there was in fact no consensus among GAC members, as DCA believed that the representative from Kenya would have objected to the advice. DCA also claimed that two ICANN Board Members had a conflict of interest at the time that the ICANN Board passed the resolution accepting the GAC Advice,[771] and that ICANN's Board failed to ensure that its staff and ICANN's constituent bodies were in compliance with ICANN's fundamental obligations.

---

768. See the application update history for application ID 1-1165-42560 at https://gtldresult.icann.org/application-result/applicationstatus/applicationchangehistory/1276.
769. Governmental Advisory Committee, *GAC Communiqué – Beijing, People's Republic of China*, 11 April 2013, https://gacweb.icann.org/display/gacweb/GAC+Announcement+Archive?preview=/27132037/30900359/Beijing%20Communique%20april2013_Final.pdf.
770. ICANN Board, *Approved Resolution 2013.06.04.NG01 – Meeting of the New gTLD Program Committee*, 4 June 2013, https://www.icann.org/resources/board-material/resolutions-new-gtld-2013-06-04-en.
771. Namely, DCA alleged that one of ICANN Board members was the treasurer and director of the ccTLD co.za, which has long been administered by UniForum, and that he was also a member of the Board of Directors of the South African Domain Names Authority which had supported the establishment of the competing applicant for .africa, South African (.za) Central Registry, a part of UniForum. Another Board Member was alleged to have been the CEO of a company

ICANN claimed that the resolution was warranted, in part because DCA's application did not have the necessary support for operating a geographic TLD.

4. Points of Procedure

a. *Arguments Discussed*

(1) Applicable Procedural Rules

DCA argued that the 'IRP is constituted under Article IV, Section 3 of ICANN's Bylaws. It is governed by two complementary sets of procedural rules, the International Dispute Resolution Procedures (the 'ICDR Rules') and ICANN's Supplementary Procedures for ICANN IRP,'[772] and that the ICDR Rules govern '[w]here there is no conflict or where the Supplementary Procedures are silent.'[773]

It argued that ICANN had made a standing offer to applicants that it would agree to be bound by the terms of the ICDR Arbitration Rules as modified by the Supplementary Procedures, and that DCA had accepted this standing offer when it initiated the IRP proceedings.[774]

DCA also argued that the IRP panel 'has the discretion to determine that the IRP is final and binding', (*see also* Nature of the IRP Declaration below) and that it 'may conduct the arbitration in *whatever manner it considers appropriate,* provided that the parties are treated with equality and that each party has the right to be heard and is given a fair opportunity to present its case.'[775]

ICANN agreed that '[t]he ICDR Rules, as supplemented by ICANN's Bylaws and Supplementary Procedures that the ICDR has adopted specially for IRP proceedings, apply here.'[776]

However, ICANN claimed that the ICDR Rules are subordinate to the Bylaws and Supplementary Procedures:

> '[W]hile ICANN has approved the use of the ICDR Rules, it has been clear that those rules are subordinate to the Bylaws and the Supplementary Procedures.'[777]

The IRP panel ruled that '[n]othing in the Supplementary Procedures either expressly or implicitly conflicts with or overrides the general and broad powers that Articles 16 [now contained in Article 20] and 36 [now contained in Article 39] of the ICDR Rules

affiliated to a company that provided consulting services with respect to the establishment of the South African (.za) Central Registry. *See* DCA Request for IRP, § 24.

772. DCA Submission on Procedural Issues, § 2.
773. DCA Submission on Procedural Issues, § 3.
774. DCA Submission on Procedural Issues, § 3.
775. DCA's Response to the Panel's questions on procedural issues, § 2.
776. ICANN's Response (*DCA*), § 26.
777. ICANN's 1st Memorandum re procedure (*DCA*), § 13.

confer upon the Panel to interpret and determine the manner in which the proceedings are to be conducted and to assure that each party is given a fair opportunity to present its case.'[778]

(2) Jurisdiction of the IRP Panel

DCA submitted that the IRP panel is competent to examine both actions and inactions of the ICANN Board, and that its remit also includes a review of ICANN Staff actions:

> 'ICANN Staff operates at the behest and direction of the Board. [...] ICANN Staff only does what they are directed to do or what they believe they can do if they do not have specific direction and are, therefore, part of the overall accountability through the mechanism of the IRP examining the actions or inaction of the Board and, thereby, ICANN and its constituent organizations.'[779]

ICANN insisted that the IRP panel is 'charged with comparing contested actions of the [ICANN] Board to the [ICANN] Articles of Incorporation and Bylaws, and with declaring whether the Board has acted consistently with the provisions of those Articles of Incorporation and Bylaws.'[780]

ICANN also argued that 'the issues in [the DCA] case are in fact extremely limited in scope. This panel is authorized only to address whether ICANN violated its Bylaws or Articles of Incorporation *in its handling of DCA's Application for .AFRICA*.'[781]

ICANN submitted that 'ICANN's Bylaws do not permit an IRP Panel to review the conduct of the GAC.'[782]

It also maintained that 'actions of ICANN staff are not reviewable in any Independent Review proceeding – ICANN's Bylaws explicitly restrict the scope of an Independent Review to actions of the ICANN Board (or NGPC acting on behalf of the Board).'[783]

Finally, it argued that 'the evaluation of ZACR's application did not involve any action by ICANN's Board (or NGPC), and is therefore not a proper basis for Independent Review.'[784]

The panel noted that '[t]he avenues of accountability for applicants that have disputes with ICANN do *not* include resort to the courts' as '[a]pplications for gTLD delegations are governed by ICANN's Guidebook, which provides that applicants waive all right to resort to the courts.'[785]

---

778. DCA Panel's Declaration on the IRP Procedure, § 50; *see also* DCA 3rd Declaration on the IRP Procedure, § 20.
779. *DCA Trust v. ICANN*, Hearing Transcripts, p. 496-497.
780. ICANN's Response to IRP (*DCA*), §§ 2 and 24; *see also* ICANN's 2nd Memorandum re procedure (*DCA*), § 2.
781. ICANN's 1st Memorandum re procedure (*DCA*), § 27.
782. ICANN's Response re merits (*DCA*), §§ 8 and 36.
783. ICANN's Response re merits (*DCA*), § 10.
784. ICANN's Response re merits (*DCA*), § 47.
785. DCA Panel's Declaration on the IRP Procedure, § 39.

It concluded that, 'assuming that the foregoing waiver of any and all judicial remedies is valid and enforceable, the ultimate 'accountability' remedy for applicants is the IRP.'[786]

(3) Nomination, Appointment, Removal and Replacement of Panelists

The appointment of panelists did not proceed smoothly in the *DCA Trust* case. ICANN complained that DCA had 'delayed the IRP proceedings by proposing a slow panelist selection process. DCA did not confirm that it was requesting a three-member panel (as opposed to a single panelist) to consider its request for independent review until early January [2014]. Soon thereafter, ICANN requested that DCA's selection of its party-appointed panelist occur "as soon as possible." With absolutely no sense of urgency, DCA instead opted to wait until the very end of January to make its initial appointment.'[787] During the course of the proceedings, the ICANN-appointed panelist passed away and was replaced. On 26 February 2015, ICANN requested the newly constituted panel to rehear the proceedings and to reconsider its decision to organize a hearing with live testimony of witnesses. On 24 March 2015, the IRP panel refused to reconsider its position, and the proceedings continued as scheduled.

(4) Written/Oral Arguments

The parties agreed that a hearing on the merits was appropriate. DCA indicated that it would agree to a video hearing, in the interest of saving time and minimizing costs.[788] Whether to organize an in-person or a video hearing was left to the discretion of the panel.

ICANN agreed that the IRP was 'one in which a telephonic or video conference would be helpful and offered to facilitate a video conference', but it did not believe that the IRP was 'sufficiently 'extraordinary' so as to justify an in-person hearing, which would dramatically increase the costs for the parties.'[789]

(5) Witnesses and Expert Witnesses

DCA argued that witnesses would need to be examined:

> 'As ICANN observes, in the event of an in-person or telephonic hearing, witness statements must be provided in advance and the hearings 'shall be' limited to 'argument only' [...] This provision does not expressly prohibit cross-examination of witnesses, however, or their questioning by the Panel. Indeed, it would be highly improper for a party to be allowed to submit witness testimony that could not then subsequently be tested, whether by opposing counsel or the Panelists. It

786. DCA Panel's Declaration on the IRP Procedure, § 40.
787. ICANN's Memorial on Interim measures (*DCA*), § 11.
788. DCA Submission on Procedural Issues, § 63.
789. ICANN's 1st Memorandum re procedure (*DCA*), § 36.

> seems impossible and implausible that this is what ICANN intended or what any Panel could allow. Untested witness testimony is ultimately not worth the paper on which it is written.'[790]

DCA pointed out that ICANN's Bylaws and Supplementary Procedures were ambiguous, as they do not expressly exclude cross-examination,[791] and that the panel had the authority to examine witnesses at the hearing, as it was entitled to conduct the arbitration in whatever manner it considered appropriate.[792]

In addition, DCA submitted that ICANN had produced witness testimony that 'purports to rely on secret documents that have not been provided', and that it was therefore important for the witness testimony 'to be fully tested by the Panel, if not by the parties.'[793]

DCA argued that the IRP panel has the power to order document production:

> '[T]he ICDR Guidelines for Arbitrators on Exchanges of Information – which apply to all proceedings commenced after 31 May 2008 – confirm that the IRP Panel has the power to order document production in this proceeding.'[794]

It argued that a claimant was entitled to adduce additional evidence to rebut ICANN's defenses:

> '[T]he Supplementary Procedures provide that [...] '[a]ll necessary evidence should' be included with the claimant's initial written submission. The use of the word 'should,' and not 'shall,' confirms that it is desirable but not required that all necessary evidence be included with the Notice of IRP [...]. Thus, nothing precludes the claimant from adducing additional evidence to rebut ICANN's defences, as DCA intends to do.'[795]

Finally, DCA argued that general principles of equality, fairness and due process weighed heavily in favor of allowing document production:

> 'General principles of equality, fairness and due process weigh heavily in favor of allowing document production, particularly where the parties do not have the ability to cross-examine witnesses and test the evidence presented against them. Document production is also important because critical information potentially dispositive of the outcome of these proceedings lies in ICANN's possession, custody and control.'[796]

ICANN argued that live witness testimony was prohibited:

> 'Both the Supplementary Procedures and ICANN's Bylaws unequivocally and unambiguously prohibit live witness testimony in conjunction with any IRP.'[797]

790. Letter from DCA of 20 April 2014, 2-3.
791. DCA Submission on Procedural Issues, § 64.
792. DCA Submission on Procedural Issues, § 65.
793. DCA Submission on Procedural Issues, § 66.
794. Letter from DCA of 17 April 2014., p. 4.
795. Letter from DCA of 20 April 2014, 2; *see also* DCA Submission on Procedural Issues, § 58.
796. DCA Submission on Procedural Issues, § 68.
797. ICANN's 1st Memorandum re procedure (*DCA*), § 15.

It claimed that 'the Panel *does not have discretion* to order live witness testimony in the face of the Bylaws' and Supplementary Procedures' clear and unambiguous prohibition of such testimony.'[798]

Furthermore, it claimed that, even if the IRP 'were a formal 'arbitration', ICANN would be entitled to limit the nature of these proceedings so as to preclude live witness testimony. The fact that this proceeding is not an arbitration further reconfirms ICANN's right to establish the rules that govern these proceedings.'[799]

On this point, ICANN relied on a ruling by the U.S. Supreme Court:

> 'The U.S. Supreme Court has explicitly held that the right to tailor unique procedural rules includes the right to dispense with certain procedures common in civil trials, including the right to cross-examine witnesses', with reference to *Mitsubishi Motors Corp. v. Soler Chrysler-Plymouth*, 473 U.S. 614, 648 n. 14 (1985).[800]

ICANN suggested that DCA, in arguing that the panel has the discretion to conduct live witness examination, 'urges the IRP Panel to apply the ICDR Rules in a manner that directly contradicts ICANN's Bylaws and the Supplementary Procedures; there is **no way** to harmonize DCA's position with the language of the Bylaws and Supplementary Procedures. [... T]he Panel simply does not have the discretion to modify or ignore the Supplementary Procedures.'[801]

ICANN argued that its witness testimony should be allowed; that 'parties are free to argue to the IRP Panel that witness testimony should be viewed in light of the fact that the rules do not permit cross-examination.'[802]

The IRP panel did then agree to allow the witness testimony. After this decision, ICANN asked that the panel send written questions to the witnesses before the hearing, and informed the panel that it would not make available its witnesses during the hearing.[803] However, ICANN was asked to reconsider its position, and ultimately it did make two of its witnesses available for examination during the hearing (Cherine Chalaby, Chair of the NGPC at the time, and Heather Dryden, Chair of the GAC at the time).

ICANN recognized that an IRP panel may order document production within the parameters set forth in the ICDR Guidelines, but objected to any attempts by DCA to propound broad discovery.[804]

ICANN had argued before that all evidence had to be part of the initial written submission:

798. ICANN's 1st Memorandum re procedure (*DCA*), § 18.
799. ICANN's 1st Memorandum re procedure (*DCA*), § 22.
800. ICANN's 1st Memorandum re procedure (*DCA*), § 20.
801. ICANN's 2nd Memorandum re procedure (*DCA*), § 18.
802. ICANN's 1st Memorandum re procedure (*DCA*), § 23.
803. Letter from ICANN of 8 April 2015.
804. ICANN's 1st Memorandum re procedure (*DCA*), § 30.

> 'A party does have the right, pursuant to the ICDR Guidelines for Arbitrators on Exchanges of Information, to request that a panel call for the production of documents. However, those documents must be 'reasonably believed to exist and to be relevant and material to the outcome of the case,' and requests must contain 'a description of specific documents or classes of documents, along with an explanation of their materiality to the outcome of the case.' [...] The ICDR rules plainly do not entitle DCA to proceed with a vague 'fishing expedition' request for any and all documents that DCA somehow believes would 'clarify the factual issues in dispute.'
>
> It should also be noted that ICANN's Supplementary Procedures explicitly state that that (sic) '*[a]ll necessary evidence* to demonstrate that the requestor's claims that ICANN violated its Bylaws or Articles of Incorporation should be part of the [initial written] submission'.'[805]

The IRP panel ruled that '[w]hile the Supplementary Procedures appear to limit both telephonic and in-person hearings to 'argument only', [...] this approach is fundamentally inconsistent with the requirements in ICANN's Bylaws for accountability and for decision making with objectivity and fairness.'[806]

It ruled it permissible for both parties at the hearing to challenge and test the veracity of statements made by witnesses.[807]

The panel found that the limitations on the conduct of hearings in ICANN's Bylaws unduly and improperly restrict the ability of an IRP panel to conduct the independent review it has been explicitly mandated to carry out in the manner it considers appropriate:

> 'Panel finds that this last sentence in Paragraph 12 of ICANN's Bylaws, unduly and improperly restricts the Panel's ability to conduct the "independent review" it has been explicitly mandated to carryout [*sic*] in Paragraph 4 of Section 3 in the manner it considers appropriate.
>
> How can a Panel compare contested actions of the Board and declare whether or not they are consistent with the provisions of the Articles of Incorporation and Bylaws, without the ability to fact find and make enquiries concerning those actions in the manner it considers appropriate?
>
> How can the Panel for example, determine, if the Board acted without conflict of interest, exercised due diligence and care in having a reasonable amount of facts in front of it, or exercised independent judgment in taking decisions, if the Panel can not [*sic*] ask the questions it needs to, in the manner it needs to or considers fair, just and appropriate in the circumstances?
>
> How can the Panel ensure that the parties to this IRP are treated with equality and that each party has the right to be heard and is given a fair opportunity to present its case with respect to the mandate the Panel has been given, if as ICANN submits, 'ICANN's Bylaws do not permit any examination of witnesses by the parties or the Panel during the hearing'?

805. ICANN's letter of 20 April 2014, p. 3; *see also* ICANN's 1st Memorandum re procedure (*DCA*), §§ 28-29.
806. DCA Panel's IRP Declaration on the IRP Procedure, § 84; *see also* DCA 2nd Declaration on IRP Procedure, § 19.
807. DCA Panel's IRP Declaration on the IRP Procedure, § 86.

> The Panel is unanimously of the view that it cannot. The Panel is also of the view that any attempt by ICANN in this case to prevent it from carrying out its independent review of ICANN Board's actions in the manner that the Panel considers appropriate under the circumstances deprives the accountability and review process set out in the Bylaws of any meaning.'[808]

It was noted that the parties agreed that there would be no cross-examination of any of the witnesses.[809]

The witnesses were required to be present and the panel noted that it would draw the necessary inferences from a witness's failure to appear at the hearing without a valid reason.[810]

Concerning document production, the panel ordered a reasonable documentary exchange, and invited the parties to agree on the documentary exchange process.[811]

The order was made on consideration that:

- 'Denying document production would be especially unfair in the circumstances of th[e] case given ICANN's reliance on internal confidential documents [...].'[812]
- 'ICANN's espoused goals of accountability and transparency would be disserved by a regime that truncates the usual and traditional means of developing and presenting a claim.'

The panel also ruled that 'while it is possible [...] that the drafters of the Supplementary Procedures may have desired to preclude the introduction of additional evidence not submitted with an initial statement of claim, [...] such a result would be inconsistent with ICANN's core values and the Panel's obligation to treat the parties fairly and afford both sides a reasonable opportunity to present their case.'

b. *Noteworthy Points for Analysis*

(1) Standing

Curiously enough, the argument of lack of standing was not raised by ICANN.

However, DCA was clearly not in a position to ask for a final resolution of the dispute. DCA could not benefit from a positive evaluation by the GNP, and DCA had lost the opportunity to show the necessary support from relevant authorities for its new gTLD application.

This suggests that DCA was not in a position to show any harm as a result of the alleged ICANN's violation of its Articles of Incorporation and Bylaws.

808. DCA 3rd Declaration on the IRP Procedure, §§ 22–26.
809. DCA 3rd Declaration on the IRP Procedure, § 34.
810. DCA 3rd Declaration on the IRP Procedure, § 37.
811. DCA Panel's IRP Declaration on the IRP Procedure, § 60.
812. DCA Panel's IRP Declaration on the IRP Procedure, § 59.

On this basis, ICANN could have argued that DCA had no standing: DCA's application had no chance of success. If it had not been for the Board's action accepting the GAC Advice, DCA's application would anyway have been refused because it lacked the necessary support to apply for a geographic TLD.

ICANN did not raise any standing arguments. It is quite remarkable that ICANN based its refusal of DCA's application on the controversial GAC Advice, and that it did not allow the GNP's evaluation procedure to conclude; DCA could never have been successful following the GNP's review.

5. Applicable Law

a. Arguments Discussed

(1) Sources

DCA argued that 'ICANN is subject to international and local law, and is required to achieve its mission in conformity with the principles expressly espoused in its Bylaws and Articles of Incorporation, including transparency, fairness, accountability, and promotion of competition with respect to the Internet's domain name system.'[813]

DCA noted that '[t]he merits of the dispute are governed by ICANN's Bylaws and Articles of Incorporation, the AGB, and international and local law, as provided in Article 4 of ICANN's Articles of Incorporation.'[814]

It then added that '[t]he version of ICANN's Articles of Incorporation and its Bylaws in effect at the time DCA filed its Request for IRP applies to these proceedings. ICANN's agreement with the DoC, National Telecommunications & Information Administration ('NTIA'), the 'Affirmation of Commitments,' is also instructive, as it explains ICANN's obligations in light of its role as regulator of the Domain Name System ('DNS').'[815]

In short, DCA submitted that '[a]ll of the obligations enumerated in these documents are to be carried out *first* in conformity with 'relevant principles of international law' and *second* in conformity with local law. As explained by Dr. Jack Goldsmith in his Expert Report submitted in *ICM v. ICANN*, the reference to 'principles of international law' in ICANN's Articles of Incorporation should be understood to include both customary international law and general principles of law.'[816]

ICANN left the issue of compliance with international and local law unaddressed and focused on compliance with its processes, as reflected in its Articles of Incorporation and Bylaws.

813. DCA Request for IRP, § 12; *see also* § 42.
814. DCA Submission on Procedural Issues, § 3.
815. DCA's Memorial on the Merits, § 30.
816. DCA's Memorial on the Merits, § 31.

The IRP panel found that ICANN had violated its Articles of Incorporation and Bylaws, and decided that it was unnecessary 'to determine who was right, to what extent and for what reasons in respect to [...] other criticisms and other alleged shortcomings of the ICANN Board identified by DCA Trust.' In other words, the IRP panel found it unnecessary to refer to any principles of international or local law, as ICANN's violation of its Articles of Incorporation and Bylaws was sufficiently clear without having to refer to general principles of law.

(2) Essential Rights and Obligations

DCA noted that ICANN had promised new gTLD applicants that it would evaluate their applications according to the Guidebook, Bylaws and Articles of Incorporation:

> 'ICANN's promise is not just evaluate the application according to the Applicant Guidebook, but to evaluate the application according to the Guidebook, the Bylaws and the Articles of Incorporation, everything that they reflect and incorporate and the promise that is thereby made to parties that are seeking to participate in the domain name system which ICANN is responsible for.'[817]

In particular, DCA claimed that ICANN had not acted in *good faith*, as it instructed the AUC how to play the new gTLD application process by becoming a voting member of the GAC:

> 'ICANN instructed the AUC – which was not a member of the GAC at the time – on how to use ICANN's objection procedures and GAC advice mechanism to 'play a prominent role in determining the outcome of any application' for .AFRICA. ICANN expressly informed the AUC that it could use the GAC 'to raise concerns that an applicant is seen as potentially sensitive or problematic, or provide direct advice to the Board'.'[818]
>
> 'ICANN's instructions to the AUC as to how to bypass ICANN's own rules for reserving names for special use breached the AGB by facilitating the AUC's avoidance of the AGB evaluation procedure and by treating the gTLD .AFRICA as a ccTLD, enabling the AUC to benefit from special treatment. In addition, ICANN's instructions violated ICANN's Articles of Incorporation and Bylaws by effecting an inequitable and inaccurate application of ICANN's AGB policies.'[819]

DCA argued that ICANN had failed to exercise *good faith* and *due diligence* in the evaluation of the GAC Advice:

> 'ICANN had a duty under principles of international law to exercise good faith and due diligence in evaluating the GAC advice rather than accepting it wholesale and without question, despite having notice of the irregular manner in which the advice was rendered. Importantly, ICANN was well aware that the AUC was using the GAC to effectively reserve .AFRICA for itself, pursuant to ICANN's own advice that it should use the GAC for that purpose and contrary to the New gTLD Program objective of enhancing competition for TLDs. The AUC's very presence on the GAC as a member rather than an observer demonstrates the extraordinary lengths

817. *DCA Trust v. ICANN*, Hearing Transcripts, p. 488.
818. DCA's Memorial on the merits, § 39.
819. DCA's Memorial on the merits, § 40.

> ICANN took to ensure that the AUC was able to reserve .AFRICA for its own use notwithstanding the new gTLD application process then underway.'[820]

DCA maintained that the ICANN Board had failed to exercise the necessary *due diligence and care* 'by giving excessive deference to the GAC advice produced thanks to the efforts of DCA's competitor, the AUC', and that the GAC was given a decision-making role instead of an advisory role.[821]

It argued that the ICANN Board had failed to exercise the necessary *due diligence and care* in accepting the BGC's recommendation to reject DCA's request to the Board that it reverse its decision rejecting DCA's application for .africa:

> 'Finally, the Board did not exercise due diligence and care in accepting the BGC's recommendation, because the BGC recommendation essentially proffered the NGPC's inadequate diligence in accepting the GAC Objection Advice in the first place, in order to absolve the NGPC of the responsibility to look into any of DCA's grievances in the context of the Request for Review. The basis for the BGC's recommendation to deny was that DCA did not state proper grounds for reconsideration, because failure to follow correct procedure is not a ground for reconsideration, and DCA did not identify the actual information an independent expert would have provided, had the NGPC consulted one. Thus, the BGC essentially found that the NGPC did not fail to take account of material information, because the NGPC did not have before it the material information that would have been provided by an independent expert's viewpoint. The BGC even claimed that if DCA had wanted the NGPC to exercise due diligence and consult an independent expert, DCA should have made such a suggestion in its Response to the GAC Objection Advice. Applicants should not have to remind the Board to comply with its Bylaws in order for the Board to exercise due diligence and care.'[822]

DCA argued that ICANN must make decisions by applying documented policies *neutrally and objectively*, with *integrity* and *fairness*.[823]

It argued that it would be *unfair* and *non-transparent* for the Board to simply accept a GAC consensus advice for which no rationale were given.[824]

DCA pointed out that ICANN is prohibited from *discriminating*:

> 'ICANN's Bylaws and Articles of Incorporation prohibit it from discriminating against any party and require it to apply its 'standards, policies, procedures or practices' equitably, unless for a 'substantial or reasonable' cause—such as the promotion of effective competition. ICANN is similarly committed to make decisions in a neutral and fair manner, without favoring any one party over another, and ICANN is required to implement its policies neutrally and objectively. Finally, ICANN has an obligation, enumerated in its governing documents and in the Affirmation of Commitments to actively promote and encourage competition in the DNS. Principles of international law, including the principle of good faith and the customary international law minimum standard of treatment of aliens, include prohibition on discrimination. Discrimination occurs when similarly placed parties

820. DCA's Memorial on the merits, § 45.
821. DCA's Request for IRP, § 46; *see also* DCA's Memorial on the merits, §§ 42 and 45.
822. DCA's Memorial on the merits, § 53.
823. DCA's Request for IRP, § 44.
824. *DCA Trust v. ICANN*, Hearing Transcripts, 504–505.

are treated differently without justification. The general principle of good faith, which includes the prohibition on abuse of rights, also requires ICANN not to abuse its authority in carrying out its activities.'[825]

It argued that ICANN had *discriminated* in this case:

> 'ICANN discriminated against DCA and abused its regulatory authority over new gTLDs by treating it differently from other new gTLD applicants without justification or any rational basis – particularly relative to DCA's competitor ZACR – and by applying ICANN's policies in an unpredictable and inconsistent manner so as to favor DCA's competitor for .AFRICA. ICANN staff repeatedly disparaged DCA and portrayed it as an illegitimate bidder for .AFRICA, and the Board failed to stop the discriminatory treatment despite protests from DCA.'[826]

DCA stated that 'the Board's failure to inquire into the actions of its staff, even when on notice of the myriad of discriminatory actions, violates its obligation to comply with its Bylaws with appropriate care and diligence.'[827]

DCA argued that ICANN is required to operate for the benefit of the Internet community as a whole, through an *open and transparent* process that enables competition and opens entry into Internet-related markets. It argued that ICANN and its constituent bodies must operate to the maximum extent feasible in an *open and transparent* manner and consistent with procedures designed to ensure fairness.[828]

DCA submitted that the ICANN Board had an obligation to investigate the rationale and support for the GAC Advice:

> 'At a bare minimum, this information put ICANN Board and staff members on notice that further investigation into the rationale and support for the GAC's decision was necessary. During the very meeting wherein the NGPC accepted the Objection Advice, the NGPC acknowledged that due diligence required a conversation with the GAC, even where the advice *was* consensus advice. The evidence shows that ICANN simply decided to push through the AUC's appointed applicant in order to allow the AUC to control .AFRICA, as it had previously requested.'[829]

Regarding *good faith*, ICANN argued that it was 'completely appropriate for ICANN to point the AU[830] member states to the publicly-stated Guidebook protections for geographic names that were put in place to address precisely the circumstance at issue here – where an application for a string referencing a geographic designation did not appear to have the support of the countries represented by the string.'[831]

It claimed that 'ICANN acted through open and transparent processes, evaluated DCA's application for .africa in accordance with the procedures set forth in the Guidebook, and followed the procedures set forth in its Bylaws in evaluating DCA's

825. DCA's Memorial on the merits, § 33.
826. DCA's Memorial on the merits, § 34.
827. DCA's Memorial on the merits, § 38.
828. DCA's Request for IRP, § 44.
829. DCA's Memorial on the merits, § 47.
830. African Union.
831. ICANN's Response re merits (*DCA*), § 15.

RfR. ICANN provided assistance to those who requested, cooperated with governmental authorities, and respected the consensus advice issued by the GAC, which speaks on behalf of the governments of the world.'

Concerning *due process*, ICANN stated that 'the GAC's consideration of DCA's application for .AFRICA followed the provisions of the Guidebook. Once the GAC issued consensus advice in opposition to DCA's application, the Guidebook made clear that "this will create a strong presumption for the ICANN Board that the application should not be approved." The Board's decision to accept the GAC Advice was fully consistent with the Guidebook, and DCA offers no basis for the Board to have acted contrary to the GAC's advice.'[832]

ICANN argued that DCA would almost certainly have failed the review by the Geographic Names Panel (GNP), as it did not have the required support, and that ICANN would be violating the Guidebook if it were to ignore the geographic names requirements.[833] On this basis, ICANN could have argued that DCA had no standing: DCA's application had no chance of success and DCA could not show any material harm. However, as mentioned above,[834] ICANN did not raise this issue to challenge DCA's standing.

ICANN claimed that the IRP is a corporate accountability mechanism, and that DCA is not entitled to *due process* or constitutional rights with respect to the IRP:

> 'First, 'constitutional' protections do not apply with respect to a *corporate accountability mechanism*. Second, 'due process' considerations (though inapplicable to corporate accountability mechanisms) were already considered as part of the design of the revised IRP.'[835]
>
> 'ICANN was not required to establish *any* internal corporate accountability mechanism, but instead did so *voluntarily*. Accordingly, DCA does not have any 'due process' or 'constitutional' rights with respect to the Independent Review process.'[836]

Regarding *fairness*, ICANN argued that '[p]ursuant to the Bylaws, reconsideration of a Board (or in this case NGPC) action is appropriate only where the NGPC took an action 'without consideration of material information' or in 'reliance on false or inaccurate material information'.'[837]

ICANN considered that DCA's request for reconsideration had been properly handled:

> 'DCA's Reconsideration Request was handled exactly in the manner prescribed by ICANN's Bylaws: the BGC – a separate Board committee charged with considering Reconsideration Requests – reviewed the material and provided a recommendation to the NGPC. The NGPC then reviewed the BGC's

832. ICANN's Response (*DCA*), § 40.
833. ICANN's Response (*DCA*), § 41.
834. *Supra*, Chapter 5.D.4.b(1).
835. ICANN's 1st Memorandum re procedure (*DCA*), § 19.
836. ICANN's 2nd Memorandum re procedure (*DCA*), § 12.
837. ICANN's Response re merits (*DCA*), § 44.

> recommendation and voted to accept it. In short, the various Board committees conducted themselves exactly as ICANN's Bylaws require.'[838]

ICANN did not accept that it had an obligation to consult with experts:

> '[T]he Guidebook is clear that the Board had the option of consulting with independent experts, not that consulting with experts was mandatory. Further, there is no reason to believe that any 'expert' could have assisted the Board in determining whether to accept the GAC's advice, and DCA did not articulate what an expert possibly could have added to ICANN's decision-making process. In short, there truly was no basis for the Board to accept DCA's Request for Reconsideration.'[839]

Furthermore, ICANN argued that '[t]he ICANN Board would have been required to develop a reasoned and well-supported rationale for not accepting the consensus GAC Advice; no such reason existed at the time the NGPC resolved to accept that GAC Advice (5 June 2013), and no such reason has since been revealed. The consensus GAC Advice against DCA's application was issued in the ordinary course, it reflected the sentiment of numerous countries on the African continent, and it was never rescinded.'[840]

The IRP panel ruled that 'ICANN is bound by its own Articles of Incorporation to act fairly, neutrally, non-discriminatorily and to enable competition.'[841]

It held that 'ICANN is also bound by its own Bylaws to act and make decisions "neutrally and objectively, with integrity and fairness".'[842]

It found ICANN to be 'bound by its Bylaws to conduct adequate diligence to ensure that it [applies] its procedures fairly.'[843]

Specifically, the IRP panel found the following actions and inactions to be inconsistent with the ICANN Articles of Incorporation and Bylaws and with ICANN's obligation to have procedures designed to ensure fairness:

- The failure to give DCA notice or an opportunity to make its position known or defend its own interests before the GAC reached consensus on the GAC Objection Advice.
- The failure of the ICANN Board to address this issue.
- The failure of the BGC to conduct a meaningful review of an ICANN Board decision that the Board was asked to reconsider.[844]

838. ICANN's Response re merits (*DCA*), § 46.
839. ICANN's Response, § 45; *see also* ICANN's Response re merits (*DCA*), §§ 42–43.
840. ICANN's Response re merits (*DCA*), § 37.
841. DCA Final IRP Declaration, § 94.
842. DCA Final IRP Declaration, § 95.
843. DCA Final IRP Declaration, § 105.
844. DCA Final IRP Declaration, §§ 107–109.

ICANN stated that it 'did not disagree that [the now replaced] Article 37 of the ICDR rules would permit DCA to seek emergency relief.'[867]

It argued, however, that 'it is generally accepted under both international and U.S. law that, in order to demonstrate entitlement to interim relief, the party seeking relief must [...] demonstrate a reasonable possibility of success on the merits.'[868]

ICANN noted that '[t]his requirement is appropriate in light of the fact that interim measures are [...] "extraordinary measures not to be granted lightly".'[869]

It also argued that 'DCA's Emergency Request should be denied because DCA has not demonstrated a reasonable possibility that it will succeed on the merits of this IRP, which the law requires DCA to demonstrate. [...] DCA does not provide any basis to demonstrate that it has a reasonable likelihood of success. DCA does not even respond to the evidence submitted by ICANN in its Response to DCA's [Request for IRP] demonstrating definitively that DCA's claims are frivolous.'[870]

ICANN complained that 'DCA has never replied to ICANN's Response or the accompanying declarations. Although any such reply would be untimely under ICANN's Bylaws and the Supplementary Procedures, DCA's Emergency Request (submitted several weeks after ICANN filed its Response) does not even hint that DCA could have any reply that would support DCA's contentions.'[871]

ICANN submitted that 'in order to show necessity [for interim relief] under international law, [DCA] must demonstrate proportionality, *i.e.* that the harm it would occur in the absence of interim relief measures would 'exceed[] greatly the damage caused to the party affected' by those measures.'[872]

It claimed that DCA's 'actual probability of harm is greatly diminished by its scant probability of success on the merits', and that account must be taken of 'the substantial potential harm [the competing applicant for .africa] could suffer if the processing of its application for, and the ultimate delegation of, .AFRICA is delayed.'[873]

Finally, it argued that DCA's delay in seeking emergency relief belied any claim of irreparable harm.[874]

The IRP panel ruled that interim relief was warranted based on the following grounds:

- It would be unfair and unjust to deny the request for interim relief when the need for such a relief arises out of ICANN's failure to follow its own Bylaws

867. ICANN's Memorial on Interim measures (*DCA*), § 7.
868. ICANN's Memorial on Interim measures (*DCA*), § 21.
869. ICANN's Memorial on Interim measures (*DCA*), § 22.
870. ICANN's Memorial on Interim measures (*DCA*), § 3.
871. ICANN's Memorial on Interim measures (*DCA*), § 18.
872. ICANN's Memorial on Interim measures (*DCA*), § 25.
873. ICANN's Memorial on Interim measures (*DCA*), § 25.
874. ICANN's Memorial on Interim measures (*DCA*), §§ 28-31.

and procedures in not selecting a standing panel which could have addressed the request for IRP as soon as it was filed.[875]

- DCA had satisfied the criteria for interim relief: urgency, necessity, protection of an existing right, and existence of a *prima facie* case on the merits or a reasonable possibility that the requesting party would succeed on the merits of the claim.[876]

The panel concluded that 'ICANN must immediately refrain from any further processing of any application for .AFRICA until [the] Panel has heard the merits of DCA Trust's Notice of Independent Review Process and issued its conclusions regarding the same.'[877]

(5) Costs

The panel held that ICANN should bear the totality of the costs of the IRP and the totality of the costs of the IRP Provider, which included the fees and expenses of the reporter associated with the hearing. Each party was to bear its own expenses and legal representation fees.[878]

b. Noteworthy Points for Analysis

The *DCA* case started after the ICANN Board accepted the controversial GAC Advice to deny DCA's application. In accepting the GAC Advice, ICANN prevented the GNP from completing its evaluation of DCA's application. If ICANN had allowed the GNP's evaluation to conclude, in all likelihood there would have been no need for the ICANN Board to react to the GAC Advice, as DCA did not in fact have the necessary government support to pass the GNP's evaluation.

However, DCA argued that the GNP's review was delayed deliberately, and that this may have occurred with the purpose of favoring ZACR.[879] If that is true, then ICANN might have discriminated against DCA and it would be difficult to undo the results of such discrimination today, unless DCA managed to obtain the necessary support for its application. With the AUC objecting to DCA's application, such support would seem to be unattainable. If ICANN positively discriminated in favor of ZACR upon instigation by the AUC, the fairest solution may have been to disqualify ZACR. However, such relief could not be granted without ZACR being given the opportunity to defend itself. ZACR requested to be present at the hearing only very late in the proceedings. DCA opposed ZACR's presence, although, ironically, having ZACR join the proceedings may

875. Emergency Declaration, §§ 29–33.
876. Emergency Declaration, §§ 35–50.
877. Emergency Declaration, § 51.
878. DCA Final IRP Declaration, §§ 144–146.
879. *See* DCA's Memorial on the merits, §§ 16, 29, 39 and following with reference to a letter from the chairman of the ICANN Board to Elham M.A. Ibrahim, Commissioner, Infrastructure and Energy Commission, AUC.

have resulted in DCA obtaining the relief that it initially asked for in its memorial on the merits, *i.e.*, a declaration that ICANN should rescind its contract with ZACR.[880] In its final request for relief, DCA no longer requested the rescission of this contract.[881]

The result of all this is that DCA's success in the IRP is ultimately something of a pyrrhic victory. The panel did not rule on the sensitive political issue of the alleged discrimination by ICANN. DCA was allowed to proceed with the remainder of the new gTLD application process, but unless DCA is able to demonstrate the necessary governmental support, DCA has little chance to succeed in the application process. Moreover, ICANN has already executed a registry agreement for .africa, and may expose itself to a claim by ZACR if it unnecessarily delays delegation of the .africa gTLD. At the time of publishing, it would seem that DCA has not managed to obtain the necessary support for its gTLD application. The *DCA* IRP decision was unable to resolve the issue, and DCA is still trying to obtain final resolution before U.S. courts.

Although the *DCA* IRP decision may not have resolved the issue of .africa, the IRP panel did make some findings that may be useful to other claimants:

- With respect to the standard of review, the panel confirmed the *Booking.com* finding that the Board's conduct should be appraised independently and without any presumption of correctness.
- The panel considered that the acceptance of GAC Advice without due consideration of the reasons behind it and the circumstances surrounding it can constitute a violation of ICANN's Articles of Incorporation and Bylaws.
- The panel declared that IRP decisions regarding new gTLD applications are binding upon ICANN.

However, the *DCA* IRP decision is maybe not the one with the clearest reasoning, and a good understanding of the context is required to pinpoint the exact nature of the violations of ICANN's Articles of Incorporation and Bylaws that the IRP panel identified. The unusual facts of this case and the way in which the decision is written limit its relevance for other IRPs.

6. Authority of the Panel

a. Arguments Discussed

Initially, DCA requested that the application for .africa by competing applicant ZACR be rejected and that DCA's application be allowed to proceed:

> 'DCA believes that, as a result of the Board's breaches of ICANN's Articles of Incorporation, Bylaws and general principles of international law, ICANN must halt the process of delegating .AFRICA to ZACR and ZACR should not be permitted

880. DCA's Memorial on the merits, §56.
881. At the hearing, DCA changed its request for relief, asking the IRP Panel to recommend that ICANN cease all preparations to delegate the .africa gTLD to ZACR (DCA Final IRP Declaration, § 46).

> to retain the rights to .AFRICA it has procured as a result of the Board's violations. Because ICANN's handling of the new gTLD application process for .AFRICA was so flawed and so deeply influenced by ICANN's relationships with various individuals and organizations purporting to represent 'the African community,' DCA believes that any chance it may have had to compete for .AFRICA has been irremediably lost and that DCA's application could not receive a fair evaluation even if the process were to be re-set from the beginning. Under the circumstances, DCA submits that ICANN should remove ZACR's application from the process altogether and allow DCA's application to proceed under the rules of the New gTLD Program, allowing DCA up to 18 months to negotiate with African governments to obtain the necessary endorsements so as to enable the delegation and management of the .AFRICA string.'[882]

During the oral hearing, DCA amended its request for relief, asking the IRP panel to:

- Declare that the Board had violated ICANN's Articles of Incorporation, Bylaws and the Applicant Guidebook.
- Declare that DCA was the prevailing party and, consequently, was entitled to the costs of the proceeding.
- Recommend a course of action for the Board to follow going forward.[883]

Regarding DCA's initial request for relief, ICANN argued that Article IV(3)(11) of the ICANN Bylaws gives the IRP panels the authority to '*declare* whether an action or inaction of the Board was inconsistent with the Articles of Incorporation or Bylaws' and '*recommend* that the Board stay any action or decision, or that the Board take any interim action, until such time as the Board *reviews and acts upon the opinion* of the IRP.'[884]

ICANN argued that IRP panels do not have authority to award affirmative relief:

> 'IRP Panels do not have authority to award affirmative relief. Rather, an IRP Panel is limited to stating its opinion as to 'whether an action or inaction of the Board was inconsistent with the Articles of Incorporation or Bylaws' and recommending (as this IRP Panel has done previously) that the Board stay any action or decision, or take any interim action until such time as the Board reviews and acts upon the opinion of the IRP Panel. The Board will, of course, give extremely serious consideration to the Panel's recommendations.'[885]

Regarding DCA's amended request for relief, ICANN objected to DCA's request for recommendations by the panel to the Board on the ground that such recommendations would be outside the panel's authority as set forth in the Bylaws.[886]

Regarding witness testimony, ICANN argued that 'the Panel exceeded its authority under the Supplementary Procedures when it held in its 14 August Order that it could

882. DCA's Memorial on the merits, § 55.
883. DCA Final IRP Declaration, § 59.
884. ICANN's 1st Memorandum re procedure (*DCA*), § 33.
885. ICANN's Response re merits (*DCA*), § 55.
886. DCA Final IRP Declaration, § 60.

"order" live testimony of witnesses despite the Panel's acknowledgment that the Supplementary Procedures expressly limit any closing argument to argument only.'[887]

The panel ruled that it had the authority to recommend affirmative relief:

> '[U]se of the word 'opinion', which means the formal statement by a judicial authority, court, arbitrator or 'Panel' of the reasoning and the principles of law used in reaching a decision of a case, is demonstrative of the point that the Panel has the authority to recommend affirmative relief. Otherwise, like in section 7 of the Supplementary Procedures, the last sentence in paragraph 11 would have simply referred to the 'declaration of the IRP'. Section 7 under the heading 'Interim Measures of Protection' says in part, that an 'IRP PANEL may recommend that the Board stay any action or decision, or that the Board take any interim action, until such time as the Board reviews and acts upon the IRP declaration'.'[888]

As a result, the panel held that 'it does have the power to recommend a course of action for the Board to follow as a consequence of any declaration that the Board acted or failed to act in a manner inconsistent with ICANN's Articles of Incorporation, Bylaws or the Applicant Guidebook.'[889]

b. *Noteworthy Points for Analysis*

The IRP panel considered that it had the authority to recommend affirmative relief. However, the panel was not entirely clear on whether such a recommendation is binding upon ICANN, or only advisory. This ambiguity in the panel's reasoning allowed the Vistaprint panel (*see below*) to consider that recommendations by an IRP panel are non-binding.

7. Nature and Value of the IRP Declaration

a. *Arguments Discussed*

(1) Binding Nature of the IRP Declaration

DCA argued that, whatever ICANN may have intended when it created the IRP, it has in fact put in place a binding mechanism for final resolution of disputes concerning ICANN Board decisions.[890] It described the IRP as the final accountability and review mechanism available to parties materially affected by ICANN Board decisions.

887. ICANN Letter of February 26, 2015, 2.
888. DCA Final IRP Declaration, § 131.
889. DCA Final IRP Declaration, § 126.
890. DCA Submission on Procedural Issues, § 15.

DCA argued that ICANN created the IRP as an alternative to allowing disputes to be resolved by the courts,[891] that the IRP is the only recourse for gTLD applicants, and that no other legal remedy is available.[892]

DCA stated that the 'powers of the IRP Panel, and the language used to describe its functions, demonstrate that it is meant to provide a final and binding decision resolving the dispute between the parties.'[893]

It further argued that 'the use of the word 'precedential' in the Bylaws means that IRP declarations are binding.'[894] It noted that the language used in the Bylaws to describe a non-binding recommendation is different from the language used to describe the IRP.[895]

DCA argued that, to the extent that the language of the various instruments drafted by ICANN and governing the IRP is ambiguous on this point, the panel should construe that language *contra proferentem*.[896]

Finally, DCA pointed out that the applicant's litigation waiver can only apply if the substitute mechanism is capable of producing a binding remedy:

> 'It is fundamentally inconsistent with California law, U.S. federal law, and principles of international law for ICANN to require applicants to waive all rights to challenge ICANN in court or any other forum and not provide a substitute accountability mechanism capable of producing a binding remedy. Such one-sided terms imposed on parties signing litigation waivers have been flatly rejected by California courts. Where California courts have considered and upheld broad litigation waivers, the alternative to court litigation provided by the parties' contract is inevitably a *binding* dispute resolution mechanism. Thus, in order for this IRP not to be unconscionable, it must be binding.'[897]

ICANN argued that '[t]he IRP Panel's declaration is not binding on the parties because the Board is not permitted to outsource its decision-making authority.'[898]

It submitted that the IRP proceedings did not amount to an arbitration:

> 'Although ICANN is using the International Center for Dispute Resolution ('ICDR') to administer these proceedings, nothing in the Bylaws can be construed as converting these proceedings into an 'arbitration,' and the Bylaws make clear that that these proceedings are not to be deemed as the equivalent of an 'international arbitration.' Indeed, the word 'arbitration' does not appear in the relevant portion of the Bylaws, and as discussed below, the ICANN Board retains full authority to accept or reject the declaration of all IRP Panels.'[899]

891. DCA Submission on Procedural Issues, § 22.
892. DCA Submission on Procedural Issues, § 22.
893. DCA Submission on Procedural Issues, § 23.
894. DCA Submission on Procedural Issues, § 27.
895. DCA Submission on Procedural Issues, § 33 and following.
896. DCA Submission on Procedural Issues, § 15.
897. DCA's Response to the Panel's questions on procedural issues, § 7.
898. ICANN's Response (*DCA*), § 27.
899. ICANN's 1st Memorandum re procedure (*DCA*), § 10.

ICANN argued that '[t]he authority of an IRP panel is not to "decide" or "rule" whether an action or inaction of the Board was inconsistent with the Articles of Incorporation or Bylaws.'[900]

Instead, it maintained that the language of the ICANN Bylaws 'makes clear that the IRP's declarations are advisory and not binding on the Board. Pursuant to the Bylaws, the Board has the discretion to consider an IRP panel's declaration and take whatever action it deems appropriate.'[901] *See also*:

> 'The direction to 'review' and 'consider' an IRP panel's declaration means that the Board has discretion as to whether to adopt and implement that declaration; if the declaration were binding, there would be nothing to review or consider, only a binding order to implement.'[902]

ICANN also submitted that the 'lengthy drafting history of ICANN's independent review process confirms that IRP panel declarations are not binding.'[903]

ICANN referred to the *ICM* IRP, which addressed the issue of binding force extensively, and noted that any references to arbitration were removed from the Bylaws, confirming that an IRP panel's declaration is not binding on ICANN's Board.[904]

ICANN claimed that a declaration could be 'both non-binding and precedential',[905] arguing that:

> '[i]n the United States ... [w]hen the prior court is the same as the subsequent court, the general rule is that precedent is not binding, even though a court may have great weigth to its own prior decisions. If the prior court is at the same level as the subsequent court but the two courts are coordinate rather than identical, as in the case of two district courts in the federal system, then stare decisis is not binding on the subsequent court.'[906]

However, the fact that *stare decisis* may be non-binding has no impact on the *res judicata* effect of a final decision. In our view, the coupling of both the terms final and precedential value in ICANN's Bylaws with the possibility for an IRP panel under Article 6 of the Supplementary Procedures to summarily dismiss a request for IRP where a prior IRP on the same issue has concluded through declaration is a clear affirmation of an IRP declaration's *res judicata* and binding effect.

The IRP panel found that '[v]arious provisions of ICANN's Bylaws and the Supplementary Procedures support the conclusion that the Panel's decisions, opinions and declarations are binding. There is certainly nothing in the Supplementary Rules that renders the decisions, opinions and declarations of the Panel either advisory or non-binding.'[907]

900. ICANN's 2nd Memorandum re procedure (*DCA*), § 4.
901. ICANN's 1st Memorandum re procedure (*DCA*), § 33.
902. ICANN's 2nd Memorandum re procedure (*DCA*), § 4.
903. ICANN's 2nd Memorandum re procedure (*DCA*), § 5.
904. ICANN's 1st Memorandum re procedure (*DCA*), § 34.
905. ICANN's 2nd Memorandum re procedure (*DCA*), § 10.
906. ICANN's 2nd Memorandum re procedure (*DCA*), § 10 and references there.
907. DCA Panel's Declaration on the IRP Procedure, § 98.

It concluded that '[o]ne of the hallmarks of international arbitration is the binding and final nature of the decisions made by the adjudicators. Binding arbitration is the essence of what the ICDR Rules, the ICDR itself and its parent, the American Arbitration Association, offer. The selection of the ICDR Rules as the baseline set of procedures for IRP's, therefore, points to a binding adjudicative process.'[908]

Indeed, the panel found that any ambiguity in ICANN's Bylaws and Supplementary Procedures would weigh against ICANN's position:

> 'Moreover, even if it could be argued that ICANN's Bylaws and Supplementary Procedures are ambiguous on the question of whether or not a decision, opinion or declaration of the IRP Panel is binding, in the Panel's view, this ambiguity would weigh against ICANN's position. The relation between ICANN and the applicant is clearly an adhesive one. There is no evidence that the terms of the application are negotiable, or that applicants are able to negotiate changes in the IRP.
>
> In such a situation, the rule of *contra proferentem* applies. As the drafter and architect of the IRP Procedure, it was open to ICANN and clearly within its power to adopt a procedure that expressly and clearly announced that the decisions, opinions and declarations of IRP Panels were advisory only. ICANN did not adopt such a procedure.'[909]
>
> The Panel also held that this finding (that IRP Panel's decisions and declarations have binding effect) is reinforced by 'the exclusive nature of the IRP' and 'the special, unique, and publicly important function of ICANN' as the 'steward of a highly valuable and important international resource.'[910]

(2) Precedential Value of the IRP Declarations and Preclusive Effect

DCA argued that the *ICM* IRP decision has no precedential value:

> 'The mere fact the Panel's decision is to have precedential effect should put an end to [ICANN]'s efforts to cut short the [IRP] proceedings; no determination resulting from the type of proceeding proposed by [ICANN] could have any sort of precedential value based on a summary, untested record.'[911]
>
> 'According to the terms of ICANN's Bylaws in effect between 2008 and 2010 and according to the *ICM* IRP Declaration itself, the *ICM* decision was *non-binding*. Accordingly, while the Panel certainly may refer to the *ICM* Declaration as a persuasive source, ICANN cannot now argue that a proceeding that was non-binding has precedential effect on this Panel.'[912]

ICANN argued that the *ICM* IRP decision did have precedential value.[913]

The IRP panel ruled that the *ICM Registry* case was not binding upon the panel:

908. DCA Panel's Declaration on the IRP Procedure, § 105.
909. DCA Panel's Declaration on the IRP Procedure, §§ 108–109.
910. DCA Panel's Declaration on the IRP Procedure, § 111.
911. Letter from DCA of 17 April 2014, p. 4.
912. Letter from DCA of 29 May 2014, p. 3.
913. ICANN's 1st Memorandum re procedure (*DCA*), § 34.

> 'Legal precedent may be either binding or persuasive. The Bylaws do not indicate which kind of precedent is intended.
>
> *Stare decisis* is the legal doctrine, which gives binding precedential effect, typically to earlier decisions on a settled point of law, decided by a higher court. The doctrine is not mandatory, as illustrated by the practice in common law jurisdictions of overruling earlier precedents deemed unwise or unworkable. In the present case there is no 'settled' law in the usual sense of a body of cases approved by a court of ultimate resort, but instead, a single decision by one panel on a controversial point, which this Panel, with respect, considers to be unconvincing.
>
> Therefore, the Panel is of the view that the ruling in the *ICM* Case is *not* persuasive and binding upon it.'[914]

b. *Noteworthy Points for Analysis*

(1) Analysis: Nature of the IRP Declaration

The IRP panel in the *DCA* case was fairly conclusive about the nature of IRP declarations. Its declaration on the IRP Procedure contains persuasive reasoning that, at least within the context of the new gTLD program, IRP declarations are binding. The IRP panel found support in the text and purpose of the applicable procedural rules. There was nothing in the Supplementary Rules that rendered the decisions, opinions and declarations of the panel either advisory or non-binding.

However, the *DCA* panel did not finally resolve the dispute. The panel considered that it could recommend a course of action for the ICANN Board to follow, but it did not specify any course of action in sufficient detail to put an end to the dispute. As a matter of fact, the panel may not have been in a position to put an end to the dispute at the time of the final determination, as ICANN had never completed its evaluation of DCA's application. This issue is closely connected with the standing issue. Had the evaluation of DCA's application been completed (in compliance with ICANN's process, Bylaws and Articles of Incorporation), it would have been clear that DCA was not affected by the ICANN Board's acceptance of the GAC Advice. DCA's application would have been rejected in any event, irrespective of the GAC Advice. Of course, in accepting the GAC Advice, the Board had already made clear that it did not want DCA's application to succeed. This put ICANN in an uncomfortable position, as any efforts by ICANN to complete the evaluation – which would likely have resulted in the application failing in any event – could easily be misinterpreted as a deliberate attempt to deny DCA's application. However, not completing the evaluation left the debate open about the ICANN Board's acceptance of the controversial GAC Advice. This may seem like a catch-22 situation, but could have been resolved by a panel that, rather than focusing on the limited issue of the GAC Advice, had been searching for a final solution to the underlying dispute. On the premise of examining the standing issue, the IRP panel could have supervised the fair and transparent handling of the evaluation by the GNP.

914. DCA Panel's Declaration on the IRP Procedure, §§ 126–128.

In all likelihood, this would have shown that DCA had no interest in pursuing the IRP, as it could not demonstrate any material harm. A more flexible approach by the parties and the IRP panel could have avoided a significant waste of resources on an IRP, which did not finally end the dispute.

8. ICANN Board's Decision Following the IRP Declaration

Following the IRP declaration, the ICANN Board decided that ICANN would continue to refrain from delegating the .africa gTLD. The ICANN Board permitted DCA's application to proceed through the remainder of the new gTLD application process, and decided to reimburse DCA for the costs of the IRP.[915] The Board also explained that it did not consider resuming the evaluation of DCA's application to be inconsistent with the GAC Advice.[916] However, if that were the case, it is curious that the evaluation was stopped in the first place, when allowing it to proceed would have saved much effort and cost. It is not surprising that DCA's application ultimately failed the evaluation of the GNP both during an initial evaluation and in an extended evaluation.[917] On 3 March 2016, the ICANN Board authorized ICANN to proceed with the delegation of .africa to ZACR.[918]

However, on 20 January 2016, DCA had initiated court proceedings,[919] which resulted in a temporary restraining order preventing ICANN from delegating the .africa gTLD pending the procedures on the merits.[920]

E. THE VISTAPRINT CASE (.WEBS/.WEB)

1. Key Notes

- IRP under the new set of applicable rules.

915. ICANN, *Approved Board Resolution 2015.07.15.01 – Special Meeting of the ICANN Board*, 16 July 2015, https://www.icann.org/resources/board-material/resolutions-2015-07-16-en.
916. ICANN, *Approved Board Resolution 2015.07.15.02 – Special Meeting of the ICANN Board*, 16 July 2015, https://www.icann.org/resources/board-material/resolutions-2015-07-16-en.
917. ICANN, *Initial Evaluation Report for Application ID 1-1165-42560*, 13 October 2015, https://newgtlds.icann.org/sites/default/files/ier/hug7f846nubabrasacu2aner/ie-1-1165-42560-en.pdf; ICANN, *Extended Evaluation Report for Application ID 1-1165-42560*, 17 February 2016, https://newgtlds.icann.org/sites/default/files/eer/co4voedroechluphiakwupo9/ee-1-1165-42560-en.pdf.
918. ICANN, *Approved Board Resolution 2016.03.03.01 – Regular Meeting of the ICANN Board*, 3 March 2016, https://www.icann.org/resources/board-material/resolutions-2016-03-03-en.
919. *DCA v. ICANN*, Complaint before the Superior Court of the State of California, City and County of Los Angeles, Case No. BC 607494, 20 January 2016, https://www.icann.org/en/system/files/files/dca-v-icann-complaint-20jan16-en.pdf.
920. *DCA v. ICANN*, Minute Order re Plaintiff's *Ex Parte* Application for TRO, Case No. CV 16-00862 RGK, 4 March 2016, https://www.icann.org/en/system/files/files/litigation-dca-minute-order-plaintiff-ex-parte-application-04mar16-en.pdf.

- Confirmation that the standard of review is an objective one, requiring the IRP panel to appraise the Board's conduct independently, and without any presumption of correctness.
- Confirmation that ICANN must act in *good faith* and with *accountability* and *transparency*, and apply documented policies *neutrally*, *objectively* and *fairly*, and must not discriminate.
- Finding that the AoC between ICANN and the U.S. Government is instructive because it explains ICANN's obligations in light of its role as regulator of the DNS.
- Confirmation that a panel's findings on the question of whether or not the ICANN Board's conduct is consistent with the Articles of Incorporation and Bylaws are in themselves binding, but that any recommendation that the panel may give to the Board is non-binding.
- Confirmation that IRP panel Declarations have precedential value.
- ICANN was the prevailing party but the panel awarded partial costs in favor of the Claimant.
- Claimant Vistaprint was found to have contributed to the public interest.
- ICANN was found not to have decided whether there was any inequitable or disparate treatment regarding Vistaprint's .webs gTLD; ICANN refused to proceed to examine this question.
- webs was delegated to Vistaprint following a successful public auction; .web was delegated to another applicant.
- Vistaprint paid USD 1 (Vistaprint was in direct contention with applicant Web.com for .web who had initially objected to the .webs application).
- The successful applicant for .web paid USD 135,000,000 (Vistaprint was in indirect contention with all other applicants for .web).
- Auction proceeds went to ICANN.

2. Introduction

This case[921] is primarily significant for its discussion of the appropriate standard of review of ICANN decisions, and for the IRP panel's ruling concerning the extent to which an IRP declaration can be considered binding. The IRP panel thoroughly examined previous IRP decisions with due regard for their precedential value, and was elaborate in its reasoning and in its interpretation of ICANN's obligations. In this respect, the *Vistaprint* panel was the first panel that explicitly referred to ICANN's Affirmation of Commitments (AoC) in order to interpret ICANN's obligations as the regulator of the DNS.

Nevertheless, the *Vistaprint* IRP declaration contains some of the same mistakes as the IRP declaration in the *Booking.com* case. *E.g.*, the panel agreed with ICANN that the time for challenging the Guidebook's standards had passed, without apparently giving

921. We acted on behalf of the claimant Vistaprint in this case.

the issue much thought. The *Vistaprint* panel also failed to resolve the dispute. The panel could not agree on the interpretation of the appropriate standard for non-discrimination, as imposed by ICANN's Bylaws, and it gave the ICANN Board the opportunity to adopt a position on the issue. Of course, the Board's adopted position would amount to a decision that could then be submitted for review by a new IRP panel to ascertain if it were consistent with ICANN's Articles of Incorporation or Bylaws. That the *Vistaprint* panel did not itself rule on the issue of discrimination – that it withheld its final decision until such time as the ICANN Board had stated its position – is in our view the main weakness of this decision.

3. Case Background

Vistaprint Limited (Vistaprint) questioned the outcome of the String Confusion Objection (SCO) procedure, conducted before the ICDR and initiated by Web.com, which resulted in the applications for .webs and .web being put in one single contention set. Vistaprint identified several procedural and substantive errors in the objection procedure, and argued that ICANN had discriminated against Vistaprint by allowing the re-evaluation of certain other SCO determinations but not of the SCO determination involving .webs and .web. ICANN denied that there were any procedural or substantive errors in the objection procedure, and maintained that Vistaprint had been treated no differently than other similarly-situated applicants.

4. Points of Procedure

a. Arguments Discussed

(1) Applicable Procedural Rules

Vistaprint argued that an IRP is to be conducted pursuant to a set of independently developed international arbitration rules (the ICDR Rules as minimally modified by the IRP Supplementary Procedures), and that ICANN conceived the IRP as an alternative to dispute resolution by courts:

> 'The IRP has all the characteristics of an international arbitration. The IRP is conducted pursuant to a set of independently developed international arbitration rules: the ICDR's International Arbitration Rules ('ICDR Rules') as minimally modified by the Supplementary Procedures for ICANN Independent Review Process ('supplementary Procedures'). The IRP is administered by a provider of international arbitration services. The decision-maker is not ICANN, but a panel of neutral individuals selected by the parties in consultation with the ICDR, and appointed pursuant to the ICDR Rules.
>
> Within its New gTLD Program, ICANN conceived the IRP as an alternative to dispute resolution by courts. To submit a new gTLD application, Vistaprint had to agree to eight pages of terms and conditions ([Applicant Guidebook], Module 6). The terms and conditions include a waiver of all of Vistaprint's rights to challenge ICANN's decisions on Vistaprint's applications in court, or in any other judicial

> forum, provided that, as an applicant, Vistaprint may utilize any accountability mechanism set forth in ICANN's Bylaws ([Applicant Guidebook], Module 6-4). '[A]ssuming that the foregoing waiver of any and all judicial remedies is valid and enforceable, the ultimate 'accountability' remedy for [Vistaprint] is the IRP'.'[922]

Using the same argument as it relied on in *Booking.com*, ICANN maintained that its Bylaws, the IRP Supplementary Procedures and the ICDR Rules apply, and that the Supplementary Procedures take precedence over the ICDR Rules. ICANN did not discuss the order of precedence between ICANN's Bylaws and the Supplementary Procedures, but mentioned the Bylaws first:

> 'This Independent Review Process ('IRP') is conducted pursuant to Article IV, Section 3 of ICANN's Bylaws, which creates a non-binding method of evaluating certain actions of ICANN's Board of Directors.'[923]

> 'ICANN has appointed the ICDR as ICANN's IRP Provider. ICANN's Bylaws and the Supplementary Procedures that the ICDR has adopted specially for ICANN IRP proceedings apply here.'[924]

> 'Absent a governing provision in ICANN's Bylaws or the ICDR's Supplemental Procedures, the ICDR Rules apply. But in the event of any inconsistency between the Supplementary Procedures and the ICDR's Rules, the Supplementary Procedures shall govern.'[925]

The IRP panel ruled that 'the three charter instruments that give the Panel its authority to act in this case [are] the Bylaws, the Supplementary Procedures, and the ICDR Rules.'[926] It clarified that:

> 'In terms of a potential interpretive hierarchy for these documents – to the extent that such hierarchy is relevant – the Bylaws can be said to have created the IRP and its terms of reference: the IRP is established as an accountability mechanism pursuant to the Bylaws, Article IV, § 3 (Independent Review of Board Actions). Article IV, § 3.8 of the Bylaws, in turn, delegates to the 'IRP Provider' the task of establishing rules and procedures that are supposed to be consistent with Article IV, § 3.'[927]

It ruled that: 'if there is a contradiction between the texts, the Bylaws and Supplemental rules would govern.'[928]

(2) Jurisdiction of the IRP Panel

Vistaprint stated that the IRP panel had to determine whether ICANN's actions or inactions are consistent with (i) the Articles of Incorporation and Bylaws and (ii) secondary rules created by ICANN, and it argued that the IRP panel's mandate includes a review of whether or not ICANN's Board has discriminated in its interventions:

922. Vistaprint Brief on *Booking.com* case (Rebuttal), §§ 27-28.
923. ICANN's Response (*Vistaprint*), § 2.
924. ICANN's Response (*Vistaprint*), § 34.
925. ICANN's Response (*Vistaprint*), § 34, n. 36.
926. Vistaprint IRP Declaration, § 130.
927. Vistaprint IRP Declaration, § 132.
928. Vistaprint IRP Declaration, § 136.

> 'In accordance with Article IV(3) of ICANN's Bylaws, an IRP Panel must determine whether the contested actions of the ICANN Board are consistent with applicable rules.
>
> As described in detail in Vistaprint's Request for IRP, the set of rules against which the actions of the ICANN Board must be assessed includes: (i) ICANN's Articles of Incorporation and Bylaws – both of which must be interpreted in light of ICANN's Affirmation of Commitments, and both of which require compliance with inter alia International law and generally accepted good governance principles – and (ii) secondary rules created by ICANN, such as the Applicant Guidebook. In setting up, implementing and supervising its policies and processes, the Board must comply with the fundamental principles embodied in these rules. That obligation includes a duty to ensure compliance with its obligations to act in good faith, transparently, fairly, and in a manner that is non-discriminatory and ensures due process.'[929]
>
> 'When the Board intervenes (or elects not to intervene) on an SCO expert determination, that action of the Board is subject to review by the IRP Panel. As explained in detail in Vistaprint's Reply, the IRP Panel must review and determine whether the contested actions of the ICANN Board are consistent with i) ICANN's AoI and Bylaws and ii) secondary rules created by ICANN. These rules require ICANN and its Board to act in good faith and in accordance with principles of international law. The IRP Panel's mandate includes a review as to whether or not ICANN's Board discriminates in its interventions on SCO expert determinations.'[930]

ICANN confirmed that the IRP panel is charged with reviewing ICANN Board actions and inactions for consistency with the Articles of Incorporation and Bylaws:

> 'This IRP Panel has one responsibility – to 'declar[e] whether the Board has acted consistently with the provisions of [ICANN's] Articles of Incorporation and Bylaws'.'[931]
>
> 'An IRP panel is limited to 'declaring whether an action or inaction of the Board was inconsistent with the Articles of Incorporation or Bylaws'.'[932]

However, ICANN argued that the IRP panel is not available as a mechanism to challenge actions or inactions by ICANN staff or third parties that may be involved with ICANN's activities.[933]

ICANN stated that an IRP 'is not a forum for challenging substantive decisions of the BGC in connection with the reconsideration process',[934] and that it 'is not intended to be an appeal mechanism to challenge the outcome of a request for reconsideration.'[935]

ICANN considered that 'the extent of the Board's discretion as a general matter is irrelevant to the Panel's task.'[936]

929. Vistaprint Reply, §§ 33–34.
930. Vistaprint brief on *Booking.com* case (Rebuttal), § 20.
931. ICANN's Response (*Vistaprint*), § 2.
932. ICANN's Reply (*Vistaprint*), § 33.
933. ICANN's Response (*Vistaprint*), § 4.
934. ICANN's Response (*Vistaprint*), § 47.
935. ICANN's Response (*Vistaprint*), § 69.
936. ICANN's Sur-Rebuttal (*Vistaprint*), § 22.

The IRP panel ruled that it was entitled to review actions and inactions of the ICANN Board for consistency with the Articles of Incorporation and Bylaws:

> 'The IRP Panel has benefited from the parties submissions on this issue, noting their agreement as to the Panel's primary task: comparing contested actions (or inactions) of ICANN's Board to its Articles and Bylaws and declaring whether the Board has acted consistently with them.'[937]

It held that the detailed listing of a defined standard cannot remove this fundamental task from the panel's remit, and that the panel may raise other questions in the performance of its task:

> 'The Panel is to focus, in particular, on whether the Board acted without conflict of interest, exercised due diligence and care in having a reasonable amount of facts in front of it, and exercised independent judgment in taking a decision believed to be in the best interests of ICANN. In the IRP Panel's view this more detailed listing of a defined standard cannot be read to remove from the Panel's remit the fundamental task of comparing actions or inactions of the Board with the Articles and Bylaws and declaring whether the Board has acted consistently or not. Instead, the defined standard provides a list of questions that can be asked, but not to the exclusion of other potential questions that might arise in a particular case as the Panel goes about its comparative work. For example, the particular circumstances may raise questions whether the Board acted in a transparent or non-discriminatory manner. In this regard, the ICANN Board's discretion is limited by the Articles and Bylaws, and it is against the provisions of these instruments that the Board's conduct must be measured.'[938]

The IRP panel considered its task to be limited to addressing challenges to the conduct of the ICANN Board and not of ICANN staff or other third parties:

> 'On a related point as to the scope of the IRP Panel's review, the Panel agrees with ICANN's point of emphasis that, because the Panel's review is limited to addressing challenges to conduct by ICANN's Board, the Panel is not tasked with reviewing the actions or decisions of ICANN staff or other third parties who may be involved in ICANN activities or provide services to ICANN (such as the ICDR or the experts in the *Vistaprint SCO*).'[939]

The IRP panel considered its task to be limited to addressing challenges to the conduct of the ICANN Board, which could include omissions:

> 'On a related point as to the scope of the IRP Panel's review, the Panel agrees with ICANN's point of emphasis that, because the Panel's review is limited to addressing challenges to conduct by ICANN's Board, the Panel is not tasked with reviewing the actions or decisions of ICANN staff or other third parties who may be involved in ICANN activities or provide services to ICANN (such as the ICDR or the experts in the *Vistaprint SCO*). With this in mind, and with the focus on the Board, the only *affirmative* action of the Board in relation to Vistaprint's .webs gTLD application was through the BGC, which denied Vistaprint's Reconsideration Request. [... H]owever, this does not eliminate the IRP Panel's consideration of whether, in the circumstances, inaction (or omission) by the BGC or the full

937. Vistaprint IRP Declaration, § 119; *see also* § 123.
938. Vistaprint IRP Declaration, § 123.
939. Vistaprint IRP Declaration, § 127.

> ICANN Board in relation to the issues raised by Vistaprint's application would be considered a potential violation of the Articles or Bylaws.
>
> As discussed below, the Panel considers that a significant question in this IRP concerns one of 'omission' – the ICANN Board, through the BGC or otherwise, did not provide relief to Vistaprint in the form of an additional review mechanism, as it did to certain other parties who were the subject of an adverse SCO determination.'[940]

The IRP panel ruled that it was not allowed to substitute its judgment for that of the ICANN Board:

> 'The Panel agrees with ICANN's statement that the Panel is neither asked to, nor allowed to, substitute its judgment for that of the Board. However, this does not fundamentally alter the lens through which the Panel must view its comparative task.'[941]

The panel decided that it did have a mandate to review whether or not the ICANN Board had discriminated against Vistaprint:

> 'The IRP Panel agrees with Vistaprint's statement that the 'IRP Panel's mandate includes a review as to whether or not ICANN's Board discriminates in its interventions on SCO expert determinations'.'[942]

(3) Nomination, Appointment, Removal and Replacement of Panelists

Vistaprint submitted that the panel should be composed of three members. As ICANN had not established the omnibus standing panel described in the Bylaws, Vistaprint suggested that each panel appoint one panelist, after which the two appointed panelists could jointly select the Chairman of the panel. However, in contrast with the *Booking-.com* case, where party-appointed panelists were nominated consecutively, Vistaprint asked for the simultaneous nomination of the party-appointed panelists.[943] And that was how the appointments were made.

(4) Standing

Vistaprint argued that an IRP is available to any person materially affected by an ICANN Board decision or action, and that the mechanism has explicitly been made available to new gTLD applicants:

> 'The IRP is not a mere "corporate accountability mechanism" aimed at ICANN's internal stakeholders. The IRP is open to *any* person materially affected by a decision or action by the Board.[944] It is made explicitly available to applicants ([Applicant Guidebook], Module 6-4), who are by definition third parties.'[945]

940. Vistaprint IRP Declaration, §§ 127–128.
941. Vistaprint IRP Declaration, § 124.
942. Vistaprint IRP Declaration, § 177.
943. Vistaprint Request for IRP, §§ 82–83.
944. Article IV(3)(2) of ICANN's Bylaws.
945. Vistaprint brief on *Booking.com* case, § 29.

Vistaprint claimed to have been harmed by ICANN's actions and decisions:

> 'Vistaprint is harmed by ICANN's unequal treatment. In addition, the substantive and procedural errors in the SCO proceedings forced Vistaprint to spend time and effort (in preparing an RfR, CEP and this IRP) in order to resolve the unreasonable outcome of the contention set determination.'[946]

ICANN argued that the IRP is only available to persons materially affected by a decision or action of the ICANN Board; not by the actions of ICANN staff or third parties:

> 'The IRP is only available to persons 'materially affected by a decision or action of the [ICANN] Board that he or she asserts is inconsistent with the Articles of Incorporation or Bylaws.' The IRP is thus limited to challenging ICANN Board conduct, and is not available as a means to challenge the conduct of third parties or the conduct of ICANN staff.'[947]

It argued that in this case there was nothing for the IRP panel to review, 'because there is no Board action or decision associated with the Expert Panel's Determination.'[948]

The panel held that an IRP is available for applicants in the case of an adverse SCO determination:

> 'In the case of an adverse SCO determination, the applicant for a new gTLD string is not left without any recourse. Module 6.6 of the Guidebook provides that an applicant *"MAY UTILIZE ANY ACCOUNTABILITY MECHANISM SET FORTH IN ICANN's BYLAWS FOR PURPOSES OF CHALLENGING ANY FINAL DECISION MADE BY ICANN WITH RESPECT TO THE APPLICATION" (no emphasis added).*'[949]

(5) Time Bar

Vistaprint argued that ICANN's processes discussed in the IRP were not yet finalized at the time of the adoption of the Guidebook, and that applicants were effectively barred from challenging the Guidebook at that time, by the fact that they could not show any harm:

> 'ICANN and the Booking.com Panel's reasoning on the timing has no merit. The Booking.com Panel ignored the fact that neither the string similarity review process nor the string confusion objection procedures had been established and implemented in their entirety at the time the Guidebook was adopted. At that time, neither Booking.com nor Vistaprint nor any other interested party could effectively challenge these, as yet unfinalized, processes. ICANN still had every opportunity to correctly implement the string confusion objection procedure in accordance with both the Guidebook and the fundamental principles in ICANN's Articles of Incorporation ("AoI") and Bylaws. The opportunity for Vistaprint to challenge the erroneous application of the Guidebook in violation of ICANN's fundamental principles only arose when the flaws in ICANN's implementation of the Guidebook

946. Vistaprint Reply, § 9.
947. ICANN's Response (*Vistaprint*), § 36; *see also* ICANN's Sur-Reply (*Vistaprint*), § 11.
948. ICANN's Response (*Vistaprint*), § 40.
949. Vistaprint IRP Declaration, § 154.

> became apparent. At the time of the adoption of the Guidebook, Vistaprint was effectively barred from challenging the Guidebook by the fact that it could not – at that time – show any harm.'[950]

Furthermore, Vistaprint pointed out that challenging the Guidebook at the time of its adoption would have harmed Vistaprint:

> 'Further, to raise an issue at that time would have required Vistaprint to reveal that it was contemplating making an application for a new gTLD, which would have encouraged opportunistic applications seeking to extract monetary value from an application by Vistaprint by applying for a TLD corresponding to the name of a product or business entity of Vistaprint or an affiliate, like ".webs".'[951]

Vistaprint argued that the *Booking.com* panel had erred in not drawing a distinction between the adoption of the general principles and their subsequent implementation:

> 'Booking.com raised similar concerns [...], but the Booking.com Panel simply did not draw the distinction between the adoption of the general principles and their subsequent implementation. The Booking.com Panel limited its review to ICANN's compliance to the letter of the Guidebook. It refrained from reviewing the Board's actions in the implementation of the Guidebook, asserting that the ICANN Board has ultimate discretion whether or not to intervene.'[952]

ICANN argued here that Vistaprint was time-barred from challenging the SCO procedure, as it had not taken the opportunity to object to the challenged aspects of the Guidebook at the time the Guidebook was implemented:

> 'Vistaprint argues for the first time in its Additional Submission that the entire string confusion objection procedure is fundamentally flawed. This argument is not only completely unsupported, but also has been time-barred for almost three years. The string confusion objection procedures have been in place since 2012 and were adopted only after extensive discussion with and input from the Internet community. The open, transparent and fair process that gave rise to the Guidebook, including the string confusion objection procedures, are completely consistent with ICANN's Articles and Bylaws. Like other members of the community, Vistaprint had the opportunity to comment on several drafts of the Guidebook and propose modifications, including to the string confusion objection procedures. It did not do so.'[953]
>
> 'Vistaprint's wholesale attack on the string confusion objection procedures is also deficient because the current version of the Guidebook was published on 4 June 2012 following an extensive review process, including public comment on multiple drafts, as set forth above. Despite having ample opportunity to do so, Vistaprint did not object to these aspects of the Guidebook at the time the Guidebook was implemented. If Vistaprint had concerns related to these issues, it should have pursued them at the time, not years later, and only after receiving an Expert Determination with which it disagreed.
>
> As the IRP Panel in *Booking.com v. ICANN* found, 'the time has long since passed for Booking.com or any other interested party to ask an IRP Panel to review the

950. Vistaprint Brief on *Booking.com* case, § 9.
951. Vistaprint Brief on *Booking.com* case, § 10.
952. Vistaprint Brief on *Booking.com* case, § 11.
953. ICANN's Sur-Reply (*Vistaprint*), § 6.

actions of the ICANN Board in relation to the establishment of the string similarity review process, including Booking.com's claims that specific elements of the process and the Board decisions to implement those elements are inconsistent with ICANN's Articles and Bylaws. Any such claims, even if they had any merit, are long since time-barred by the 30-day limitation period set out in Article IV, Section 3(3) of the Bylaws.' While the Guidebook process at issue in this case is different—the string confusion objection process rather than the string similarity review process—the Booking.com Panel's reasoning applies equally. Because both processes were developed years ago, as part of the development of the Guidebook, challenges to both are time-barred.'[954]

ICANN also argued that 'Vistaprint's fears that other potential applicants might have guessed what gTLD(s) Vistaprint might apply for and then maybe apply for the same string, does not constitute a valid reason to disregard the unambiguous thirty-day IRP filing deadline.'[955]

The IRP panel decided that the time for challenging the Guidebook's standard for evaluating SCOs had passed. The panel did not rule on the possibility to challenge the policies or their implementation:

> 'ICANN has argued that the time for Vistaprint to have objected to the Guidebook and its SCO policy has long since passed. Vistaprint has responded that it contests the *implementation* of the Guidebook and its *policies*, not just the policies themselves. Even assuming that the Guidebook's policies could be challenged at this point, the IRP Panel finds that the relevant polices, such as the standard for evaluating String Confusion Objections, do not violate any of ICANN's Articles or Bylaws reflecting principles such as good faith, fairness, transparency and accountability. However, the Panel does agree with ICANN that the time for challenging the Guidebook's standard for evaluating String Confusion Objections – which was developed in an open process and with extensive input – has passed.'[956]

As was also the case in the Booking.com IRP, the IRP panel disregarded that the thirty-day limitation period was only introduced on 11 April 2013, *i.e.*, long after the new gTLD application window closed.[957] Nor did the IRP panel comment on the consideration that the objection procedures had not been established and implemented in their entirety at the time the Guidebook was adopted. In our view, no applicant, nor any other interested party, could have effectively challenged these processes at that time, because they had not yet been finalized.[958]

954. ICANN's Sur-Reply (*Vistaprint*), §§ 27–28.
955. ICANN's Sur-Rebuttal (*Vistaprint*), § 18.
956. Vistaprint IRP Declaration, § 172.
957. The application window closed on 30 May 2012 (*see* Akram Atallah, *New gTLD update*, 30 May 2012, https://newgtlds.icann.org/en/announcements-and-media/announcement-3-30may12-en).
958. *Supra* Chapter 5.C.4.a(5) and Chapter 5.C.4.b(4); *infra* Chapter 5.E.4.b(1).

(6) Written/Oral Arguments

Vistaprint requested a hearing, preferably in person. However, Vistaprint did not insist on an in-person hearing, and the parties mutually agreed to organize a telephone hearing.

ICANN finally agreed to a telephone hearing, despite initially wanting to limit the proceedings to Vistaprint's Request for IRP and ICANN's Response:

> 'ICANN disagrees that Vistaprint has any "rights to rebut," but will reserve discussion on that topic unless and until Vistaprint seeks leave to place additional information before the IRP Panel.'[959]

In its first procedural order, the IRP panel granted Vistaprint the opportunity to file a written reply to ICANN's response, and ICANN was given a right to sur-reply. One day after Vistaprint submitted its written reply, the final declaration intervened in the *Booking.com* IRP. In its sur-reply, ICANN referred to the *Booking.com* IRP declaration to support its arguments. As Vistaprint wanted to comment on ICANN's reading of the *Booking.com* IRP declaration, Vistaprint sought leave for an additional submission. ICANN objected, but Vistaprint was nevertheless permitted to file a rebuttal to discuss the *Booking.com* IRP declaration and the post-hearing material and communications that were exchanged in that case. ICANN was permitted to submit a sur-rebuttal.[960] A telephone hearing took place on 28 May 2015.

(7) Witnesses and Expert Witnesses

Vistaprint submitted an expert report by Prof. Dr. Piet Desmet[961] showing that .webs and .web cannot be considered confusingly similar. Vistaprint also submitted a testimonial by Kurt Pritz, ICANN's former Chief Strategy Officer and Senior Vice President of Stakeholders Relations, showing the lack of appropriately qualified experts in the SCO procedure and a failure by ICANN to ensure consistency in the objection rulings, which resulted in discrimination.

ICANN briefly commented on Vistaprint's expert witness:

> 'Professor Desmet's disagreement with the Expert's conclusion does not demonstrate that the Expert erred, and definitely does not demonstrate that *ICANN's Board* violated its Bylaws in determining that the Expert had properly applied the Guidebook standard in upholding the Objections to Vistaprint's Applications.'[962]

959. ICANN's Response (*Vistaprint*), § 34, n. 38.
960. Vistaprint Panel, Procedural Order No. 2, 19 April 2015.
961. Prof. Dr. Piet Desmet is Professor of Applied Linguistics at the KU Leuven University, Belgium. He was also asked to prepare a report in the *Booking.com* case.
962. ICANN's Sur-Reply (*Vistaprint*), § 30.

ICANN expressed similar comments on the testimonial by Kurt Pritz and considered that his 'after-the-fact critique – in an adversarial proceeding – of the work he and his now former ICANN colleagues performed years ago should be seen for precisely what it is and be given no weight.'[963]

The IRP panel did not comment on the expert report by Prof. Dr. Piet Desmet. The panel limited itself to stating that it agreed with the ICANN Board's rejection of Vistaprint's claim that the SCO expert incorrectly applied both the burden of proof and the substantive criteria for evaluating the SCO.[964]

The IRP panel did mention the testimonial by Kurt Pritz, but it could not agree on whether ICANN's failure to ensure consistency and its Board's selective interventions met the standard of non-discrimination imposed by ICANN's Bylaws.[965]

(8) Costs

The IRP panel showed significant sympathy for Vistaprint's arguments by allocating 40% of the IRP costs to ICANN despite declaring it to be the prevailing party. In doing so, the panel took account of the significant issues raised by Vistaprint and its contribution to the public interest in connection with the New gTLD Program and the IRP:

> 'The IRP Panel also recognizes that Vistaprint, through its Request and submissions, raised certain complex and significant issues and contributed to the 'public interest' involving the New gTLD Program and the Independent Review Process. It is therefore appropriate and reasonable to divide the IRP costs over the parties in a 60% (Vistaprint) / 40% (ICANN) proportion.'[966]

b. Noteworthy Points for Analysis

(1) Time Bar

The IRP panel failed to take into consideration that the time limit for challenging an ICANN Board decision was not introduced until April 2013, and should surely not have been applied retroactively.

The panel only discussed the time bar in relation to the establishment of the SCO standard in the Guidebook. However, in this respect, the question of the time bar was a non-issue. We agree with the panel that the definition of the SCO standard in itself does not violate ICANN's Articles of Incorporation or Bylaws. But Vistaprint did not challenge the SCO standard itself; it challenged the inconsistent and discriminatory application of the standard. In our view, in its assessment of the SCO standard, the

963. ICANN's Sur-Reply (*Vistaprint*), §26.
964. Vistaprint IRP Declaration, § 166.
965. Vistaprint IRP Declaration, § 189, n. 232.
966. Vistaprint IRP Declaration, § 197.

panel put too much emphasis on the standard as described in the Guidebook. The Guidebook was only one instrument in the implementation of the GNSO's policy on new gTLDs. Other ICANN materials (which were presented to potential applicants) explained how the Guidebook's standard had to be applied. As ICANN promised to work with appropriately qualified experts only, one would have expected these experts to be fully informed about these materials. However, the fact that these experts looked at the SCO standard only as it was formulated in the Guidebook was apparently not seen as a problem by the IRP panel.[967]

The panel did not base its decision on the question of time bar, but considered that there was no violation of the Articles of Incorporation or Bylaws in the Board's consideration of Vistaprint's arguments as set out in its reconsideration request. While it is unfortunate that, in making this assessment, the panel only considered the SCO standard as it is formulated in the Guidebook, the panel's *obiter dictum* on the time bar must be seen precisely within that context.

The panel did not decide on Vistaprint's most crucial argument, *i.e.*, its concerns about inconsistent decisions in SCO proceedings and ICANN's discriminatory treatment in addressing these concerns.[968] However, it did consider that the argument was raised in a timely manner,[969] and considered itself competent to rule on the Board's actions or omissions in the area of alleged non-discriminatory treatment.[970] The panel's reasoning in this respect seems to confirm that the discriminatory application of a pre-established policy can be challenged any time the discrimination occurs, irrespective of the policy's age. In our view this strengthens the argument that the panel's *obiter dictum* that 'the time for challenging the Guidebook's standard for evaluating string confusion objections [...] has passed' is of limited application.

5. Applicable Law

a. Arguments Discussed

(1) Sources

Vistaprint argued that the applicable law for the proceedings is contained in ICANN's Articles of Incorporation and Bylaws, which must be interpreted in light of the fact that ICANN is subject to both local and international law and must act in compliance with general principles of international law.[971]

967. Vistaprint IRP Declaration, § 170.
968. Vistaprint IRP Declaration, § 189 and following.
969. Vistaprint IRP Declaration, § 186.
970. Vistaprint IRP Declaration, § 179–180.
971. Vistaprint Request for IRP, § 55.

It added that ICANN has obligations under its AoC and under the policies it has established, provided the implementation of these policies is consistent with ICANN's fundamental obligations.[972]

ICANN did not comment on this. However, in discussing the drafting history of its Bylaws, ICANN itself referred to its AoC, stating that it had 'committed to "maintain and improve robust mechanisms for public input, accountability and transparency".'[973]

The IRP panel agreed with Vistaprint and ruled that the following procedural rules apply:

- ICDR Rules (version of 1 June 2009).
- ICDR Supplementary Rules for IRP.
- Articles of Incorporation.
- Bylaws (version of 11 April 2013).

It also accepted Vistaprint's submission that the procedural rules must be interpreted in view of ICANN's AoC:

> 'This Affirmation of Commitments is instructive, as it explains ICANN's obligations in light of its role as regulator of the DNS.'[974]

(2) Essential Rights and Obligations

Vistaprint argued that ICANN must act in *good faith*, ensure *fairness*, *non-discrimination*, *openness* and *transparency*, *accountability* and the promotion of *competition*:

> 'ICANN is a Californian non-profit public benefit corporation, responsible for administering technical aspects of the Internet's domain name system (DNS). Core to its mission is increasing competition and fostering choice in the DNS. ICANN's Articles of Incorporation require ICANN to act "for the benefit of the Internet community as a whole" and "in conformity with the relevant principles of international law and local law" ([Articles of Incorporation], Article 4). ICANN's fundamental principles, which are reiterated numerous times in ICANN's governance documents and other policies, require ICANN to act in good faith, to ensure fairness, non-discrimination, openness and transparency, accountability, and the promotion of competition.'[975]

Vistaprint submitted that ICANN's obligation to act in *good faith* is a universal rule which must guide ICANN's substantial and procedural rules, and which includes an obligation to ensure procedural *fairness*:

> 'Many of the guiding substantive and procedural rules in ICANN's Articles and Bylaws – including the rules involving transparency, fairness, and non-

972. Vistaprint Request for IRP, §§ 6, 7, 57 ; Vistaprint Reply, §§ 34, 36; Vistaprint Rebuttal, § 30.
973. ICANN's Sur-Reply, §40, n. 55.
974. Vistaprint IRP Declaration, § 67.
975. Vistaprint Request for IRP, § 13.

> discrimination – are so fundamental that they appear in some form in virtually every legal system in the world. One of the reasons they are so universal is because they arise from the general principle of good faith, which is considered to be the foundation of all law and convention. As stated by the ICJ, the principle of good faith is "[o]ne of the basic principles governing the creation and performance of legal obligations."
>
> The principle of good faith includes an obligation to ensure procedural fairness by, *inter alia*, adhering to substantive and procedural rules, avoiding arbitrary action, and recognizing legitimate expectations. ICANN's core values require ICANN to obtain informed input from those entities most affected by ICANN's decisions ([Bylaws], Art. I, §2(9)).'[976]

Vistaprint argued that ICANN's new gTLD Applicant's Guidebook was established with the purpose of ensuring *legal certainty*:

> 'The purpose of the Applicant Guidebook was to ensure that prospective applicants understood what was required of them when applying for a new gTLD and what they could expect at each stage of the evaluation process.'[977]

Vistaprint argued that applicable general principles of international *due process* include equal and fair treatment of the parties, fair notice and a fair opportunity to present one's case:

> 'As noted above, the international law standard of good faith encompasses an obligation to ensure procedural fairness and due process. General principles of 'international due process' self-evidently include equal and fair treatment of the parties, fair notice, and a fair opportunity to present one's case. These requirements are basic principles that inform transnational public policy with regard to procedure. They are more than just formalistic procedural requirements. The opportunity must be meaningful: the party must be given adequate notice of the relevant rules and be given a full and fair opportunity to present its case. And the mechanisms for redress must be both timely and effective.'[978]

It submitted that ICANN's Board is ultimately responsible, and must ensure that third party vendors respect its policies and fundamental principles:

> 'ICANN's Board ultimately has responsibility for ensuring that ICANN policies are respected. [...]
>
> ICANN failed to show that it has done any investigation into Vistaprint's fundamental questions about the Panel's arbitrariness, lack of independence, partiality, inappropriate qualification, the DRSP's and the Panel's disregard of the applicable rules and policies, etc. As it is ICANN's responsibility to ensure that its policies and fundamental principles are respected by its third party vendors,'[979]
>
> 'The fact that the ICANN Board may rely on third parties for advice does not alter the Board's responsibility. The Board remains ICANN's decision-making body. This means that the ICANN Board cannot blindly accept advice by third parties or

976. Vistaprint Request for IRP, §§ 59–60.
977. Vistaprint Request for IRP, § 16.
978. Vistaprint Request for IRP, § 69.
979. Vistaprint Request for IRP, §§ 51–52.

> expert determinations. The ICANN Board must always verify compliance with its Articles of Incorporation and Bylaws, particularly when the third party advice or expert determination is questioned.'[980]

Vistaprint pointed out that ICANN must apply policies *neutrally, fairly and without discrimination*:

> 'ICANN is subject to a fundamental obligation to act fairly and apply established policies neutrally and without discrimination. Not only does this obligation arise from general principles of international law, it is also repeatedly in ICANN's governing documents. Article 2(3) of ICANN's Bylaws provides that:
>
>> "ICANN shall not apply its standards, policies, procedures, or practices inequitably or single out any party for disparate treatment unless justified by substantial and reasonable cause..."
>
> The above obligation is further elaborated in ICANN's Core Values, which require ICANN to make "decisions by applying documented policies neutrally and objectively, with integrity and fairness."'([ICANN's Bylaws], Art. I, §2)[981]

Vistaprint argued that the ICANN Board's latitude in its decision making is limited, and that the Board's obligations are reinforced by the standard of review for the IRP process:

> 'The ICANN Board's latitude in its decision making does not bestow the Board with "an unfettered discretion in making decisions. [...] The decision or action [of the ICANN Board] should be based on a reasoned judgment of the Board, not on an arbitrary exercise of discretion"'[...]. The limitation to the ICANN Board's discretion is explicitly mentioned in the ICANN Bylaws [...]
>
> The obligations of the ICANN Board in its decision making are "reinforced by the standard of review for the IRP process [...] when the action of the Board is compared to the requirements under the [AoI] and Bylaws. The standard of review includes a consideration of whether the Board exercised due diligence and care in having a reasonable amount of facts before them and also whether the Board exercised its own independent judgement" [...].'[982]

Furthermore, Vistaprint argued that the Board may not treat applicants *inequitably* nor *discriminate* when considering a particular application:

> 'When the ICANN Board individually considers an application, it must make sure that it does not treat applicants inequitably and that it does not discriminate among applicants. Article II, Section 3 of ICANN's Bylaws provides that "ICANN shall not apply its standards, policies, procedures, or practices inequitably or single out any particular party for disparate treatment unless justified by substantial and reasonable cause, such as the promotion of effective competition" ([Bylaws]). However, with regard to the SCO proceedings, the ICANN Board has done the exact opposite. It created the opportunity for some aggrieved applicants to participate in an appeals process, while denying others.

980. Vistaprint Reply, § 30.
981. Vistaprint Request for IRP, §§ 61-62.
982. Vistaprint brief on *Booking.com* case, §§ 16-17.

> As explained above, there is no justification for this disparate treatment, and the ICANN Board has not given any substantial and reasonable cause that would justify this discrimination.'[983]

Vistaprint requested that ICANN guarantee *openness* in its decision-making, as it is required to do by Article 4 of the Articles of Incorporation, Article III of ICANN's Bylaws, as supplemented by the Bylaws 'Core Values'.[984]

ICANN argued that there was no procedure foreseen by which ICANN or its Board could or should conduct a substantive review of the results in a SCO:

> 'The Guidebook does not provide for any procedure by which ICANN (or anyone else) is to conduct a substantive review of the Expert Panel's results.'[985]

> 'While Vistaprint may disagree with the ICDR's decision to accept the Objector's challenge, it is not the BGC's role to second guess the ICDR's discretion, and it was not a violation of the ICANN Articles or Bylaws for the BGC to deny reconsideration on this ground, particularly given that Vistaprint provided no basis to believe that the ICDR's decision was in violation of the ICDR's policies.'[986]

ICANN argued that its refusal to reconsider the substance of the SCO result was not a failure to act in *good faith*:

> '[T]he only reason Vistaprint asserts ICANN failed to act in good faith is in 'refus[ing] to reconsider the substance' of the Determination or to 'act with independent judgment[.]' The absence of an appeal mechanism by which Vistaprint might challenge the Determination does not form the basis for an IRP because there is nothing in ICANN's Bylaws or Articles of Incorporation requiring ICANN to provide one.'[987]

It submitted that the ICANN Board was under no obligation to investigate the impartiality of an expert panel:

> 'Vistaprint cites no obligation in the Articles or Bylaws that the ICANN Board affirmatively investigate the impartiality of an Expert Panel, outside of the requirement that the ICDR follow its policies on conflicts, which the ICDR did.'[988]

ICANN claimed that there was no discrimination, because '[c]laiming that other applicants have not suffered adverse determinations does not convert the Expert panel's Determination into a 'discriminatory ICANN Board act'.'[989]

It claimed that no disparate treatment can exist if the ICANN Board finds that established policies and procedures have been followed:

> 'Vistaprint's 'disparate treatment' argument fails to recognize that in considering Vistaprint's Reconsideration Request, the ICANN Board (via the BGC) did evaluate

983. Vistaprint Reply, §§ 31–32.
984. Vistaprint Request for IRP, §§ 63–66.
985. ICANN's Response (*Vistaprint*), § 21.
986. ICANN's Response (*Vistaprint*), § 60.
987. ICANN's Response (*Vistaprint*), § 71.
988. ICANN's Response (*Vistaprint*), § 73.
989. ICANN's Response (*Vistaprint*), § 72.

whether the Expert had followed established policies and procedures with respect to the Expert Determination, and found that he had.'[990]

It further argued that the ICANN Board had unfettered discretion whether or not to individually consider an application for a new gTLD:

> 'As the *Booking.com* IRP Panel found, "the fact that the ICANN Board enjoys [the] discretion [to individually consider an application for a New gTLD] and may choose to exercise it at any time does not mean that it is bound to exercise it, let alone at the time and in the manner demanded by [a claimant]".'[991]

ICANN disputed the suggestion that it should post all IRP correspondence (even if that correspondence contained substantive legal arguments):

> 'Vistaprint cites no Article or Bylaws provision requiring that every email from an IRP claimant be publicly posted, and none exists.'[992]

In any event, ICANN stated that its failure to post IRP correspondence could not be remedied via an IRP:

> '[T]he allegation that ICANN has not comprehensively posted all such correspondence is not a matter that could even potentially be remedied via an IRP.'[993]

It also stated that it did not accept that a claimant is harmed by ICANN's failure to post IRP correspondence if its counsel has had access to the information:

> '[G]iven the fact that Vistaprint's counsel also serves as counsel for *Booking.com*, Vistaprint has had access to all of the Booking.com post-hearing communications. Thus, it is unclear how Vistaprint is harmed if a few pieces of email correspondence in another IRP proceeding that its counsel has access to are not posted on ICANN's website.'[994]

The IRP panel ruled that the ICANN Board has no affirmative duty to consider new gTLD applications *sua sponte* in the absence of a party's recourse to an accountability mechanism:

> 'Although the Guidebook provides in § 5.1 that ICANN's Board of Directors has ultimate responsibility for the New gTLD Program, there is no affirmative duty stated in the Articles, Bylaws or Guidebook that the Board must to review the result in each and every SCO case.'[995]

> 'While Guidebook, § 5.1 permits ICANN's Board to individually consider new gTLD applications, such as through the RFR mechanism, it does not require that the Board do so in each and every case, *sua sponte*.'[996]

990. ICANN's Sur-Reply (*Vistaprint*), § 5.
991. ICANN's Sur-Reply (*Vistaprint*), § 17.
992. ICANN's Sur-Rebuttal (*Vistaprint*), § 5.
993. ICANN's Sur-Rebuttal (*Vistaprint*), § 12.
994. ICANN's Sur-Rebuttal (*Vistaprint*), § 13.
995. Vistaprint IRP Declaration, § 153.
996. Vistaprint IRP Declaration, § 156.

> 'The IRP Panel determines that in the absence of a party's recourse to an accountability mechanism such as the RFR, the ICANN Board has no affirmative duty to review the result in any particular SCO case.'[997]

The panel considered that the ICANN Board could have done a more thorough investigation in the issues raised by Vistaprint, but that it was not required to do so:

> 'Vistaprint also argued that the BGC conducted no investigation as to the nature of the new conflict that confronted the First Expert and instead 'developed baseless hypotheses for the other reasons that could have led to this Panel stepping down.' In this respect, perhaps the BGC could have sought to develop evidence on this issue by inquiring with the ICDR about the circumstances concerning the First Expert. Article IV, § 2.13 of the Bylaws provides the BGC 'may also request information relevant to the request from third parties,' but it does not require that the BGC do so. However, it would not have changed the outcome, as noted above.'[998]

The IRP panel held that ICANN must act in *good faith* and with *accountability* and *transparency*, and apply documented policies *neutrally*, *objectively* and *fairly*.[999]

The panel held that the lack of an appeal mechanism to contest the merits of a SCO was not a violation of the Articles of Incorporation or Bylaws:

> 'The IRP Panel finds that the lack of an appeal mechanism to contest the merits of the Third Expert's SCO determination is not, in itself, a violation of ICANN's Articles or Bylaws. ICANN's commitment through its Articles and Bylaws to act in good faith and with accountability and transparency, and to apply documented policies neutrally, objectively and fairly, does not require that it must have designed the SCO mechanism so that the result of a string confusion determination would be subject to a right of appeal. Other significant dispute resolution systems – such as the international legal regime for commercial arbitration regarding awards as final and binding – do not normally provide for a right of appeal on the merits.'[1000]

The panel found that Vistaprint had been given a *fair* opportunity to present its case:

> 'The IRP Panel denies Vistaprint's claim that Vistaprint was not given a fair opportunity to present its case; was deprived of procedural fairness and the opportunity to be heard by an independent panel applying the appropriate rules; and was not given any meaningful opportunity for remedy or redress once the SCO determination was made, even in the RFR procedure.'[1001]

Although it held that ICANN must apply its policies *neutrally*, *objectively* and *fairly*, it rejected Vistaprint's claim that the challenged SCO determination was contrary to ICANN's policy as established in the Guidebook:

> 'Vistaprint claims ICANN failed to comply with its obligation under Article I § 2.8 to neutrally, objectively and fairly apply documented policies as established in the Guidebook and Bylaws. As discussed above, the IRP Panel rejects Vistaprint's

997. Vistaprint IRP Declaration, § 157.
998. Vistaprint IRP Declaration, § 162.
999. Vistaprint IRP Declaration, §174.
1000. Vistaprint IRP Declaration, § 174.
1001. Vistaprint IRP Declaration, § 175.

> claim that the Vistaprint SCO determination – finding that the .webs and .web gTLD strings are confusingly similar – is contradictory to ICANN's policy for String Confusion Objections as established in the Guidebook.'[1002]

The panel held that the ICANN Board's right to individually consider an application must be exercised in a *non-discriminatory* fashion:

> 'As discussed above, in the Guidebook, § 5.1, ICANN has reserved the right to individually consider an application for a new gTLD to determine whether approval would be in the best interest of the Internet community [...]
>
> However, as a counterbalance against this reserved power to individually consider new gTLD applications, the ICANN Board must also comply with Article II, § 3 of ICANN's Bylaws, providing for non-discriminatory treatment [...].
>
> As Vistaprint maintains in its First Additional Submission, '[w]hen the ICANN Board individually considers an application, it must make sure that it does not treat applicants inequitably and that it does not discriminate among applicants.'[1003]

It confirmed that the ICANN Board's exercise of its discretion to individually consider an application must bear the scrutiny of *independent* and *objective* review, without any presumption of correctness:

> '[T]he IRP Panel considers that the Board's actions or omissions in this area of alleged non-discriminatory treatment bear the scrutiny of independent and objective review, without any presumption of correctness. Moreover, ICANN's Bylaws in Article I, § 2 set out its core values that should guide the decisions and actions of ICANN, including the requirement, when balancing among competing core values, to exercise judgment to determine which core values are the most relevant and how they apply to the specific circumstances at hand.'[1004]

The IRP panel found that the ICANN Board had not yet had the opportunity to exercise its independent judgment on the issue:

> 'The Panel finds that, contrary to what ICANN has stated above, ICANN's Board did not have an opportunity to 'exercise its independent judgment' – in particular, in view of its decisions to implement an additional review mechanism for certain other inconsistent SCO expert determinations – to consider specifically whether it should intervene with respect to the adverse SCO expert determination involving Vistaprint's .webs applications.'[1005]
>
> 'In accordance with Article 1, § 2 of the Bylaws, the Board shall exercise its judgment to determine which competing core values are most relevant and how they apply to arrive at a defensible balance among those values in relation to the case at hand. Given the timing of Vistaprint's Reconsideration Request, and the timing of ICANN's consultation process for potential review mechanisms to address inconsistent SCO expert determinations, this exercise of judgment by the Board has not yet occurred in the case of Vistaprint's .webs gTLD applications.
>
> Here, ICANN is subject to the requirements of Article II, § 3 of its Bylaws regarding nondiscriminatory treatment, providing that it shall not apply its 'standards,

1002. Vistaprint IRP Declaration, § 175.
1003. Vistaprint IRP Declaration, § 177-179.
1004. Vistaprint IRP Declaration, § 180.
1005. Vistaprint IRP Declaration, § 185.

policies, procedures, or practices inequitably or single out any particular party for disparate treatment unless justified by substantial and reasonable cause.' ICANN has provided additional relief to certain gTLD applicants who were subject to adverse decisions in String Confusion Objection cases. In those cases, the differences in the gTLD strings at issue were not too dissimilar from the *.webs/.web* gTLD strings.'[1006]

The IRP panel could not agree on whether it would be *discriminatory* if the Board refused to expand the scope of the review mechanism that was installed for other SCOs:

> 'This IRP Panel, among its three members, could not agree – in regards to the specific circumstances of Vistaprint's gTLD applications – whether the reasons offered by ICANN in its Resolution 2014.10.12.NG02 for refusing the 'to expand the scope of the proposed review mechanism to include other [SCO] Expert Determinations' would meet the standard of non-discrimination imposed by Article II, § 3 of the Bylaws, as well as the relevant core values in Article 1, § 2 of the Bylaws (e.g., applying documented policies neutrally and objectively, with integrity and fairness). For instance, one view is that limiting the additional review mechanism to only those SCO cases in which there were inconsistent decisions is a sufficient reason for intervening in these cases, but not in other SCO cases involving similar singular vs. plural gTLD strings were the applicant received an adverse decision. On the other hand, another view is that the real focus should be on the developments involving single vs. plural gTLDs strings, including the inconsistency of decisions and the offering of additional review mechanism in certain cases, and the delegation of so many other single/plural variations of the same gTLD strings, which are, at least in this way, similarly situated to the circumstances of the *.webs/.web* strings.'[1007]

(3) Standard of Review

Vistaprint argued that the standard of review is non-deferential, and that a restrictive interpretation of the standard of review would be inappropriate:

> 'In its Response to the Request for IRP, ICANN submits that its "Bylaws specify that a deferential standard of review be applied when evaluating the actions of the ICANN Board". This is simply wrong. No such specification is made in ICANN's Bylaws or elsewhere, and a restrictive interpretation of the standard of review would be inappropriate. It would fail to ensure accountability on the part of ICANN and would be incompatible with ICANN's commitment to maintain (and improve) robust mechanisms for accountability, as required by Article 9.1 of ICANN's Affirmation of Commitments ([...]) and ICANN's core values, which require ICANN to "remain accountable to the Internet community through mechanisms that enhance ICANN's effectiveness ([Bylaws], Article I(2)(10))".'[1008]

ICANN argued that IRP panels must apply a deferential standard of review:

1006. Vistaprint IRP Declaration, §§ 187–188.
1007. Vistaprint, IRP Declaration, § 189.
1008. Vistaprint Reply, § 36.

> breached its obligations under its AoI, Bylaws and the Applicant Guidebook. To offer effective redress to applicants, the IRP Panel may indicate what action ICANN must take to cease violating these obligations. The point is all the stronger here, as ICANN conceived the IRP to be the sole dispute resolution mechanism available to new gTLD applicants [...].'[1015]

Vistaprint argued that a claimant was entitled to such relief as it would put an end to the inconsistency of ICANN's decision with the Articles of Incorporation and Bylaws:

> 'Any relief ordered must be sufficient to avoid another unfair, arbitrary and discriminatory decision.'[1016]

In Vistaprint's view, any relief that allowed the disputed contention set to remain would leave ICANN in ongoing violation of the fundamental principles that bind it:

> 'Any outcome that allows the contention set between .webs and .web to remain would leave ICANN in ongoing violation of the fundamental principles that bind it, because, since this case began, ICANN has delegated various strings that are at least as similar to each other as .webs and .web. [...]ICANN should therefore delegate both .webs and .web. If the decision to put .webs and .web in a single contention set is upheld, then ICANN should also revoke the delegation of those gTLDs with at least equal string similarities. Any other outcome would result in Vistaprint continuing to suffer discrimination. ICANN would also remain in violation of its contractual obligations and continue to deprive registry operators of legal certainty and their legitimate expectations. The only way in which ICANN can act in accordance with its Articles of Incorporation and Bylaws is to reject the determination that .webs and .web are confusingly similar and to dissolve the resulting contention set.'[1017]

At the very least, Vistaprint argued, ICANN should organize a new SCO procedure:

> 'In the alternative, ICANN must reject the determination that .webs and .web are confusingly similar and organize a new and independent and impartial SCO procedure, as specified in Vistaprint's request for IRP. However, being an ICDR panel, there is no reason why this IRP Panel could not serve as the panel in said SCO procedure.'[1018]

ICANN argued that the IRP panel had no authority to grant affirmative relief, as its authority was limited to issuing opinions as to whether an action or inaction of the Board was inconsistent with the Articles of Incorporation or Bylaws and recommending interim actions or the stay of any action or decision:

> 'Any request that the IRP Panel grant affirmative relief goes well beyond the IRP Panel's authority. An IRP Panel is limited to 'declaring whether an action or inaction of the Board was inconsistent with the Articles of Incorporation or Bylaws' and *recommending* that the Board stay any action or decision or take any interim action until such time as the Board reviews and acts upon the opinion of

1015. Vistaprint Brief on *Booking.com* case (Rebuttal), § 24.
1016. Vistaprint Reply, § 39.
1017. Vistaprint Reply § 40.
1018. Vistaprint Brief on *Booking.com* case (Rebuttal), §26.

> the IRP Panel. This IRP Panel simply does not have the authority to award affirmative relief or to require ICANN to undertake specific conduct.'[1019]

In particular, ICANN submitted that the IRP panel could not perform a substantive review of an evaluation panel's decision:

> 'Neither ICANN's Board nor this IRP Panel is tasked with determining—or competent to determine—who should prevail in a battle of linguistic experts. Again, this IRP Panel is tasked solely with declaring its opinion as to whether the Board acted 'without conflict of interest and with due care' and in a manner 'consistent with the Articles of Incorporation or Bylaws [or] the Guidebook.' The Board did just that in carefully considering the arguments Vistaprint raised regarding the standard applied by the Expert and issuing a reasoned determination denying Vistaprint's Reconsideration Request.'[1020]

It argued that an IRP panel 'simply does not have the authority to award affirmative relief or to require ICANN to undertake specific conduct.'[1021]

In short, ICANN stated that the IRP panel was authorized neither to substitute its judgment for that of the Board nor to deviate from the procedures set forth in the Guidebook:

> '[T]he rules are clear that the IRP Panel is neither asked to, nor allowed to, substitute its judgment for that of the Board.'[1022]

> 'As the IRP Panel in *Booking.com v. ICANN* recently confirmed, IRP panels are expressly limited to "compare[ing] contested actions of the *Board* to ICANN's Articles [] and Bylaws" and are "neither asked to, nor allowed to, substitute [their] judgment for that of the Board.'[1023]

> 'Vistaprint offers only one new variation as to its demand for a declaration requiring specific relief: it asks that this *IRP Panel itself* adjudicate its string confusion objection. To take Vistaprint's suggestion would contravene the Guidebook, the Bylaws and the new gTLD Program itself in multiple ways, as the Guidebook sets out distinct procedures for the appointment of string confusion expert panelists whereas the Bylaws set forth different procedures for the constitution of IRP panels.'[1024]

The IRP panel ruled that it had no authority to award affirmative relief, but could recommend the Board to take, or refrain from taking, actions or decisions:

> '*Authority to award affirmative relief:* The IRP Panel's analysis on this issue is closely related to, and dependent upon, its analysis of the binding vs. non-binding issue immediately above. To the extent that the IRP Panel renders any form of relief whereby the Panel would direct the Board to take, or refrain from taking, any action or decision, that relief must be "recommend[ed]" to the Board, which then "reviews and acts upon the opinion of the IRP," as specified in § 3.11(d) of the

1019. ICANN's Response (*Vistaprint*), § 78; *see also* ICANN's Response, § 56 and ICANN's Sur-Reply, § 46 in the *Booking.com* case.
1020. ICANN's Sur-Reply (*Vistaprint*), § 31.
1021. ICANN's Sur-Reply (*Vistaprint*), § 33.
1022. ICANN's Response (*Vistaprint*), § 33.
1023. ICANN's Sur-Reply (*Vistaprint*), § 7.
1024. ICANN's Sur-Rebuttal (*Vistaprint*), § 28.

> Bylaws. Relatedly, Supplementary Rule 7 provides that an "IRP Panel may recommend that the Board stay any action or decision, or that the Board take any interim action, until such time as the Board reviews and acts upon the IRP declaration." Consequently, the IRP Panel finds that it does not have authority to render affirmative relief requiring ICANN's Board to take, or refrain from taking, any action or decision.'[1025]

The panel considered that the ICANN Board would risk violating its Bylaws if it did not exercise its judgment on the question of disparate treatment as recommended by the panel:

> 'The IRP Panel is mindful that it should not substitute its judgment for that of ICANN's Board. The Board has not yet considered Vistaprint's claim of disparate treatment, and the arguments that ICANN makes through its counsel in this IRP do not serve as a substitute for the exercise of independent judgment by the Board. Without the exercise of judgment by ICANN's Board on this question of whether there is any inequitable or disparate treatment regarding Vistaprint's .webs gTLD applications, the Board would risk violating its Bylaws, including its core values.'[1026]

> 'Accordingly, it follows that in response to Vistaprint's contentions of disparate treatment in this IRP, ICANN's Board – and not this Panel – should exercise its independent judgment on this issue, in light of all of the foregoing considerations.'[1027]

b. *Noteworthy Points for Analysis*

The IRP panel considered that it was not entitled to render affirmative relief, on the basis that it was *only* permitted to recommend that the Board stay or take any action or decision.[1028] However, neither the Bylaws nor the Supplementary Rules provide that the panel may 'only' recommend such actions. It may have been more consistent with the ICDR Rules to interpret Article IV(3)(11) of the Bylaws as providing a non-exhaustive list of the authority of the panel.

Moreover, in our view, a recommendation can also be a binding recommendation. The precise nature of a recommendation flows from its context: 'while "recommendations" often connotes advice or information which the recipient may disregard, the term might also refer to directions or orders which are binding.'[1029] This is no different with respect to IRPs. In response to two requests for interim relief, the emergency IRP panelist has issued recommendations, ordering that ICANN refrain from certain

1025. Vistaprint IRP Declaration, § 149.
1026. Vistaprint IRP Declaration, § 190.
1027. Vistaprint IRP Declaration, § 191.
1028. Vistaprint IRP Declaration, § 136.
1029. *Thomson v. Canada* (Deputy Minister of Agriculture), [1992] 1 SCR 385, 1992 CanLII 121 (SCC), http://www.canlii.org/en/ca/scc/doc/1992/1992canlii121/1992canlii121.html.

actions.[1030] In our view, the language of these 'recommendations' that effectively prescribed what ICANN was (not) to do, is a clear indication of their binding nature.

The *Vistaprint* panel recognized that a 'recommendation' could be intended to be binding on the parties, but considered that, in the context of the IRP, 'the word "recommend" conveys that the panel's direction of any action or inaction on the part of the Board is a non-binding reference.'[1031] However, the panel did not explain why 'in the context of the IRP' a recommendation should be considered non-binding. The absence of a detailed explanation on this point is unfortunate, given that the *Vistaprint* panel referred to the use of the word 'recommend' in Article 47 of the ICSID Convention[1032] as an example of when it could refer to a binding order, and this Article 47 contains language very similar to that used in ICANN's Bylaws and in Article 7 of the ICDR Supplementary Rules for IRP. The purpose behind both provisions is also very similar. They are both intended to protect the rights of parties during the pendency of the proceedings: Article 47 of the ICSID Convention foresees provisional measures 'to preserve the respective rights of either party'; Article 7 of the ICDR Supplementary Rules for IRP is entitled 'interim measures of protection'.

Of course, it is clear that the possibility to render affirmative relief gives IRP panel's significant authority that must be exercised with great caution. The *Vistaprint* panel was 'mindful that it should not substitute its judgment for that of ICANN's Board.'[1033] However, this caveat should not prevent an IRP panel from indicating what actions or inactions are contrary to ICANN's Articles of Incorporation and Bylaws and what actions would comply with ICANN's fundamental obligations. The primary focus of an IRP panel should be on resolving the dispute, and this purpose cannot be achieved if the IRP panel limits itself to issuing non-binding recommendations.

7. Nature and Value of the IRP Declaration

a. *Arguments Discussed*

(1) Binding Nature of the IRP Declaration

Vistaprint argued that IRP Declarations are binding:

> 'The outcome of the IRP is binding upon ICANN. Since ICANN's amendment of its Bylaws on 11 April 2013, IRP declarations have precedential value ([Bylaws], Article IV(3)(21), *in fine*). The precedential value – and binding force – of IRP declarations was recently confirmed in an IRP Panel declaration that itself has precedential effect. It follows that the IRP declaration requested in this case by

1030. *Dot Registry case*, Interim Declaration on Emergency Independent Review Panelist's Order on Request for Emergency Measures of Protection, 23 December 2014, p. 19; *GCC* case, Interim Declaration on Emergency Request for Interim Measures of Protection, 12 February 2015, § 96.
1031. Vistaprint IRP Declaration, § 138, n. 192.
1032. Vistaprint IRP Declaration, § 138, n. 192.
1033. Vistaprint IRP Declaration, § 190.

Vistaprint would be binding upon ICANN. Any other outcome would effectively grant ICANN arbitrary and unlimited power. It would make ICANN virtually untouchable, something which was never intended and it would be incompatible with ICANN's obligation to maintain and improve robust mechanisms for accountability (*E.g.*, [Affirmation of Commitments], Article 9.1 and [Bylaws], Article I(2)(10)).'[1034]

It submitted that ICANN's Articles of Incorporation and Bylaws would be put into question if an IRP were not considered binding, and that the applicable procedural rules call for a binding IRP:

'The IRP cannot be an effective and robust mechanism for accountability – as required under ICANN's Affirmation of Commitments ([Affirmation of Commitments], Article 9.1) and ICANN's Bylaws ([Bylaws], Article I(2)(10) – unless it is binding upon ICANN. Otherwise, the ICANN Board's discretion would indeed be unfettered and ICANN's AoI and Bylaws would be moot.

As mentioned in Vistaprint's Reply, a previous IRP Panel ruled that "[v]arious provisions of ICANN's Bylaws and the Supplementary Procedures support the conclusion that the [IRP] Panel's decisions, opinions and declarations are binding" *and that* "[t]here is certainly nothing in the Supplementary Rules that renders the decisions, opinions and declarations of the [IRP] Panel either advisory or non-binding" [...].

Indeed, as per Article IV(3)(8) of the ICANN Bylaws, the ICANN Board has given its approval to the ICDR to establish a set of operating rules and procedures for the conduct of the IRP. The operating rules and procedures established by the ICDR are the ICDR Rules as referred to in the preamble of the Supplementary Procedures [...]. The Supplementary Procedures *supplement* the ICDR Rules (Supplementary Procedures, Preamble and Section 2). The preamble of the ICDR Rules provides that "[a] dispute can be submitted to an arbitral tribunal for a final and binding decision'. Article 30 of the ICDR Rules specifies that '[a]wards shall be made in writing by the arbitral tribunal and shall be final and binding on the parties". No provision in the Supplementary Procedures deviates from the rule that the Panel's decisions are binding. On the contrary, Section 1 of the Supplementary Procedures defines an IRP Declaration as a decision/opinion of the IRP Panel. Section 10 of the Supplementary Procedures requires that IRP Declarations i) are made in writing, and ii) specifically designate the prevailing party. Where a decision must specifically designate the prevailing party, it is inherently binding. Moreover the binding nature of IRP Declarations is further supported by the language and spirit of Section 6 of the Supplementary Procedures and Article IV(3)(11)(a) of the ICANN Bylaws. Pursuant to these provisions, the IRP Panel has the authority to summarily dismiss requests brought without standing, lacking in substance, or that are frivolous or vexatious. Surely, such a decision, opinion or declaration on the part of the IRP Panel would not be considered advisory [...].

Finally, even if ICANN's Bylaws and Supplementary Procedures are ambiguous – *quod non* – on the question of whether or not an IRP Declaration is binding, this ambiguity would weigh against ICANN. The relationship between ICANN and Vistaprint is clearly an adhesive one. In such a situation, the rule of *contra proferentem* applies. As the drafter and architect of the IRP Procedure, it was possible for ICANN, and clearly within its power, to adopt a procedure that

1034. Vistaprint Reply, § 37.

expressly and clearly announced that the decisions, opinions and declarations of IRP Panels were advisory only. ICANN did not adopt such a procedure [...].

For all these reasons, the IRP Declaration is binding upon ICANN.'[1035]

ICANN argued that the IRP is a specific form of dispute resolution, which is non-binding:

> 'An IRP is not an arbitration process, but rather a means by which entities that participate in ICANN's processes can seek an independent review of decisions made by ICANN's Board of Directors. Specifically, the IRP, when invoked, calls for the IRP Panel to consider and then declare whether the IRP Panel believes an action or decision of ICANN's Board of Directors was consistent with ICANN's Articles of Incorporation ('Articles') or Bylaws. The ICANN Board then considers that declaration. The declaration is not binding on the ICANN Board but, of course, ICANN takes the IRP seriously and the Board will consider the declaration at the first opportunity.'[1036]

It claimed that the language of the IRP provisions in ICANN's Bylaws and their drafting history made clear that IRP declarations were not binding on ICANN:

> 'The plain language of the IRP provisions set forth in Article IV, Section 3 of ICANN's Bylaws, as well as the drafting history of the development of the IRP provisions, make clear that IRP panel declarations are not binding on ICANN.
>
> First, the Bylaws charge an IRP panel with "comparing contested actions of the Board to the Articles of Incorporation and Bylaws, and with declaring whether the Board has acted consistently with the provisions of those Articles of Incorporation and Bylaws." The Board is then obligated to "review[]" and "consider" an IRP panel's declaration at the Board's next meeting "where feasible." The direction to "review" and "consider" an IRP panel's declaration means that the Board has discretion as to whether it should adopt that declaration and whether it should take any action in response to that declaration; if the declaration were binding, there would be nothing to review or consider, only a binding order to implement.
>
> Second, the lengthy drafting history of ICANN's independent review process confirms that IRP panel declarations are not binding. Specifically, the Draft Principles for Independent Review, drafted in 1999, state that "the ICANN Board should retain ultimate authority over ICANN's affairs — after all, it is the Board ... that will be chosen by (and is directly accountable to) the membership and supporting organizations." And when, in 2001, the Committee on ICANN Evolution and Reform (ERC) recommended the creation of an independent review process, it called for the creation of "a process to require non-binding arbitration by an international arbitration body to review any allegation that the Board has acted in conflict with ICANN's Bylaws." The individuals who actively participated in the process also agreed that the review process would not be binding. As one participant stated: IRP "decisions will be nonbinding, because the Board will retain final decision-making authority." The amendments to the Bylaws, which occurred following a community process on proposed IRP revisions, added, among other things, a sentence stating that "declarations of the IRP Panel, and the Board's subsequent action on those declarations, are final and have precedential value." Vistaprint argues that this new language, which does not actually use the word

1035. Vistaprint brief on the *Booking.com* case (Rebuttal), §§ 30–34.
1036. ICANN Response (*Vistaprint*), § 2; *see also* ICANN Response (*Vistaprint*), § 35.

"binding," nevertheless provides that IRP panel declarations are binding, trumping years of drafting history, the sworn testimony of those who participated in the drafting process,[53] and the plain text of the Bylaws. This argument is meritless.

First, relying on the use of the terms "final" and "precedential" is unavailing—a declaration clearly can be both non-binding and also final and precedential [...].

Second, the language Vistaprint references was added to ICANN's Bylaws to meet recommendations made by ICANN's Accountability Structures Expert Panel (ASEP). The ASEP was comprised of three world-renowned experts on issues of corporate governance, accountability, and international dispute resolution, and was charged with evaluating ICANN's accountability mechanisms, including the Independent Review process. The ASEP recommended, among other things, that an IRP should not be permitted to proceed on the same issues as presented in a prior IRP. The ASEP's recommendations in this regard were raised in light of the second IRP constituted under ICANN's Bylaws, where the claimant presented claims that would have required the IRP Panel to reevaluate the declaration of the IRP Panel in the ICM IRP. To prevent claimants from challenging Board action taken in direct response to a prior IRP panel declaration, the ASEP recommended that "[t]he declarations of the IRP, and ICANN's subsequent actions on those declarations, should have precedential value." The ASEP's recommendations in this regard did not convert IRP panel declarations into binding decisions. One of the important considerations underlying the ASEP's work was the fact that ICANN, while it operates internationally, is a California non-profit public benefit corporation subject to the statutory law of California as determined by United States courts. As Graham McDonald, one of the three ASEP experts, explained, because California law requires that the board "retain responsibility for decision-making," the Board has "final word" on "any recommendation that . . . arises out of [an IRP]." The ASEP's recommendations were therefore premised on the understanding that the declaration of an IRP panel is not "binding" on the Board.'[1037]

The IRP panel ruled that its findings on the question of whether or not the ICANN Board's conduct is consistent with the Articles of Incorporation and Bylaws are in themselves binding, but that any recommendation that the panel may give to the Board is non-binding:

> 'The Panel views that it is important to distinguish between (i) the findings of the Panel on the question of whether the ICANN Board's conduct is consistent (or not) with the Articles and Bylaws, and (ii) any consequent remedial measures to be considered as a result of those findings, at least insofar as those measures would direct the Board to take or not take any action or decision. The Panel considers that, as to the first point, the findings of the Panel on whether the Board has acted in a manner that is consistent (or not) with the Articles or Bylaws is akin to a finding of breach/liability by a court in a contested legal case. This determination by the Panel is 'binding' in the sense that ICANN's Board cannot overrule the Panel's declaration on this point or later decide for itself that it disagrees with the Panel and that there was no inconsistency with (or violation of) the Articles and Bylaws. However, when it comes to the question of whether or not the IRP Panel can *require* that ICANN's Board implement any form of redress based on a finding of violation, here, the Panel believes that it can only raise remedial measures to be considered by the Board in an advisory, non-binding manner. The Panel concludes that this distinction – between a "binding" declaration on the violation question

1037. ICANN's Sur-Reply (*Vistaprint*), §§ 34–41; *see also* ICANN's Sur-Rebuttal (*Vistaprint*), § 29.

> and a "non-binding" declaration when it comes to recommending that the Board stay or take any action – is most consistent with the terms and spirit of the charter instruments upon which the Panel's jurisdiction is based, and avoids conflating these two aspects of the Panel's role.'[1038]
>
> '[A]ny form of relief whereby the IRP Panel *would direct the Board* to take, or refrain from taking, any action or decision, as specified in § 3.11(d), must be "recommend[ed]" to the Board, which then "reviews and acts upon the opinion of the IRP." The Panel's authority is thus limited (and in this sense non-binding) when it comes to providing ICANN's Board with potential courses of action or inaction in view of Board's non-compliance with the Articles or Bylaws.'[1039]

The panel found that the hybrid nature of IRP declarations (partly binding, partly advisory) is consistent with the applicable rules and their drafting history:

> 'The IRP Panel shares some of Vistaprint's concerns about the efficacy of the IRP as an accountability mechanism if any affirmative relief that might be considered appropriate by the Panel is considered non-binding on ICANN's Board (see discussion below); nevertheless, the Panel determines on the basis of the charter instruments, as well as the drafting history of those documents, that its declaration is binding only with respect to the finding of compliance or not with the Articles and Bylaws, and non-binding with respect to any measures that the Panel might recommend the Board take or refrain from taking.'[1040]

It considered that the IRP panel in the *ICM Registry* case did not conclusively address this issue, and that nothing in the Bylaws, Supplementary Rules or ICDR Rules suggests that the IRP panel's declaration is non-binding with respect to the panel's core task of deciding whether the Board did, or did not, comply the Articles or Bylaws:

> 'The IRP panel in the *ICM Registry Final Declaration* stressed that the IRP panel's task is to "declare", not to "decide" or to "determine". However, the word "declare", alone, does not conclusively answer the question of whether the IRP's declaration (or any part of it) is binding or not. "To declare" means *"to announce or express something clearly and publicly, especially officially."* Declarations can and do serve as the predicate for binding or non-binding consequences in different contexts. For example, a declaratory relief action – in which a court resolves legal uncertainty by determining the rights of parties under a contract or statute without ordering anything be done or awarding damages – can have a binding result because it may later preclude a lawsuit by one of the parties to the declaratory lawsuit. Further, in a non-legal context, "declaring" a state of emergency in a particular state or country can have binding consequences. Thus, the word "declare," in itself, does not answer the issue.
>
> Moreover, nothing in the Bylaws, Supplementary Procedures or ICDR Rules suggests that the IRP Panel's declaration is non-binding with respect to the Panel's core task of deciding whether the Board did, or did not, comply [with] the Articles or Bylaws. There is no provision that states the ICANN Board can reconsider this independent and important declaration. To the contrary, the ICDR Rules, which apply to the IRP proceedings, can be read to suggest that *both* the Panel's finding of compliance (or not) by ICANN's Board, *and* the Panel's possible reference to

1038. Vistaprint IRP Declaration, § 130.
1039. Vistaprint IRP Declaration, § 138.
1040. Vistaprint IRP Declaration, § 131.

> any remedial measures, are binding on ICANN. As Vistaprint indicates, the preamble of the ICDR Rules provide that "[a] dispute can be submitted to an arbitral tribunal for a *final and binding decision*,' and Article 30(1) of those Rules specifies that '[a]wards shall be made in writing by the arbitral tribunal and shall be final and binding on the parties" *(emphasis added)*.'[1041]

The IRP panel found that several provisions of the Bylaws and Supplementary Procedures indicate the areas in which an IRP panel may issue binding decisions, namely summary dismissals, designation of the prevailing party, decisions on costs and procedural aspects, and the panel's findings on consistency with the Articles of Incorporation and Bylaws:

> 'Several other provisions of the Bylaws and Supplementary Procedures can be fairly read to relate to decisions of the IRP panel that would be considered binding, even as to ICANN's Board. Article IV, § 3.18 provides "[t]he IRP Panel shall make its declaration based solely on the documentation, supporting materials, and arguments submitted by the parties, and in its declaration shall specifically designate the prevailing party." There is no mechanism for the Board to overrule the IRP panel's designation as to which party is the prevailing party. Article IV, § 3.20 provides "[t]he IRP Panel may, in its discretion, grant a party's request to keep certain information confidential, such as trade secrets." A fair reading of this provision is that the IRP panel's decision concerning such questions of confidentiality would be binding on all parties (including ICANN) in the IRP procedure. Consolidating IRP requests and determining the timing for each IRP proceeding are also decisions of the panel that are binding and not subject to review. Finally, Supplemental Procedures, Rule 11, directs that "[t]he IRP Panel shall fix costs in its Declaration." Here too, this decision of the IRP panel can be fairly read to be binding on the parties, including the Board.'[1042]
>
> 'Thus, the IRP Panel's authority to render binding or non-binding decisions, orders or relief can be considered in relation to four basic areas:
>
> (i) *summary dismissals* by the IRP Panel (for different reasons as stated in the Bylaws and Supplementary Procedures) are final and binding on the parties. There is no mechanism for appeal of such dismissals and they have precedential value.
> (ii) *the designation of prevailing party, fixing costs for the IRP, and other orders in support of the IRP proceedings* (e.g., timing of proceedings, confidentiality, requests for additional submissions, consolidation of IRP cases) are binding decisions of the IRP Panel, with no review by the Board or any other body.
> (iii) *the IRP Panel's declaration of whether or not the Board has acted consistently with the provisions of the Articles and Bylaws* is final and binding, in the sense that there is no appeal on this point to ICANN's Board or any other body; it is a final determination and has precedential value.
> (iv) *any form of relief in which the IRP Panel would direct the Board to take, or refrain from taking, any action or decision* is only a recommendation to the Board. In this sense, such a recommendation is not binding on the Board. The Bylaws and Supplementary Procedures provide specific and detailed guidance in this key area – i.e., relief that would require the Board to take or refraining

1041. Vistaprint IRP Declaration, §§ 134–135.
1042. Vistaprint IRP Declaration, § 139.

> from taking any action or decision – where the IRP Panel's decisions *would not* be binding on the Board, but would serve only as a recommendation to be reviewed and acted upon by the Board.

The other decisions of the IRP panel, as outlined above and including the declaration of whether or not the Board violated the Articles and Bylaws, would be binding, consistent with the Bylaws, Supplementary Procedures and ICDR Rule Article 30(1). This approach provides a reading that harmonizes the terms of the three charter instruments. It also provides interpretive context for Article IV, § 3.21 of the Bylaws, providing that "[w]here feasible, the Board shall consider the IRP panel declaration at the Board's next meeting." The IRP panel in the ICM Registry Final Declaration stated that "[t]his relaxed temporal proviso to do no more than 'consider' the IRP declaration, and to do so at the next meeting of the Board 'where feasible', emphasizes that it is not binding." However, consistent with the analysis above, the IRP panel here reads this statement in the ICM Registry Final Declaration to relate only to an IRP panel's decision to "recommend" that the Board take, or refrain from taking, any action or decision. It does not relate to the other decisions or duties of the IRP panel, as explained above.

Vistaprint contends that the second sentence in Article IV, § 3.21 – providing "[t]he declarations of the IRP panel, and the Board's subsequent action on those declarations, are final and have precedential value" – which was added in April 2013 after the issuance of ICM Registry Final Declaration, was a change that supports the view that the IRP panel's outcome, including any references to remedial relief, is binding. However, the panel agrees with ICANN's view that "a declaration clearly can be both non-binding and also final and precedential." Further, the preparatory work and drafting history for the relevant provisions of the Bylaws relating to the IRP procedure indicate the intention for a non-binding procedure with respect to the panel's authority to advise the Board to take, or refrain from taking, any action or decision. As summarized in ICANN's contentions above, ICANN has submitted evidence that those who were initially involved in establishing the IRP considered that it should be an advisory, non-binding procedure in relation to any policies that the Board might be requested to consider and implement by the IRP panel.

Thus, the Bylaws and the Supplementary Procedures draw a line: when the measures that an IRP panel might consider as a result of its core task require that the Board take or refrain from taking any action or decision, the panel may only "recommend" this course of action. On the other hand, if the IRP panel decides that the Board had violated its Articles or Bylaws, or if the panel decides to dismiss the IRP request, designate a prevailing party, set conditions for confidentiality, consolidate IRP requests, request additional written submissions or fix costs, a fair reading of the Bylaws, Supplementary Procedures and ICDR Rules relevant to these determinations would be that the IRP panel's decisions on these matters are binding on both parties, including ICANN.'[1043]

1043. Vistaprint IRP Declaration, §§ 140–143; *see also* Vistaprint IRP Declaration, §§ 147–148.

(2) Precedential Value of IRP Declaration

The IRP panel ruled that its findings on the standard of review (see above) have precedential value and are now settled.[1044]

It held that its declaration would have precedential value:

> 'The Panel's Declaration will have "precedential value" and will possibly be made publicly available on ICANN's website. Thus, the declaration of violation (or not), even without the ability to order binding relief vis-à-vis ICANN's Board, will carry more weight than would be the case if the IRP was a confidential procedure with decisions that carried no precedential value.'[1045]

b. Noteworthy Points for Analysis

(1) Binding Nature of the IRP Declaration

Although the IRP panel was seemingly clear on which part of its ruling could be considered binding, there are complexities to be considered here. The panel found that the ICANN Board would risk violating its Bylaws if it did not exercise its judgment on the question of whether there were any inequitable or disparate treatment regarding Vistaprint's .webs gTLD. If the panel's recommendation to the Board on this point were to be considered non-binding, and ICANN were then not to follow the recommendation, the result could be that a subsequent IRP panel review the inaction and rule it to be a violation of the Bylaws. In this way, the recommendation would become *de facto* binding. Thus, the panel's statement seems logically at odds with its finding that although it could issue a binding declaration on the question of whether ICANN violated its Articles of Incorporation and/or Bylaws, any recommendation by the IRP panel to the Board would be non-binding only.

However, the panel's findings on the non-binding nature of recommendations must be seen in conjunction with its findings concerning its lack of authority to render affirmative relief or substitute its own judgment for that of ICANN's Board. In other words, the panel considered that it could not impose specific actions on the Board, but that it could review whether the Board's actions or inactions were consistent with ICANN's Articles of Incorporation and Bylaws. The IRP panel did not recommend a specific and well-framed action to the ICANN Board. Instead, it gave the Board the opportunity to exercise its independent judgment on the issue, and ruled that a failure of the Board to exercise this discretion would risk violating ICANN's Bylaws. In this way, the IRP panel abstained from telling the ICANN Board how to exercise its discretion, but maintained its right to scrutinize the Board's exercise of its discretion or the Board's refusal to exercise its discretion.

1044. Vistaprint IRP Declaration, § 126.
1045. Vistaprint IRP Declaration, § 131.

8. ICANN Board's Decision Following the IRP Declaration

On 22 October 2015, the ICANN Board accepted the panel's findings and the panel's recommendation that the Board exercise its independent judgment on the question of 'whether an additional review mechanism is appropriate to re-evaluate the Third Expert's determination in the Vistaprint SCO, in view of ICANN's Bylaws concerning core values and non-discriminatory treatment, and based on the particular circumstances and developments noted in [the IRP] Declaration.'[1046] As a result, the ICANN Board was obliged to reassess the case and consider whether or not Vistaprint was discriminated against. However, in our view the ICANN Board misquoted the IRP Declaration in stating that the IRP panel 'found that ICANN did not discriminate against Vistaprint in not directing a re-evaluation of the Expert Determination.'[1047] As explained above, the IRP panel did not in fact decide on this issue, as it could not agree whether ICANN's refusal '"to expand the scope of the proposed review mechanism to include other [SCO] Expert Determinations" would meet the standard of non-discrimination imposed by Article II, § 3 of the Bylaws, as well as the relevant core values in Article 1, § 2 of the Bylaws (e.g., applying documented policies neutrally and objectively, with integrity and fairness).'[1048] The panel considered that the ICANN Board had not yet considered Vistaprint's claim of disparate treatment, and that the Board would risk violating its Bylaws, including its core values, if it refused to exercise its independent judgment on the question.[1049]

In any event, the ICANN Board did agree to consider Vistaprint's claim of disparate treatment, and, when it finally did so on 3 March 2016, it concluded that 'the Vistaprint SCO Expert Determination is not sufficiently "inconsistent" or "unreasonable" such that the underlying objection proceedings resulting in the Expert Determination warrants re-evaluation.'[1050] It added that it found 'as it has previously found, that ICANN's Bylaws concerning core values and non-discriminatory treatment and the particular circumstances and developments noted in the Final Declaration do not support re-evaluation of the objection proceedings leading to the Vistaprint SCO Expert Determination.'[1051]

The phrase 'as it has previously found' is puzzling. The IRP panel established that the ICANN Board had not yet considered Vistaprint's claim of disparate treatment. The ICANN Board did not reject or deny this statement by the IRP panel, and it considered

1046. ICANN, *Approved Resolutions 2015.10.22.17-2015.10.22.18 – Regular Meeting of the ICANN Board*, 22 October 2015, https://www.icann.org/resources/board-material/resolutions-2015-10-22-en.
1047. ICANN, *Preamble to Approved Resolutions 2015.10.22.17-2015.10.22.18 – Regular Meeting of the ICANN Board*, 22 October 2015, https://www.icann.org/resources/board-material/resolutions-2015-10-22-en.
1048. Vistaprint IRP Declaration, § 189.
1049. Vistaprint IRP Declaration, § 190.
1050. ICANN, *Approved Board Resolution 2016.03.03.02 – Regular Meeting of the ICANN Board*, 3 March 2016, https://www.icann.org/resources/board-material/resolutions-2016-03-03-en.
1051. ICANN, *Approved Board Resolution 2016.03.03.03 – Regular Meeting of the ICANN Board*, 3 March 2016, https://www.icann.org/resources/board-material/resolutions-2016-03-03-en.

Vistaprint's discrimination claim for the first time at its meeting of 3 March 2016. Moreover, it is doubtful that the Board's conclusion that the Vistaprint SCO Expert Determination was not 'sufficiently' inconsistent or unreasonable is satisfactory as a justification for denying a re-evaluation. After all, the reasoning in the Vistaprint SCO Expert Determination was based upon a case which the ICANN Board had found to be sufficiently inconsistent and unreasonable as to merit a re-evaluation process.

9. What Happened Thereafter?

In our view, there were grounds to initiate a new claim against ICANN and to have an IRP panel review the ICANN Board's denial of a re-evaluation for consistency with ICANN's Articles of Incorporation and Bylaws. However, a new IRP involves renewed efforts and delays in bringing the gTLD to market with no guarantee that it would resolve the dispute. *E.g.*, if the panel in a new IRP decided that the ICANN Board violated its Bylaws in failing to provide a reasonable justification, it could still consider that it should not substitute its judgment for that of the ICANN Board and refer the matter back to ICANN. In such a scenario, it seems unlikely that the ICANN Board would reconsider its position; it would merely be likely to try to provide a better justification for its disparate treatment and conclude, 'as it has previously found', that it did not discriminate Vistaprint. The parties would end up in a deadlock situation that could only be resolved by an IRP panel granting affirmative relief.

In the meantime, ICANN had clarified the rules for solving indirect contention sets. Indirect contention existed when two applications were in direct contention with a third application, but not with one another.[1052] The existence of direct contention related to applications and not necessarily to strings, as was stated in the Applicant Guidebook.[1053] For Vistaprint, this meant that, following the SCO Expert Determination, its application for .webs was in direct contention with the application for .web by Web.com, the party that raised the SCO. However, Vistaprint's application for .webs was only in indirect contention with the other applicants for .web. This meant that unless the .web gTLD was awarded to Web.com, .webs and .web could both be delegated. Vistaprint had figured out that the auction scheme developed by ICANN for resolving indirect contention sets favored the delegation of multiple strings. Simply put, Vistaprint's bid for .webs would be added to the highest bid for .web by any applicant other than Web.com. If the combined bids for .webs and .web were higher than Web.com's bid, Web.com's application for .web was going to be eliminated. The auction took place on 27 and 28 July 2016. Vistaprint prevailed in the auction with a USD 1 bid. The .web gTLD was auctioned for USD 135,000,000.[1054]

1052. *See* ICANN, *New gTLD Applicant Guidebook 4 June 2012*, https://newgtlds.icann.org/en/applicants/agb/guidebook-full-04jun12-en.pdf, Module 4-3.

1053. *See* ICANN, *New gTLD Applicant Guidebook 4 June 2012*, https://newgtlds.icann.org/en/applicants/agb/guidebook-full-04jun12-en.pdf, Module 4-3.

1054. ICANN, *New gTLD Auction Results*, https://gtldresult.icann.org/application-result/applicationstatus/auctionresults.

In retrospect, Vistaprint's auction bid to resolve the contention set was a small price to pay for avoiding a possible deadlock situation. However, the Internet community would have been better served by an IRP declaration that avoided such a situation arising. In this respect, it is unfortunate that the *Vistaprint* IRP panel was unable to reach consensus on the applicable standard for non-discrimination, and that it did not proceed on the basis of an interim decision, withholding its final decision until the ICANN Board had exercised its independent judgment on the question of inequitable and disparate treatment. The pressure of an impending review of the Board's exercise of independent judgment might have incentivized the Board to reflect more thoroughly on the question of whether disparate treatment was justified, and bring about a welcome improvement in ICANN's accountability.

F. THE MERCK CASE (.MERCK/.MERCKMSD)

1. Key Notes

- IRP under the new set of applicable rules.
- Written arguments only.
- Confirmation that the standard of review is non-deferential.
- Finding that ICANN's RfR process is of limited scope.

2. Introduction

This is a case that, like the *DCA* case, should not have been initiated.[1055] The claimant challenged ICANN's appraisal of an expert determination in objection proceedings. However, both ICANN and the expert made a correct assessment of the facts and the applicable rules.

The claimant had a difficult case to make, and provided limited guidance to the IRP panel as it restricted the debate to written arguments only. The IRP panel did not examine the existing IRP case law in its decision, and deviated from settled case law without a thorough analysis of the issue. We expect that the *Merck* case will stand on its own and will be of little relevance to future IRP panels.

3. Case Background

In this case Merck KGaA (Merck) questioned the outcome of the Legal Rights Objection (LRO) procedure conducted before WIPO that denied Merck's LRO to the application for .merck and .merckmsd by Merck & Co., Inc. (MSD).

Merck and MSD both have rights in the MERCK trade mark. The companies agreed on a territorial differentiation of rights: MSD has exclusive rights in the MERCK trade mark

1055. We were not involved as counsel for either party in this case.

within North America; throughout the rest of the world, Merck has the exclusive rights. Both Merck and MSD applied for the .merck gTLD. Based on a lack of affirmative assurances in MSD's applications, Merck concluded that MSD was going to infringe Merck's trade marks, and therefore asked that MSD's applications be disqualified. The WIPO expert panel considered that it was not its place to anticipate all the possible types of use MSD could make of its applied-for gTLDs and noted that, if MSD did in fact infringe Merck's trade marks, Merck was not precluded from enforcing its rights by taking legal action.

As ICANN accepted the WIPO panel's expert determination, Merck then made a RfR. Merck argued that ICANN was wrong to accept the expert determination and asked the ICANN Board to reconsider this decision. The ICANN Board rejected Merck's RfR, arguing that the WIPO panel had applied the correct standard and procedure.

4. Points of Procedure

a. Arguments Discussed

(1) Jurisdiction of the IRP Panel

Merck argued that its 'IRP is not itself an attempt to appeal the LRO panel's substantive assessment, but rather, is an assertion that the ICANN Board did not correctly apply its own policies and processes when considering Merck's [request for reconsideration].'[1056]

ICANN argued that an IRP is to be conducted pursuant to Article IV(3) of the ICANN Bylaws.[1057]

Specifically, it argued that the IRP panel 'has one responsibility: to provide its opinion as to 'whether the [ICANN] Board has acted consistently with the provisions of [ICANN's] Articles of Incorporation and Bylaws'.'[1058]

In this case, according to ICANN, Merck's IRP Request 'does not challenge Board action, but rather improperly challenges the determination of an independent expert, designated by an independent third party dispute resolution provider,'[1059] and ICANN therefore argued that there was no Board action for the IRP panel to review.[1060]

The IRP panel ruled that it was mandated to undertake an analysis of comparison, namely that it must compare a contested action or inaction of the Board to the Articles of Incorporation and Bylaws 'to ascertain whether there is consistency.'[1061]

1056. Merck's Reply, § 42.
1057. ICANN's Response (*Merck*), § 4.
1058. ICANN's Response (*Merck*), § 4.
1059. ICANN's Response (*Merck*), § 4.
1060. ICANN's Response (*Merck*), §§ 9 and 12.
1061. Merck IRP Declaration, § 17.

It held that '[n]one of [the] three bases for the Request for Reconsideration process requires or even permits [the IRP] Panel to provide for a substitute process for exploring a different conclusion on the merits.'[1062]

It further added that, because of the precise and limited jurisdiction of an IRP panel the panel did not have the power to second guess the determination by the ICANN Board that the WIPO Panel Expert did not in fact apply the wrong standards.[1063]

(2) Time Bar

Merck considered the challenge to be timely because:

- Merck could not reasonably expect to be materially harmed by ICANN's decision regarding the availability of relief mechanisms until such time as it received its materially erroneous LRO determination.[1064]
- The ICANN Board had the ability to modify the objection procedure; its refusal to do so (by denying Merck's request for reconsideration) was an inaction which Merck challenged at the earliest possible time.[1065]

ICANN argued that the time had long passed for challenging the absence of appeal and review mechanisms in the Guidebook beyond those already provided.[1066] It urged the IRP panel to reach the same conclusion as in the *Booking.com* case on this issue.[1067]

In particular, ICANN submitted that 'IRPs must be initiated within 30 days [following] 'the posting of the minutes of the Board meeting' and that 'Merck did not object to the Guidebook procedures at the time the Guidebook was implemented, and did not raise any objection for several years.'[1068]

The IRP panel did not explicitly rule on the issue. However it considered that the IRP was neither initiated nor capable of being initiated 'to challenge, in substance, the policy decision of ICANN in 2012 to include the Auction of Last Resort.'[1069]

(3) Written/Oral Arguments

Merck asked the IRP panel to decide the case on the basis of written arguments only.

ICANN indicated that it believed that a telephone hearing would be useful.

As Merck had indicated that it considered a hearing unnecessary, the IRP panel determined that no hearing was necessary.

1062. Merck IRP Declaration, § 47.
1063. Merck IRP Declaration, § 49.
1064. Merck's Reply, § 75.
1065. Merck's Reply, §§ 76–77.
1066. ICANN's Response (*Merck*), § 52.
1067. ICANN's Sur-Reply (*Merck*), § 9.
1068. ICANN's Sur-Reply (*Merck*), § 46.
1069. Merk IRP Declaration, § 41.

b. *Noteworthy Points for Analysis*

(1) Jurisdiction of the IRP Panel

The IRP panel had a very limited view on its jurisdiction, considering that it did not have the authority to second guess the determination by the ICANN Board that the WIPO Panel Expert did not in fact apply the wrong standards. It is unclear how the panel came to this decision. Moreover, the decision seems at odds with the panel's task to review the Board's decisions for compliance with ICANN's Articles of Incorporation and Bylaws. As ICANN's Bylaws prescribe a fair and equitable application of ICANN's standards and policies, the IRP panel's task should include whether the Board ensured a correct application of those standards.

With its limited view on the jurisdiction of IRP panels, the *Merck* IRP declaration did not contribute to the improvement of ICANN's accountability mechanisms. The decision did not consider any of the previous IRP declarations, and its limited rationale may be related to the underlying nature of the case and the way in which the case was handled. Merck had initiated an LRO for a dispute that did not match the limited purpose of an LRO. The purpose of an LRO was to ensure that a new gTLD string did not 'infringe the existing legal rights of others that are recognized or enforceable under generally accepted and internationally recognized principles of law.'[1070] An LRO was not designed to block the delegation of a new gTLD because of a possible future violation of trade mark rights through a particular use by a gTLD applicant, especially if (as was the case in *Merck*) the applicant also had rights in the trade mark corresponding to the gTLD.[1071] The dispute between Merck and MSD should never have been the subject of an LRO, and it is therefore understandable that the IRP panel wanted to make short shrift of the issues presented in the IRP. The panel's findings on its jurisdiction must be seen within this context.

(2) Time Bar

In an *obiter dictum*, the IRP panel considered that an IRP could not be initiated 'to challenge, in substance, the policy decision of ICANN in 2012 to include the Auction of Last Resort.'[1072] The panel gave neither reasoning nor explanation for this finding. Was it because the panel considered the policy decision to be fundamentally fair, or because the panel considered that the time to challenge this policy decision had passed? In any event, in making this side comment – the panel's observation was made between

1070. *See* ICANN, *New gTLD Applicant Guidebook 4 June 2012*, https://newgtlds.icann.org/en/applicants/agb/guidebook-full-04jun12-en.pdf, Module 3-18.
1071. *See* ICANN, *New gTLD Applicant Guidebook 4 June 2012*, https://newgtlds.icann.org/en/applicants/agb/guidebook-full-04jun12-en.pdf, Module 3-19, consideration factors 6 and 7.
1072. Merck IRP Declaration, § 41.

parentheses[1073] – the panel did not look into the issue of the late introduction of the time bar and the issue of retroactive application.[1074]

(3) Written/Oral Arguments

It is puzzling why Merck asked the IRP panel to decide the case on the basis of written arguments only. When Merck initiated this request, there was almost no IRP case law in existence. We would have expected any claimant to want to furnish the panel with as much information as possible concerning the context of ICANN's new gTLD program, and to give the IRP panel the opportunity to ask questions during a hearing to make sure it had fully grasped the debate. We find it surprising that a party would restrict its own right to present its case. Without a doubt, Merck's decision in this regard contributed to the cursory nature of the IRP decision.

5. Applicable Law

a. *Arguments Discussed*

(1) Essential Rights and Obligations

Merck argued that ICANN had not provided a mechanism for reviewing erroneous decisions, after having explicitly drafted its dispute resolution procedure to exclude the possibility of court proceedings.[1075]

It stated that ICANN had an obligation to provide some process for relief in accordance with the minimum basic requirements for such dispute resolution processes.[1076]

Merck claimed that it did not have the option to take the matter against MSD to court, as the LRO panel had suggested.[1077]

It claimed that the LRO panelist had not taken sufficient time in reviewing the parties' pleadings and had disregarded the applicable LRO standards when he refused to consider the intended global use of MSD's applied-for gTLD strings.[1078]

Merck argued that ICANN had not exercised *due diligence and care* in the acceptance of the LRO determination.[1079]

1073. Merck IRP Declaration, § 41.
1074. *Supra* Chapter 5.C.4.b(4) and Chapter 5.E.4.b(1).
1075. Merck's Request for IRP, §§ 18 and 102.
1076. Merck's Reply, § 74.
1077. Merck's Request for IRP, § 112.
1078. Merck's Request for IRP, §§ 29–30.
1079. Merck's Request for IRP, § 48.

It claimed that the ICANN Board, by accepting the erroneous expert determination, prevented Merck from receiving an expert determination applying the LRO standards in accordance with the Applicant Guidebook.[1080]

It argued that the ICANN Board was required to assess whether Merck had received *due process* in the LRO procedure,[1081] and that Merck's RfR required 'substantive assessment of certain questions of law relating to the application of legal standards', a process which the ICANN Board could not itself engage in as it lacked expertise in intellectual property disputes.[1082] It argued that because the ICANN Board was not competent to address the substantive questions posed by Merck, it had, by doing so, failed to exercise *due diligence and care* when it made its determination to deny Merck's RfR. And therefore, that the ICANN Board should have taken steps to address Merck's concerns in an appropriate manner, such as by seeking the advice of an independent legal advisor.[1083]

Merck also argued that ICANN's Articles of Incorporation and Bylaws require ICANN to provide a certain minimum level of relief in its dispute resolution processes.[1084]

Concerning *fairness*, Merck argued that the ICANN Board improperly disposed of Merck's RfR, as ICANN made an incorrect assessment and failed to take into account the global use of the gTLD by MSD.[1085] It argued that the ICANN Board had completely neglected to assess the potential use argument raised by Merck and had confined its discussion to the application of the standard by WIPO's panel; and that this was incorrect and misleading.[1086]

It argued that ICANN had a clear and significant financial interest in denying Merck's RfR, which put ICANN's real or perceived *neutrality* in deciding the substantive issues raised by Merck into question.[1087] According to Merck, there was a 'very real and substantial likelihood that should the resolution of the .MERCK contention set not occur through objection procedures, ICANN would directly receive in the tens of millions of dollars as a result of the Auction of Last Resort' which ICANN installed for resolving string contention.[1088]

It also argued that, when the ICANN Board denied Merck's RfR, it was the ICANN Board that was responsible for the LRO determinations and not ICANN's staff.[1089]

Merck argued that ICANN *discriminated* against Merck by providing the possibility for third-party review to certain applicants in relation to other *prima facie* erroneous expert

1080. Merck's Request for IRP, § 72.
1081. Merck's Request for IRP, § 79.
1082. Merck's Reply, §§ 48–53.
1083. Merck's Request for IRP, § 82; *see also* Merck's Reply, § 6.
1084. Merck's Reply, § 8.
1085. Merck's Request for IRP, § 46.
1086. Merck's Request for IRP, § 93.
1087. Merck's Request for IRP, § 88.
1088. Merck's Request for IRP, § 97.
1089. Merck's Reply, § 7.

determinations while denying this third party review to Merck.[1090] It argued that 'ICANN has entertained substantive review of certain errors for only a subset of all complaining parties, with no discernable basis for its discrimination between similarly-situated complaining parties. It is improper for the ICANN Board to subjectively determine for itself, without independent or expert assessment, which claims for which [*sic*] it will permit substantive review.'[1091]

With regards to *transparency*, Merck argued that the WIPO panel had provided insufficient reasoning to justify its expert determination.[1092]

ICANN argued that ICANN's Articles of Incorporation and Bylaws do not contain a requirement for the Board to review the decision on the merits of an ICANN-designated dispute resolution provider.[1093]

It stated that 'the Bylaws provide that reconsideration of staff (or D[ispute] R[esolution S[ervice] P[rovider]) is appropriate only where that action 'contradict[ed] established ICANN policy(ies),' and do not provide for a substantive review of expert determinations.'[1094]

In this case, ICANN considered that WIPO's expert had 'clearly applied the LRO standard from the Guidebook, and the [ICANN Board] correctly determined that he did.'[1095]

ICANN argued that 'the Guidebook purposely does *not* require the Board to sit as an "appellate panel" and insert itself into the thousands of third-party determinations and reviews conducted in conjunction with the New gTLD Program.'[1096] Equally, it considered that the ICANN Board 'was not required to engage in any 'substantive' assessment of the LRO or UDRP standards, and the [ICANN Board] did not need the help of an independent legal expert to determine that the Expert followed the Guidebook's procedures.'[1097]

ICANN claimed that the ICANN Board had 'examined each of Merck's contentions regarding the process followed by the Expert and issued a reasoned analysis properly concluding that the Expert had not violated any established policy in rendering the Expert Determinations.'[1098]

ICANN denied that Merck had any basis to claim that the ICANN Board was biased or financially motivated.[1099]

1090. Merck's Request for IRP, § 46.
1091. Merck's Reply, § 71.
1092. Mercks' Request for IRP, § 62.
1093. ICANN's Response (*Merck*), §§ 4 and 9.
1094. ICANN's Response (*Merck*), § 40; ICANN's Sur-Reply (*Merck*), § 5.
1095. ICANN's Sur-Reply (*Merck*), § 25.
1096. ICANN's Sur-Reply (*Merck*), § 6.
1097. ICANN's Sur-Reply (*Merck*), §§ 27.
1098. ICANN's Sur-Reply (*Merck*), § 34.
1099. ICANN's Response (*Merck*), §§ 43–44; ICANN's Sur-Reply (*Merck*), §§ 30–32.

The IRP panel held that it was under an obligation to review whether there was 'a neutral and objective application, with integrity and fairness, by the [ICANN] Board of documented policies.'[1100] However, the IRP panel also held that (i) ICANN's RfR process is 'of limited scope, with Article IV, Section 2.2 [of ICANN's Bylaws], delineating that jurisdiction'[1101] and (ii) it did not have the power to second guess the determination by the ICANN Board (in the reconsideration process) that the WIPO Panel Expert did not in fact apply the wrong standards.[1102]

(2) Standard of Review

Merck argued that it 'is not requesting that the IRP [Panel] undertake a de novo review of LRO Determinations or replace the LRO Determinations with their own decision. Rather, Merck's purpose in discussing the errors of the LRO Panel is to provide the basis for its discussion of the violations of the ICANN Board in its evaluation of Merck's [request for reconsideration] and its decisions regarding the implementation and administration of the dispute resolution process in the New gTLD Program.'[1103]

Merck argued that the IRP panel should review the actions of the ICANN Board in accordance with an objective and non-deferential standard of review, as had been decided in the *Booking.com* case.[1104]

ICANN argued that ICANN's Bylaws specifically identify a deferential standard of review that the IRP panel must apply when evaluating the actions of the ICANN Board, and that the IRP panel is neither asked, nor allowed, to substitute its judgment for that of the Board.[1105]

The panel found that '[n]othing in the language of Article IV, Section 3.4 [of the Bylaws] suggests that there be any deference afforded to the contested action', but that '[d]iscussion as regards whether the Panel should engage in a *de novo* standard of review is also apt to mislead.'[1106]

The panel added that the contesting party 'bears the burden of persuasion.'[1107]

The panel was clear that it 'may not substitute its own view of the merits of the underlying dispute.'[1108]

1100. Merck IRP Declaration, § 38.
1101. Merck IRP Declaration, § 47.
1102. Merck IRP Declaration, § 49.
1103. Merck's Reply, § 4.
1104. Merck's Reply, §§ 10–12.
1105. ICANN's Response (*Merck*), § 28; *see also* ICANN's Sur-Reply (*Merck*), §§ 10–11.
1106. Merck IRP Declaration, §§ 20–21.
1107. Merck IRP Declaration, § 22.
1108. Merck IRP Declaration, § 21.

b. *Noteworthy Points for Analysis*

(1) Essential Rights and Obligations

The IRP panel correctly held that it had to review whether there was 'a neutral and objective application, with integrity and fairness, by the [ICANN] Board of documented policies.' However, the panel's views on its jurisdiction and on the limited scope of the RfR process in fact prevented the panel from performing this review. It considered that it did not have the power to second guess the Board's determination about the application of ICANN's policies. Thus, although the IRP panel recognized that ICANN had fundamental obligations, it allowed for these to be easily set aside in a case where the ICANN Board determines that an ICANN contractor has correctly applied ICANN's policies.

The panel's reasoning reaffirms ICANN's narrow view of the RfR process as an accountability mechanism. As discussed in Chapter 3.D, adherence to this interpretation of the RfR has resulted in ICANN missing out on an opportunity to improve its accountability towards gTLD applicants. Unlike the *Vistaprint* panel, the *Merck* panel did not review ICANN's obligations in light of its role as the regulator of the DNS.

(2) Standard of Review

Every other IRP panel that has ruled on the issue of the standard of review has decided – on the basis of a thorough analysis – that the standard of review to be applied by an IRP panel is 'a de novo, objective and independent one, which does not require any presumption of correctness.'[1109] The *Vistaprint* panel considered that the issue was settled and left no room for doubt that its findings on the standard of review should be adopted by future IRP panels.[1110] However, the *Merck* IRP panel adopted its own reasoning on the issue with no reference to previous case law. It confirmed that the standard of review was non-deferential. However, its finding that application of a *de novo* standard is apt to mislead is not supported by any in-depth analysis, and it is unclear why the *Merck* panel disregarded settled case law on this issue.

1109. ICM IRP Declaration, § 136; DCA Final IRP Declaration, § 76; Booking.com IRP Declaration, § 111; Vistaprint IRP Declaration, § 124.
1110. *Supra* Chapter 5.E.5.a(3) and Chapter 5.E.5.b(3).

6. Authority of the Panel

a. Arguments Discussed

Merck requested the IRP panel to order ICANN to appoint a new panel to decide upon Merck's LRO.[1111]

ICANN argued that an IRP panel does not have the authority to award affirmative relief.[1112]

The panel held that it is not open to the IRP panel to create a referral or appeal process for LRO decisions:

> 'Merck's arguments are unavailing. If this Panel were to find that the BGC and Board are incompetent to assess the propriety of a Panel determination under the LRO this would effectively require a referral or appeal process for LRO Decisions. Such a mechanism was not included in the delegation, challenge and dispute resolution process adopted by ICANN and it is not open to this Panel to create it.'[1113]

b. Noteworthy Points for Analysis

The panel may have been correct in finding that it was not allowed to create a referral or appeal process for LRO Decisions, and the underlying facts of the case did not support the creation of such process. However, that does not mean that the absence of a referral or appeal process cannot be considered a violation of ICANN's Articles of Incorporation or Bylaws. *E.g.*, if ICANN had created an appeal process for similarly situated applicants, an IRP panel could have found that ICANN's failure to make this appeal process available to other applicants amounts to an illegal discrimination. In this case, however, it seems that Merck failed to show that similarly situated applicants had been treated differently. In this respect, the IRP panel noted that 'in *different* cases, the [ICANN] Board [is] entitled to pursue different options depending upon the nature of the case at issue' and that '[i]t is insufficient to ground an argument of discrimination simply to note that on *different* occasions the Board has pursued different options among those available to it.'[1114] Indeed, if a situation is dissimilar, a different treatment may be justified.

1111. Merck's Request for IRP, § 112.
1112. ICANN's Response (*Merck*), § 55; ICANN's Sur-Reply (*Merck*), § 49.
1113. Merck IRP Declaration, § 60.
1114. Merck IRP Declaration, § 61 (emphasis added).

7. Nature and Value of the IRP Declaration

a. *Arguments Discussed*

(1) Binding Nature of the IRP Declaration

ICANN argued that the IRP is a unique, non-binding process.[1115] Merck did not comment on the nature of the IRP declaration, and the IRP panel did not consider the issue.

(2) Precedential Value of the IRP Declaration

Merck argued that the decision in the *Booking.com* case regarding the standard of review has precedential value and should be followed.[1116]

ICANN did not comment on the precedential value of previous IRP declarations. The panel did not discuss the issue, and ignored previous IRP decisions, which had been declared to have precedential value.[1117]

b. *Noteworthy Points for Analysis*

Merck was not in a position to bring forward clear indications of unfairness, non-transparency or discrimination, as the claimants in the *Booking.com* and *Vistaprint* cases had been able to do. However, Merck did bring forward valid points about the standard of review and about the ICANN Board's obligations of due diligence and care in reviewing third party expert determinations. It is unfortunate that the IRP panel did not examine these issues more thoroughly, and that it did not take the time to analyze existing case law in its declaration. Although it is highly unlikely that a more thorough analysis of these issues would have changed the outcome for Merck, a more comprehensive review would have contributed to the IRP jurisprudence. Of course, Merck's claim that the proceedings should be limited to written argument only, probably encouraged the panel to favor speed over an extensive analysis of all issues presented in this case. Such a pragmatic approach may be recommended for future IRP panels, once there is a clear body of settled jurisprudence. However, in the meantime, the Internet community may be better served by more detailed IRP decisions.

1115. ICANN's Response (*Merck*), § 28.
1116. Merck's Reply, § 12, n.6.
1117. *Supra* Chapter 5.F.5.b(2).

8. ICANN Board's Decision Following the IRP Declaration

The *Merck* IRP panel had named ICANN the prevailing party and made no recommendations for the ICANN Board to consider. The ICANN Board accepted the IRP declaration in its meeting of 3 February 2016.[1118]

G. THE CASES OF DESPEGAR ONLINE SRL, DONUTS INC., FAMOUS FOUR MEDIA LIMITED, FEGISTRY LLC, AND RADIX FZC V. ICANN (.HOTEL) & LITTLE BIRCH LLC AND MINDS + MACHINES GROUP LIMITED V. ICANN (.ECO) (DESPEGAR ET AL.)

1. Key Notes

- IRP under the new set of applicable rules.
- Agreement to consolidate two requests for IRPs.
- Rejection of a request to join the proceedings, which was made after the IRP panel was appointed, on the basis that it was time-barred.
- Confirmation that a determination by the ICANN Board should be a procedural one not a substantive one.
- Confirmation that the ICANN Board should review how external experts and ICANN staff apply the standard, and that the ICANN Board must have a reasonable degree of assurance that the policy has been applied correctly.
- Confirmation that ICANN should apply principles like transparency and administrative due process.
- Finding that the ICANN Board should seek to ensure that ICANN's staff comply with ICANN's Articles of Incorporation and Bylaws, and that a failure of the Board to ensure such compliance is a failure of the Board itself.
- Finding that principles of openness and transparency require ICANN to investigate serious allegations of misconduct properly and to make public the fact of the investigation and the result thereof
- ICANN was the prevailing party but the panel found partially in favor of the Claimants (on cost allocation).

2. Introduction

The *Despegar et al.* case is the first case in which two requests for IRPs were consolidated.[1119]

1118. ICANN, *Approved Board Resolution 2016.02.03.10 – Regular Meeting of the ICANN Board*, 3 February 2016, https://www.icann.org/resources/board-material/resolutions-2016-02-03-en.

1119. We acted on behalf of the claimants in these cases.

The decision by the IRP panel is to be welcomed for its interpretation of ICANN's obligations and the role of the ICANN Board in supervising its staff. However, the IRP panel did not address certain important arguments and points of law (*e.g.*, on the binding nature of the decision and on the Board's discriminatory interventions). The IRP panel did also not address part of the claimants' request, namely their claims regarding the legitimacy of the CPE process as organized by ICANN.

The IRP panel focused on the Board's handling of the claimants' DIDP requests and RfRs. In its examination of the DIDP requests and RfRs, it seems that the IRP panel took some of the statements by the ICANN Board for granted, treating the ICANN Board with deference. However, recent developments suggest that material information was not disclosed to the IRP panel. In our view, the panel would perhaps give less deference to the ICANN Board if it were asked to rule on the issue today.

Finally, the Board decided not to rule on the unlawful access to the TLD application platform that occurred during the IRP proceedings, and to leave the issue open for adjudication by a future IRP panel. This decision is surprising. The IRP panel gave clear indications on how the ICANN Board should have dealt with the situation to avoid a violation of its Articles of Incorporation and Bylaws. It also added that, if no appropriate action had been taken by the date of the IRP Declaration, the failure of the Board to act could well amount to unjustified inaction on its part. In the light of this, the IRP panel might have been expected to keep jurisdiction on this issue and retain authority to reassess the situation after its initial findings. This it did not do.

3. Case Background

Within the new gTLD program, applicants were entitled to designate their new gTLD applications as either standard or community-based. A community-based application was to be operated for the benefit of a clearly delineated community. If a community-based application was made for a gTLD for which other applicants had made standard applications, the community-based applicant was then invited to elect to proceed to Community Priority Evaluation (CPE). During CPE, an application was evaluated according to four criteria, each criterion being worth a maximum of four points. To prevail in CPE, the application had to receive a score of 14 or more points out of a maximum of 16. An applicant who prevailed in CPE would proceed to the next stage of the evaluation, and other standard applications for the same gTLD would not proceed because the community-based application would be considered to have achieved priority.

ICANN appointed an external provider, the Economist Intelligence Unit (EIU), to constitute the CPE panel. The EIU evaluated the CPE criteria for all community-based applicants who elected CPE and issued a recommendation to ICANN, which ICANN typically accepted without any review by its Board.

One applicant for .hotel and another for .eco submitted that they were entitled to community priority. The EIU issued reports, which determined that the community-based application for .hotel should receive fifteen points and that the community-based application for .eco should receive fourteen points. The applicants who submitted standard applications for .hotel and .eco (hereinafter referred to as Despegar et al.) considered that the EIU's evaluation was erroneous and inconsistent with other determinations by the EIU. Despegar et al. asked that the ICANN Board reconsider ICANN's decision to accept the EIU's determination. The ICANN Board rejected Despegar et al.'s RfR.

In the course of the IRP, ICANN revealed that the user credentials of an individual associated with the community-based applicant for .hotel were used to obtain sensitive and confidential business information concerning several of the standard .hotel applicants. All claimants in the IRP asked ICANN for full transparency on the issue and requested that the ICANN Board respond appropriately to this theft of trade secrets. The ICANN Board did not respond to the claimants' request before the end of the IRP proceedings.

4. Points of Procedure

a. Arguments Discussed

(1) Jurisdiction of the IRP Panel

Despegar et al. argued that the IRP has all the characteristics of an international arbitration:

> 'The IRP has all the characteristics of an international arbitration. The IRP is conducted pursuant to a set of independently developed international arbitration rules: the ICDR's International Arbitration Rules ('ICDR Rules') as minimally modified by the Supplementary Procedures for ICANN's Independent Review Process ('supplementary Procedures'). The IRP is administered by a provider of international arbitration services. The decision-maker is not ICANN, but a panel of neutral individuals selected by the parties in consultation with the ICDR, and appointed pursuant to the ICDR Rules.'[1120]

They argued that the IRP panel must decide whether or not actions or inactions of the Board are compatible with ICANN's fundamental principles:

> 'The IRP Panel has authority to decide whether or not actions or inactions on the part of the ICANN Board are compatible with [ICANN's fundamental] principles. The most recent versions of ICANN's Bylaws[1121] – which had not been introduced at the time of Claimants' submissions of its applications[1122] – also require the IRP

1120. Dot Hotel Reply, § 10.
1121. Adopted on 11 April 2013 and subsequently amended on 7 February 2014; *see also* ICANN's Bylaws as amended on 16 March 2012, Article IV(3).
1122. In 2012.

> Panel to focus on whether the ICANN Board was free from conflicts of interest and exercised an appropriate level of due diligence and independent judgment in its decision making.'[1123]

Notably, Despegar et al. argued that an IRP panel's task is not limited to a purely procedural review; the IRP panel must also review the substance and examine whether standards have been applied consistently to ensure fairness and non-discrimination:

> 'To assess whether ICANN has applied its standards, policies and procedures in a fair, equitable and non-discriminatory fashion, it is imperative that the IRP Panel reviews the application of standards, policies and procedures in detail. One cannot investigate whether a standard was applied fairly and correctly without looking into how the standard was applied. A review of the substance is required, and it must be examined whether standards have been applied consistently to ensure fairness and non-discrimination.'[1124]

> 'As the IRP Panel's task includes a review as to whether ICANN discriminated in the application of its policies and standards, the IRP Panel is obliged to consider how the standards were applied in different cases.'[1125]

ICANN argued that the IRP panel is tasked with providing its opinion as to whether the challenged Board actions violated ICANN's Articles or Bylaws:

> 'The IRP is a unique, non-binding process available under ICANN's Bylaws for persons or entities that claim to have been materially and adversely affected by a decision or action of the ICANN Board, and only to the extent that Board action was inconsistent with ICANN's Articles or Bylaws. The IRP Panel is tasked with providing its opinion as to whether the challenged Board actions violated ICANN's Articles or Bylaws.'[1126]

It argued that the IRP panel is only entitled to evaluate Board actions, and that IRPs are not a vehicle for second-guessing either the judgment of a third-party CPE panel or the Board's judgment that no further intervention was warranted with respect to the CPE panel's decision:

> '[A]s discussed herein and made clear in ICANN's Bylaws, IRPs are not a forum for challenging third party expert reports, which involve no Board action whatsoever.'[1127]

> '[T]here was <u>no</u> Board action with respect to the CPE Report, and the Claimants' disagreement with that report is <u>not</u> a basis for independent review.'[1128]

> 'In the end, the only Board actions properly reviewable in this IRP are the BGC's denial of Claimants' reconsideration requests.'[1129]

1123. Dot Hotel Request for IRP, § 32.
1124. Dot Hotel Reply, § 39.
1125. Dot Hotel Reply, § 45.
1126. ICANN's Response (*Dot Hotel*), § 30.
1127. ICANN's Response (*Dot Hotel*), § 34.
1128. ICANN's Response (*Dot Hotel*), § 55.
1129. ICANN's Sur-Reply (*Dot Hotel*), § 8.

> 'Just as the Board was not properly tasked with second-guessing the judgment of the CPE Panel, this IRP panel is not tasked with second-guessing the Board's independent judgment that no further intervention was warranted with respect to the CPE Report.'[1130]

ICANN submitted that the IRP was an internal corporate accountability mechanism:

> 'ICANN's independent review process is an internal corporate accountability mechanism that ICANN voluntarily established via its Bylaws. California law expressly authorizes California non-profit public benefit corporations, such as ICANN, to establish such mechanisms and to define the scope and form of those mechanisms.[...] Pursuant to this explicit authority, ICANN defined the procedures and standard of review that would govern the independent review process.'[1131]

The IRP panel considered itself to be charged with comparing the actions of the ICANN Board with the Articles of Incorporation and Bylaws, and declaring whether the Board had acted consistently with the provisions of those Articles of Incorporation and Bylaws.[1132] For the panel, the review also related to inactions, as it identified the relevant provisions of ICANN's Articles of Incorporation and Bylaws 'against which the actions, or inactions, of the Board should be compared.'[1133] The panel also ruled that a failure by the ICANN Board to investigate serious allegations or to publish the results of its investigation could 'amount to Board inaction and fall within the remit of the panel.'[1134]

(2) Time Bar

Despegar et al. argued that because there was no time limit for bringing a request for IRP at the time when they filed their new gTLD applications, they were entitled to challenge all ICANN actions and inactions that led to ICANN granting community priority for .hotel and .eco:

> 'Claimants are entitled to challenge all ICANN actions and inactions that have led to ICANN granting community priority to .hotel and .eco, and there is no time bar for doing so.
>
> Indeed, when Claimants filed their applications in 2012, there was no time limit for bringing a request for IRP [...]. Prospective applicants, who considered that they risked being materially affected by ICANN's application of the Guidebook in contravention of the AoI and/or Bylaws, could legitimately expect to challenge the Guidebook as well as ICANN's implementation thereof.
>
> ICANN's decision to introduce a time bar for challenging Board decisions was introduced on 11 April 2013, *i.e.*, long after the new gTLD application window closed (compare Article IV(3)(3) of the previous Bylaws [...] with Article IV(3)(3) of the amended Bylaws of 11 April 2013 [...]). As a result, the time bar can only

1130. ICANN's Sur-Reply (*Dot Hotel*), § 15.
1131. ICANN's Sur-Reply (*Dot Hotel*), § 28.
1132. Despegar et al. IRP Declaration, § 58.
1133. Despegar et al. IRP Declaration, § 58.
1134. Despegar et al. IRP Declaration, §§ 134–135.

> apply to actions taken after 11 April 2013 (See *United States v. Security Indus. Bank*, 459 U.S. 79 (1982)), and Claimants have timely challenged the ICANN's Board actions taken after 11 April 2013 with respect to their individual applications. As a result, the IRP Panel is authorized to scrutinize all of ICANN's actions and inactions regarding Claimants' applications for consistency with ICANN's AoI and Bylaws.'[1135]

Despegar et al. argued that the opportunity to challenge the deficiencies of the CPE process only emerged after the CPE process was established and implemented:

> 'ICANN's and the Booking.com Panel's reasoning on the timing has no merit. The Booking.com Panel ignored the fact that neither the string similarity review process nor the CPE process had been established and implemented in their entirety at the time the Guidebook was adopted. At that time, it was not possible for Booking.com, Claimants, or any other interested party, to effectively challenge these, as yet unfinalized, processes. ICANN still had every opportunity to correctly implement the CPE process in accordance with the applicable policy, the Guidebook and the fundamental principles in ICANN's Articles of Incorporation ('AoI') and Bylaws. The opportunity for Claimants to challenge the erroneous application of the policy for the new gTLD program in violation of ICANN's fundamental principles only arose when the flaws in ICANN's implementation of the policy became apparent. At the time of the adoption of the policy or the Guidebook, Claimants were effectively barred from challenging the Guidebook because they could not – at that time – show any harm. The policy still needed to be implemented, which can be seen, *inter alia*, from the following facts: the Economist Intelligence Unit published its final CPE guidelines only on 27 September 2013 [...]; community-based applicants had yet to decide whether they wanted to elect the CPE; CPE panels still needed to be appointed in all transparency; the CPE panels had yet to apply the CPE standards and issue their recommendations to ICANN; ICANN had still to perform a quality review and assess the recommendations; the ICANN Board had yet to exercise the necessary due diligence before deciding if it accepted the CPE Panel's recommendation(s).'[1136]

ICANN argued that any IRP challenge regarding the selection of the EIU as the CPE panel had to be made within thirty days of the announcement of the selection:

> 'ICANN's retention of the EIU was announced in 2011, meaning that any IRP challenge to that selection would have had to be filed within 30 days thereafter pursuant to ICANN's Bylaws.'[1137]
>
> 'Even if the ICANN staff's selection of the EIU were a basis for Independent Review, Claimants' argument is time-barred. ICANN's call for Expressions of Interest was issued in 2009, and ICANN announced that it had selected the EIU in October 2011. Both the selection process and the criteria for selection (set forth in detail in the call for Expressions of Interest) were made public. If Claimants had concerns with the selection process or with the selection of the EIU, they were obligated to have raised those concerns at the time, not years later and only after

1135. Dot Hotel Answers to Panel Questions, Response to Question # 2.
1136. Dot Hotel Reply, § 7.
1137. ICANN's Response (*Dot Hotel*), § 12.

> the issuance of a CPE Report with which they disagree. ICANN's Bylaws require that IRPs be initiated within 30 days of the Board decision to be reviewed, not over four years later.'[1138]

It added that Despegar et al. had not objected to the CPE process in a timely manner:

> 'Despite having ample opportunity to do so, Claimants did not object to CPE process at the time the Guidebook was implemented. If Claimants had concerns related to these issues, they were properly pursued at the time.'[1139]

Finally, ICANN stated that previous panels had found that challenges to procedures set out in the AGB were time-barred:

> '[A]ny challenges to the procedures set out in the Guidebook are long since time-barred because challenges to the Guidebook were due 30 days following its adoption. Indeed, the only two IRP panels to consider whether challenges to procedures set out in the Guidebook were proper, have found that such challenges are time-barred.'[1140]

During the hearing ICANN clarified that the claimants (with the exception of Minds + Machines Group Limited (Minds + Machines) in the .hotel IRP)[1141] were not time-barred from seeking IRP of ICANN's denials in the RfRs.[1142] The panel considered that '[g]iven the confirmation by ICANN, that a time bar is not being raised in relation to the substantive issues in this IRP, the panel does not have to discuss this question save for when it considers Minds + Machines' attempt to join in the .hotel IRP.'[1143]

(3) Consolidation and the Joining of Parties

As the object of both IRPs was the same, parties discussed the consolidation of the two IRPs. However, Minds + Machines had not initially joined the claimants in the claim on .hotel. A question rose as to whether the consolidation could mean that Minds + Machines would become a party in the case on .hotel as it was already a co-claimant in the case on .eco.

In the end, the parties agreed to consolidate the cases on .hotel and .eco. However, ICANN opposed Minds + Machines joining the .hotel IRP. ICANN argued that no additional party could be joined after the appointment of any panelist, unless all parties otherwise agreed. It added that it did not consent to the joinder of an additional party:

> 'Minds + Machines Limited ('Minds + Machines') is not a claimant in this proceeding but, nevertheless, signed the Reply and now seeks to join as an additional claimant. Article 7 of the International Center for Dispute Resolution's International Dispute Resolution Procedures explicitly provides that '[n]o additional party may be joined after the appointment of any [neutral], unless *all parties*, including the additional party, otherwise agree.'[...] ICANN does not

1138. ICANN's Response (*Dot Hotel*), § 37.
1139. ICANN's Response (*Dot Hotel*), § 45.
1140. ICANN's Sur-Reply (*Dot Hotel*), § 19; *see also* ICANN's Sur-Reply (*Dot Hotel*), § 4.
1141. *Infra Chapter 5.G.4.a(3).*
1142. Despegar et al. IRP Declaration, § 60.
1143. Despegar et al. IRP Declaration, § 62.

> consent to the joinder of Minds + Machines because any claims Minds + Machines may have with respect to the CPE Report or ICANN's response to that Report are time-barred.'[1144]

The panel ruled that Minds + Machines was time-barred from doing so. The panel did not see any reason why Minds + Machines could not have joined the claimants bringing the .hotel IRP at an earlier stage.[1145]

b. *Noteworthy Points for Analysis*

(1) Jurisdiction of the IRP Panel

The IRP panel confirmed the findings of the Booking.com and Vistaprint IRP panels and ruled that it was entitled to review both actions and inactions of the ICANN Board. This issue seems now settled.

(2) Time Bar

The IRP panel considered that it did not have to rule on the time bar issue, because in its view the time bar argument was not relevant for an evaluation of ICANN's arguments in the RfRs in this case. Indeed, with the exception of Minds + Machines (with respect to the .hotel application), it was not contested that the claimants had challenged ICANN's refusal in time.

However, in our view, the IRP panel's refusal to look more broadly at the question of time-bar was a missed opportunity. It would have been helpful if the panel had considered ICANN's obligation to implement the CPE process in the light of all applicable rules, the hierarchy of norms and fundamental legal principles.[1146] (*See also* our discussion of this in the *Booking.com* case).

The absence of a ruling on this issue is unfortunate for two reasons. First, the panel did not rule on one of the claimants' core arguments, namely that the ICANN Board should at all times guarantee compliance with its Articles of Incorporation and Bylaws, and that the legality of a policy may be questioned any time it is implemented. Second, the panel was given detailed arguments to explain why the findings in the *Booking.com* case on the time bar issue were unconvincing, and why the *obiter dictum* on this issue in the *Vistaprint* case could be disregarded. During the hearing members of the IRP panel seemed to indicate that the panel would try not to second guess decisions made by previous IRP panels. This comment was made during a discussion on the time bar issue in connection with the claimants' wider claims. It could indicate that the panel wanted to avoid making a ruling on claimants' wider claims, possibly out of fear for a spill-over effect for other applications. However, in our view, there is no risk of such a

1144. ICANN's Sur-Reply (*Dot Hotel*), § 35.
1145. Despegar et al. IRP Declaration, §§ 139–142.
1146. Dot Hotel Reply, § 35.

spill-over effect. The time bar rule would still require that any illegal implementation of a policy be challenged in time, and parties not electing to challenge an adverse decision in time would still be considered to have abandoned their right to challenge the illegality.

(3) Consolidation and Joining of Parties

The IRP panel's reasoning in its decision not to allow Minds + Machines to join the proceedings with respect to the .hotel application followed from its line of argument concerning the abandonment of a right to challenge (mentioned above). In the circumstances of the case, the panel's view may seem somewhat formalistic, but correct. Indeed, whether or not Minds + Machines joined the proceedings, its application remained part of the same contention set and it was going to be impacted by the outcome of the .hotel IRP proceedings in any event. The attempt of Minds + Machines to join the proceedings was an important signal that all standard applicants for .hotel challenged the CPE determination.

Moreover, it seems that the IRP panel, in its decision not to have Minds + Machines join the proceedings, focused only on the claimants' challenge to ICANN's refusal of the RfRs. Minds + Machines raised the issue of the illegal access to competing applications by an individual associated with Hotel Top Level Domain (HTLD) together with the other applicants for .hotel, and with respect to this issue, none of the .hotel applicants was time barred. However, the IRP panel left the issue of illegal access open for adjudication by a future panel, with the possibility that a failure by the ICANN Board to act appropriately could be challenged by all applicants.

5. Applicable Law

a. Arguments Discussed

(1) Sources

Despegar et al. argued that the ICANN Board's actions and inactions must be assessed in the light of international law, ICANN's Articles of Incorporation and Bylaws and secondary rules created by ICANN:

> 'In accordance with Article IV(3) of ICANN's Bylaws, an IRP Panel must determine whether the contested actions of the ICANN Board are consistent with applicable rules. The set of rules against which the actions of the ICANN Board must be assessed includes: (i) ICANN's Articles of Incorporation and Bylaws – both of which must be interpreted in light of ICANN's Affirmation of Commitments, and

> both of which require compliance with *inter alia* International law[1147] and generally accepted good governance principles – and (ii) secondary rules created by ICANN, such as the Applicant Guidebook.'[1148]

ICANN argued that 'ICANN has appointed the International Centre for Dispute Resolution ('ICDR') as ICANN's IRP Provider. ICANN's Bylaws and the Supplementary Procedures that the ICDR has adopted specifically for ICANN IRP proceedings apply here.'[1149]

(2) Essential Rights and Obligations

Despegar et al. argued that ICANN should be as *non-interventionist* as possible:

> 'In performing its mission, ICANN must depend to the largest possible extent on market mechanisms to promote and sustain a competitive environment. ICANN must be as non-interventionist as possible and its activities are limited to matters requiring, or significantly benefiting from, global coordination.'[1150]

It maintained that the ICANN Board must comply with fundamental principles, which includes 'a duty to ensure compliance with its obligations to act in *good faith*, *transparently*, *fairly*, and in a manner that is *non-discriminatory* and ensures *due process*.'[1151]

In its view, the ICANN Board had ultimate responsibility for the new gTLD Program and the responsibility to supervise and assure the compliance of that program with ICANN's fundamental obligations:

> 'Since ICANN's Board has ultimate responsibility for the New gTLD Program, it is required to supervise and assure the compliance of that program (and its implementation) with ICANN's fundamental obligations under its Articles of Incorporation and Bylaws. The Applicant Guidebook explicitly calls on the Board to individually consider an application under an ICANN accountability mechanism ([Applicant Guidebook], Module 5-4), such as a Request for Reconsideration ([ICANN Bylaws], Article IV(2)).'[1152]
>
> 'In establishing the selection criteria for evaluation panels, and in making selections, the ICANN Board had a duty to ensure compliance with ICANN's fundamental obligations.'[1153]

Despegar et al. argued that ICANN and its Board was not entitled to adopt a purely process-focused position, but that they must review the compliance of ICANN's processes and their implementation with ICANN's fundamental obligations:

1147. 'In particular, Article IV charges ICANN "*with acting consistently with relevant principles of international law, including the general principles of law recognized as a source of international law*" ([...], Declaration of the Independent Review Panel in ICDR Case No. 50 117 T 00224 08, § 140)'.
1148. Dot Hotel Request for IRP, § 31.
1149. ICANN's Response (*Dot Hotel*), § 32.
1150. Dot Hotel Request for IRP, § 40.
1151. Dot Hotel Request for IRP, § 31.
1152. Dot Hotel Request for IRP, § 64.
1153. Dot Hotel Request for IRP, § 44.

> 'It is unsustainable for ICANN to adopt a purely process-focused position. The ICANN Board has an overriding responsibility to make fair, reasoned and non-discriminatory decisions under conditions of full transparency. Simply following the processes and procedures developed by ICANN cannot alone be sufficient grounds for declining to review a decision. If the requirements of fairness, reasoned decision-making, non-discrimination and transparency have not been met in the implementation of the process and procedures, the ICANN Board must, when invited to do so, conduct a meaningful review ([...]). Claimants understand that the ICANN Board may be required to take advice and recommendations from its constituent bodies or third party experts into consideration; however, the Board is not obliged to follow those recommendations ([...]). Also, when the ICANN Board receives an advice or recommendation, it is expected to (at the very least) investigate the matter before taking a decision ([...]), and conduct a meaningful review when reviewing a challenged decision ([...]).'[1154]

Despegar et al. argued that 'ICANN is subject to a fundamental obligation to act *fairly* and apply established policies *neutrally* and without discrimination. Not only does this obligation arise from general principles of international law, it is also laid down repeatedly in ICANN's governing documents.'[1155]

They argued that a policy which is inconsistent with fundamental legal principles cannot be applied, irrespective of the policy's age:

> 'It is not too late to challenge either applicable policy or the Guidebook, if implementation is inconsistent with the AoI and Bylaws. According to established case law of the U.S. Supreme Court, a policy's age or the age of an implementing regulation cannot be used as an excuse for clear inconsistency with fundamental legal principles.[1156] Even if a statute of limitations is imposed on challenges to a specific policy, it does not prevent those affected by the application of the policy to challenge that application on the grounds that the policy conflicts with a more fundamental legal principle.[1157]'[1158]

Despegar et al. submitted that ICANN must safeguard *due process* rights and ensure that the parties involved know the identity of the adjudicator:

> 'ICANN's obligation to safeguard due process rights covers the right to be heard by an independent and impartial adjudicator.[1159] That right is violated if the adjudicator remains anonymous.[1160] The right to know the identity of the adjudicator – with a view to knowing whether there might be grounds for challenging or removing them – is a fundamental requirement.[1161]'[1162]

They argued that a policy or process cannot be implemented if it derogates from fundamental *due process* rights:

1154. Dot Hotel Reply, § 30.
1155. Dot Hotel Request for IRP, § 33.
1156. 'See *e.g.*, *Brown v. Gardner*, 513 U.S. 115, 122 (1994) ([...]); *Rapanos v. United States*, 547 U.S. 715, 752 (2006) ([...]).'
1157. '*Weaver v. Federal Motor Carrier Safety Admin.*, 744 F. 3d 142, 145 (D.C. Cir. 2014) ([...]).'
1158. Dot Hotel Reply, § 35.
1159. '*E.g.*, Article 14 ICCPR ([...]).'
1160. 'IAComHR, *Lindo et al. v. Peru*, Case 11.182, Report No. 49/00, paras. 115-118 ([...]).'
1161. '*See* IAComHR, *Lindo et al. v. Peru*, Case 11.182, Report No. 49/00, paras. 116 ([...]).'
1162. Dot Hotel Request for IRP, § 57.

> 'Moreover, even if a published policy or process were to explicitly derogate from fundamental due process rights (which is not the case here), ICANN could not implement that policy or process without violating its Articles of Incorporation and Bylaws, regardless of the contents of the Applicant Guidebook.'[1163]

Despegar et al. argued that ICANN had created a reasonable expectation that the CPE process would respect principles of *fairness* and *due process*:

> 'The international law standard of good faith encompasses an obligation to ensure procedural fairness and due process. General principles of "international due process" include equal and fair treatment of the parties, fair notice, and a fair opportunity to present one's case. These requirements are basic principles that inform transnational procedural public policy. They are more than just formalistic procedural requirements. Compliance must be meaningful: parties must be given adequate notice of the relevant rules and a full and fair opportunity to present their case. The mechanisms for redress must be both timely and effective. In view of ICANN's general obligations and the selection criteria for the CPE Panel established by ICANN, new gTLD applicants could reasonably expect that the CPE would, at a minimum, (i) act in accordance with a plan for *"ensuring fairness, nondiscrimination and transparency"*, (ii) reach conclusions that were *"compelling and defensible"* and (iii) *"document the way in which [the CPE performed evaluations] in each case"*.'[1164]

They further argued that ICANN must ensure *openness* in its decision making:

> 'The principle of transparency arises from, and is generally seen as an element of, the principle of good faith. Indeed, transparency has itself obtained the position of a fundamental principle in international economic relations, especially in the regulatory and/or standard-setting space that ICANN occupies. The core elements of transparency include clarity of procedures, the publication and notification of guidelines and applicable rules, and the duty to provide reasons for actions taken. The coupling of the terms *'open'* and *'transparent'*, and a consideration of the context within which the term has been included, confirms that ICANN intended the term to denote the most developed dimension of transparency, namely openness in decision-making.'[1165]

To summarize, the claimants argued that ICANN's fundamental obligations constitute an integral part of the CPE process and that such was confirmed in the information ICANN made available to claimants (and new gTLD applicants in general).[1166] However, ICANN did not comply with its fundamental obligations in the implementation of the CPE process, and the process was not organized in the transparent, fair and non-discriminatory manner, ensuring consistency of approach and scoring, as was promised to prospective applicants, according to claimants. According to the claimants, the CPE process was not illegal per se, as it could have been implemented in a way

1163. Dot Hotel Request for IRP, § 66.
1164. Dot Hotel Request for IRP, § 48.
1165. Dot Hotel Request for IRP, § 38.
1166. *See* Dot Hotel Reply, § 7 with reference to EIU, *CPE Guidelines of 27 September 2013*, available at http://newgtlds.icann.org/en/announcements-and-media/announcement-27sep13-en which contain the promise on p. 22 that the CPE process would 'respect the principles of fairness, transparency, avoiding potential conflicts of interest, and non-discrimination', and that '[c]onsistency of approach in scoring Applications [was going to] be of particular importance'.

that took into account ICANN's fundamental obligations of transparency, fairness and non-discrimination. But the claimants nevertheless requested that, insofar as ICANN's *contra legem* interpretation of the CPE process and AGB is upheld, it be declared that the CPE process and the Applicant Guidebook are inconsistent with the Articles of Incorporation and Bylaws. In this respect, claimants had argued that parties affected by the application of a policy are entitled to challenge that application on the grounds that the policy conflicts with a more fundamental legal principle.[1167]

ICANN argued that the evaluation procedures set forth in the AGB are in compliance with ICANN's Articles of Incorporation and Bylaws:

> '[T]he evaluation procedures set forth in the Guidebook were developed as part of an extended, transparent process involving the reasoned judgment of ICANN's Board and the Internet community. Nothing about those procedures violates ICANN's Articles or Bylaws, and the Claimants' time to challenge those procedures has long since passed.'[1168]

It argued that the ICANN Board may decide independently whether or not it elects to intervene with respect to a CPE Report:

> 'Claimants similarly have identified no Article or Bylaws provision violated by the ICANN Board in exercising its independent judgment not to intervene further with respect to the CPE Report. As the *Booking.com* IRP Panel found, 'the fact that the ICANN Board enjoys [the] discretion [to individually consider an application for a New gTLD] and may choose to exercise it at any time does not mean that it is bound to exercise it, let alone at the time and in the manner demanded by [a claimant]'.'[1169]

ICANN submitted that the ICANN Board was not obliged to perform a substantive review of CPE Reports, but that it must only review whether the actions of the third-party evaluators contradicted established ICANN policies:

> '[A]s the BGC pointed out in its Determination, 'the reconsideration process does not call for the BGC to perform a substantive review of CPE Reports,'[...] which would involve exactly the sort of comprehensive appellate review that the Board (and the community) determined it would not undertake. The BGC did, however, address each of Claimants' complaints with the CPE Panel's scoring of HOTEL TLD's Application, noting that in each case, Claimants' complaint was that the number of points awarded by the Panel was 'wrong,' not that the CPE Panel had violated any ICANN policy or procedure in scoring the Application.'[1170]
>
> 'Claimants do not identify any ICANN Article or Bylaws provision that the BGC allegedly violated in reviewing their First Reconsideration Request. Claimants simply object to the BGC's adherence to the standard for Reconsideration Requests, which calls for the BGC to review only whether the actions of the third-party evaluators 'contradict[ed] established ICANN policy(ies).'[...] The

1167. Dot Hotel Reply, § 35.
1168. ICANN's Response (*Dot Hotel*), § 50.
1169. ICANN's Response (*Dot Hotel*), § 52.
1170. ICANN's Response (*Dot Hotel*), § 49.

> BGC plainly did not violate any Article or Bylaws provision in adhering to the Bylaws standard for Reconsideration Requests.'[1171]

> 'ICANN's Board has not taken *any* action that violates any provision of ICANN's Articles or Bylaws. ICANN's Board was not involved in the creation of the CPE Report and did not substantively review that report. Instead, the Board properly limited its review on reconsideration to assessing whether the CPE Panel had violated established policy and procedure, and correctly concluded that it had not.'[1172]

> 'The BGC did not conduct a substantive evaluation of the CPE Report because doing so is outside of the Board's mandate on reconsideration.'[1173]

> 'Even though ICANN's Board has extended reconsideration to Third Party Providers (reasoning that they are essentially acting in place of ICANN staff), in no way did it expand the scope of the review, which is still limited to whether the Third Party Providers' actions contradicted established policies.'[1174]

ICANN argued that the decision not to perform a substantive review of third party evaluators' reports reflected a considered decision of the ICANN Board at the time of the establishment of the New gTLD Program:

> 'It is not the role of the BGC (or, for that matter, this IRP Panel) to second-guess the substantive determinations of independent, third-party evaluators. The decision not to have ICANN (much less ICANN's Board) perform substantive reviews of third party evaluators' reports reflects a considered decision of ICANN's Board, made after significant public input and comment, that third party experts (and not ICANN) should be resolving these types of issues with respect to the hundreds of gTLD applications that were expected and the 1,930 applications that ICANN in fact received.'[1175]

Regarding the data exposure issue, ICANN stated that the Board was not obliged to address this issue:

> 'The only Board action (or inaction) that Claimants vaguely allude to in their Reply is that the Board did not directly respond to a letter addressed to both ICANN Board and staff requesting disclosure of information regarding the Portal Configuration issue.[...] But, it was not the Board's responsibility to do so, and ICANN's Articles and Bylaws do not mandate that the Board reply to every letter it receives. Indeed, that letter was also submitted through ICANN's Documentary Information Disclosure Policy ('DIDP') and pursuant to the DIDP procedure,[...] ICANN staff was tasked with and did evaluate and respond to the request, providing further details regarding the Portal Configuration issue.[...] Even if Claimants did not like ICANN staff's response to their letter, or to the DIDP request, that is not the basis for independent review. The ICANN Board took no action (and was not required to take action under either the ICANN Articles or Bylaws) with respect to Claimant's letter and DIDP request.'[1176]

1171. ICANN's Response (*Dot Hotel*), § 51.
1172. ICANN's Sur-Reply (*Dot Hotel*), § 5.
1173. ICANN's Sur-Reply (*Dot Hotel*), § 9.
1174. ICANN's Sur-Reply (*Dot Hotel*), § 10.
1175. ICANN's Response (*Dot Hotel*), § 53.
1176. ICANN's Sur-Reply (*Dot Hotel*), § 24.

ICANN argued that although the principle of *transparency* is a fundamental safeguard in the public benefit, it is not always available to specific interested parties:

> 'ICANN considers the principle of transparency to be a fundamental safeguard in assuring that its bottom-up, multistakeholder operating model remains effective and that outcomes of its decision making are in the public benefit and are derived in a manner accountable to all stakeholders. As the BGC noted in its determination, the DIDP is not a litigation tool designed to 'make pieces of information available to specific interested parties.'[…] Rather, it is 'intended to ensure that information contained in documents concerning ICANN's operational activities, and within ICANN's possession, custody, or control, is made available to the public unless there is a compelling reason for confidentiality.'[1177]

It maintained that '[a]ll of the policy development work, implementation, and decision-making that culminated in the current version of the AGB was open, fair and transparent; it led to clear and predictable procedures. All of this work and the results of this work are fully consistent with ICANN Articles and Bylaws.'[1178]

It also claimed that ICANN staff had followed the process in determining that certain documents were subject to nondisclosure conditions:

> 'The BGC's determination on the Second Reconsideration Request addressed each of Claimants' arguments and concluded that ICANN staff had followed the DIDP in determining that certain documents related to the CPE Report were subject to Nondisclosure Conditions, and that the public interest in disclosing those documents did not outweigh the harm that might be caused by such disclosure.'[1179]

At the hearing, ICANN submitted that it was not subject to a due process obligation either pursuant to its Articles of Incorporation and Bylaws, or pursuant to general international legal principles.[1180]

The IRP panel commented that it found this statement 'most surprising in the context of the role ICANN fulfils and the language of Article 4 [of ICANN's Articles of Incorporation] itself.'[1181] The panel opined that 'Article 4 of the Articles of Incorporation refers to the principles of international law and local law and to the use of open and transparent processes to enable competition and open entry in Internet markets' and invited the Board to affirm that 'transparency and due process should be applicable.'[1182]

The IRP panel ruled that the ICANN Board should look into how a relevant policy or procedure was actually applied in practice, and, in the process, decide whether the ICANN Board could have a reasonable degree of assurance that the policy or procedure was in fact being applied correctly.[1183]

1177. ICANN's Response (*Dot Hotel*), § 60.
1178. ICANN's Response (*Dot Hotel*), § 44.
1179. ICANN's Response (*Dot Hotel*), § 59.
1180. Despegar et al. IRP Declaration, § 145.
1181. Despegar et al. IRP Declaration, § 145.
1182. Despegar et al. IRP Declaration, § 145.
1183. Despegar et al. IRP Declaration, §§ 83 and 115.

It further held that the ICANN Board 'should seek to ensure that ICANN's staff comply with the Articles of Incorporation and Bylaws of ICANN, and that a failure of the Board to ensure such compliance is a failure of the Board itself.'[1184]

Concerning the DIDP requests regarding the CPE process, the IRP panel's view was that there was an impression given that a process was not properly conducted if ICANN simply responded that, '*to the extent*' ICANN had documents, these documents were not disclosable, for a variety of reasons, without there being any attempt made to link categories of document to particular conditions for nondisclosure.[1185]

The panel felt that, although it was not possible for it to judge whether the policy for nondisclosure had been correctly applied,[1186] the ICANN Board's determination in response to a reconsideration request 'provides the requisite degree of confirmation that the correct procedure was actually followed, that the [ICANN Board] did, properly, consider whether the relevant policy or procedure was actually applied by the ICANN staff and whether, in doing so, the [ICANN Board] could have a reasonable degree of assurance that the ICANN staff had correctly applied the policy or procedure.'[1187]

Concerning the allegation of association between HTLD and the person who allegedly fraudulently obtained trade secrets of competing applicants, the IRP panel held that *openness and transparency* required ICANN (i) to investigate the allegation of association between HTLD and such person, and (ii) to make public the fact of the investigation and the result thereof.[1188]

(3) Standard of Review

Despegar et al. argued that IRP panels must apply a de novo, objective and independent standard of review without any presumption of correctness:

> 'IRP panels are required 'to 'objectively' determine whether or not the Board's actions are in fact consistent with the [AoI], Bylaws and Guidebook' ([...]). They must appraise the Board's conduct 'independently, and without any presumption of correctness.' ([...]). Consequently, the standard of review in an IRP is 'a de novo, objective and independent one, which does not require any presumption of correctness.' ([...]).'[1189]

ICANN argued that previous panels had found that IRP panels were not intended to substitute their judgment for that of the ICANN Board:

> 'As the IRP panels in *Booking.com* and *Vistaprint* each found, this defined standard of review reflects the fact that IRP panels are not intended to substitute their judgment for the independent judgment of ICANN's Board.'[1190]

1184. Despegar et al. IRP Declaration, § 104.
1185. Despegar et al. IRP Declaration, § 100.
1186. Despegar et al. IRP Declaration, § 97.
1187. Despegar et al. IRP Declaration, § 110.
1188. Despegar et al. IRP Declaration, § 134.
1189. Dot Hotel Reply, § 37.
1190. ICANN's Sur-Reply (*Dot Hotel*), § 30.

The IRP panel declared that ICANN's Bylaws required a defined standard of review to be applied.[1191] It held that the review of the CPE determination to be undertaken by the ICANN Board should be a procedural one, not a substantive one.[1192] It also held that the ICANN Board needed to look into how the EIU / ICANN staff applied the standard, and that the ICANN Board must have a reasonable degree of assurance that the EIU / ICANN staff had applied the policy correctly.[1193]

b. *Noteworthy Points for Analysis*

(1) Sources

The parties agreed on the application of the ICDR Rules, Supplementary Rules and ICANN's Bylaws, but they disagreed on the applicability of general international legal principles. This may seem surprising, given that the *ICM Registry* panel had already conclusively ruled that ICANN was bound by general principles of international law, and given that ICANN had accepted the *ICM Registry* panel's findings. The *Despegar et al.* panel expressed surprise at the position taken by ICANN. However, it did not go on to explicitly confirm the findings of the *ICM Registry* panel. Instead, it simply invited the ICANN Board to affirm that transparency and due process should be applied (even though this would seem self-evident). In any event, the ICANN Board did later affirm 'that, as appropriate, ICANN will continue to ensure that its activities are conducted through open and transparent processes in conformance with Article IV of ICANN's Articles of Incorporation.'[1194] In our view, the obvious result of this should be that ICANN can in the future no longer argue that it is not bound by general principles of international law. However, as ICANN claimed not to be bound by these fundamental principles prior to this affirmation (which was particularly surprising in light of its role as the responsible regulator of the DNS and the express provisions in the Bylaws) it remains to be seen if this point is now settled.

(2) Essential Rights and Obligations

The parties fundamentally disagreed about ICANN's interpretation of the CPE process, with the claimants criticizing the CPE process as a whole (complaining that the ICANN Board had failed to establish, implement and supervise a fair and transparent process) and ICANN considering that it had correctly followed the process and that any legal complaint concerning the process was time-barred.

Unfortunately, the IRP panel did not address the broader issue of the CPE process itself and explicitly refused to make a declaration concerning (i) the selection process of the

1191. Despegar et al. IRP Declaration, §§ 64, 88 and 113.
1192. Despegar et al. IRP Declaration, §§ 66–67.
1193. Despegar et al. IRP Declaration, §§ 69, 90 and 115.
1194. ICANN, *Approved Board Resolution 2016.03.10.11 – Regular Meeting of the ICANN Board*, 10 March 2016, https://www.icann.org/resources/board-material/resolutions-2016-03-10-en.

CPE panel by ICANN, (ii) the CPE process as a whole, (iii) whether that process breached ICANN's Articles of Incorporation or Bylaws, and (iv) whether the Guidebook breached ICANN's Articles of Incorporation or Bylaws.[1195] Surprisingly, the panel apparently considered that relief in respect of these wider issues had not been requested.[1196] In our view, that was not correct. As the panel itself recognized, such relief was referred to by the claimants in their response to the panel's questions of 2 December 2015,[1197] and it was confirmed at the oral hearing. We are of the opinion that, in refusing to address the claimants' criticism of the CPE process as a whole, the IRP panel made an *infra petita*[1198] decision.

Although the IRP panel did not rule on the CPE process as a whole, the panel did share some of the claimants' concerns with the process, finding that there 'needs to be a system in place that ensures the marks are allocated on a consistent and predictable basis by different individual evaluators' and feeling strongly that 'there needs to be a consistency of approach in making CPE evaluations' and that a 'quality review or quality control procedure needs to be in place to ensure consistency, both of approach and marking, by evaluators.'[1199] So why did the IRP panel refuse to review the CPE process as a whole? As mentioned above, this may have been out of a fear of creating a spill-over effect regarding other applications that had already been delegated by ICANN.[1200] The panel apparently considered that there was little that could still be done, given that the CPE process for the round of gTLDs was almost at an end.[1201] In our view, this premise was not entirely correct. The ICANN Board could still have undone the results of the CPEs for .eco and .hotel and asked for a re-evaluation without there being any risk of a spill-over effect. The claimants had requested the panel to make a ruling *inter partes*, not *erga omnes*;[1202] neither the ICANN Board nor the panel had been asked to find a solution for any third-party applicants who had elected not to challenge an inconsistent CPE determination.

It is possible that a finding by the IRP panel concerning the CPE process would have had a broader effect than that originally desired by the claimants. However, the decision whether to apply any corrections to the CPE process retroactively towards other applicants would have been a decision for ICANN, and the overall status of the gTLD round should not serve as an excuse for ICANN not to act in any individual file.

The IRP panel provided the Board with some guidelines on how it should act. First, it stated that the Board should seek 'to ensure that ICANN's staff comply with the Articles of Incorporation and Bylaws of ICANN.'[1203] A 'failure of the Board to ensure such

1195. Despegar et al. IRP Declaration, §§ 46–47.
1196. Despegar et al. IRP Declaration, §§ 44–50.
1197. Despegar et al. IRP Declaration, § 43.
1198. Less than what was requested.
1199. Despegar et al. IRP Declaration, § 147.
1200. *Supra* Chapter 5.G.4.b(2).
1201. ICDR Case No. 01-15-0002-8061, *Despegar Online SRL et al. v. ICANN*, Final Declaration, § 147.
1202. Opposable to or valid against all persons.
1203. Despegar et al. IRP Declaration, § 104.

compliance is a failure of the Board itself.'[1204] However, the IRP panel applied a different reasoning with respect to third parties. Despite the IRP panel's questioning why the EIU was not mandated to apply ICANN's core values in making its determinations, the panel fell short of ordering this to be done, and merely suggested that the ICANN Board ensure that there be a flow-through of the application of ICANN's core values to entities such as the EIU.[1205] The distinction made by the IRP panel between ICANN staff and third parties is unfortunate, especially in view of the fact that ICANN had argued that its third party providers were essentially acting in place of ICANN staff.[1206] Moreover, there are some indications that ICANN may have misrepresented the extent of the involvement of its staff in the evaluation by the EIU,[1207] and this may have had a material impact on the outcome of the case.

(3) Standard of Review

The IRP panel made no reference to settled case law on the standard of review. The panel merely considered that it needed to apply a defined standard of review. In its examination of the DIDP requests and RfRs, it seems that the IRP panel took some of the statements by the ICANN Board for granted, treating the ICANN Board with deference. This is most apparent in the discussion of the DIDP requests. The IRP panel criticized the response by ICANN's staff to the DIDP requests, as ICANN did not indicate which documents it actually had, nor which specific conditions for nondisclosure applied to which specific documents or category of documents. As a consequence, the IRP panel held that 'it is not possible to judge whether the policy for nondisclosure has been correctly applied.'[1208] The panel considered that 'the ICANN staff could, and should, have been more explicit as to the process they had followed in refusing disclosure.'[1209] The panel then continues that the determination by ICANN's Board Governance Committee (BGC) – *i.e.*, a division of the ICANN Board – 'provides the requisite degree of confirmation that the correct procedure was actually followed, that the BGC did, properly, consider whether the relevant policy or procedure was actually applied by the ICANN staff and whether, in doing so, the BGC could have a reasonable degree of assurance that the ICANN staff had correctly the [*sic*] applied the policy or procedure.'[1210]

However, the IRP panel did not verify whether the 'reasonable degree of assurance' by the BGC was justified. It did not examine the underlying facts, and, thus, was not in a position to judge whether the determination by the BGC was correct. As a result, the IRP panel did not review the BGC's action objectively and independently, without any presumption of correctness, as required according to settled case law.

1204. Despegar et al. IRP Declaration, § 104.
1205. Despegar et al. IRP Declaration, § 150.
1206. ICANN's Sur-Reply (*Dot Hotel*), § 10.
1207. *Infra* Chapter 5.G.9.
1208. Despegar et al. IRP Declaration, §§ 94, 97.
1209. Despegar et al. IRP Declaration, § 110.
1210. Despegar et al. IRP Declaration, § 110.

Moreover, as stated above, developments in a more recent case[1211] show that the IRP panel might have been misled not only as to the involvement of ICANN staff, but also regarding material information that was not disclosed to the panel. In light of this, it is possible that the panel would give less deference to the ICANN Board if asked to rule on this issue today.

6. Authority of the Panel

a. *Arguments Discussed*

Despegar et al. argued that the IRP panel was obliged to order relief that finally resolves the dispute and offers effective redress:

> 'The right to an independent review is 'a significant and meaningful one under the ICANN's Bylaws. This is so particularly in light of the importance of ICANN's global work in overseeing the DNS for the Internet and also the weight attached by ICANN itself to the principles of accountability and review which underpin the IRP process' ([...], para. 59). The IRP Panel's authority is not limited to a simple declaration that ICANN breached its obligations under its AoI, Bylaws and the Applicant Guidebook. The task of an IRP panel is to resolve the dispute: the applicable ICDR Rules (as supplemented by the Supplementary Procedures) are designed to resolve a dispute between the parties; the panel is instructed to arbitrate and to render final and binding awards. (See Preamble of ICDR Rules: 'These Procedures are designed to provide a complete dispute resolution framework for disputing parties.'; Article 20(2) ICDR Rules: 'The tribunal shall conduct the proceedings with a view to expediting the resolution of the dispute.'; Article 30(1) ICDR Rules: 'Awards shall be made in writing by the arbitral tribunal and shall be final and binding on the parties.').
>
> To resolve the dispute and to offer effective redress to applicants, the IRP Panel may issue a binding recommendation regarding what action ICANN must take in order to cease violating its obligations. Indeed, IRP panels 'have the power to recommend a course of action for the Board to follow as a consequence of any declaration that the Board acted or failed to act in a manner inconsistent with ICANN's Articles of Incorporation, Bylaws or the Applicant Guidebook.' ([...], para. 126, emphasis added). The point is all the stronger here, as ICANN created the IRP specifically to be the sole dispute resolution mechanism available to new gTLD applicants (supra).
>
> Previous IRP panels have given binding recommendations to ICANN: [...].
>
> As a result, the applicable rules and the jurisprudence clearly establish that an IRP panel is authorized to grant affirmative relief.'[1212]

Despegar et al. submitted that the IRP panel in the *Vistaprint* case did not act in accordance with the ICDR Rules because it did not finally resolve the dispute.[1213]

1211. *Infra, Dot Registry case.*
1212. Dot Hotel Reply, §§ 20–23.
1213. Dot Hotel Reply, § 24.

It also argued that '[a]ny relief ordered must effectively avoid another unfair, arbitrary and discriminatory decision.'[1214]

ICANN argued that IRP panels have no authority to award affirmative relief:

> 'An IRP Panel, however, is explicitly limited to stating its opinion as to 'whether an action or inaction of the Board was inconsistent with the Articles of Incorporation or Bylaws' and recommending, if requested, that the Board stay any action or decision or take any interim action until such time as the Board reviews and acts upon the opinion of the IRP Panel.[...] Even if there were a basis for some kind of relief here (which there is not), neither this Panel nor any IRP panel has the authority to award affirmative relief.'[1215]

It argued that it is the ICANN Board's action following the IRP decision that finally resolves the dispute:

> 'Claimants argue that IRP panels do have the authority to grant affirmative relief, and that the *Vistaprint* IRP panel '[d]id not act in accordance with the ICDR Rules, as it did not finally resolve the dispute.'[...] The *Vistaprint* IRP panel 'recommend[ed] that the ICANN Board exercise its judgment on the question of whether an additional review mechanism [was] appropriate to re-evaluate the [expert declaration at issue in *Vistaprint*].'[...] This recommendation was exactly the type of 'relief' that an IRP panel has authority to issue – a recommendation of how the Board should proceed. ICANN's Board considers and acts upon the recommendation of all IRP panels, and it is that action by ICANN's Board that, in conjunction with the declaration of the IRP panel, finally resolves the dispute between the parties. Even though Claimants cite to the final declaration of the IRP panel in *DotConnectAfrica* and the declarations of emergency panelists in other IRPs,[...] affirmative relief was not 'awarded' or 'mandated' by those IRP panels but rather by ICNN's Board, which considered and then accepted the recommendations contained in those panel determinations.'[1216]

The panel noted that the claimants had requested relief neither with respect to their criticism of the CPE process as a whole, nor for the ICANN Board's failure to establish, implement and supervise a fair and transparent CPE process.[1217]

The panel decided that it should not make a declaration on the violation of trade secrets by an individual associated to HTLD, as the issue was still under investigation by the ICANN Board, but that the issue should remain open to be considered by a future IRP.[1218]

The panel trusted that the ICANN Board would give due consideration to the concerns raised by the claimants and shared by the panel.[1219]

1214. Dot Hotel Reply, § 47.
1215. ICANN's Response (*Dot Hotel*), § 62; *see also* ICANN's Sur-Reply (*Dot Hotel*), § 33.
1216. ICANN's Sur-Reply (*Dot Hotel*), § 34.
1217. Despegar et al. IRP Declaration, §§ 44–47.
1218. Despegar et al. IRP Declaration, §§ 137–138.
1219. Despegar et al. IRP Declaration, § 144.

The panel also invited the ICANN Board 'to affirm that, to the extent possible, and compatible with the circumstances and the objects to be achieved by ICANN, transparency and administrative due process should be applicable.'[1220]

b. Noteworthy Points for Analysis

As explained above, the IRP panel did not rule on important claims with respect to the CPE process as a whole. It considered that the claimants had abandoned their requests in this regard and, as a result, the panel did not need to discuss the extent of its authority. The panel did not find that ICANN had violated its Articles of Incorporation and Bylaws in its consideration of the claimants' RfRs, and, thus, the panel did not need to examine whether upholding the refusal by ICANN to grant the relief requested by the claimants in their RfRs constituted a continued violation of the Articles of Incorporation and Bylaws.

The IRP panel required that the ICANN Board investigate the allegations of association between HTLD and the person who fraudulently obtained trade secrets of competing applicants, and that ICANN make public the fact of the investigation and the result thereof.[1221] The panel added that a failure of the Board to take appropriate action could well amount to inaction on its part,[1222] making it clear that not taking appropriate action was not an option.

Although the panel left the issue of the data exposure open for adjudication by a future IRP panel, it considered that ICANN's failure to investigate the issue, to publish the results and to take appropriate action could amount to a reviewable inaction of the Board. The IRP panel also recognized the seriousness of the allegations with respect to the data exposure issue. As the IRP panel made clear that not taking appropriate action was not a viable option for the ICANN Board, it seems that the IRP panel considered itself competent to require specific action from the ICANN Board. Therefore, we fail to understand why the IRP panel reserved this issue for a future IRP. Instead, the panel could have issued an interim decision and reserved final adjudication only. Such a decision would have been procedurally more economic and would have obliged the ICANN Board to take appropriate action.

Finally, the IRP panel also gave a strong signal that ICANN should change its process going forward. Indeed, the fact that it ruled that the fees and expenses of the IRP proceedings be split equally between ICANN and Despegar et al. indicates that the panel considered the claimants to have raised important issues which gave cause for concern. The panels in the *Booking.com* and *Vistaprint* cases had ruled in the same way.

1220. Despegar et al. IRP Declaration, § 145.
1221. Despegar et al. IRP Declaration, § 134.
1222. Despegar et al. IRP Declaration, § 136.

7. Nature of the IRP Declaration

a. Arguments Discussed

(1) Binding Nature of the IRP Declaration

Despegar et al. argued that '[t]he IRP Panel has the jurisdiction to render decisions that are binding upon ICANN and that resolve the dispute.'[1223]

They argued that the IRP was created to be a binding dispute resolution mechanism within the new gTLD Program, as confirmed in the applicable rules and by most IRP panels:

> 'Within its New gTLD Program, ICANN created the IRP so as to provide an alternative to dispute resolution by courts. To submit a new gTLD application, Claimants had to agree to eight pages of terms and conditions ([...]). The terms and conditions include a waiver of all Claimants' rights to challenge ICANN's decisions on Claimants' applications in court, or in any other judicial forum, provided that, as an applicant, Claimants may utilize any accountability mechanism set forth in ICANN's Bylaws ([...]). Assuming that the foregoing waiver of any and all judicial remedies is valid and enforceable, the ultimate accountability remedy for Claimants is the IRP ([...]).
>
> The IRP is not a mere 'corporate accountability mechanism' aimed at ICANN's internal stakeholders. The IRP is open to *any* person materially affected by a decision or action by the Board (Article IV(3)(2) of ICANN's Bylaws). It is made explicitly available to applicants such as Claimants ([...]), who are by definition third parties.
>
> The IRP cannot fulfil its role as an effective and robust mechanism for accountability (as required by ICANN's Affirmation of Commitments ([...], Article 9.1) and ICANN's Bylaws ([...], Article I(2)(10)) unless it be binding upon ICANN. Otherwise, the ICANN Board's discretion would indeed be unfettered and ICANN's AoI and Bylaws would be called into question.
>
> A previous IRP panel ruled that "[v]arious provisions of ICANN's Bylaws and the Supplementary Procedures support the conclusion that the [IRP] Panel's decisions, opinions and declarations are binding' and that '[t]here is certainly nothing in the Supplementary Rules that renders the decisions, opinions and declarations of the [IRP] Panel either advisory or non-binding" ([...], para. 98).
>
> Indeed, as per Article IV(3)(8) of the ICANN Bylaws, the ICANN Board has given its approval to the ICDR to establish a set of operating rules and procedures for the conduct of the IRP. The operating rules and procedures established by the ICDR are the ICDR Rules as referred to in the preamble of the Supplementary Procedures ([...], para. 101). The Supplementary Procedures *supplement* the ICDR Rules (Supplementary Procedures, Preamble and Section 2). The preamble of the ICDR Rules provides that "[a] dispute can be submitted to an arbitral tribunal for a final and binding decision'. Article 30 of the ICDR Rules specifies that '[a]wards shall be made in writing by the arbitral tribunal and shall be final and binding on the parties". No provision in the Supplementary Procedures deviates from the idea

1223. Dot Hotel Reply, § 4.

that the Panel's decisions are binding. On the contrary, Section 1 of the Supplementary Procedures defines an IRP Declaration as a decision/opinion of the IRP Panel. Section 10 of the Supplementary Procedures requires that IRP Declarations i) are made in writing, and ii) specifically designate the prevailing party. Where a decision must specifically designate the prevailing party, it is inherently binding. Moreover the binding nature of IRP Declarations is further supported by the language and spirit of Section 6 of the Supplementary Procedures and Article IV(3)(11)(a) of the ICANN Bylaws. Pursuant to these provisions, the IRP Panel has the authority to summarily dismiss requests that are brought without standing, are lacking in substance, or are frivolous or vexatious. It is clear that such a decision, opinion or declaration on the part of the IRP Panel would not be considered advisory only ([...], para. 107).

Finally, even if ICANN's Bylaws and Supplementary Procedures were considered to be ambiguous (*quod non*) regarding the question of whether or not an IRP Declaration is binding, this ambiguity would weigh against ICANN. The relationship between ICANN and Claimants is clearly one of an adhesion contract. In such a situation, the rule of *contra proferentem* applies. As the drafter and architect of the IRP Procedure, it was possible for ICANN, and clearly within its power, to adopt a procedure that expressly and clearly announced that the decisions, opinions and declarations of IRP panels were advisory only. ICANN did not adopt such a procedure ([...], paras. 108-109).

An IRP panel in a recent decision, the *Vistaprint* decision, made a distinction between i) an IRP panel's finding on whether or not the Board has acted consistently with the AoI and Bylaws and ii) the form of relief that the IRP panel can provide by directing the ICANN Board either to take, or to refrain from taking, any action or decision. According to the panel in the *Vistaprint* decision, the former is binding; the latter would serve only as a recommendation to be reviewed and acted upon by the ICANN Board ([...], para. 140). Said IRP Panel attempted to support its reasoning by reference to a statement made by a former Chair of the ICANN Board, who advocated, in 2009, that an IRP panel's recommendations be advisory ([...], para. 142).

However, the panel in the *Vistaprint* decision disregarded the fact that the IRP procedure has been modified to make ICANN more accountable, and that for the New gTLD Program the IRP procedure was conceived by ICANN as the ultimate dispute resolution mechanism (*supra*, para. 11). Maybe more importantly, the panel in the *Vistaprint* case made an erroneous reading of Article IV(3)(11) of ICANN's Bylaws, when it stated that the Panel may *only* recommend that the ICANN Board stay or take any action or decision ([...], paras. 136 and 143). Nothing in the ICANN Bylaws or the Supplementary Procedures suggests that the examples of an IRP panel's authority given in Article IV(3)(11) impose limits on the IRP Panel's authority. A recommendation can be a binding recommendation. No provision (be it in the Supplementary Procedures, in the ICANN Bylaws or elsewhere) limits the IRP Panel's task pursuant to the ICDR Rules of resolving the dispute with a final and binding decision (*infra*). This has been the interpretation of most IRP panels appointed in the context of the New gTLD Program (*infra*; [...]).

For all these reasons, the IRP Declaration is binding upon ICANN.'[1224]

1224. Dot Hotel Reply, §§ 11–19.

ICANN argued that the ICANN Board would give serious consideration to the IRP panel's opinion:

> 'Consistent with ICANN's Bylaws, the IRP Panel is to issue a written declaration designating, among other things, the prevailing party.[...] The Board will give serious consideration to the IRP Panel's opinion and, 'where feasible,' shall consider the IRP Panel's declaration at the Board's next meeting.'[1225]

It claimed that IRP decisions were not binding, but that ICANN had always taken IRP decisions seriously and that, to date, it had adopted the recommendations of all IRP declarations:

> 'ICANN's Bylaws are clear that ICANN's Board is required to 'review[]' and 'consider' the declaration, thereby exercising its discretion as to whether and in what manner to adopt and implement that declaration.[...] This is precisely what happened in all four IRPs that have gone to a final declaration to date—following the issuance of the final declarations in the *ICM, Booking.com, DotConnectAfrica,* and *Vistaprtint* IRPs, the ICANN Board promptly reviewed and ultimately determined to adopt the relevant portions of the panels' declarations.[...]
>
> ICANN recognizes that a single IRP panel in the *DotConnectAfrica* matter issued a finding that its declaration would be legally binding, in contrast to the findings made by the panels in the *Vistaprint* and *ICM* matters that their declarations were not legally binding.[...] As ICANN has emphasized repeatedly to all IRP panels, the ICANN Board has announced that it will take (and is required by the Bylaws to take) any declarations of IRP panels seriously and to date has adopted the recommendations of all IRP declarations.'[1226]

The IRP panel's Declaration contains no explicit reasoning on the binding nature of the IRP Declaration. The panel merely designated ICANN as the prevailing party, and declared that the fees and expenses of the IRP panel members and the ICDR be born half by Despegar et al. and half by ICANN. The panel did, however, state that its 'Final Declaration may be executed in any number of counterparts, each of which shall be deemed an original, and all of which together shall constitute the Final Declaration of this IRP Panel.'[1227]

b. Noteworthy Points for Analysis

(1) Binding Nature of the IRP Declaration

Although the IRP Declaration contains no explicit reasoning on its binding nature, in our view the decision suggests that the IRP panel agreed with the claimants that IRP declarations have binding effect. We find this clear from the operative part of the IRP Declaration that states that it may be 'executed'. If the IRP panel considered its declaration to have no binding effect, it would not have mentioned that the declaration could be executed – as there would be nothing to execute.

1225. ICANN's Response (*Dot Hotel*), § 33.
1226. ICANN's Sur-Reply (*Dot Hotel*), § 32.
1227. Despegar et al. IRP Declaration, operative part.

8. ICANN Board's Decisions Following the IRP Declaration

On 10 March 2016, the ICANN Board accepted the IRP Declaration.[1228] It asked that the new gTLD program review 'take into consideration the issues raised by the Panel as they relate to the consistency and predictability of the CPE process and third-party provider evaluations.'[1229] The ICANN Board also affirmed that 'ICANN will continue to ensure that its activities are conducted through open and transparent processes in conformance with Article IV of ICANN's Articles of Incorporation.'[1230] Finally, the ICANN Board called for the completion of the 'investigation of the issues alleged by the .hotel Claimants regarding the portal configuration as soon as feasible and to provide a report to the Board for consideration following the completion of that investigation.'[1231]

9. What Happened Thereafter?

The claimants asked ICANN to clarify whether the review of the new gTLD program would involve a re-evaluation of the challenged CPE results and to specify what measures ICANN was going to take to ensure that a re-evaluation remained meaningful.[1232] However, it transpired that ICANN did not anticipate a re-evaluation of the CPE results,[1233] and ICANN then proceeded with the delegation of the .eco gTLD to the 'community-based' applicant.[1234]

With respect to .hotel, it seems that ICANN started investigations concerning the alleged theft of trade secrets after the IRP panel's declaration that ICANN's failure to take appropriate action by the date of the IRP Declaration could well amount to inaction of the ICANN Board. On 23 February 2016, ICANN asked the claimants for more information about the alleged affiliation between the person who accessed confidential and proprietary information and HTLD. The claimants expressed their surprise at this sudden request, as ICANN's own file on HTLD showed this affiliation.[1235] On 16 March 2016, ICANN acknowledged that the individual concerned had

1228. ICANN, *Approved Board Resolution 2016.03.10.10 – Regular Meeting of the ICANN Board*, 10 March 2016, https://www.icann.org/resources/board-material/resolutions-2016-03-10-en.
1229. ICANN, *Approved Board Resolution 2016.03.10.11 – Regular Meeting of the ICANN Board*, 10 March 2016, https://www.icann.org/resources/board-material/resolutions-2016-03-10-en.
1230. ICANN, *Approved Board Resolution 2016.03.10.11 – Regular Meeting of the ICANN Board*, 10 March 2016, https://www.icann.org/resources/board-material/resolutions-2016-03-10-en.
1231. ICANN, *Approved Board Resolution 2016.03.10.11 – Regular Meeting of the ICANN Board*, 10 March 2016, https://www.icann.org/resources/board-material/resolutions-2016-03-10-en.
1232. E-mail by Claimants of 27 April 2016, https://www.icann.org/en/system/files/correspondence/petillion-to-atallah-icann-board-27apr16-en.pdf.
1233. ICANN, *Letter from Christine Willett of 11 May 2016*, https://www.icann.org/en/system/files/correspondence/willett-to-petillion-11may16-en.pdf.
1234. ICANN, *.eco Registry Agreement*, 8 July 2016, https://www.icann.org/resources/agreement/eco-2016-07-08-en.
1235. E-mail by Travel Reservations SRL of 1 March 2016, https://www.icann.org/en/system/files/correspondence/petillion-to-atallah-01mar16-en.pdf; E-mail by Claimants of 8 March 2016, https://www.icann.org/en/system/files/correspondence/petillion-to-atallah-08mar16-en.pdf.

indeed accessed and downloaded confidential information with respect to applications of competitors and that he appeared to have specifically searched for such information.[1236] ICANN had also discovered that multiple business connections existed between HTLD and the individual concerned.[1237] After being informed that ICANN was apparently taking the matter seriously, HTLD made changes in its management and ownership structure.[1238] The claimants pointed out to ICANN that HTLD had waited for almost a year before terminating its relationship with the individual concerned, and that it had done so only at ICANN's specific request. They argued that, if awarded the .hotel gTLD, HTLD would have an unfair advantage over competing registry operators, because of its access to this sensitive business information.[1239] Nevertheless, on 9 August 2016, the ICANN Board decided that cancellation of HTLD's application for .hotel was not warranted and allowed the further processing of HTLD's application.[1240]

The ICANN Board decision revealed that the user credentials of HTLD's CEO at the time were also 'responsible for numerous instances of suspected intentional unauthorized access to other applicants' confidential information' for a protracted period of time.[1241] Also, on 9 August 2016, ICANN accepted an IRP declaration in the *Dot Registry* case.[1242] The claimants in the .hotel matter considered that the ICANN Board's acceptance of the Dot Registry IRP Declaration was incompatible with the ICANN Board's acceptance of the Despegar et al. IRP Declaration.[1243] The claimants have raised both these issues in an RfR which is currently pending.[1244]

H. THE DONUTS CASE (.SPORTS/.RUGBY)

1. Key Notes

- IRP under the new set of applicable rules.

1236. ICANN, *Letter from Christine Willet of 16 March 2016*, https://www.icann.org/en/system/files/correspondence/willett-to-lenz-hawliczek-16mar16-en.pdf.
1237. ICANN, *Letter from Christine Willet of 16 March 2016*, https://www.icann.org/en/system/files/correspondence/willett-to-lenz-hawliczek-16mar16-en.pdf.
1238. HTLD, *Letter from Philip Grabensee of 23 March 2016*, https://www.icann.org/en/system/files/correspondence/grabensee-to-willett-23mar16-en.pdf.
1239. E-mail by Claimants of 12 May 2016, https://www.icann.org/en/system/files/correspondence/petillion-to-icann-board-et-al-12may16-en.pdf.
1240. ICANN, *Approved Board Resolutions 2016.08.09.14-2016.08.09.15 – Special Meeting of the ICANN Board*, 9 August 2016, https://www.icann.org/resources/board-material/resolutions-2016-08-09-en.
1241. ICANN, *Approved Board Resolutions 2016.08.09.14-2016.08.09.15 – Special Meeting of the ICANN Board*, 9 August 2016, https://www.icann.org/resources/board-material/resolutions-2016-08-09-en, rationale.
1242. *Infra*; ICANN, *Approved Board Resolutions 2016.08.09.11-2016.08.09.13 – Special Meeting of the ICANN Board*, 9 August 2016, https://www.icann.org/resources/board-material/resolutions-2016-08-09-en.
1243. For a detailed analysis of the incompatibility, *see* Chapter 4.I.8.
1244. *Travel Reservations SRL et al. v. ICANN, Request for Reconsideration 16-11*, 25 August 2016, https://www.icann.org/en/system/files/files/reconsideration-16-11-trs-et-al-request-redacte
d-25aug16-en.pdf.

- ICANN agreed to stay the delegation of the gTLDs relevant to the IRP pending the proceedings.
- The majority of the panel concluded that it could review acts and omissions by third parties, if those acts could be attributed to the ICANN Board, but considered that the claimant had failed to prove such attribution.
- Confirmation that the standard of review is non-deferential.
- Finding that discrimination can only exist when disparate treatment occurs in like circumstances.
- Due regard for precedential value of IRP declarations.
- Finding that an appeals mechanism for expert determinations might add predictability of outcome and produce greater satisfaction among new gTLD applicants.
- Finding by the majority of the panel that the ICANN Board's failure to intervene must be considered in light of the range of possible actions available to applicants affected and in view of an applicant's decision to forgo a RfR.
- ICANN was the prevailing party. However, in a well-reasoned dissenting opinion, one panelist explained why he would have partially granted Donuts' request for IRP.

2. Introduction

The claimant in this case had a strong case on the merits.[1245] The claimant's applications had been subjected to expert determinations which arguably applied an erroneous standard and went against the stated purpose of the new gTLD program. Although there was no demonstrable action or inaction by the ICANN Board, the claimant nonetheless filed a request for IRP.

Indeed, the claimant gave the ICANN Board little opportunity to redress the alleged short comings in the expert determinations. The claimant decided to forgo the option to file a RfR with the ICANN Board, arguing that an RfR would have been futile for the purpose of solving the issue. It is true that ICANN Board responses to comparable RfRs in other cases seem to back up the claimant's point of view[1246] and an RfR would probably not in itself have brought final resolution of the issues. However, it would have required the Board to exercise its independent judgment on the issue and to take a decision based on a thorough examination of the facts and the claimant's arguments. In this way, an RfR would likely have put the claimant in a more comfortable position in arguing its case before the IRP panel. As it was, the claimant had to jump a difficult

1245. We were not involved as counsel for either party in this case.

1246. *See Dot Sport Limited v. ICANN*, BGC Determination on Reconsideration Request 13-16, 8 January 2014, errata added 28 July 2014, https://www.icann.org/en/system/files/files/determination-sport-08jan14-en.pdf; *Dot Rugby Limited v. ICANN*, BGC Determination on Reconsideration Request 14-6, 16 March 2014, https://www.icann.org/en/system/files/files/determination-rugby-13mar14-en.pdf; *Dot Sport Limited v. ICANN*, ICANN Board Resolution - Meeting of the New gTLD Program Committee 2014.07.18.NG01, 18 July 2014, https://www.icann.org/resources/board-material/resolutions-new-gtld-2014-07-18-en.

hurdle, arguing that the ICANN Board should have intervened *sua sponte*. As a result, this IRP must be seen in view of the claimant's decision not to file an RfR, and much of the discussion revolved around this topic.

The majority of the panel took a rather narrow view of its authority and was criticized severely by the dissenting panelist, who would have partially[1247] granted the request for IRP. The majority of the panel agreed that the dissenting opinion was a sensible one, but maintained its more narrow view concerning the panel's authority. The decision is relevant for its views on precedential value and its confirmation of the standard of review. The IRP panel also examined ICANN's non-discrimination obligation, but its analysis seems somewhat undiscerning and one-sided.

3. Case Background

Donuts, Inc. (Donuts) is the parent company of numerous new gTLD applicants, including Steel Edge, LLC (an applicant for .sports), Wild Lake LLC (an applicant for .ski) and Atomic Cross, LLC (an applicant for .rugby). On 13 March 2013, SportAccord, the International Ski Federation (FIS) and the International Rugby Board (IRB) respectively challenged the applications by Donuts' subsidiaries on the basis of a community objection with the International Chamber of Commerce (ICC).[1248] The appointed experts upheld the community objections against all three applications and advised ICANN to reject the applications by Donuts' subsidiaries.

On 24 March 2014, Donuts sought assistance from the ICANN Ombudsman in connection with the objection rulings. However, the Ombudsman decided that his competency was limited to considering certain matters of procedural fairness. He considered that he was not authorized to review the complaint or the interpretation of the Guidebook principles and applicable law. Donuts then filed for an IRP with the ICDR to challenge the determinations issued by the experts upholding the community objections.

On 14 July 2015, counsel to Donuts informed the IRP panel that it no longer sought relief with respect to .ski.[1249] With respect to .sports and .rugby, Donuts complained that the ICC experts had misapplied the grounds for community objections. Donuts also argued that the expert appointed in the .sports case had failed to disclose fully his relationship with organizations affiliated with the objector.

1247. The dissenting Panelist would have reversed and denied the expert determination on .sports, which is one of the expert determinations that were challenged by Donuts. The dissenting Panelist considered that the integrity and fairness of the system was compromised in the matter involving .sports. However, he was unable to conclude that a violation of fundamental principles or covenants took place in the matter involving .rugby, and agreed with the Panel's majority not to grant relief regarding .rugby.

1248. This objection ground allows formal objections to be filed by parties with standing if there is substantial opposition to the gTLD application from a significant portion of the community to which the gTLD string may be explicitly or implicitly targeted. https://community.icann.org/display/newgtldrg/community+objection+grounds.

1249. Donuts IRP Procedural Order No. 1, § 10.

4. Points of Procedure

a. *Arguments Discussed*

(1) Jurisdiction of the IRP Panel

In its IRP request, Donuts challenged the objection rulings on .sports and .rugby as well as ICANN's 'failure to correct them'.[1250] According to Donuts, 'both the objection rulings themselves and the Board's failure to correct them constitute Board "action" and "inaction".'[1251] Donuts requested that the IRP panel 'exercise its express authority to declare whether such "action or inaction of the Board was inconsistent with the Articles [of Incorporation] ... or Bylaws".'[1252]

According to ICANN, the IRP panel 'has one (and only one) responsibility – to, in its opinion, "declar[e] whether the Board has acted consistently with the provisions of [ICANN's] Articles of Incorporation and Bylaws."[1253]'[1254] ICANN submitted that IRPs are 'limited to addressing actions of the ICANN Board' and that they 'were not established to evaluate the conduct of ICANN staff, much less third party providers that have contracted with ICANN to provide services to the corporation.'[1255]

The panel opined that it was able to examine both actions and certain inactions of the ICANN Board, but the majority of the panel considered that its mandate was strictly limited:

> 'As more fully discussed below in connection with the Panel's Analysis of the Parties' arguments, the Panels mandate is highly limited. The Panel is called upon to evaluate only acts (and certain failures to act) of the ICANN Board. The Panel is asked to judge such conduct against ICANN's Bylaws and Articles [of Incorporation ...].'[1256]

The majority of the panel considered that it could not review acts and omissions by other actors, unless they could be attributed to the ICANN Board:

> 'As more fully developed below, this proceeding is instituted to allow an independent panel to compare the actions and certain inactions of the ICANN Board to the obligations attaching to it under ICANN's Articles [of Incorporation], its Bylaws and potentially other documents central to the new gTLD program. This Panel is not authorized to assess acts and omissions by other actors unless those can be attributed to the Board on some basis. A core disagreement between the parties is the extent to which any Board action or inaction cognizable by this Panel has been demonstrated by Donuts. Because the Board ordinarily is not directly involved in processing objections, Donuts has faced a difficult obstacle – the need to show an equivalency between the activities of the ICC and its appointed experts on the one

1250. Donuts' IRP Request, § 30.
1251. Donuts' IRP Request, § 30.
1252. Donuts' IRP Request, § 30.
1253. 'Bylaws, [...] Art. IV, §3.4.'
1254. ICANN's Response (*Donuts*), § 3; *See also*, ICANN's Sur-Reply (*Donuts*), § 1.
1255. ICANN's Response (*Donuts*), §4.
1256. Donuts IRP Declaration, § 8.

hand, and the Board on the other, or alternatively, to show inaction by the Board that is inconsistent with the Articles [of Incorporation] or Bylaws.'[1257]

(2) Standing

Donuts argued that it was 'materially affected' by acts and omissions of ICANN's Board contrary to its Bylaws and Articles. In Donuts' opinion, the Board had divested Donuts of its right to compete for valuable Internet 'real estate' in the form of new gTLDs.[1258]

ICANN asked for the summary dismissal of the IRP, on the basis that Donuts had not challenged any Board action, but only the conduct of a third party contractor:

> 'IRPs, however, are limited to addressing actions of the ICANN Board. IRPs were not established to evaluate the conduct of ICANN staff, much less third party providers that have contracted with ICANN to provide services to the corporation. Absent Board action, there simply is nothing for the IRP Panel to evaluate. Because Donuts does not challenge Board action, but rather challenges determinations made by an independent third party dispute resolution provider, this IRP can be summarily resolved in ICANN's favor.'[1259]

However, the panel did not summarily dismiss Donuts' request for IRP. In the course of the proceedings, ICANN had agreed to a stay with respect to the gTLDs that were the subject of the IRP proceedings.[1260] As a result, ICANN's claim for summary dismissal was weakened, and the proceedings followed their normal course.

(3) Time Bar

Donuts considered that its request for IRP was timely.[1261]

ICANN did not object, but argued that, objections to the community objection process and 'any objection to the selection of the ICC [were] time-barred.'[1262]

The panel ruled that there was a time bar to challenge the process as developed, but not the way in which it was conducted:

> 'Finally, complaints about the community objection process as adopted, however well-founded, must be viewed in light of the time bar established in the Bylaws[[1263]] and applied by other Panels.[[1264]] That said, this Panel believes that it may not always be improper to consider *the manner* in which the process, as

1257. Donuts IRP Declaration, § 57.
1258. Donuts' IRP Request, § 1.
1259. ICANN's Response (*Donuts*), § 4; *See also* ICANN's Sur-Reply (*Donuts*), § 7.
1260. Email from counsel to ICANN to counsel to Donuts of 21 November 2014.
1261. Donuts' IRP Request, § 59.
1262. ICANN's Response (*Donuts*), § 58.
1263. 'See ICANN Bylaws, Article IV, Sec 3(3).'
1264. 'See Booking.com IR[P] Declaration, at para. 129 [...].'

> established by ICANN, was conducted, and in particular the extent to which relevant actors deviated from that process.[1265]'[1266]

As such, the panel considered that Donuts was in a position to challenge the community objection expert's failure to disclose a potential conflict of interest, finding that:

> 'At least arguably, moreover, no time bar would operate because the complaint is not about the system as installed by ICANN, but rather concerns a failure of the system as designed to be followed in this particular case.'[1267]

(4) Written/Oral Arguments

The panel organized an in-person hearing. The hearing was limited to argument only.

(5) Witnesses and Expert Witnesses

Donuts produced an expert opinion and a witness statement by a former ICANN employee. There is no indication that any of the parties requested the examination of witnesses. In any event, it is doubtful that the Panel would have accepted the examination or cross-examination of witnesses, as the Panel was of the opinion that 'rather limited fact-finding [...] can be pursued in an IRP'.[1268]

However, ICANN commented on the expert opinion and the witness statement in writing, and the panel took account of both statements.

(6) Costs

The parties did not develop arguments about the costs of the proceedings, but requested that the non-prevailing party paid the costs.

The majority of the panel did not find that the circumstances of the case warranted 'departing from the general rule that, ordinarily, "the party not prevailing in an IRP shall ... be responsible for bearing all costs of the proceedings".'[1269] The majority of the panel recognized that the claimant might have contributed to the public interest, but that this contribution had been 'offset by the tenuousness of some of [the claimant's] positions.'[1270]

The panel also held that Article 34 of the ICDR Rules accorded it 'discretion to hear the parties on the question of legal fees and to make an award of such fees in whole or in

1265. 'This was the approach taken by the Bookings.com [*sic*] Panel. See, e.g., para. 163 [...].'
1266. Donuts IRP Declaration, § 136; *See also* Donuts IRP Declaration, § 179.
1267. Donuts IRP Declaration, § 200.
1268. Donuts IRP Declaration, § 135.
1269. Donuts IRP Declaration, § 233.
1270. Donuts IRP Declaration, § 234.

part.'[1271] Nevertheless, the panel recognized the apparent tendency of previous IRP panels to leave each party responsible for its own legal fees. '[I]n keeping with that trend', the panel unanimously decided that 'each side should bear its own legal fees and similar costs.'[1272]

b. *Noteworthy Points for Analysis*

(1) Jurisdiction of the IRP Panel

The majority of the panel had a somewhat narrow view concerning its own jurisdiction. It considered the panel to be able only to review actions and inactions proven to be attributable to the ICANN Board. However, the panel's majority disregarded the fact that it was the ICANN Board that installed a system whereby community objections were examined by third-party contractors, and that the purpose of this system was to assist the ICANN Board in its selection of new gTLD operators. If the advice by a third-party contractor was ill-founded or contrary to ICANN's essential obligations, nothing would prevent ICANN from rejecting that advice. We would even go further and suggest that ICANN is obliged to reject recommendations that go against ICANN's essential obligations.

The final decision whether or not to delegate a new gTLD string to a specific applicant is a decision that should always be attributable to the ICANN Board. Indeed, the ICANN Board is the only entity that can be held responsible for ICANN's actions. Article I(1) of ICANN's Bylaws provides that ICANN's business and affairs are conducted by, or under the direction of, the ICANN Board, and, in the context of the new gTLD Program, the Guidebook explicitly confirms that 'ICANN's Board of Directors has ultimate responsibility for the New gTLD Program.'[1273] The term 'responsibility' would be meaningless if the ICANN Board were allowed to escape its responsibility simply by relying completely on third party expert advice, irrespective of how seriously impaired that advice may be.

That was also the view of the dissenting panelist in the *Donuts* case. He was extremely critical of the majority's reliance on 'agency theory' and appears to have believed that his fellow panelists were abdicating their responsibilities.[1274] The dissenting panelist qualified their attempt to draw a narrow distinction between whether delegated decision-making is the work of an agent or an independent contractor as merely a 'technical nicety'. He added that such a technical nicety 'would not be acceptable in the simplest workers compensation case, much less acceptable in a matter of extraordinary public interest.'[1275] He opined that 'it disserves the integrity of the system for an

1271. Donuts IRP Declaration, § 237.
1272. Donuts IRP Declaration, § 238.
1273. ICANN, *New gTLD Applicant Guidebook 4 June 2012*, https://newgtlds.icann.org/en/applicants/agb/guidebook-full-04jun12-en.pdf, Module 5-4.
1274. Donuts IRP Declaration, Dissenting Opinion, p. 5.
1275. Donuts IRP Declaration, Dissenting Opinion, p. 5.

opinion to rely upon whether the delegated decision-maker is an agent of the Board, a staff member reporting to the Board, a Board member, or an "independent contractor" of the Board.'[1276]

The dissenting panelist – rightfully, in our view – did not dissociate his views on the IRP panel's jurisdiction from the IRP's general purpose. He considered:

> 'It is the independence of judgment, transparency, and accountability, which ensure fairness and which lay the basic foundation of ICANN's vast regulation authority. These essential principles, in this Member's opinion, should be at the forefront of this Panel's review, because ICANN's position in this review seeks a rubberstamping of decision-making that was not independent, that was not transparent, and that has not been held accountable.'[1277]

We believe that the dissenting panelist saw through ICANN's attempt to shield its Board from being held accountable by delegating 'decisions' to 'independent' contractors. Such behavior would directly conflict with ICANN's fundamental commitment of ensuring transparency and accountability, and IRP panels should adopt a broad view on their jurisdiction. While it is encouraging that an IRP panelist showed such a clear understanding of what is at stake here, and that he made the effort to write a sound and well-reasoned dissenting opinion, it remains worrisome that he was unable to convince his fellow panelists who denied the request for IRP on the basis of a technical fiction, created by ICANN itself.

(2) Time Bar

In our view, ICANN's argument on time bar is another technicality created by ICANN to limit its accountability. On the time bar issue, the (majority of the) IRP panel adopted the same erroneous reasoning as the *Booking.com* and *Vistaprint* panels without given the issue any more thought. The IRP panel majority found that while it could consider challenges to the manner in which ICANN's processes were conducted, it could not consider challenges to the process itself. The IRP panel did not consider any arguments concerning when the time bar was introduced, *i.e.*, long after ICANN had adopted the processes related to the new gTLD program, and that it should not be applied retroactively. The majority's finding on the time bar highlights the danger of relying too heavily on previous case law; the same error can get repeated, giving the impression that the issue has been 'settled'. As said once by a cynic: 'Some doctors make the same mistake for twenty years and call it clinical experience.'[1278] We can only hope that what we consider to be a mistaken view regarding this time bar issue gets corrected quickly, so that this quote cannot be said to be true in this instance.

1276. Donuts IRP Declaration, Dissenting Opinion, p. 5.
1277. Donuts IRP Declaration, Dissenting Opinion, p. 1.
1278. Sydney Walker, *A Dose of Sanity: Mind, Medicine, and Misdiagnosis*, 1997 Wiley, p. 27.

(3) Costs

The majority of the IRP panel followed the usual trend in IRP jurisprudence on costs. However, it considered that the contribution to the public interest that Donuts might otherwise have been seen to have made was offset by the tenuousness of some of Donuts' positions. *E.g.*, the panel's majority was critical about the fact that Donuts apparently directed the panel to documents that proved not to give the asserted justification for Donuts' arguments.[1279]

However, this does not change the fact that Donuts had a strong grievance in this case, and that the majority of the panel qualified the dissenting opinion of their fellow panelist, who would have partially granted Donuts' request for IRP, as 'cogent' and 'forceful'.[1280] In these circumstances, it seems harsh to have given Donuts full responsibility for all the costs of the proceedings. To use the words of the dissenting panelist, it would seem that it 'discourages justifiable challenges to ICANN in the future.'[1281]

5. Applicable Law

a. Arguments Discussed

(1) Essential Rights and Obligations

Donuts argued that the ICANN Board violated the legitimate expectations of applicants and singled out Donuts for disparate treatment:

> 'Donuts and others applied for new gTLDs legitimately expecting that ICANN would honor the Guidebook. For its sizable investment, Donuts depends upon predictability and consistency in decision-making. Erratic application of Guidebook standards and divergent results in like cases undermine the system. The results have singled out Donuts for disparate treatment in violation of the Bylaws' anti-discrimination creed. The Board's refusal to use its power to impose some sort of review to create uniformity exacerbates the violation, undercuts ICANN's credibility, and threatens future applications for new gTLDs.'[1282]

According to Donuts, the ICANN Board allowed for the erroneous application of ICANN policy:

> 'The Board must "apply[] documented policies neutrally and objectively, with integrity and fairness." Yet, it has allowed the .SPORTS, .SKI and .RUGBY panels to exceed their authority and violate this mandate, and failed to provide for review in cases of inconsistent results and clear violations of the Guidebook. For example, each panel finds 'material detriment' on the perception that Donuts is not as valid a 'steward' of the respective 'communities' described by the strings as the

1279. Donuts IRP Declaration, § 209, n. 226; § 234, n. 240.
1280. Donuts IRP Declaration, § 201.
1281. Donuts IRP Declaration, Dissenting Opinion, p. 8.
1282. Donuts' IRP Request, § 9.

> objectors themselves – a ground which the Guidebook expressly forbids, and one not followed by other objection panelists.'[1283]

According to Donuts, the Board was responsible for the erroneous and discriminatory application of ICANN's policy as the Board failed (i) to provide for adequate training of the experts, (ii) to install a review mechanism, and (iii) to act remedially. Donuts argued that ICANN had been given ample notice of the failures of the community objection process, and that Donuts was not required to first file a reconsideration request:

> 'First, the Bylaws do not make reconsideration a prerequisite to IRP.[1284] ICANN concedes this, yet contends it would be "appropriate" nonetheless to saddle Donuts *ex post facto* with that obligation.[1285] ICANN's subjective position directly opposes the Bylaws, which make reconsideration and IRP separate, independent accountability methods.[1286]
>
> Second, Donuts had sought reconsideration in prior other objection cases.[1287] It met the same fate as all but one of over a hundred requestors whose cases the BGC had rejected by that time.[1288] In both decisions, the Board committee ruling on Donuts' requests ended up simply "punting" to the Ombudsman stating that it would not consider reconsideration of an objection result.[1289] Neither the Bylaws nor common sense required Donuts to keep traveling the "dead-end" reconsideration road.
>
> Third, Donuts did take ICANN up on its invitation to explore Ombudsman investigation and invoked that additional accountability procedure. The Bylaws establish an Ombudsman appointed by, and who reports to, the Board.[1290] Shortly after the .SPORTS and .RUGBY rulings, Donuts lodged a complaint with the Ombudsman,[1291] who in a report to Donuts and the Board determined that he did not have jurisdiction. Donuts then invoked the "cooperative engagement process" provided under the Bylaws prior to instigating this IRP.[1292]
>
> ICANN appears to assert that all aggrieved parties are bound to have requested the futile reconsideration process before initiating an IRP. In this case, lack of a

1283. Donuts' IRP Request, § 8.
1284. '*See* Bylaws [...] at Art. IV, Sections 2 and 3.'
1285. '*See* Transcr. at 140: "And then finally a question of whether it's a prerequisite to file a reconsideration motion. [Counsel to Donuts] is absolutely correct. There's nothing that requires an applicant to file a reconsideration request. But if you have a problem with a procedure that wasn't followed, that's the appropriate thing to do, it's the logical thing to do."'
1286. 'Indeed, as noted in Donuts' Opening Brief, the Board amended the Bylaws (including IRP provisions in Article IV) after the *ICM* decision, but for whatever reason chose ***not*** to tie Reconsideration to IRP. *See* Opening Brief at 5.'
1287. '*See* https://www.icann.org/resources/pages/14-3-2014-01-30-en (re: .CHARITY) and https://www.icann.org/resources/pages/13-23-2014-02-14-en (re: .HOSPITAL).'
1288. '*See* IRP Req. [§] 20.'
1289. '*See, e.g.*, https://www.icann.org/en/system/files/files/determination-ruby-pike-05feb14-en.pdf at 15: "If the Requester believes that it has somehow been treated unfairly in the process, the Requester is free to ask the Ombudsman to review this matter."'
1290. 'Bylaws [...] Art. V §§ 1.2, 1.4, 2, 3.1, 4.4.'
1291. 'Nevett Stmt. [§] 18.
1292. '*Id.* [§] 19; Transcript at 56.'

> reconsideration request is a complete non-issue. Donuts has demonstrated ample notice to the Board, which provided it with the opportunity to act […]'[1293]

ICANN maintained that the acts and omissions about which Donuts complained were not acts or omissions of the Board, and that they could therefore not properly fall within the scope of an IRP:

> 'It cannot be a violation of the Bylaws or Articles [of Incorporation] for the Board to "fail" to do something that the Board is not required to do, and should not do.'[1294]

> 'Understanding that the ICANN Board played no role, Donuts is forced to argue that the ICANN Board violated its Bylaws by its "lack of action."[1295] But the "lack of action" is more appropriately characterized as "no action to take" because the Guidebook does not call for the Board to review the ICC's decision about selected panelists' alleged conflicts of interest, and such review similarly is not required by any provision of the Bylaws or Articles [of Incorporation].'[1296]

> '[T]here is no requirement that ICANN's Board review expert determinations […]. Pursuant to the Guidebook, the "findings of the panel <u>will</u> be considered an expert determination and advice that ICANN <u>will</u> accept within the dispute resolution process."[1297] Following receipt of expert determinations, ICANN <u>staff</u> is tasked with taking the next step of accepting it, not the Board.'[1298]

ICANN argued that no Board action was required for dealing with purported inconsistencies, as different outcomes by different expert panels were to be expected:

> 'However, contrary to Donuts' allegations, no ICANN Board action was the cause of the purported inconsistencies. Different outcomes by different independent expert panels related to different gTLD applications was to be expected, and is hardly evidence that the Board violated its "standards, policies, procedures, or practices." Donuts asserts that the three Determinations at issue here "single Donuts out for disparate and adverse treatment,"[1299] but it offers no support for that statement other than the fact that it lost whereas other applicants prevailed.[1300]'[1301]

ICANN's line of defense was based almost exclusively on the fact that no Board action took place:

> 'Even if a breach of the covenant of good faith and fair dealing could form the basis of an IRP, no breach occurred here because Donuts does not challenge any Board action and, in any event, identifies no violation of the ICANN Bylaws or Articles [of Incorporation].'[1302]

1293. Donuts' Post Hearing Submission, §§ 18–21.
1294. ICANN's Response (*Donuts*), § 5.
1295. '[Donut's IRP Request, §] 68.'
1296. ICANN's Response (*Donuts*), § 49.
1297. 'Guidebook, [...] § 3.4.6 (emphasis added).'
1298. ICANN's Response (*Donuts*), § 54.
1299. '[Donuts'] Request [for IRP, §] 77'.
1300. 'Indeed, to take Donuts at its word and create an appellate review process for all objection determinations would call into question the finality of the objection proceeding in which Donuts prevailed.'
1301. ICANN's Response (*Donuts*), § 55.
1302. ICANN's Response (*Donuts*), § 56.

ICANN argued that no Board conduct was required to accept the expert determination on the community objection, and that there was no obligation for the ICANN Board to be involved in the implementation of the community objection process:

> 'Here, the Board did not conduct any review of the expert determinations that Donuts complains of, nor do the Bylaws or the Guidebook require the Board to conduct such a review. Donuts tries to obscure this distinction by arguing that ICANN must "accept" the expert determinations issued by the panelists appointed by the ICC;[1303] however, this "acceptance" involves no conduct – affirmative or otherwise – by the Board.
>
> [...] Nothing in the Guidebook provides for the Board to be involved in any way in the panel selection process, and the Guidebook does not provide any procedure by which ICANN (or anyone else) is to conduct a substantive review of the expert panels' results. Donuts' generalized reference to the Board's "ultimate authority over the new gTLD program"[1304] cannot mask the fact that the Bylaws do not require the Board to consider expert determinations resulting from objection proceedings administered by the ICC – in stark contrast to the Bylaws' clear requirement that the Board consider GAC advice.'[1305]

ICANN submitted that Donuts could have asked the ICANN Board to consider the issue by filing a request for reconsideration. However, Donuts elected not to do so, and that as a result there was no requirement for the ICANN Board to consider Donuts' complaints:

> 'Donuts, however, did not file requests for reconsideration, instead opting to proceed directly to an IRP. As a result, there literally was not a single time that the ICANN Board (or any of its committees) evaluated, or was required to evaluate, the expert determinations that are at issue in this IRP.'[1306]

ICANN argued that its Board had no obligation to act *sua sponte*, that it was entitled to take action on expert determinations in only a very limited situation, and had no obligation to address the expert determinations involving Donuts' applications:

> 'Donuts has not identified an Article or Bylaws provision that the ICANN Board violated by exercising its independent judgment to intervene with respect to these inconsistent string confusion objection expert determinations, much less by exercising its independent judgment not to intervene with respect to the community objection expert determinations on Donuts' Applications. Inasmuch as the Board had no obligation to address any of these matters, the fact that the Board elected to act in a very limited situation, but not to act with respect to Donuts' Applications, is not a violation of the Articles or Bylaws.'[1307]

Finally, ICANN argued that the Bylaws' provisions, invoked by Donuts, on the Board's retention of experts for policy guidance 'are wholly inapplicable' as the expert determinations in question were not related to the development of ICANN policies.[1308]

1303. '[Donuts' Reply, §] 28.
1304. [Donuts' Reply, §] 28.
1305. ICANN's Sur-Reply (*Donuts*), §§ 13–14.
1306. ICANN's Sur-Reply (*Donuts*), § 15.
1307. ICANN's Sur-Reply (*Donuts*), § 25.
1308. ICANN's Sur-Reply, § 29.

The panel was mindful of ICANN's status as the regulatory authority of the DNS and the framework within which ICANN's essential obligations had to be reviewed:

> 'As stated by the *ICM Registry* Panel, "ICANN is no ordinary non-profit California corporation. The Government of the United States vested regulatory authority of vast dimension and pervasive global reach in ICANN."[1309]'[1310]

The panel agreed with ICANN, that an IRP panel's task is to examine actions that are attributable to the ICANN Board, and examined whether the actions of the ICC and its experts on community objections were indeed attributable to the ICANN Board. The majority of the panel found that they were not, ruling that Donuts failed to supply the panel with a precise basis on which to find an agency relationship between the ICANN Board and the ICC (and the experts of the latter):

> 'Had the agency theory been more fully addressed by the parties,[1311] the propriety of imputing directly to the Board the acts of the ICC and its experts would most likely depend on how the relationship between the ICC and ICANN is characterized; under the general principles of law known to the Panel that would probably turn upon the level of control that ICANN exerts or is entitled to exert over the ICC's operations in respect of objection proceedings.
>
> Given that the matter was not elaborated upon by Donuts, let alone briefed by the parties, the Panel will not do more than suggest why it considers that, on balance, there is not enough evidence of control in the record to attribute the acts of the ICC and its experts to the ICANN Board. [...]
>
> The notion that administering institutions, such as the ICC, are third-party service providers, and not "constituent entities" of ICANN generally or alter egos of the ICANN Board in particular is consistent with most of what one finds in the reasoning [of] other IR[P] Panels.'[1312]

When addressing Donuts' argument that the dispute resolution process regarding .sports was 'materially defective by virtue of the expert's failure to make sufficient disclosures,'[1313] the panel's majority considered, that if the conduct of the ICC experts could be seen as attributable to the ICANN Board, then it would 'struggle with those prongs of the Standard of Review requiring independent, conflict-free decision making.'[1314] Thus, it seems that the panel would have considered there to be a violation of ICANN's Bylaws, if the expert's failure to make sufficient disclosures was attributable to ICANN. In any event, according to the majority of the panel, Donuts did not establish a basis for attribution.[1315]

The panel then examined whether the ICANN Board had a duty to intervene, as under some circumstances a failure to act is actionable and can be challenged:

1309. 'ICM Registry IR[P] Declaration of Feb. 19, 2010, para. 136.'
1310. Donuts IRP Declaration, § 7.
1311. 'An antecedent step in elaborating such an argument would be to determine what body of law should be consulted by the Panel.'
1312. Donuts IRP Declaration, §§ 155–159.
1313. Donuts IRP Declaration, § 164.
1314. Donuts IRP Declaration, § 165.
1315. Donuts IRP Declaration, § 165.

> 'It seems to have become common ground between the parties to this IR[P] that under some circumstances the requester may legitimately complain of the Board's failure to take action as well as its affirmative acts. Other Panels are in accord.[1316] Not all inaction is actionable, however. Rather, in the Panel's view, "actionable inaction" is a failure that is inconsistent with a duty to act, whether that duty is formally established by ICANN's constitutive documents, generated by some other explicit or clearly implied undertaking by the Board, or, powerfully suggested by all the circumstances present. In assessing alleged failures to act, the question is not whether the Board has the power to act, or whether to act would be consistent with the Articles [of Incorporation] and Bylaws, but whether the Board must act given all the circumstances.'[1317]

Where no specific obligation to act existed, the panel favored the application of a three-factor test to consider whether the circumstances required Board action:

> 'It follows that not every circumstance in which the Board might be empowered to act gives rise to a duty to act. In particular, when the complaining party points not to an explicit promise to act or a specific obligation to act substantiated in ICANN's constituent documents, but rather relies on the circumstances and more general sources of obligation, actionable inaction would seem to assume circumstances: 1] that are, or ought be, known to the Board; 2] that forcefully impinge on relevant values and principles; and 3] that could reasonably have been expected to be mitigated by Board action. Importantly, even when the three factors just enumerated are present, the inaction must be judged in light of the Standard of Review (that is: it might be that determined inaction is well-informed, independent and conflict-free).'[1318]

On the alleged absence of adequate training of experts, the panel considered that 'the Board is not specifically required by any consitituent [*sic*] document known to the Panel to institute training; nor has it represented that it would perform such training.'[1319] The majority of the panel also found that some variation between expert determinations on community objections was to be expected:

> '[I]t is to be expected given the Guidebook's multi-factor tests, diversity of factual patterns and the role of advocates that variations in way experts frame issues and apply the governing factors will be perceived; these may or may not reflect genuine differences of approach or the deficiency of one approach compared to another. As a general matter, it would be surprising if among the corpus of reasoned objections to have been issued thus far that a somewhat diverse marketplace of ideas had not developed; some variation is to be expected.'[1320]

But, the panel did not exclude 'the possibility that jurisprudential disarray might become so acute and prolonged with respect to community objections that the Board would be required to act to improve upon the original manner of equipping experts; Donuts has not demonstrated that such a state of affairs exists, however.'[1321] And although the panel considered that an appeal mechanism might be beneficial to avoid

1316. 'See e.g., Vistaprint IR[P] Declaration, paras. 127-128 [...].'
1317. Donuts IRP Declaration, § 129; *see also* Donuts IRP Declaration, § 168.
1318. Donuts IRP Declaration, § 169.
1319. Donuts IRP Declaration, § 172.
1320. Donuts IRP Declaration, § 176.
1321. Donuts IRP Declaration, § 178.

jurisprudential disarray, it did not identify an absolute need for the ICANN Board to add another layer of adjudication or review:

> 'The Panel believes that to install some sort [of] appeals mechanism might add predictability of outcome and produce greater satisfaction with the process by some. The Panel assumes, without opining, that the Board has the power to institute such a mechanism, and it believes that to do so in a sound fashion after careful study would be consistent with ICANN's Articles [of Incorporation] and Bylaws.
>
> Equally, however, absent jurisprudential disarray so urgently in need of a top-down remedy that the Board would not be entitled to establish other priorities, it may indeed refrain from exercising the power it has already exercised in connection with certain string similarity cases.
>
> [...] In the Panel's view, absent compelling facts to the contrary, the Board need not rush into adding another layer of adjudication or review, whether or not urged to do so by Donuts and others.'[1322]

The panel commended the Board's prudent approach in responding to *ad hoc* petitions to intervene, and considered that the Board's inaction must be seen in the context of the available accountability mechanisms:

> '[A] hypothetical Board policy of ordinarily not responding to ad hoc petitions to intervene with respect to individual applications would seems [*sic*] prudent on its face.
>
> Accordingly, the Panel agrees with the Vistaprint Panel, who ruled that "the ICANN Board has no affirmative duty to review the result in any particular ... case."[1323] As Donuts does in this case, Vistaprint had relied upon the Guidebook's reference to individual Board consideration of applications. As the Vistaprint Panel observed, however, the Guidebooks example of "exceptional circumstances" that involve individual assessment by the Board is when the disappointed applicant engages the Board through an accountability process such as the RFR.[1324]
>
> True, the RFR example, being only that, does not preclude an ad hoc intervention by the Board; it does however remind one of context, and to consider Board inaction in light of the other grievance mechanisms available to applicants, most notably in this case the RFR option.'[1325]

Regarding the community objection expert's failure to disclose information on a possible conflict of interest, the panel's majority also found no violation of ICANN's Articles of Incorporation or Bylaws. The majority of the panel found no basis for considering the ICC or the expert to be a partner or agent of the ICANN Board.[1326] Equally, the majority of the panel found no evidence of formal Board consideration of the expert's conduct, and considered that the claimant did not 'point to a Board undertaking, or other formal source, that expressly or by clear implication requires the

1322. Donuts IRP Declaration, §§ 181-183.
1323. 'Vistaprint IR[P] Declaration, para. 157.'
1324. 'Id., para. 156 ("For example, the Board might individually consider an application as a result ... of the use of an ICANN accountability mechanism.").'
1325. Donuts IRP Declaration, §§ 184–186.
1326. Donuts IRP Declaration, § 203.

Board to exercise oversight with respect to individual ICC appointments or the sufficiency of an expert's disclosure (although the RFR process arguably provides access to such oversight).'[1327] The expert's disclosure in the community objection on .sports was considered 'seemingly insufficient'. However, the majority of the panel found the Board was not required to intervene *sua sponte*:

> 'Ultimately, on the question of the Board's alleged failure to act to ameliorate the consequences of Mr. Taylor's seemingly insufficient disclosure, the majority concludes that the circumstances did not so powerfully suggest a need to act that the Board's failure to do so transgresses the Articles [of Incorporation] or the Bylaws or otherwise raises doubts under the Standard of Review. Those circumstances include but are not limited to the availability to Donuts of the RFR process and the Board's apparent lack of knowledge of any conflicts potentially impairing [the expert]'s impartiality that remained both undisclosed and unknown to Donuts.'[1328]

The RfR would have been the appropriate vehicle by which to address an expert's seemingly insufficient disclosure, according to the panel's majority:

> 'In the view of this Panel's majority, however, even if the alleged biases of a particular expert are made known to ICANN officers in the ordinary course of interacting with the ICC, or because ICANN was petitioned by an applicant asking it to intervene, the Board's failure to intervene would have to be considered in light of the range of defensible options available to it and the existing ICANN mechanisms that offer a complaining applicant potential redress. Chief among these alternatives to ad hoc Board intervention is the RFR mechanism, which Donuts elected to forgo in this case.
>
> Without purporting to predict the likely outcome of the RFR forgone by Donuts, the majority of this Panel does believe that it would have been an appropriate vehicle by which to address an expert's seemingly insufficient disclosure. The RFR process would have allowed an organ of the Board, with certain fact finding powers, to evaluate Mr. Taylor's conduct, and the ICC's handling of it, to determine if it amounted to: "one or more staff actions or inactions that contradict established ICANN policy(ies)", to quote from RFR grounds for seeking reconsideration.
>
> Had Donuts pursued an RFR, not only might some relief have been forthcoming (perhaps obviating this IR[P]) but any RFR recommendation and subsequent processing of it would involve activities likely to fall within the jurisdiction of an IR[P] Panel. Indeed, the RFR path is the one routinely taken by other disappointed applicants before resorting to the IR[P] machinery. The Board was entitled to expect that Donuts would do likewise given the architecture in place. Correspondingly, in the view of this Panel's majority, the Board simply was not required to pursue some other form application-specific interevention [*sic*] in the process.'[1329]

While the majority of the panel considered that the alleged insufficient disclosure could be addressed appropriately, it nevertheless had a limited view on the scope of RfR proceedings:

1327. Donuts IRP Declaration, § 206.
1328. Donuts IRP Declaration, § 216.
1329. Donuts IRP Declaration, §§ 211–213.

> 'Donuts is no doubt correct that it is not required to pursue an RFR. It is also correct that to the extent it sought a review of the merits, the RFR process would not be appropriate, and to that extent would be futile. The same cannot be so easily said when there is alleged conduct directly implicating the fairness and transparency of ICANN "staff".'[1330]

Finally, the panel examined the issue of alleged discrimination. The panel considered that discrimination could be said to occur only if differences in treatment occur in like circumstances. The panel found no evidence that the expert determinations on community objections suffered from the same consistency issues as the expert determinations on string confusion:

> 'By its terms, Article II, Section 3 [of ICANN's Bylaws] is not violated if ICANN is justified in its line drawing by "substantial and reasonable" cause. Albeit with a slight different application of the principle, the Panel agrees with [the] Vistaprint IR[P] Panel that temporal context is important. It is obvious that a fresh phase of study begins when a regime with the many operational features of the new gTLD program moves from planning to implementation. There having been extensive study and stakeholder participation before implementation of the gTLD program, the Board is more likely to violate its duties if acting precipitously rather than with deliberateness.
>
> The benefits of deliberateness will in the majority's view often constitute "substantial and reasonable cause" for selective application of new policies and new mechanisms. Moreover, in the majority's opinion, the only differences in treatment that implicate Bylaws Article II, Section 3 are those which occur in like circumstances. The record does not allow the Panel to conclude that the considerable consistency issues raised in connection with string similarity case have emerged in connection with community objection cases as a whole, or with respect to the two expert decisions giving rise to this IR[P].
>
> On the contrary, the materials produced in this case afford ample justification for giving a priority to the string confusion case,[[1331]] which readily give the impression of containing a certain percentage of irreconcilable outcomes. The opprobrium raised among observers, stakeholders and others in reaction to the string confusion cases, correspondingly, seems to have been of a kind and a degree not occurring with respect to community objections.[[1332]]'[1333]

(2) Standard of Review

Relying on the *Booking.com* case, Donuts considered that 'an IRP panel must appraise the Board's conduct "objectively" and "independently, and without any presumption of correctness".'[1334] Donuts argued that the panel must apply a *de novo* standard of review, 'that is, it must decide whether the matter under review in fact conformed with ICANN governing principles – *not* whether the Board reasonably *believed* it did.'[1335]

1330. Donuts IRP Declaration, § 214.
1331. 'See, e.g., Booking.com IR[P] Declaration, paras. 119-30.'
1332. 'Cf. Vistaprint IR[P] Declaration, paras. 188-92.'
1333. Donuts IRP Declaration, §§ 219–221.
1334. Donuts' Reply, § 9.
1335. Donuts' Reply, § 9.

Moreover, Donuts claimed that, even under a limited standard of review, the IRP panel had the power to declare that the Board violated the Bylaws and Articles and to direct the Board either to reverse the rulings or empower properly trained and unbiased experts to rehear the objections:

> 'Even under the limited standard of review with which ICANN has constrained it, this Panel has the power to declare that the objection rulings and the Board's refusal to act on them violate the Bylaws and Articles. It should direct the Board either to reverse the rulings or empanel properly trained and unbiased experts to rehear the objections.'[1336]

ICANN argued that the IRP panel had to apply a deferential standard of review, maintaining that 'ICANN's Bylaws specifically identify the deferential standard of review that the IRP panel must apply when evaluating the actions of the ICANN Board.'[1337]

The panel ruled that it was 'asked to judge [the ICANN Board's] conduct against ICANN's Bylaws and Articles [of Incorporation], and to do so in light of a prescribed standard of review.'[1338] The panel considered itself duty-bound to answer the three questions identified in ICANN's Bylaws and the ICDR IRP Supplementary Procedures:

> 'Additionally, as an IR[P] Panel, we are duty-bound to focus on three questions (the "Standard of Review"), as underscored by the Merck Panel in its Declaration [...]:
>
> 1] Did the Board act without conflict of interest in taking its decision;
> 2] Did the Board exercise due diligence and care in having a reasonable amount of facts in front of them; and
> 3] Did the Board members exercise independent judgment in taking the decision, believed to be in the best interests of the company?
>
> The ICDR Supplemental IRP Rules replicate the Bylaws as to the above focus questions, but add:
>
>> 8. Standard of Review. ./ .... If a requestor demonstrates that the ICANN Board did not make a reasonable inquiry to determine it had sufficient facts available, ICANN Board members had a conflict of interest in participating in the decision, or the decision was not an exercise in independent judgment, believed by the ICANN Board to be in the best interests of the company, after taking account of the Internet community and the global public interest, the requestor will have established proper grounds for review.'[1339]

The panel recognized that several IRP panels had already addressed the question of the standard of review, and found the declarations made by those panels sufficiently persuasive:

> 'The several Panels to have already addressed the question, however, have done so with relative consistency. In their view, IR[P] Panels are not to accord normal Business Judgment Rule style deference to the work of the ICANN Board, but

1336. Donuts' IRP Request, § 13.
1337. ICANN's response, § 38.
1338. Donuts IRP Declaration, § 8.
1339. Donuts IRP Declaration, §§ 126–127.

> rather are to purse "objective" review.[1340] This conclusion results from the implications of the word "independent", the explicit standard of review to which the Panel is already bound (which functions in place of the more general Business Judgment Rule jurisprudence) and related justifications. This Panel finds those Declarations sufficiently persuasive that it need not depart from what seems to be the established trend and general approach.'[1341]

However, the panel considered that in reviewing the ICANN Board's actions, it may not 'base its determinations on what it, itself, might have done, had it been the Board,'[1342] and considered that its review was limited by ICANN's Bylaws, as they afford ICANN an element of discretion, or 'margin of appreciation' regarding Board action and inaction:

> 'First, whatever label one uses to describe the approach (e.g., "objective," "de novo," or "independent") that approach does not allow the Panel to base its determinations on what it, itself, might have done, had it been the Board. The explicit standard of review – for better or worse – is much narrower than that. [...]
>
> As did the Booking.com Panel, this Panel finds that, in the absence of a demonstrable conflict of interest, affording a margin of appreciation to Board action and inaction is to some extent dictated by the Bylaws themselves. [... T]hose Bylaws contemplate that ICANN bodies are expected to assess relevance and strive for "an appropriate and defensible balance among competing values" [...].
>
> Second, a measure of self-restraint is also dictated by the Standard of Review to which this Panel is bound, expressed as it is in terms of whether the Board made "a reasonable inquiry" as opposed to, for example, an "exhaustive" inquiry to determine if it had "sufficient facts available."[1343] Relatedly, to the extent possible given what may be the rather limited fact-finding that can be pursued in an IR[P], due account ought to be given to such contextual factors as the actual information available to the Board at the relevant time and the array of competing considerations with which it was faced.'[1344]

(3) Emergency Proceedings

Donuts also filed a request for emergency relief because it was of the opinion that (i) ICANN had not appointed an "Omnibus Standing Panel" of trained experts and (ii) that the objections of International Rugby Board, Fédération Internationale de Ski and SportAccord against Donuts' applications eliminated all other applicants from competing for those strings. Since RIB, FIS and SA also applied for the respective strings and because ICANN could at any time sign registry agreements with each objector affected

1340. 'See Vistaprint IR[P] Declaration, para. 126 [...].'
1341. Donuts IRP Declaration, § 131.
1342. IRP Final declaration, § 133.
1343. 'See ICDR Supplemental Procedures for ICANN Independent Review Process, Article 8 (essentially restating the Standard of Review set forth in ICANN Bylaws, Article IV, Section 3.4).'
1344. Donuts IRP Declaration, §§133–135.

by Donuts' IRP request, Donuts was of the opinion that emergency relief was needed to preserve the remedies sought in the IRP proceeding and to prevent irreparable harm to Donuts.[1345]

ICANN claimed that Donuts' request for emergency relief was not warranted because Donuts did not demonstrate any likelihood of success on the merits:

> 'In its Emergency Request, Donuts does not propose any particular legal standard that should apply to determine whether emergency relief is warranted. Further, Donuts' IRP Request does not demonstrate any likelihood of success on the merits, and in fact fails to set forth even a *prima facie* case that IRP relief is warranted. As a result, no emergency relief should be provided.'[1346]

Nevertheless, in the course of the proceedings, ICANN agreed to a stay with respect to the gTLDs that were subject to the IRP proceedings. Donuts withdrew its request for emergency relief, which had become redundant.[1347]

b. *Noteworthy Points for Analysis*

(1) Essential Rights and Obligations

There was little disagreement about the fact that ICANN was obliged to act transparently and apply its policies fairly and non-discriminatorily. Instead, much of the discussion in this case revolved around the question of whether the alleged violations were attributable to the ICANN Board, especially in view of Donuts' decision to forgo RfR proceedings. In our view, Donuts was correct in stating that an RfR was not a prerequisite to starting IRP proceedings. However, without an RfR, it was more difficult – although not impossible, as shown by the reasoning in the dissenting opinion – to attribute wrongful conduct to the ICANN Board. Donuts' decision not to pursue an RfR is understandable, as past experience had shown RfRs not to be very effective in resolving issues with expert determinations. In our view, this is largely because of the limited view ICANN takes of RfRs; ICANN has focused on whether the process, as laid out in its policies, was followed, rather than on whether the standards, as laid out in its policies, were applied correctly and fairly.[1348] In its consideration of RfRs, the ICANN Board has not examined whether defined standards were applied consistently throughout the process, but has rather looked at whether the standards were correctly quoted in the expert determinations. In other words, ICANN has not investigated whether its policies allowed for discriminatory treatment in their application.

1345. Donuts Inc.'s Request for Emergency Relief.
1346. ICANN's Response, § 37; *see also* ICANN's Response, § 11.
1347. Email from counsel to ICANN to counsel to Donuts of 21 November 2014.
1348. *Supra* Chapter 3.D.2, Chapter 4.A.2, Chapter 4.C.2.c, Chapter 4.C.4.b, Chapter 5.C.5.a(2), Chapter 5.C.5.b(1), Chapter 5.G.5.a(2) and Chapter 5.G.5.b(2).

In an *obiter dictum*, the majority of the IRP panel seemed to approve ICANN's limited view on the scope of RfR proceedings, finding that the RfR process would not be appropriate for those seeking a review of the merits. While, on the face of it, this statement is correct, much depends on how a review of the 'merits' gets qualified. We can accept that an appointed expert is sovereign in his or her appraisal of the facts. However, when it comes to applying those facts to the policy, the ICANN Board must be able to assess whether this application is correct, fair and non-discriminatory. In our view, the RfR is an appropriate vehicle to make the ICANN Board perform such assessment. And if the ICANN Board refuses to make the assessment, or if the Board errs in its review, the Board's mistake can be corrected in an IRP.

To perform a meaningful review, IRP panels must have a thorough understanding of ICANN's transparency and other obligations and of ICANN's prohibition to discriminate. The Donuts IRP panel had a somewhat limited view on non-discrimination. It considered that discrimination can only exist when like circumstances are treated differently. However, the prohibition to discriminate has different facets. Put simply, like circumstances must be treated alike and different circumstances must be treated differently. A difference in treatment must be justified by substantial and reasonable cause. In our view, good governance and ICANN's transparency obligations require that ICANN communicates openly about its justification for treating some applications differently from others.

Thus, when ICANN ordered a re-evaluation of certain expert determinations on SCOs, it did so because the inconsistencies between them were deemed to be obvious. Although the inconsistencies between the expert determinations on community objections may have appeared less obvious, that does not make them less worthy of being addressed. We disagree with the *Donuts* IRP panel's findings that there was 'ample justification for giving a priority to the string confusion cases.'[1349] The mere fact that the inconsistencies between the SCO expert determinations were more apparent, or that they were criticized more broadly, does not in itself provide a reasonable and substantial cause, justifying disparate treatment. Indeed, it is our view that it was merely coincidental that certain inconsistencies were more readily apparent than others: it so happened that multiple objections were raised against the same gTLD string and resulted in a different outcome. We believe that mere coincidence cannot be the basis of the 'substantial and reasonable cause' needed in order to treat similar situations differently. We find it regrettable that the *Donuts* IRP panel was not more rigorous in its appreciation of what constitutes a substantial and reasonable cause.

(2) Standard of Review

The *Donuts* panel's findings on the applicable standard of review are in line with the findings of previous IRP panels. The panel rejected ICANN's argument that IRP panels must adopt a deferential standard of review. However, the panel limited itself to the

1349. Donuts IRP Declaration, § 221.

'focus questions' that are explicitly taken up in ICANN's Bylaws and the Supplementary Procedures. In our view, these focus questions are non-exhaustive, and an IRP panel is not 'duty-bound' to limit its review to these questions only. We share the criticism of the dissenting panelist against the too narrow interpretation of an IRP panel's mandate by the majority.[1350]

In our view, the 'confinement' of the IRP panel's mandate is not 'redoubled by the standard of review.'[1351] On the contrary, Article 8 of the Supplementary Procedures explains that a claimant will have established proper grounds for review if he or she demonstrates a conflict of interest, a failure to exercise independent judgment or a failure to exercise due diligence as defined in the standard of review's focus questions.

The dissenting panelist made the following observation about the focus question on conflict of interest:

> '[W]hether the Board action or inaction is "without conflict of interest," is a flawed inquiry in the context of this case. Every time the Board or its agents or delegated decision-makers consider action or inaction of any kind, in addressing the decision of the Board's delegated decision-maker, the Board is acting with and not without conflict of interest. If the Board promulgates or leaves in place a procedure or standard of review, stacked in favor of its delegated decision-maker, the Board is acting with and not without a conflict of interest. If ICANN's argument is that the standard of review only refers to "certain kinds of conflicts of interests," that is not an apparent conclusion to draw from the language of the Guidebook or the Articles. Not only should no deference be accorded the decision under review, but also the basic principles justifying ICANN's authority – independent judgment, transparency and accountability – mandate that the procedures and standards for review not be stacked in any way in favor of ICANN's delegated decision-maker, or applied in a manner that suggests that they are.'[1352]

The observation that one must interpret 'conflict of interest' broadly is certainly interesting, but it is doubtful whether such a broad interpretation is workable in view of the precept in Article 8 of the ICDR IRP Supplementary Procedures stating that proper grounds for review are established once a conflict of interest is shown. If a decision must be reviewed simply because the ICANN Board, by definition, has a conflict of interest when considering a determination by a delegated decision-maker, then all of ICANN's decisions on RfRs must be reviewed. Indeed, an RfR deals either with actions or inactions by delegated 'decision-makers' or with actions or inactions by the Board itself. If the ICANN Board has a conflict of interest when assessing the actions of delegated decision-makers, then it certainly has one when considering its own actions or inactions. However, such inevitable 'conflict of interest' should not result automatically in the finding that the claimant has established proper grounds for review. If, however, a conflict of interest is avoidable, the existence of such conflict should be a sufficient ground for finding a violation of ICANN's Articles of Incorporation and Bylaws.

1350. Donuts IRP Declaration, Dissenting Opinion, p. 3.
1351. *See* Donuts IRP Declaration, § 202.
1352. Donuts IRP Declaration, Dissenting Opinion, pp. 3–4.

6. Authority of the Panel

a. *Arguments Discussed*

Donuts requested the IRP panel to recommend that ICANN reject the expert determinations on the community objections, and permit Donuts' applications to proceed through the remainder of the application process.[1353] According to Donuts, the IRP panel was entitled to '"recommend" that the objection rulings not stand or the proceedings be redone.'[1354] Donuts claimed that the ICANN Board was ultimately responsible for the new gTLD Program 'in its entirety', and that '[s]uch pervasive involvement [made] the Board responsible for the transgressions raised' in the IRP.[1355] Consequently, the ICANN Board and the IRP panel were entitled to examine the correctness of the expert determinations.

ICANN argued that 'to delve into the correctness' of the rationale in the expert determination on the community objections 'is far outside the scope of any IRP.'[1356]

The panel considered that it was not authorized to act as a plenary review body concerned with errors of fact or the correct application of substantive standards:

> 'Even if this Panel deemed itself authorized as Independent Reviewers to equate the work of ICC experts in their rulings on objections to that of the Board, however, it would stop well short of acting as a plenary review body concerned with errors of fact or the correct application of substantive standards. We would be required to consult the explicit Standard of Review to which we are bound.'[1357]
>
> 'The Panel is not entitled under the guise of an IR[P] to propose an authoritative construction of the Guidebook's community objection standards.'[1358]

With respect to an IRP panel's authority to recommend that the Board stay any action or decision, or that the Board take any interim action, the panel considered it was allowed to give advice to ICANN:

> 'There is precedent for taking a broad view of this prerogative.[[1359]] Even though an IR[P] is an accountability mechanism, it also has the potential to serve an advisory function, inasmuch as it represents the view of three independent neutrals.'[1360]

The majority of the panel gave ICANN the following advice:

> 'The majority believes that rather than using single expert panels, the community objection might to advantage [*sic*] employ panels composed of three experts. In such circumstances, partisans can only do limited damage and, correspondingly, any party concerned about the prospect of biased expert determinations should be

1353. Donuts Reply, § 37.
1354. Donuts Post-Hearing Submission, § 33.
1355. Donuts Post-Hearing Submission, § 6.
1356. ICANN's Response (*Donuts*), § 50; *see also ibid.*, §53.
1357. Donuts IRP Declaration, § 160.
1358. Donuts IRP Declaration, § 177, n. 202.
1359. 'See Booking.com IR[P] Declaration, para. 4; Vistaprint IR[P] Declaration, paras. 186-90.'
1360. Donuts IRP Declaration, § 227.

> reassured to a considerable extent by three-person tribunals. In the majority's view, even with the added costs involved, it would be economically justifiable in the long term and not inconsistent with ICANN's values and principles to adopt a three-neutral model as the default in community objection cases.
>
> Concerning the community objection proceeding brought by SportAccord in connection with .SPORTS, the majority believes it would not be inconsistent with ICANN's values and principles to provide for a rehearing of that objection, by a different expert (or three experts).'[1361]

The panel was also sensitive to the tensions created by ICANN's policy on community objections, and the majority of the panel suggested 'that the assumptions and policies that lead to this kind of tension warrant further study.'[1362]

But, ultimately, the panel considered there was no violation of ICANN's Articles of Incorporation or Bylaws. Consequently, it did not grant affirmative relief to Donuts.

b. *Noteworthy Points for Analysis*

In view of the findings of the IRP panel's majority that ICANN did not violate its essential obligations, it is logical that the IRP panel provided no remedy for Donuts. However, not all the panel members agreed on the absence of a violation of ICANN's Articles of Incorporation and Bylaws. The dissenting panelist considered that ICANN's 'promise of independent judgment, transparency and accountability, as to decision-making that is essentially judicial in nature, regarding matters of extreme public import and interest, should not be set aside by resort to technical rules of construction contrary both to equity and to applicable principles of law.'[1363] This panel member considered that a remedy was warranted, and stated that he would 'reverse and deny' the community objection regarding .sports.[1364] He reasoned: 'If there is no remedy for [...] fundamental failure[s] of the independence, transparency and accountability requirements, then this is a systemic defect that required and requires Board action.'[1365] The dissenting panelist considered that his conclusion that the objection should be denied was 'reasonable and consistent with the goals and responsibilities of independence, accountability and transparency.'[1366] In our view, such remedy would not only be consistent with these goals and responsibilities, the remedy would also put an end to the dispute, as required by the ICDR Rules.

By contrast, the advisory opinion of the panel's majority that a rehearing of the .sports community objection would not be contrary to ICANN's Articles of Incorporation and Bylaws has the potential to intensify the dispute; indeed, if the advice is interpreted –

1361. Donuts IRP Declaration, §§ 229–230.
1362. Donuts IRP Declaration, § 231.
1363. Donuts IRP Declaration, Dissenting Opinion, p. 4.
1364. Donuts IRP Declaration, Dissenting Opinion, p. 6.
1365. Donuts IRP Declaration, Dissenting Opinion, p. 2 (emphasis omitted).
1366. Donuts IRP Declaration, Dissenting Opinion, p. 7.

as it was by the dissenting panelist[1367] – as advice to Donuts to seek a rehearing, this would seem to be encouraging Donuts to take the matter further.

7. Nature and Value of the IRP Declaration

a. *Arguments Discussed*

(1) Binding Nature of the IRP Declaration

Donuts considered that IRP declarations are binding,[1368] and ICANN considered them advisory only.[1369] The panel did not pronounce itself on the issue.

(2) Precedential Value of the IRP Declaration

The panel gave a summary of previous decisions as a background to the panel's analysis.[1370] The panel took account of previous decisions, and considered it should seek consistency with previous decisions to the extent warranted:

> 'This is not the first IR[P] proceeding to have arisen out of the new gTLD program. Several declarations have been issued by other Panels. They are to enjoy "precedential value" according to ICANN's Bylaws.[1371] The Panel takes that to mean that it should take account of the reasoning of other Panels in pursuing its own analysis, and should, to the extent warranted, seek consistency.'[1372]

8. ICANN Board's Decisions Following the IRP Declaration

On 25 June 2016, the ICANN Board accepted the IRP Declaration, and considered that 'nothing in the Final Declaration supports re-review of the .SPORTS Expert Determination, nor is it sufficiently "inconsistent" or "unreasonable" such that it warrants re-evaluation.'[1373]

1367. Donuts IRP Declaration, Dissenting Opinion, p. 3.
1368. Donuts, Request for IRP, § 23.
1369. ICANN's Response (*Donuts*), § 3.
1370. Donuts IRP Declaration, §§ 76 and following.
1371. 'Article IV, Section 3.21 states, in part: "The declarations of the IRP Panel, and the Board's subsequent action on those declarations, are final and have precedential value."'
1372. Donuts IRP Declaration, § 76.
1373. ICANN, *Approved Board Resolutions 2016.06.25.06-2016.06.25.09 – Regular Meeting of the ICANN Board*, 25 June 2016, https://www.icann.org/resources/board-material/resolutions-2016-06-25-en.

I. THE DOT REGISTRY LLC CASE (.INC/.LLC/.LLP)

1. Key Notes

- IRP under the new set of applicable rules.
- Claimant, Dot Registry, was the prevailing party.
- Finding by the panel's majority that ICANN cannot avoid its responsibilities by contracting out its obligations to a third party.
- Finding that ICANN had presented no real evidence that its Board had exercised independent judgment in reaching its decisions to deny reconsideration requests (rather than relying entirely on recommendations of ICANN staff).
- The panel declined to substitute its judgment for the judgment of the CPE panel as to whether Dot Registry was entitled to community priority.

2. Introduction

This IRP is similar to the *DCA* case in that, in our view, it is questionable why this case was ever initiated.[1374] The claimant, Dot Registry LLC (Dot Registry), was the applicant for .inc, .llc and .llp and had requested community priority. In view of the strict criteria for community priority, it seems that Dot Registry never had a chance of succeeding in a Community Priority Evaluation (CPE). Of course, like any other applicant, Dot Registry is entitled to initiate whatever procedure it likes in order to ensure that ICANN respects its Articles of Incorporation and Bylaws. However, to date it has not been proven, in our view, that Dot Registry has been materially harmed by ICANN's violation of the Articles of Incorporation and Bylaws. Indeed, a refusal to grant Dot Registry community priority would seem to be in line with the CPE criteria, as the purpose of community-based applications has never been to eliminate competition among applicants for a generic word TLD or to pick winners and losers from within a diverse commercial industry. The CPE criteria were specifically developed to prevent 'undue priority [being given] to an application that refers to a "community" construed merely to get a sought-after generic word as a gTLD string.'[1375] As a result, an IRP was unlikely ever to afford Dot Registry anything more than a pyrrhic victory.

Nevertheless, the IRP Declaration contains interesting reasoning about ICANN's obligations and about the ICANN Board's task in examining RfRs. The IRP panel's majority considered that ICANN's use of contractors did not vitiate the requirement to comply with ICANN's Articles of Incorporation and Bylaws. The panel's majority also disapproved of the ICANN Board's apparent practice of blindly following draft decisions prepared by its legal staff. In this respect, the majority of the panel was critical about ICANN exercising its litigation privileges in not disclosing communications

1374. We were not involved as counsel for either party in this case.
1375. ICANN, *New gTLD Applicant Guidebook 4 June 2012*, https://newgtlds.icann.org/en/applicants/agb/guidebook-full-04jun12-en.pdf, Module 4-9.

between the ICANN Board and its legal staff. However, the IRP panel refused to substitute its judgment for the judgment of the CPE panel, and limited itself to concluding that the ICANN Board's reconsideration decisions were made in violation of ICANN's Articles of Incorporation and Bylaws.

Finally, the IRP Declaration contains an important dissenting opinion, which submits that the majority's declaration committed 'a fundamental error by disregarding the weakness of Dot Registry's underlying CPE Applications.'[1376] This finding in the dissenting opinion gets to the heart of the matter. Dot Registry's 'success' in the IRP in no way strengthened its request for community priority nor did it put Dot Registry in a better position. It would seem that the IRP proceedings were pointless in any practical sense, or – to use the words of counsel to Dot Registry – they have 'ultimately done nothing but spin [their] wheels.'[1377]

3. Case Background

ICANN had denied Dot Registry's CPE applications for .inc, .llc and .llp, following an unequivocal recommendation by the Economist Intelligence Unit (EIU). As explained under the *Despegar et al.* case, an application had to receive a score of 14 or more points out of a maximum of 16 to prevail in CPE. An applicant who prevailed in CPE would then proceed to the next stage of the evaluation, and other standard applications for the same gTLD would not be allowed to proceed because the community-based application would be considered to have achieved priority. ICANN's CPE policy explained that this was 'a fundamental reason for very stringent requirements for qualification of a community-based application,' and that the CPE criteria were specifically developed to prevent 'undue priority [being given] to an application that refers to a "community" construed merely to get a sought-after generic word as a gTLD string.'[1378] In the case of Dot Registry's CPE applications, the EIU seems to have adhered to the stringent evaluation criteria. All three of Dot Registry's CPE applications received a consistent low score of 5 out of 16.

Despite the seemingly logical outcome of the CPE, Dot Registry challenged the denial of community priority in an RfR to ICANN's BGC. The BGC denied Dot Registry's RfR. Dot Registry submitted a request for IRP, asking the IRP panel to rule that its applications satisfied the CPE criteria, or in the alternative, to order ICANN to permit the reevaluation of its CPE applications by newly constituted panels not under the direction of the EIU.

1376. Dot Registry IRP Declaration, Dissenting Opinion, § 3.
1377. Dot Registry IRP Transcripts, p. 239.
1378. ICANN, *New gTLD Applicant Guidebook 4 June 2012*, https://newgtlds.icann.org/en/applicants/agb/guidebook-full-04jun12-en.pdf, Module 4-9.

In the course of the IRP proceedings, ICANN informed Dot Registry that it planned to proceed with auctioning the rights to the gTLD strings that were the subject of the IRP proceedings, unintentionally spurring Dot Registry to ask for interim relief to preserve the *status quo*.

4. Points of Procedure

a. Arguments Discussed

(1) Applicable Procedural Rules

According to Dot Registry, 'general principles of law and principles of international law, including principles of international arbitration, govern ICANN and are applicable in [IRP] proceeding[s]'.[1379] With reference to the *ICM Registry* case, Dot Registry argued that previous IRP panels had conclusively decided this, with precedential effect.[1380] Dot Registry also emphasized that, in electing the ICDR as IRP provider, ICANN had opted for dispute settlement before an international arbitration institution.[1381]

Dot Registry recognized that parties are allowed to modify the rules and the ICANN's Supplementary Procedures had modified certain of the ICDR Rules. However, Dot Registry submitted that 'it is still incumbent on a tribunal to ensure that the parties are accorded their fundamental rights' and that the Supplementary Procedures had 'not limited the Panel's powers to fashion a proceeding that is appropriate for the rights at stake and the issues that have to be decided.'[1382]

ICANN submitted that general principles of international dispute resolution apply to IRPs 'only insofar as those principles are incorporated into the ICDR Procedures.' However, in case of inconsistency between those general principles and the Supplementary Procedures, ICANN submitted that the Supplementary Procedures would apply.[1383]

The panel declared 'that the principles of laws applicable to the [IRP] proceeding are ICANN's Articles of Incorporation, its Bylaws, the laws of the State of California, the Supplemental Rules, and the ICDR Rules of Arbitration. The Panel [did] not find that there are "relevant principles of international law and applicable international conventions" that would assist it in the task [...] before it.'[1384]

(2) Jurisdiction of the IRP Panel

Dot Registry submitted a request for IRP to seek relief from the harm it had suffered as a result of the actions, inaction and decisions of the ICANN Board of Directors:

1379. Dot Registry's Response to IRP Panel's questions of 12 October 2015, §6.
1380. Dot Registry's Response to IRP Panel's questions of 12 October 2015, §6.
1381. Dot Registry's Response to IRP Panel's questions of 12 October 2015, §§ 18, 25.
1382. Dot Registry's Response to IRP Panel's questions of 12 October 2015, § 25.
1383. ICANN's Response to IRP Panel's questions of 12 October 2015 (*Dot Registry*), pp. 2-3.
1384. Dot Registry IRP Declaration, § 67.

'Dot Registry, LLC ("Dot Registry") hereby submits this Request for Independent Review

Process ("IRP"), [...] in order to seek relief from the harm it has suffered as a result of the actions, inaction and decisions of the ICANN Board of Directors (the "Board"), in violation of ICANN's Articles of Incorporation, Bylaws, gTLD Applicant Guidebook ("AGB") and principles of international law, relating to Dot Registry's applications to ICANN to operate the generic Top-Level Domains ("gTLDs") .INC, .LLC and .LLP.'[1385]

ICANN argued that the IRP panel had only one responsibility:

'This IRP Panel has one (and only one) responsibility: to provide its views as to "whether the Board has acted consistently with the provisions of [ICANN's] Articles of Incorporation and Bylaws".'[1386]

ICANN agreed that the term "action" also 'encompasses inactions by the ICANN Board [...]. However, the notion of Board "inaction" leading to a decision that is reviewable by an IRP Panel must involve a situation where the Board was required to, but did not, act.'[1387]

However, according to ICANN, IRPs 'are not a vehicle for challenging the substance of determinations made by third-party experts in the context of the New gTLD Program. Instead, an IRP is an accountability mechanism intended solely to assess whether ICANN's Board acted in conformance with ICANN's Articles [of Incorporation] and Bylaws.'[1388] ICANN argued:

'Dot Registry is generally correct that boards of corporations have ultimate legal responsibility for the actions of the corporation, including the actions of the corporation's employees,[1389] but this does not mean that the scope of an IRP – a process that ICANN uniquely adopted in its Bylaws and that does not exist in other corporate bylaws – is somehow expanded to include every decision that any person at ICANN makes. In addition, while Dot Registry is also correct that ICANN has ultimate authority for CPE results and the EIU acts as a contracter within the New gTLD Program,[1390] these facts have no bearing on whether independent review, an accountability mechanism created and defined by ICANN's Bylaws, extends to actions of ICANN's staff or third parties.[1391]'[1392]

The panel confirmed its jurisdiction:

1385. Dot Registry's Request for IRP, § 1.
1386. ICANN's Response (*Dot Registry*), § 5.
1387. ICANN's Response to IRP Panel's questions of 12 October 2015 (*Dot Registry*), p. 6.
1388. ICANN's Sur-Reply (*Dot Registry*), § 7.
1389. '[Dot Registry's Reply, §§] 12-14.'
1390. '[Dot Registry's Reply, §§] 18-20.'
1391. 'Dot Registry argues that the fact that that litigation waiver signed by New gTLD applicants covers ICANN staff and third parties such as the EIU somehow converts the IRP into a mechanism for review of staff and third party actions. ([Dot Registry's Reply, §§] 15-17). This is wrong. No entity is entiled to or has the right to a new gTLD, and thus every entity that applies understands that it is bound by the rules set forth in the Applicant Guidebook. Applicants were aware of the scope of the litigation waiver at the time they applied, and they were also aware of the scope of ICANN's accountability mechanisms.'
1392. ICANN's Sur-Reply, § 10.

> 'An IRP Panel is tasked with declaring whether the ICANN Board has, by its action or inaction, acted inconsistently with the Articles and Bylaws. It is not asked to declare whether the applicant who sought reconsideration should have prevailed.'[1393]

(3) Standing

Dot Registry argued that it had standing because it was directly and materially affected:

> 'As the applicant for the .INC, .LLC and .LLP gTLD strings, Dot Registry is directly and materially affected by the actions, inaction and decisions of the Board described herein relating to these strings and the contention sets for each string. Dot Registry has invested substantial time, funds and effort to obtain the rights to operate these strings, including $621,000 in applications fees alone.'[1394]

Dot Registry considered it had 'suffered harm as a result of the EIU's inconsistent and inequitable interpretation and application of the CPE criteria, and the [ICANN] Board's failure to ensure that the EIU is complying with its policies and procedures.'[1395] According to Dot Registry, ICANN's rejection of community priority status for the applications of .inc, .llc and .llp 'effectively guts Dot Registry's business model, and as a consequence the objectives and desires of the communities intended to be served.'[1396]

ICANN requested that Dot Registry's request for IRP 'be summarily denied because the ICANN Board has not taken any action that violates any provision of ICANN's Articles or Bylaws.'[1397] However, ICANN did not dispute that Dot Registry had standing to bring the IRP.[1398]

Given ICANN's agreement that Dot Registry had standing, the IRP panel did not have to rule on this issue.

(4) Time Bar

ICANN argued that 'any challenges to the Board's delegation of authority via the Guidebook are long since time-barred because the Guidebook was published in 2012, and IRP challenges to Board decisions must be filed within 30 days of the posting of the minutes of the Board meeting reflecting the challenged Board action or inaction.'[1399] But, as stated by the Panel, ICANN 'has never argued [...] that Dot Registry failed

1393. Dot Registry IRP declaration, § 70.
1394. Dot Registry's Request for IRP, § 56.
1395. Dot Registry's Amendment to Request for IRP, § 6.
1396. Dot Registry's Reply, § 10.
1397. ICANN's Response (*Dot Registry*), § 6.
1398. ICANN's Sur-Reply (*Dot Registry*), § 46, n. 50.
1399. ICANN's Response to IRP Panel's Questions of 12 October 2015 (*Dot Registry*), p. 4.

timely or properly to raise claims of *inter alia* disparate treatment/unjustified discrimination, lack of transparency or other alleged breaches of Articles, Bylaws, or AGB by the BGC.'[1400]

As a result, ICANN's time bar argument was a non-issue and did not need to be considered by either the claimant or the IRP panel.

(5) Written/Oral Arguments

Dot Registry requested a hearing, either by videoconference or in-person. ICANN recognized that its 'Bylaws and the Supplementary Procedures governing [the] IRP do not prohibit the holding of an in-person hearing', but emphasized that the Bylaws 'strongly encourage' IRP panels to reserve in-person hearings for extraordinary circumstances only.[1401] The IRP panel decided to organize a hearing by videoconference.

(6) Witnesses and Expert Witnesses

Both Parties submitted witness statements. ICANN also agreed to produce documents with assurances of confidentiality and protection by Dot Registry.[1402] ICANN considered that IRP proceedings are 'not subject to the same presumption of openness that one finds in U.S. and other courts.'[1403]

ICANN also submitted that the Supplementary Procedures and the Bylaws 'are dispositive and expressly prohibit live witness testimony.' ICANN argued 'IRP panels do not have the discretion to modify or ignore such express provisions of the Supplementary Procedures' and 'that it would be contrary to both the Bylaws and the Supplementary Procedures for an IRP Panel to order that any of the potential witnesses be subjected to live examination.'[1404]

Dot Registry nevertheless insisted that witnesses be examined during an in-person hearing, and considered that the IRP panel had the authority to allow for this,[1405] in spite of any provisions to the contrary in ICANN's Bylaws and the Supplementary Procedures:

> 'Streamlining IRP proceedings is in the interests of both aggrieved claimants and ICANN to a point; however, when the process becomes so truncated that a claimant does not have the right to be heard fully nor a fair opportunity to present its case, then Dot Registry submits that it is appropriate for the Panel to exercise its discretion to structure the proceeding in such a way to address these shortcomings.

1400. Dot Registry IRP Declaration, § 62.
1401. ICANN's Response to IRP Panel's Questions of 12 October 2015 (*Dot Registry*), p. 6.
1402. Letter from counsel to ICANN of 15 April 2015 (*Dot Registry*); Dot Registry IRP Procedural Order No. 3.
1403. Letter from counsel to ICANN of 15 April 2015 (*Dot Registry*).
1404. ICANN's Response to IRP Panel's Questions of 12 October 2015 (*Dot Registry*), p. 6.
1405. Dot Registry's Response to IRP Panel's Questions of 12 October 2015, § 96.

> This is particularly important because the IRP is the final accountability mechanism and only opportunity ICANN provides applicants for independent third-party review. ICANN not only designed this accountability mechanism, but it can modify it at any time. Furthermore, it has done so and to its own advantage. ICANN not only controls the application process, but strictly controls what information about it is released to applicants. To further limit the IRP such that neither the parties nor the panelists may request the appearance of and question persons whose testimony would aid the panelists in reaching a fair decision, would be, as the *DotConnectAfrica Trust v. ICANN* Panel found, "fundamentally inconsistent with the requirements in ICANN's Bylaws for accountability and decision making with objectivity and fairness."[...]
>
> For these reasons, Dot Registry urges the Panel to exercise its authority under the ICDR Rules, to structure the proceeding such that the Panel or the parties may request that witnesses appear (whether in-person, by videoconference or by teleconference) for questioning at the future hearing on the merits.'[1406]

The panel decided not to allow live fact or expert witness testimony of any kind at the hearing.[1407] Nevertheless, Dot Registry allegedly tried to introduce a fact witness at the hearing[1408] and was heavily criticized for doing so by the dissenting panelist in the IRP.

(7) Costs

Dot Registry asked to be awarded its cost for the IRP proceedings, including all legal fees and expenses. Dot Registry considered an award of cost was 'particularly appropriate [...] given that ICANN failed to participate [...] in the CEP[1409] with Dot Registry'.[1410]

ICANN argued that each party should bear its own expenses, according to the ICANN's Bylaws:

> 'Dot Registry also asks that it be awarded "its costs in this proceeding, including, without limitation, all legal fees and expenses." This request directly contradicts ICANN's Bylaws, which provide that "[e]ach party to the IRP Proceeding shall bear its own expenses".'[1411]

The panel declared that Dot Registry is the prevailing party and that ICANN is to bear all the fees and expenses of the ICDR:

> '[...] the Panel declares that Dot Registry is the prevailing party. The administrative fees and expenses of the International Centre for Dispute Resolution ("ICDR") totaling $4,600.00 and the compensation and expenses for the Panelists totaling $461,388.70 shall be borne entirely by ICANN. Therefore, ICANN shall pay to Dot

1406. Dot Registry's Response to IRP Panel's Questions of 12 October 2015, §§ 99–101.
1407. Dot Registry IRP Panel's Order No. 11, § 2; Dot Registry IRP Panel's Order No. 12, § 2.
1408. Dot Registry IRP Hearing Transcript, pp. 37–42.
1409. Cooperative Engagement Process.
1410. Dot Registry's Reply, § 40.
1411. ICANN's response (*Dot Registry*), § 50.

> Registry, LLC $235,294.37 representing said fees, expenses and compensation previously incurred by Dot Registry, LLC upon demonstration that these incurred costs have been paid in full.'[1412]

The panel did not rule in relation to any other fees and expenses that Dot Registry may have incurred for legal representation in the IRP proceedings.

b. *Noteworthy Points for Analysis*

(1) Standing

In our view, it is surprising that ICANN did not dispute Dot Registry's standing. Even if the ICANN Board did not handle Dot Registry's RfRs correctly (*infra*), it remains questionable that Dot Registry was materially harmed by this violation of ICANN's Articles of Incorporation and Bylaws. This point was raised by ICANN when Dot Registry applied for interim relief, and in our view, the dissenting panelist was correct in considering that Dot Registry's CPE applications 'never had a chance of succeeding.'[1413] He considered that Dot Registry had 'quite boldly gamed the system, seeking CPEs which all of the other 21 applicants for the three gTLDs in issue thought were obviously unattainable, since they ventured no such applications, in hopes of outflanking, hence defeating, all of them by bulldozing ICANN in the [IRP] proceeding.'[1414] Therefore it seems that even if the ICANN Board had investigated all the possible facts and acted with complete transparency in its examination of Dot Registry's RfRs, it would not have changed the fact that Dot Registry never had a chance of succeeding.

5. Applicable Law

a. *Arguments Discussed*

(1) Sources

Dot Registry argued that the substantive applicable law(s) to be applied in this proceeding are ICANN's Articles of Incorporation and Bylaws, relevant principles of international law (such as good faith) and the doctrine of legitimate expectations, applicable international conventions, the laws of the State of California and the Applicant Guidebook.[1415]

ICANN essentially agreed on the applicability of these rules, but considered that principles of international law or international dispute resolution applied only insofar as those principles are incorporated in ICANN's processes.[1416]

1412. Dot Registry IRP declaration, § 154.
1413. Dot Registry IRP Declaration, Dissenting Opinion, § 3.
1414. Dot Registry IRP Declaration, Dissenting Opinion, § 35.
1415. Dot Registry's Response to IRP Panel's Questions of 12 October 2015.
1416. ICANN's Response to IRP Panel's Questions of 12 October 2015 (*Dot Registry*), p. 2.

The panel considered that there were no '"relevant principles of international law applicable international conventions" that would assist it in the task [...] before it.'[1417]

(2) Essential Rights and Obligations

Dot Registry argued that '[t]he ICANN Board violated its obligation to comply with principles of international law and its obligations to transparency and accountability to the Internet community by ignoring and perpetuating a pattern of behavior undertaken by ICANN staff in violation of those principles.'[1418] According to Dot Registry, the ICANN Board acted to Dot Registry's detriment without making a 'reasonable inquiry', and failed to 'employ proper care, skill and diligence.'[1419] It considered that ICANN's BGC had breached its obligations to ensure fair and equitable, reasonable and non-discriminatory treatment.[1420]

Dot Registry also alleged that the ICANN Board had violated its obligations under the Bylaws by not ensuring either the competence of the third parties relied upon, or the absence of a conflict of interest:

> 'ICANN's Bylaws explicitly require ICANN to ensure that its policies are implemented accurately and in a transparent, unbiased manner. In addition, pursuant to its obligation to act transparently and accountably and in accordance with relevant principles of international law, ICANN must ensure that anyone it delegates authority to is competent to exercise that authority and will likewise implement ICANN's policies in compliance with the principles expressed in ICANN's governing documents. Finally, ICANN is required to ensure a lack of conflicts of interest among its affiliated parties and independent experts. As the only entity within ICANN authorized to contract on behalf of ICANN and the ultimate authority for such contracts, the ICANN Board violated these obligations [...].'[1421]

Dot Registry further submitted that ICANN remained responsible for the acts of the EIU, since the EIU can only recommend to ICANN and ICANN has complete discretion as to whether or not to follow the EIU's recommendations.[1422] Specifically, ICANN's 'Board is responsible for the actions of ICANN staff and its contracted third-party evaluators, because the Board is ultimately responsible for conducting and directing the business and affairs of ICANN.'[1423] Dot Registry argued that 'accepting ICANN's exceedingly limited view of the Board's collective accountability for the implementation of the [new gTLD] program the Board itself established would mean that there could be no possibility of independent, third-party review of actions taken in the course of implementing the New gTLD Program' and that such is 'entirely contradictory [to] ICANN's commitments to transparency and accountability.'[1424]

1417. Dot Registry IRP Declaration, § 67.
1418. Dot Registry's Request for IRP, § 61.
1419. Dot Registry Post-Hearing Brief, § 9.
1420. *See* Dot Registry IRP Declaration, § 52.
1421. Dot Registry's Request for IRP, § 62.
1422. Dot Registry's Reply, § 18.
1423. Dot Registry's Reply, § 12.
1424. Dot Registry's Reply, § 14.

According to Dot Registry the BGC also failed to exercise appropriate due diligence and care in considering its Reconsideration Requests:

> 'Furthermore, the Determination mischaracterized Dot Registry's claims as "challeng[ing] the substantive determinations of the Panels," rather than acknowledging that the CPE panels violated established policies and procedures.'[1425]

Moreover, Dot Registry considered that ICANN had failed to appoint a competent evaluator and failed to provide any evidence that it vetted the evaluators performing the CPEs.[1426]

Finally, Dot Registry submitted that the EIU had engaged in unjustified discrimination:[1427]

> ICANN argued that Dot Registry had failed to show that the BGC actions were not in accordance with ICANN's Articles of Incorporation and Bylaws.[1428] ICANN was of the opinion that Dot Registry had failed to identify any provision that had been violated by the BGC:
>
> > 'While Dot Registry disagrees with the BGC's determination denying reconsideration, Dot Registry fails to identify <u>any</u> provision of ICANN's Articles or Bylaws that was allegedly violated by the BGC in making its determination on Dot Registry's Reconsideration Requests.'[1429]

For ICANN, there was only one Board action to be reviewed by this IRP, namely the review by the BGC of the RfRs that Dot Registry had filed challenging the CPE Reports.[1430] ICANN argued that the BGC did not violate ICANN's Articles of Incorporation or Bylaws in its consideration of Dot Registry's RfRs.

ICANN submitted that the ICANN staff and the EIU did not need to adhere to the Bylaws in relation to the CPE:

> 'The language of the EOI did not, however, obligate the EIU, an independent, third-party provider, to adhere to ICANN's Articles or Bylaws. Indeed, the EIU does not reference the Articles or Bylaws. Instead, each candidate was required to "*warrant* that the candidate, if selected, will operate under ICANN's non-disclosure agreement and standard consulting agreement, and that neither the candidate nor any individual who might be engaged to work on this project . . . has a known conflict of interest."[...]
>
> Similarly, ICANN's contract with the EIU does not contain any statement requiring the EIU to comply with ICANN's Articles or Bylaws or with the values or principles contained therein, however it does explicitly require that the EIU ensure that its panelists comply with ICANN's Conflict of Interest and Code of Conduct Guidelines.[...] Accordingly, nothing in either the EOI or ICANN's contract with the EIU required the EIU to comply with ICANN's Articles or Bylaws.'[1431]

1425. Dot Registry's Request for IRP, § 50; Dot Registry's Reply, §§ 27-31.
1426. Dot Registry's Reply, § 35.
1427. *See* Dot Registry's Reply, §§ 24-25.
1428. ICANN's Sur-Reply (*Dot Registry*), § 21.
1429. ICANN's Response (*Dot Registry*), § 40.
1430. ICANN's Sur-Reply (*Dot Registry*), § 8.
1431. ICANN's Post-Hearing Brief (*Dot Registry*), §§ 7 and 8.

ICANN effectively argued that actions of ICANN staff or of the EIU were not subject to IRP review:

> '[...] the Board was not involved in the selection of the EIU; ICANN staff selected third-party providers, including the EIU, via a public solicitation of Expressions of Interest. As such, the selection of the EIU is not a basis for Independent Review.'[1432]

According to ICANN the Bylaws made it clear that the IRP review did not extend to actions of ICANN staff or of third parties acting on behalf of ICANN staff, such as the EIU.[1433]

ICANN insisted that there was no challengeable ICANN Board conduct:

> '[...] neither the creation nor the acceptance of the CPE Panel Reports regarding Dot Registry's Applications for .INC, .LLC, or .LLP constitutes ICANN Board action; nor does the appointment of the EIU by ICANN staff – not the ICANN Board – following a public request for applications from interested firms. When the Board did act, in responding to GAC advice and denying Dot Registry's Reconsideration Requests, it followed ICANN policies and processes at every turn.'[1434]
>
> 'As to the majority of Dot Registry's IRP filing, there simply is no ICANN Board conduct that could result in a finding that the Board violated its Articles of Incorporation or Bylaws.'[1435]

ICANN saw 'the BGC's review as properly limited to whether the CPE Panels followed the appropriate policies and procedures in rendering the CPE Reports':

> 'Even if the CPE Panels allegedly "got it wrong," this was not an issue for the BGC to review unless the BGC also determined that the CPE Panels acted inconsistently with established ICANN policy or procedure in completing their work.'[1436]

Making a 'substantive evaluation of whether the CPE Panels "got it right"' would be 'outside of the Board's mandate,' according to ICANN.[1437]

Furthermore, ICANN considered there to be no due process requirement for the delegation of new gTLDs:

> 'As for the Panel's question regarding "due process," ICANN is a nonprofit corporation, not a government entity or actor, and neither California nor relevant international law imposes any sort of "due process" requirement on ICANN with respect to its determinations regarding the delegation of specific new gTLDs.[1438] In any event, inasmuch as the Bylaws and Articles [of Incorporation] do not create "due process" rights on behalf of gTLD applicants,

---

1432. ICANN's Response (*Dot Registry*), § 26.
1433. ICANN's Sur-Reply (*Dot Registry*), §§ 7, 14, 19.
1434. ICANN's Response (*Dot Registry*), § 7.
1435. ICANN's Response (*Dot Registry*), § 51.
1436. ICANN's Sur-Reply (*Dot Registry*), § 19.
1437. ICANN's Sur-Reply (*Dot Registry*), § 27.
1438. '*See, e.g., Jackson v. Metropolitan Edison Co.*, 419 U.S. 345, 349 (1974) (the Constitution's due process protections are limited to "state action").'

> it is not within the scope of this IRP to determine whether Dot Registry was accorded "due process" in the processing of its applications.'[1439]

The IRP panel did not accept ICANN's argument that the ICANN Board could avoid its obligations under the Articles of Incorporation and Bylaws simply by using third-party vendors. First, the IRP panel observed that ICANN had agreed with the EIU that ICANN would remain solely responsible for all legal matters in the new gTLD application process:

> '[...] EIU was "not a gTLD decision-maker but simply a consultant to ICANN." "The parties [*i.e.*, EIU and ICANN] agreed that EIU, while performing its contracted functions, would operate largely in the background, and that ICANN would be solely responsible for all legal matters pertaining to the application process."'[1440]

The panel took note of the fact that the decisions on community priority were ICANN's decisions:

> '[...] "ICANN will be free in its complete discretion to decide whether or not to follow [EIU's] determination," that "ICANN will be solely responsible to applicants ... for the decisions it decides to issue," and that "each decision must be issued by ICANN in its own name only".'[1441]

The panel also observed that ICANN's staff was intimately involved in the CPE process:

> 'Moreover, EIU did not act on its own in performing the CPEs that are the subject of this proceeding. ICANN staff was intimately involved in the process. The ICANN staff supplied continuing and important input on the CPE reports [...].'[1442]

The panel concluded that both ICANN staff and the EIU were obligated to comply with ICANN's Articles and Bylaws:

> 'The facts that ICANN staff was intimately involved in the production of the CPE and that ICANN staff was obligated to follow the Articles and Bylaws, further support the Panel majority's finding that ICANN staff and the EIU were obligated to comply with ICANN's Articles and Bylaws [...].'[1443]

Moreover, the majority of the panel decided that ICANN could not avoid its responsibilities by contracting with a third party to perform ICANN's obligations:

> 'The Panel majority further declares that the contractual use of the EIU as the agent of ICANN does not vitiate the requirement to comply with ICANN's Articles and Bylaws, or the Board's duty to determine whether ICANN staff and the EIU complied with these obligations. ICANN cannot avoid its responsibilities by contracting with a third party to perform ICANN's obligations. It is the responsibility of the BGC in its reconsideration to insure such compliance. Indeed, the CPEs themselves were issued on the letterhead of ICANN, not that

1439. ICANN's Response to IRP Panel's Questions of 12 October 2015 (*Dot Registry*), p. 2.
1440. Dot Registry IRP Declaration, § 15.
1441. Dot Registry IRP Declaration, § 92.
1442. Dot Registry IRP Declaration, § 93.
1443. Dot Registry IRP Declaration, § 101.

> of the EIU, and Module 5 of the Applicant Guidebook states that "ICANN's Board of Directors has ultimate responsibility for the New gTLD Program." AGB, Module 5, at 5-4.'[1444]

However, the IRP panel did not examine whether ICANN staff or the EIU had themselves failed to comply with obligations under ICANN's Articles of Incorporation, Bylaws, or the AGB. Rather, it assessed the decision by the BGC to deny the Reconsiderations Requests:

> 'The Panel majority emphasizes that, in reaching these conclusions, the Panel is not assessing whether ICANN staff or the EIU failed themselves to comply with obligations under the Articles, the Bylaws, or the AGB. There has been no implicit foundation or hint one way or another regarding the substance of the decisions of ICANN staff or the EIU in the Panel majority's approach. Rather the Panel majority has concluded that, in making its reconsideration decisions, the Board (acting through the BGC) failed to exercise due diligence and care in having a reasonable amount of facts in front of them and failed to fulfill its transparency obligations (including both the failure to make available the research on which the EIU and ICANN staff purportedly relied and the failure to make publically available the ICANN staff work on which the BGC relied). The Panel majority further concludes that the evidence before it does not support a determination that the Board (acting through the BGC) exercised independent judgment in reaching the reconsideration decisions.'[1445]

The panel's majority considered that the BGC had the obligation to examine and determine whether the CPE panel and ICANN staff had respected ICANN's essential obligations, and it concluded that the BGC had not done so:

> 'Accordingly, the Panel majority declares that in performing its duties of Reconsideration, the BGC must determine whether the CPE (in this case the EIU) and ICANN staff respected the principles of fairness, transparency, avoiding conflicts of interest, and non-discrimination as set out in the ICANN Articles, Bylaws and AGB. These matters were clearly raised in Dot Registry's submissions. The Panel majority declares that the BGC failed to make the proper determinations as to compliance by ICANN staff and the EIU with the Articles, Bylaws, and AGB, let alone to undertake the requisite due diligence or to conduct itself with the transparency mandated by the Articles and Bylaws in the conduct of the reconsideration process.'[1446]

Indeed, the majority of the panel considered that the BGC had failed to address adequately the assertions of Dot Registry in relation to the CPE and, thus, that the BGC had violated the Bylaws:

> 'Yet, the BGC failed to address any of these assertions, other than to recite that Dot Registry had failed to identify any "established policy or procedure" which had been violated.
>
> Article IV, Section 3.4 of the Bylaws calls upon this Panel to determine whether the BGC, in making its Reconsideration Decision "exercise[d] due diligence and care in having a reasonable amount of facts in front of them" and "exercise[d]

1444. Dot Registry IRP Declaration, § 89.
1445. Dot Registry IRP Declaration, § 152.
1446. Dot Registry IRP Declaration, § 88.

independent judgment in taking the decision believed to be in the best interests of the company." Consequently, the Panel must consider whether, in the face of Dot Registry's Reconsideration Requests, the BGC employed the requisite due diligence and independent judgment in determining whether or not ICANN staff and the EIU complied with Article, Bylaw, and AGB obligations such as transparency and non-discrimination.

Indeed, the BGC admittedly did not examine whether the EIU or ICANN staff engaged in unjustified discrimination or failed to fulfill transparency obligations. It failed to make any reasonable investigation or to make certain that it had acted with due diligence and care to be sure that it had a reasonable amount of facts before it.'[1447]

Furthermore, the majority of the panel considered that the fact that ICANN was not capable of providing any evidence of an independent deliberative process showed that the BGC had failed to exercise independent judgment in deciding to deny Dot Registry's RfRs:

> 'ICANN has presented no real evidence to this Panel that the BGC exercised independent judgment in reaching its decisions to deny the Reconsideration Requests, rather than relying entirely on recommendations of ICANN staff. Thus, the Panel is left highly uncertain as to whether the BGC "exercise[d] due diligence and care in having a reasonable amount of facts in front of them" and "exercise[d] independent judgment in taking the decision." And, by shielding from public disclosure all real evidence of an independent deliberative process at the BGC (other than the pro forma meeting minutes), the BGC has put itself in contravention of Bylaws IV.2.11 and IV.2.14 requiring that ICANN staff work on which it relies be made public".'[1448]

(3) Standard of Review

Dot Registry submitted that the standard of review for an IRP is *de novo*; it referred to the general meaning of the term 'independent' in 'independent review', and to the findings of the *ICM*, *Booking.com* and *DCA Trust* panels.[1449]

ICANN argued that ICANN's Bylaws set out a 'defined standard of review' and that the IRP is 'neither asked to, nor allowed to, substitute its judgment for that of the [ICANN] Board'.[1450] According to ICANN, the 'plain language of this standard [of review] restricts the IRP panel's assessment of the Board's "due diligence and care" to an assessment of whether the Board's action was taken in reliance on a "reasonable amount of facts".'[1451]

1447. Dot Registry IRP Declaration, §§ 109–111.
1448. Dot Registry IRP Declaration, § 150.
1449. Dot Registry Reply, §§ 4–6.
1450. ICANN's Sur-Reply (*Dot Registry*), § 11.
1451. ICANN's Response to IRP Panel's Questions of 12 October 2015 (*Dot Registry*), p. 3.

However, at the hearing, ICANN conceded that the Bylaws do not give a strict definition of the standard of review, and that the questions of the 'defined' standard of review, as formulated in the Bylaws, are not exclusive.[1452]

The panel agreed with the *Vistaprint* panel that the ICANN Board's conduct is to be reviewed and appraised by the IRP panel using an objective and independent standard without any presumption of correctness and concluded 'that neither the California business judgment rule nor any other applicable provision of law or charter documents compels the Panel to defer to the BGC's decisions.'[1453]

(4) Emergency Proceedings

After Dot Registry had submitted its request for IRP, ICANN informed the claimant that it planned to proceed with auctioning the rights to the gTLD strings that were the subject of the IRP proceedings. Dot Registry considered that no auction was warranted and requested emergency interim relief.[1454] Dot Registry argued that 'an order enjoining ICANN form [*sic*] auctioning or delegating .INC, .LLC and .LLP [was] necessary in order to protect Dot Registry's procedural rights in the IRP, to protect the integrity of the IRP process an[d] to preserve the *status quo* at the time Dot Registry filed the IRP.'[1455]

ICANN argued that no interim relief was warranted, as Dot Registry could not demonstrate a reasonable likelihood of success on the merits.[1456] Moreover, ICANN argued that Dot Registry had not demonstrated that the harm it would suffer in the absence of interim relief outweighed the potential harm to others, particularly given the fact that 'Dot Registry's IRP is frivolous and unlikely to succeed on the merits.'[1457]

The ICDR appointed an Emergency panelist, who subsequently granted Dot Registry's request for interim relief. The Emergency panelist found 'the preservation of the IRP as a process that is capable of providing an effective remedy in the IRP to be a substantial right.'[1458] According to the Emergency panelist, the need for interim measures was 'urgent to prevent the imminent dissipation of substantial rights.'[1459] The potential harm to Dot Registry – the irrevocable loss of priority registration rights – 'would not be compensable by monetary damages,' the panelist considered.[1460] The panelist was also of the opinion that the interim measures sought were 'rather modest' and that 'ICANN ha[d] not identified any concrete harm that would result from the relatively short delay required for the IRP panel to complete its review.'[1461] Finally, the

1452. Dot Registry IRP Transcript, pp. 248–249.
1453. Dot Registry IRP Declaration, §§ 68–69.
1454. Dot Registry Request for Emergency Relief, § 2.
1455. Dot Registry Request for Emergency Relief, § 25.
1456. ICANN's Response to Request for Emergency Relief (*Dot Registry*), §§ 17–23.
1457. ICANN's Response to Request for Emergency Relief (*Dot Registry*), §§ 24–26.
1458. Dot Registry IRP Order on Request for Emergency Measures of Protection, § 46.
1459. Dot Registry IRP Order on Request for Emergency Measures of Protection, § 49.
1460. Dot Registry IRP Order on Request for Emergency Measures of Protection, § 51.
1461. Dot Registry IRP Order on Request for Emergency Measures of Protection, § 54.

Emergency panelist considered that Dot Registry had raised "substantial questions going to the merits" which "will be for the IRP panel to determine".'[1462]

b. *Noteworthy Points for Analysis*

(1) Essential Rights and Obligations

The panel's majority agreed with the views of the claimants in the *Booking.com*, *Vistaprint* and *Despegar et al.* cases, and of the dissenting panelist in the *Donuts* case, and decided – in our view correctly – that the use of contractors does not vitiate ICANN's requirement to ensure that its essential obligations are complied with. ICANN cannot avoid its responsibilities by contracting with a third party who then performs ICANN's obligations.

In the *Despegar et al.* case, the same shortcomings of the CPE process were discussed as in the *Dot Registry* case. However, the Despegar *et al.* IRP panel concluded that these shortcomings did not amount to a violation of ICANN's Articles of Incorporation, Bylaws and core values. The *Despegar et al.* panel's conclusion was based upon the premise that the EIU was not mandated to apply ICANN's core values,[1463] and upon the premise that the EIU's determinations are presumed to be final[1464] and were made independently by the EIU, without ICANN's active involvement. In this respect, ICANN 'had informed' the claimants and the IRP panel in the *Despegar et al.* case that '[b]ecause of the EIU's role as the panel firm, ICANN does not have any communications (nor does it maintain any communications) with the evaluators that identify the scoring of any individual CPE.'[1465] The *Despegar et al.* panel concluded: 'That is a clear and comprehensive statement that such documentation does not exist',[1466] and the IRP panel proceeded upon this premise. However, the *Dot Registry* IRP Declaration has shown that this finding was unreliable.

Indeed, the findings in the *Dot Registry* IRP Declaration reveal that ICANN staff was 'intimately involved in the CPE' and 'in the production of the CPE [result]'[1467] 'The ICANN staff supplied continuing and important input on the CPE reports.'[1468] As the CPE reports identify the scoring of CPEs, ICANN *did* communicate with the evaluators who scored the individual CPEs.

Moreover, ICANN's description in the *Despegar et al.* IRP of the EIU as the 'panel firm' or independent evaluator, making 'presumptively final' determinations was arguably misleading. Because of ICANN's staff intimate involvement in the process, the EIU cannot be qualified as a 'panel firm' or independent evaluator. The findings of the *Dot*

1462. Dot Registry IRP Order on Request for Emergency Measures of Protection, § 60.
1463. Despegar IRP Declaration, §§ 148-151.
1464. Despegar IRP Declaration, §§ 148-151.
1465. Despegar IRP Declaration, § 95.
1466. Despegar IRP Declaration, § 95.
1467. Dot Registry IRP Declaration, §§ 93, 101.
1468. Dot Registry IRP Declaration, § 93.

Registry IRP panel also revealed that the EIU was 'simply a consultant to ICANN', and that ICANN had agreed with the EIU that the EIU 'would operate largely in the background, and that ICANN would be solely responsible of all legal matters pertaining to the application process.'[1469] ICANN was 'solely responsible to applicants ... for the decisions it decide[d] to issue', and 'each decision [had to] be issued by ICANN in its own name only.'[1470]

In our view, the intimate involvement of ICANN staff, and the fact that ICANN had to issue decisions in its own name was material to the IRP Determinations in the *Despegar et al.* and *Dot Registry* cases. Both IRP panels agreed,[1471] and ICANN acknowledged,[1472] that ICANN staff is bound to conduct itself in accordance with ICANN's AoI and Bylaws. The *Despegar et al.* IRP panel considered:

> 'The Panel is, of course, charged with reviewing the action of ICANN's Board, rather than its staff, but the Panel wishes to make clear that, in carrying out its activities, the Board should seek to ensure that ICANN's staff comply with the Articles of Incorporation and Bylaws of ICANN, and that a failure of the Board to ensure such compliance is a failure of the Board itself.'[1473]

Therefore, in our view, the *Despegar et al.* panel's reliance on the incorrect information that the EIU served as an independent panel, without the intimate involvement of ICANN staff, was material to the IRP Declaration. Indeed, the factual finding by the *Dot Registry* panel that the ICANN staff was intimately involved seems to be the main reason why the IRP panels in both cases came to different conclusions. In short, it is doubtful that the *Despegar et al.* panel would have denied the request for IRP had it (i) been aware of the details concerning the relationship between ICANN and the EIU, and (ii) been correctly informed about the intimate involvement of ICANN staff in the CPE.

(2) Emergency Proceedings

ICANN's attempt to push ahead with auctioning the .llc, .llp and .inc gTLDs pending the IRP seems a curious strategic decision. By doing this, ICANN effectively treated Dot Registry's applications differently from other applications that were the subject of IRPs – where further developments regarding the gTLDs remained on hold pending the outcome of the proceedings. As a result, it was only to be expected that Dot Registry would file a request for emergency relief. As all similar requests for emergency relief have been granted in IRPs, ICANN could have anticipated that Dot Registry had a good chance of succeeding in its request, even if Dot Registry had a weak case on the underlying merits.

By engaging in emergency proceedings for interim relief, Dot Registry's case, arguably weak on the underlying merits, may actually have gained credibility. ICANN argued

1469. Dot Registry IRP Declaration, § 91.
1470. Dot Registry IRP Declaration, § 92.
1471. Despegar IRP Declaration, § 104; Dot Registry IRP Declaration, §§ 88, 100.
1472. Dot Registry IRP Declaration, § 100.
1473. Despegar IRP Declaration, § 104.

that Dot Registry's IRP was frivolous and unlikely to succeed on the merits, but the Emergency panelist considered that Dot Registry had raised 'substantial questions going to the merits.'[1474] This finding seems to be inspired by the Emergency panelist's finding that 'the balance of hardships [tipped] decidedly in favor of [Dot Registry]', allowing for a somewhat 'relaxed' showing of a reasonable possibility that the requesting party would succeed on the merits of the claim.[1475] Proceeding with the auction would indeed have made the IRP proceedings meaningless, and, in these circumstances, it seems only logical that the request for interim relief was granted. However, the preliminary finding that Dot Registry had raised substantial questions going to the merits may have been detrimental to ICANN's argument that Dot Registry's IRP was frivolous.

6. Authority of the Panel

a. Arguments Discussed

Dot Registry specifically sought review of the actions by the ICANN Board related to the handling and treatment of the CPEs and the Determination of the BGC on Dot Registry's Reconsideration Requests:

> 'Specifically, Dot Registry seeks review of the Board's actions relating to ICANN's handling and treatment of the Community Priority Evaluations ("CPEs") performed by the Economist Intelligence Unit ("EIU") and the Determination of the ICANN Board Governance Committee ("BGC") on Dot Registry's Reconsideration Request Nos. 14-30 (.LLC), 14-32 (.INC) and 14-33 (.LLP), dated July 24, 2014 (the "Determination").'[1476]

ICANN considered that 'any argument that proposes to re-evaluate the CPE panel's analysis and scoring is not material to [the] IRP.'[1477]

The panel declined to substitute its judgment for the judgment of the CPE panel as to whether Dot Registry was entitled to community priority:

> 'The Panel majority declines to substitute its judgment for the judgment of the CPE as to whether Dot Registry is entitled to Community priority. The IRP Panel is tasked specifically "with comparing contested actions of the Board to the Articles of Incorporation and Bylaws, and with declaring whether the Board has acted consistently with the provisions of those Articles of Incorporation and Bylaws." Bylaws, Art. IV, §3.4. This is what the Panel has done.'[1478]

1474. Dot Registry IRP Order on Request for Emergency Measures of Protection, § 60.
1475. Dot Registry IRP Order on Request for Emergency Measures of Protection, § 59.
1476. Dot Registry's Request for IRP, § 2.
1477. ICANN's Sur-Reply (*Dot Registry*), § 13.
1478. Dot Registry IRP Declaration, § 153.

b. *Noteworthy Points for Analysis*

The IRP panel's refusal to substitute its judgment for the judgment of the CPE panel did not bring the dispute any closer to its resolution. In our view, the IRP panel had sufficient elements to assess whether the EIU's recommendation on Dot Registry's applications was consistent with ICANN's policy on community priority and with the other CPE determinations. At a minimum, the panel could have advised ICANN on how ICANN's acceptance or rejection of a community priority application could be made in line with ICANN's Articles of Incorporation and Bylaws.

To us it is clear that IRP panelists should be chosen on the basis of their expertise in the subject-matter of the IRP, and they should therefore be perfectly comfortable with assessing all the aspects of the underlying dispute. IRP panelists should not shy away from interpreting ICANN's policy, and examining whether or not ICANN's standards and policies have been applied fairly, equitably and non-discriminatorily.

7. Nature of the IRP Declaration

a. *Arguments Discussed*

(1) Binding Nature of the IRP Declaration

Dot Registry made extensive arguments that IRP Declarations must be final and binding on both parties.[1479]

ICANN 'believed that further discussion of this issue [of the binding nature of IRP declarations] would not be particularly useful.'[1480]

The panel decided not to express its views on whether the IRP Declaration was binding or not:

> 'The question has arisen in some prior Declarations of IRP Panels whether Panel declarations are "binding" or "non-binding." While this question is an interesting one, it is clear beyond cavil that this or any Panel's decision on that question is not binding on any court of law that might be called upon to decide this issue.'[1481]

The panel considered a determination on whether or not its declaration is binding unnecessary, as such determination would not be binding on any reviewing court:

> 'Since any declaration we might make on this issue would not be binding on any reviewing court, the Panel does not purport to determine whether its declaration is binding or non-binding.'[1482]

1479. Dot Registry's Response to IRP Panel's Questions of 12 October 2015, §§ 85–95.
1480. ICANN's Response to IRP Panel's Questions of 12 October 2015 (*Dot Registry*), p. 5.
1481. Dot Registry IRP Declaration, § 71.
1482. Dot Registry IRP declaration, § 78.

b. Noteworthy Points for Analysis

(1) Binding Nature of the IRP Declaration

While it is correct that a determination on the binding nature of an IRP declaration is not binding on any reviewing court, such a determination by the IRP panel would nevertheless have been useful to facilitate the declaration's execution.

8. ICANN Board's Decisions Following the IRP Declaration

On 9 August 2016, the ICANN Board accepted the Dot Registry IRP Declaration that named Dot Registry as the prevailing party because the ICANN Board 'failed to exercise due diligence and care in having a reasonable amount of facts in front of them and failed to fulfill its transparency obligations' in ICANN's handling of the CPE process.[1483] In our view, the ICANN Board's acceptance of the Dot Registry IRP Declaration is incompatible with the ICANN Board's acceptance of the Despegar et al. IRP Declaration. Both IRPs criticized the shortcomings of ICANN's handling of the CPE process. But the *Dot Registry* IRP panel considered that these shortcomings amounted to a violation of ICANN's Articles of Incorporation and Bylaws, whereas the *Despegar et al.* IRP panel came to the opposite conclusion (on the basis of a misrepresentation of facts (*supra*)). The close relationship between these two IRP Declarations makes them an indivisible whole, and the ICANN Board should have considered them together to avoid the risk of irreconcilable decisions.

We are of the opinion that the Board can only reconcile these two IRP Declarations by addressing the shortcomings of the CPE process, as recommended in the Despegar et al. IRP Declaration, namely by (i) putting 'a system in place that ensures that marks are allocated on a consistent and predictable basis by different individual evaluators,'[1484] (ii) ensuring 'consistency, both of approach and marking,'[1485] and (iii) affirming that 'transparency and administrative due process' are applicable.[1486] It remains to be seen how the ICANN Board will resolve this situation.

1483. ICANN, *Approved Board Resolutions 2016.08.09.11–2016.08.09.13 – Special Meeting of the ICANN Board*, 9 August 2016, https://www.icann.org/resources/board-material/resolutions-2016-08-09-en.
1484. Despegar et al. IRP Declaration, § 147.
1485. Despegar et al. IRP Declaration, § 147.
1486. Despegar et al. IRP Declaration, § 145.

CHAPTER 6
Lessons Learned

A. INTRODUCTION

The previous chapter, Chapter 5, contains a detailed description and analysis of the IRP cases as well as a consideration of unresolved, pending cases. All IRPs have been initiated by dissatisfied applicants in the various application rounds for generic Top Level Domains (gTLDs). This chapter first provides a brief historical overview of the application rounds so as to be able to put the subsequent gTLD disputes into context. It then describes the major issues, main trends and unresolved problems that have come to light in the past and pending IRPs where an interim or final decision has been taken.

In the next chapter, Chapter 7, we discuss the action points that we believe must be addressed for the proper future functioning of the regulatory framework governing IRPs. New bylaws have now been adopted, and in Chapter 8, we will discuss whether and to what extent these new bylaws address these action points and resolve the problems that we have highlighted here.

B. CONTEXT

As mentioned above (Chapter 2), in 2000, ICANN organized a so-called proof of concept round for new gTLDs. The goal was very precise: to organize a limited round to test the impact on the security and stability of the DNS and to enhance its utility. This first round was a 'beauty contest.' It resulted in newly approved gTLDs .biz, .name, .info, .pro, .aero, .coop and .museum which joined the already existing gTLDs .com, .org, .net, .edu, .gov and .mil.

In 2004, ICANN organized a second round of applications for so-called sponsored TLDs (sTLDs). This time the goal was to extend the system to include TLDs sponsored by a 'community', whether or not that community was already established at the time. This round resulted in ICANN's approval of the sTLDs .post (UPU), .cat (Catalonia), .asia, .jobs, .mobi, .tel, .travel, and – after a lengthy IRP – .xxx.

The third and last round was approved in 2011 after several years of preparation. On this occasion, the goal was to hold a full-blown competition for gTLDs with some exceptional protection mechanisms to protect legal rights, community interests, limited public interests, and applicants of existing or newly applied for TLDs challenging string confusion. This round generated 1,930 applicants for 1,409 unique strings, including 116 Internationalized Domain Names (IDNs), and resulted in an increased number of litigious proceedings related to certain distinct issues.

There were no IRP cases related to the first round, because the IRP as an alternative dispute regulation mechanism did not yet exist. The IRP was introduced in 2002, and was first applied in the second round.

Two parties started an IRP in the second round: ICM Registry, an applicant in the first and second round, and Manwin International, an applicant in the first round.

In the latest round, sixteen IRPs were initiated. To date, only nine IRPs have come to a final resolution (*Booking.com* on *.hotels/.hoteis*; *DCA* on *.africa*; *Vistaprint* on *.webs/.web*; *Merck* on *.merck; Despegar et al.* in two consolidated cases on *.hotel* and *.eco; Donuts* on .sports/.rugby; *Dot Registry* on *.inc/.llc/.llp*; *Corn Lake* on *.charity*[1487]). One case was clearly time-barred and is said to have been 'settled' (*Better Living Management* on *.thai*); the application did not result in a delegation of the TLD. Two other cases were withdrawn (*Afilias* and *Tin Dale* on *.radio,* and *Commercial Connect* on *.shop*). All other IRPs (*Gulf Cooperation Council* (*GCC*) on *.persiangulf*; *dot Sport Limited* on *.sport*; *Asia Green IT Systems* on *.islam/.halal*; another *Commercial Connect* on *.shop*; *Amazon* on *.amazon*) are pending. In two cases, an interim decision has been taken (*GCC* on *.persiangulf*; *Dot Registry* on *.inc/.llc/.llp*).

ICANN's arguments in the latest IRPs have so far – with a very few exceptions – focused on only the latest application round cases, possibly in an attempt to prevent applicants from understanding the historical context of the ADR mechanism and to obfuscate ICANN's variable approach and its decision to amend certain rules. For future IRPs, it is vital to understand the whole historical picture, in particular regarding the involvement of the GAC and the serious issues that have been raised as a result.

1487. For the reasons mentioned in Chapter 5, we find it inappropriate to comment on the *Corn Lake* case at this juncture.

C. MAJOR ISSUES: TRENDS IN IRPS, UNRESOLVED ISSUES

1. Points of Procedure

a. *Applicable Procedural Rules*

Although the IRP mechanism was already contemplated in ICANN's original Bylaws of 6 November 1998, it was not introduced until the adoption of ICANN's new Bylaws of 15 December 2002.

On 19 April 2004, ICANN decided that the IRPs were to be administered by the ICDR of the AAA.[1488]

The IRPs are governed by ICANN's Bylaws and the ICDR Rules. The ICDR establishes the operating rules and procedures.[1489] The ICDR introduced specific Supplementary Procedures for IRPs in 2007. Below, we refer to the Bylaws, the ICDR IRP Supplementary Procedures, and the ICDR Rules as 'the Procedural Rules.'

Order of priority of the Procedural Rules

The Procedural Rules apply generally in the following descending order of priority:

(1) The ICANN Bylaws.
(2) The ICDR IRP Supplementary Procedures.
(3) The ICDR Rules.

The order of priority follows from the principle of procedural party autonomy in international arbitration and ADR. The parties to an arbitration or IRP may agree upon the procedural rules, and ICANN has made use of this ability by introducing a standard offer of an IRP in its Bylaws. ICANN's Bylaws contain specific procedural rules governing the conduct of IRP proceedings, and these rules should be followed by any claimant initiating a request for an IRP. The claimant and ICANN can agree to deviate from certain aspects of the IRP proceedings, *e.g.*, as a result of pre-litigation discussions. In such cases, the specific agreement between the parties should prevail over the ICANN Bylaws.

Contents of the Procedural Rules

'The principal exception to the parties' ultimate procedural autonomy is where the parties' agreement on arbitral procedures violates mandatory rules of procedural fairness and equality, denying one party the opportunity to be heard.'[1490] The choice of institutional rules may also limit the parties' procedural autonomy, and grant procedural power to the arbitral tribunal or panel. For procedures administered by the ICDR,

1488. ICANN Board Resolutions 04.33 – 04.34, 19 April 2004, https://www.icann.org/resources/board-material/resolutions-2004-04-19-en; ICANN, Bylaws as adopted effective 15 December 2002, Article IV(3)(4); ICANN, Bylaws as amended on 11 April 2013, Article IV(3)(7).
1489. ICANN, Bylaws as amended on 11 April 2013, Article IV(3)(8).
1490. G. Born, *International Commercial Arbitration: Volume II, International Arbitral Procedures*, 2nd ed. 2014 Wolters Kluwer Law & Business, p. 2142.

Article 20.1 of the ICDR Rules provides that the panel may 'conduct the arbitration in whatever manner it finds appropriate, provided that the parties are treated with equality and that each party has the right to be heard and is given a fair opportunity to present its case.'[1491] Thus, IRP panels have broad discretion to structure the proceedings in the manner best suited to provide each party the right to be heard and a fair opportunity to present its case. Neither the Supplementary Procedures nor the Bylaws contain a provision to the contrary. In rare circumstances, an IRP panel may set aside procedural agreements between the parties, *e.g.*, if the panel considers that these agreements do not give the necessary assurance that each party will be given a fair opportunity to present its case. The *DCA* panel made use of this authority to set aside the limitations ICANN tried to impose via its Bylaws on the conduct of oral hearings.[1492]

The ICDR Rules have been updated from time to time, but no substantial changes have been made that would impact IRPs. More controversially, dramatic changes to the IRP's Procedural Rules were made in the Bylaws during the evaluation phase related to applications for New gTLDs and, thus, *after* applicants had filed applications for new gTLDs and *before* disputes could arise. ICANN also introduced a so-called CEP in its Bylaws[1493] and specific rules for CEPs were laid down in a separate document.[1494] Many of these changes are also reflected in the updated ICDR IRP Supplementary Procedures.[1495]

The applicable Procedural Rules were considered in detail in the decision on *.webs/.web*.[1496] The panel in that case revealed inconsistent language between the three documents constituting the Procedural Rules and it attempted to give a consistent interpretation of all the applicable rules (*see* below, *Binding nature of the IRP declaration*).

b. *Jurisdiction of the IRP Panel*

(1) Mission of the IRP panel

Ever since the creation of the IRP, the task of an IRP panel has been to check contested actions by the ICANN Board against the obligations set out in ICANN's Articles of

1491. International Centre for Dispute Resolution, *International Arbitration Rules*, Article 20.1 (1 June 2014).
1492. DCA Declaration on IRP Procedure, § 84; DCA 3rd Declaration on IRP Procedure, §§ 30, 33–34, 38; *infra* Chapter 6.C.1.i.
1493. ICANN, Bylaws as amended on 11 April 2013, Article IV(3)(14) – IV(3)(17).
1494. ICANN, *Cooperative Engagement Process – Requests for Independent Review*, 11 April 2013, https://www.icann.org/en/system/files/files/cep-11apr13-en.pdf.
1495. According to the website of the ICDR, the ICDR IRP Supplementary Procedures were adapted on 21 December 2011. But this updated version refers to changes that were in fact introduced only with the Bylaws change in 2013. As a result, it is doubtful that the date of December 2011 is correct, and it is unclear when the updated version was posted and became applicable.
1496. Vistaprint IRP Declaration, §§ 132 and 133.

Incorporation and Bylaws, and to declare whether or not the Board has acted consistently with the provisions of the Articles of Incorporation and the Bylaws.[1497]

IRP panels have consistently accepted that their independent review covers both actions and inactions of the ICANN Board.[1498] Doubt remains as to what constitutes an actionable inaction, in particular when third parties have been involved in the decision-making process. The *Vistaprint* IRP panel ruled that it was not tasked with reviewing the actions or decisions of ICANN staff or other third parties who may have been involved in ICANN activities or have provided services to ICANN.[1499] The *Despegar et al.* IRP panel ruling was more nuanced and held that the ICANN Board was responsible for ensuring compliance by ICANN staff with ICANN's Articles of Incorporation and Bylaws,[1500] but that there was not necessarily a flow-through of ICANN's obligations to third parties essentially acting on ICANN's behalf.[1501] In the *Donuts* case, the majority of the panel considered that it could not review acts and omissions by other actors, unless they could be attributed to the ICANN Board.[1502] However, the view of the dissenting panelist in the *Donuts* case – namely that ICANN could not avoid its responsibility simply by contracting out its obligations – was followed by the majority in the *Dot Registry* case.[1503] It seems that the decision by the *Dot Registry* IRP panel was inspired by the specific contractual relationship between ICANN and its third-party evaluators, however, and although these recent decisions are encouraging, case law is not yet settled on the issue of whether the ICANN Board remains responsible for actions by third parties who are assisting ICANN in the performance of its mission.

(2) Waiver of Rights by the Applicants

New gTLD applicants in the latest round were required to agree to the TLD application terms and conditions which imposed a waiver of the applicants' rights to challenge ICANN's decisions on applications in court, or in any other judicial forum, and which instead allowed applicants to use the IRP for the purposes of challenging any final decision made by ICANN with respect to their application(s).[1504]

Applicants could possibly argue that the waiver is unenforceable, as it could be considered unconscionable or contrary to public policy, and a California court can refuse to enforce a contract that is unconscionable or contrary to public policy. A court

1497. Bylaws as adopted effective 15 December 2002 (https://www.icann.org/resources/unthemed-pages/bylaws-2002-12-15-en), Article IV(3); Current ICANN Bylaws, Article IV(3).
1498. *See e.g.*, Booking.com IRP Declaration, § 53; DCA Final IRP Declaration, §§ 107–109; Vistaprint IRP Declaration, § 119; *see also* § 123; Merck IRP Declaration, § 17; Despegar et al. IRP Declaration, § 58; Donuts IRP Declaration, § 8; Dot Registry IRP Declaration, § 70.
1499. Vistaprint IRP Declaration, § 127.
1500. Despegar et al. IRP Declaration, § 104.
1501. Despegar et al. IRP Declaration, § 150.
1502. Donuts IRP Declaration, § 57.
1503. Dot Registry IRP Declaration, § 89.
1504. ICANN, *New gTLD Applicant Guidebook 4 June 2012*, https://newgtlds.icann.org/en/applicants/agb/guidebook-full-04jun12-en.pdf, Module 6-4.

will find a contract unconscionable if it is both procedurally and substantively unconscionable. The waiver (and the indemnification provisions) in the ICANN application terms and conditions could be considered unconscionable because the contract is a contract of adhesion with substantive results that greatly favor ICANN. A court will find a contract contrary to public policy if it violates an express statute, or if the interest in its enforcement is outweighed by the public policy interest against enforcement of the provision. Finally, an applicant could argue fraudulent inducement by alleging that ICANN failed to accurately inform the applicant of its decision-making procedures and criteria and that, had it done so, the applicant would not have agreed to the waiver and indemnification provisions. In this respect, applicants could claim that they were not sufficiently informed about ICANN's accountability mechanisms and the changes that occurred during the evaluation period. They could argue that they could not have predicted that ICANN was going to restrictively interpret its obligations under the RfR process by refusing to verify compliance with its overall obligations under its Articles of Incorporation and Bylaws.

To date, in a case where the claimant alleged fraudulent actions by ICANN, one California court has held that there are serious questions regarding the enforceability of ICANN's waiver.[1505]

The question of whether or not the waiver is enforceable should have no impact on the binding nature of the IRP. Only California courts are competent to rule on the issue. An IRP panel cannot make a declaration on the validity of the waiver, but should rule according to its own competence, and has jurisdiction to decide the validity and effect of the dispute resolution clause. Indeed, the existence of the waiver gives applicants an additional basis to argue that the IRP constitutes binding arbitration: the inclusion of the waiver should help IRP panels to understand ICANN's intention to have the IRP as an alternative to court proceedings. Where an ADR mechanism serves as an alternative to court proceedings, the proceedings must comply with minimum standards and international due process considerations, and constitutional rights come into play. (*See* Chapter 6.C.4.a below, *Binding nature of the IRP declaration*)

c. *Nomination, Appointment, Removal and Replacement of Panelists*

Since 11 April 2013, the Bylaws have provided that there should be an omnibus standing panel from which each specific IRP panel is to be selected. Either party is allowed to request that the IRP be considered by a one- or three-member panel. The chair of the standing panel is to determine the size of each IRP panel, taking into account the wishes of the parties and the complexity of the issues presented.[1506]

1505. *DCA v. ICANN & ZA Central Registry*, In Chambers Order re Plaintiff's Motion for Preliminary Injunction, Case No. 16-CV-00862 RGK, 12 April 2016.
1506. ICANN, Bylaws as amended on 11 April 2013, Article IV(3)(9) ; ICDR IRP Supplementary Procedures, Article 3.

Although ICANN has talked to several individuals with a view to listing them for the standing panel, the omnibus standing panel itself is not (yet) in place. Consequently, IRP panelists are appointed in accordance with the ICDR Rules, which grant a large freedom to the parties to agree upon a procedure for appointing panelists. If no agreement is reached, the ICDR will decide whether the IRP panel should be a one- or three-member panel, and parties will be invited to mutually designate the panelist(s).[1507] If the nomination(s) are not made in time, the ICDR will appoint the panelists after consultation with the parties.[1508]

In some cases, ICANN has expressed its preference for a one-member panel. However, in all IRPs to date, ICANN has accepted that a three-member panel be appointed.

In two IRPs (*ICM* and *Booking.com*) the co-panelists were nominated successively by first the claimant and then ICANN. It is not public knowledge how the co-panelists were nominated in the *Manwin* case.

In the *Vistaprint*, *Despegar et al.* and *dot Sport Limited* cases, the claimants proposed the simultaneous nomination of the co-panelists by both the claimant and ICANN within an agreed deadline. ICANN accepted this appointment procedure without significant discussion.

In theory, the nomination process is achieved within forty-five days,[1509] and ICANN has agreed on shorter nomination procedures. ICANN was itself granted an extension in the *Booking.com* case and three consecutive extensions in the *Vistaprint* case.

In the majority of cases, ICANN agreed that the nomination of the chair should occur within twenty days following the nomination of the two party-appointed co-panelists. However, once again, in practice, extensions have been granted.

In cases where we have been personally involved, we have always agreed to extensions so as to avoid a situation in which the ICDR (as a fallback solution) appoints both one of the co-panelists and the chair. Parties have every interest in knowing who the panel members are so as to prevent the appointment of people lacking sufficient knowhow or experience.

So far, no panel members have been removed from their panel. One panel member in the *DCA* case died and had to be replaced, but this occurred without any complications. Also, the replacement had no impact on the orders that the panel had already released.

In the *Dot Sport Limited* case, ICANN nominated a panelist who then withdrew because of a conflict of interest. As a result of the withdrawal, ICANN had the advantage of knowing the identity of the claimant's appointed panelist before it nominated its replacement panelist.

1507. ICDR Rules, Article 11; ICANN, Bylaws as amended on 11 April 2013, Article IV(3)(6); ICDR IRP Supplementary Procedures, Article 3.
1508. ICDR Rules, Article 12(4).
1509. ICDR Rules, Article 12.

Assistance from the ICDR has sometimes been required for the selection of the panel's chair. In the *Booking.com* case, the co-panelists were unable to agree on a chair on the basis of the candidates they proposed. The ICDR proposed a shortlist from which the co-panelists chose the chair. In the *Vistaprint* case, the ICDR was asked to choose from a two-person shortlist proposed by the co-panelists. In the *Despegar et al.* and the *Dot Sport Limited* cases, the co-panelists agreed on a chair without assistance from the ICDR. There is no publicly available information on nomination issues in other cases.

Overall, it seems that the nomination of panelists has occurred smoothly, and has resulted in the appointment of appropriately qualified panelists. ICANN has nominated some panelists more than once. Other panelists were appointed more than once by different parties in different cases.

d. *Standing*

Any person materially affected by a decision or action by the ICANN Board may submit a request for an IRP.[1510] With the Bylaws of 11 April 2013, ICANN clarified what is required for a person to be considered 'materially affected':

> 'In order to be materially affected, the person must suffer injury or harm that is directly and causally connected to the Board's alleged violation of the Bylaws or the Articles of Incorporation, and not as a result of third parties acting in line with the Board's action.'[1511]

The Applicant Guidebook for the third round (AGB) provides that any applicant may use ICANN's accountability mechanisms, which includes IRPs, to challenge any final decision made by ICANN with respect to the application.[1512] IRP panels seem to accept that new gTLD applicants have standing, but most panels have limited the scope of their independent review to the actions and inactions of the ICANN Board.[1513]

The IRP panel has the authority to summarily dismiss any requests that are without standing, lacking in substance, or that are frivolous or vexatious.[1514]

The second version of the ICDR IRP Supplementary Procedures provides that a claim may also be summarily dismissed if a request is querulous, or where a prior IRP on the same issue has been concluded with a declaration.[1515] The latter addition seems to have been inspired by ICANN's position in the *Manwin* case, where the claimant arguably sought to overturn the results of a previous IRP decision. However, a situation such as this has not presented itself since.

1510. ICANN, Bylaws as amended on 11 April 2013, Article IV(3)(2).
1511. ICANN, Bylaws as amended on 11 April 2013, Article IV(3)(2), *in fine*.
1512. ICANN, *New gTLD Applicant Guidebook 4 June 2012*, https://newgtlds.icann.org/en/applicants/agb/guidebook-full-04jun12-en.pdf, Module 6-4.
1513. *See* Chapter 6.C.1.b(1) *supra*.
1514. ICANN, Bylaws as amended on 11 April 2013, Article IV(3)(11).
1515. ICDR IRP Supplementary Procedures, Article 6.

Conversely, there have been cases in which we would argue the claimants were not materially affected because of the weakness of their underlying case. A weak case on the underlying merits means that a claimant is unlikely to succeed in the underlying dispute – even if it prevailed in the IRP. We find it surprising that in cases such as these, ICANN has not stressed the claimants' lack of standing; such a claimant could not argue that it was materially affected, even though there might have been procedural irregularities. While allowing such cases to proceed may benefit the public interest, for the claimant, and for ICANN, these cases are largely a waste of resources.[1516]

e. *Time Bar*

The Bylaws of 11 April 2013 introduced the time bar rule, providing that a request for an IRP must be filed within thirty days of the posting of the minutes of the Board meeting that allegedly demonstrate a violation by ICANN of its Articles of Incorporation or Bylaws.[1517]

However, following the initiation of a CEP, the deadline for filing a request for IRP may be extended. A request for CEP must be filed within fifteen days of the posting of the minutes of the Board meeting. The time to file a request for IRP is extended for each day of the CEP. In the absence of mutual written agreement, the extension cannot be more than fourteen days.[1518] In practice, while the deadline has been extended almost indefinitely in some cases, in others ICANN has insisted that an IRP be initiated.

In one case, the claimant did not start a CEP and waited almost six months after the posting of the minutes of the Board meeting before initiating a request for IRP. ICANN invoked the time bar, and the matter was closed shortly after the filing of ICANN's response brief.[1519]

ICANN has also relied on the time bar rule to argue that certain claims, made in IRPs in the latest round and challenging ICANN's policy, were time-barred. The IRP panels in the *Booking.com* and *Vistaprint* cases confirmed that these particular claims were indeed time-barred. The *Donuts* IRP panel adopted the reasoning of the *Booking.com* and *Vistaprint* panels without further debate. The issue was not discussed in any detail in the *DCA*, the *Merck*, the *Despegar et al.* and the *Dot Registry* cases; the panels in those cases focused on the implementation of ICANN's policy.

However, in our view there is an outstanding issue regarding the time bar rule. When claimants in the latest round filed their applications for a gTLD in 2012, there was no time limit for bringing a request for IRP. Applicants who considered that they risked being materially affected by ICANN's application of the AGB in contravention of the Articles of Incorporation and/or Bylaws, had a legitimate expectation that they would

1516. *See e.g.*, DCA IRP and Dot Registry IRP.
1517. ICANN, Bylaws as amended on 11 April 2013, Article IV(3)(3).
1518. ICANN, *Cooperative Engagement Process – Requests for Independent Review*, 11 April 2013, https://www.icann.org/en/system/files/files/cep-11apr13-en.pdf.
1519. Better Living Management Co, Ltd. IRP, Letter of Closure, 17 July 2014.

be able to challenge the AGB as well as ICANN's implementation thereof. ICANN's decision to introduce a time bar for challenging Board decisions was introduced long after the new gTLD application window closed (compare Article IV(3)(3) of the previous Bylaws with Article IV(3)(3) of the amended Bylaws of 11 April 2013). As a result, the time bar rule can, in our opinion, only apply to Board actions taken after 11 April 2013,[1520] and IRP panels are authorized to scrutinize all of ICANN's actions and inactions regarding claimants' applications for consistency with ICANN's Articles of Incorporation and Bylaws.

We consider IRP case law not to be settled on this issue. In the *Booking.com* case, the panel took the narrow view that a process should have been challenged within thirty days following the first implementation of the AGB.[1521] In the *Vistaprint* case, the panel considered, in an *obiter dictum*, that the time for challenging a Guidebook standard had passed, but the panel did not rule on the possibility to challenge the Guidebook's policies or its implementation.[1522]

These decisions did not take into account the fact that the time bar was introduced only after the final version of the Guidebook was published and did not exist at the time applicants filed an application for a new gTLD.

In addition, the panels' reasoning in the *Booking.com* and *Vistaprint* cases seems at odds with the finding of the emergency arbitrator in the *GCC* case, who considered that a decision remains subject to possible review by the IRP panel even if it was made entirely pursuant to the Guidebook.[1523] The interim decision in the *GCC* case seems in line with established case law of the U.S. Supreme Court, according to which a policy's age or the age of an implementing regulation cannot be used as an excuse for clear inconsistency with fundamental legal principles.[1524]

When applying these principles to the standards and policies in the Guidebook, it should be possible to challenge the legality of these standards and policies in view of ICANN's more fundamental obligations. The time that has lapsed since the adoption of the Guidebook should not serve as an excuse for the violation of fundamental rules in individual cases. Hence, it should be possible to question the legality of the Guidebook's standards and policies as well as the legality of the Guidebook's implementation. At the hearing in the *Despegar et al.* case, ICANN conceded that no time bar argument was raised with respect to the Guidebook's implementation, but only in relation to challenges to the legality of the Guidebook's provisions. The *Despegar et al.* IRP panel and the IRP panels in subsequent cases focused on ICANN's implementation of policies, effectively making the time bar argument a non-issue.

1520. *See United States v. Security Indus. Bank*, 459 U.S. 79 (1982).
1521. Booking.com IRP Declaration, § 129.
1522. Vistaprint IRP Declaration, § 172.
1523. GCC Interim Declaration, § 79.
1524. *See e.g., Brown v. Gardner*, 513 U.S. 115, 122 (1994); *Rapanos v. United States*, 547 U.S. 715, 752 (2006).

f. Emergency Proceedings

Under the previous ICDR Rules, Article 12 of the ICDR IRP Supplementary Procedures explicitly excluded the possibility of emergency procedures and the appointment of an emergency arbitrator. However, since the ICDR's adoption of new Rules on 1 June 2014, Article 12 of the ICDR IRP Supplementary Procedures is no longer consistent with the ICDR Rules. Indeed, before the 2014 change in the ICDR Rules, the framework for interim or emergency measures was unclear: Article IV(3)(11)(d) of the ICANN Bylaws[1525] provides that the IRP panel may recommend that the ICANN Board stay any action or decision, or that the Board take any interim action. Article 7 of the ICDR IRP Supplementary Procedures adds that the chair of the omnibus standing panel may provide a recommendation on the stay, if the IRP panel is not yet compromised. However, there is currently no omnibus standing-panel in place and no chair has been appointed. As a result, in cases where the IRP panel has not yet been appointed, it is not clear to whom a request for urgent interim relief should be addressed.

In practice, both before and after the change in the ICDR Rules on 1 June 2014, ICANN has accepted that applicants can use the emergency proceedings. For example, a request for emergency relief was addressed to the IRP panel in the *DCA* case before the change in the Rules. In that case, the IRP panel was already in place when the claimant expressed its request for emergency relief, and ICANN explicitly agreed to the possibility of emergency proceedings. After the change in the ICDR Rules, ICANN has agreed in different IRPs to the possibility of emergency proceedings and to the appointment of an emergency arbitrator by the ICDR.

Interim measures were granted in the *DCA*, *GCC* and *Dot Registry* cases.[1526] In the *Donuts* case concerning .sports, .rugby and .ski, the request for emergency relief was withdrawn after ICANN agreed to stay the delegation of these gTLDs.[1527] In the *Commercial Connect* case concerning .shop, the claimant withdrew its request for emergency relief within one week. No other requests for interim measures or emergency relief have been made, nor are we aware of any circumstances that would have required interim relief in any of the other cases, as there were no indications that ICANN was going to take any action that would impede the handling or the usefulness of the IRP. (*E.g.*, in the *Booking.com*, *Vistaprint* and *Despegar et al.* cases, ICANN maintained the contention sets that could be impacted by the outcome of the IRP.)

1525. Article 4(3)(o) in the Amended Bylaws of 1 October 2016.
1526. DCA IRP Decision on Interim Measures of Protection; GCC IRP Interim Declaration on Emergency Request for Interim Measures of Protection; Dot Registry IRP Emergency Independent Review Panelist's Recommendation on Request for Emergency Measures of Protection.
1527. Donuts IRP Resolution of Request for Emergency Relief.

g. *Written/Oral Arguments*

The 2013 ICANN Bylaws and the ICDR IRP Supplementary Procedures favor the handling of proceedings in writing and without oral argument.[1528] The request for IRP and ICANN's response must each be limited to twenty-five pages, double-spaced, using a 12-point font.[1529] Parties may submit an unlimited amount of documentary evidence supporting their positions.[1530] There is no pre-established page limit for additional submissions.

In practice, IRP panels have discussed the admissibility and the length of additional submissions in preliminary hearings. With the exception of the *DCA* and *Dot Registry* cases in which lengthy submissions were admitted, additional submissions have tended not to exceed ten to twenty-five pages.

h. *Hearings*

The focus of the IRP remains on cost-efficient and straightforward proceedings. Both the ICDR IRP Supplementary Procedures and the Bylaws as amended on 11 April 2013 recognize the possibility of telephone or in-person hearings. They specify however that such hearings should be the exception, and should be limited to argument only.[1531] The previous version of the Bylaws did not explicitly provide for the possibility of in-person hearings. However, that did not prevent the IRP panel in the *ICM* case from organizing in-person hearings.

In all cases, with the exception of the *Merck* case, oral hearings have been requested by claimants. It is difficult to understand the claimant's position in the *Merck* case. The absence of an oral hearing deprived the IRP Panel of the opportunity for an in-depth debate, involving the questioning of the parties or the parties' representatives. Experience has shown that oral hearings are most helpful for both parties and panels, especially in view of the fact that IRPs involve complex legal issues for which there is little or no precedent.

ICANN has always agreed to participate in an oral hearing. However, it has on occasion insisted that the hearing be a telephone hearing only. Requests for interim relief have always been discussed in telephone hearings.[1532] Hearings on the merits have been conducted via telephone, via video conference and in person. The following table summarizes the nature of the hearings on the merits in all past IRPs:

1528. ICANN, Bylaws as amended on 11 April 2013, Article IV(3)(12); ICDR IRP Supplementary Procedures, Article 4.
1529. ICANN, Bylaws as amended on 11 April 2013, Article IV(3)(5).
1530. ICANN, Bylaws as amended on 11 April 2013, Article IV(3)(5).
1531. ICANN, Bylaws as amended on 11 April 2013, Article IV(3)(12); ICDR IRP Supplementary Procedures, Article 4.
1532. DCA IRP Decision on Interim Measures of Protection, § 25; GCC IRP Interim Declaration on Emergency Request for Interim Measures of Protection, § 4; Dot Registry IRP Emergency Independent Review Panelist's Recommendation on Request for Emergency Measures of Protection, § 7.

IRP Case	*Telephone Hearing*	*Video Conference*	*In-Person Hearing*
ICM			✓
Manwin	✓[1533]		
Booking.com	✓		
DCA			✓ [1534]
Vistaprint	✓		
Better Living Management Co, Ltd.	N/A	N/A	N/A[1535]
Merck	N/A	N/A	N/A
Dot Registry		✓	
Donuts			✓
GCC	✓ [1536]		
Despegar et al.	✓		
Dot Sport Limited		✓	
Corn Lake		✓	
Afilias et al.	N/A	N/A	N/A[1537]
Asia Green	tbd[1538]	tbd	tbd
Commercial Connect	✓		
Amazon			✓

Since the amendments of 11 April 2013, oral hearings have been limited to telephone hearings in the majority of the cases. These telephone hearings have lasted between 2.5 and 3 hours. It should be noted that claimants in the *Booking.com*, *Vistaprint* and *Despegar et al.* cases expressly agreed to telephone hearings. We are not aware of any case in which an IRP panel has decided to organize a telephone hearing in the face of a claimant's opposition to such a hearing.

In the *Dot Sport Limited* case, the claimant maintained its request for an in-person hearing even after the panel had expressed its provisional view that the most efficient way to proceed was with a telephone hearing. The panel ultimately decided to hold a video conference hearing, with all the panel members attending from one location.

1533. The hearing was limited to arguments on standing and preclusion. The proceedings were stopped before a hearing on the merits was organized.
1534. The claimants requested an oral hearing via videoconference, but the IRP Panel preferred in-person hearings.
1535. The matter was closed on 17 July 2014 before the issuance of a procedural order.
1536. A preliminary hearing took place on 6 January 2016. A final hearing has been scheduled for 17 May 2016. It is not known whether that hearing will be via telephone or otherwise.
1537. The claimants withdrew their request for IRP on 18 May 2016, *i.e.*, before a procedural order was made on the course of proceedings.
1538. To be determined.

In the *DCA* case, the claimant requested a hearing via video conference. However, the IRP panel preferred an in-person hearing.

In-person hearings have typically lasted much longer than telephone hearings: five days in the *ICM* case, two days in the *DCA* case and 3.25 hours in the *Donuts* case.

In the *Dot Registry* case, an 8-hour hearing via video conference has been scheduled. The video conference hearing in the *Dot Sport Limited* case lasted for about three hours.

Hearings via telephone or video conference are cost-efficient and provide the means for a focused debate. They require the panel to be very well prepared. However, there is a potential disadvantage in reduced communication between the parties. *E.g.*, it is more difficult for a claimant to observe the panel's attention level than during an in-person hearing. Indeed, in telephone hearings, the panel's attention level can only be deduced from the questions asked by the different panelists. Furthermore, there is also a greater risk of misunderstandings between the parties involved. In the *Booking.com* case, the panel considered that Booking.com's claim concerning discrimination was largely unexpressed during the hearing. In our view, that was not the case. Also, the panel in the *Despegar et al.* case mischaracterized the claimants' request for relief on the basis of its interpretation of the oral argument. There is a chance that these misunderstandings could have been avoided had there been an in-person hearing; in any event, these examples demonstrate the importance of transcripts and post-hearing submissions.

i. Witnesses and Expert Witnesses

Since the amendments made on 11 April 2013, the ICANN Bylaws and the ICDR IRP Supplementary Procedures state that all evidence, including witness statements, must be submitted in writing and in advance, and that hearings will be limited to arguments only (*i.e.*, without witness testimony).[1539]

Written witness statements and expert testimony has been produced by claimants in the majority of the cases, and its admissibility has never been the subject of discussion.

In the *DCA* case, the claimant requested that witnesses be examined at the hearing, but agreed with ICANN that no cross-examination was necessary. The *DCA* IRP panel decided to allow live witness testimony at the hearing, permitting the panel to examine the witnesses and counsel to the parties to ask follow-up questions in relation to the questions posed by the panel.[1540] In other words, the panel allowed for limited cross-examination. The *DCA* panel also required certain identified witnesses to be

1539. ICANN, Bylaws as amended on 11 April 2013, Article IV(3)(12); ICDR IRP Supplementary Procedures, Article 4.

1540. DCA Declaration on IRP Procedure, § 84; DCA 3rd Declaration on IRP Procedure, §§ 30, 33–34, 38.

physically present at the hearing, stating that failure to attend would entitle the panel to draw the necessary inferences and reach the appropriate conclusions regarding that witness's declaration.[1541]

The *DCA IRP* panel did not consider itself bound by the limitations on oral hearings set forth in the ICANN Bylaws and Supplementary Procedures. The panel determined that it had 'the power to interpret and determine the IRP Procedure'[1542] and that '[n]othing in the Supplementary Procedures either expressly or implicitly conflicts with or overrides the general and broad powers that [...] the ICDR Rules confer upon the panel to interpret and determine the manner in which the IRP proceedings are to be conducted and to assure that each party is given a fair opportunity to present its case.'[1543] The panel took the unanimous view that it was unable to 'ensure that the parties [in an] IRP are treated with equality and that each party has the right to be heard and is given a fair opportunity to present its case with respect to the mandate the panel has been given, if as ICANN submits, "ICANN's Bylaws do not permit any examination of witnesses by the parties or the Panel during the hearing".'[1544]

In the *Dot Registry* case, the claimant tried to introduce a witness of fact at the hearing. The claimant intended to call on its executive director to present the factual background to the pleadings.[1545] ICANN objected, arguing that the rules did not permit witnesses to testify.[1546] In our view, refusing a party's executive the right to present its case seems a disproportionate and unnecessary limitation on a party's right to be heard.

j. Document Production

The Procedural Rules provide very few requirements on document production that are specific to IRPs. The ICDR IRP Supplementary Procedures state that '[a]ll necessary evidence to demonstrate the requestor's claims that ICANN violated its Bylaws or Articles of Incorporation should be part of the submission.'[1547] 'The submission' in this provision arguably refers to a claimant's initial written submission. However, it may not always be possible to submit all the evidence with the initial written submission. *E.g.*, evidence may be withheld by ICANN, new facts may arise later, and evidence which was not considered necessary to demonstrate the initial claims may become necessary to counter ICANN's arguments.

1541. DCA 3rd Declaration on IRP Procedure, § 37.
1542. DCA Declaration on IRP Procedure, §§ 20, 129.
1543. DCA Declaration on IRP Procedure, § 50; *see also* DCA Declaration on IRP Procedure, § 51: 'To the contrary, the Panel finds support in the 'Independent Review Process Recommendations' filed by ICANN, which indicate that the Panel has the discretion to run the IRP proceedings in the manner it thinks appropriate.'
1544. DCA 3rd Declaration on IRP Procedure, §§ 25–26.
1545. Dot Registry IRP Hearing Transcript, pp. 37–42.
1546. Dot Registry IRP Hearing Transcript, pp. 40–41.
1547. ICDR IRP Supplementary Procedures, Article 5.

The ICANN Bylaws and the ICDR IRP Supplementary Procedures do not satisfactorily deal with situations such as these, where the production of additional evidence may be required in order for the parties to be treated fairly and to afford both sides a reasonable opportunity to present their case. Consequently, the general provisions of Articles 20 and 21 of the ICDR Rules should apply. Article 20(4) of the ICDR Rules provides the general rule that, at any time during the proceedings, the tribunal may order the parties to produce documents, exhibits, or other evidence it deems necessary or appropriate. Article 21 of the ICDR Rules sets forth the standard principles for documentary exchange.[1548] These principles give the panel a broad discretion regarding how it organizes documentary exchange and they are comparable to the rules on documentary exchange taken up in the International Bar Association (IBA) Rules on the Taking of Evidence in International Arbitration.[1549]

In practice, ICANN has not challenged requests to produce new evidence with additional submissions. However, ICANN has objected to the forced production of evidence, claiming that the requested documents were either not sufficiently detailed or were irrelevant to the outcome of the case. In cases where claimants have requested the forced production of evidence, these requests have been granted by the IRP panel, despite ICANN's objections.[1550] However, ICANN has been allowed to invoke litigation privilege for communications with its legal staff and outside counsel. ICANN has been criticized for the overuse of this litigation privilege, which some suspect has been employed as a means of preventing the disclosure of relevant information.[1551]

k. *Timing for the Decision*

Article 30(1) of the ICDR Rules provides that, '[u]nless otherwise agreed by the parties, specified by law, or determined by the Administrator, the final award shall be made no later than 60 days from the date of the closing of the hearing.' As there is no deviating rule in the ICANN Bylaws or the ICDR IRP Supplementary Procedures, the final IRP declaration must be made within sixty days from the date of the closing of the hearing. To date, we are not aware of any IRP declaration in which the panel did not comply with this rule, or of a panel's non-compliance giving rise to any issues. However, in the *Vistaprint* case, the IRP panel requested two extensions. The first request for extension was granted by the parties without any discussion. Upon the second request for extension, the claimant requested that the extension be limited to a few days. The IRP panel and the ICDR responded positively to this request.

1548. The default principles for documentary exchange were not included in the ICDR Rules before 1 June 2014. However, Article 21 of the ICDR Rules merely incorporates the ICDR Guidelines for Arbitrators concerning Exchanges of Information which apply in all international cases administered by the ICDR commenced after 31 May 2008.

1549. International Bar Association, *IBA Rules on the Taking of Evidence in International Arbitration, adopted by a resolution of the IBA Council*, 29 May 2010.

1550. DCA IRP Declaration on the IRP Procedure, §§ 59–60; Dot Registry IRP Procedural Order No. 3; Corn Lake IRP Procedural Order No. 2.

1551. Dot Registry IRP Declaration, § 128.

l. Duration

There is no overall maximum duration given for an IRP. However, since 11 April 2013, the Bylaws state that the IRP panel should strive to issue its written declaration no later than six months after the filing of the request for IRP.[1552] In practice, the shortest case duration exceeds eleven months.[1553] One case that was without oral hearing and had only limited additional submissions took almost seventeen months.[1554] So far, the longest case duration exceeded twenty months.[1555]

m. Costs

The party not prevailing according to the IRP declaration is ordinarily responsible for bearing all the costs of the IRP Provider.[1556] These costs include the costs of the ICDR and of the IRP panel members.

Each party to IRP proceedings bears its own expenses.[1557] This means that each party is liable to pay its own fees for representation. However, the IRP panel is obliged to award ICANN all reasonable fees and costs incurred by ICANN in the IRP, including legal fees, if a claimant who is subsequently unsuccessful in the IRP did not first, in good faith, avail itself of the cooperative engagement or conciliation process.[1558] To our knowledge, ICANN has never claimed the reimbursement of its reasonable fees and costs for this reason.

In exceptional cases, the IRP panel may allocate up to half of the costs of the IRP Provider to the prevailing party depending on the circumstances, including a consideration of the reasonableness of the parties' positions and their contribution to the public interest.[1559] IRP panels have availed themselves of this opportunity in three cases. In the *Booking.com* and *Despegar et al.* cases, ICANN was held responsible for half the costs of the IRP Provider. In the *Vistaprint* case, ICANN was held responsible for 40% of these costs.

The allocation of costs may also be influenced by the parties' conduct in the proceedings. In accordance with Article 20(7) of the ICDR Rules, the IRP panel may allocate

1552. ICANN, Bylaws as amended on 11 April 2013, Article IV(3)(18).
1553. In the *Despegar et al.* case, the Requests for IRP were filed on 4 and 13 March 2015, and the IRP Declaration was issued on 11 February 2016.
1554. The *Merck* case was filed in July 2014 and the IRP Declaration was issued on 10 December 2015.
1555. In the *DCA* case a deficient notice of IRP was filed on 24 October 2013, and the Final IRP Declaration was issued on 9 July 2015; in the *Dot Registry* case, the notice of IRP was filed on 22 September 2014, and the IRP Declaration was issued on 29 July 2016.
1556. ICANN, Bylaws as amended on 11 April 2013, Article IV(3)(18); *see also* ICDR IRP Supplementary Procedures, Article 11.
1557. ICANN, Bylaws as amended on 11 April 2013, Article IV(3)(18).
1558. ICANN, Bylaws as amended on 11 April 2013, Article IV(3)(16); ICDR IRP Supplementary Procedures, Article 11.
1559. ICANN, Bylaws as amended on 11 April 2013, Article IV(3)(18); *see also* ICDR IRP Supplementary Procedures, Article 11.

costs to protect the efficiency and integrity of the arbitration. According to the *Corn Lake* IRP panel, it can use the power to allocate costs to address unreasonable requests for disclosure as well as unreasonable objections or failures to fully perform reasonable requests for disclosure.[1560] A failure to comply with an order for information exchange may be taken into account in allocating costs.[1561] To date, no IRP panel has allocated costs in relation to unreasonable requests for disclosure or a failure to comply with an interim order.

In the *Donuts* case, the majority of the panel penalized the claimant for making tenuous arguments by allocating all the costs of the proceedings to the claimant, despite the contribution of the case to the public interest.[1562] This decision was severely criticized by the dissenting panelist.[1563]

2. Applicable law

a. *Sources*

ICANN is a non-profit public benefit corporation that was established under the laws of the State of California on 30 September 1998.

ICANN is obliged to ensure that it continues to operate as a non-profit corporation in accordance with the California Corporations Code, and it is duty-bound to devote primary attention to the promotion of its social mission. However, California corporate law does not, as ICANN argues, prevent the organization from submitting its decisions to binding independent review on the basis that the Board should 'retain responsibility for decision-making.' By virtue of Article 5132 of the California Corporations Code a corporation's articles of incorporation and bylaws may limit the Board's decision-making authority. ICANN did exactly that when it introduced the IRP into its Bylaws.

According to its Articles of Incorporation, ICANN must act 'for the benefit of the Internet community as a whole' and 'in conformity with relevant principles of international law and applicable international conventions and local law and, to the extent appropriate and consistent with these Articles and its Bylaws, through open and transparent processes that enable competition and open entry in Internet-related markets.'[1564]

California law can also help in interpreting ICANN's fundamental obligations. *E.g.*, the obligation to act in good faith is a general principle of law that is found in both international law and in the corporate law of California.[1565]

1560. Corn Lake IRP Procedural Order No. 2.
1561. ICDR Rules, Article 21(9).
1562. Donuts IRP Declaration, § 209, n. 226; § 234, n. 240.
1563. Donuts IRP Declaration, Dissenting Opinion, p. 8.
1564. Articles of Incorporation, Article 4.
1565. Nuclear Tests (*Austl. v. Fr.*), 1974 I.C.J. 253, 268 (20 Dec.) (merits); *see also* Land and Maritime Boundary (*Cameroon v. Nig.*), 1998 I.C.J. 275, 296 (11 June) (good faith is a 'well established principle of international law'); U.S. and California law, like almost all

ICANN's Bylaws declare ICANN's mission: to coordinate the global Internet's systems of unique identifiers, and in particular to ensure their stable and secure operation.[1566]

b. *Essential Rights and Obligations*

In performing its mission, ICANN's core values[1567] should guide the decisions and actions of ICANN.[1568] They contain specific obligations for ICANN, such as the obligation to operate in an open and transparent manner and consistent with procedures to ensure fairness.[1569] They forbid ICANN to apply its standards, policies, procedures, or practices inequitably or single out any particular party for disparate treatment unless justified by substantial and reasonable cause.[1570]

Any ICANN body making a recommendation or decision must exercise its judgment to determine which core values are most relevant and how they apply to the specific circumstances of the case at hand, and to determine, if necessary, an appropriate and defensible balance among competing values.[1571]

ICANN's Bylaws and Articles of Incorporation are supplemented with soft law instruments, such as the Code of Conduct Guidelines (CCG), the Conflicts of Interest Policy (CoIP), and the Board Governance Guidelines (BGG). As ICANN engages itself to apply its standards, policies, procedures and practices neutrally, objectively and fairly,[1572] these instruments have the potential to become governing instruments.

ICANN also limited its authority by affirming key commitments in an agreement with the DoC: the Affirmation of Commitments (AoC). ICANN *inter alia* committed to take specific actions to ensure accountability, transparency and to preserve the interests of global Internet users.[1573] The *Vistaprint* IRP panel explicitly took ICANN's AoC into account when interpreting ICANN's obligations as the regulator of the DNS.[1574] In our view, Internet users and Internet stakeholders may be seen as third-party beneficiaries of ICANN's AoC. The most recent version of ICANN's Bylaws confirms this idea, as

jurisdictions, recognize obligations to act in good faith and ensure procedural fairness. The requirement of procedural fairness has been an established part of the California common law since before the turn of the 19th century. (*See Pinsker v. Pacific Coast Society of Orthodontists*, 526 P.2d 550-553 (Cal. 1974); Carma Developers (Cal.), *Inc. v. Marathon Development California*, Inc. (1992) 2 Cal.4th 342, 371–372 [6 Cal.Rptr.2d 467, 826 P.2d 710], internal citations omitted.).

1566. ICANN, Bylaws as amended on 11 April 2013, Article I(1).
1567. *E.g.*, promoting competition, applying policies neutrally, objectively and fairly, remaining accountable.
1568. ICANN, Bylaws as amended on 11 April 2013, Article I(2).
1569. ICANN, Bylaws as amended on 11 April 2013, Article III(1).
1570. ICANN, Bylaws as amended on 11 April 2013, Article II(3).
1571. ICANN, Bylaws as amended on 11 April 2013, Article I(2).
1572. ICANN, Bylaws as amended on 11 April 2013, Articles I(2)(8) and II(3).
1573. Affirmation of Commitments, Articles 3, 9.1 and 9.2.
1574. Vistaprint IRP Declaration, § 67.

ICANN has now transposed those commitments contained in its agreement with the DoC for the benefit of the Internet community, following the termination of the U.S. oversight role.[1575]

How exactly ICANN's obligations should apply to particular circumstances has given rise to many debates, *e.g*:

(1) Is there a statute of limitations for challenging a standard, policy or process that is not designed to ensure fairness?
(2) Do the obligations apply to all ICANN staff, constituencies and the ICANN Board?
(3) Do the obligations apply to third party vendors, appointed by ICANN?

The IRP case law is not yet settled on these issues.

ICANN's transparency and fairness obligations and its prohibition on discrimination and the inequitable application of its standards, policies, procedures or practices have existed since ICANN's founding and have never changed. ICANN's obligations as set out in its Articles of Incorporation have also remained unchanged.

(1) Good Faith

ICANN's obligation to act in conformity with the relevant principles of international law includes the obligation to act consistently with 'general principles of law recognized as a source of international law.'[1576] The obligation to act in good faith is a general principle of law which is found in both international law and the corporate law of California.[1577]

ICANN does not deny that it must act in good faith. However, ICANN considers that its good faith must be presumed,[1578] and that a refusal to reconsider the substance of an expert determination is not a failure to act in good faith.[1579]

ICANN's obligation to act in good faith is recognized explicitly in the *ICM Registry* and the *Vistaprint* cases.[1580] One can argue that the obligation is recognized implicitly in the *Booking.com*[1581] and *DCA* cases.[1582]

The *Dot Registry* panel considered that there were no '"relevant principles of international law (*sic*) applicable international conventions" that would assist it in the task

1575. ICANN, *Bylaws for Internet Corporation for Assigned Names and Numbers*, as amended 1 October 2016, https://www.icann.org/resources/pages/governance/bylaws-en.
1576. ICM IRP Declaration, § 140; *see also* Booking.com IRP Declaration, §§ 112–113; Vistaprint IRP Declaration, §§ 125–126; Despegar et al. IRP Declaration, § 145.
1577. *Supra* n. 1565.
1578. ICANN's Response (*ICM Registry* IRP), § 91.
1579. ICANN's Response (*Vistaprint* IRP), § 71.
1580. ICM IRP Declaration, §§ 141, 152; Vistaprint IRP Declaration, § 174.
1581. Booking.com IRP Declaration, § 115, n. 99; §§ 117 and following.
1582. DCA Final IRP Declaration, §§ 32, 67, 94, 105.

[...] before it.'[1583] In our view, the panel did not mean by this that there were no relevant principles of international law that applied to ICANN; rather, we take it to mean that the panel considered the relevant principles of international law to be already included in the more specific rules of ICANN's Articles of Incorporation and Bylaws.

(2) Due Process

Ensuring an applicant's right to due process forms part of ICANN's obligation to act in good faith. IRP panels have recognized ICANN's obligation to ensure due process either implicitly or explicitly. *E.g.*, the *DCA* panel considered that ICANN is 'bound by its Bylaws to conduct adequate diligence to ensure that it [applies] its procedures fairly.'[1584] However, IRP panels have ruled that the lack of an appeal mechanism to contest the merits of a case was not a violation of ICANN's obligations, and, according to some panels, an applicant can be time-barred from challenging the absence of due process rights:[1585]

(1) In the *Booking.com* case, the panel criticized the fact that the Guidebook provided no means for applicants to be fully heard on the substantive question of their applied-for gTLD strings.[1586] However, as that panel considered that Booking.com was time-barred from challenging the Guidebook,[1587] the panel ruled that the simple fact that an established process was followed was a fundamental obstacle to *Booking.com*'s case.[1588]
(2) The *Vistaprint* panel recognized ICANN's obligation to ensure due process, but considered that Vistaprint had been given a fair opportunity to present its case and that the lack of an appeal mechanism to contest the merits of a SCO was not, in itself, a violation of the Articles of Incorporation or Bylaws.[1589]
(3) The panel in the *Merck* case came to a similar conclusion, ruling that it was not up to an IRP panel to create a referral or appeal process for LROs.[1590]

We agree that a lack of an appeal mechanism to contest the merits of a case is not necessarily a due process violation. However, new gTLD applicants were entitled to a meaningful review to establish whether ICANN's standards were applied correctly and consistently. Indeed, ICANN's Bylaws warrant that ICANN shall apply its standards,

1583. Dot Registry IRP Declaration, § 67.
1584. DCA Final IRP Declaration, § 105.
1585. As discussed in Chapter 6.C.1.e, we are of the view that the consideration that an applicant can be time-barred from raising due process issues is without merit.
1586. Booking.com IRP Declaration, § 117.
1587. As mentioned above, this consideration did not take into account the fact that the time bar was introduced only after the final version of the Guidebook was published and did not exist at the time applicants filed an application for a new gTLD (Chapter 5.C.4.b(4)).
1588. Booking.com IRP Declaration, § 132.
1589. Vistaprint IRP Declaration, §§ 174–175.
1590. Merck IRP Declaration, § 60.

policies and procedures fairly and equitably, and they provide for accountability mechanisms to ensure compliance with this obligation. While an appeal as to the merits may not be required, it is our view that ICANN should respect due process rights and offer judicial review to ensure the correct application of its standards and policies.

The *Despegar et al.* panel invited the ICANN Board to affirm that transparency and due process should be applied (even though this would seem self-evident). The ICANN Board agreed to make this affirmation, and, as a result, it should no longer be possible for ICANN to claim that it is not bound by general principles of international law and administrative due process. Nevertheless, as ICANN has historically tried to minimize its obligations under international law, it remains to be seen if this point is now settled.

(3) Fairness

IRP panels have consistently shared the view that ICANN must act and make decisions neutrally, objectively and fairly.[1591] However, there seems no consensus on what constitutes a fair decision.

The *Booking.com* panel refused to rule explicitly on whether or not the application process was fair. Instead, it limited its review to whether the process was applied correctly.[1592] The *Despegar et al.* panel adopted a similar approach, and decided – incorrectly in our view – not to address the claimants' challenges to ICANN's process.[1593]

Conversely, the *Vistaprint* and *DCA* panels did not limit their review to a correct application of the process. Both these panels agreed that an applicant must be given a meaningful opportunity to present its case.[1594] According to the respective panels, such an opportunity was given to Vistaprint, but not to DCA.

(4) Non-discrimination

ICANN's prohibition on discrimination has been raised in all IRPs, and the principle has been accepted in all IRP decisions. However, most IRP panels have failed to examine the issue thoroughly:

(1) The *ICM* Registry panel found that although there might have been grounds for a finding of disparate treatment, the facts were not fully coherent in this regard.[1595]

1591. *See e.g.*, Vistaprint IRP Declaration, § 175; DCA Final IRP Declaration, §§ 94–95.
1592. Booking.com IRP Declaration, §§ 117, 132.
1593. Despegar et al. IRP Declaration, §§ 46–50.
1594. Vistaprint IRP Declaration, § 175; DCA Final Declaration, §§ 107–109.
1595. ICM IRP Declaration, § 152.

(2) The *Booking.com* panel limited its examination of the claim for discrimination to a review of the application process. The result of the string similarity process was insufficient to show that Booking.com had been treated differently, according to the panel.[1596]
(3) The *DCA* panel did not assess the discrimination arguments, as it had already found a violation of ICANN's Articles of Incorporation and Bylaws.[1597]
(4) In the Merck case, the claimant did not develop its discrimination argument thoroughly. The *Merck* panel ruled that it is 'insufficient to ground an argument of discrimination simply to note that on different occasions the Board has pursued different options among those available to it.'[1598]

The *Vistaprint* panel was the first IRP panel that gave meaning to ICANN's prohibition on discrimination, by deciding that the ICANN Board's right to individually consider an application must be exercised in a non-discriminatory fashion.[1599] However, the *Vistaprint* panel could not agree on the criteria to assess the discrimination or its justification.[1600] The panel decided to give the ICANN Board the opportunity to exercise its independent judgment on the question of discriminatory treatment.

The ICANN Board decided on a narrow interpretation of disparate treatment, and found that the challenged decision was not sufficiently 'inconsistent' or 'unreasonable' to warrant a re-evaluation, such as it had ordered in similar situations.[1601] However, it is unclear what the ICANN Board meant by *sufficiently* inconsistent or unreasonable. For the most part, consistency between decisions is not a question of gradation: they are either consistent or not. If ICANN nevertheless wants to use different scales of consistency and reasonableness to justify differences in its decision-making, good governance would, in our view, require that the difference in scaling be justified. The opposite view would open the door to arbitrary decisions and discrimination. However, for the claimant in the *Vistaprint* case, it was no longer expedient to challenge the ICANN Board's view on disparate treatment.[1602]

The issue of non-discrimination was also raised in the *Donuts* case, but the IRP panel did not take the opportunity to rectify ICANN's narrow interpretation. The *Donuts* IRP panel considered that discrimination can only exist when like circumstances are treated differently.[1603] This opinion does not seem sufficiently nuanced, as the prohibition to discriminate has different facets. Put simply, like circumstances must be treated alike and different circumstances must be treated differently. In essence, it

1596. Booking.com IRP Declaration, § 140.
1597. *See* DCA Final IRP Declaration, § 117.
1598. Merck IRP Declaration, § 61.
1599. Vistaprint IRP Declaration, §§ 177–179.
1600. Vistaprint IRP Declaration, § 189.
1601. ICANN, *Approved Board Resolution 2016.03.03.02 – Regular Meeting of the ICANN Board*, 3 March 2016, https://www.icann.org/resources/board-material/resolutions-2016-03-03-en.
1602. *Supra*, Chapter 5.E.9.
1603. Donuts IRP Declaration, §§ 219–221.

seems that the *Donuts* IRP panel concluded that there was not sufficient inconsistency in the case to require the ICANN Board to act.[1604]

In our view, this decision must be seen together with the panel majority's findings that the ICANN Board was not required to intervene outside the framework of a formal RfR, even when serious issues were raised.[1605] This conflicts with the panel decision in the *Despegar et al.* case, which found that there were circumstances in which the ICANN Board would be required to take action in view of serious allegations made outside a formal reconsideration request.[1606]

In any event, the *Donuts* IRP panel found no discrimination on the basis of the record of the case. With respect to one of the challenged community objection decisions (concerning .sports), the panel's majority stated its belief that 'it would not be inconsistent with ICANN's values and principles to provide for a rehearing of that objection.'[1607] The *Donuts* decision contains no similar statement about the other challenged community objection (concerning .rugby), and the panel expressed the view that, 'absent compelling facts to the contrary, the [ICANN] Board need not rush into adding another layer of adjudication or review.'[1608] However, it is not readily apparent from the majority's decision whether the possible distinction between the .sports and the .rugby objection was deliberate or on what basis the distinction was made.

In summary, it seems that the assessment by IRP panels of ICANN's actions in the light of ICANN's prohibition on discrimination remains underdeveloped.

(5) Transparency

ICANN's obligation to be open and transparent in its decision-making is broadly acknowledged.[1609] Some IRP panels have ordered that ICANN produce documents in the interest of transparency and accountability.[1610] The transparency obligation does not apply to the ICANN Board only; it must also be guaranteed by ICANN's constituent bodies, including the GAC.[1611] When the ICANN Board considers GAC Advice, the Board is expected, at a minimum, to investigate the matter in the light of the clear transparency provisions to be found in ICANN's Bylaws.[1612]

1604. Donuts IRP Declaration, §§ 219–221.
1605. Donuts IRP Declaration, § 216.
1606. Despegar et al. IRP Declaration, §§ 130 and following.
1607. Donuts IRP Declaration, § 230.
1608. Donuts IRP Declaration, § 183.
1609. ICM IRP Declaration, §§ 3, 5, Booking.com IRP Declaration, § 138; DCA IRP Declaration, § 113; Vistaprint IRP Declaration, §§ 123, 174.
1610. DCA IRP Declaration on the IRP Procedure, §§59–60; Other panels have also granted document production requests, *see* Dot Registry Amended Procedural Order No. 2 and Procedural Order No. 3; Donuts Procedural Order No. 4; Corn Lake Procedural Order No. 2.
1611. DCA IRP Declaration, § 102.
1612. DCA IRP Declaration, § 113.

In the *Booking.com* case, the claimant objected to the lack of transparency in the string similarity review process both during the selection process and the implementation of the process, and with respect to ICANN's control over the process. Booking.com *inter alia* criticized the use of anonymous evaluators. The IRP panel agreed with Booking-.com that there was a lack of transparency in the string similarity review process.[1613] Greater transparency existed with respect to the objection processes. Both the *Vistaprint* and *Merck* Panel considered the objection processes not to lack transparency.[1614]

In the *Despegar et al.* case, the IRP panel evaluated ICANN's transparency obligations in the light of ICANN's Documentary Information Disclosure Policy (DIDP). The claimants challenged the fact that ICANN had failed to disclose information regarding the CPE process. The IRP panel decided that it was unable to judge whether the DIDP had been correctly applied.[1615] This position may seem logical: without access to the underlying information, it is indeed impossible to judge whether there were good reasons to deny access to the requested information. However, we question whether it was correct for the IRP panel to then decide that the ICANN Board's determination in response to the claimants' reconsideration request 'provides the requisite degree of confirmation that the correct procedure was actually followed, that the [ICANN Board] did, properly, consider whether the relevant policy or procedure was actually applied by the ICANN staff and whether, in doing so, the [ICANN Board] could have a reasonable degree of assurance that the ICANN staff had correctly applied the policy or procedure.'[1616] In other words, the IRP panel was prepared simply to accept the ICANN Board's judgment on the issue. Taking the ICANN Board's judgment for granted in this way seems to us to be at odds with settled case law on the standard of review[1617] and with the IRP panel's obligation to provide an independent review of the ICANN Board's actions (or inactions).

The IRP panel in the *Despegar et al.* case also looked into ICANN's transparency obligations in relation to ICANN's investigation of a data exposure issue concerning an individual associated to a competing applicant who had accessed confidential information belonging to some of the claimants. In this respect, the IRP panel ruled that openness and transparency required that ICANN: (i) investigate the allegation of association between the individual and the competing applicant, and (ii) make public the fact of the investigation and the result thereof.[1618] In doing so, the IRP panel made clear that the ICANN Board had only limited discretion regarding keeping information confidential. In our view, the IRP panel's recognition of ICANN's limited discretion conflicts with their decision simply to accept, without any review of the underlying information, the ICANN Board's finding that the DIDP was correctly applied. Indeed, there is now some doubt that the ICANN Board's finding was correct: there are some indications that, in its response to the DIDP request and during the IRP proceedings,

1613. Booking.com IRP Declaration, §§ 117, 129.
1614. Vistaprint IRP Declaration; Merck IRP Declaration.
1615. Despegar et al. IRP Declaration, § 97.
1616. Despegar et al. IRP Declaration, § 110.
1617. *Infra*, Chapter 6.C.2.c.
1618. Despegar et al. IRP Declaration, §134.

ICANN may have misrepresented the extent of the involvement of its staff in the evaluation by the EIU. If nothing else, the decision in the *Despegar et al.* case shows that the practical application of ICANN's transparency obligations is still very much open to debate.

The question of transparency was largely ignored in the *Donuts* IRP Declaration. The dissenting panelist – rightfully in our view – condemned ICANN's attempt to rubber-stamp decision-making that was 'not independent, that was not transparent, and that has not been held accountable.'[1619] However, he was unable to convince his fellow panelists, who did not seek to examine ICANN's specific transparency obligations.

The panel's majority in the *Dot Registry* case considered that ICANN had clear transparency obligations that required the ICANN Board to be transparent about its decision-making when addressing reconsideration requests.[1620] The *Dot Registry* IRP panel considered transparency to be one of the most essential obligations of ICANN and its staff, and 'one that [ICANN's] contractor, EIU, had pledged to follow in its work for ICANN.'[1621] The panel's majority was also critical about ICANN's apparent use of 'the attorney-client privilege and the litigation work-product privilege to shield staff work from disclosure to the Panel.'[1622] According to the majority of the panel, ICANN's exercise of its litigation privileges (by passing information from ICANN staff through legal counsel) allowed ICANN to breach its obligatory transparency requirements.[1623] As a result, the panel inferred that the ICANN Board had not exercised due diligence, care and independent judgment.[1624]

c. *Standard of Review*

In April 2013, ICANN introduced a defined standard of review to be applied by IRP panels.[1625] IRP panels were obliged to focus on the following questions:

(1) Did the Board act without conflict of interest in taking its decision?
(2) Did the Board exercise due diligence and care in having a reasonable amount of facts in front of them? and
(3) Did the Board members exercise independent judgment in taking the decision, believed to be in the best interests of the company?

Before this defined standard of review was introduced, ICANN had argued that its Board's decisions were entitled to deference, and that there had to be a strong presumption that the Board's decisions were not at odds with ICANN's Articles of

1619. Donuts IRP Declaration, Dissenting Opinion, p. 1.
1620. Dot Registry IRP Declaration, § 88.
1621. Dot Registry IRP Declaration, §§ 117–122.
1622. Dot Registry IRP Declaration, § 128.
1623. Dot Registry IRP Declaration, § 149.
1624. Dot Registry IRP Declaration, § 148.
1625. ICANN, Bylaws as amended on 11 April 2013, Article IV(3)(4).

Incorporation and Bylaws.[1626] However, ICANN's views were rejected in IRP.[1627] It was settled that IRP panels were to review and appraise the judgments of the ICANN Board objectively, not deferentially.[1628]

With the introduction of the defined standard of review, ICANN argued that this standard had been introduced to make clear that its Board was entitled to deference.[1629] However, nothing in the Bylaws or the ICDR IRP Supplementary Procedures specifies that the IRP panel's review must be founded on a deferential standard. The introduction of a deferential standard of review would have undermined the IRP panel's goal of ensuring accountability, and would have been incompatible with ICANN's commitment to maintain and improve robust mechanisms for accountability, as required by ICANN's AoC, Bylaws and core values.[1630] Since the introduction of the defined standard of review, IRP panels have consistently rejected ICANN's argument.[1631]

The *Vistaprint* panel considered that the ICANN Board's conduct should be reviewed and appraised objectively and independently, without any presumption of correctness, and it recognized that there was unanimity on this point in the decisions of the three IRP panels that had previously considered the issue.[1632] As the decisions of those panels have precedential value, the *Vistaprint* panel considered this issue to be settled.[1633]

The *Vistaprint* case confirmed that the detailing of a defined standard did not remove from the panel's remit its fundamental obligation to compare actions or inactions of the Board with the Articles of Incorporation and Bylaws. Instead, the defined standard provided a non-exhaustive list of questions that can be asked and does not exclude the possibility that other potential questions might arise in a particular case.[1634] In short, the obligations of the ICANN Board in relation to its decision-making are reinforced by the introduction of a defined standard of review, not reduced by it.[1635]

The recommendations that led to the introduction of the standard of review seem to confirm that, for a claimant to have proper grounds for review of a Board action, it is sufficient for the claimant to demonstrate 'that the Board did not make a reasonable inquiry to determine it had sufficient facts available, Board members had a conflict of interest in participating in the decision, or the decision was not an exercise in independent judgment, believed by the Board to be in the best interests of the

1626. ICANN's Response (*ICM*), § 87.
1627. ICM IRP Declaration, § 136.
1628. ICM IRP Declaration, § 136.
1629. ICANN's Response re merits (*DCA*), § 12; *see also* ICANN's Response (*Booking.com*), § 24; ICANN's Response (*Vistaprint*), § 33.
1630. Vistaprint IRP Declaration, § 124.
1631. Booking.com IRP Declaration, § 111; DCA Final IRP Declaration, 76; Vistaprint IRP Declaration, §§ 124–126; Merck IRP Declaration, § 20; Despegar et al. IRP Declaration, §§ 64, 88 and 113; Donuts IRP Declaration, § 131; Dot Registry IRP Declaration, §§ 68–69.
1632. ICM IRP Declaration, § 136; Booking.com IRP Declaration, § 111; DCA Final IRP Declaration, § 76.
1633. Vistaprint IRP Declaration, § 126.
1634. Vistaprint IRP Declaration, § 123.
1635. *See* GCC Interim IRP Declaration, §§ 76–77.

company, after taking account of the Internet community and the global public interest.'[1636] The ICDR IRP Supplementary Procedures also provide that a claimant will have established proper grounds for review if it demonstrates that the Board fails any of these requirements. The existence of any one of these factors would thus be sufficient to justify an ICANN Board decision being reviewed. However, in our view, they are not the only possible bases for a review. Any other violation of the Articles of Incorporation or Bylaws could also result in a review of the decision.

Nonetheless, the three IRP decisions immediately following the *Vistaprint* decision seem to limit the panels' independent review to the questions detailed in the defined standard of review.[1637] These decisions make no reference to the above analysis and two of them fail to mention the *Vistaprint* decision. This could mean that there is still some doubt surrounding this issue. However, the *Dot Registry* panel seems once again to have ascribed to the reasoning of the *Vistaprint* case.[1638]

3. Authority of the Panel

a. *Relevant Provisions*

Article IV(3)(11) of the 2013 ICANN Bylaws provides that IRP panels have the authority to:

(1) Summarily dismiss requests brought without standing, lacking in substance, or that are frivolous or vexatious;
(2) Request additional written submissions from the party seeking review, the Board, the SOs, or from other parties;
(3) Declare whether an action or inaction of the Board was inconsistent with the Articles of Incorporation or Bylaws;
(4) Recommend that the Board stay any action or decision, or that the Board take any interim action, until such time as the Board reviews and acts upon the opinion of the IRP;
(5) Consolidate requests for independent review if the facts and circumstances are sufficiently similar; and
(6) Determine the timing for each proceeding.

Article IV(3)(18) of the 2013 ICANN Bylaws specifies that the IRP panel shall make its declaration based solely on the documentation, supporting materials, and arguments submitted by the parties, and that it must specifically designate the prevailing party in its declaration. This is confirmed by Article 10 of the ICDR IRP Supplementary Procedures.

1636. Report by Accountability Structures Expert Panel (ASEP), 26 October 2012, https://www.icann.org/en/system/files/files/report-26oct12-en.pdf, p. 48.
1637. Merck IRP Declaration, §§ 20–22; Despegar et al. IRP Declaration, §§ 64, 88, 113; Donuts IRP Declaration, §§ 126 and following.
1638. Dot Registry IRP Declaration, §§ 68–69.

Pursuant to Article 11 of the ICDR IRP Supplementary Procedures, the IRP panel must also fix costs in its declaration.[1639]

b. *The Panel's Main Task*

The fundamental task for an IRP panel is to evaluate ICANN Board actions and inactions for consistency with the Articles of Incorporation and Bylaws.[1640] All ICANN Board actions and inactions are subject to review, and the panel must determine whether they are consistent with: (i) ICANN's Articles of Incorporation and Bylaws, and (ii) secondary rules created by ICANN, such as the policy introducing the New gTLD Program or the Applicant Guidebook. The panel's review should include a consideration of whether or not ICANN and its Board have acted in good faith, in accordance with principles of international law and without discrimination.[1641]

c. *Limits to the Panel's Authority*

The question has arisen whether the authority of IRP panels is limited to the measures that are listed explicitly under Article IV(3)(11) of the ICANN Bylaws, or whether IRP panels have a broader authority to end a dispute. In our opinion, the list in Article IV(3)(11) is not exhaustive. Nothing in the ICANN Bylaws or the ICDR IRP Supplementary Procedures would seem to detract from the main purpose of the ICDR Rules, which is to resolve/to arbitrate the dispute.[1642] The ICDR Rules are designed to provide a final and binding resolution of the dispute.

If an IRP panel is authorized to declare that an action or inaction is inconsistent with the Articles of Incorporation or Bylaws, it should also be authorized to declare that upholding a certain action or inaction is inconsistent with the Articles of Incorporation or Bylaws. In so deciding, IRP panels could effectively render affirmative relief by giving ICANN only one option to put an end to the violation of its Articles of Incorporation or Bylaws.

The IRP panel in the *ICM Registry* case adopted this approach when it found that there was no violation of the Bylaws in the Board's decision that ICM's application met the sponsorship criteria, and that there was a violation in the Board's reconsideration of that decision.[1643]

1639. For a detailed overview of the Panel's authority in allocating costs, *see* Chapter VI.C.1.m *supra*.
1640. ICANN, Bylaws as amended on 11 April 2013, Article IV(3)(4) *juncto* Article IV(3)(11)(c); Booking.com IRP Declaration, § 53; DCA Final IRP Declaration, § 109; Vistaprint IRP Declaration, §§ 119, 123; Merck IRP Declaration, § 17; Despegar et al. IRP Declaration, § 58.
1641. ICANN Articles of Incorporation, Article 4; ICANN, Bylaws as amended on 11 April 2013, Article II(3) *juncto* Article IV(3); Vistaprint IRP Declaration, § 180.
1642. ICDR Rules, Introduction, Article 1, Article 19, Article 20 and Article 30.
1643. ICM IRP Declaration, § 152.

Also in the new gTLD round, IRP panels have given clear instructions to the ICANN Board:

(1) The emergency arbitrator in the *Dot Registry* case 'ORDERED that ICANN refrain from scheduling an auction for the new gTLDs .INC, .LLP and .LLC';[1644]
(2) The emergency arbitrator in the *GCC* case made the 'order by way of an interim declaration and recommendation to the ICANN Board that [...] ICANN shall refrain from taking any further steps towards the execution of a registry agreement for .PERSIANGULF, with Asia Green or any other entity, until the IRP is completed, or until such other order of the IRP panel when constituted';[1645]
(3) The IRP panel in the *DCA* case issued a recommendation that 'ICANN continue to refrain from delegating the.AFRICA gTLD and permit DCA Trust's application to proceed through the remainder of the new gTLD application process.'[1646]

In these cases, the IRP panels appear to have left ICANN with no maneuvering room: it was obliged to abide by these instructions.

However, other IRP panels have struggled with their authority to render affirmative relief:

(1) The *Booking.com* panel decided that it could neither substitute its judgment for that of the ICANN Board, nor appraise the policies and procedures established by ICANN.[1647] The panel nevertheless encouraged ICANN to consider: (i) Booking.com's legitimate concerns regarding the string similarity process for the future, and (ii) whether approval of both the .hotels and .hoteis TLD would be in the best interest of the Internet community.[1648] In fact, the ICANN Board considered the first recommendation, but ignored the second;[1649]
(2) The *Vistaprint* panel considered that it had no authority to award affirmative relief, but that it could instead recommend that the ICANN Board take, or refrain from taking, actions or decisions.[1650] The panel recommended that the

1644. Dot Registry Interim IRP Declaration, p. 19.
1645. GCC Interim IRP Declaration, § 96.
1646. DCA IRP Declaration, § 149.
1647. Booking.com IRP Declaration, §§ 115, 128.
1648. Booking.com IRP Declaration, § 154.
1649. ICANN, *Board Resolutions 2015.04.26.14 – 2015.04.26.16*, 26 April 2016, https://www.icann.org/resources/board-material/resolutions-2015-04-26-en#2.b; Booking.com B.V. and Travel Reservation SRL's Request for Reconsideration 15-7, 13 May 2015, https://www.icann.org/en/system/files/files/reconsideration-request-15-7-booking-bv-travel-reservations-srl-annexes-13mar15-en.pdf; ICANN, *BGC Recommendation on Reconsideration Request 15-7*, 20 June 2015, https://www.icann.org/en/system/files/files/recommendation-15-7-booking-bv-travel-reservations-srl-20jun15-en.pdf; ICANN, *Board Resolution 2015.07.28.08*, 28 July 2015, https://www.icann.org/resources/board-material/resolutions-2015-07-28-en#2.b.
1650. Vistaprint IRP Declaration, § 149.

> Board consider Vistaprint's claim of disparate treatment,[1651] and added that, without the exercise of judgment by ICANN's Board on this question, the Board would risk violating its Bylaws.[1652] The panel stated that the Board's actions or omissions in this area bore the scrutiny of independent and objective review, without any presumption of correctness.[1653]

The *Vistaprint* decision is interesting because the IRP panel gave the ICANN Board the opportunity to exercise its discretion while at the same time acknowledging that an IRP panel could later review, and therefore exercise control over, the use of that discretion. In this way, it would be possible for an IRP panel to decide that ICANN had violated its Articles of Incorporation and Bylaws either: (i) by failing to consider whether there had been disparate treatment, or (ii) by failing to justify disparate treatment by substantial and reasonable cause.[1654] However, the *Vistaprint* panel nonetheless issued a final decision before the ICANN Board had had the chance to follow its recommendation, in our view terminating the IRP proceedings too soon. The *Vistaprint* panel could have issued an interim decision, reserving its final decision until the ICANN Board had had the opportunity to consider the issue. This would have potentially allowed the IRP to finally resolve the dispute. However, the *Vistaprint* panel could not agree among its three members what would constitute discrimination in the context of reviewing expert determinations,[1655] and left the issue undecided.

The panel in the *Merck* case considered its authority to be limited. The panel decided that it had no authority to create a referral or appeal process for expert determinations in LROs.[1656] In our view, this is a correct finding. However, we believe that the *Merck* panel would have had the authority to rule that ICANN's failure to create such a process constituted a violation of ICANN's Articles of Incorporation or Bylaws. It is our understanding that the *Merck* panel refrained from making such a finding in view of the palpable weaknesses in *Merck*'s case.

Nevertheless, we consider it unfortunate that the *Merck* panel also expressed the view that it did not have the authority to second-guess the appropriateness of the ICANN Board's determination that the LRO panelist had applied the correct standard in making his expert determination.[1657] This finding is incompatible with previously settled case law that IRP panels must review and appraise the judgments of the ICANN Board objectively, without any presumption of correctness.[1658] No provision exists that prevents an IRP panel from reviewing the ICANN Board's determinations.

The panel in the *Despegar et al.* case avoided a discussion on the extent of its authority, by deciding not to rule on claims with respect to the CPE process as a whole. By

1651. Vistaprint IRP Declaration, § 196.
1652. Vistaprint IRP Declaration, § 190.
1653. Vistaprint IRP Declaration, § 180.
1654. ICANN, Bylaws as amended on 11 April 2013, Article II(3).
1655. Vistaprint IRP Declaration, § 189.
1656. Merck IRP Declaration, § 60.
1657. Merck IRP Declaration, § 49.
1658. *Supra*, Chapter 6.C.2.c.

considering that the claimants had abandoned their requests in this regard, and by naming ICANN as the prevailing party in the other claims, the panel avoided having to examine whether upholding the policy in question constituted a continued violation of the Articles of Incorporation and Bylaws.

ICANN also prevailed in the *Donuts* case, making it unnecessary for the panel in that case to decide on its authority to grant affirmative relief. The dissenting panelist in the *Donuts* case considered, however, that the objection concerning .sports, which was challenged by the claimant, should indeed be denied.[1659] This opinion implies that at least the dissenting panelist considered that IRP panels are competent to grant affirmative relief going to the merits of the case.

Interestingly, the dissenting panelist in the *Dot Registry* case also wanted the panel to take due account of the underlying merits when making its assessment. He considered that IRP panels are 'empowered to make recommendations to the [ICANN] Board', and he was critical of the majority IRP Declaration for not touching on the merits of the case.[1660] His position contrasts with that of the panel's majority, which intentionally avoided 'any recommendations to the [ICANN] Board as to how it should respond to th[e IRP] Declaration.'[1661]

In our view, nothing prevents IRP panels from recommending how ICANN should avoid a further violation of ICANN's Articles of Incorporation and Bylaws. In cases where there is effectively only one way to avoid or bring to an end a violation of ICANN's essential obligations - and as the panel's declaration should be considered binding - such a recommendation will effectively grant affirmative relief. In cases where more options are available, IRP panels should indeed not substitute their judgment for that of the ICANN Board, although nothing would prevent a panel from giving an advisory recommendation. In any event, we consider that IRP panels should strive to bring disputes to final resolution, as that remains their primary task under the ICDR Rules.

4. Nature of the IRP Declaration

a. *Binding Nature of the IRP Declaration*

So far, only three IRP panels have explicitly ruled on the issue of the binding nature of IRP declarations. Under the rules in place at the time, the *ICM Registry* panel considered that IRP declarations were advisory in nature.[1662] The *DCA* panel and the *Vistaprint* panel decided, under the rules applying to the New gTLD Program, that IRP declarations were binding.[1663]

1659. Donuts IRP Declaration, Dissenting Opinion, p. 2 and 7.
1660. Dot Registry IRP Declaration, Dissenting Opinion, § 37.
1661. Dot Registry IRP Declaration, Dissenting Opinion, § 37.
1662. ICM IRP Declaration, § 134.
1663. DCA Final IRP Declaration, § 23; Vistaprint IRP Declaration, § 130 and following.

The *Vistaprint* decision is the most detailed decision on the subject. The *Vistaprint* panel is the only panel to have made a distinction between what it considered to be the panel's core task, and what recommendations an IRP panel may give. The *Vistaprint* panel considered panel findings on the question of whether the ICANN Board's conduct is consistent with the Articles of Incorporation and Bylaws to be binding, and any recommendations that the panel may give to the Board to be non-binding.[1664] The *Vistaprint* panel also considered IRP panels authorized to issue binding decisions on summary dismissals, the designation of the prevailing party, and on decisions regarding costs and procedural aspects.[1665] However, its finding that an IRP panel's recommendation is non-binding seems at odds with the recommendation the *Vistaprint* panel itself gave to the ICANN Board. As mentioned above, the *Vistaprint* panel recommended that the ICANN Board exercise its judgment concerning whether there was any inequitable or disparate treatment regarding Vistaprint's .webs gTLD[1666] and added that:

(1) The Board would risk violating its Bylaws if it did not exercise its judgment on this issue,[1667] and that;
(2) The issue of disparate treatment can be brought to IRP for a binding decision on whether the Board's exercise of its judgment is consistent with ICANN's Articles of Incorporation and Bylaws.[1668]

In other words, the panel found that if the ICANN Board chose not to accept the *Vistaprint* panel's recommendation, that decision could in itself be brought before an IRP panel for independent and binding review. And, if the ICANN Board considered the issue but came to a decision that Vistaprint still found to be discriminatory, then Vistaprint could again submit the issue to an IRP panel.[1669]

Other IRP panels have not explicitly ruled on the issue of the binding nature.[1670] The *Dot Registry* IRP panel considered it unnecessary to give a determination on whether or not its declaration were binding, as such a determination would not be binding on any reviewing court.[1671] However, the *Dot Registry* and other IRP panels have been sufficiently affirmative in their decisions on this point to allow us to conclude that the panelists intended their decisions to have binding effect – at least with respect to decisions that relate to the panels' core tasks and costs. *E.g.*, the *Despegar et al.* panel designated the prevailing party, denied certain claims, ordered that ICANN reimburse the claimants and that its IRP declaration be executed in any number of counterparts.[1672] In our view, the explicit mention that the IRP declaration may be executed

1664. Vistaprint IRP Declaration, §§ 130, 138.
1665. Vistaprint IRP Declaration, § 139.
1666. Vistaprint IRP Declaration, § 191.
1667. Vistaprint IRP Declaration, § 190.
1668. Vistaprint IRP Declaration, §§ 177–179, 188.
1669. As explained in Chapter 5.E.9, it was no longer expedient for Vistaprint to challenge the Board's decision in this respect.
1670. *See e.g.*, Despegar et al IRP Declaration; Donuts IRP Declaration.
1671. Dot Registry IRP Declaration, § 78.
1672. Despegar et al. IRP Declaration, p. 40.

seems to confirm its binding nature. The language used by the *Despegar et al.* panel in relation to the data exposure issue also seems to confirm its binding nature. The panel 'concluded it should not make a declaration on this issue in [the] IRP, but that it should remain open to be considered at a future IRP should one be commenced in respect of this issue.'[1673] This language seems conclusive and dispositive of the question whether the data exposure issue can be raised in a future IRP.

Although no explicit reference is made to the *Vistaprint* case, the *Despegar et al.* IRP Declaration seems to follow the reasoning of the *Vistaprint* panel. The *Despegar et al.* panel made a (seemingly) binding decision with respect to the panel's 'core task' and made non-binding recommendations with respect to ICANN's general due process obligations and its dealings with third party service providers. Nevertheless, some statements are very affirmative, which could imply that the main decision of the IRP panel might have been different if the claimants had already put forward their arguments on the more general issues in their requests for reconsideration. The *Despegar et al.* panel affirmatively stated that 'there needs to be a system in place that ensures that marks are allocated on a consistent and predictable basis by different individual evaluators.'[1674]

b. *Precedential Value of IRP Declarations*

Since the amendments of 11 April 2013, ICANN's Bylaws have provided that the declarations of the IRP panel, and the Board's subsequent action resulting from those declarations, are final and have precedential value.[1675] This specification in the Bylaws seems to have been inspired by the *Manwin* case, where ICANN argued that a matter that was previously handled in an IRP must have preclusive effect and should not be re-litigated in another IRP.[1676] ICANN's concern that an IRP declaration must have preclusive effect seems to be reflected in Article 6 of the ICDR IRP Supplementary Procedures, which provides that a request for IRP may be summarily dismissed if a prior IRP on the same issue has concluded in an IRP declaration. This provision, together with ICANN's position in the *Manwin* case, seems to corroborate that the intent is for IRP declarations to create binding legal precedent.

However, the applicable rules provide little guidance on what kind of precedential value is being referred to here. Legal precedent may be either binding or persuasive,

1673. Despegar et al. IRP Declaration, § 138.
1674. Despegar et al. IRP Declaration, § 147.
1675. ICANN Bylaws as amended on 11 April 2013, Article IV(3)(21). In the amended Bylaws of 1 October 2016 creating legal precedent is mentioned as one of the purposes of the IRP, but it no longer mentions as affirmatively that IRP declarations have precedential value (Amended Bylaws, Article 4(3)(a)).
1676. ICANN's Response (*Manwin*), §§ 4, 129–130; ICANN brief re standing (*Manwin*), pp. 1, 3, 4; ICANN's Supplementary brief (*Manwin*), pp. 4–7.

and, according to one IRP panel, the Bylaws do not indicate which kind of precedent is intended.[1677] IRP case law is not yet settled on the nature of the legal precedent of IRP declarations.

It is clear that IRP declarations which pre-date the 2013 amendments should not create binding precedent. Prior to the 2013 amendments, there was no provision stipulating that IRP declarations had precedential value, let alone binding precedential value. In this respect, the *Booking.com* panel rightly ruled that it was in no way bound by the IRP declaration in the *ICM* case[1678] (a case which pre-dated the 2013 amendments). The *DCA* panel considered the ruling in the *ICM Registry* case, that IRP declarations are merely advisory, to be unpersuasive and not binding upon it.[1679] The *Vistaprint* panel recognized that the rules were different under the *ICM* case,[1680] but nevertheless tried to reconcile its decision concerning the binding nature of IRP declarations with the decision in the *ICM Registry* case.[1681]

Of course, IRP declarations from before 2013 may be referred to as a persuasive source. The *Booking.com* and *Vistaprint* panels took this approach in their reasoning on the applicable standard of review.[1682] The *ICM Registry* case can also serve as a persuasive source in relation to the *ICM Registry* panel's findings on the applicable norms of international law. The panel's findings were based on extensive expert evidence, and the majority decision was rendered by eminent authorities in public international law. The panel's Chair, Judge Schwebel, is the former President of the International Court of Justice (ICJ). ICANN's fundamental obligations have not changed since the *ICM Registry* case. As a result, the findings of the *ICM Registry* panel with respect to these fundamental obligations should have greater persuasive value than the *ICM Registry* panel's findings on procedural matters, for which the rules have since been changed.

For IRP declarations which post-date the 2013 amendments, it is unclear if a binding precedent rule is workable. All IRP panels are on the same footing: there are no lower IRP panels which must follow the rulings of higher IRP panels, and there is no opportunity to appeal IRP decisions. Panelists are often appointed for specific subject-matter expertise. As is often the case in international arbitration, a panel in one case may have its own views and be unconvinced by another panel's reasoning in a different case. The value of IRP declarations may therefore have to remain largely persuasive as towards other IRP panels.

Settled case law could emerge on certain issues. For example, the *Vistaprint* panel considered the issue on the applicable standard of review to be settled in view of the fact that three different IRP panels had previously considered the issue and had reached the same conclusion (namely that the ICANN Board's conduct is to be reviewed and appraised by IRP panels using an objective and independent standard, without any

1677. DCA Declaration on IRP Procedure, § 126.
1678. Booking.com IRP, § 113.
1679. DCA Declaration on IRP Procedure, §§ 126-128.
1680. Vistaprint IRP Declaration, § 142.
1681. Vistaprint IRP Declaration, § 141.
1682. Booking.com IRP Declaration, §§ 111-113; Vistaprint IRP Declaration, § 125.

presumption of correctness).[1683] Against this, more recent decisions have made no reference to settled case law with respect to the standard of review. Without any reference to previous case law, the *Merck* IRP panel considered that it could not substitute its own view on the merits of the underlying dispute, and that the standard of review is neither deferential nor *de novo*.[1684] The *Despegar et al.* IRP panel did not rule on the question of whether the standard of review was a deferential or objective one, but with respect to the ICANN Board's review of ICANN staff's compliance with its transparency obligations, the *Despegar et al.* IRP panel effectively accorded deference to the ICANN Board.[1685]

The panel in the *Donuts* case considered that 'it should take account of the reasoning of other panels in pursuing its own analysis, and should, to the extent warranted, seek consistency.'[1686]

In view of the above, it seems that the effect of previous IRP decisions remains largely persuasive even if some panels considered that settled case law exists on specific issues.

1683. Vistaprint IRP Declaration, § 126.
1684. Merck IRP Declaration, §§ 19–21.
1685. Despegar et al. IRP Declaration, § 97 *juncto* § 110.
1686. Donuts IRP Declaration, § 76.

CHAPTER 7
Action Points

A. INTRODUCTION

In Chapter 6 we identified various problems with ICANN's regulatory framework and highlighted important issues encountered in the implementation process. In Chapter 5 we considered the practical manifestation of some of these issues through a detailed examination of the IRP cases initiated against ICANN. Then, in Chapter 6, we listed the lessons to be learned from these IRP cases.

In this chapter, we give an overview of the issues that have been raised, making a distinction between those that have been resolved and those that remain unsettled. We give our opinion on how ICANN could improve its regulatory framework in order to prevent the problems experienced in the past new gTLD rounds recurring in the future.

In the last two rounds introducing new gTLDs, IRP panels have recognized inconsistencies in ICANN's decision-making as well as a lack of fairness and transparency in some of ICANN's processes. However, only a few IRP panels have been able to offer applicants a final resolution to the dispute, and it remains to be seen whether parties affected by ICANN's actions would be able to apply to court effectively regarding violations of ICANN's fundamental obligations under its Articles of Incorporation and Bylaws. In any event, such a step would doubtless prove cumbersome and expensive.

Our experience strongly suggests a need for clarification in ICANN's fundamental obligations, in particular regarding the hierarchy of norms that applies to these obligations (see Section B, below). We also believe that the procedural rules governing an IRP require clarification and amendment to allow for a genuine judicial review of ICANN's actions and inactions (see Section C, below).

Alongside our own evaluation of the situation, the ICANN community has been following the IRP cases and has shown interest in the issues raised and the concerns of the applicants. This has resulted in the community making concrete proposals to ICANN, which led to the adoption by the Board of amendments to the ICANN Bylaws (which entered into force on 1 October 2016), following the IANA functions transition.

The ICANN community review started in December 2014 (*i.e.*, before the first IRP on new gTLDs had concluded), when ICANN established a working group, consisting of its existing stakeholder groups and called the Cross Community Working Group (CCWG), to develop a set of proposed enhancements to ICANN's accountability to the global Internet community.[1687] The CCWG's main priority was to enhance ICANN's accountability mechanism to support the transition of the United States' stewardship of the IANA functions to ICANN, which was expected, at the time, to take place by the end of September 2015.[1688] The U.S. Government granted more time to improve ICANN's accountability mechanisms,[1689] and, as a result, the CCWG had the opportunity to consider the issues raised in the first IRP Declarations. Yet, the CCWG focused mainly on the interests of stakeholders already represented within ICANN, and on the structural improvement of their position within the organization.

The CCWG focused on establishing new specific powers for the ICANN community and on specific ways for the community to enforce these powers, *inter alia* by:

- Rejecting ICANN Budgets, IANA Budgets or Strategic/Operating Plans.
- Rejecting changes to ICANN's Standard Bylaws.
- Approving changes to new Fundamental Bylaws, Articles of Incorporation and ICANN's sale or other disposition of all or substantially all of ICANN's assets.
- Removing an individual ICANN Board Director.
- Recalling the entire ICANN Board.
- Rejecting ICANN Board decisions relating to reviews of the IANA functions, including the triggering of Post-Transition IANA separation.
- Making use of rights of inspection and investigation.[1690]

1687. ICANN, *Transcripts of CCWG on Enhancing ICANN Accountability Meeting #1*, 9 December 2014, https://community.icann.org/pages/viewpage.action?pageId=50823987&preview=/50823987/51576985/Meeting1_10Dec.pdf.

1688. ICANN, *Charter of the Cross Community Working Group on Enhancing ICANN Accountability*, 3 November 2014, https://community.icann.org/display/acctcrosscomm/Charter.

1689. Lawrence E. Strickling (NTIA), *Reflections on the IANA Stewardship Transition Process*, 23 September 2015, https://www.ntia.doc.gov/blog/2015/reflections-iana-stewardship-transition-process.

1690. *See* CCWG-Accountability, *Initial Draft Proposal for Public Comment*, 4 May 2015, https://community.icann.org/pages/viewpage.action?pageId=52897394&preview=/49348770/54002041/CCWG-Draft-Proposal-clean.pdf#; CCWG-Accountability, *2nd Draft Proposal on Work Stream 1 Recommendations*, 3 August 2015, https://community.icann.org/pages/viewpage.action?pageId=53783460; CCWG-Accountability, *3rd Draft Proposal on Work Stream 1 Recommendations*, 30 November 2015, https://community.icann.org/pages/viewpage.action?pageId=56145016; CCWG-Accountability, CCWG-Accountability, *Supplemental Final Proposal on Work Stream 1 Recommendations*, 23 February 2016, https://community.icann.org/display/acctcrosscomm/Final+Report.

While the ICANN community's review is to be welcomed, it is important to understand its limitations. We have not focused on the same issues. Rather, our assessment of the deficiencies in ICANN's accountability framework has been inspired by the first-hand experience we have had representing relative newcomers to the ICANN community, who have been faced with the complexities of this organization and who have needed to address shortcomings in the ICANN decisions and processes that affected them. The CCWG's review of the IRP also seems largely inspired by the ICANN community's wish to have more efficient and cost-effective internal accountability mechanisms. However, the proposed cost-saving efficiencies for community-based action may be unavailable for individual actors who are affected by ICANN's actions and who are not backed by a significant part of the ICANN community. These individual actors may find themselves in a weaker position from the beginning, and there are possible scenarios where a majority of the community would benefit from singling out an individual actor for disparate treatment. Also, it remains to be seen whether the cost savings to the community at large will not negatively impact the position of individual actors.

In this chapter, we will examine and evaluate the amendments brought about in light of these proposals. We will also look further at how ICANN can improve its accountability in dealing with third parties.

B. CLARIFYING THE HIERARCHY OF NORMS GOVERNING ICANN'S FUNDAMENTAL OBLIGATIONS

1. Why a Clear Hierarchy of Norms is Important

ICANN has committed itself to the fundamental obligations of good faith, fairness, transparency and non-discrimination, etc. These obligations are enunciated in ICANN's governing documents and have been confirmed in IRP case law. However, the extent of these obligations and their concrete implementation has given rise to much debate, and may not have been appropriately addressed in past new gTLD rounds. It is our view that ICANN is committed to continuously maintaining and improving robust mechanisms to support the most developed notion of transparency.[1691] However, many of ICANN's processes related to the delegating of new gTLDs have remained distinctly non-transparent: specific selection criteria for evaluators and their identities have remained largely undisclosed; inconsistent decisions have been accepted with no clear rationale; ICANN has been secretive about the involvement of its staff in the evaluation by 'independent' evaluators; etc.

When applicants have raised these issues with ICANN in the past, ICANN's standard response has been that it followed the process, and that if the applicant had issues with the process it should have challenged the process at the time of its adoption. It seems clear that such a response is unsatisfactory from the viewpoint of ICANN's accountability.

1691. *Supra* Chapter 2.B.3.c.

At the time when the various processes were first adopted, applicants could not predict how ICANN was going to implement these processes, and applicants may not have been in a position to challenge them. Nevertheless, IRP panels have been reluctant to set aside processes which were deemed unfair and non-transparent. As a result, there is a need to clarify how ICANN should ensure compliance with its fundamental obligations at all times, irrespective of when those processes were adopted, and there cannot be such clarity without there also being a clear hierarchy of norms governing the working of ICANN.

2. How to Achieve a Clear Hierarchy of Norms

a. Confirming That International Law Prevails Over Domestic Law

ICANN is subject to both international and local California law. ICANN's Articles of Incorporation mention international law first in recognition of the fundamental principle that international law prevails over domestic law.[1692] In case of a conflict between a substantive norm of international law and domestic law, ICANN cannot invoke a rule of domestic law to escape its obligations under international law. ICANN has nevertheless tried to do so in IRP proceedings.[1693] Therefore, a confirmation by ICANN that its international law obligations prevail over its obligations under California law would help to avoid unnecessary discussions in this respect in the future.

b. Reconciling Competing Rules: Respecting the Natural Hierarchy Between the Different Sources of Law

Even if one accepts – as one should – the pre-eminence of ICANN's obligations under international law, there may be conflicts in substantive norms, which require the reconciliation or prioritization of competing rules. It is commonplace in liberal democracies to give constitutional status to the most fundamental values of society, and to give constitutional rules precedence over secondary legislation in case of a normative conflict. By the same token, administrative rules or policies must conform to legislative norms and general good governance principles.

ICANN's Articles of Incorporation and Bylaws seem to embrace the same logic. The Articles of Incorporation reflect ICANN's fundamental obligations to operate for the benefit of the Internet community as a whole, to comply with principles of

1692. *See e.g.*, PCIJ, *Interpretation of the Convention between Greece and Bulgaria respecting reciprocal emigration, signed at Neuilly-sur-Seine on November 27th, 1919 (Question of the Greco-Bulgarian 'communities')*, Advisory Opinion of 31 July 1930, *P.C.I.J. Rep., Series B*, No. 17, 32; PCIJ, *Treatment of Polish nationals and other persons of Polish origin or speech in the Danzich territory*, Advisory Opinion of 4 February 1932, *P.C.I.J. Rep., Series A/B*, No. 44, 24; ICJ, *Applicability of the Obligation to Arbitrate under Section 21 of the United Nations Headquarters Agreement of 26 April 1947*, Advisory Opinion of 26 April 1988, *I.C.J. Rep* 1988, 12, § 57.

1693. *E.g., supra* Chapter 5.A.5.a and Chapter 5.C.5.a(2).

international and local law, and ICANN's commitment toward openness, transparency and enabling competition and open entry. These values can be said to have 'constitutional' status, as these fundamentals cannot be changed without a supermajority of at least two-thirds of ICANN's Board members, and 'when' ICANN has members, any amendment to the Articles of Incorporation must be ratified by a two-thirds majority of the members voting.[1694],[1695]

The ICANN Bylaws also require a two-thirds majority of ICANN's Board members for amendments. In addition, some of the Bylaws' provisions reflect rules that are more fundamental than others, in our view. For example, the prohibition of discrimination and ICANN's obligation to apply standards, policies, procedures and practices fairly and equitably have always been included in ICANN's Bylaws and have never been changed. These principles must govern ICANN's actions, policies and administrative decisions.

In our view, there is no pressing need to change these fundamental obligations in ICANN's Articles of Incorporation or Bylaws. A contemporary and liberal approach towards ICANN's non-discrimination, fairness and transparency obligations reflects quite well the core commitments one may expect from an organization such as ICANN. If ICANN is committed to abide by the rule of law, compliance with these fundamental obligations should afford adequate protection to the Internet community's stakeholders.

However, the problem lies in the restrictive interpretation of these rules by ICANN. As already explained, ICANN has often put process before content in its decision-making, refusing to adapt previously adopted processes in spite of serious fairness and transparency concerns. When ICANN applies its processes, standards or policies to a particular case, it should always be possible to challenge the legality of these processes, standards and policies in view of ICANN's more fundamental obligations. In developing and applying secondary rules, policies and processes, ICANN must always warrant the 'constitutionality' of these secondary rules with respect to ICANN's fundamental obligations of good faith, non-discrimination, fairness, transparency and due process. We consider that ICANN has failed in this respect, and that its accountability mechanisms have not always been adequate. We believe it is of paramount importance that ICANN: (i) recognize explicitly the precedence of its fundamental obligations over the application of its processes, standards and policies, and (ii) accept that any process, standard or policy which violates a more fundamental rule is inapplicable.

c. *Reconciling Competing Rules: Balancing the Fundamental Values Within a Single Source of Law*

In our view, it has always been clear that some values within ICANN's Bylaws were more fundamental than others. Since the original version of its Bylaws, ICANN has

1694. ICANN, Articles of Incorporation, Article 9.
1695. As ICANN has never had any 'members', this ratification requirement has no practical effect.

been committed to non-discrimination, fairness, openness and transparency. These obligations have been established in separate provisions, using affirmative language. These provisions have never been changed, which is indicative of the importance of these obligations for ICANN.

With its amended Bylaws of 15 December 2002, ICANN introduced a number of 'core values' which were intended to guide the decisions and actions of ICANN. However, these core values are guidance factors only. As a result, they should not be relied upon as grounds to deviate from ICANN's fundamental obligations, which are stated more affirmatively in ICANN's Articles of Incorporation and Bylaws. According to ICANN's Bylaws, ICANN must find an 'appropriate and defensible balance' among competing values.[1696] Much discretion was given to the ICANN Board in making this balancing exercise. ICANN has tried to rely on the discretion granted by its Bylaws to argue that the authority of IRP panels was limited. However, some IRP panels considered (rightly, in our opinion) that the ICANN Board's discretion is not unfettered. Nevertheless, clearer provisions limiting the ICANN Board's discretion in relation to the application of ICANN's most fundamental values would be a welcome addition to ICANN's Bylaws.

3. How the Hierarchy of Norms Is Addressed Under ICANN's New Bylaws, and How It Can Be Improved

a. *International Law Prevails Over Domestic Law*

ICANN's new Bylaws reaffirm ICANN's commitment to carry out its activities in conformity with relevant principles of international law, international conventions and applicable local law (in that order).[1697] At first glance, the inclusion of this commitment in ICANN's Bylaws adds nothing to ICANN's existing commitment under its Articles of Incorporation. However, in our view, the inclusion in ICANN's Bylaws must be seen as an affirmation of the applicable hierarchy of norms, and the fact that ICANN's obligations under international law prevail over its obligations under domestic law. As a result, there should be no future discussion about the pre-eminence of ICANN's obligations under international law.

b. *Reconciling Competing Rules: Respecting the Natural Hierarchy Between the Different Sources of Law*

ICANN's new Bylaws have left the issue of normative conflicts between its Articles of Incorporation, Bylaws and secondary rules unaddressed. This is unfortunate, as compliance with fundamental rules at all times is essential to improve accountability. Without a clear provision stating that policies and processes should be set aside if they

1696. ICANN, Bylaws as amended on 15 December 2002, Article I(2).
1697. ICANN, Bylaws as amended on 1 October 2016, Article 1(2)(a).

are inconsistent with ICANN's fundamental obligations, parties risk facing some of the same issues in this regard as arose in the IRPs of the last round of gTLDs.

c. *Reconciling Competing Rules: Balancing the Fundamental Values Within a Single Source of Law*

The precedence of some fundamental values over others has become clearer with the adoption of the new Bylaws of 1 October 2016. ICANN's new Bylaws distinguish between 'commitments' and 'core values.' The 'commitments' take precedence over ICANN's stated 'core values', which remain guidance factors only.[1698] The commitments are said to 'reflect ICANN's fundamental compact[[1699]] with the global Internet community and are intended to apply consistently and comprehensively to ICANN's activities.'[1700] ICANN must *comply* with the 'commitments', whereas it must simply *respect* its 'core values.'[1701] Also, the ICANN 'commitments' are stated first, and, contrary to ICANN's 'core values',[1702] they leave no room for a balancing exercise.

Some of ICANN's fundamental values, which were previously part of ICANN's 'core values', have now become 'commitments', indicating that these values take precedence over ICANN's core values. Not surprisingly, these 'commitments' include ICANN's obligation regarding openness and transparency and to 'apply[...] documented policies consistently, neutrally, objectively, and fairly, without singling out any particular party for discriminatory treatment.'[1703] These obligations also remain as specific obligations in separate affirmative Bylaws articles.[1704]

ICANN has now also transposed in its new Bylaws its good governance obligations which existed under the AoC between ICANN and the DoC.[1705] However, stating principles of administrative good governance is not a difficult task; applying and interpreting good governance obligations in a coherent, continuous and sound manner is more complicated.

In any event, it seems that ICANN has accepted the natural hierarchy of norms, and that it has clarified the relationship between the fundamental values that are mentioned in ICANN's Bylaws.

However, we would argue that some provisions in ICANN's new Bylaws are inadequately drafted. For example, Article 1(2)(a)(v) appears to define discriminatory

1698. ICANN, Bylaws as amended on 1 October 2016, Article 1(2)(b).
1699. A compact is a formal agreement between two or more parties.
1700. ICANN, Bylaws as amended on 1 October 2016, Article 1(2)(c).
1701. ICANN, Bylaws as amended on 1 October 2016, Article 1(2).
1702. With respect to the balancing of core values, ICANN's new Bylaws further curtail ICANN's discretionary power, as the Bylaws now specify that 'the result of the balancing must serve a policy developed through the bottom-up multistakeholder process or otherwise best serve ICANN's Mission.' (ICANN, Bylaws as amended on 1 October 2016, Article 1(2)(c)).
1703. ICANN, Bylaws as amended on 1 October 2016, Article 1(2)(b).
1704. ICANN, Bylaws as amended on 1 October 2016, Articles 2(3) and 3.
1705. ICANN, Bylaws as amended 1 October 2016; *see also* Chapter 6.C.2.b.

treatment as 'making an unjustified prejudicial distinction between or among different parties.' If interpreted narrowly, this definition does not cover all facets of objectionable discriminatory treatment. For example, it does not cover the eventuality that different situations may need to be treated differently. As discussed above, the assessment by IRP panels of ICANN's prohibition on discrimination already seems underdeveloped.[1706] The adoption of a seemingly narrow definition of discriminatory treatment risks curtailing the little progress made thus far in this area.

Similarly, ICANN seems not to have adequately affirmed its commitment to respect (non-derogable) human rights.[1707] In its new Bylaws, ICANN apparently conditions the respect of human rights upon the approval of the ICANN Board.[1708] Moreover, 'respecting internationally recognized human rights as required by applicable law' is taken up as a core value and not as a formal commitment under Article 1(2) of ICANN's Bylaws. According to the text of the new Bylaws, this '[c]ore [v]alue does not obligate ICANN to enforce its human rights obligations, or the human rights obligations of other parties, against other parties.'[1709] It is not entirely clear what is meant with the phrase 'against other parties.' However, if the provision is intended to mean that ICANN is not obliged to enforce its human rights obligations, it is doubtful whether this interpretation of the provision would be enforceable (it might be considered contrary to more fundamental principles of international law). Clearly, peremptory norms of international law cannot be made dependent on the approval of an executive body, and ICANN cannot function as an accountable organization if it does not ensure compliance with such peremptory norms.

In our view, ICANN should settle for nothing less than the interpretation of human rights that exists in all liberal democracies of the developed world. When it comes to evaluating ICANN's obligations, there is, in our view, no room for cultural relativism or diversity regarding the protection of the universal rights of individual stakeholders. Article 27(2) of ICANN's new Bylaws calls for the introduction of a framework of interpretation for human rights. We understand that ICANN may wish to establish an enlightened framework for interpreting human rights in order to advance the progressive realization of better protection of human rights within ICANN. However, such a framework would be of little use if it does not have to be respected. As a result, we would recommend that ICANN does not limit itself to establishing an enlightened framework for interpreting its human rights obligations, but rather that it also makes clear that this framework is obligatory for ICANN. ICANN's observance of human rights should be a firm 'commitment' instead of a 'core value' subject to ICANN's discretion.

1706. *See* Chapter 6.C.2.b(4).
1707. *See e.g.*, the statement by counsel to ICANN in the *Despegar et al.* case (Despegar et al. IRP Declaration, § 145).
1708. ICANN, Bylaws as amended on 1 October 2016, Article 27(2) *juncto* Article 1(2)(b)(viii).
1709. ICANN, Bylaws as amended on 1 October 2016, Article 1(2)(b)(viii).

C. CLARIFYING AND AMENDING THE IRP'S PROCEDURAL RULES

In this section, we concentrate on the IRP procedural rules, looking at each issue from three different angles. First we explain why there is a need for action; then we suggest what action should be taken; lastly we look at how, if at all, the issue has been addressed by ICANN's new Bylaws (in force since October 2016) and how we would address remaining issues.

1. Ensuring Consistency Between the Various Applicable Procedural Rules

a. Need for More Consistency: The Troubled Relationship Between the Different Procedural Rules

ICANN unilaterally fixed the procedural rules that govern the IRP. The rules that apply are those set out in the ICANN Bylaws, the ICDR IRP Supplementary Procedures and the ICDR Rules (in that order). Experience has shown that certain inconsistencies between these three sets of rules have been a cause of problems.

Some of the provisions set out in the IRP procedural documents – *e.g.*, with respect to the nature of IRP declarations – contain inconsistent language, creating difficulties for IRP panels in applying these rules. Panels have been required to look into the historic context of some of the Bylaws' provisions in order to be able to interpret the text.

Amendments to the ICDR Rules have also led to inconsistencies. *E.g.*, Article 12 of the ICDR IRP Supplementary Procedures, which refers to 'Emergency Measures of Protection', currently states that 'Article 37 of the [ICDR] RULES will not apply.' However, this reference to Article 37 is out of date. Under a previous version of the ICDR Rules, Article 37 related to emergency measures. However, since June 2014, the ICDR has changed its procedures on emergency measures, and Article 37 of the ICDR rules no longer relates to emergency measures, but to confidentiality. In addition, ICANN did not provide for a viable alternative to emergency measures under the old Article 37. The ICDR IRP Supplementary Procedures provide that a claimant requiring urgent interim relief can request that ICANN stay an action or decision with the Chair of the IRP standing panel.[1710] However, to date, no IRP standing panel has been in place. Applicants in the new gTLD Program also had to agree on an advance waiver from seeking recourse in court. As a result, it has become unclear where claimants should address their requests for emergency measures.

Fortunately, in various IRPs – initiated both before and after June 2014 – ICANN has accepted the appointment of an emergency arbitrator in accordance with the ICDR Rules, and emergency measures of protection have been imposed upon ICANN. Nevertheless, without ICANN's explicit approval that the ICDR Rules on emergency measures apply, ambiguity remains about the legal framework that applies to emergency measures.

1710. ICDR IRP Supplementary Procedures, Article 7.

There is also a potential for inconsistent IRP panel decisions with regards to certain procedural limitations that ICANN has sought to impose through its Bylaws. In our view, some of the procedural limitations can be said to violate the due process requirements of international arbitration, and we would recommend them being changed.[1711] The intended limitations seem to contrast quite sharply with the aim of the ICDR Rules: (i) to provide for balanced and flexible arbitration procedures and (ii) to grant extensive authority to the arbitration (IRP) panel to structure the proceedings in the manner best suited for the case under review.[1712]

In the past, IRP panels have generally found ways to interpret the procedural rules in a balanced and fair manner. In certain cases, panels have decided to set aside the Bylaws' procedural limitations, where they considered that these limitations prevented the parties from being treated equally or from being heard. ICANN has complied with the instructions of the panels in individual cases, and these findings demonstrate an IRP panel's ability to interpret the applicable procedural rules in a sound fashion. However, the ability of one panel to interpret inconsistent rules in a balanced and fair manner does not guarantee that future panels will do so.

In short, while the applicability of these rules and their order of priority may not in itself cause a problem as long as IRP panels interpret the rules so as to give pre-eminence to the fundamental principles of international arbitration, a better approach would be to make the rules clearer and more consistent so as to enhance legal certainty in the IRP.

b. *How to Ensure Consistency Within the IRP Procedural Rules*

A consistent interpretation of procedural rules does not imply that all IRPs should be structured in the same way. Party autonomy and the circumstances of a case, as well as the experience and personality of the appointed panelists, may make one procedure quite different from another. This flexibility in organizing the procedures is considered to be one of the major advantages of international arbitration. The procedure can be adapted to the needs of the parties and the particularities of each case. To guarantee a consistent interpretation of the IRP procedural rules, it is important that the rules allow for sufficient flexibility in managing the procedures and that they make it clear that the fundamentals of international arbitration must always be respected. Some of the existing procedural limitations relating to the IRP and imposed by ICANN's Bylaws and the ICDR IRP Supplementary Procedures (such as the limitations on the organization of oral hearings and witness testimony) could simply be removed.

As institutional rules for arbitration, such as the ICDR Rules, are updated from time to time, it would be advisable to check the consistency of the ICDR Rules with ICANN's Bylaws and the ICDR IRP Supplementary Procedures in a timely fashion. ICANN should require that its IRP service provider keeps ICANN informed about impending

1711. *See further infra* Chapter 7.A.6 and Chapter 7.A.7.
1712. *See* ICDR Rules, Article 20.

changes to the rules of arbitration. This would allow the changes to be discussed openly within the Internet community and help ensure that all applicable rules are checked for consistency, and adapted where necessary. Should the ICDR not be in a position to change the Supplementary Procedures following an update of the ICDR Rules, ICANN could ask for a transition period during which IRPs would be considered under the old rules. Ultimately, ICANN must be able to opt for a similar approach, were it to decide to replace the ICDR by another IRP provider.

c. *Critical Appraisal of How ICANN's New Bylaws Address Consistency Between the IRP Procedural Rules*

ICANN's new Bylaws call for IRP procedural rules that 'conform with international arbitration norms', 'are streamlined, easy to understand and apply fairly to all parties.'[1713] ICANN's explicit recognition of these norms and principles is a positive development.

However, much work remains to be done. ICANN's new Bylaws do not address the existing inconsistencies between the various procedural rules. Furthermore, they anticipate the development of specific new rules of procedure at some future point in time. Thus, issues that were covered under the previous Bylaws, such as the length of an IRP request and the time limit within which it must be submitted, will now only be addressed in still-to-be-developed rules of procedure. As ICANN's Bylaws do not contain transitional provisions laying down the IRP procedural rules that apply pending the development of these new rules, the introduction of ICANN's new Bylaws may have added to the legal uncertainty regarding the applicable procedural rules for pending proceedings or newly initiated proceedings.

In addition, it is questionable whether overly specific rules of procedure for IRPs are desirable. While the case can be made for establishing rules that are tailored to ICANN's unique mission and purpose, the question remains whether it would not be possible for ICANN simply to opt for pre-existing institutional arbitration rules, which have been in existence for many years and which have a proven worth in the settling of a variety of disputes. ICANN could for example ask IRP panels to apply the IBA Rules on the Taking of Evidence in International Arbitration[1714] with due regard for ICANN's transparency obligations. Developing procedural rules which are too specific may jeopardize the flexibility that may be essential to the efficient administration of justice adapted to the specific circumstances of a particular case.

1713. ICANN, Bylaws as amended on 1 October 2016, Article 4(3)(n)(i).
1714. International Bar Association, *IBA Rules on the Taking of Evidence in International Arbitration, adopted by a resolution of the IBA Council*, 29 May 2010.

2. Clarifying and Amending the Jurisdiction of IRP Panels

a. *Need for Clarifying the Jurisdiction of IRP Panels*

In various cases during the last round of new gTLDs, the limits on an IRP panel's jurisdiction has been a subject of debate.[1715] The question was raised whether IRP panels can review both ICANN actions and inactions. IRP panels seem to have generally accepted that they are entitled to examine actionable inaction for consistency with the Articles of Incorporation and Bylaws.[1716] But questions remain as to whether panels are limited to examining decisions of the ICANN Board or can also examine the acts of ICANN staff and third parties working for ICANN?

In this respect, the extent of the control the ICANN Board must exercise over its staff and third-party contractors remains subject to discussion. This lack of certainty is unhelpful and inappropriate given ICANN's obligation to enhance its accountability on a continuous basis. If ICANN's accountability can be avoided simply by outsourcing its decision-making, ICANN's essential obligations and accountability mechanisms risk becoming meaningless. It should not be possible for ICANN to hide behind third-party advisors in order to avoid its responsibilities for actions that have negatively impacted applicants.[1717]

b. *How to Clarify the Rules on the Jurisdiction of IRP Panels*

Clear rules on outsourcing and on the (expanded) jurisdiction of IRP panels are needed to ensure that ICANN's essential obligations do not become meaningless. As the dissenting panelist in the *Donuts* case observed, ICANN should not be able to seek a 'rubberstamping of decision-making that was not independent, that was not transparent, and that has not been held accountable.'[1718] While ICANN may certainly use expert advice to support its decisions, ICANN and its Board must remain responsible for all decisions being made in a fair, transparent and non-discriminatory fashion. In addition, no decisions which relate to ICANN's core tasks should be outsourced to third parties; these should be taken by ICANN and its Board.

As a safeguard against ICANN outsourcing decisions relating to its core tasks without due regard for compliance with ICANN's fundamental obligations, IRP panels must have clear jurisdiction to review such outsourced decision-making.

1715. *See e.g.*, *Booking.com* case, *Vistaprint* case, *Merck* case, *Despegar et al.* case and *Donuts* case.
1716. *See e.g.*, Booking.com IRP Declaration, § 53; DCA Final IRP Declaration, §§ 107–109; Vistaprint IRP Declaration, § 119; *see also* § 123; Merck IRP Declaration, § 17; Despegar et al. IRP Declaration, § 58; Donuts IRP Declaration, § 8; Dot Registry IRP Declaration, § 70.
1717. ICANN also invoked a procedural time bar to shield its acceptance of third-party advice from being challenged. *See also* Chapter 7.A.5 *infra*.
1718. Donuts IRP Declaration, Dissenting Opinion, p. 1.

c. *Critical Appraisal of How ICANN's Bylaws Address the Jurisdiction of IRP Panels*

The ICANN community has focused on the possible expansion of the IRP panel's jurisdiction. Indeed, the CCWG recognized that the IRP should not only hear and resolve claims that ICANN, through its Board of Directors or staff, has acted (or has failed to act) in violation of its Articles of Incorporation or Bylaws, but should also investigate any violation of the Bylaws resulting from action taken in response to advice or input from any SO or Advisory Committee (AC).[1719] It advocated that IRP panels be given competence to rule, *inter alia*, on claims regarding inconsistent DIDP decisions or expert panel decisions.[1720] This explicit inclusion of examples such as DIDP decisions and expert panel decisions is helpful so long as it is not taken to imply an exhaustive list.

Following the community discussions, ICANN introduced new provisions on the scope of IRPs in its Bylaws. ICANN's Bylaws now include a non-exhaustive list of disputes that can be submitted to an IRP panel. However, in our view the jurisdiction of an IRP panel could have been defined more clearly. Indeed, the Bylaws' description of the IRP panel's scope contains circular definitions, in that its definition for 'Covered Actions' under an IRP refers to the defined term 'Dispute', and *vice versa*.[1721]

In any event, the IRP panel's scope now seems to include 'any actions or failures to act by or within ICANN committed by the Board, individual Directors, Officers or Staff members' in violation of the Articles of Incorporation or Bylaws.[1722] 'Staff members' includes 'employees and individual long-term paid contractors serving in locations where ICANN does not have the mechanisms to employ such contractors directly.'[1723] Despite this reference to 'long-term paid contractors', it is our view that ICANN's new definition of the scope of IRPs does not completely rule out the possibility of future discussion regarding ICANN's accountability for outsourced decisions. It is true that ICANN's new Bylaws seem to reflect the CCWG's intention. Indeed, Article 4(3)(b)(iii)(A)(3) of ICANN's new Bylaws provides that IRP panels may examine ICANN actions or inactions that 'resulted from decisions of process-specific expert panels that are claimed to be inconsistent with the Articles of Incorporation or Bylaws.' However, it remains to be seen how broadly the new text will be interpreted.[1724]

1719. CCWG-Accountability, *Supplemental Final Proposal on Work Stream 1 Recommendations*, 23 February 2016, https://www.icann.org/en/system/files/files/ccwg-accountability-supp-proposal-work-stream-1-recs-23feb16-en.pdf, p. 34.
1720. CCWG-Accountability, *Supplemental Final Proposal on Work Stream 1 Recommendations*, 23 February 2016, https://www.icann.org/en/system/files/files/ccwg-accountability-supp-proposal-work-stream-1-recs-23feb16-en.pdf, p. 34.
1721. ICANN, Bylaws as amended on 1 October 2016, Article 4(3)(b)(ii) *juncto* Article 4(3)(b)(iii).
1722. ICANN, Bylaws as amended on 1 October 2016, Article 4(3)(b) (ii) *juncto* Article 4(3)(b)(iii)(A).
1723. ICANN, Bylaws as amended on 1 October 2016, Article 4(2)(a).
1724. Indeed, in the light of past experience, we cannot exclude the possibility that ICANN might argue that a claimant is time barred from challenging inconsistencies with the Articles of Incorporation or Bylaws which may have resulted from ICANN's earlier adoption of a specific (potentially problematic) process. *E.g.*, ICANN could adopt a process *contra legem* that

In view of the above, we would welcome an amendment which further clarifies the scope of an IRP panel's jurisdiction and which removes any circular definitions.

3. Maintaining Party Autonomy in the Nomination of IRP Panelists

a. *Why the Current System of Nominating IRP Panelists Works*

In view of the fact that ICANN did not have in place the IRP omnibus standing panel which was envisioned in ICANN's Bylaws of 11 April 2013, parties had to fall back on the appointment procedure of the ICDR Rules.[1725] The ICDR Rules grant considerable freedom to the parties to agree upon a procedure for appointing panelists.[1726] In our experience, the parties' involvement in the appointment procedure contributes to the smooth running of proceedings. If the parties are able to contribute to the composition of the panel, they have greater confidence in the competence, independence and impartiality of the panelists than when a panel is appointed with no or very little involvement by either of the parties. A major advantage of *ad hoc* appointments is that the parties have more freedom in finding the panelists that are best suited for the case.

One appointment procedure, proposed by the majority of claimants and accepted by ICANN, has been for each party simultaneously to nominate one panelist, leaving the two party-appointed co-panelists to agree on the nomination of the chair.[1727] The ICDR Rules allow the party-appointed co-panelists to discuss the potential chair candidates with the party that appointed them.[1728] Such discussions can be helpful to avoid a chair's nomination being later challenged by one of the parties. However, these discussions should remain limited in our view, as it would be desirable for the party appointing a co-panelist to trust that panelist's judgment in selecting a chair. Another option may be for the parties to agree between themselves on the appointment of a chair. However, the party-appointed co-panelists should not become negotiating proxies for the parties appointing them, as, in such circumstances, the involvement of the co-panelists might impede rather than facilitate the appointment process.

In the cases in which we have been involved, the nomination and appointment of panelists has occurred smoothly, apart from the fact that some time extensions were requested, and granted, when ICANN required more time to nominate co-panelists.[1729]

---

provides for ICANN's automatic acceptance of a decision by an expert panel, and subsequently argue that a claimant challenging ICANN's acceptance of the expert's decision is time barred, as the claimant should have objected to the process of automatic acceptance at the time of its adoption. In our view, such an interpretation would be inconsistent with the meaning of the text. Moreover, if the scope of what an IRP panel is entitled to examine could be impacted by a time bar, it is curious why the discussion on possible time bars was reserved to a later stage. (*See also* Chapter 7.A.5 *infra*).

1725. *Supra* Chapter 6.C.1.c.
1726. ICDR Rules, Article 12.
1727. *Supra* Chapter 6.C.1.c.
1728. ICDR Rules, Article 13(6).
1729. *Supra* Chapter 6.C.1.c.

b. *How to Improve the Current System of Nominating IRP Panelists*

ICANN, as the party involved in all IRPs, could perhaps be expected to have a list of pre-selected individuals for nomination as co-panelists. Having a prior list of interested panelists and formalizing the appointment procedure with the simultaneous nomination of co-panelists could contribute to even more efficiency in establishing IRP panels in a timely fashion.

However, it is important that ICANN's list of interested panelists be sufficiently broad. ICANN has had a tendency to nominate the same panelist for multiple cases.[1730] This practice can be problematic, as it could, in the eyes of claimant parties, give rise to doubts as to an arbitrator's impartiality and independence. This is why, absent any practice in certain types of arbitration to draw arbitrators from a smaller or specialized pool of individuals, the IBA Guidelines on Conflicts of Interest in International Arbitration provide for the disclosure of the fact that an arbitrator has been appointed by one of the parties on two or more occasions within the past three years.[1731] If parties decide to adhere to these Guidelines, the other party may veto the appointment of such arbitrator.[1732] In our view, there is no reason why ICANN should nominate the same panelist more than twice in IRPs or why ICANN should not adhere to the IBA Guidelines on Conflict of Interest in International Arbitration.

c. *Critical Appraisal of How ICANN's Bylaws Address the Nomination of IRP Panelists*

Although ICANN has no actual experience with the appointment of a standing panel or with dispute resolution by such panel, the ICANN community favored the institution of an omnibus standing panel for IRPs.[1733] It is not clear how the community would benefit from the institution of an omnibus standing panel as opposed to relying on more liberal appointment methods, which have worked well until now.

We understand the benefits to ICANN of a standing panel, as it would be easier to guide a small group of panelists who are supposed to serve for five years. ICANN's new Bylaws provide that the members of the standing panel will receive training provided by ICANN on the workings and management of the Internet's unique identifiers.[1734] However, there is a risk that panelists could be prejudiced by ICANN's interpretation of its obligations as a result of these trainings. It is difficult to see how a standing panel, trained by one party to the IRP proceedings, would improve ICANN's accountability,

1730. *See Booking.com*, *Merck* and *Amazon* IRP cases.
1731. International Bar Association, *IBA Guidelines on Conflicts of Interest in International Arbitration, adopted by resolution of the IBA Council*, 23 October 2014, Part II, Section 3.1.3.
1732. International Bar Association, *IBA Guidelines on Conflicts of Interest in International Arbitration, adopted by resolution of the IBA Council*, 23 October 2014, Part II, Section 3.
1733. CCWG-Accountability, *Supplemental Final Proposal on Work Stream 1 Recommendations*, 23 February 2016, https://www.icann.org/en/system/files/files/ccwg-accountability-supp-proposal-work-stream-1-recs-23feb16-en.pdf, p. 35.
1734. ICANN, Bylaws as amended on 1 October 2016, Article 4(3)(j)(i).

especially in view of the fact that the system of *ad hoc* appointments has been shown to work and gives parties the opportunity to appoint a balanced panel.

As mentioned above, the absence of an omnibus standing panel has not been an impediment to the appointment of appropriately qualified IRP panelists. In our view, there is no pressing need to limit the pool of individuals who can serve as IRP panelists. Significant legal expertise is one of the most important qualifications required of an IRP panelist – particularly in international law, corporate governance, and regulatory and administrative processes – as is experience in dispute resolution and arbitration. A strong understanding of the DNS is obviously a prerequisite, but experience shows that open-minded panelists can quickly make up for an initially limited knowledge of the DNS. It is much more important to have independent and impartial panelists with an open mind than to have a DNS subject-matter expert who may be involved with various ICANN stakeholder groups or advisory committees.

4. Enforcing the Standing Requirements in an IRP

a. Need for Enforcing the Standing Requirements in an IRP

Only persons or entities materially affected by an ICANN action or inaction in violation of ICANN's Articles of Incorporation and/or Bylaws may submit a request for IRP.[1735] However, that has not prevented parties with an arguably weak case on the merits from seeking 'relief' through IRP. In our view, too little attention has been given to the question of whether those claimants were 'materially affected' by the alleged violation of ICANN's Articles of Incorporation and/or Bylaws. When the party bringing a request for IRP is not materially affected by the alleged violation, the IRP is unlikely to resolve the dispute, as the claimant will normally not benefit materially once the violation has been redressed. At most, such a claim may serve as an *actio popularis*, which could serve the interest of the international Internet community, but not the individual claimant.

When an individual claimant brings an IRP request without the possibility for it to end in personal benefit, it is a waste of ICANN's resources. Therefore, we would recommend that an analysis of the standing requirement be made at the outset of proceedings.

b. How to Handle Claims That Are Brought Without Personal Interest

IRPs are not suited to handle claims that are brought without a personal interest. An *actio popularis*[1736] type of claim may make sense, as it could incite ICANN to apply

1735. ICANN, Bylaws as amended on 11 April 2013, Article IV(3)(2); ICANN, Bylaws as amended on 1 October 2016, Article 4(3)(b)(i).
1736. A lawsuit brought by a third party in the interest of the public as a whole.

greater care in its decision-making. However, in our view, an *actio popularis* is best addressed in very straightforward proceedings, specifically designed for that purpose.

c. *Critical Appraisal of How ICANN's New Bylaws Address the IRP Standing Requirements*

The standing requirements for bringing an individual request for IRP have not changed significantly under ICANN's new Bylaws.[1737] However, there is a need for increased attention to the application of these standing requirements and for analyzing them more thoroughly at the start of the IRP proceedings.

At the request of the ICANN community, ICANN has introduced a so-called empowered community, which is entitled to bring IRPs on behalf of the public interest. ICANN's empowered community is deemed to be materially affected by an ICANN action or inaction, and will thus have standing to bring a request for IRP.[1738] The empowered community is a non-profit association formed under the laws of the State of California consisting of the ASO,[1739] the ccNSO, the GNSO, the ALAC and the GAC.[1740] Apart from the authority to bring IRPs, the empowered community, *inter alia*, has the authority to appoint and remove individual Board members or to recall the entire Board and to reject or approve amendments to the ICANN Bylaws and Articles of Incorporation.[1741]

ICANN shall bear all costs associated with an IRP brought by the empowered community on behalf of the Internet community.[1742] However, the procedure to make the empowered community act on behalf of the public interest may prove cumbersome,[1743] and time will tell if the empowered community will truly represent the interests of the international Internet community. Furthermore, once it has been accepted that the empowered community can bring an IRP on behalf of the international Internet community, it is conceivable that the right to initiate IRP proceedings should be given to anyone acting in the interests of the global Internet community, regardless of his or her affiliation with the ICANN stakeholder group. As indicated above, we believe that such *actio popularis* would be better addressed in more straightforward proceedings, specifically designed for that purpose.

1737. *Compare* ICANN, Bylaws as amended on 11 April 2013, Article IV(3)(2) *with* ICANN, Bylaws as amended on 1 October 2016, Article 4(3)(b)(i).
1738. ICANN, Bylaws as amended on 1 October 2006, Article 4(3)(b)(i)(A).
1739. The ASO is an organization with ICANN which advises the ICANN Board with respect to policy issues relating to the operation, assignment, and management of Internet addresses (ICANN, Bylaws as amended on 1 October 2016, Article 9(1)).
1740. ICANN, Bylaws as amended on 1 October 2016, Article 6.
1741. ICANN, Bylaws as amended on 1 October 2016, Article 6(2).
1742. ICANN, Bylaws as amended on 1 October 2016, Article 4(3)(r).
1743. *See* ICANN, Bylaws as amended on 1 October 2016, Annex D.

5. Clarifying and Amending the Time Bar Requirement for Submitting a Request for IRP

a. *Need for Clarifying ICANN's Time Bar Requirement*

ICANN's introduction of a time bar during the evaluation phase of its new gTLD Program has been the subject of many debates that could have been avoided. ICANN has tried to impose this time bar retroactively to prevent previously adopted policies and processes from being challenged in an IRP.[1744] However, when parties applied for new gTLDs, they did so with the expectation that they could challenge the policies and process for consistency with the Articles of Incorporation and Bylaws if they were harmed by their application.

b. *How to Amend ICANN's Time Bar Requirement*

In our view, new rules should explicitly state that a time bar cannot be applied retroactively, and that a claimant can never be barred from invoking the inconsistency of an ICANN policy with fundamental legal principles or ICANN's essential obligations, irrespective of the policy's age. It is perfectly possible for a party not to be materially affected by an illegal or inconsistent ICANN policy at the time of its adoption, but for that party to be affected by the very same policy when that policy is implemented or applied to the party's detriment. The fact that the policy was not challenged before should not prevent an IRP panel from evaluating the consistency of the policy with ICANN's Articles of Incorporation and Bylaws. The time bar should not be used to justify a policy that contradicts ICANN's essential obligations.

c. *Critical Appraisal of How ICANN's New Bylaws Address the Time Bar Requirement*

The time bar issue has hardly been debated by the CCWG.[1745] ICANN's new Bylaws no longer contain the provision which required a claimant to file a request for IRP within thirty days of the posting of the minutes of the relevant Board meeting. They now provide that new IRP rules of procedure – which are to be developed at a future date – must address the time within which a claim must be filed after a claimant 'becomes aware or reasonably should have become aware of the action or inaction giving rise to the Dispute.'[1746]

As a result, ICANN's new Bylaws have removed the existing time bar provision with the intention of replacing it sometime in the future with a new rule yet to be agreed

1744. *See e.g.*, Chapter 5.C.4.a(5) *supra*.
1745. CCWG-Accountability, *Supplemental Final Proposal on Work Stream 1 Recommendations*, 23 February 2016, https://www.icann.org/en/system/files/files/ccwg-accountability-supp-proposal-work-stream-1-recs-23feb16-en.pdf, pp. 33–36.
1746. ICANN, Bylaws as amended on 1 October 2016, Article 4(3)(n)(iv)(A).

upon. However, for pending cases or for claims that are initiated between now and the adoption of the IRP rules of procedure, it is unclear if a time bar applies or how long it would be. This situation creates legal uncertainty about an essential part of the procedural rules. In our view, until the adoption of new rules on the time bar, IRP claimants should benefit from the fact that there currently is no time bar rule.

6. Ensuring Flexibility in the Rules on Written and Oral Arguments

a. Need for Flexible Rules on Written and Oral Arguments: The Balance Between Streamlining Proceedings and Procedural Equality

In 2013, ICANN tried to streamline the IRP proceedings by introducing page limits on requests for IRPs and by recommending that the proceedings be conducted by email and otherwise via the Internet to the maximum extent feasible.[1747] While it is defensible to focus on cost-efficient and straightforward proceedings, this should not be at the expense of procedural equality and a claimant's right to be given a fair opportunity to present its case.

In practice, oral argument has been deemed useful in almost all IRP cases, as a way to facilitate a thorough debate on the complex legal and factual issues of the case.[1748] In most cases, opening statements can be relatively succinct. The main value of oral arguments lies in the interactive debate, which both allows IRP panels to ensure that they have understood the parties' respective positions, and can be useful in uncovering any flaws in a party's reasoning.

Oral argument may not be necessary in less complex cases. However, with relatively little jurisprudence and in view of the important issues that may be at stake in an IRP, it is to be expected that oral hearings will be appropriate in most cases. As a result of the limitations ICANN has tried to impose on the organization of in-person hearings, many IRP panels have favored holding the hearing via telephone or video conference.[1749] However, as explained in Chapter 6.C.1.h, there is a potential disadvantage attached to the reduced communication in such hearings (as opposed to in-person hearings), because of the greater risk of misunderstandings between the parties involved.

b. How to Create Rules on Written and Oral Arguments

In our view, it is important that IRP panels retain sufficient flexibility to structure the proceedings in the manner best suited for each individual case. A fixed page limit for

1747. ICANN, Bylaws as amended on 11 April 2013, Article IV(3)(12).
1748. *Supra* Chapter 6.C.1.h.
1749. *Supra* Chapter 6.C.1.h.

a request for IRP is acceptable as long as there is flexibility concerning additional submissions and their length. Straightforward cases may not require lengthy submissions or extensive oral argument. It generally benefits the procedure if the parties can agree on the length of the submissions and the organization of oral hearings. In the absence of an agreement, the IRP panel should be able to rule on the issue. However, it is important that IRP panels accept that ICANN's preference for short submissions and limited oral hearing is not a sacrosanct principle.

In the absence of agreement between the parties, we generally favor clear instructions by the IRP panel about the number of submissions and their length. Of course, there can be reasons to deviate from the initial schedule. However, when there is a clear schedule from the outset, this generally leads to a more focused, more expedient and hence cheaper process. Clear page limit instructions also help to avoid the filing of overly extensive written submissions, which may only frustrate the panel and increase costs.[1750]

c. *Critical Appraisal of How ICANN's New Bylaws Address Written and Oral Arguments*

The rules governing written and oral arguments are no longer covered in the ICANN Bylaws themselves. ICANN's new Bylaws require that the IRP procedural rules address the length of statements, the number of supplemental statements, the required elements of a claim, limits on content, the time for filing, etc.[1751] However, the detailed development of these rules has been left for a future date, which at present creates uncertainty about these aspects of the proceedings.

In our view, it is doubtful whether the Internet community will be served by overly-rigid procedural rules. As explained, some matters may require fewer submissions and fixed rules on the number of submissions might encourage parties to 'play safe' and submit additional statements that are not strictly necessary. For more complex matters, predefined rules on the number and content of supplemental statements may be inadequate and a disproportionate limitation to a party's right to present its case. In our view, pre-established limits can be imposed on the length of the request for IRP and its response. However, the rules on additional submissions are better determined on an ad hoc basis by the parties and the IRP panel.

1750. For a panelist criticizing a party's procedural behavior, *see* Dot Registry IRP Declaration, Dissenting Opinion, § 11.
1751. ICANN, Bylaws as amended on 1 October 2016, Article 4(3)(n)(iv).

7. Ensuring Flexibility in the Rules on Allowing Witnesses and Expert Witnesses

a. *Need for Flexible Rules on Allowing Witnesses and Expert Witnesses*

ICANN's Bylaws of 11 April 2013 arguably excluded the possibility of live witness testimony.[1752] However, this provision was set aside by one IRP panel as it was considered to be in violation of a party's right to be heard and to be given a fair opportunity to present its case.[1753] Other panels have been very reluctant to admit the examination of witnesses or examining expert testimony.[1754] Clearly, the Bylaws' provision that oral hearings must be limited to argument only has influenced panels considering whether or not to admit the examination or cross-examination of witnesses.

b. *How to Deal with Witness Testimony*

In our view, and in the absence of party agreement, IRP panels must be able to adopt a flexible approach and should be given a large amount of discretion to decide whether to admit factual and expert witness testimony. Flexibility is one of the main advantages of arbitration, as it allows the parties and the panel to structure the proceedings in accordance with the particulars of the case. Some cases can do well without witness testimony. There is no need to corroborate undisputed facts or facts that are not relevant to the resolution of the case with testimonial evidence. Likewise, if a party does not dispute the contents of a statement filed by the opposing party, there is no need to call the witness for examination or cross-examination. If, on the other hand, testimonial evidence is crucial for deciding the outcome of the case, the examination or cross-examination of witnesses should be allowed as necessary. If a party fails to make witnesses available for cross-examination or for examination by the panel, this should lead to the possibility of adverse inference or the exclusion of written testimonials.

There are various ways of dealing with witnesses and experts, and it is important that witnesses know in advance what is expected of them, to avoid valuable time being lost during the hearing. An increasingly popular method of examining witnesses and experts is known as 'hot-tubbing', 'witness conferencing' or 'concurrent evidence.' The practice consists of a simultaneous joint hearing of all witnesses and experts involved in the procedure. A joint hearing such as this, if properly conducted, can be very effective, both from a timing and fact-finding perspective. The technique is especially valued in arbitrations with a particularly technical content, and it could lend itself well to IRP disputes involving complex DNS policy issues. Pre-hearing

1752. ICANN, Bylaws as amended on 11 April 2013, Article IV(3)(12).
1753. DCA Panel's IRP Declaration on the IRP Procedure, §§ 84, 86; *see also* DCA 2nd Declaration on IRP Procedure, § 19.
1754. *See e.g.*, Dot Registry IRP Panel's Order No. 11, § 2; Dot Registry IRP Panel's Order No. 12, § 2.

conferences can also be useful, *e.g.*, to reduce voluminous expert testimony by eliminating those areas on which the experts agree and leaving only the disputed facts on the table.

The question of whether witness or expert witness testimony is necessary largely depends on the circumstances of each case and the expertise of the panel. In our view, IRP panels should be selected in light of their expertise regarding the questions of law that must be addressed. Unnecessary time and resources need not be spent on expert legal testimony if the legal arguments can be advanced by the parties and assessed by an appropriately qualified panel. However, parties must remain free to structure their legal argument as they see fit and to call on legal expert opinion if this strengthens their position. Therefore, whether live witness testimony should be admitted in a particular case is best left to the discretion of the panel in question; it is not something that can be decided once and for all by rigid procedural rules.

c. *Critical Appraisal of How ICANN's New Bylaws Address the Admission of Witness Testimony*

With ICANN's new Bylaws of 1 October 2016, the possibility of live witness testimony is no longer explicitly excluded from the Bylaws. However, ICANN plans to establish specific procedural rules regarding the admission of evidentiary support.[1755]

In our view, there is no need to develop a separate set of rules to this end. The current version of the ICDR Rules contains specific rules regarding witnesses and the admissibility of written statements.[1756] ICANN could also choose to adopt the IBA Rules on the Taking of Evidence in International Arbitration.[1757] They provide an efficient, economical and fair process for the taking of evidence in international arbitration and include flexible mechanisms for the presentation of witnesses and experts. The IBA Rules take account of the international nature of the arbitration and are especially useful if the parties come from different legal cultures. They reflect procedures in use in many different legal systems, and their international nature would make them particularly suited to the international nature of ICANN's mission.

8. Maintaining Efficient Document Disclosure Proceedings

a. *Why the Current Rules on Document Disclosure Can Work*

In 2014, the ICDR adopted standard principles for documentary exchange, which are comparable to the rules on documentary disclosure in the IBA Rules on the Taking of Evidence in International Arbitration.[1758] Both sets of rules provide for efficient and

1755. ICANN, Bylaws as amended on 1 October 2016, Article 4.3(n)(iv)(C).
1756. ICDR Rules, Article 23.
1757. IBA Rules on the Taking of Evidence, *supra* n. 1714.
1758. ICDR Rules, Articles 20 and following; IBA Rules on the Taking of Evidence, *supra* n. 1714.

flexible mechanisms to request and obtain the disclosure of documents that are relevant to the dispute and material to its outcome.

One of the advantages of the IBA Rules – or of the ICDR Rules which seem largely inspired by the IBA Rules – is that they were developed taking into account cultural differences in an international context, and building on the traditions of both civil and common law systems. Their adoption generally allows the parties to avoid extensive and time-consuming U.S.-style discovery proceedings.[1759] At the same time, the claimants in an IRP would have access to efficient and balanced methods for document production.

b. *How to Ensure Stability in the Rules Governing Document Disclosure*

There is no need for ICANN to develop a new set of rules on documentary exchange in IRP proceedings. It would be appropriate for it simply to make clear the application of the ICDR Rules or the IBA Rules on the Taking of Evidence in International Arbitration. In our view, it would be best for ICANN to select the IBA Rules on the Taking of Evidence in International Arbitration, so as to ensure stability. It is possible for ICANN to change its IRP provider, or invite other DRSPs to submit a proposal for administering IRPs. By adopting documentary disclosure rules that are not specifically linked to one particular DRSP, ICANN would avoid the possibility of problems arising in relation to evidentiary rules should it change its IRP administrator.

c. *Critical Appraisal of How ICANN's New Bylaws Address Document Disclosure*

ICANN's new Bylaws do not address procedures for document disclosure. The issue is left for resolution in the procedural rules still to be developed.[1760] In the absence of other specific rules on the issue, the ICDR Rules on document disclosure will presumably apply.

9. Addressing the Costs of IRP Proceedings

a. *Need to Address the Costs of IRP Proceedings*

The costs associated with IRP proceedings may have acted as a deterrent for parties impacted by an ICANN action or inaction in violation of the Articles of Incorporation or Bylaws. The majority of the IRP panelists who have so far been nominated are eminent international arbitrators, and some may charge relatively high fees. This element of cost, combined with the various procedural obstacles that ICANN created for IRP

1759. The ICDR Rules explicitly exclude the possibility of U.S.-style discovery proceedings. ICDR Rules, Article 21(10) provides: 'Depositions, interrogatories, and requests to admit as developed for use in U.S. court procedures generally are not appropriate procedures for obtaining information in an arbitration under these Rules.'
1760. ICANN, Bylaws as amended on 1 October 2016, Article 4(3)(n)(iv)(d).

claimants, has made some IRP panels conclude that claimants have faced an uphill battle.[1761] It may also explain why IRPs have only been initiated in a small number of cases, several of which had a potentially significant financial impact, as can be seen by looking at the value of certain TLDs in public auctions organized by ICANN.

The declarations made by IRP panels have shown that, unless a claimant prevails - which would imply that a claimant succeeds in leaping all the procedural hurdles created by ICANN –, it is impossible under the current rules (even for claimants with a strong case on the underlying merits) to recover more than half of the costs of the IRP provider. Moreover, no prevailing party has succeeded in recovering its costs for legal representation in an IRP.

Since the 2013 changes to the Bylaws, ICANN has been entitled to a refund of all reasonable fees and costs incurred by ICANN in the IRP, including legal fees, if a claimant does not participate in good faith in the CEP and ICANN is the prevailing party in the IRP.[1762] There is no reciprocal clause in favor of the claimant, however. Apparently, ICANN's good faith participation in CEPs is to be presumed. We do not agree with this approach, especially as ICANN's obligation to act in good faith must be appraised objectively and independently by IRP panels, without any presumption of correctness.

b. *How to Address the Costs of IRP Proceedings*

We believe that it should be easier for claimants with a strong case on the underlying merits to recover their costs. However, this should not be achieved by any significant amendment to the provisions on the costs of IRP proceedings; it should mainly be done by removing the procedural burdens for bringing an IRP. In our view, the main burdens that require removal are the ambiguity about the panel's jurisdiction, its authority, and ICANN's reliance on the time bar to justify policies which may contradict ICANN's essential obligations.[1763]

The only change to the rules on procedural costs we consider advisable would allow IRP panels to rule on the recovery of costs for legal representation. The possibility to recover legal fees (in extraordinary circumstances) should not be given to ICANN only.

c. *Critical Appraisal of How ICANN's New Bylaws Address the Costs of IRP Proceedings*

ICANN has changed the cost structure of IRP proceedings dramatically with respect to the administrative costs and the panelist fees. ICANN's new Bylaws provide that ICANN will bear 'all the administrative costs of maintaining the IRP mechanism,

1761. *See e.g.*, Booking.com IRP Declaration, § 141.
1762. ICANN, Bylaws as amended on 12 April 2013, Article IV(3)(16).
1763. *Supra* Chapter 7.A.2 and Chapter 7.A.5; *Infra* Chapter 7.A.11

including compensation of Standing Panel members.'[1764] Hence, it seems that ICANN is prepared to cover all IRP expenses, if it may appoint the IRP Standing Panel. As discussed above, we do not favor the introduction of a Standing Panel,[1765] and ICANN's willingness to pay for such a panel is not a positive development.

In the absence of exceptional circumstances, and if the idea of a Standing Panel is indeed maintained, there will be no change in costs of legal representation and each party will still have to bear its own legal expenses. If an IRP panel deems a losing party's claim or defense to be frivolous or abusive, it may order the losing party to pay the administrative costs and/or fees of the prevailing party.[1766] ICANN is also entitled to a refund of all reasonable fees and costs incurred by ICANN in the IRP, including legal fees, if a claimant does not participate in good faith in the CEP and ICANN is the prevailing party in the IRP.[1767] There is still no reciprocal clause in favor of the claimant. As mentioned above, we believe there should be, given that ICANN's obligation to act in good faith must be appraised objectively and independently by IRP panels, without any presumption of correctness.

10. Confirming the Applicable Standard of Review

a. Need for Confirming the Applicable Standard of Review

ICANN has long tried to convince IRP panels that the ICANN Board is entitled to deference, and that IRP panels need to apply a reasonable business judgment rule. However, the idea of a reasonable business judgment rule is not adapted to ICANN's important role as the global regulator of the DNS.

b. How to Address the Standard of Review

Following the *Vistaprint* case the question of the applicable standard of review seemed settled, as the panel made clear that there was unanimity among IRP panels that ICANN's conduct should be reviewed and appraised objectively and independently, without any presumption of correctness.[1768] However, later panels seem to have given *de facto* deference to the ICANN Board's decisions.[1769] As a result, a clear recognition by ICANN of the *Vistaprint* case law on the applicable standard of review seems appropriate.

1764. ICANN, Bylaws as amended on 1 October 2016, Article 4(3)(r).
1765. *Supra* Chapter 7.A.3.
1766. ICANN, Bylaws as amended on 1 October 2016, Article 4(3)(r).
1767. ICANN, Bylaws as amended on 1 October 2016, Article 4(3)(r) *juncto* Article 4.3(e)(ii).
1768. *Supra* Chapter 6.C.2.c.
1769. *E.g.*, Despegar et al. IRP Declaration (*supra* Chapter 5.G.b.3); *see also* Chapter 6.C.2.c.

c. Critical Appraisal of How ICANN's New Bylaws Address the Standard of Review

With its new Bylaws, ICANN finally seems to have agreed with the settled case law on this issue. Article 4(3)(i) now provides that each IRP panel 'shall conduct an objective, *de novo* examination of the Dispute.'

Nevertheless, ICANN's new Bylaws also provide that for claims 'arising out of the Board's exercise of its fiduciary duties, the IRP Panel shall not replace the Board's reasonable judgment with its own so long as the Board's action or inaction is within the realm of reasonable business judgment.'[1770] The ICANN Bylaws do not define the nature and extent of the ICANN Board's fiduciary duties. As a result, it remains to be seen whether ICANN will try to impose the reasonable business judgment rule as the standard of review on future IRP panels which are asked to rule on issues of global importance.

To avoid unnecessary discussions in this respect, we think it would be advisable for ICANN to draw up an exhaustive list of the ICANN Board's fiduciary duties that may be assessed according to a reasonable business judgment rule.

11. Adopting a Broad View on the Authority of IRP Panels

a. Need for Adopting a Broad View on the Authority of IRP Panels

The extent of an IRP panel's authority has repeatedly been a point of controversy. We have always been of the opinion that the panel's authority is not limited to measures that are explicitly listed in ICANN's Bylaws. It is our view that nothing in the ICANN Bylaws or the ICDR IRP Supplementary Procedures may detract from the main purpose of the ICDR Rules, which is to resolve and arbitrate the dispute.[1771]

However, many IRP panels have struggled with their authority to render affirmative relief. Some panels have issued recommendations to the ICANN panel, but they did not maintain their jurisdiction in the case until after the ICANN Board had acted upon the panel's recommendation.[1772] Therefore, these decisions did not assure a final resolution of the dispute, and, consequently, there is the risk that the IRP as an efficient dispute resolution mechanism is compromised.

b. How to Address the Authority of IRP Panels

To put an end to the discussion about the extent of the IRP panel's authority, it would be advisable for ICANN to include a provision in its Bylaws explicitly stating that the list of possible measures is illustrative and not exhaustive.

1770. ICANN, Bylaws as amended on 1 October 2016, Article 4(3)(i)(iii).
1771. *Supra*, Chapter 6.C.3.c.
1772. *See* Vistaprint IRP Declaration; Despegar et al. IRP Declaration.

In addition, it should be made clear that the primary task of an IRP panel is to bring disputes to final resolution. To avoid that a claimant must initiate new proceedings whenever ICANN acts erroneously (or fails to act) upon a recommendation of an IRP panel, an IRP panel could envisage maintaining its jurisdiction until after ICANN has acted upon the panel's recommendation, effectively making the recommendation an interim decision.[1773] Moreover, it should be made clear that IRP panels are entitled to render affirmative relief in cases where there is in practice only one way to avoid or bring to an end a violation of ICANN's essential obligations.

c. *Critical Appraisal of How ICANN's New Bylaws Address the Authority of IRP Panels*

With its new Bylaws, ICANN simply made the list of possible IRP measures longer without clarifying the illustrative nature of the list.[1774] The list now mentions *inter alia* that IRP panels may '[c]onsolidate Disputes if the facts and circumstances are sufficiently similar, and take such other actions as are necessary for the efficient resolution of Disputes.'[1775] It is not clear whether the last part of this phrase may be taken as a recognition by ICANN that IRP panels may order whatever measures they deem fit for the effective resolution of the dispute. It could be that the panel's authority in this respect is intended to be limited to orders of a procedural nature only. In view of ICANN's obligation to enhance its accountability mechanisms on a continuous basis, we would favor the former interpretation. However, it would have been helpful if ICANN had been more explicit about the panel's authority in its new Bylaws.

12. Confirming the Binding Nature of IRP Declarations

a. *Why it is Useful to Confirm the Binding Nature of IRP Declarations*

The nature of the IRP declaration is extremely important from an accountability perspective. There would be little value for the Internet community in creating complex dispute resolution mechanisms and a body of normative rules and regulations if the most important among those dispute resolution mechanisms (*i.e.*, the IRP) is unable to enforce compliance with these rules. Nevertheless, the binding nature of IRP declarations has given rise to significant debate.

1773. An embryonic version of such approach can be found in the *Vistaprint* and the Despegar et al. IRP Declarations.
1774. ICANN, Bylaws as amended on 1 October 2016, Article 4(3)(o).
1775. ICANN, Bylaws as amended on 1 October 2016, Article 4(3)(o)(v).

b. How to Address the Need to Confirm the Binding Nature of IRP Declarations

Although the majority of IRP case law seems to have settled the issue in favor of the binding nature of IRP declarations, a clear provision reaffirming that IRP declarations are binding would be helpful.

c. Critical Appraisal of How ICANN's Bylaws Address the Binding Nature of IRP Declarations

ICANN's new Bylaws provide that the IRP is intended to hear and resolve disputes for the purpose of '[l]ead[ing] to binding, final resolutions consistent with international arbitration norms that are enforceable in any court with proper jurisdiction.'[1776] In view of previous debates on the issue, we believe that this provision should be interpreted as a clear affirmation of the binding nature of IRP declarations.

13. Maintaining and Strengthening the Precedential Value of IRP Declarations

a. Need for Maintaining and Strengthening the Precedential Value of IRP Declarations

Since the amendments of 11 April 2013, ICANN's Bylaws have provided that the declarations of the IRP panel, and the Board's subsequent action resulting from those declarations, are final and have precedential value.[1777] However, as explained above, IRP case law is not settled on the nature of the legal precedent of IRP declarations.[1778] Whether persuasive or binding, precedential value of IRP declarations can contribute to the enhancement of ICANN's accountability. Persuasive reasoning could guide ICANN in its decision-making processes, making ICANN's decisions more predictable and sound. Increased predictability and fairer decision-making would obviously contribute to the advancement of the Internet community and reduce the number of disputes.

b. How to Strengthen the Precedential Value of IRP Declarations

In our view, the precedential value of IRP declarations should be persuasive only, as all IRP panels appointed according to our guidelines are on an equal footing (there is no court hierarchy for IRPs). Nevertheless, IRP panels should seek consistency between IRP declarations, to the extent warranted. This means that an IRP panel cannot simply ignore the reasoning of other panels, but should take account of previous decisions in its own analysis.

1776. ICANN, Bylaws as amended on 1 October 2016, Article 4(3)(a)(viii).
1777. ICANN Bylaws as amended on 11 April 2013, Article IV(3)(21).
1778. *Supra* Chapter 6.C.4.b.

c. *Critical Appraisal of How ICANN's New Bylaws Address the Precedential Value of IRP Declarations*

The purpose of '[r]educing [d]isputes by creating precedent to guide and inform the [ICANN] Board', as well as other ICANN constituencies and the global Internet community 'in connection with policy development and implementation' has been recognized in ICANN's amended Bylaws of 1 October 2016. Nevertheless, the creation of legal precedent is mentioned now as one of the purposes of the IRP, but the new Bylaws no longer mention as affirmatively that IRP declarations have precedential value.[1779] In our view, this does not mean that ICANN intended to reduce the precedential value of IRP declarations. Instead, ICANN has clarified the purpose of the creation of precedential value through IRP. ICANN's new provisions on the binding nature of IRP declarations must also be seen within this context.

14. An Appeal Procedure: Yes or No?

a. *No Need for an Appeal Procedure*

The possibility of an appeal procedure for IRPs has never been a topic for discussion under ICANN's previous Bylaws. It is unclear how parties in an IRP under those rules would benefit from an appeal procedure. Indeed, in many cases, parties opt for arbitration without the possibility to appeal the arbitral award. The reasoning is that the parties were involved in the selection process of the arbitrators or panelists, and that they want to obtain in an expedited fashion an enforceable award which finally resolves the dispute. Some institutional arbitration centers offer optional appeal procedures. However, if the purpose of the appeal is simply to redo the proceedings and give the parties another shot, then there is little merit in organizing an appeal. Why would the first panel of arbitrators be less well positioned to render an award than the appeals panel?

The situation would be different if the power of one of the parties in the arbitrators' selection process was curtailed to the benefit of another party. As ICANN is planning to appoint an omnibus standing panel for IRPs, the involvement of an IRP claimant in the panel's selection process will be reduced to a minimum. In such cases, it may well be advisable to organize an *en banc* appeal process to restore the procedural balance.

b. *Critical Appraisal of How ICANN's Bylaws Address the Appeal Procedure*

ICANN's new Bylaws provide for an *en banc* appeal process in limited circumstances (which are yet to be defined).[1780] ICANN's choice for an appeal process is understandable in view of ICANN's choice of working with an omnibus standing panel. However,

1779. *Compare* ICANN Bylaws as amended on 11 April 2013, Article IV(3)(21) *with* ICANN, Bylaws as amended on 1 October 2016, Article 4(3)(a).
1780. ICANN, Bylaws as amended on 1 October 2016, Article 4(3)(x).

we do not favor the introduction of an appeal process, as organizing an appeal risks prolonging disputes. Moreover, an appeal process would not have been necessary had ICANN abandoned the idea of having an omnibus standing panel, as it should have.[1781]

15. Mediation: Yes or No?

a. *The Limited Success of Voluntary Conciliation within ICANN*

With its Bylaws of 11 April 2013, ICANN introduced a voluntary CEP and a voluntary conciliation process.[1782] The CEP was aimed at the parties negotiating an agreement to resolve the issue, narrowing the issues for IRP, or bringing the matter to the ICANN Board's attention.[1783] However, only few CEPs have resulted in a resolution of the issue.[1784] And while confidentiality during the CEP may be a prerequisite to successful negotiations, there seem to be no reasons for ICANN to be secretive about why a particular CEP led to resolution.

b. *How to Make Mediation a Success*

In our view, transparency as to the reasons of a resolution through CEP might contribute to the success of CEPs. Unfortunately, transparency seems to be lacking here, and we believe more disputes could have been resolved through CEP, were it a more transparent process. CEPs and mediation will only work if parties do not approach the issue from the angle of their legal position, but instead try to find agreement about the underlying interest. In our experience, ICANN has taken on a more legalistic approach.

c. *Critical Appraisal of How ICANN's New Bylaws Address Mediation*

With the new Bylaws, ICANN puts further emphasis on the amicable resolution of IRPs, and allows for the appointment of a mediator following CEP.[1785] Mediation has the advantage that an independent mediator might facilitate the resolution of the issue and might help the parties to focus on the underlying interests rather than on their legal position. It remains to be seen whether mediation will be successful.

1781. *Supra* Chapter 7.A.3.
1782. ICANN, Bylaws as amended on 11 April 2013, Article IV(3)(16).
1783. ICANN, *Cooperative Engagement Process – Requests for Independent Review*, 11 April 2013, https://www.icann.org/en/system/files/files/cep-11apr13-en.pdf.
1784. For an example of a CEP that resulted in a resolution of the issue, *see* ICANN, *Approved Board Resolutions 2016.02.03.12 – 2016.02.03.13 – Regular meeting of the ICANN Board*, 3 February 2016, https://www.icann.org/resources/board-material/resolutions-2016-02-03-en.
1785. ICANN, Bylaws as amended on 1 October 2016, Article 4(3)(e).

D. LITIGATION WAIVERS: YES OR NO?

1. ICANN's Introduction of a Litigation Waiver

ICANN introduced a broad litigation waiver in the new gTLD Program. Even though arguments exist to consider the litigation waiver unconscionable[1786] – and thus unenforceable – its mere existence may discourage parties from asserting their rights in court, as the waiver creates an additional hurdle that a claimant will need to overcome. The mere existence of a waiver is not necessarily problematic, provided the waiver is not used to exempt ICANN from responsibility for its own wrongful acts and provided ICANN offers an effective alternative to court litigation.

2. How to Address Litigation Waivers

One possibility would be to prohibit ICANN adopting broad litigation waivers in future application processes. However, that would not be necessary if ICANN offers the possibility of efficient IRP proceedings which take into account the action points included in this chapter.

In any event, a waiver should not be invoked as a defense against an enforcement action of an arbitral award or IRP declaration. Also, a waiver should not prevent a party from obtaining a temporary restraining order to preserve its rights and interests, if there is no assurance that interim relief can be obtained efficiently and in a timely fashion via IRP emergency proceedings.[1787]

3. Critical Appraisal of ICANN's New Bylaws on Litigation Waivers

The possibility to include a waiver in future rounds has not been discussed within the CCWG, and ICANN's new Bylaws do not exclude the possibility of introducing a broad waiver for the future introduction of new gTLDs. The Bylaws simply mention as one of the purposes of the IRP, that it is to provide a mechanism for the resolution of disputes, as an alternative to legal action in the civil courts of the United States or other jurisdictions.[1788] In our view, this provision is not meant to exclude court action, but is merely an expression of ICANN's intention to favor IRP proceedings over court proceedings. In our view, a litigation waiver is reasonable if ICANN accepts a judicial review through arbitration and is committed to the enforcement of the award or IRP declaration.

1786. *Supra* Chapter 6.C.1.b(2).
1787. *Supra* Chapter 7.A.1.
1788. ICANN, Bylaws as amended on 1 October 2016, Article 4(3)(a)(ix).

CHAPTER 8

Proposed Way Forward

Our main focus in this book is on the need for judicial review through arbitration of ICANN's decisions concerning the opening of the market in Internet extensions to newcomers.

We have demonstrated the need for more power to be given to IRP panels. The recently amended ICANN Bylaws show that ICANN understands that the arguments raised in this regard were appropriate. However, it took a lengthy review process for the Board to ultimately accept this reality. And, although the need for a greater role for IRP panels has been expressly recognized, some major issues remain unresolved, as we explained in the previous chapter.

Our reflections in this section are not meant to offer a final and fully worked-out solution; rather they are meant to spur the debate and to inspire the Internet community to continue its work towards improving ICANN's accountability on the basis of wide support for proposed changes to ICANN's accountability framework. In our view, important work remains to be done to improve the balance of power between ICANN stakeholders, the ICANN Board and the IRP panels, and to improve the way rules and policies are adopted, implemented and reviewed. We were somewhat surprised that neither the CCWG nor the U.S. Government's administration raised these matters when discussing the recent relinquishment of the U.S. Government's oversight role. And, while it is of course never too late to work towards better and more balanced decision-making processes, this relinquishment of the U.S. Government's oversight role may now make it more difficult to implement the necessary changes to ICANN's structure and accountability framework. We hope that common sense will prevail.

A. BALANCING THE POWERS

ICANN does not have members, even though this was anticipated at the time of its creation.[1789] Instead, the ICANN Board is assisted in its decision-making by a highly complex, multi-layer group of stakeholders, advisory committees, third-party experts and staff. While ICANN's decisions must benefit the Internet community as a whole,[1790] this group has become extremely diverse and is dispersed throughout the world. Today's Internet community is far removed from the initial groups of engineers who worked on the ARPANET and NSFNET research projects.[1791] The interests of the different stakeholders that form the worldwide Internet community are not always aligned. For example, private sector stakeholders may be looking for large operational freedom, whereas certain governments are interested in ways to control, monitor and even censor Internet activity. IP rights holders have an interest in protecting their corporate image on the Internet, whereas individuals and consumer organizations want to preserve their freedom of expression. These obvious tensions are difficult to manage within a single state, let alone within the global Internet community.

Running parallel to all these individual interests is the global public interest of maintaining the operational stability of the Internet and a need for ICANN to abide by the rule of law.[1792] Although observance of these fundamental principles may guide ICANN's actions to some extent, they provide no answer to the question of how exactly the interests of different stakeholders must be balanced.

At present, the balance of the different stakeholders' interests is largely decided by the composition of the ICANN Board. Since its foundation, ICANN has operated through the actions of its Board. The Board serves as ICANN's executive branch. However, the Board also holds a great deal of legislative and judicial authority, as all of ICANN's substantive policies and procedures must be approved by the Board, and the Board reviews complaints against actions and inactions of both ICANN's staff and the Board itself.

1. The Relationship Between the Executive and the Legislative

ICANN's substantive rules, policies and procedures are drafted by the SOs recognized by the ICANN Board.[1793] The authority of ICANN's SOs has long been limited. They serve as either advisory bodies or nomination or selection bodies of a number of the

1789. ICANN, Articles of Incorporation, Article 9.
1790. ICANN, Articles of Incorporation, Article 4.
1791. *Supra* Chapter 2.A.2.
1792. *Supra* Chapter 2.A and Chapter 7.B.
1793. ICANN, Original Bylaws of 6 November 1998, https://www.icann.org/resources/unthemed-pages/bylaws-1998-11-06-en, Articles V(2) and VI; ICANN, Bylaws as amended on 21 November 1998, https://www.icann.org/resources/unthemed-pages/bylaws-1998-11-23-en, Article V(2) and VI.

ICANN Board's Directors.[1794] Since the introduction of the 'empowered community' in 2016, ICANN's SOs and advisory committees together have been given the authority, *inter alia*, to reject or approve amendments to the ICANN Bylaws and Articles of Incorporation.[1795] Although in some ways ICANN's SOs can be seen as a parliament, they are not entitled to enact legislation, but only to propose rules, policies and procedures to the Board.

As a result, the extent of their prerogative in nominating Directors may be of crucial importance to the ultimate enactment of their own proposed rules, policies and procedures.

The three SOs which are recognized by the ICANN Board were originally entitled to select three Directors each.[1796] Nine other Directors were selected by the Internet community 'at large' in accordance with a process developed by ICANN's initial Board.[1797] ICANN's Board was then comprised of these eighteen Directors and a President, the latter being elected by the Board.[1798] The first Directors selected by ICANN's SOs were installed in November 1999.[1799] They were added to the nine Directors of ICANN's first interim Board, which was selected in a rather secretive manner, but which included people from different geographic locations.[1800] The replacement of the nine initial Directors gave rise to ample discussion. In October 1999, ICANN's Bylaws envisioned the existence of at least 5,000 members of the corporation, who would establish the selection process for the council responsible for selecting those Directors elected from the community 'at large' from among ICANN's members.[1801] However, this process was never implemented. In 2000, ICANN's Board

1794. ICANN, Original Bylaws of 6 November 1998, https://www.icann.org/resources/unthemed-pages/bylaws-1998-11-06-en, Articles V(2) and VI; ICANN, Bylaws as amended on 21 November 1998, https://www.icann.org/resources/unthemed-pages/bylaws-1998-11-23-en, Article V(2) and VI.
1795. ICANN, Bylaws as amended on 1 October 2016, Article 6.
1796. ICANN, Original Bylaws of 6 November 1998, https://www.icann.org/resources/unthemed-pages/bylaws-1998-11-06-en, Articles V(2) and VI; ICANN, Bylaws as amended on 21 November 1998, https://www.icann.org/resources/unthemed-pages/bylaws-1998-11-23-en, Article V(2) and VI.
1797. ICANN, Original Bylaws of 6 November 1998, https://www.icann.org/resources/unthemed-pages/bylaws-1998-11-06-en, Article V(4); ICANN, Bylaws as amended on 21 November 1998, https://www.icann.org/resources/unthemed-pages/bylaws-1998-11-23-en, Article V(4); ICANN, *Board Resolutions 99.116 – 99.117*, 29 October 1999, https://www.icann.org/resources/board-material/consent-1999-10-29-en; ICANN, Bylaws as amended and restated on 29 October 1999, https://www.icann.org/resources/unthemed-pages/bylaws-1999-10-29-en.
1798. ICANN, Original Bylaws of 6 November 1998, https://www.icann.org/resources/unthemed-pages/bylaws-1998-11-06-en, Article V; ICANN, Bylaws as amended on 21 November 1998, https://www.icann.org/resources/unthemed-pages/bylaws-1998-11-23-en, Article V.
1799. ICANN, *Los Angeles Meetings: Details, Schedules and Agendas*, 1-4 November 1999, https://archive.icann.org/en/meetings/losangeles99/; ICANN, *Biographical Data on New Directors*, 28 October 1999, http://archive.icann.org/en/general/new-director-bios-28oct99.htm.
1800. *Supra* Chapter 2.A.2.b(3)(d).
1801. ICANN, Bylaws as amended and restated on 29 October 1999, https://www.icann.org/resources/unthemed-pages/bylaws-1999-10-29-en, Articles II(6) – II (8); ICANN, *Board Resolutions 99.116 – 99.117*, 29 October 1999, https://www.icann.org/resources/board-material/consent-1999-10-29-en.

observed that there remained a considerable diversity of views concerning the 'at large' membership and the electoral structures for appointing 'at large' Directors.[1802] In June 2000, the Board established a temporary 'nominating committee', mainly populated by Directors of ICANN, to nominate the corporation's 'at large' Directors.[1803]

In 2002, following the recommendation by a special-purpose committee that 'a broad-based Nominating Committee is the preferred way to select a majority of the ICANN Board',[1804] ICANN installed a more permanent nominating committee with delegates selected by different ICANN constituencies, advisory committees and specific Internet-related organizations.[1805] The nominating committee selected eight Directors, and ICANN's SOs selected two Directors each (instead of the three they had elected before).[1806] Nevertheless, the SOs and their constituencies provide the majority of the voting delegates of the nominating committee.[1807]

Today, ICANN's Board comprises sixteen Directors: each SO is entitled to nominate two Directors; the community 'at large' nominates one Director; eight Directors are nominated by ICANN's nominating committee; and ICANN's President continues to serve as an *ex officio* Director. Apart from the President, all Directors of the ICANN Board are designated by ICANN's 'empowered community'.[1808] In addition to the voting Directors, ICANN's Board also comprises non-voting liaisons of ICANN advisory committees.

The balance between the interests of stakeholders largely depends on the choices made by the nominating committee. Given the powers vested in the ICANN Board, striking the right balance in the nomination process is crucial for ICANN's legitimacy towards the Internet community as a whole. After all, the decisions that shape the Internet's global policies are taken by sixteen people, 50% of whom are nominated by a committee of twenty or twenty-one persons with fifteen voting members.

As the Internet community is constantly evolving, it is important for ICANN's structure and nomination processes to evolve accordingly. The large-scale introduction of new

1802. ICANN, *Meeting of the Board Minutes*, 10 March 2000, https://www.icann.org/resources/board-material/minutes-2000-03-10-en.
1803. ICANN, *Board Resolution 00.52, Regular Meeting of the Board Minutes*, 16 July 2000, https://www.icann.org/resources/board-material/minutes-2000-07-16-en; ICANN, Bylaws as amended on 16 July 2000, https://www.icann.org/resources/unthemed-pages/bylaws-2000-07-16-en, Article II(4).
1804. ICANN, *Final Implementation Report and Recommendations of the Committee on ICANN Evolution and Reform*, 2 October 2002, http://archive.icann.org/en/committees/evol-reform/final-implementation-report-02oct02.htm.
1805. ICANN, Bylaws as adopted effective 15 December 2002, https://www.icann.org/resources/unthemed-pages/bylaws-2002-12-15-en, Article VII; ICANN, *Board Resolution 02.146, Fourth Annual Meeting of the Board Minutes*, 15 December 2002, https://www.icann.org/resources/board-material/minutes-annual-meeting-2002-12-15-en.
1806. ICANN, Bylaws as adopted effective 15 December 2002, https://www.icann.org/resources/unthemed-pages/bylaws-2002-12-15-en, Article VI(2).
1807. ICANN, Bylaws as adopted effective 15 December 2002, https://www.icann.org/resources/unthemed-pages/bylaws-2002-12-15-en, Article VII; ICANN, Bylaws as amended on 1 October 2016, Article 8.
1808. ICANN, Bylaws as amended on 1 October 2016, Article 7.

gTLDs has the potential significantly to reshape the DNS landscape and the needs of the Internet community. The future will tell if ICANN is able to adapt to these changing circumstances, and if the existing balance between ICANN's stakeholders will be tenable.

2. ICANN's Relationship with the Judiciary

ICANN, through its Board, has sole responsibility for the adoption of rules and policies affecting the DNS. It combines both a legislative and an executive role, accepting, refusing and reconsidering the implementation of those rules and policies. For this reason, a strong 'judiciary' is required to provide a check and balance to ICANN's power.

ICANN and the Internet community have now understood that ICANN's relationship with the 'judiciary' needs to be changed. As demonstrated in this book, ICANN's existing accountability mechanisms have so far been unable to ensure that ICANN's fundamental obligations in its dealings with third parties (and applicants in particular) were respected. Therefore, much attention has been given to how ICANN's accountability mechanisms should be strengthened. However, as explained above, ICANN's involvement in shaping the rules of the IRP and in the training and appointment of IRP panelists risks making the IRP less effective as a judicial review mechanism than the Internet community originally intended.[1809]

ICANN's reshaped 'judiciary' seems to be focused almost exclusively on providing mechanisms to resolve disputes. However, a judiciary can, and should, also play an important role in preventing conflicts from arising. A well-developed process of judicial review can invalidate rules and policies which are shown to be incompatible with fundamental norms before these rules and policies give rise to a conflict.

In our view, there is room for improvement in ICANN's relationship with the judiciary. In Section B below, we discuss how this improvement could be realized, and how such an improvement would contribute positively to ICANN's decision-making and review processes.

B. IMPROVING ICANN'S DECISION-MAKING ADOPTION, IMPLEMENTATION, APPLICATION, AND REVIEW PROCESSES

We see a need for three distinct mechanisms for judicial review if ICANN's decision-making process is to be properly supported. These mechanisms can be distinguished on the basis of when they should be brought into play during the decision-making process, *i.e.*, (i) prior to the adoption of new rules and policies, (ii) within a specific time period after such adoption, or (iii) at the time of their implementation and application. At the moment, there is a formal mechanism for (iii) only – the IRP.

1809. *Supra* Chapter 7.C.3.

1. Judicial Review Prior to the Adoption of New Rules and Policies

First, we propose the creation of a new independent advisory body, designed to perform a judicial review of newly proposed rules and policies. This independent body would advise ICANN and its Board on the legality of the newly proposed rules and policies in view of ICANN's primary norms, the provisions of its Bylaws and Articles of Incorporation, and its obligations under domestic and International law. An advance review mechanism such as this, usually involving constitutional or administrative courts, is commonplace in multiple liberal democracies. It can be either mandatory or optional, and either advisory or binding. For the ICANN Board, we would support the introduction of a mandatory advisory system.

The introduction of a mandatory advisory system would imply that, absent exceptional circumstances, the ICANN Board would have to seek the advice of the independent advisory body, but the Board would be free either to accept or reject the advice. The ICANN Board would remain responsible for adopting rules, policies, amendments, etc. However, a formal mandatory advisory system would contribute to enhanced decision-making and encourage a more developed rationale.

To prevent the system blocking the adoption of new rules and policies, we would recommend the introduction of a set period of time within which the review authority would be required to issue its advice (*e.g.*, two or three months following receipt of the draft policy by the Board[1810]). Were no advice to be given within the set time period, the Board would be free to proceed without it.

The success and stature of an independent advisory body such as this very much depends on the independence, impartiality and competences of its members. In our view, members of the advisory body should have no other role within ICANN. The advisory body should be made up of eminent legal scholars from different continents and legal traditions, appointed either for life or for a significant period of time, and selected through objective and transparent procedures. We would have no objection to including *former* active members from stakeholder groups in the advisory body.

2. Judicial Review upon the Adoption of New Rules and Policies

Second, we propose the creation of a new independent review body; this time empowered to annul rules and policies at the time of their adoption, if those rules and policies conflict with fundamental principles. Such a body is again quite common in many jurisdictions, where a constitutional or administrative court is tasked with this

1810. Adjustments can be made to particular circumstances. Some policies may require additional time for review; for others it may be clear from the outset that no negative advice will be issued. The independent review body could adopt a screening method to estimate the time needed to issue its advice on a particular policy and allow for emergency advice proceedings, if circumstances so require.

review. This would allow anyone affected to request the annulment of the rule or policy in question. If the independent review body agreed to grant the annulment, it would apply *erga omnes*.

An independent review body such as this is necessary in addition to the independent advisory body described above. A party negatively affected by a rule or policy must have the opportunity to raise a challenge and request annulment. ICANN and its Board should be aware that the adoption of a new rule may violate a higher value or fundamental norm, even if the independent advisory body (described above) did not identify the fact.

An independent review body such as this has significant power (*i.e.*, the annulment *erga omnes*), and the conditions laid down for requesting such a review should be strict, well defined and limited. Also, there should be a time limit for requesting the annulment. This would help prevent there being a lack of legal certainty that would clearly not be in the interests of the Internet community.

Furthermore, the importance of the independent review body's office makes it imperative that great care be taken in the appointment of unbiased and experienced legal scholars, whose loyalty to the rule of law and independent judgment must be beyond reproach. In our view, the selection process and the tenure of these independent judicial reviewers should resemble those of the independent advisory body, however, the two bodies must be kept entirely separate and independent.

3. Judicial Review in the Implementation and Application of Rules and Policies

Third, we recommend that the authority of the IRP panels be increased. IRP panels should have the power to annul any specific implementation (*e.g.*, a new applicant guidebook and its relevant policies) and application (*e.g.*, a decision whether or not to delegate) of rules and policies that violate ICANN's Bylaws or Articles of Incorporation with regard to a particular party. In our view, a ruling by an IRP panel should generate effects *inter partes* only, although it may create an incentive for ICANN to amend its rules and policies immediately or in the future with a view to avoiding disparate treatment.

Of course, a judicial review of the implementation and application of rules and policies will always take place in adversarial proceedings, and claimants must be able to show actual or potential real harm. Because of the adversarial context, and because the circumstances of each case can be quite different, IRPs are best dealt with through arbitration. Our recommendations on the organization of (adversarial) IRPs have been detailed in the previous chapter, and we will not repeat them here.

In our proposed scenario, this third judicial review mechanism, the IRP, would be independent of the two mechanisms described above. Any party with standing should have the right to initiate an IRP regardless of whether or not an independent advisory or review body has previously advised against or annulled the rule or policy in question. In other words, an individual IRP panel should be able to set aside a given rule as regards a particular claimant, and that ruling should be binding for ICANN and have precedential value.

CHAPTER 9
Epilogue

We started this book with an analysis of ICANN's role and we reiterate here that without an organization such as ICANN the Internet would be unmanageable. In many ways, ICANN is to be applauded for its work. However, we have also shown that ICANN has not always acted in accordance with either the rules imposed on it by the U.S. Government, or those adopted by the multi-stakeholder community that it represents. It is disturbing, to say the least, that the ICANN Board relied on its right to change the application rules in such a way that they were fundamentally altered after the application window in the third and last round had closed. This was much to the detriment of the applicants and it caused a good deal of commotion and legal uncertainty.

The ICANN Board has also attempted to conceal many of its actions, inactions and actionable inactions, relying on the argument that it only had to comply with a process-driven approach. In our view, it is primarily this attitude and behavior that has led to the IRPs described in this book, and several IRP panels were, we believe, rather too accepting of ICANN's argument that an IRP should never deal with the merits of a case. Much time, energy and funds have been invested in these IRPs that could have been better spent elsewhere.

We have pointed out that ICANN is the ultimate decision maker through its Board and we have discussed the changes that we consider necessary. But there is more. We have demonstrated that if ICANN is in effect accountable only to itself, there is a real danger that despite any professed general principles to the contrary, Internet governance will not be protected from capture, arbitrariness, discrimination and the unwarranted restriction of competition. For as long as the IANA functions contract remained in place, the U.S. Government retained its external control mechanism and its ability to encourage ICANN to improve its internal and external accountability. With the U.S. Government relinquishing its oversight of ICANN's operation of the IANA functions, ICANN's self-supervision, and the risks associated with it, have become a reality.

ICANN's job is far from over. ICANN still has to achieve one of its major goals: enhancing competition at the registry level. Although this is one of ICANN's essential obligations, the question is how ICANN stakeholders will be able to force ICANN's hand after the recent relinquishment of U.S. Government control. Unfortunately, the U.S. stewardship role over the IANA functions was relinquished without any transition or test period for ICANN's 'new' accountability framework. If the transition is not carried out properly, the global Internet community could face a largely introspective and unaccountable ICANN and a situation where established groups could endeavor to effectively block new entrants from entering the market.

The other major issue worth mentioning here concerns ICANN's international persona. We are rapidly approaching the milestone of two decades of ICANN leadership supported by one dominant commercial partner (Verisign); both ICANN and Verisign are U.S. based. It is not unusual that ICANN, like many other inventions that have become essential facilities on an international scale, can be historically linked to a particular country, and its historical link with the U.S. is undeniable (although much of the Internet's development happened internationally).

However, is this link still relevant? International agreements are made and organizations are created to set standards and agreements on the entry into a market and the use of facilities (such as aviation and postal services) and it is fair to say that the world is extending this internationalized approach to other basic facilities (water, air – or, in one word, climate). In our view, it is questionable whether the existence of ICANN under California law continues to be essential or even appropriate. Is it correct to maintain the California courts as the sole and ultimate jurisdiction where ICANN can be reminded of the rules according to which it must operate? Is it right for applicants that are treated unfairly by ICANN to be forced to initiate court cases in California? ICANN has an indisputable advantage 'playing at home'. Non-U.S. applicants – who might increasingly come from less developed parts of the world – would need to have deep pockets to start U.S. court proceedings, not to mention a large amount of patience. In this sense, the withdrawal of U.S. Government oversight, and a weakening of the historical link to the U.S. could be seen as an opportunity.

ICANN has certainly shown its intention to involve other regions of the world in the development of the Internet, and this is to be supported. Indeed, the organization should open further offices on continents that have undoubtedly contributed to what the DNS has become. However, care needs to be taken here, and it is arguable whether ICANN should have opened a second office in a country that is democratically unstable, and a third office in a country that is very stable but undemocratic.

In the last round, ICANN generated a considerable amount of cash and, proportionally, even more through auctions than through applications. The organization has created lucrative jobs. Some people on the Board clearly enjoy the state-like aspects of the organization and some of its positions. Meetings have become mega shows.

Is now not the time to raise questions about the global enforceability of an allegedly geo-present entity that is expected to serve the whole world's public interests? Should

ICANN and the international community not rethink some crucial decisions made in the past even if the U.S. Government is no longer there to look over the shoulder of trusted key decision-makers? Is now not the time to show some worldmanship?

To summarize, while the past seventeen years have shown no reason why ICANN should not continue to oversee technical Internet functions, it remains to be seen whether ICANN will be able to operate in an appropriate and accountable manner. We are left with some basic questions that the Internet community will want answered in order to prevent the discussions and disputes of the past muddying the waters of the future.

Timeline

Date	*Event*
1951	The U.S. Air Force commissioned MIT to design an early-warning network to guard against a Soviet nuclear bomber attack
1961	Publication of the first paper on the so-called packet switching theory
1965	First long distance communication between a computer at the Massachusetts Institute of Technology (MIT) and a computer in California, using a low speed dial-up telephone line
1967	Publication of the first plan for communication network ARPANET
September 1969	Connection of the first packet switch, called Interface Message Processor (IMP), and a host computer at UCLA
October 1969	Connection of a second host computer and IMP at the Stanford Research Institute (SRI)
29 October 1969	The first successful host-to-host message sent from UCLA to SRI using the ARPANET
December 1970	Development of a communication protocol, called the Network Control Protocol or "NCP"
1972	Introduction of email that quickly became one of the most popular applications on the ARPANET, allowing researchers to communicate better over long distances
1972	Development of the File Transfer Protocol, allowing the efficient and reliable transfer of files between host computers at remote locations and creating the possibility to store and access files at remote locations
1972	First proposal of system connecting computers on the network using a unique numbering system, by Jon Postel

Timeline

Date	*Event*
1974	Start of the development of the first version for a universal "inter-networking protocol", named "Transmission Control Protocol/Internet Protocol" or "TCP/IP"
Mid-1970s	Emerging of many other computer networks like NASA's computer network
1981	Launch of idea to create a hierarchical name-space and to partition the name-space into different domains
1982–1983	Deployment of TCP/IP on military networks
1983	Jon Postel handed over the assigning authority of IP addresses to fellow researcher Joyce Reynolds in 1983
1988	Mention of the Internet Assigned Numbers Authority ("IANA") for the first time in a publication
1989	Invention of the World Wide Web by English scientist Tim Berners-Lee
1990	Implementation of the World Wide Web when Tim Berners-Lee wrote the first web browser while employed at CERN in Switzerland
1991–1992	Growth of the National Science Foundation ("NSF") Net ("NSFNET"), going from connecting over 3,500 networks to over 6,000 networks
31 December 1992	NSF enters into a cooperative agreement with Network Solutions, Inc. ("NSI")
13 September 1995	NSF allows NSI to charge user fees for the registration of domain names
May 1997	U.S government indicates that it will not support the gTLD-MoU
July 1997	Clinton administration begins privatization efforts in an attempt to increase competition and to promote international participation in the DNS
20 February 1998	Publication of the Green Paper
1998	Publication of the White Paper
September 1998	Incorporation of ICANN
30 September 1998	Initial date of expiration of the cooperative agreement between the NSF and NSI
7 October 1998	U.S. Government extends the cooperative agreement with NSI, and NSI accepted that the U.S. Government transitioned its DNS obligations under the cooperative agreement to a new corporation
16 October 1998	Death of Jon Postel
25 October 1998	ICANN installs its first interim Board, Chairman, President and CEO
6 November 1998	Adoption of ICANN's original Bylaws

Date	*Event*
8 February 1999	U.S. Government authorizes that ICANN perform the IANA functions
26 February 1999	U.S. Department of Commerce officially recognizes ICANN as the new corporation that was envisioned in the White Paper, and authorized that ICANN take over obligations of the U.S. Government under the cooperative agreement with NSI - U.S. Government effectively grants management authority over the DNS to ICANN.
August 1999	ICANN adopts the Uniform Domain Name Dispute Resolution Policy ("UDRP")
June 2000	ICANN releases second status report
11 September 2000	Extension of the MOU with one year
30 September 2000	Original MOU was scheduled to terminate
24 September 2001	Extension of the MOU with one year
20 September 2002	Extension of the MOU with one year
5 December 2005	GNSO issues report on starting a PDP on the introduction of new gTLDs
7 August 2007	GNSO issues Final Report on introduction of new gTLDs
6 June 2008	Notice of IRP in .xxx by ICM Registry
26 June 2008	Board adopts GNSO recommendations for the introduction of new gTLDs
2009	Original MOU is no longer in place
30 September 2009	Affirmation of Commitments by the United States Department of Commerce ("DOC") and ICANN
19 February 2010	IRP Declaration in .xxx
16 March 2010	IOC proposes meeting with ICANN to discuss new gTLD program, the protection of its intellectual property and "the status of the development of the new extension '.sport'."
13-18 March 2010	ICANN meeting in San Francisco (ICANN 40) ICANN and IOC have confidential meetings
23 March 2010	Letter from ICANN (R. Beckstrom and J. Jeffrey) to IOC confirming that ICANN is open for discussion
5–10 December 2010	ICANN meeting in Cartagena (ICANN 39) ICANN and IOC have confidential meetings
20 June 2011	ICANN's Board approves the gTLD Applicant Guidebook
19-24 June 2011	ICANN meeting in Singapore (ICANN 41) ICANN and IOC have confidential meetings
19 September 2011	ICANN confirms that it has granted protection to the IOC in AGB, version 8
16 November 2011	Notice of IRP in .xxx by Manwin
12 January 2012–30 May 2012	Application period Extension of application window due to bug

<table>
<tr><th>Date</th><th>Event</th></tr>
<tr><td>16 March 2012</td><td>Amended Bylaws:
– New voting requirements for GNSO
– Changes to organization of public comments</td></tr>
<tr><td>4 June 2012</td><td>Final version of the Guidebook introducing batching system for dealing with large numbers of applications</td></tr>
<tr><td>5 September 2012</td><td>Introduction of new gTLD Change Request process and criteria</td></tr>
<tr><td>10 October 2012</td><td>Introduction of new gTLD prioritization draw – removal of batching system</td></tr>
<tr><td>20 December 2012</td><td>Amended Bylaws:
– Changes to terms of directors</td></tr>
<tr><td>5 February 2013</td><td>PICs
ICANN organizes Public Comment: Revised New gTLD Registry Agreement Including Additional Public Interest Commitments Specification
PICs DRP finalized on 19 December 2013</td></tr>
<tr><td>28 February 2013</td><td>ICANN sets the deadline for filing objections on 13 March 2013, although the Initial Evaluation period had not yet ended.
The Guidebook provided that the objection filing period would close following the end of the Initial Evaluation period, with a two-week window of time between the posting of the Initial Evaluation results and the close of the objection filing period
The Initial Evaluation period ended on 30 August 2013.</td></tr>
<tr><td>11 April 2013</td><td>Amended Bylaws:
– Changes to accountability mechanisms
– Introduction of a defined standard of review for IRP Panel
– Introduction of standing panel
– Introduction of page limit
– Introduction of CEP
– Introduction of precedential value of IRP Declarations
– Changes to Root Server System Advisory Committee (RS-SAC)</td></tr>
<tr><td>8 May 2013</td><td>Joint Letter of Dismissal of IRP in .xxx by Manwin and ICANN</td></tr>
<tr><td>25 June 2013</td><td>Introduction of PICs</td></tr>
<tr><td>25 June 2013</td><td>De facto prohibition of Closed generic TLDs (exclusive access TLDs)
Later on: only applicants who accepted to open up TLD were admitted to proceed with delegation
Outcome for those who do not accept remains unclear</td></tr>
<tr><td>23 August 2013</td><td>ICANN receives first complaints about inconsistent and unreasonable Expert Determinations</td></tr>
</table>

Date	Event
4 September 2013	ICANN receives complaint about unreasonable expert determination involving .shop/.通販
10 October 2013	BGC orders ICANN staff to prepare report, setting out the options for dealing with the situation of differing expert determination outcomes in similar disputes
24 October 2013	Notice of and Request for IRP in .africa by DCA Trust
9 November 2013	Staff deadline to submit report to the ICANN Board, setting out the options for dealing with the situation of differing expert determination outcomes in similar disputes
5 February 2014	ICANN Board intervenes with Expert Determinations on .car/.cars and .com/.cam, directing staff to investigate
7 February 2014	Amended Bylaws: – Removal of non-voting liaison appointed by Technical liaison group
14 March 2014	NTIA announces the U.S. Government's renewed intent to transition out of its oversight role and to conclude the privatization efforts which had started in 1997
18 March 2014	Notice of and Request for IRP in .hotels/.hoteis by Booking.com
26 March 2014	Introduction of new category of gTLDs: NGPC approves Registry Agreement Specification 13 for Brand Category of Applicants
10 April 2014	Execution of the first registry agreement involving a gTLD string that had been subject to a (reasonable and consistent) expert determination (.direct)
11 June 2014	Notice of and Request for IRP in .webs/.web by Vistaprint
21 June 2014	ICANN Board rejects the expert determination on the community objection regarding .med
17 July 2014	Request for IRP in .merck by Merck KGaA
30 July 2014	Amended Bylaws: – Compensation for non-voting liaisons with the exception of GAC representative
22 September 2014	Notice of and Request for IRP in .INC, .LLC and .LLP by Dot Registry, LLC
30 September 2014	ICANN updates Application Change Request Process
12 October 2014	ICANN Board orders re-evaluation of specific inconsistent and unreasonable expert determinations (.cam/.com and .shop/.通販, and directs evaluation panel how it should proceed
13 October 2014	Notice of and Request for IRP in .sports and .rugby by Donuts Inc.

Timeline

Date	*Event*
5 December 2014	Notice of and Request for IRP in .persiangulf by Gulf Cooperation Council
3 March 2015	Final Declaration in .hotels/.hoteis
10 March 2015	Notice of and Request for IRP in .hotel by Despegar Online SRL, Donuts Inc., Famous Four Media Limited, Fegistry LLC, and Radix FZC
19 March 2015	Notice of and Request for IRP in .sport by dot Sport Limited
24 March 2015	Notice of and Request for IRP in .eco by Little Birch and Minds + Machines Group Limited
7 April 2015	Notice of and Request for IRP in .charity by Corn Lake, LLC
12 May 2015	Consolidation of the IRPs in .hotel and .eco
9 July 2015	Final Declaration in .africa
9 October 2015	Final Declaration in .webs/.web
11 December 2015	Final Declaration in .merck
16 December 2015	Notice of and Request for IRP in .islam/.halal by Asia Green IT Systems Bilgisayar San. ve Tic. Ltd. Sti.
3 February 2016	ICANN Board orders re-evaluation of .hospital
10 February 2016	Request for IRP in .shop by Commercial Connect, LLC
12 February 2016	Final Declaration in .hotel and .eco
2 March 2016	Notice of and Request for IRP in .amazon by Amazon EU S.à.r.l.
12 May 2016	Final Declaration in .sports and .rugby
29 July 2016	Final Declaration in .INC, .LLC and .LLP
17 October 2016	Final Declaration in .charity

Bibliography

Legislative and Regulatory Materials

Memorandum of Understanding between the U.S. Department of Commerce and Internet Corporation for Assigned Names and Numbers (MOU). 25 November 1998 Available at https://www.ntia.doc.gov/other-publication/1998/memorandum-understanding-between-us-department-commerce-and-internet-corporat.

MOU. Amendment 1, 10 November 1999. Available at https://www.ntia.doc.gov/page/1999/icann-ammendment-1.

MOU. Amendment 2, 11 September 2000. Available at https://www.ntia.doc.gov/page/2000/icann-ammendment-2.

MOU. Amendment 3, 25 May 2001. Available at https://www.ntia.doc.gov/page/2001/icann-ammendment-3.

MOU. Amendment 4, 24 September 2001. Available at https://www.ntia.doc.gov/page/2001/icann-ammendment-4.

MOU. Amendment 5, 20 September 2002. Available at https://www.ntia.doc.gov/page/2002/icann-ammendment-5.

MOU. Amendment 6, Article II, introducing the new Article V(C)(8). Available at https://www.ntia.doc.gov/page/2003/icann-ammendment-6.

Joint Project Agreement between the U.S. Department of Commerce and the ICANN Corporation for Assigned Names and Numbers. 29 September 2006. Available at https://www.ntia.doc.gov/files/ntia/publications/signedmou290906.pdf.

Annex A to the Joint Project Agreement between the U.S. Department of Commerce and the ICANN Corporation for Assigned Names and Numbers. 29 September 2006. Available at https://www.ntia.doc.gov/files/ntia/publications/signedmou290906.pdf.

Affirmation of Commitments by the United States Department of Commerce and the Internet Corporation for Assigned Names and Numbers. 30 September 2009. Available on https://www.icann.org/resources/pages/affirmation-of-commitments-2009-09-30-en.

ICANN. *Draft Articles of Incorporation of Internet Corporation for Assigned Names and Numbers*. Available at https://www.ntia.doc.gov/legacy/ntiahome/domainname/proposals/icann/Articles.htm.

ICANN. *Draft Articles of Incorporation – Fifth Iteration: Articles of Incorporation of Internet Corporation for Assigned Names and Numbers*. Available at http://forum.icann.org/iana/comments/formation/,,articles5.html.

ICANN. *Articles of Incorporation of Internet Corporation for Assigned Names and Numbers.* As Revised 21 November 1998. Available on https://www.icann.org/resources/pages/articles-2012-02-25-en.

ICANN. *Amended and Restated Articles of Incorporation of Internet Corporation for Assigned Names and Numbers, Draft as of 25 May 2016*. May 2016. Available at https://www.icann.org/en/system/files/files/draft-restated-articles-incorporation-25may16-en.pdf.

ICANN. *Draft Articles of Incorporation of new IANA*. Available at http://forum.icann.org/iana/comments/formation/,,articles1.html.

ICANN. *Draft Bylaws for the Internet Corporation for Assigned Names and Numbers – A California Nonprofit Public Benefit Corporation*. 1998. Available at https://www.ntia.doc.gov/legacy/ntiahome/domainname/proposals/icann/Bylaws.htm.

ICANN. *Original Bylaws for the Internet Corporation for Assigned Names and Numbers – A California Nonprofit Public Benefit Corporation* effective 6 November 1998. Available on https://www.icann.org/resources/unthemed-pages/bylaws-1998-11-06-en.

ICANN. *Bylaws for the Internet Corporation for Assigned Names and Numbers – A California Nonprofit Public Benefit Corporation* as adopted effective 21 November 1998. Available on https://www.icann.org/resources/unthemed-pages/bylaws-1998-11-23-en.

ICANN. *Bylaws for the Internet Corporation for Assigned Names and Numbers – A California Nonprofit Public Benefit Corporation* as adopted effective 31 March 1999. Available on https://www.icann.org/resources/unthemed-pages/bylaws-1999-03-31-en.

ICANN. *Bylaws for the Internet Corporation for Assigned Names and Numbers – A California Nonprofit Public Benefit Corporation* as adopted effective 27 May 1999. Available on https://www.icann.org/resources/unthemed-pages/bylaws-1999-05-27-en.

ICANN. *Bylaws for the Internet Corporation for Assigned Names and Numbers – A California Nonprofit Public Benefit Corporation* as adopted effective 12 August 1999. Available on https://www.icann.org/resources/unthemed-pages/bylaws-1999-08-12-en.

ICANN. *Bylaws for the Internet Corporation for Assigned Names and Numbers – A California Nonprofit Public Benefit Corporation* as adopted effective 26 August 1999. Available on https://www.icann.org/resources/unthemed-pages/bylaws-1999-08-26-en.

ICANN. *Bylaws for the Internet Corporation for Assigned Names and Numbers – A California Nonprofit Public Benefit Corporation* as adopted effective 27 September 1999. Available on https://www.icann.org/resources/unthemed-pages/bylaws-1999-09-27-en.

ICANN. *Bylaws for the Internet Corporation for Assigned Names and Numbers – A California Nonprofit Public Benefit Corporation* as adopted effective 29 October 1999. Available on https://www.icann.org/resources/unthemed-pages/bylaws-1999-10-29-en.

ICANN. *Bylaws for the Internet Corporation for Assigned Names and Numbers – A California Nonprofit Public Benefit Corporation* as adopted effective 10 March 2000. Available on https://www.icann.org/resources/unthemed-pages/bylaws-2000-03-10-en.

ICANN. *Bylaws for the Internet Corporation for Assigned Names and Numbers – A California Nonprofit Public Benefit Corporation* as adopted effective 16 July 2000. Available on https://www.icann.org/resources/unthemed-pages/bylaws-2000-07-16-en.

ICANN. *Bylaws for the Internet Corporation for Assigned Names and Numbers – A California Nonprofit Public Benefit Corporation* as adopted effective 12 February 2002. Available on https://www.icann.org/resources/unthemed-pages/bylaws-2002-02-12-en.

ICANN. Bylaws as adopted effective 15 December 2002 ("New Bylaws" as a result of 2002 Evolution and Reform Process). Available on https://www.icann.org/resources/unthemed-pages/bylaws-2002-12-15-en.

ICANN. *Bylaws for the Internet Corporation for Assigned Names and Numbers – A California Nonprofit Public Benefit Corporation* as adopted effective 25 February 2003. Available on https://www.icann.org/resources/unthemed-pages/bylaws-2003-02-25-en.

ICANN. *Bylaws for the Internet Corporation for Assigned Names and Numbers – A California Nonprofit Public Benefit Corporation* as adopted effective 25 March 2003. Available on https://www.icann.org/resources/unthemed-pages/bylaws-2003-03-25-en.

ICANN. *Bylaws for the Internet Corporation for Assigned Names and Numbers – A California Nonprofit Public Benefit Corporation* as adopted effective 2 June 2003. Available on https://www.icann.org/resources/unthemed-pages/bylaws-2003-06-02-en.

ICANN. *Bylaws for the Internet Corporation for Assigned Names and Numbers – A California Nonprofit Public Benefit Corporation* as adopted effective 26 June 2003 (includes ccNSO). Available on https://www.icann.org/resources/unthemed-pages/bylaws-2003-06-26-en.

ICANN. *Bylaws for the Internet Corporation for Assigned Names and Numbers – A California Nonprofit Public Benefit Corporation* as adopted effective 13 October 2003. Available on https://www.icann.org/resources/pages/bylaws-2003-10-13-en.

ICANN. *Bylaws for the Internet Corporation for Assigned Names and Numbers – A California Nonprofit Public Benefit Corporation* as adopted effective 19 April 2004. Available on https://www.icann.org/resources/pages/bylaws-2004-04-19-en.

ICANN. *Bylaws for the Internet Corporation for Assigned Names and Numbers – A California Nonprofit Public Benefit Corporation* as adopted effective 8 April 2005. Available on https://www.icann.org/resources/pages/bylaws-2005-04-08-en.

ICANN. *Bylaws for the Internet Corporation for Assigned Names and Numbers – A California Nonprofit Public Benefit Corporation* as adopted effective 28 February 2006. Available on https://www.icann.org/resources/pages/bylaws-2006-02-28-en.

ICANN. *Bylaws for the Internet Corporation for Assigned Names and Numbers – A California Nonprofit Public Benefit Corporation* as adopted effective 15 February 2008. Available on https://www.icann.org/resources/pages/bylaws-2008-02-15-en.

ICANN. *Bylaws for the Internet Corporation for Assigned Names and Numbers – A California Nonprofit Public Benefit Corporation* as adopted effective 29 May 2008. Available on https://www.icann.org/resources/pages/bylaws-2008-05-29-en.

ICANN. *Bylaws for the Internet Corporation for Assigned Names and Numbers – A California Nonprofit Public Benefit Corporation* as adopted effective 20 March 2009. Available on https://www.icann.org/resources/pages/bylaws-2009-03-20-en.

ICANN. *Bylaws for the Internet Corporation for Assigned Names and Numbers – A California Nonprofit Public Benefit Corporation* as adopted effective 27 August 2009. Available on https://www.icann.org/resources/pages/bylaws-2009-08-27-en.

ICANN. *Bylaws for the Internet Corporation for Assigned Names and Numbers – A California Nonprofit Public Benefit Corporation* as adopted effective 30 September 2009. Available on https://www.icann.org/resources/pages/bylaws-2009-09-30-en.

ICANN. *Bylaws for the Internet Corporation for Assigned Names and Numbers – A California Nonprofit Public Benefit Corporation* as adopted effective 25 June 2010. Available on https://www.icann.org/resources/pages/bylaws-2010-06-25-en.

ICANN. *Bylaws for the Internet Corporation for Assigned Names and Numbers – A California Nonprofit Public Benefit Corporation* as adopted effective 5 August 2010. Available on https://www.icann.org/resources/pages/bylaws-2010-08-05-en.

ICANN. *Bylaws for the Internet Corporation for Assigned Names and Numbers – A California Nonprofit Public Benefit Corporation* as adopted effective 28 October 2010. Available on https://www.icann.org/resources/pages/bylaws-2010-10-28-en.

ICANN. *Bylaws for the Internet Corporation for Assigned Names and Numbers – A California Nonprofit Public Benefit Corporation* as adopted effective 25 January 2011. Available on https://www.icann.org/resources/pages/bylaws-2011-01-25-en.

ICANN. *Bylaws for the Internet Corporation for Assigned Names and Numbers – A California Nonprofit Public Benefit Corporation* as adopted effective 18 March 2011. Available on https://www.icann.org/resources/pages/bylaws-2011-03-18-en.

ICANN. *Bylaws for the Internet Corporation for Assigned Names and Numbers – A California Nonprofit Public Benefit Corporation* as adopted effective 24 June 2011. Available on https://www.icann.org/resources/pages/bylaws-2011-06-24-en.

ICANN. *Bylaws for the Internet Corporation for Assigned Names and Numbers – A California Nonprofit Public Benefit Corporation* as adopted effective 8 December 2011. Available on https://www.icann.org/resources/pages/bylaws-2011-12-08-en.

ICANN. *Bylaws for the Internet Corporation for Assigned Names and Numbers – A California Nonprofit Public Benefit Corporation* as adopted effective 16 March 2012. Available on https://www.icann.org/resources/pages/bylaws-2012-12-21-en.

ICANN. *Bylaws for the Internet Corporation for Assigned Names and Numbers – A California Nonprofit Public Benefit Corporation* as adopted effective 20 December 2012. Available on https://www.icann.org/resources/pages/bylaws-2013-04-12-en.

ICANN. *Bylaws for the Internet Corporation for Assigned Names and Numbers – A California Nonprofit Public Benefit Corporation* as adopted effective 11 April 2013. Available on https://www.icann.org/resources/pages/bylaws-2014-04-04-en.

ICANN. *Bylaws for the Internet Corporation for Assigned Names and Numbers – A California Nonprofit Public Benefit Corporation* as adopted effective 7 February 2014. Available on https://www.icann.org/resources/pages/bylaws-2014-10-06-en.

ICANN. *Bylaws for the Internet Corporation for Assigned Names and Numbers – A California Nonprofit Public Benefit Corporation* as adopted effective 30 July 2014. Available on https://www.icann.org/resources/pages/bylaws-2012-02-25-en.

ICANN. *Bylaws for the Internet Corporation for Assigned Names and Numbers – A California Nonprofit Public Benefit Corporation* as adopted effective 11 February 2016. Available on https://www.icann.org/resources/pages/bylaws-2016-02-16-en.

ICANN. *Future Bylaws for Internet Corporation for Assigned Names and Numbers, a California Nonprofit Public-Benefit Corporation, adopted by ICANN Board on 27 May 2016*. Available at https://www.icann.org/en/system/files/files/adopted-bylaws-27may16-en.pdf.

ICANN. *Bylaws for the Internet Corporation for Assigned Names and Numbers – A California Nonprofit Public Benefit Corporation* as adopted effective 1 October 2016. Available on https://www.icann.org/resources/pages/governance/bylaws-en.

ICANN. *Cooperative Engagement Process – Requests for Independent Review*. 11 April 2013. Available on https://www.icann.org/en/system/files/files/cep-11apr13-en.pdf.

ICANN. *ICDR Supplementary Procedures for Internet Corporation for Assigned Names and Numbers (ICANN) Independent Review Process*. Available on https://www.adr.org/aaa/ShowPDF?doc=ADRSTG_002001.

ICDR. *INTERNATIONAL DISPUTE RESOLUTION PROCEDURES (Including Mediation and Arbitration Rules)*. 1 June 2014. Available on https://www.icdr.org/icdr/ShowProperty?nodeId=/UCM/ADRSTAGE2020868&revision=latestreleased.

ICANN. *Documentary Information Disclosure Policy*. Available at https://www.icann.org/resources/pages/didp-2012-02-25-en.

ICANN. *Criteria for Assessing TLD Proposals*. 15 August 2000. Available at http://archive.icann.org/en/tlds/tld-criteria-15aug00.htm.

ICANN. *Final Report of the New TLD Evaluation Process Planning Task Force*. 31 July 2002. Available at http://archive.icann.org/en/committees/ntepptf/final-report-31jul02.htm.

ICANN. *Establishment of new sTLDs: Request for Proposals (Draft for public comment)*. 24 June 2003. Available at http://archive.icann.org/en/tlds/new-stld-rfp/new-stld-rfp-24jun03.htm.

ICANN. *New TLD Application Instructions*. 15 August 2000. Available at https://archive.icann.org/en/tlds/new-tld-application-instructions-15aug00.htm.

ICANN. *New sTLD Application – Explanatory Notes and Selection Criteria*. 15 December 2003. Available on https://archive.icann.org/en/tlds/new-stld-rfp/new-stld-application-parta-15dec03.htm.

ICANN Generic Names Supporting Organization. *Final Report - Introduction of New Generic Top-Level Domains Part A*. 8 August 2007. Available at http://gnso.icann.org/en/issues/new-gtlds/pdp-dec05-fr-parta-08aug07.htm.

ICANN. *New gTLD Program: Draft Applicant Guidebook (Draft RFP)*, version 1. 24 October 2008. Available on http://archive.icann.org/en/topics/new-gtlds/draft-rfp-24oct08-en.pdf.

ICANN. *Draft Applicant Guidebook, Version 2*. 18 February 2009.

ICANN. *New gTLD Draft Applicant Guidebook-Version 2: Analysis of Public Comment*. 31 May 2009. Available on http://archive.icann.org/en/topics/new-gtlds/agv2-analysis-public-comments-31may09-en.pdf.

ICANN. *New gTLD Applicant Guidebook 11 January 2012*. Available at https://newgtlds.icann.org/en/applicants/agb/guidebook-full-11jan12-en.pdf.

ICANN. *New gTLD Applicant Guidebook 4 June 2012*. Available at https://newgtlds.icann.org/en/applicants/agb/guidebook-full-04jun12-en.pdf.

NSF Act of 1950. Pub. L. 81-507 (codified at 42 U.S.C. 1862).

Scientific and Advanced-Technology Act of 1992, Pub. L. 102–476 section 4(9), 106 Stat. 2297, 2300 (codified at 42 U.S.C. 1862).

U.S. House of Representatives. *H Con Res* 268 (16 November 2005).

U.S. Senate. *S Res* 323 (18 November 2005).

NTIA. *A Proposal to Improve Technical Management of Internet Names and Addresses – Discussion Draft*. 30 January 1998. Available at https://www.ntia.doc.gov/files/ntia/publications/dnsdrft.txt.

NTIA. *Federal Register Online: Improvement of Technical Management of Internet Names and Addresses*. 20 February 1998. Available at https://www.ntia.doc.gov/files/ntia/publications/022098fedreg.txt.

NTIA. *Statement of Policy on the Management of Internet Names and Addresses*. 5 June 1998. Available at https://www.ntia.doc.gov/federal-register-notice/1998/statement-policy-management-internet-names-and-addresses.

NTIA. *Management of Internet Names and Addresses: statement of policy*. 10 June 1998. Available at https://www.ntia.doc.gov/files/ntia/publications/6_5_98dns.pdf.

Network Information Services Manager(s) for NSFNET and the NREN. *INTERNIC Registration Services Cooperative Agreement No.NCR-9218742*. 1 January 1993. Available at http://archive.icann.org/en/nsi/coopagmt-01jan93.htm.

ICANN. *Amendment 4 to Cooperative Agreement Between NSI and U.S. Government*. Available at https://archive.icann.org/en/nsi/coopagmt-amend4-13sep95.htm.

ICANN. *Amendment 11 to Cooperative Agreement Between NSI and U.S. Government*. Available at http://archive.icann.org/en/nsi/coopagmt-amend11-07oct98.htm.

ICANN. *Amendment 14 to the DOC/NSI Cooperative Agreement of 15 June 1999*. 15 June 1999. Available at https://www.ntia.doc.gov/legacy/ntiahome/domainname/amends/amend14rev.htm.

ICANN. *Amendment 15 to the DOC/NSI Cooperative Agreement of 15 July 1999*. 15 July 1999. Available at https://www.ntia.doc.gov/legacy/ntiahome/domainname/amends/amend15rev.htm.

ICANN. *Amendment 16 to the DOC/NSI Cooperative Agreement of 10 August 1999*. 10 August 1999. Available at https://www.ntia.doc.gov/legacy/ntiahome/domainname/amends/amend16.htm.

ICANN. *Amendment 18 to the DOC/NSI Cooperative Agreement of 5 October 1999*. 5 October 1999. Available at (https://www.ntia.doc.gov/legacy/ntiahome/domainname/amends/amend18.htm).

ICANN. *Amendment 34 to DOC/Verisign Cooperative Agreementof 20 October 2016*. 20 October 2016. Available at https://www.ntia.doc.gov/files/ntia/publications/amendment_34.pdf.

ICANN. *USC/ICANN Transition Agreement*. May 2000. Available at https://www.icann.org/resources/unthemed-pages/usc-icann-transition-2012-02-25-en.

NTIA. *IANA Functions Contract of 8 February 1999*. Available at https://www.ntia.doc.gov/files/ntia/publications/ianacontract.pdf.

NTIA. *IANA Functions Contract of 21 March 2001*. Available at https://www.ntia.doc.gov/page/iana-functions-purchase-order.

NTIA. *IANA Functions Contract of 13 March 2003*. Available at https://www.ntia.doc.gov/page/iana-functions-purchase-order.

NTIA. *IANA Functions Contract of 11 August 2006*. Available at https://www.ntia.doc.gov/page/iana-functions-purchase-order.

NTIA. *IANA Functions Contract of 2 July 2012*. Available at https://www.ntia.doc.gov/page/iana-functions-purchase-order.

NTIA. *Amendment Modification No. 0001 to the IANA Function Contract*. 1 October 2012. Available at http://www.ntia.doc.gov/page/iana-functions-purchase-order.

NTIA. *Amendment Modification No. 0002 to the IANA Function Contract*. 30 April 2013. Available at http://www.ntia.doc.gov/page/iana-functions-purchase-order.

NTIA. *Amendment Modification No. 0003 to the IANA Function Contract*. 4 August 2015. Available at http://www.ntia.doc.gov/page/iana-functions-purchase-order.

NTIA. *Amendment Modification No. 0004 to the IANA Function Contract*. 17 September 2015. Available at http://www.ntia.doc.gov/page/iana-functions-purchase-order.

NTIA. *Amendment Modification No. 0005 to the IANA Function Contract*. 2 February 2016. Available at http://www.ntia.doc.gov/page/iana-functions-purchase-order.

NTIA. *Contract Close-out*. 21 October 2016. Available at http://www.ntia.doc.gov/page/iana-functions-purchase-order.

NTIA. *First Status Report to the Department of Commerce*. 15 June 1999. Available at https://www.ntia.doc.gov/report/1999/first-status-report-department-commerce-icann.

NTIA. *Second Status Report to the Department of Commerce*. 30 June 1999. Available at https://www.ntia.doc.gov/report/2000/second-status-report-department-commerce-icann.

NTIA. *Third Status Report to the Department of Commerce*. 3 July 2001. Available at https://www.ntia.doc.gov/report/2001/third-status-report-department-commerce-icann.

ICANN. *Minutes of Organizational Meeting October 25, 1998*. Available at https://www.icann.org/resources/board-material/minutes-1998-10-25-en.

ICANN. *Minutes of Special Meeting October 29, 1998*. Available at https://www.icann.org/resources/board-material/minutes-1998-10-29-en.

ICANN. *Minutes of Special Meeting 6 November 1998*. Available at https://www.icann.org/resources/board-material/minutes-1998-11-06-en.

ICANN. *Minutes of Special Meeting 21 November 1998*. Available at https://www.icann.org/resources/board-material/minutes-1998-11-21-en.

ICANN. *Resolution 99.48*. Minutes of Meeting of 27 May 1999. Available at https://www.icann.org/resources/board-material/minutes-1999-05-27-en.

ICANN. *Resolution 00.47*, Regular Meeting of the Board Minutes. 16 July 2000. Available at https://www.icann.org/resources/board-material/minutes-2000-07-16-en.

ICANN. *Resolution 00.89 – Minutes of Second Annual Meeting (in Marina Del Rey)*. 16 November 2000. Available at https://www.icann.org/resources/board-material/minutes-annual-meeting-2000-11-16-en.

ICANN. *Resolutions 01.52 – 01.59 – Special Meeting of the Board Minutes*. 7 May 2001. Available on https://www.icann.org/resources/board-material/minutes-2001-05-07-en.

ICANN. *Resolution 01.79 – Regular Meeting of the Board Minutes*. 10 September 2001. Available on https ://www.icann.org/resources/board-material/minutes-2001-09-10-en.

ICANN. *Resolution 02.152*. 15 December 2002. Available at https://www.icann.org/resources/board-material/minutes-annual-meeting-2002-12-15-en.

ICANN. *Resolution 02.97A*. 23 August 2002. Available at https://www.icann.org/resources/board-material/minutes-2002-08-23-en.

ICANN. *Board Resolution 03.166-168 and rationale*. 31 October 2003. Available at https://www.icann.org/news/advisory-2003-10-31-en.

ICANN. *Resolutions 03.169-171*. 31 October 2003. Available at https://www.icann.org/news/advisory-2003-10-31-en.

ICANN. *Resolution 04.33 adopted at Special ICANN Board Meeting*. 19 April 2004. Available on https://www.icann.org/resources/board-material/resolutions-2004-04-19-en.

ICANN. *Minutes – Special Meeting of the Board*. 18 October 2004. Available on https://www.icann.org/resources/board-material/minutes-2004-10-18-en.

ICANN. *Resolutions 04.123 – 04.126 – Special Meeting of the Board*. 13 December 2004. Available on https://www.icann.org/resources/board-material/minutes-2004-12-13-en.

ICANN. *Minutes – Special Meeting of the Board*. 3 May 2005. Available on https://www.icann.org/resources/board-material/minutes-2005-05-03-en.

ICANN. *Board Resolution 06.71*. 25 September 2006. Available at https://www.icann.org/resources/board-material/minutes-2006-09-25-en.

ICANN. *Voting Transcript of Board Meeting of 25 September 2006*. Available at https://www.icann.org/resources/board-material/voting-transcript-2006-09-25-en.

ICANN. *Adopted Resolution 07.18 from ICANN Board Meeting*. 30 March 2007. Available on https://www.icann.org/resources/board-material/resolutions-2007-03-30-en.

ICANN. *Adopted Board Resolutions | New Delhi*. 15 February 2008. Available at http://www.icann.org/en/minutes/resolutions- 15feb08.htm#_Toc64545917.

ICANN. *ICANN Board Resolution 2008.06.26.02*. Available at https://www.icann.org/resources/board-material/resolutions-2008-06-26-en.

ICANN. *ICANN Board Resolution 2008.06.26.02-03*. Available at https://www.icann.org/resources/board-material/resolutions-2008-06-26-en.

ICANN. *ICANN Board Resolution 2009.06.26.23*. Available at https://www.icann.org/resources/board-material/resolutions-2009-06-26-en.

ICANN. *Adopted Board Resolutions 2009.03.06.07 – 2009.03.06.08 – Mexico*. 6 March 2009. Available on https://www.icann.org/resources/board-material/resolutions-2009-03-06-en.

ICANN. *Adopted Board Resolution 2010.12.10.22 – Cartagena*. 10 December 2010. Available on https://www.icann.org/resources/board-material/resolutions-2010-12-10-en.

ICANN, *Adopted Board Resolutions 2010.09.25.02 – 2010.09.25.03*. Available on https://www.icann.org/resources/board-material/resolutions-2010-09-25-en.

ICANN. *Adopted Board Resolutions 2011.03.18.23 – 2011.03.18.25 – Silicon Valley / San Francisco*. 18 March 2011. Available on https://www.icann.org/resources/board-material/resolutions-2011-03-18-en.

ICANN. *Approved Board Resolutions 2011.06.20.01 – 2011.06.20.03 – Singapore.* 20 June 2011. Available on https ://www.icann.org/resources/board-material/resolutions-2011-06-20-en.

ICANN. *Board Rationales for the Approval of the Launch of the New gTLD Program,* Available at http://www.icann.org/en/groups/board/documents/rationale-board-approval-new-gtld-program-launch-20jun11-en.pdf.

ICANN. *Rationale: Remaining areas of difference between ICANN's Board and Governmental Advisory Committee regarding implementation of the New gTLD Program.* 20 June 2011. Available on https ://www.icann.org/en/system/files/bm/rationale-gac-response-new-gtld-20jun11-en.pdf.

ICANN. *Board workshop: new gTLD Program discussion topics.* 20 June 2011. Available on https://www.icann.org/en/system/files/bm/briefing-materials-20jun11-en.pdf.

ICANN. *Approved Resolutions 2012.04.10.NG4 – 2012.04.10.NG5 – Meeting of the New gTLD Program Committee.* 10 April 2012. Available on https://www.icann.org/resources/board-material/resolutions-new-gtld-2012-04-10-en.

ICANN. *Rationale for Resolutions 2012.12.20.17 – 2012.12.20.19.* 20 December 2012. Available at https://www.icann.org/resources/board-material/resolutions-2012-12-20-en.

ICANN. *Rationale for Resolution 2013.04.11.06.* 11 April 2013. Available at https://www.icann.org/resources/board-material/resolutions-2013-04-11-en.

ICANN. *Approved Board Resolutions 2013.05.18.08 – 2013.05.18.11 – Regular Meeting of the ICANN Board.* 18 May 2013. Available on https://www.icann.org/resources/board-material/resolutions-2013-05-18-en.

ICANN. *Approved Resolution 2013.06.04.NG01 – Meeting of the New gTLD Program Committee.* 4 June 2013. Available on https ://www.icann.org/resources/board-material/resolutions-new-gtld-2013-06-04-en.

ICANN. *Approved Resolution 2013.06.25.NG07 – Meeting of the New gTLD Program Committee.* 25 June 2013. Available on https ://www.icann.org/resources/board-material/resolutions-new-gtld-2013-06-25-en.

ICANN. *Approved Resolution 2013.09.10.NG03 – Meeting of the New gTLD Program Committee.* 10 September 2013. Available on https://www.icann.org/resources/board-material/resolutions-new-gtld-2013-09-10-en.

ICANN. *Minutes of the Meeting of the New gTLD Program Committee.* 10 September 2013. Available at https://www.icann.org/resources/board-material/minutes-new-gtld-2013-09-10-en.

ICANN. *Approved Resolution 2014.05.14.NG03 – Meeting of the New gTLD Program Committee.* 14 May 2014. Available on https://www.icann.org/resources/board-material/resolutions-new-gtld-2014-05-14-en.

ICANN. *ICANN Board New gTLD Program Committee Resolutions 2014.10.12.NG02 – 2014.10.12.NG03*, 12 October 2014. Available on https://www.icann.org/resources/board-material/resolutions-new-gtld-2014-10-12-en.

ICANN. *Board Resolutions 2015.04.26.14 – 2015.04.26.16.* 26 April 2016. Available on https://www.icann.org/resources/board-material/resolutions-2015-04-26-en#2.b.

ICANN. *Approved Resolution 2015.06.21.NG02 – Meeting of the New gTLD Program Committee*. 21 June 2015. Available on https ://www.icann.org/resources/board-material/resolutions-new-gtld-2015-06-21-en.

ICANN. *Board Resolution 2015.07.28.08*. 28 July 2015. Available on https://www.icann.org/resources/board-material/resolutions-2015-07-28-en#2.b.

ICANN, *Approved Board Resolutions 2016.02.03.12 – 2016.02.03.13 – Regular Meeting of the ICANN Board*. 3 February 2016. Available on https://www.icann.org/resources/board-material/resolutions-2016-02-03-en.

ICANN. *Approved Board Resolution 2016.03.03.02 – Regular Meeting of the ICANN Board*. 3 March 2016. Available on https://www.icann.org/resources/board-material/resolutions-2016-03-03-en.

ICANN. *Approved Board Resolutions 2016.08.09.14-2016.08.09.15 – Special Meeting of the ICANN Board*. 9 August 2016. Available on https://www.icann.org/resources /board-material/resolutions-2016-08-09-en, rationale.

ICANN. *Notes from October 31 conference call between several members of the ICANN board and representatives of the Boston Working Group and Open Root Server Confederation*. 31 October 1998. Available at https://www.icann.org/resources /board-material/notes-1998-10-31-en.

ICANN. *Public meeting of 14 November 1998 (Berkman Center for Internet and Society) – ICANN Public Meeting Transcript* 7. 14 November 1998. Available at http://cyber.law.harvard.edu/icann/cambridge-1198/archive/transintro.html.

ICANN. *Public Meeting Transcript, Meeting Held in Cambridge, Massachusetts Saturday, November 14, 9:00 am – 4:00 pm*. 14 November 1998. Available at http://cyber.law.harvard.edu/icann/cambridge-1198/archive/transtransparenc y.html.

ICANN. *ICANN Yokohama Meeting Topic: Introduction of New Top-Level Domains*. 13 June 2000. Available at https://archive.icann.org/en/meetings/yokohama/new -tld-topic.htm.

ICANN. *Report on TLD Applications*. 9 November 2000. Available at http://archive.icann.org/en/tlds/report/.

Stuart, Lynn. *A Plan for Action Regarding New gTLDs*. 18 October 2002 (published 8 November 2002). Available at https://archive.icann.org/en/committees/ntepptf /new-gtld-action-plan-18oct02.htm.

ICANN. *ICANN Rio de Janeiro Meeting Topic: Criteria to be used in the Selection of New Sponsored TLDs*. 25 March 2003. Available at http://archive.icann.org/en/meetings/riodejaneiro/stld-rfp-topic.htm.

ICANN GNSO Council Montreal Meeting on 24 June 2003 – minutes. Available at http://www.dnso.org/dnso/notes/20030624.GNSOmontreal-minutes.html.

ICANN. *ICANN Launches Broad Strategic Initiative for New Generic Top-Level Domain*. 31 October 2003. Available at https://www.icann.org/news/announcement-200 3-10-31-en.

ICANN. *Status Report on sTLD Application Process*. 19 March 2004. Available at https://archive.icann.org/en/tlds/stld-apps-19mar04/PostsTLDStatusRpt.pdf.

ICANN. *ICANN Meetings in Kuala Lumpur – ICANN Public* Forum. 22 July 2004. Available at http://archive.icann.org/meetings/kualalumpur/captioning-public-forum-23jul04.htm.

ICANN. *Announcement: ICANN Moves Forward in First Phase Commercial & Technical Negotiations with Two sTLD Applicants*. 27 October 2004. Available on https://www.icann.org/news/announcement-2004-10-27-en.

ICANN. *ICANN Accountability & Transparency Frameworks and Principles*. 2008. Available at https://www.icann.org/en/system/files/files/acct-trans-frameworks-principles-10jan08-en.pdf.

ICANN. *Address by ICANN Chairman to Public Meeting on the Midterm Review of the JPA*. 28 February 2008. Available at https://archive.icann.org/en/jpa/chairman-address.html.

ICANN. *Summary and analysis of second IIC comment period (18 September to 20 October 2008)*. Available at https://archive.icann.org/en/jpa/iic/summary-iic-second-public-comment-period-en.pdf.

ICANN. *Draft Implementation Plan for Improving Institutional Confidence*. 26 February 2009. Available at https://archive.icann.org/en/jpa/iic/draft-iic-implementation-26feb09-en.pdf.

ICANN. *Summary and analysis of third IIC comment period (12 March 2009 to 11 May 2009)*. Available at https://archive.icann.org/en/jpa/iic/summary-iic-third-public-comment-period-en.pdf.

ICANN. *Announcement: Evaluators Selection for the New gTLD Program Continues*. 25 October 2009. Available on https://www.icann.org/news/announcement-2009-10-25-en.

ICANN. *.post Sponsored TLD Agreement*. 11 December 2009. Available on https://www.icann.org/resources/unthemed-pages/post-2015-10-30-en.

ICANN. *Report on Status of Independent Review Nominating Committee*. March 2010. Available at https://archive.icann.org/en/meetings/accra/indrev-topic.htm.

ICANN. *Accountability and Transparency Review Team – Selection of Independent Expert and Update on ATRT Review*. 10 August 2010. Available at https://www.icann.org/news/announcement-2010-08-10-en.

ICANN SSAC. *Invalid Top Level Domain Queries at the Root Level of the Domain Name System*. 15 November 2010. Available on https://www.icann.org/en/system/files/files/sac-045-en.pdf.

ICANN. *Unredacted version of Board Workshop Paper on IOC/Red Cross Protection*. 20 June 2011. Released on 28 August 2012. Available on https://www.icann.org/en/system/files/bm/briefing-materials-unredacted-20jun11-en.pdf.

ICANN. *Transcripts of Dakar New gTLD Program Update*. 26 October 2011. Available on http://archive.icann.org/en/meetings/dakar2011/bitcache/Transcript_%20DAKAR%20New%20gTLD%20Program%20Update-vid=30087&disposition=attachment&op=download.pdf.

ICANN. *New gTLD Program Update*. Dakar. 26 October 2011. Available on http://dakar42.icann.org/node/26953.

Maher, David W., Chair (RySG). *Comments of the RySG on the IOC/RC Names at the Top Level*. 7 March 2012. Available on http://forum.icann.org/lists/ioc-rcrc-proposal/msg00010.html.

ICANN At-Large Advisory Committee (ALAC). *ALAC Statement on the Reservation of Olympic and Red Cross Namesin the gTLD Application Procedure*. 23 March 2012. Available on http://forum.icann.org/lists/ioc-rcrc-proposal/pdfogYOred2Fb.pdf.

ICANN. *GNSO Council Resolution 20120326-1*. 26 March 2012. Available on http://gnso.icann.org/en/council/resolutions#201203.

ICANN. *New gTLD Update on the close of the TLD Application system*. 30 May 2012. Available at http://newgtlds.icann.org/en/announcements-and-media/announcement-3-30may12-en.

ICANN. *Report by Accountability Structures Expert Panel (ASEP)*. 26 October 2012. Available on https://www.icann.org/en/system/files/files/report-26oct12-en.pdf.

ICANN. *New gTLD Program: String Similarity Contention Sets*. 26 February 2013. Available on https://newgtlds.icann.org/en/announcements-and-media/announcement-26feb13-en.

ICANN. *ICANN Public Forum Beijing*. 11 April 2013. 13:30 to 18:00. Available on http://archive.icann.org/en/meetings/beijing2013/bitcache/Transcript_%20ICANN%20Public%20Forum-vid = 49407&disposition = attachment&op = download.pdf.

ICANN. *Transcription ICANN Durban Meeting, NCUC Workshop Wednesday 17 July 2013 at 13:30 local time*. 17 July 2013. Available on http://archive.icann.org/en/meetings/durban2013/bitcache/Transcript_%20NCUC%20-%20The%20Debate%20on%20%27Closed%27%20Generic%20Top%20Level%20Domains-vid = 52845&disposition = attachment&op = download.pdf.

ICANN. *Announcement: New gTLD Applicant and GDD Portal Update*. 1 March 2015. Available on https://www.icann.org/news/announcement-2015-03-01-en.

ICANN. *Announcement Update – New gTLD Applicant and GDD Portal Back Online*. 2 March 2015. Available on https://www.icann.org/news/announcement-3-2015-03-02-en.

ICANN. *Announcement: New gTLD Applicant and GDD Portals Update*. 27 May 2015. Available on https://www.icann.org/news/announcement-2015-05-27-en.

ICANN. *Information on the Applicant Guidebook*. Available at http://newgtlds.icann.org/en/applicants/agb.

ICANN. *CPE Results*. Available on https://newgtlds.icann.org/en/applicants/cpe.

ICANN. *Program Implementation Review*. 29 January 2016. Available on https://www.icann.org/en/system/files/files/program-review-29jan16-en.pdf.

ICANN. *Recommendation of the Committee on Reconsideration Request 00-8*. 5 March 2001. Available on https://archive.icann.org/en/committees/reconsideration/rc00-8.htm.

ICANN. *Recommendation of the Committee on Reconsideration Request 00-9*. 30 April 2001. Available on https://archive.icann.org/en/committees/reconsideration/rc00-9.htm.

ICANN. *Recommendation of the Committee on Reconsideration Request 00-10*. 5 March 2001. Available on https://archive.icann.org/en/committees/reconsideration/rc00-10.htm.

ICANN. *Recommendation of the Committee on Reconsideration Request 00-11*. 16 March 2001. Available on https://archive.icann.org/en/committees/reconsideration/rc00-11.htm.

ICANN. *Recommendation of the Committee on Reconsideration Request 00-12*. 16 March 2001. Available on https://archive.icann.org/en/committees/reconsideration/rc00-12.htm.

ICANN. *Recommendation of the Committee on Reconsideration Request 00-13*. 16 March 2001. Available on https://archive.icann.org/en/committees/reconsideration/rc00-13.htm.

ICANN. *Recommendation of the Committee on Reconsideration Request 00-14*. 16 March 2001. https://archive.icann.org/en/committees/reconsideration/rc00-14.htm.

ICANN. *Recommendation of the Committee on Reconsideration Request 00-16*. 30 April 2001. Available on https://archive.icann.org/en/committees/reconsideration/rc00-16.htm.

ICANN. *Recommendation of the Committee on Reconsideration Request 01-2*. 30 April 2001. Available on https://archive.icann.org/en/committees/reconsideration/rc01-2.htm.

ICANN. *Recommendation of the Committee on Reconsideration Request 00-8*. 5 March 2001. Available on https://archive.icann.org/en/committees/reconsideration/rc00-8.htm.

ICANN. *Recommendation of the Committee on Reconsideration Request 00-9*. 30 April 2001. Available on https://archive.icann.org/en/committees/reconsideration/rc00-9.htm.

ICANN. *Revised Recommendation of the Committee on Reconsideration Request 00-15*. 7 September 2001. Available on https ://archive.icann.org/en/committees/reconsideration/rc00-15-1.htm.

ICANN. *BGC Determination on Reconsideration Request 14-5*. 27 February 2014. Available on https://www.icann.org/en/system/files/files/determination-vistaprint-27feb14-en.pdf.

ICANN. *BGC Recommendation on Reconsideration Request 15-7*. 20 June 2015. Available on https ://www.icann.org/en/system/files/files/recommendation-15-7-booking-bv-travel-reservations-srl-20jun15-en.pdf.

ICANN. *Independent Evaluators of sTLD proposals*. Available on http://archive.icann.org/en/tlds/new-stld-rfp/panel.htm.

ICANN. *Call for Expressions of Interest (EOIs) – New gTLD Process: Application Evaluation Temas (Technical and Financial Evaluation)*. 25 February 2009. Available on https://archive.icann.org/en/topics/new-gtlds/eoi-app-eval-25feb09-en.pdf.

ICANN. *Call for Expressions of Interest (EOIs) – New gTLD Process: Application Evaluation Temas (Technical and Financial Evaluation)*. 31 July 2009. Available on https://archive.icann.org/en/topics/new-gtlds/eoi-app-eval-31jul09-en.pdf.

ICANN. *Call for Expressions of Interest (EOIs) for a New gTLD Comparative Evaluation Panel.* 25 February 2009. Available on https://archive.icann.org/en/topics/new-gtlds/eoi-comparative-evaluation-25feb09-en.pdf.

ICANN. *Call for Expressions of Interest (EOIs) for a New gTLD Community Priority Evaluation Panel – formerly Comparative Evaluation Panel.* 31 July 2009. Available on https://archive.icann.org/en/topics/new-gtlds/eoi-commun-priority-31jul09-en.pdf.

ICANN. *Call for Expressions of Interest (EOIs) for a New gTLD Geographic Names Panel.* 25 February 2009. Available on https://archive.icann.org/en/topics/new-gtlds/eoi-geonames-25feb09-en.pdf.

ICANN. *Call for Expressions of Interest (EOIs) for a New gTLD Geographic Names Panel.* 31 July 2009. Available on https://archive.icann.org/en/topics/new-gtlds/eoi-geo-names-31jul09-en.pdf.

ICANN. *Call for Expressions of Interest (EOIs) for New gTLD String Similarity Examiners.* 25 February 2009. Available on https://archive.icann.org/en/topics/new-gtlds/eoi-string-sim-25feb09-en.pdf.

ICANN. *Call for Expressions of Interest (EOIs) for New gTLD String Similarity Examiners.* 31 July 2009. Available on https://archive.icann.org/en/topics/new-gtlds/eoi-string-sim-31jul09-en.pdf.

ICANN *GAC Principles for the Delegation and Administration of Country Code Top Level Domains.* 23 February 2000. Available on https://archive.icann.org/en/committees/gac/gac-cctldprinciples-23feb00.htm.

ICANN GAC. *GAC Principles regarding New gTLDs.* 28 March 2007. Available on https://archive.icann.org/en/topics/new-gtlds/gac-principles-regarding-new-gtlds-28mar07-en.pdf.

ICANN GAC. *GAC Comments on the Applicant Guidebook (15 April 2011 version).* 26 May 2011. Available on https://gacweb.icann.org/download/attachments/28278837/GAC%20Comments%20on%20the%20new%20gTLDs%20-%2026%20May%202011.pdf?version = 1&modificationDate = 1312360275000&api = v2.

ICANN GAC. *GAC Communiqué – Paris.* 26 June 2008. Aailable on https://gacweb.icann.org/download/attachments/27131940/GAC_32_Paris_Communique.pdf?version = 1&modificationDate = 1312228254000&api = v2.

ICANN GAC. *GAC Communiqué – Beijing, People's Republic of China.* 11 April 2013. Available on https://gacweb.icann.org/download/attachments/28278854/Beijing%20Communique%20april2013_Final.pdf?version = 1&modificationDate = 1367607354000&api = v2.

ICANN GAC. *GAC Communiqué – Durban, South Africa.* 18 July 2013. Available on https://gacweb.icann.org/download/attachments/28278854/Final_GAC_Communique_Durban_20130718.pdf?version = 1&modificationDate = 1375798225000&api = v2.

ICANN. *Statement from the first meeting of the IANA stewardship transition coordination group.* 18 July 2014. Available at https://www.icann.org/en/system/files/files/draft-icg-statement-18jul14-en.pdf.

ICANN. *IANA Stewardship Transition Coordination Group Process Timeline*. 8 September 2014. Available at https://www.icann.org/en/system/files/files/icg-process-timeline-08sep14-en.pdf.

ICANN. *Charter for the IANA Stewardship Transition Coordination Group*. 27 August 2014. Available at https://www.icann.org/ en/system/files/files/charter-icg-27aug14-en.pdf.

ICANN. *Charter Cross Community Working Group on Enhancing ICANN Accountability*. 4 November 2014. Available at https://community.iicann.org/display/acctcrosscomm/Charter.

Cross Community Working Group (CCWG). *Accountability Initial Draft Proposal for Public Comment*. 4 May 2015. Available at https://community.icann.org/pages/viewpage.action?pageId=52897394.

CCWG-Accountability. *2nd Draft Proposal on Work Stream 1 Recommendations*. 3 August 2015. Available at https://community.icann.org/pages/viewpage.action?pageId=53783460.

ICANN GNSO Business Constituency. *Comment on Cross Community Working Group on Enhancing ICANN Accountability (CCWG) 2nd Draft Report (Work Stream 1)*. 12 September 2015. Available at https://community.icann.org/download/attachments/56136438/62.%20%20Business%20Constituency%20%28BC%29%20Comments.pdf?api=v2.

ICANN. *Impact Analysis of CCWG-Accountability Second Draft Proposals by external counsel*. Available at https://community.icann.org/download/attachments/56136438/43.%20f%29%20%20ICANN%20Board%20Submission%20of%20Jones%20Day%20Impact%20Analysis.pdf?api=v2.

CCWG-Accountability. *3rd Draft Proposal on Work Stream 1 Recommendations*. 30 November 2015. Available at https://community.icann.org/pages/viewpage.action?pageId=56145016.

ICANN. *Letter from ICANN to NTIA*. 10 March 2016. Available at https://www.icann.org/en/system/files/correspondence/crocker-to-strickling-10mar16-en.pdf.

ICANN. *IANA Stewardship Transition Proposal and Enhancing ICANN Accountability Recommendations*. 10 March 2016. Available on https://www.icann.org/en/system/files/files/iana-stewardship-transition-package-10mar16-en.pdf.

GAO. *Letter regarding Relationship with the Internet Corporation for Assigned Names and Numbers*. Available at http://www.gao.gov/new.items/og00033r.pdf.

Open Letter to Congress from U.S. Business. Available at http://blogs.intel.com/policy/files/2016/04/Business-Open-Letter-supporting-IANA-Transition-VersionV.pdf.

Civil Society Statement of Support for IANA Transition. Available at https://www.accessnow.org/cms/assets/uploads/2016/05/CSstatementonIANAtransitionMay2016-1.pdf.

ICANN. *ICANN Letter to Mr. Lawrence E. Strickling, Assistant Secretary for Communication and Information and Administrator of NTIA*. 12 August 2016. Available at https://www.icann.org/en/system/files/correspondence/marby-to-strickling-12aug16-en.pdf.

ICANN. *IANA Stewardship Transition Proposal Implementation Planning Status Report*. 12 August 2016. Available at https://www.icann.org/en/system/files/files/iana-stewardship-implementation-planning-status-12aug16-en.pdf.

NTIA. *Registration and Administration of Internet Domain Names – Summary of Comments*. 18 August 1997. Available at https://www.ntia.doc.gov/other-publication/1997/registration-and-administration-internet-domain-names-summary-comments-docket.

NTIA. *Domain Name Comments Index*, Available at https://www.ntia.doc.gov/legacy/ntiahome/domainname/email/list.htm.

NTIA Archive. *Comment on "green paper" (Pat Forrestal)*. 31 January 1998. Available at https://www.ntia.doc.gov/legacy/ntiahome/domainname/130dftmail/01_31_98.htm.

NTIA Archive. *A proposal to improve technical management of internet names and addresses (Robert M. Rutherford)*. 31 January 1998. Available at https://www.ntia.doc.gov/legacy/ntiahome/domainname/130dftmail/01_31_98.htm.

NTIA Archive. *Oversight of the Non-Profit Corp. (Amit Mehrotra)*. 2 February 1998. Available at https://www.ntia.doc.gov/legacy/ntiahome/domainname/130dftmail/02_02_98.htm.

NTIA Archive. *Comments on support of monopolies in the Green Paper (Kent Crispin)*. 9 February 1998. Available at https://www.ntia.doc.gov/legacy/ntiahome/domainname/130dftmail/02_09_98.htm.

NTIA Archive. *Get out of the way! (Matthias Tschakert)*. 11 February 1998. Available at https://www.ntia.doc.gov/legacy/ntiahome/domainname/130dftmail/02_11_98.htm.

NTIA Archive. *Our comments in opposition to exclusive ownership of generic Top Level Domains (Paul Stahura)*. 11 February 1998. Available at https://www.ntia.doc.gov/legacy/ntiahome/domainname/130dftmail/02_11_98.htm.

NTIA Archive. *Comments on the US Dept. of Commerce Green Paper on Internet Names (European Telecommunication Standards Institute)*. 12 February 1998. Available at https://www.ntia.doc.gov/legacy/ntiahome/domainname/130dftmail/02_12_98.htm.

NTIA Archive. *I Support CORE (Paul Preston)*. 12 February 1998. Available at https://www.ntia.doc.gov/legacy/ntiahome/domainname/130dftmail/02_12_98.htm.

NTIA Archive. *Global administration for a global net (Carsten Reinke)*. 16-17 February 1998. Available at https://www.ntia.doc.gov/legacy/ntiahome/domainname/130dftmail/02_16_98.htm, https://www.ntia.doc.gov/legacy/ntiahome/domainname/130dftmail/02_17_98.htm.

NTIA Archive. *Comments on US Government Draft (Shaun Dolan)*. 18 February 1998. Available at https://www.ntia.doc.gov/legacy/ntiahome/domainname/130dftmail/02_18_98.htm.

NTIA Archive. *Domain Farce (Louis Fischer)*. 18 February 1998. Available at https://www.ntia.doc.gov/legacy/ntiahome/domainname/130dftmail/02_18_98.htm.

NTIA Archive. *Domains (Norman Fall)*. 23 February 1998. Available at https://www.ntia.doc.gov/legacy/ntiahome/domainname/130dftmail/02_23_98.htm.

NTIA Archive. *Comments on the Green Paper (Simon White)*. 24 February 1998. Available at https://www.ntia.doc.gov/legacy/ntiahome/domainname/130dftmail/02_24_98.htm.

NTIA Archive. *1/30/98 U.S. Gov. proposal (Tom Murphy)*. 26 February 1998. Available at https://www.ntia.doc.gov/legacy/ntiahome/domainname/130dftmail/02_26_98.htm.

NTIA Archive. *The plan to wreck the Internet (J. Williams)*. 27 February 1998. Available at https://www.ntia.doc.gov/legacy/ntiahome/domainname/130dftmail/02_26_98.htm.

NTIA Archive. *Comments on the Technical Management of Internet Domain Names (Eurotel GmbH Internom)*. 2 March 1998. Available at https://www.ntia.doc.gov/legacy/ntiahome/domainname/130dftmail/03_02_98.htm.

NTIA Archive. *Name proposal (Nikolaj Nyholm)*. 2 March 1998. Available at https://www.ntia.doc.gov/legacy/ntiahome/domainname/130dftmail/03_02_98.htm.

NTIA Archive. email of Leonard Werbes to NTIA. 4 March 1998. Available at https://www.ntia.doc.gov/legacy/ntiahome/domainname/130dftmail/03_04_98.htm.

NTIA Archive. *Unbelievelable? [sic] (Denis Bucher)*. 4 March 1998. Available at https://www.ntia.doc.gov/legacy/ntiahome/domainname/130dftmail/03_04_98.htm.

NTIA Archive. *Do not ignore Core (Bradley Jacobsen)*. 5 March 1998. Available at https://www.ntia.doc.gov/legacy/ntiahome/domainname/130dftmail/03_05_98.htm.

NTIA Archive. *Give freedom a chance (Donald Smits)*. 5 March 1998. Available at https://www.ntia.doc.gov/legacy/ntiahome/domainname/130dftmail/03_05_98.htm.

NTIA. *Response to Green Paper From Demon Internet (Stuart Berman)*. 5 March 1998. Available at https://www.ntia.doc.gov/legacy/ntiahome/domainname/130dftmail/03_05_98.htm.

NTIA Archive. *Where is the CORE of your proposal? (Richard Fromme)*. 6 March 1998. Available at https://www.ntia.doc.gov/legacy/ntiahome/domainname/130dftmail/03_06_98.htm.

NTIA Archive. *Re: discussion draft (Monica Crawford)*. 6 March 1998. Available at https://www.ntia.doc.gov/legacy/ntiahome/domainname/130dftmail/03_06_98.htm.

NTIA Archive. *New gTLD input (Phillip Davies)*. 6 March 1998. Available at https://www.ntia.doc.gov/legacy/ntiahome/domainname/130dftmail/03_06_98.htm.

NTIA Archive. *Comment to discussion draft (Site Leader, Inc.)*. 8 March 1998. Available at https://www.ntia.doc.gov/legacy/ntiahome/domainname/130dftmail/03_08_98.htm.

NTIA Archive. *Re: TLDs (Mark Kavana)*. 9 March 1998. Available at https://www.ntia.doc.gov/legacy/ntiahome/domainname/130dftmail/03_09_98.htm.

NTIA Archive. *Mediafusion's response on the Green Paper (Jacques Bernier)*. 9 March 1998. Available at https://www.ntia.doc.gov/legacy/ntiahome/domainname/130dftmail/03_09_98.htm.

NTIA Archive. *Please correct your Green Paper (Albert Y. Boud)*. 10 March 1998. Available at https://www.ntia.doc.gov/legacy/ntiahome/domainname/130dftmail/03_10_98.htm.

NTIA Archive. *Green Paper response (Capital Networks)*. 10 March 1998. Available at https://www.ntia.doc.gov/legacy/ntiahome/domainname/130dftmail/03_09_98.htm.

NTIA Archive. *Support the CORE plan (John Mozena)*. 12 March 1998. Available at https://www.ntia.doc.gov/legacy/ntiahome/domainname/130dftmail/03_12_98.htm.

NTIA Archive. *Green Paper comments (Joe Angiolillo)*. 13 March 1998. Available at https://www.ntia.doc.gov/legacy/ntiahome/domainname/130dftmail/03_13_98.htm.

NTIA Archive. *Proposal to improve T.M.I.N.A. (Robert Ridgeway)*. 13 March 1998. Available at https://www.ntia.doc.gov/legacy/ntiahome/domainname/130dftmail/03_13_98.htm.

NTIA Archive. *Listen to the Internet community (Joseph Yeung)*. 13 March 1998. Available at https://www.ntia.doc.gov/legacy/ntiahome/domainname/130dftmail/03_13_98.htm.

NTIA Archive. *Re: Draft on Technical Management of Internet Domain Names (Angelo González*. 16 March 1998. Available at https://www.ntia.doc.gov/legacy/ntiahome/domainname/130dftmail/03_16_98.htm.

NTIA Archive. *Reasons why I support CORE (Charles Liu)*. 16 March 1998. Available at https://www.ntia.doc.gov/legacy/ntiahome/domainname/130dftmail/03_16_98.htm.

NTIA Archive. *Comments of the Internet Society in regards to the Department Of Commerce National Telecommunications and Information Administration 15 CFR Chapter XXIII [Docket No. 980212036-8036-01] Improvement of Technical Management of Internet Names and Addresses ("Green Paper")*. 17 March 1998. Available at https://www.ntia.doc.gov/legacy/ntiahome/domainname/130dftmail/03_17_98.htm.

NTIA Archive. *MIT's Analysis of the Domain Name System Policy by a Private Institution*. 17 March 1998. Available at https://www.ntia.doc.gov/legacy/ntiahome/domainname/130dftmail/03_17_98.htm.

NTIA Archive. *Comments of the Generic Top Level Domain Memorandum of Understanding Policy Advisory Body on Green Paper*. 20 March 1998. Available at https://www.ntia.doc.gov/legacy/ntiahome/domainname/130dftmail/03_20_98.htm.

NTIA Archive. *Disney Online Response to NTIA's Green Paper*. 20 March 1998. Available at https://www.ntia.doc.gov/legacy/ntiahome/domainname/130dftmail/scanned/Disney.htm.

NTIA Archive. *CORE solution (Jeffrey Masters)*. 20 March 1998. Available at https://www.ntia.doc.gov/legacy/ntiahome/domainname/130dftmail/03_20_98.htm.

NTIA Archive. *MARQUES response to the US discussion draft of 30 January 1998 entitled "Proposal to improve technical management of Internet names and addresses"*. 20 March 1998. Available at https://www.ntia.doc.gov/legacy/ntiahome/domainname/130dftmail/03_20_98.htm.

NTIA Archive. *Domain Names (Garth Krock)*. 21 March 1998. Available at https://www.ntia.doc.gov/legacy/ntiahome/domainname/130dftmail/03_21_98.htm.

NTIA Archive. *FICPI Discussion Draft on 'A Proposal to Improve Technical Management of Internet Names and Addresses'*. 21 March 1998. Available at https://www.ntia.doc.gov/legacy/ntiahome/domainname/130dftmail/03_21_98.htm.

NTIA Archive. *Comments on Green Paper--- For Development of the Internet Governance (Internet Association of Japan)*. 22 March 1998. Available at https://www.ntia.doc.gov/legacy/ntiahome/domainname/130dftmail/03_21_98.htm.

NTIA Archive. *Comments by IBM Corporation on Docket Entitled 'Improvement of Technical Management of Internet Names and Addresses'*. 22 March 1998. Available at https://www.ntia.doc.gov/legacy/ntiahome/domainname/130dftmail/03_22_98.htm.

NTIA Archive. *U.S. Civil Liberties Organizations Response to NTIA's Green Paper*. 23 March 1998. Available at https://www.ntia.doc.gov/legacy/ntiahome/domainname/130dftmail/03_23_98-8.htm.

NTIA Archive. *Comments of the US Council for International Business to the Department of Commerce on the 'Proposal to Improve Technical Management of Internet Names and Addresses*. 23 March 1998. Available at https://www.ntia.doc.gov/legacy/ntiahome/domainname/130dftmail/03_23_98-10.htm.

NTIA Archive. *Comments on NTIA's green paper by Ministry of Posts and Telecommunications of Japan*. 23 March 1998. Available at https://www.ntia.doc.gov/legacy/ntiahome/domainname/130dftmail/03_23_98-2.htm.

NTIA Archive. *Australian Internet Industry Response to NTIA's Green Paper*. 23 March 1998. Available at https://www.ntia.doc.gov/legacy/ntiahome/domainname/130dftmail/03_23_98-1.htm.

NTIA Archive. *Asia Network Research Response to NTIA's Green Paper*. 6 April 1998. Available at https://www.ntia.doc.gov/legacy/ntiahome/domainname/130dftmail/04_06_98.htm.

NTIA. *Press Conference Remarks by Becky Burr*. 5 June 1998. Available at https://www.ntia.doc.gov/files/ntia/publications/DNSBURR.pdf.

Commission of the European Communities. *Internet governance, management of Internet names and addresses, Analysis and assessment from the European Commission of the United States Department of Commerce White Paper*. COM (1998). 29 July 1998.

NTIA Archive. *INTA Response to the U.S. Government Paper on the Improvement of Technical Management of Internet Names and Addresses*. Available at https://www.ntia.doc.gov/legacy/ntiahome/domainname/130dftmail/scanned/INTA.htm.

NTIA Archive. *Letter from Jon Postel to NTIA regarding Management of Internet Names and Addresses*. 2 October 1998. Available at https://www.ntia.doc.gov/legacy/ntiahome/domainname/proposals/icann/Letter.htm.

NTIA Archive. *Comments on the Proposals for a New Corporation to Manage Internet Domain Name System Functions*. between 30 September 1998 and 15 October

1998. Available at https://www.ntia.doc.gov/legacy/ntiahome/domainname/proposals/comments/comments.html.

NTIA. *Becky Burr, Associate Administrator of NTIA for International Affairs sends letter to the Internet Corporation for Assigned Names and Numbers*. 20 October 1998. Available at https://www.ntia.doc.gov/press-release/1998/becky-burr-associate-administrator-ntia-international-affairs-sends-letter-intern.

NTIA. *NTIA Reviewing ICANN November 6 Submission*. 10 November 1998. Available at https://www.ntia.doc.gov/press-release/1998/ntia-reviewing-icann-november-6-submission.

NTIA. *Letter from J. Beckwith Burr to Network Solutions, Inc. regarding Cooperative Agreement No. NCR-921874, as amended*. 26 February 1999. Available at https://www.ntia.doc.gov/legacy/ntiahome/domainname/icannnewco.htm.

NTIA, U.S. Department of Commerce. *Statement regarding extension of Memorandum of Understanding with ICANN (Amendment 5)*. Available at https://www.ntia.doc.gov/page/2002/statement-regarding-extenstion-memorandum-understanding-icann-ammendment-5.

NTIA, U.S. Department of Commerce. *Statement regarding extension of Memorandum of Understanding with ICANN (Amendment 6)*. Available at https://www.ntia.doc.gov/page/2003/statement-regarding-extension-mou-icann-ammendment-6.

NTIA Archive. *Comments received by the NTIA*, published at *NTIA Seeks Public Comments Regarding Joint Project Agreement with ICANN*. 29 October 2007. Available at https://www.ntia.doc.gov/other-publication/2007/ntia-seeks-public-comments-regarding-joint-project-agreement-icann.

NTIA. *Statement on the Mid-Term Review of the Joint Project Agreement (JPA) Between NTIA and ICANN*. 2 April 2008. Available at https://www.ntia.doc.gov/press-release/2008/statement-mid-term-review-joint-project-agreement-jpa-between-ntia-and-icann.

NTIA. *Notice of Inquiry: Assessment of the Transition of the Technical Coordination and Management of the Internet's Domain Name and Addressing System [docket no. 090420688-9689-01]*. 24 April 2009. Federal Register Vol. 74, No. 78.

NTIA Archive. Internet Society. *Comments submitted to the U.S. Department of Commerce, National Telecommunications and Information Administration, Notice of Inquiry "Assessment of the Transition of the Technical Coordination and Management of the Internet's Domain Name and Addressing System [Docket No. 090420688-9689-01]"*. Available at https://www.ntia.doc.gov/files/ntia/comments2009/012.pdf.

NTIA Archive. *Letter from SIDN regarding Request for Comment on the Transition of the Technical Coordination and Management of the DNS*. 5 June 2009. Available at https://www.ntia.doc.gov/files/ntia/comments2009/014.pdf.

NTIA Archive. *Letter from The International AntiCounterfeiting Coalition regarding NTIA-Assessment of the Transition of the Technical Coordination and Management of the Internet's Domain Name and Addressing System*. 5 June 2009. Available at https://www.ntia.doc.gov/files/ntia/comments2009/015.pdf.

NTIA Archive. *Comments of Thomas M. Lenard and Lawrence J. White. ICANN at a crossroads: A proposal for better governance and performance*. 5 June 2009. Available at https://www.ntia.doc.gov/files/ntia/comments2009/017.pdf.

NTIA Archive. Roberts, Michael M. *The ICANN Accountability Dilemma – A Response to the 2009 ICANN Notice of Inquiry Issued by the National Telecommunications and Information Administration*. 8 June 2009. Available at https://www.ntia.doc.gov/files/ntia/comments2009/034.pdf.

NTIA. *NTIA Announces Intent to Transition Key Internet Domain Name Functions*, 14 March 2014, Available at https://www.ntia.doc.gov/press-release/2014/ntia-announces-intent-transition-key-internet-domain-name-functions.

NTIA. Strickling, Lawrence E. Assistant Secretary of Commerce for Communications and Information. *PLI/FCBA Telecommunications Policy & Regulation Institute*. Washington, DC. 4 December 2014. Available at https://www.ntia.doc.gov/speechtestimony/2014/remarks-assistant-secretary-strickling-plifcba-telecommunications-policy-regula.

NTIA. *Remarks of Lawrence E. Strickling Assistant Secretary of Commerce for Communications and Information ICANN Meeting*. 21 June 2015. Available at https://www.ntia.doc.gov/speechtestimony/2015/remarks-lawrence-e-strickling-assistant-secretary-commerce-communications-and-i.

NTIA. *Testimony of Assistant Secretary Strickling on 'Internet Governance Progress After ICANN 53*. 8 July 2015. Available at https://www.ntia.doc.gov/speechtestimony/2015/testimony-strickling-internet-governance-progress-after-icann-53.

NTIA. *NTIA Finds IANA Stewardship Transition Proposal Meets Criteria to Complete Privatization*. 9 June 2016. Available at https://www.ntia.doc.gov/press-release/2016/iana-stewardship-transition-proposal-meets-criteria-complete-privatization.

NTIA. *NTIA Letter to Congress Transmitting NTIA's Assessment of IANA Transition Proposal*. 9 June 2016. Available at https://www.ntia.doc.gov/files/ntia/publications/ntia_letter_to_congress_transmitting_ntias_assessment_of_iana_transition_proposal_06.09.16.pdf.

NTIA. *NTIA Letter to Senators Thune and Rubio on IANA Transition*. 9 June 2016. Available at https://www.ntia.doc.gov/files/ntia/publications/ntia_letter_to_senators_thune_and_rubio_on_iana_transition_06.09.16.pdf.

NTIA. *NTIA Assistant Secretary Responds to Senators Rubio, Blunt, Johnson, Heller, and Sullivan Regarding the Transition of the U.S. Government's Stewardship of Key Internet Domain Name Functions*. 27 June 2016. Available at https://www.ntia.doc.gov/files/ntia/publications/20160627_-_ntia_response_iana_-_rubio.pdf.

NTIA. *NTIA Letter to Mr. Göran Marby, President and CEO of ICANN*. 16 August 2016. Available at https://www.ntia.doc.gov/files/ntia/publications/20160816marby.pdf.

Network Working Group Request for Comments

Arkko, J. and F. Baker. *Guidelines for Using IPv6 Transition Mechanisms during IPv6 Deployment*. Internet Engineering Task Force Request for Comments # 6180. May 2011. Available at https://tools.ietf.org/html/rfc6180.

Bhushan, Abay, Ken Pogran, Ray Tomlinson and Jim White. *Standardising Network Mail Headers*. Request for Comments # 561. Available at https://tools.ietf.org/html/rfc561.

Bhushan, Abay. *The File Transfer Protocol*. Request for Comments # 354. Available at https://tools.ietf.org/html/rfc354.

Camarillo, G., K. El Malki and V. Gurbani. *IPv6 Transition in the Session Initiation Protocol (SIP)*. Internet Engineering Task Force Request for Comments # 6157. April 2011. Available at https://tools.ietf.org/html/rfc6157.

Cheshire, S., M. Krochmal and Apple Inc. *Multicast DNS*. Internet Engineering Task Force Request for Comments # 6762. February 2013. Available at https://tools.ietf.org/html/rfc6762.

Davies, E., S. Krishnan and P. Savola. *IPv6 Transition/Coexistence Security Considerations*. Network Working Group Request for Comments # 4942. September 2007. Available at https://www.ietf.org/rfc/rfc4942.txt.

Deering, S. and R. Hinden. *Internet Protocol, Version 6 (IPv6) Specification*. Network Working Group Request for Comments # 2460. Available at https://www.ietf.org/rfc/rfc2460.txt.

Huitema, C., R. Austein, S. Satapati and R. Van Der Pol. *Unmanaged Networks IPv6? Transition Scenarios*. Network Working Group Request for Comments # 3750. April 2004. Available at https://www.ietf.org/rfc/rfc3750.txt.

Internet Engineering Task Force. *Request for Comments # 1083*. Available at http://www.ietf.org/rfc/rfc1083.txt (accessed 22 April 2016).

Jiang, D., D. Guo and B. Carpenter. *An Incremental Carrier-Grade NAT (CGN) for IPv6 Transition*. Internet Engineering Task Force Request for Comments # 6264. June 2011. Available at https://tools.ietf.org/html/rfc6264.

Klensin, J. *Role of the Domain Name System (DNS)*. Network Working Group Request for Comments # 3467. February 2003. Available at https://tools.ietf.org/html/rfc 3467.

Li, X., C. Bao, M. Chen, H. Zhang and J. Wu. *The China Education and Research Network (CERNET) IVI Translation Design and Deployment for the IPv4/IPv6 Coexistence and Transition*. Internet Engineering Task Force Request for Comments # 6219. May 2011. Available at https://tools.ietf.org/html/rfc6219.

Livingood, Jason. *Considerations for Transitioning Content to IPv6*. Internet Engineering Task Force Request for Comments # 6589. April 2012. Available at https://tools.ietf.org/html/rfc6589.

Mills, D.L. *Internet Name Domains*, Network Working Group Request for Comments # 799. Sept. 1981. Available at https://tools.ietf.org/html/rfc799.

Mockapetris, Paul. *Domain names – concepts and facilities*, Network Working Group Request for Comments # 882. November 1983. Available at https://tools.ietf.org/html/rfc882.

Mockapetris, Paul. *Domain Names – Concepts and Facilities*, Network Working Group Request For Comments # 1034. November 1987. Available at http://www.ietf.org/rfc/rfc1034.txt.

Mockapetris, Paul. *Domain names – implementation and specification*, Network Working Group Request for Comments # 883. November 1983. Available at https://tools.ietf.org/html/rfc883.

Mockapetris, Paul. *Domain Names – Implementation and Specification*, Network Working Group Request For Comments # 1035. November 1987. Available at http://www.ietf.org/rfc/rfc1035.txt.

Neigus, Nancy and Jon Postel. *Socket Number List*. Network Working Group Request For Comments # 503. 13 April 1973. http://www.ietf.org/rfc/rfc0503.txt.

Network Working Group. FYI on "What is the Internet?" Request for Comments 1462 (May 1993).

Normark, E. and R. Gilligan. *Basic Transition Mechanisms for IPv6 Hosts and Routers*. Network Working Group Request for Comments # 4213. October 2005. Available at https://tools.ietf.org/html/rfc4213.

Postel, Jon and Nancy Neigus. *Socket Number List*. Network Working Group Request for Comments # 433. 22 December 1972. Available at https://www.ietf.org/rfc/rfc0433.txt.

Postel, Jon and Nancy Neigus. *Socket Number List*. Network Working Group Request for Comments # 433, 22 December 1972. Available at https://www.ietf.org/rfc/rfc0433.txt.

Postel, Jon. (ed.). *Internet Protocol DARPA Internet Program Protocol Specification*. Request for Comments # 791. Available at http://www.ietf.org/rfc/rfc0791.txt.

Postel, Jon. and James Vernon. *Assigned Numbers*. Network Working Group Request For Comments # 820. January 1983. Available at http://www.ietf.org/rfc/rfc0820.txt.

Postel, Jon. *Assigned Link* Numbers. Network Working Group Request For Comments # 604. 26 December 1973. http://www.ietf.org/rfc/rfc0604.txt.

Postel, Jon. *Assigned Numbers*. Network Working Group Request For Comments # 739. Available at http://www.ietf.org/rfc/rfc0739.txt.

Postel, Jon. *Assigned Numbers*. Network Working Group Request For Comments # 750. 26 September 1978, Available at http://www.ietf.org/rfc/rfc0750.txt.

Postel, Jon. *Assigned Numbers*. Network Working Group Request For Comments # 755. 3 May 1979. Available at http://www.ietf.org/rfc/rfc0755.txt.

Postel, Jon. *Assigned Numbers*. Network Working Group Request For Comments # 758. August 1979. Available at http://www.ietf.org/rfc/rfc0758.txt.

Postel, Jon. *Assigned Numbers*. Network Working Group Request For Comments # 762. January 1980. Available at http://www.ietf.org/rfc/rfc0762.txt.

Postel, Jon. *Assigned Numbers*. Network Working Group Request For Comments # 770. September 1980. Available at http://www.ietf.org/rfc/rfc0770.txt.

Postel, Jon. *Assigned Numbers.* Network Working Group Request For Comments # 776. January 1981. Available at http://www.ietf.org/rfc/rfc0776.txt.

Postel, Jon. *Assigned Numbers.* Network Working Group Request For Comments # 790. September 1981. Available at http://www.ietf.org/rfc/rfc0790.txt.

Postel, Jon. *Domain Name System Structure and Delegation.* Network Working Group Request for Comments # 1591. March 1994. https://www.ietf.org/rfc/rfc1591.txt.

Postel, Jon. *IAB official protocol standards.* Network Working Group Request for Comments # 1083. December 1988. Available at http://www.ietf.org/rfc/rfc1083.txt.

Postel, Jon. *New Registries and the Delegation of International Top Level Domains.* June 1996. Available at https://tools.ietf.org/html/draft-postel-iana-itld-admin-01.

Postel, Jon. *New Registries and the Delegation of International Top Level Domains.* May 1996. Available at https://tools.ietf.org/html/draft-postel-iana-itld-admin-00.

Reynolds, Joyce (ed.). *Assigned Numbers: RFC 1700 is Replaced by an On-line Database.* Network Working Group Request For Comments # 3232. January 2002. Available at http://www.ietf.org/rfc/rfc3232.txt.

Reynolds, Joyce and Jon Postel. *Assigned Numbers.* Network Working Group Request For Comments # 870. October 1983. Available at http://www.ietf.org/rfc/rfc0870.txt.

Reynolds, Joyce and Jon Postel. *Assigned Numbers.* Network Working Group Request For Comments # *923.* October 1984. Available at http://www.ietf.org/rfc/rfc0923.txt.

Reynolds, Joyce and Jon Postel. *Assigned Numbers.* Network Working Group Request For Comments # 943. April 1985. Available at http://www.ietf.org/rfc/rfc0943.txt.

Reynolds, Joyce and Jon Postel. *Assigned Numbers.* Network Working Group Request For Comments # 960. December 1985. Available at http://www.ietf.org/rfc/rfc0960.txt (accessed 22 April 2016).

Reynolds, Joyce and Jon Postel. *Assigned Numbers.* Network Working Group Request For Comments # 990. November 1986. Available at http://www.ietf.org/rfc/rfc0990.txt.

Reynolds, Joyce and Jon Postel. *Assigned Numbers.* Network Working Group Request For Comments # 1010. May 1987. Available at http://www.ietf.org/rfc/rfc1010.txt.

Reynolds, Joyce and Jon Postel. *Assigned Numbers.* Network Working Group Request For Comments # *1700.* October 1994. Available at http://www.ietf.org/rfc/rfc1700.txt.

Reynolds, Joyce and Jon Postel., *Assigned Numbers.* Network Working Group Request For Comments # *900.* June 1984. Available at http://www.ietf.org/rfc/rfc0900.txt.

Shin, M-K. (ed.), Y-G. Hong, J. Hagino, P. Savola and E. M. Castro. *Application Aspects of IPv6 Transition.* Network Working Group Request for Comments # 4038. March 2005. Available at https://www.ietf.org/rfc/rfc4038.txt.

Su, Zaw-Sing and Jon Postel. *The Domain Naming Convention for Internet User Applications*. Network Working Group Request For Comments # 819. August 1982. Available at http://www.ietf.org/rfc/rfc819.txt.

Su, Zaw-Sing. *A Distributed System for Internet Name Service*. Network Working Group Request For Comments # 830. October 1982. Available at http://www.ietf.org/rfc/rfc830.txt (accessed 22 April 2016).

Wiljakka, J. (ed.). *Analysis on IPv6 Transition in Third Generation Partnership Project (3GPP) Networks*. Network Working Group Request for Comments # 4215. October 2005. Available at https://tools.ietf.org/html/rfc4215.

Yasuda, A. and T. Thompson. *TELNET Data Entry Terminal Option DODIIS Implementation*. Network Working Group Request for Comments # 1043. February 1988. Available at http://www.ietf.org/rfc/rfc1043.txt.

Case Materials

PCIJ. *Interpretation of the Convention between Greece and Bulgaria respecting reciprocal emigration, signed at Neuilly-sur-Seine on November 27th, 1919 (Question of the Greco-Bulgarian 'communities')*. Advisory Opinion of 31 July 1930. *P.C.I.J. Rep., Series B*, No. 17, 32.

PCIJ. *Treatment of Polish nationals and other persons of Polish origin or speech in the Danzich territory*. Advisory Opinion of 4 February 1932. *P.C.I.J. Rep., Series A/B*, No. 44, 24.

U.S. Supreme Court. *Pinsker v. Pacific Coast Society of Orthodontists*, 526 P.2d 550-553 (Cal. 1974).

ICJ Nuclear Tests (*Austl. v. Fr.)*. 20 December 1974. Merits.

U.S. Supeme Court. *United States v. Security Indus. Bank*, 459 U.S. 79 (1982).

ICJ *Applicability of the Obligation to Arbitrate under Section 21 of the United Nations Headquarters Agreement of 26 April 1947*. Advisory Opinion of 26 April 1988. *ICJ Rep* 1988, 12, § 57.

U.S. Supreme Court. *Carma Developers (Cal.), Inc. v. Marathon Development California, Inc.* 6 Cal.Rptr.2d 467 (1992).

U.S. Supreme Court. *Brown v. Gardner*. 513 U.S. 115, 122 (1994).

ICJ. Nuclear Tests (*Austl. v. Fr.*), 1974 ICJ 253, 268 (20 December) (merits) Land and Maritime Boundary (*Cameroon v. Nig.*), 1998 ICJ 275, 296 (11 June).

OLG Frankfurt am Main. decision from 29.04.2008, case number 11 U 32/04 ("VW.de") and LG Frankfurt am Main, decision from 14.10.1998, case number 2/06 O 283/98 ("Ambiente").

U.S. Court of Appeals. Ninth Circuit. *DotConnectAfrica Trust v. ICANN, et al. and ZA Central Registry, NPC*. Memoranda. No. 2:16-CV-00862-RGK. Available at https://www.icann.org/resources/pages/litigation-dca-v-icann-appellate-2016-09-13-en.

U.S. District Court. Eastern District of Missouri Easter Division. *Economic Solutions, Inc. v. ICANN*. Order Denying Temporary Restraining Order. 13 November 2000.

Case No. 4:00CV1785-DJS. Available at https://www.icann.org/resources/unthemed-pages/esi-v-icann-2000-11-13-en.

Superior Court of California. County of Los Angeles. *Karl Auerbach v. ICANN.* Advisory: Court Ruling in Auerbach v. ICANN Lawsuit. 29 July 2002. Available at https://www.icann.org/news/advisory-2002-07-29-en.

U.S. District Court. C.D. California. *Dotster, Inc., et al. v. ICANN.* Order Denying Plaintiff's Motion for Preliminary Injunction. 10 November 2003. Case No. CV 03-5045-JFW (MANx). Available at https://www.icann.org/en/system/files/files/order-denying-dotster-pi-13nov03-en.pdf.

U.S. District Court. C.D. California. *Dotster, Inc., et al. v. ICANN.* Dismissal with Prejudice. 4 December 2003. Case No. CV 03-5045-JFW (MANx). Available at https://www.icann.org/en/system/files/files/dismissal-04dec03-en.pdf.

U.S. Court of Appeals. Second Circuit. *Register.com, Inc. v. Verio, Inc.* Decision Affirming the Injunction. 23 January 2004. Docket No. 00-9596. Available at https://www.icann.org/en/system/files/files/decision-23jan04-en.pdf.

U.S. District Court. C.D. California. *Registersite.com, et al. v. ICANN, et al.* Court's Order re Motion to Dismiss. 12 July 2004. Case No. CV 04-1368 ABC (CWx). Available at https://www.icann.org/en/system/files/files/court-order-mtd-12jul04-en.pdf.

U.S. District Court. C.D. California. *VeriSign, Inc. v. ICANN.* Final Judgment. 21 September 2004. Case No. CV 04-1292 AHM (CTx). Available at https://www.icann.org/en/system/files/files/revised-final-judgment-21sep04-en.pdf.

Superior Court of California. County of Los Angeles. *VeriSign, Inc. v. ICANN.* Minute Order Denying ICANN's Motion to Stay. 18 January 2005. Case No. BC320763. Available at https://www.icann.org/en/system/files/files/court-order-18jan05-en.pdf.

U.S. Supreme Court. *Rapanos v. United States*. 547 U.S. 715, 752 (2006).

Superior Court of California. County of Los Angeles. *VeriSign, Inc. v. ICANN.* Dismissal with Prejudice of State Court Proceedings. 11 December 2006. Case No. BC 320 763. Available at https://www.icann.org/en/system/files/files/icann-dismissal-11dec06-en.pdf.

U.S. Court of Appeals. Ninth Circuit. *VeriSign, Inc. v. ICANN.* Order Dismissing Ninth Circuit Appeal. 22 December 2006. Case No. 04-56761. Available at https://www.icann.org/en/system/files/files/order-dismissing-appeal-la-422355-1-22dec06-en.pdf.

U.S. District Court. Middle District of North Carolina. *Anne Martinez v. RegisterFly, Inc., et al.* Court Order Denying TRO and Unsealing Record. 23 March 2007. Case No. 1:07CV00188. Available at https://www.icann.org/en/system/files/files/deny-tro-unseal-record-23mar07-en.pdf.

U.S. District Court. Middle District of North Carolina. *Anne Martinez v. RegisterFly, Inc., et al.* Notice of Dismissal as to Defendant ICANN. 7 May 2007. Civil Action No 07-cv-188. Available at https://www.icann.org/en/system/files/files/notice-dismissal-07may07-en.pdf.

U.S. District Court. Northern District of California San Jose Division. *Coalition for ICANN Transparency Inc. v. VeriSign, Inc.* Judgment in favor of VeriSign. 14 May

2007. No. C-05-04826 RMW. Available at https://www.icann.org/en/system/files/files/judgement-favor-verisign-14may07-en.pdf.

Superior Court of California. County of Los Angeles. *Karl Auerbach v. ICANN*. Judgment. 5 August 2007. Case No. BS 074771. Available at https://www.eff.org/nl/document/auerbach-judgment.

U.S. District Court. C.D. California. *ICANN v. RegistryFly.Com, Inc., et al.* Default Judgment Entered Against RegisterFly. 24 September 2007. Case No. CV 07-2089 R (PLAx). Available at https://www.icann.org/en/system/files/files/rf-default-judgment-24sep07-en.pdf.

U.S. District Court. Northern District of Alabama Western Division. *Michael Moore et al. v. Enom, Inc., et al.* Court Order Dismissing ICANN for Lack of Jurisdiction. 9 November 2007. Case no. 7:07-CV-1153-RDP. Available at https://www.icann.org/en/system/files/files/dismissal-09nov07-en.pdf.

U.S. Court of Appeals. Ninth Circuit. *Coalition for ICANN Transparency Inc. v. VeriSign, Inc.* Order Reversing Opinion on VeriSign's Motion to Dismiss Second Amended Complaint. 5 June 2009. No. 07-16151. Available at https://www.icann.org/en/system/files/files/order-reversing-opinion-on-verisign-motion-to-dismiss-second-amended-complaint-05jun09-en.pdf.

U.S. District Court. Northern District of California San Jose Division. *Coalition for ICANN Transparency Inc. v. VeriSign, Inc.* Order on Stipulation for Dismissal with Prejudice. 31 May 2011. No. 5:05-CV-04826 (RMW) HRL. Available at https://www.icann.org/en/system/files/files/order-stipulation-dismissal-31may11-en.pdf.

Common Pleas Court. Franklin County, Ohio. *Ann. M. Yeager v. Go Daddy Group, Inc. et al.* Order Granting in Part Go Daddy's Motion to Dismiss and Staying Discovery. 20 June 2011. Case No. 11 CVC-04-4434. Available at https://www.icann.org/en/system/files/files/order-granting-go-daddy-motion-to-dismiss-20jun11-en.pdf.

Common Pleas Court. Franklin County, Ohio. *Ann. M. Yeager v. Go Daddy Group, Inc. et al.* Decision and Entry Dismissing Plaintiff's Complaint without Prejudice. 11 October 2011. Case No. 11 CVC-04-4434. Available at https://www.icann.org/en/system/files/files/dismissing-plantiff-complaint-11oct11-en.pdf.

U.S. District Court. Southern District of Florida. *John Zuccarini v. Network Solutions, LLC, et al.* Order Granting Network Solution and NameJet's Motions to Dismiss. 8 December 2011. Case No. 11-14052-CIV-MARTINEZ/LYNCH. Available at https://www.icann.org/en/system/files/files/order-granting-defendant-motion-to-dismiss-08dec11-en.pdf.

U.S. District Court. Southern District of Florida. *John Zuccarini v. Network Solutions, LLC, et al.* Order Granting ICANN's Motion to Dismiss. 9 December 2011. Case No. 11-14052-CIV-MARTINEZ/LYNCH. Available at https://www.icann.org/en/system/files/files/order-granting-icann-motion-to-dismiss-09dec11-en.pdf.

U.S. District Court. Northern District of Texas Dallas Division. *Netsphere, Inc. et al. v. Jeffrey Baron and Ondova Limited Company*. Second Order Granting Receiver's

Second Motion to Enforce Stay. 10 January 2012. Civil Action No. 3:09-CV-0988-F. Available at https://www.icann.org/en/system/files/files/second-order-granting-receivers-second-motion-to-enforce-stay-10jan12-en.pdf.

U.S. District Court. Northern District of Texas Dallas Division. *Netsphere, Inc. et al. v. Jeffrey Baron and Ondova Limited Company*. Order Clarifying and Revising 10 January 2012 Order. 18 January 2012. Civil Action No. 3:09-CV-0988-F. Available at https://www.icann.org/en/system/files/files/order-clarifying-and-revising-10jan12-order-18jan12-en.pdf.

ICC. *Employ Media v. ICANN*. Settlement Agreement. 11 December 2012. Available at https://www.icann.org/en/system/files/files/settlement-agreement-11dec12-en.pdf.

ICC. *Employ Media v. ICANN*. Employ Media's Letter of Withdrawal of Arbitration. 14 December 2012. Available at https://www.icann.org/en/system/files/files/employ-media-letter-of-withdrawal-14dec12-en.pdf.

U.S. District Court. C.D. California. *Image Online Design, Inc. v. ICANN*. Order Granting ICANN's Motion to Dismiss Complaint. 7 February 2013. Case No. CV 12-08968 DDP (JCx). Available at https://www.icann.org/en/system/files/files/order-granting-motion-dismiss-07feb13-en.pdf.

U.S. District Court. C.D. California. *Manwin Licensing International S.A.R.L., et al. v. ICM Registry, LLC, et al.* Order Granting Defendants' Motion to Dismiss and Motion to Strike Against ICM. 26 February 2013. Case No. CV 11-9514 PSG (JCGx). Available at https://www.icann.org/en/system/files/files/order-granting-defendant-motion-to-dismiss-and-strike-26feb13-en.pdf.

U.S. District Court. C.D. California. *Name.Space, Inc. v. ICANN*. Order Dismissing Name.Space Complaint. 19 March 2013. Case CV 12-8676 PA (PLAx). Available at https://www.icann.org/en/system/files/files/order-dismissing-namespace-19mar13-en.pdf.

U.S. District Court. C.D. California. *Manwin Licensing International S.A.R.L., et al. v. ICM Registry, LLC, et al.* Dismissal with Prejudice. 10 May 2013. Case No. CV 11-9514 PSG (JCGx). Available at https://www.icann.org/en/system/files/files/dismissal-prejudice-10may13-en.pdf.

U.S. Court of Appeals. Fourth Circuit. *Graham Schreiber v. Lorraine Lesley Dunabin et al.* Judgment. 17 September 2013. No. 13-1812 (1:12-cv-00852-GBL-JFA). Available at https://www.icann.org/en/system/files/files/judgment-17sep13-en.pdf.

U.S. District Court. C.D. California. *Del Monte International GmbH v. Del Monte Corporation*. 995 F.Supp.2d 1107 (C.D. Cal. 2014).

U.S. Court of Appeals. Ninth Circuit. *Name.Space, Inc. v. ICANN*. Opinion Affirming Dismissal of Name.Space Complaint. 31 July 2015. D.C. No. 2:12-cv-08676-PA-PLA. Available at https://www.icann.org/en/system/files/files/namespace-ninth-circuit-affirming-dismissal-31jul15-en.pdf.

ICDR. *OpenTLD, B.V. v. ICANN*. Emergency Award. 24 Aug. 2015. Case No. 01-15-0004-1379. Available at https://www.icann.org/en/system/files/files/emergency-award-24aug15-en.pdf.

AAA. *OpenTLD, B.V. v. ICANN*. Joint Stipulation for Dismissal with Prejudice. 9 November 2015. Case No. 01-15-0004-1379. Available at https://www.icann.org

/en/system/files/files/litigation-opentld-joint-stipulation-dismissal-prejudice-redacted-09nov15-en.pdf.

U.S. District Court. C.D. California. *DotConnectAfrica Trust v. ICANN*. Minute Order re Plaintiff's *Ex Parte* Application for TRO. 4 March 2016. Case CV 16-00862 RGK (JCx). Available at https://www.icann.org/en/system/files/files/litigation-dca-minute-order-plaintiff-ex-parte-application-04mar16-en.pdf.

U.S. District Court. C.D. California. *DotConnectAfrica Trust v. ICANN*. Court Order Denying Application to File Under Seal. 9 March 2016. Case CV 16-00862 RGK (JCx). Available at https://www.icann.org/en/system/files/files/litigation-dca-court-order-Denying-application-under-seal-09mar16-en.pdf.

U.S. District Court. C.D. California. *DotConnectAfrica Trust v. ICANN*. Order re: Plaintiff's Motion for Preliminary Injunction. 12 April 2016. Case CV 16-00862 RGK (JCx). Available at https://www.icann.org/en/system/files/files/litigation-dca-icann-motion-prelim-injunction-12apr16-en.pdf.

U.S. District Court. Western District of Kentucky Louisville Division. *Commercial Connect, LLC v. ICANN, et al.* Order Granting ICANN's Motion to Dismiss Complaint. 28 April 2016. Case 3:16CV-00012-JHM. Available at https://www.icann.org/en/system/files/files/litigation-cc-order-granting-motion-to-dismiss-28apr16-en.pdf.

U.S. District Court. C.D. California. *DotConnectAfrica Trust v. ICANN*. Order Granting ZACR's Motion to Dismiss. 14 June 2016. Case CV 16-00862 RGK (JCx). Available at https://www.icann.org/en/system/files/files/litigation-dca-zacr-motion-to-dismiss-14jun16-en.pdf.

U.S. District Court. C.D. California. *Ruby Glen, LLC v. ICANN*. Complaint. 22 July 2016. Available at https://www.icann.org/en/system/files/files/litigation-ruby-glen-complaint-22jul16-en.pdf.

U.S. Court of Appeals. District of Columbia Circuit. *Susan Weinstein, individually as Co-Administrator of the Estate of Ira William Weinstein, and as natural guardian of plaintiff David Weinstein (minor), et al. v. Islamic Republic of Iran, et al.* Order and Judgment. 2 August 2016. No. 14-7193. Available at https://www.icann.org/en/system/files/files/litigation-haim-et-al-order-judgment-02aug16-en.pdf.

U.S. Court of Appeals. District of Columbia Circuit. *Susan Weinstein, individually as Co-Administrator of the Estate of Ira William Weinstein, and as natural guardian of plaintiff David Weinstein (minor), et al. v. Islamic Republic of Iran, et al.* Opinion for the U.S. Court of Appeals for the D.C. 2 August 2016. No. 14-7193. Available at https://www.icann.org/en/system/files/files/litigation-haim-et-al-opinion-court-appeals-circuit-02aug16-en.pdf.

U.S. Court of Appeals. District of Columbia Circuit. *Susan Weinstein, individually as Co-Administrator of the Estate of Ira William Weinstein, and as natural guardian of plaintiff David Weinstein (minor), et al. v. Islamic Republic of Iran, et al.* Order Denying Appellants' Petition for Panel Rehearing. 19 September 2016. No. 14-7193. Available at https://www.icann.org/en/system/files/files/litigation-haim-et-al-order-denying-appellants-petition-rehearing-19sep16-en.pdf.

U.S. Court of Appeals. District of Columbia Circuit. *Susan Weinstein, individually as Co-Administrator of the Estate of Ira William Weinstein, and as natural guardian of plaintiff David Weinstein (minor), et al. v. Islamic Republic of Iran, et al.* Order Denying Appellants' Petition for Rehearing En Banc. 19 September 2016. No. 14-7193. Available at https://www.icann.org/en/system/files/files/litigation-haim-et-al-order-denying-appellants-petition-rehearing-en-banc-19sep16-en.pdf.

U.S. District Court Southern District of Texas Galveston Division. *State of Arizona et al. v. NTIA et al.* Complaint for Declaratory and Injunctive Relief and Application for Temporary Restraining Order and Preliminary Injunction. 28 September 2016. Case 3:16-cv-00274. Available at https://www.icann.org/en/system/files/files/litigation-states-various-complaint-application-tro-injunction-28sep16-en.pdf.

U.S. District Court Southern District of Texas Galveston Division. *State of Arizona et al. v. NTIA et al.* Court Order Denying Plaintiff's Motion for Temporary Restraining Order and Preliminary Injunction. 3 October 2016. Case 3:16-cv-00274. Available at https://www.icann.org/en/system/files/files/litigation-defendants-denying-motion-for-injunction-30sep16-en.pdf.

U.S. District Court. C.D. California. *Ruby Glen, LLC v. ICANN.* Judgment. 28 November 2016. Case cv 16/5505 PA (Asx). Available at https://www.icann.org/en/system /files/files/litigation-ruby-glen-judgment-28nov16-en.pdf.

Doctrine and Studies

Aaronson, Susan Ariel and Rob Maxim. *Data Protection and Digital Trade in the Wake of the NSA Revelations.* 48(5) Intereconomics. 281–285 (September 2013).

Aaronson, Susan Ariel. *Trade and the Internet.* International Economy. 75–77 (Winter 2012).

Alves, Sergio Jr. Jr. *Internet Governance 2.0.1.4: The Internet Balkanization Fragmentation* (29 June 2014).

Anderson, Janna and Lee Rainee. *The Internet of Things Will Thrive by 2025.* Pew Research Internet Project (14 May 2014).

Atallah, Akram. *Root Zone Management Transition Update: Preservation of Security, Stability and Resiliency.* ICANN Blog. 28 June 2016. Available at https://www.icann.org/news/blog/root-zone-management-transition-update-preservation-of-security-stability-and-resiliency.

Baird, Stacy. *The Government at the Standards Bazaar.* 18 Stanford Law & Policy Review (2007).

Balkin, Jack. *The Future of Free Expression in a Digital Age.* 36 Pepperdine Law Review (29 January 2009).

Barlow, J.P. *A Declaration of the Independence of Cyberspace* (February 1996).

Benkler, Yochai. *A Free Irresponsible Press: Wikileaks and theBattle Over the Soul of the Networked Fourth Estate.* 46 Harvard Civil Rights – Civil Liberties Law Review 311 (2011).

Berners-Lee, Tim. *Weaving the Web: The original design and ultimate destiny of the World Wide Web, by its inventor*, 1999.

Bilgil, Melih. *History of the Internet.* Youtube (4 January 2009).

Blum, Andrew. *Tubes: A Journey to the Centre of the Internet*. Chapter 1. Ecco, May 2013.

Border Gateway Protocol. *Analysis Report*. Available at http://bgp.potaroo.net/index-bgp.html.

Born, G. *International Commercial Arbitration: Volume II, International Arbitral Procedures*. 2nd ed. 2014 Wolters Kluwer Law & Business, 2014.

Boyd, Danah and Kate Crawford. *Six Provocations for Big Data A Decade in Internet Time*. Symposium on the Dynamics of the Internet and Society (September 2011).

Boyle, James and Jennifer Jenkins. *Intellectual Property: Law & the Information Society*. Cases & Materials: An Open Casebook: 2014 Edition. Duke Center for the Study of the Public Domain. Chapter 22 ("A Creative Commons?"), 773–784.

Boyle, James. *Why Intellectual Property?*. In *The Public Domain – Enclosing the commons of the Mind*. Yale University Press, 2008.

Brousseau, Eric, Meryem Marzouki and Cécile Méadel. *Governance, Regulation, and Powers on the Internet*. Cambridge University Press, Cambridge, 2012.

Brown, Ian and Douwe Korff. *Digital Freedoms in International Law*. Report prepared by the Global Network Initiative (14 June 2012).

Burkert, Herbert and Urs Gasser. *Accountability and transparency at ICANN – an independent review – Memorandum: Transparency and internal decision making*. Available at: https://newgtlds.icann.org/en/about/program.

Burri, Mira. *Re-Conceptualizing the Global Digital Divide*. 2(3) Journal of Intellectual Property: Information Technology and E-Commerce Law. 217–225 (6 December 2011).

Busch, Lawrence. *Standards and Democracy*. In *Standards: Recipes for Reality*. MIT Press, 2011.

Cabell, Diane. *Foreign Domain Name Disputes 2000*. 17(10) The Computer & Internet Lawyer. 5–17 (October 2000).

Centre for Democracy and Technology. *Shielding the Messenger: Protecting Platforms for Expression* and Innovation (2012).

Cerf, Vinton and Robert Kahn. *A Protocol for Packet Network Interconnection*. Vol. COM-22 V 5 IEEE Transactions on Communications Technology 1974.

Chan, Patty. *Safer (cyber)sex with.XXX: The case for first amendment zoning of the internet*. 39 Loyola of Los Angeles Law Review 1299 (December 2006).

Chik, Warren B. *Lord of you domain, but master of none: The need to harmonize and recalibrate the domain name regime of ownership and control*. 16 International Journal of Law and Information Technology 8 (Spring 2008).

Coglianese. *Globalization and the Design of International Institutions*. In J. Nye and J. Donahue. *Governance in a Globalizing World*. Brookings Institution Press, 2000.

Crawford, Susan P. *The ICANN Experiment*. 12 Cardozo Journal of International Comparative Law. 409 (Fall 2004).

Curran, James, et al. *Rethinking internet history*. In *Misunderstanding the Internet*. New York Routledge, 2012.

DelBianco, Steve and Braden Cox. *ICANN Internet governance: Is it working?*. Symposium--I Think I Can, I Think ICANN: Regulating the Internet… or Not. 21 Pacific McGeorge Global Business & Development Law Jouranl 27 (2008).

DeNardis, Laura. *Chapter 1: The Internet Governance Oxymoron*. In *The Global War for Internet Governance*. Yale University Press, January 2014.

DeNardis, Laura. *Internet Points of Control as Global Governance*. Paper No. 2 Internet Governance Papers (August 2013).

DeNardis, Laura. *Scarcity and Internet Governance* and *Protocol Select as Power Selection*. In *Protocol Politics: The Globalization of Internet Governance*. MIT Press, 2009.

DeNardis, Laura. *The Emerging Field of Internet Governance*. In William H. Dutton (ed.), *The Oxford Handbook of Internet Studies*, 2013.

Donahey, M. Scott. *Part IV. Intellectual Property Issues. Chapter 16. ICANN Dispute Resolution Guidelines*. 1 Internet Law and Practice § 16:3 (July 2008).

Dutta, Soumitra, William H. Dutton and Ginette Law. *The New Internet World: A Global Perspective on Freedom of Expression, Privacy, Trust and Security Online*. No. 2011/89/TOM INSEAD Working Paper (24 August 2011).

Epstein, Dmitry. *Constructing the Information Society: The Binding Nature of Nonbinding Debates About Internet Governance*. TPRC (15 August 2010).

Forrest, Heather. *Protection of Geographic Names in International Law and Domain Name System Policy*. Wolters Kluwer Law International, 2013.

Frischmann, Brett M. *Infrastructure: the Social Value of Shared Resources*. In *Infrastructure: The Social Value of Shared Resources*. Oxford University Press, 2012.

Froomkin, Michael. *Wrong Turn in Cyberspace: Using ICANN to Route Around the APA and the Constitution*. 50 Duke Law Journal 17 (2000).

Fuller, Kathleen E. *Media & Communications. An interview with Michael Froomkin*. 2001 Duke Law & Technology Review 1 (28 February 2001).

Goldsmith, Jack and Tim Wu. *Who Controls the Internet? Illusions of a Borderless World*. Oxford University Press, 2008.

Google White Paper. *Enabling Trade in the Era of Information Technologies: Breaking Down Barriers to the Free Flow of Information* (2011).

Grimmelman, James. *Internet Law: Cases and Problems 4.0*. Semaphore Press, 2014.

Grimmelmann, James. *Saving Facebook*. 94 Iowa Law Review 1137 (2009).

Guobin, Yang. *The Power of the Internet in China: Citizen Activism Online*. Columbia University Press, 2011.

Hafner, Katie and Matthew Iyon. *Where wizards stay up late: The Origins of the Internet* (1996).

Hill, Jonah Force. *Internet Fragmentation: Highlighting the Major Technical, Governance and Diplomatic Challenges for U.S. Policy Makers*. Paper, Science, Technology, and Public Policy Program. Belfer Center for Science and International Affairs, Harvard Kennedy School (May 2012).

Internet Governance Forum Watch (23 September 2011).

Internet Society. *A Ten Year Tribute to Jon Postel*. 16 October 2008. Available at http://www.internetsociety.org/what-we-do/grants-and-awards/awards/postel-service-award/ten-year-tribute-jon-postel.

Internet Society. *IANA's Statement on Postel Service Award*. 2008. Available at http://www.isoc.org/postel/iana.shtml.

ITU-D Study Group 1 (International Telecommunications Union). *Final Report: Question 22-1/1: Securing Information and Communication Networks: Best Practices for Developing a Culture of Cybersecurity* (March 2014).

Janssen, Jan. *Istanboel is Constantinopel niet (Onrechtmatige registratie van domeinnaam).* 3 Computerr. 125 (2009).

Janssen, Jan. *Houd de cybersquatter!*. 18 RABG 1330 (2011).

Janssen, Jan. *Identificatie op het Internet: een nieuw begin.* 12 RABG 846 (2013).

Janssen, Jan. *ICANN Dispute Resolution Procedures.* GTDT (2015).

Janssen, Jan. *ICANN Dispute Resolution Procedures.* GTDT (2016).

Jeffery, Simon et. al. *When was the Internet invented? A People's history of the internet – A people's history of the internet.* The Guardian (23 October 2009).

Johnson, David R. and David Post. *Law and Borders- The Rise of Law in Cyberspace.* 48 Stanford Law Review 1367 (1995).

Katz, Michael L., Gregory L. Rosston and Theresa Sullivan. *An Economic Framework for the Analysis of the Expansion of Generic Top-Level Domain Names.* June 2010. Available on https://archive.icann.org/en/topics/new-gtlds/economic-analysis-of-new-gtlds-16jun10-en.pdf.

Katz, Michael L., Gregory L. Rosston and Theresa Sullivan. *Economic Considerations in the Expansion of Generic Top-Level Domain Names – Phase II Report: Case Studies prepared for ICANN.* December 2010. Available on https://archive.icann.org/en /topics/new-gtlds/phase-two-economic-considerations-03dec10-en.pdf.

Kleinrock, L. *Information Flow in Large Communication Nets.* M.I.T. RLE Quarterly Progress Report. July 1961. Available at http://www.lk.cs.ucla.edu/data/files/ Kleinrock/Information%20Flow%20in%20Large%20Communication%20Nets0 .pdf.

Kleinwachter, Wolfgang. *The History of Internet Governance.* In *Governing the Internet: Freedom and Regulation in the OSCE Region.* OSCE, Vienna, 2007.

Koppell, Jonathan G.S. *Introduction: The Organization of Global Rulemaking.* and *Accountability and Legitimacy-Authority Tension in Global Governance.* In *World Rule: Accountability, Legitimacy, and the Design of Global Governance.* University of Chicago, 2010.

Kotera, A. *Regulatory Transparency. In* P. Muchlinski, F. Ortino and C. Schreuer. *Oxford Handbook of International Investment Law.* Oxford University Press, 2008.

Kreimer, Seth F. *Censorship by Proxy: The first amendment, internet intermediaries and the problem of the weakest link.* 155 University of Pennsylvania Law Review 11 (2006).

Kruger, Lennard G. *Internet domain names: Background and policy issues.* 7 NO. E-Commerce Law Report 4 (September 2005).

Kurbalija, Jovan. *An Introduction to Internet Governance (6th Edition) The Online Companion to the Book, An Introduction to Internet Governance.* Diplo Foundation, Geneva, 2012.

Kurbalija, Jovan. *International inviolability for the root zone?.* 9 December 2013. Available at http://www.diplomacy.edu/blog/international-inviolability-root-zone.

Kurbalija, Jovan. *There is a practical solution for global inviolability of the Internet root zone*. DiploFoundation Policy Brief. October 2014. Available at http://www.diplomacy.edu/sites/default/files/DiploFoundation%20Policy%20Brief%20No%204%20WEB%20v1.pdf.http://www.diplomacy.edu/sites/default/files/DiploFoundation0PolicyBriefNo4WEBv1.pdf.

La Rue, Frank. *Report of the Special Rapporteur on the promotion and protection of the right to freedom of opinion and expression*. UN Doc. A/HRC/17/27 (2011).

Lacey, Simon B.C. *Trade Rules and Their Limits: Internet Restrictions as Actionable Trade Barriers* (15 May 2012).

Leiner, Barry M. et al. *A Brief History of the Internet*. Available at http://www.internetsociety.org/internet/what-internet/history-internet/brief-history-internet.

Lemley, Mark A., David S. Levine and David G. Post. *Don't Break the Internet*. 64 Stanford Law Review Online 34 (3 January 2012).

Lemly, Mark A. and Lawrence Lessig. *The End of End-to-End: Preserving the Architecture of the Internet in the Broadband Era*. 48 UCLA Law Review 925 (2001).

Lindsay, David. *International Domain Name Law: ICANN and the UDRP*. Hart Publishing, 2007.

Little, Brent A. and Cheryl B. Preston. *ICANN can: Contracts and porn sites--Choosing "to play Internet ball in American cyberspace"*. Symposium--I Think I Can, I Think ICANN: Regulating the Internet… or Not. 21 Pacific McGeorge Global Business & Development Law Journal 79 (2008).

Lynn, Stuart. *A Plan for Action Regarding New gTLDs*. 18 October 2002 (published 8 November 2002). https://archive.icann.org/en/committees/ntepptf/new-gtld-action-plan-18oct02.htm.

MacKinnon, Rebecca. *Consent and Sovereignty*. In *Consent of the Networked: The World-wide Struggle for Internet Freedom*. Basic, New York, 2012.

Malcolm, Jeremy. *Where to develop Internet policy: ITU, G8, OECD or an empowered IGF?*.

Manheim, Karl M. and Lawrence B. Solum. *An economic analysis of domain name policy*. 25 Hastings Committee & Entertainment Law Jouranl 359 (Spring-Summer 2003).

Mathiason, John, Milton Mueller, Hans Klein, Marc Holitscher and Lee McKnight. *Internet Governance: The State of Play* (September 2004).

Mathiason, John. *The ICANN Experiment*. In *Internet Governance: The New Frontier of Global Institutions*. Routledge, London, 2008.

Mathiason, John. *What is the Internet and What is Governance?*. In *Internet Governance: The New Frontier of Global Institutions*. Routledge, London, 2008.

Mayer-Schönberger, Viktor and Malte Ziewitz. *Jefferson rebuffed: The United States and the future of Internet governance*. 8 Columbia Science & Technology. Law Review 188 (2006-2007).

McCarthy, J. Thomas. *McCarthy on Trademarks and Unfair Competition, Fourth Edition*.

Morozov, Evgeny. *The Google Doctrine*. In *The Net Delusion: How Not to Liberate The World*. Allen Lane, London, 2011.

Mueller, Milton, Hans Klein, Jeanette Hofmann, Lee McKnight and Derrick L. Cogburn. *Political Oversight of ICANN: A Briefing for the WSIS Summit – Concept Paper by the Internet Governance Project*. 1 November 2005. Available at http://www.internetgovernance.org/wordpress/wp-content/uploads/political-oversight.pdf.

Mueller, Milton. *Chapter 11: Ideologies and Visions*. In *Networks and States: The Global Politics of Internet Governance*. MIT Press, 2010.

Mueller, Milton. *Do Networks Govern?*. In *Networks and States: The Global Politics of Internet Governance (Information Revolution and Global Politics)*. MIT Press, Cambridge, 2010.

Mueller, Milton. *Ruling the Root : Internet Governance and the Taming of Cyberspace*. MIT Press, 2002.

Mueller, Milton. *The Root as Resource*. In *Ruling the Root: Internet Governance and the Taming of Cyberspace*. MIT. Cambridge, MA, 2002.

Murino, John and Emily Alban. *Application for New gTLDs and Domain Names*. GTDT (2015).

Murino, John and Emily Alban. *Application for New gTLDs and Domain Names*. GTDT (2014).

Nafziger, Jamie N. *Internet governing body ICANN approves next generation of Top Level Domain Names*. 7 NO. 8 E-Commerce Law Report 8 (August 2005).

National Science Foundation. *The Launch of NSFNET*. Available at https://www.nsf.gov/about/history/nsf0050/internet/launch.htm (accessed 11 May 2016).

NETMundial Multistakeholder Statement. NETMundial Global Multistakeholder Meeting on the Future of Internet Governance (24 April 2014).

Nissenbaum, Helen. *Privacy in context of technology, policy and the integrity of Social Life*. Stanford Law books (2009).

Nye, Joseph S. *The Regime Complex for Managing Global Cyber Activities*. Paper Series No. 1. Center for International Governance Innovation (CIGI), Global Commission on Internet Governance (20 May 2014).

OECD High Level Meeting. *Communique on Principles for Internet Policy-Making*. Paris, France (28-29 June 2011).

OECD. *Generic Top Level Domain Names: Market Development and Allocation Issues*. OECD Digital Economy Papers No. 84 OECD Publishing, Paris, 2004.

OECD. *Internet Domain Names: Allocation Policies*. OECD Document GD(97)207. Paris 1997. Available at https://www.oecd.org/sti/2091363.pdf.

Palfrey, John. *The end of the experiment: How ICANN's foray into global Internet democracy failed*. 17 Harvard Journal of Law & Technology 409 (Spring 2004).

Palfrey John and Urs Gasser. *Introduction: "Why Interop Matters."*. In *Interop: the Promise and Perils of Highly Interconnected Systems*. Basic Books, New York, 2012.

Penney, Jonathan W. *Internet Access Rights: A Brief History and Intellectual Origins*. 38.1 William Mitchell Law Review 10 (2011).

Perry Barlow, John. *Declaration of the Independence of Cyberspace* (8 February 1996).

Petillion, Flip. *De actualiteiten inzake het Internetrecht*. Actua in Internet Law. Kluwer. Berchem, Belgium (10 February 2011).

Petillion, Flip. *Nieuwe Top-Level Domains,* Actua Intellectuele eigendomsrechten. Kluwer. La Hulpe, Belgium (24 February 2011).

Petillion, Flip. *Virtual Realities: Game Changer.* Intellectual Property Magazine (March 2011).

Petillion, Flip. *Le droit de l'Internet: points d'actualité.* Actua Droits Intellectuels. Kluwer. Brussels, Belgium (5 May 2011).

Petillion, Flip. *Le Programme des Nouveaux gTLDs après Singapour.* AFNIC webinar (28 June 2011).

Petillion, Flip. *On your marks for the great gTLD brand race.* World Trademark Review (August-September 2011).

Petillion, Flip. *ICC seminar addresses top level domain names.* ICC. Paris, France (1 September 2011).

Petillion, Flip. *The Changing Domain Name Landscape and New gTLDs, Avoiding and countering trademark abuse and infringement.* ICC. Paris, France (30 September 2011).

Petillion, Flip. *De Actualiteiten Inzake Het Internetrecht.* Actua Intellectuele eigendomsrechten. Kluwer. Berchem, Belgium (30 November 2011).

Petillion, Flip. *Le droit de l'Internet: Points D'actualité.* Actua Droits Intellectuels. Kluwer. Brussels, Belgium (8 December 2011).

Petillion, Flip. *The Status of the New gTLD Applications.* WIPO Annual Meeting. Genève, Switzerland (22 October 2012).

Petillion, Flip. *Challenges in the Extended Internet: How to Defend Your Interests and Addressing the Competition in the New gTLDs, Whether You Applied or Not.* ICC/Cepani Seminar. Brussels, Belgium (22 June 2012).

Petillion, Flip. *Claims on the Internet.* 20th Alumni day of Leuven University. Leuven, Belgium (8 March 2013).

Petillion, Flip. *Claims on the Internet. VRG-Alumniboek* (8 March 2013).

Petillion, Flip. *Des marques et des lettres dans les nouvelles extensions Internet. IRDI* (January 2014).

Petillion, Flip. *Domain Names and New Generic Top-Level Domains*. ICC Concise notes on intellectual property issues for business (2014).

Petillion, Flip. *Domains and Domain Names – Global Overview* Getting The Deal Through (2014).

Petillion, Flip. *The ICC Intellectual Property Roadmap. Current and Emerging Issues for Business and Policy Makers* (12th edn.) (2014).

Petillion, Flip. *Filling the NTIA void.* Trademarks Brands Online (May 2014).

Petillion, Flip. *Domains and Domain Names – Global Overview.* Getting The Deal Through (2015).

Petillion, Flip. *Has .SUCKS set a dangerous precedent?.* Trademarks & Brands Online (July 2015).

Petillion, Flip. *Restricted Access*. Trademarks & Brands Online (February 2015).

Petillion, Flip. *Domains and Domain Names – Global Overview.* Getting The Deal Through (2016).

Petillion, Flip. *Internet Governance.* National CLE Conference. Vail, Colorado (6–10 January 2016).

Petillion, Flip and Jan Janssen. *A critical assessment of litigation in the new domain name landscape.* 5 Computerrecht (2013).

Petillion, Flip and Jan Janssen. *ICANN Dispute Resolution Procedures.* GTDT (2014).

Petillion, Flip and Jan Janssen. *Litigation on top-level domains.* GTDT (2016).

Petillion, Flip and Jan Janssen. *Can self-regulation do the job?.* TBO (2016).

Petillion, Flip, John Murino, Jan Janssen and Emily Alban. *Lessons from the cases against Icann.* 227 Managing Intellectual Property 30 (March 2013).

Phillips, Jennifer D. *The seamy side of the seamy side: Potential danger of cyberpiracy in the proposed ".XXX" Top Level Domain.* 7 North Carolina Journal of Law & Technology 233 (Fall 2005).

Prechal, Sacha and Madeleine de Leeuw. *Dimensions of Transparency: The Building Blocks for a New Legal Principle?.* Review of European Administrative Law (2007).

Rafert, Greg and Catherine Tucker. *Phase II Assessment of the Competitive Effects Associated with the New gTLD Program.* 28 September 2016. Available on https://newgtlds.icann.org/en/reviews/cct/competitive-effects-phase-two-assessment-11oct16-en.pdf.

Report by the Panel on Global Internet Governance Ecosystem. *Towards a Collaborative, Decentralized Internet Governance Ecosystem* (May 2014).

Resnick, Pete. *RFC 7282: On Consensus and Humming in the IETF.* Internet Engineering Task Force (June 2014).

Roberts, David E. *Top Level Domain reorganization: A constitutional solution to legislative attempts at Internet regulation.* 36 Indian Law Review 883 (2003).

Roman, Reece. *What if ICANN can't?: Can the United Nations really save the Internet?.* 15 Syracuse Science & Technology Law Report 27 (Spring 2007).

Rony Ellen and Peter Rony, *The Domain Name Handbook: High Stakes and Strategies in Cyberspace.* 1998 R&D Books.

Ryan, S., *Governing Cyberspace: ICANN a Controversial Internet Standards Body.* 1 October 1999. Available at http://www.fed-soc.org/publications/detail/governing-cyberspace-icann-a-controversial-internet-standards-body).

Sacha Wunsch-Vincent and Arno Hold. *Towards coherent rules for digital trade: Building on efforts in multilateral versus preferential trade negotiations.* Working Paper No 2011/64 Swiss National Centre of Competence and Research: Trade Regulation (July 2011).

Salazar, Michael. *Preparing Evaluators for the New gTLD Application Process.* 22 November 2011. Available on https://newgtlds.icann.org/en/blog/preparing-evaluators-22nov11-en.

Savio, Jessica. *Browsing history: A heritage site has been set up in Boelter Hall 3420, the room the first Internet message originated in.* Daily Bruin. 4 April 2011. Available at http://dailybruin.com/2011/04/01/browsing_history/.

Schauer, Frederick. *Internet Privacy and the Public-Private Distinction.* 38 Jurimetrics Journal 555 (1998).

Secretary of State Hillary Clinton. *Remarks on Internet Freedom.* Speech. Newseum, Washington, D.C. (10 January 2010).

Secretary of State Hillary Rodham Clinton. *Conference on Internet Freedom*. Speech. Fokker Terminal, The Hague, Netherlands (8 December 2011).

Shahan, Travis D. *The world summit on the information society and the future of Internet governance*. 10 Computer Law Review & Technology Journal 325 (Summer 2006).

Simonelis, Alex. *A Concise Guide to the Major Internet Bodies*. Ubiquity: Information Everywhere (February 2005).

Smith Ekstrand, Victoria. *Unmasking Jane and John Doe: Online Anonymity and the First Amendment*. 405 Communication Law and Policy 8(4) (2003).

Solove, Daniel. *A Taxonomy of Privacy*. 154 University of Pennsylvania Law Review 477 (2006).

Solum, Lawrence and Minn Chung. *The Layers Principle: Internet Architecture and the Law*. Paper No. 55 University of San Diego Public Law Research (June 2003).

Sonbuchner, Scott P. *Master of your domain: Should the U.S. government maintain control over the Internet's root?*. 17 Minnesota Journal of International Law 183 (Winter 2008).

Summit Strategies International. *Evaluation of the New gTLDs: Policy and Legal Issues – prepared for the Internet Corporation for Assigned Names and Numbers (ICANN)*. Available on https://archive.icann.org/en/tlds/new-gtld-eval-31aug04.pdf.

Tene, Omer. *What Google knows: Privacy and Internet Search Engines*. 4 Utah Law Review 1433 (2008).

The Economist Intelligence Unit. *Community Priority Evaluation Panel and its Processes*. 6 August 2014. Available on https://newgtlds.icann.org/en/applicants/cpe/panel-process-07aug14-en.pdf.

The Institute (IEEE). *Special Report: The Internet of Things* (March 2014).

Turner, Fred. *From Counterculture to Cyberculture*. Chicago Press, 2016, Chapter 1. *Working definition of Internet governance*. In *Report of the Working Group on Internet Governance*, June 2000.

Van Schewick, Barbara. *Internet Architecture and Innovation*. MIT Press, Cambridge, 2010.

Verhulst, Stefaan. *Net Neutrality and the Media*. Open Society Foundation (August 2011).

Verisign. *The Domain Name Industry Brief*. Volume 13 – Issue 3. September 2016. Available on https://www.verisign.com/assets/domain-name-report-sept2016.pdf.

Vint, Cerf, Patrick S. Ryan and Max Senges. *Internet Governance is Our Shared Responsibility. I/S: A Journal of Law and Policy for the Information Society*. 10 ISJLP 1 (2014).

Waldrop, Mitch. *DARPA and the Internet revolution*. Available at http://www.darpa.mil/attachments/%282O15%29%20Global%20Nav%20-%20About%20Us%20-%20History%20-%20Resources%20-%2050th%20-%20Internet%20%28Approved%29.pdf.

Weinberg, Jonathan. *ICANN and the Problem of Legitimacy*. 50 Duke Law Journal 187–198 (2000).

White, Jim. *A Proposed Mail Protocol* RFC # 524. Available at https://tools.ietf.org/html/rfc524 (accessed 5 April 2016).

Whitman, James Q. *The Two Western Cultures of Privacy: Dignity versus Liberty*. 113 Yale Law Journal (April 2004).

WIPO Press Release. *Cybersquatting Cases Up in 2015, Driven by New gTLDs*. 18 March 2016. Available on http://www.wipo.int/pressroom/en/articles/2016/article_0003.html.

WIPO. *The Management of Internet Names and Addresses: Intellectual Property Issues – Final Report of the WIPO Internet Domain Name Process*. 30 April 1999. Available at http://www.wipo.int/export/sites/www/amc/en/docs/report-final1.pdf.

WTO. A report prepared by the World Trade Organization. *15 Years of the Information Technology Agreement: Trade, innovation and global production networks*. Geneva (2012).

Wu, Felix T. *Collateral Censorship and the Limits of Intermediary Immunity*. 87 Notre Dame Law Review 293 (2011–2012).

Wu, Felix T. *Defining Privacy and Utility in Data Sets*. 84 University of Colorado Law Review 1117 (2013).

Wu, Tim. *Network Neutrality, Broadband discrimination*. Journal of Telecommunications and High Technology Law 2141 (2003).

Wu, Tim. *Why You Should Care About Network Neutrality: The future of the internet depends on it!*. Slate Magazine (1 May 2006).

Ziewitz, Malte and Ian Brown. *A Prehistory of Internet Governance*. In Ian Brown (ed.), *Research Handbook on Governance Of The Internet*. Edward Elgar, Cheltenham, 2012.

Zittrain, Janathan. *The Generative Internet*. 119 Harvard Law Review 1974 (May 2006).

Zittrain, Jonathan and John Palfrey. *Internet Filtering: The Politics and Mechanisms of Control, Access Denied: The Practice and Policy of Global Internet Filtering*. MIT Press, Cambridge, 2008.

Zittrain, Jonathan. Conclusion in *The Future of the Internet - And How to Stop It*. Yale University Press, Penguin UK/Allen Lane, Oxford Legal Studies Research Paper No. 36/2008.

Zittrain, Jonathan. *Freedom and Anonymity: Keeping the Internet Open*. Scientific American (15 February 2011).

Zwillenberg, Paul, Dominic Field and David Dean. *Greasing the Wheels of the Internet Economy*. Boston Consulting Group (20 January 2014).

Miscellaneous

NTIA. *Telecommunications: Glossary of Telecommunication Terms*. Business & Economics (1997).

The GovLab. *A Report by the ICANN Strategy Panel on Multistakeholder Innovation. The Quest for a 21st Century ICANN*. May 2014.

CERN. *The birth of the web*. Available at http://home.cern/topics/birth-web.

Table of Referenced IRP Case Material

Note: * indicates that the document has not been referenced in this edition of the book.

ICM v. ICANN (.xxx)

Full Reference	*Shortened Reference*
ICDR Case No. 50 117 T 00224 08, *ICM v. ICANN*, ICM's Request for Independent Review Process, 6 June 2008, **139**	ICM's Request for IRP
ICDR Case No. 50 117 T 00224 08, *ICM v. ICANN*, ICANN's Response to ICM's IRP Request, 8 September 2008, **137, 138, 140–143, 344, 351**	ICANN's Response (*ICM)*
ICDR Case No. 50 117 T 00224 08, *ICM v. ICANN*, ICM Memorial on the Merits, 22 January 2009, **137, 139, 140, 143**	ICM's Reply
ICDR Case No. 50 117 T 00224 08, *ICM v. ICANN*, Expert Report of Jack Goldsmith, 22 January 2009, **39**	Expert Report of Jack Goldsmith, *in* ICDR Case No. 50 117 T 00224 08, 22 January 2009
ICDR Case No. 50 117 T 00224 08, *ICM v. ICANN*, ICANN's Response to ICM's Memorial on the Merits, 8 May 2009, **141–143**	ICANN's Sur-Reply (*ICM*)
ICDR Case No. 50 117 T 00224 08, *ICM v. ICANN*, ICM Post-Hearing Brief, 13 October 2009	ICM Post-Hearing Brief*
ICDR Case No. 50 117 T 00224 08, *ICM v. ICANN*, ICANN Post-Hearing Brief, 13 October 2009	ICANN Post-Hearing Brief (*ICM*)*
ICDR Case No. 50 117 T 00224 08, *ICM v. ICANN*, ICANN Letter to Panel re ICM Post-Hearing Submission, 14 October 2009	ICANN Letter re Post-Hearing Submission (*ICM*)*

Full Reference	*Shortened Reference*
ICDR Case No. 50 117 T 00224 08, *ICM v. ICANN*, IRP Declaration, 19 February 2010, **137, 139, 140, 143, 144, 145, 205, 251, 344, 346, 348, 351, 353, 356**	ICM IRP Declaration

Manwin Licensing International v. ICANN (.xxx)

Full Reference	*Shortened Reference*
ICDR Case No. 50 117 T 00812 11, *Manwin Licensing International s.a.r.l. v. ICANN*, Manwin's Request for Independent Review Proceeding, 16 November 2011, **158**	Manwin Request for IRP
ICDR Case No. 50 117 T 00812 11, *Manwin Licensing International s.a.r.l. v. ICANN*, ICANN's Response to Manwin's Request for Independent Review, 4 May 2012, **151–153, 155–158, 358**	ICANN's Response (*Manwin)*
ICDR Case No. 50 117 T 00812 11, *Manwin Licensing International s.a.r.l. v. ICANN*, Manwin's Brief on Standing to Maintain IRP, 15 October 2012, **150, 151, 153, 155**	Manwin's brief re standing
ICDR Case No. 50 117 T 00812 11, *Manwin Licensing International s.a.r.l. v. ICANN*, ICANN's Response to Manwin's Response on Standing, 16 November 2012), **149, 152–155, 158–160**	ICANN's brief re standing (*Manwin)*
ICDR Case No. 50 117 T 00812 11, *Manwin Licensing International s.a.r.l. v. ICANN*, Manwin Supplemental Brief on Standing, 7 January 2013, **149, 150, 154, 156, 157**	Manwin's Supplemental brief
ICDR Case No. 50 117 T 00812 11, *Manwin Licensing International s.a.r.l. v. ICANN*, ICANN's Response to Manwin's Supplemental Brief on Standing, **148, 149, 153, 155**	ICANN's Supplemental brief (*Manwin)*
ICDR Case No. 50 117 T 00812 11, *Manwin Licensing International s.a.r.l. v. ICANN*, Joint Letter of Dismissal of IRP, 8 May 2013, **408**	Joint Letter of Dismissal (*Manwin*)

Booking.com v. ICANN (.hotels)

Full Reference	*Shortened Reference*
ICDR Case No. 50-20-1400-0247, *Booking.com v. ICANN*, Booking.com's Request for IRP, 18 March 2014, **163, 164, 169, 170, 172–175**	Booking.com's Request for IRP
ICDR Case No. 50-20-1400-0247, *Booking.com v. ICANN*, Expert Report, Letter from Prof. Dr. Piet Desmet to Flip Petillion, 10 March 2014, Claimant's Annex 20, **118, 119**	Expert Report, Letter from Prof. Dr. Piet Desmet to Flip Petillion, 10 March 2014, *Booking.com* IRP, Claimant's Annex 20
ICDR Case No. 50-20-1400-0247, *Booking.com v. ICANN*, ICANN's Response to Booking.com's Request for IRP, 25 April 2014), **109, 110, 162–164, 171–173, 175, 177, 351**	ICANN's Response (*Booking.com*)
ICDR Case No. 50-20-1400-0247, *Booking.com v. ICANN*, Booking.com's Additional Submission, Reply to ICANN's Response, 6 October 2014, **164, 170, 173, 174, 177**	Booking.com's Reply
ICDR Case No. 50-20-1400-0247, *Booking.com v. ICANN*, ICANN's Response to Claimant Booking.com's Reply Brief, 20 November 2014, **163, 165, 171, 172, 175, 178**	ICANN's Sur-Reply (*Booking.com*)
ICDR Case No. 50-20-1400-0247, *Booking.com v. ICANN*, Booking.com's reply to ICANN's additional exhibits, 13 December 2014, **165**	Booking.com's post-hearing submission, email of 13 December 2014
ICDR Case No. 50-20-1400-0247, *Booking.com v. ICANN*, Final IRP Declaration, 3 March 2015, **163, 165–167, 169, 172, 173, 175, 176, 178, 181, 217, 251, 329, 334, 344–349, 351, 353, 354, 359, 372, 384**	Booking.com IRP Declaration

DCA Trust v. ICANN (.africa)

Full Reference	*Shortened Reference*
ICDR Case No. 50 117 T 1083 13, *DCA Trust v. ICANN*, DCA Trust's Notice of Independent Review, 24 October 2013, **199, 341**	DCA Notice of IRP
ICDR Case No. 50 117 T 1083 13, *DCA Trust v. ICANN*, DCA Trust's Amended Notice of Independent Review, 10 January 2014, **183, 190**	DCA Request for IRP
ICDR Case No. 50 117 T 1083 13, *DCA Trust v. ICANN*, ICANN's Response to Claimant's Amended Notice, 10 February 2016, **183, 194, 196, 203**	ICANN's Response (*DCA*)
ICDR Case No. 50 117 T 1083 13, *DCA Trust v. ICANN*, DCA's Request for Interim Relief, 28 March 2014, **197**	DCA Request for Interim Measures
ICDR Case No. 50 117 T 1083 13, *DCA Trust v. ICANN*, ICANN's Response to DCA's Request for Interim Relief, 4 April 2014, **185, 198**	ICANN's Memorial on Interim Measures (*DCA*)
ICDR Case No. 50 117 T 1083 13, *DCA Trust v. ICANN*, ICANN's Memorandum Regarding Procedural Issues, 5 May 2014, **183–188, 194, 201, 203–205**	ICANN's 1st Memorandum re procedure (*DCA*)
DCA's Submission on Procedural Issues, 5 May 2014, **183, 185, 186, 190, 202, 203**	DCA Submission on Procedural Issues
ICDR Case No. 50 117 T 1083 13, *DCA Trust v. ICANN*, Panel Decision on Interim Measures of Protection, 12 May 2014, **335, 336**	DCA IRP Decision on Interim Measures of Protection
ICDR Case No. 50 117 T 1083 13, *DCA Trust v. ICANN*, ICANN's Futher Memorandum Regarding Procedural Issues, 20 May 2014, **184, 187, 194, 204**	ICANN's 2nd Memorandum re procedure (*DCA*)
ICDR Case No. 50 117 T 1083 13, *DCA Trust v. ICANN*, DCA's Response to the Panel's Questions on Procedural Issues, 20 May 2014, **183, 203**	DCA's Response to the Panel's questions on procedural issues
ICDR Case No. 50 117 T 1083 13, *DCA Trust v. ICANN*, ICANN's Response to the Panel's 12 May 2014 Decision and Request for Partial Reconsideration, 20 May 2014	ICANN's Partial Reconsideration Request (*DCA*)*

Full Reference	*Shortened Reference*
ICDR Case No. 50 117 T 1083 13, *DCA Trust v. ICANN*, DCA's Response to ICANN's Request for Partial Reconsideration, 28 May 2014	DCA's Response to ICANN's Partial Reconsideration Request*
ICDR Case No. 50 117 T 1083 13, *DCA Trust v. ICANN*, DCA's Supplemental Letter Brief, 29 May 2014, **186, 205**	Letter from DCA of May 29, 2014
ICDR Case No. 50 117 T 1083 13, *DCA Trust v. ICANN*, ICANN's Supplemental Letter Brief, 2 June 2014	ICANN's Supplemental Letter Brief*
ICDR Case No. 50 117 T 1083 13, *DCA Trust v. ICANN*, Panel Decision on ICANN's Request for Partial Consideration, 4 June 2014	DCA Declaration on Partial Consideration Request*
ICDR Case No. 50 117 T 1083 13, *DCA Trust v. ICANN*, Panel Declaration on the IRP Procedure, 14 August 2014, **328, 338, 339, 359**	DCA Declaration on IRP Procedure
ICDR Case No. 50 117 T 1083 13, *DCA Trust v. ICANN*, DCA's Memorial on the Merits, 3 November 2014, **190–193, 196, 199–201**	DCA's Memorial on the merits
ICDR Case No. 50 117 T 1083 13, *DCA Trust v. ICANN*, ICANN's Response to DCA's Memorial on the Merits, 3 December 2014, **184, 193–196, 201, 351**	ICANN's Response re merits (*DCA*)
ICDR Case No. 50 117 T 1083 13, *DCA Trust v. ICANN*, Letter from ICANN to IRP Panel, 26 February 2015, **185**	Letter from ICANN to DCA IRP Panel, 26 February 2015
ICDR Case No. 50 117 T 1083 13, *DCA Trust v. ICANN*, DCA's Response to ICANN's Request to Rehear the Proceedings, 5 March 2015, **185**	DCA's Response to ICANN's Request to Rehear the Proceedings
ICDR Case No. 50 117 T 1083 13, *DCA Trust v. ICANN*, Panel Declaration on ICANN's Request for Revisiting of the 14 August 2014 Panel Declaration on the IRP Procedure Following the Replacement of Panel Member, 24 March 2015, **188, 381**	DCA 2nd Declaration on the IRP Procedure
ICDR Case No. 50 117 T 1083 13, *DCA Trust v. ICANN*, Letter from ICANN to IRP Panel, 8 April 2015, **187**	Letter from ICANN to IRP Panel, 8 April 2015 (*DCA*)

Full Reference	*Shortened Reference*
ICDR Case No. 50 117 T 1083 13, *DCA Trust v. ICANN*, Third Panel Declaration of IRP Procedure, 20 April 2015, **184, 189, 328, 338, 339**	DCA 3rd Declaration on the IRP Procedure
ICDR Case No. 50 117 T 1083 13, *DCA Trust v. ICANN*, Hearing Transcript, 23 May 2015, **184, 191, 192**	Hearing Transcripts (*DCA*)
ICDR Case No. 50 117 T 1083 13, *DCA Trust v. ICANN*, Final Declaration of IRP Procedure, 9 July 2015, **174, 195–197, 199–202, 251, 329, 344–347, 351, 353, 356, 372**	DCA Final IRP Declaration

Vistaprint v. ICANN (.webs)

Full Reference	*Shortened Reference*
ICDR Case No. 01-14-0000-6505, *Vistaprint Limited v. ICANN*, Vistaprint Limited's Request for IRP, 11 June 2014, **213, 219–223**	Vistaprint Request for IRP
ICDR Case No. 01-14-0000-6505, *Vistaprint Limited v. ICANN*, ICANN's Response to Vistaprint's Request for Independent Review, 21 July 2014, **210, 211, 214, 217, 223, 228, 231, 344, 351**	ICANN's Response (*Vistaprint*)
ICDR Case No. 01-14-0000-6505, *Vistaprint Limited v. ICANN*, Vistaprint's Additional Submission in Support of Its Request for IRP, 2 March 2015, **211, 214, 220, 222, 223, 227, 230, 234**	Vistaprint Reply
ICDR Case No. 01-14-0000-6505, *Vistaprint Limited v. ICANN*, ICANN's Response to Vistaprint's Additional Submission in Support of Vistaprint's Request for IRP, 2 April 2015, **214–218, 224, 228, 231, 236**	ICANN's Sur-Reply (*Vistaprint*)
ICDR Case No. 01-14-0000-6505, *Vistaprint Limited v. ICANN*, Vistaprint's Second Additional Submission in Accordance with Procedural Order No. 2, 24 April 2015, **210, 211, 213, 215, 222, 230, 235**	Vistaprint Brief on Booking.com case (Rebuttal)
ICDR Case No. 01-14-0000-6505, *Vistaprint Limited v. ICANN*, ICANN's Response to Claimant's Second Additional Submission, 1 May 2015, **211, 216, 224, 231, 236**	ICANN's Sur-Rebuttal (*Vistaprint*)
ICDR Case No. 01-14-0000-6505, *Vistaprint Limited v. ICANN*, Final Declaration of the Independent Review Panel, 9 October 2015, 40, **145, 174, 208, 210, 212–214, 216, 218–220, 224–229, 232, 233, 237–241, 251, 328, 329, 334, 343–349, 351, 353–357, 359, 360, 372, 386**	Vistaprint IRP Declaration

Merck KGaA v. ICANN (.merck)

Despegar et al. (.hotel, .eco)

Full Reference	*Shortened Reference*
ICDR Case No. 01-14-0001-5004 (consolidated Case No. 01-15-0002-8061), *Despegar Online SRL et al. v. ICANN*, Claimants' Request for IRP, 4 March 2015, **256, 257, 263–265**	Dot Hotel Request for IRP
ICDR Case No. 01-15-0002-8906 (consolidated Case No. 01-15-0002-8061), *Little Birch LLC et al. v. ICANN*, Claimants' Request for IRP, 13 March 2015	Dot Eco Request for IRP*
ICDR Case No. 01-14-0001-5004 (consolidated Case No. 01-15-0002-8061), *Despegar Online SRL et al. v. ICANN*, ICANN's Response to Claimants' Request for IRP, 17 April 2015, **257, 259, 260, 263, 266–268, 274, 278**	ICANN's Response (*Dot Hotel*)
ICDR Case No. 01-15-0002-8906 (consolidated Case No. 01-15-0002-8061), *Little Birch LLC et al. v. ICANN*, ICANN's Response to Claimants' IRP Request, 27 April 2015	ICANN's Response (*Dot Eco*)*
ICDR Case No. 01-15-0002-8061 (consolidated Case No. 01-15-0002-8061), *Despegar Online SRL et al. v. ICANN*, Additional Submission Reply to ICANN's Response, 19 October 2015, **256, 257, 259, 261, 264–266, 269, 273, 274, 276, 277**	Dot Hotel Reply
ICDR Case No. 01-15-0002-8906 (consolidated Case No. 01-15-0002-8061), *Little Birch LLC et al. v. ICANN*, Additional Submission Reply to ICANN's Response, 19 October 2015	Dot Eco Reply*
ICDR Case No. 01-15-0002-8061 (consolidated Case No. 01-15-0002-8061), *Despegar Online SRL et al. v. ICANN*, ICANN's Sur-Reply to the Reply of Despegar Online SRL et al. (.HOTEL), 10 November 2015, **257, 258, 260, 261, 267, 269, 272, 274, 278**	ICANN's Sur-Reply (*Dot Hotel*)
ICDR Case No. 01-15-0002-8906 (consolidated Case No. 01-15-0002-8061), *Little Birch LLC et al. v. ICANN*,	ICANN's Sur-Reply (*Dot Eco*)*

Full Reference	*Shortened Reference*
ICANN's Sur-Reply to the Reply of Little Birch LLC et al. (ECO), 10 November 2015	ICANN's Sur-Reply (*Dot Eco*)*
ICDR consolidated Case No. 01-15-0002-8061, *Despegar Online SRL et al. v. ICANN* and *Little Birch LLC et al. v. ICANN*, Claimant's Answers to the Panel Questions, 4 December 2015, **259**	Dot Hotel Answers to Panel Questions
ICDR consolidated Case No. 01-15-0002-8061, *Despegar Online SRL et al. v. ICANN* and *Little Birch LLC et al. v. ICANN*, ICANN's Answers to the Panel Questions, 4 December 2015	ICANN's Answers to Panel Question (*Dot Hotel*)*
ICDR consolidated Case No. 01-15-0002-8061, *Despegar Online SRL et al. v. ICANN* and *Little Birch LLC et al. v. ICANN*, Final Declaration, 11 February 2016, **129, 258260, 261, 268, 269–272, 274, 275, 278, 280, 320, 321, 324, 329, 344, 346, 348, 349, 351–353, 357, 358, 360, 368, 372, 385–387**	Despegar et al. IRP Declaration

Donuts Inc. v. ICANN (.sports, .rugby)

Full Reference	*Shortened Reference*
ICDR Case No. 01-14-0000-1579, *Donuts Inc. v. ICANN*, Donuts' Request for Emergency Relief, 13 October 2014, **299**	Donuts' Request for Emergency Relief
ICDR Case No. 01-14-0001-6263, *Donuts Inc. v. ICANN*, Donuts' Request for Independent Review Process, 13 October 2014, **283, 284, 288, 289, 297, 299**	Donuts' IRP Request
ICDR Consolidated Cases No. 01-14-0000-1579 and No. 01-14-0001-6263, *Donuts Inc. v. ICANN*, ICANN's Consolidated Response to Claimant Donuts Inc.'s Request for Independent Review Process and Request for Emergency Relief, 14 November 2014, **283, 284, 290, 302, 304**	ICANN's Response (*Donuts*)
ICDR Case No. 01-14-0000-1579, *Donuts Inc. v. ICANN*, Donuts' Additional Submission in Further Support of Its Request for Emergency Relief, 17 November 2014	Donuts' Reply Request for Emergency Relief*
ICDR Case No. 01-14-0000-1579, *Donuts Inc. v. ICANN*, Email Re Resolution of Donuts' Request for Emergency Relief Re .RUGBY, .SPORTS and .SKI, 21 November 2014, **284, 299**	Email from counsel to ICANN to counsel to Donuts of 21 November 2014
ICDR Case No. 01-14-0001-6263, *Donuts Inc. v. ICANN*, Procedural Order No. 1, 17 July 2015, **282**	Donuts IRP Procedural Order No. 1
ICDR Case No. 01-14-0001-6263, *Donuts Inc. v. ICANN*, Donuts Inc's Letter Brief Re: Document Requests, 10 August 2015	Donuts' Document Request*
ICDR Case No. 01-14-0001-6263, *Donuts Inc. v. ICANN*, ICANN's Letter Brief Re: Donuts Inc.'s Request for Documents, 10 August 2015	ICANN's Response to Document Request (*Donuts*)*
ICDR Case No. 01-14-0001-6263, *Donuts Inc. v. ICANN*, Donuts' Supplemental Memorandum in Further Support of Request for Independent Review Process Re New gTLD Applications for .SPORTS and .RUGBY, 20 August 2015, **291, 296, 302**	Donuts Reply

Full Reference	*Shortened Reference*
ICDR Case No. 01-14-0001-6263, *Donuts Inc. v. ICANN*, ICANN''s Response to Donuts' Supplemental Memorandum in Support of Request for Independent Review Process, 21 September 2015, **283, 284, 291**	ICANN's Sur-Reply (*Donuts*)
ICDR Case No. 01-14-0001-6263, *Donuts Inc. v. ICANN*, Hearing Transcript, 8 October 2015	Donuts Hearing Transcript*
ICDR Case No. 01-14-0001-6263, *Donuts Inc. v. ICANN*, Donuts' Post-Hearing Brief in Support of Request for Independent Review Process Re New gTLD Applications for .SPORTS and .RUGBY, 29 October 2015, **290, 302**	Donuts Post-Hearing Submission
ICDR Case No. 01-14-0001-6263, *Donuts Inc. v. ICANN*, ICANN's Post-Hearing Brief in Response to Donuts' Request for Independent Review Process, 29 October 2015	ICANN's Post-Hearing Submission (*Donuts*)*
ICDR Case No. 01-14-0001-6263, *Donuts Inc. v. ICANN*, Final Declaration of the Panel, 5 May 2015, **283–288, 292–298, 300–304, 329, 342, 347, 348, 350–352, 356, 357, 360, 372**	Donuts IRP Declaration

Dot Registry LLC v. ICANN (.inc, .ltd, .llp)

Full Reference	*Shortened Reference*
ICDR Case No. 01-14-0001-5004, *Dot Registry LLC v. ICANN*, Dot Registry, LLC's Request for Independent Review Process, 22 September 2014, **308, 309, 313, 314, 322**	Dot Registry's Request for IRP
ICDR Case No. 01-14-0001-5004, *Dot Registry LLC v. ICANN*, ICANN's Response to Dot Registry, LLC's Request for Independent Review, 27 October 2014, **308, 309, 311, 314, 315**	ICANN's Response (*Dot Registry)*
ICDR Case No. 01-14-0001-5004, *Dot Registry LLC v. ICANN*, Dot Registry, LLC's Request for Emergency Panelist and Interim Measures of Protection, 19 November 2014, **319**	Dot Registry's Request for Emergency Relief
ICDR Case No. 01-14-0001-5004, *Dot Registry LLC v. ICANN*, ICANN's Response to Dot Registry's Request for Emergency Relief, 8 December 2014, **319**	ICANN's Response to Emergency Relief (*Dot Registry*)
ICDR Case No. 01-14-0001-5004, *Dot Registry LLC v. ICANN*, Emergency Independent Review Panelist Order on Request for Emergency Measures of Protection, 23 December 2014, **233, 319, 320, 322, 335, 336**	Dot Registry IRP Order on Request for Emergency Measures of Protection
ICDR Case No. 01-14-0001-5004, *Dot Registry LLC v. ICANN*, Amendment to Dot Registry LLC's Request for IRP, 4 February 2015, **309**	Dot Registry's Amendment to Request for IRP
ICDR Case No. 01-14-0001-5004, *Dot Registry LLC v. ICANN*, ICANN Letter to IRP Panel Regarding Discovery Matter, 15 April 2015, **310**	Letter from counsel to ICANN of 15 April 2015 (*Dot Registry*)
ICDR Case No. 01-14-0001-5004, *Dot Registry LLC v. ICANN*, Additional Submission of Dot Registry, LLC, 13 July 2015, **308, 309, 311, 313, 314**	Dot Registry's Reply

Full Reference	*Shortened Reference*
ICDR Case No. 01-14-0001-5004, *Dot Registry LLC v. ICANN*, ICANN's Response to Dot Registry, LLC's Additional Submission, 10 August 2015, **308, 309, 314, 315, 318, 322**	ICANN's Sur-Reply (*Dot Registry*)
ICDR Case No. 01-14-0001-5004, *Dot Registry LLC v. ICANN*, ICANN's Response to Procedural Order No. 8, 12 October 2015, **307–310, 312, 316, 318, 323**	ICANN's Response to IRP Panel's questions of 12 October 2015 (*Dot Registry*)
ICDR Case No. 01-14-0001-5004, *Dot Registry LLC v. ICANN*, Dot Registry's Response to Procedural Order No. 8, 12 October 2015, **307, 310–312, 323**	Dot Registry's Response to IRP Panel's questions of 12 October 2015
ICDR Case No. 01-14-0001-5004, *Dot Registry LLC v. ICANN*, Procedural Order No. 11, 13 January 2016, **311, 381**	Dot Registry IRP Panel's Order No. 11
ICDR Case No. 01-14-0001-5004, *Dot Registry LLC v. ICANN*, Procedural Order No. 12, 25 February 2016, **311, 381**	Dot Registry IRP Panel's Order No. 12
ICDR Case No. 01-14-0001-5004, *Dot Registry LLC v. ICANN*, IRP Final Hearing Transcript, 29 March 2016, **306, 319**	Dot Registry IRP Transcript
ICDR Case No. 01-14-0001-5004, *Dot Registry LLC v. ICANN*, Claimant's Post-Hearing Brief, 8 April 2016, **313**	Dot Registry Post-Hearing Brief
ICDR Case No. 01-14-0001-5004, *Dot Registry LLC v. ICANN*, ICANN's Post-Hearing Brief, 8 April 2016, **314**	ICANN's Post-Hearing Brief (*Dot Registry*)
ICDR Case No. 01-14-0001-5004, *Dot Registry LLC v. ICANN*, Declaration of the Independent Review Panel, 29 July 2016, **280, 306, 307, 309, 310, 312, 313, 316–324, 329, 340, 345, 350–352, 356, 357, 372, 380**	Dot Registry IRP Declaration

Corn Lake, LLC v. ICANN (.charity)

Full Reference	*Shortened Reference*
ICDR Case No. 01-15-0002-9938, *Corn Lake, LLC v. ICANN*, Request for Independent Review Process By Corn Lake, LLC Re New gTLD Application for .charity, 24 March 2015, **410**	Corn Lake Request for IRP
ICDR Case No. 01-15-0002-9938, *Corn Lake, LLC v. ICANN*, ICANN's Response to Claimant Corn Lake, LLC's Request for Independent Review Process, 15 May 2015	ICANN's Response (*Corn Lake*) *
ICDR Case No. 01-15-0002-9938, *Corn Lake, LLC v. ICANN*, Reply Memorandum of Claimant Corn Lake, LLC in Further Support of Request for Independent Review Process Re New gTLD Application for .charity, 10 December 2015	Corn Lake Reply*
ICDR Case No. 01-15-0002-9938, *Corn Lake, LLC v. ICANN*, ICANN's Sur-Reply to the Reply of Claimant Corn Lake, LLC, 8 January 2016	ICANN Sur-Reply (*Corn Lake*) *
ICDR Case No. 01-15-0002-9938, *Corn Lake, LLC v. ICANN*, Supplemental Submission of Claimant Corn Lake, LLC Concerning February 3, 2016 Board Resolution Re .hospital (as Requested by Panel at February 8, 2016 Hearing), 16 February 2016	Corn Lake Rebuttal*
ICDR Case No. 01-15-0002-9938, *Corn Lake, LLC v. ICANN*, ICANN's Supplemental Submission as Requested by Panel at 8 February 2016 Hearing, 16 February 2016	ICANN's Sur-Rebuttal (*Corn Lake*) *
ICDR Case No. 01-15-0002-9938, *Corn Lake, LLC v. ICANN*, ICANN's Brief Concerning the Final Declaration Issued in the *Donuts, Inc. v. ICANN* IRP Proceeding, 19 May 2016	ICANN's Submission re Donuts IRP (*Corn Lake*)*

Full Reference	*Shortened Reference*
ICDR Case No. 01-15-0002-9938, *Corn Lake, LLC v. ICANN*, Additional Submission of Claimant Corn Lake, LLC Concerning the Final IRP Declaration in *Donuts v. ICANN*, 26 May 2016	Corn Lake Response re Donuts IRP*
ICDR Case No. 01-15-0002-9938, *Corn Lake, LLC v. ICANN*, Supplemental Submission of Claimant Corn Lake, LLC Concerning the July 29, 2016 IRP Declaration in *Dot Registry v. ICANN*, 15 August 2016	Corn Lake Submission re Dot Registry IRP*
ICDR Case No. 01-15-0002-9938, *Corn Lake, LLC v. ICANN*, ICANN's Response to the Supplemental Submission of Corn Lake, LLC Concerning the July 29, 2016 IRP Declaration in *Dot Registry v. ICANN*, 19 August 2016	ICANN's Response re Dot Registry IRP (*Corn Lake*) *
ICDR Case No. 01-15-0002-9938, *Corn Lake, LLC v. ICANN*, Final Declaration, 17 October 2016, **134, 326, 337, 340, 342**	Corn Lake IRP Declaration

Gulf Cooperation Council (GCC) v. ICANN (.persiangulf)

Full Reference	*Shortened Reference*
ICDR Case No. 01-14-0002-1065, *Gulf Cooperation Council (GCC) v. ICANN*, GCC's Request for Emergency Relief, 5 December 2014	GCC's Request for Interim Relief*
ICDR Case No. 01-14-0002-1065, *Gulf Cooperation Council (GCC) v. ICANN*, GCC's Request for Independent Review Process, 5 December 2014, **410**	GCC's Request for IRP
ICDR Case No. 01-14-0002-1065, *Gulf Cooperation Council (GCC) v. ICANN*, ICANN's Response to GCC's Request for Emergency Relief, 17 December 2014	ICANN's Response re Interim Relief (*GCC*)*
ICDR Case No. 01-14-0002-1065, *Gulf Cooperation Council (GCC) v. ICANN*, GCC's Reply in Support of Its Request for Emergency Arbitrator and Interim Measures of Protection, 22 December 2014	GCC's Reply re Interim Relief*
ICDR Case No. 01-14-0002-1065, *Gulf Cooperation Council (GCC) v. ICANN*, ICANN's Response to GCC's Request for Independent Review Process, 20 January 2015	ICANN's Response (*GCC*)*
ICDR Case No. 01-14-0002-1065, *Gulf Cooperation Council (GCC) v. ICANN*, Panel Interim Declaration on Emergency Request for Interim Measures of Protection, 12 February 2015, **233, 334–337, 351, 354**	GCC Interim (IRP) Declaration
ICDR Case No. 01-14-0002-1065, *Gulf Cooperation Council (GCC) v. ICANN*, GCC's Supplementary Request for Independent Review, 12 February 2016	GCC's Supplementary Request*
ICDR Case No. 01-14-0002-1065, *Gulf Cooperation Council (GCC) v. ICANN*, ICANN's Supplementary Response to GCC's Supplementary Request, 14 March 2016	ICANN's Supplementary Response (*GCC*)*
ICDR Case No. 01-14-0002-1065, *Gulf Cooperation Council (GCC) v. ICANN*, GCC's Reply to ICANN's Response, 28 March 2016	GCC's Reply*

Full Reference	*Shortened Reference*
ICDR Case No. 01-14-0002-1065, *Gulf Cooperation Council (GCC) v. ICANN*, ICANN's Sur-Response to GCC's Reply, 11 April 2016	ICANN's Sur-Reply (*GCC*)*

Index

C

D

E

J

L

M

N

O